HANDBOOK OF REGIONAL
AND URBAN ECONOMICS
VOLUME I

HANDBOOKS
IN
ECONOMICS

7

Series Editors

KENNETH J. ARROW
MICHAEL D. INTRILIGATOR

NORTH-HOLLAND
AMSTERDAM · NEW YORK · OXFORD · TOKYO

HANDBOOK OF REGIONAL AND URBAN ECONOMICS

VOLUME I
REGIONAL ECONOMICS

Edited by

PETER NIJKAMP
Free University, Amsterdam

1986

NORTH-HOLLAND
AMSTERDAM · NEW YORK · OXFORD · TOKYO

ISBN North-Holland for this volume 0 444 87969 2
ISBN North-Holland for this set 0 444 87971 4

Publishers
ELSEVIER SCIENCE PUBLISHERS B.V.
P.O. Box 1991
1000 BZ Amsterdam
The Netherlands

Sole distributors for the U.S.A. and Canada
ELSEVIER SCIENCE PUBLISHING COMPANY, INC.
52 Vanderbilt Avenue
New York, N.Y. 10017
U.S.A.

Library of Congress Cataloging-in-Publication Data

Handbook of regional and urban economics.

   (Handbooks in economics; 7)
   Includes bibliographies.
   Contents: v. 1. Regional economics.
   1. Regional economics– Handbooks, manuals, etc.
2. Urban economics – Handbooks, manuals, etc. I. Nijkamp,
Peter. II. Series.
HT391.3.H36   1986   330.9172′2   86-16538
ISBN 0-444-87971-4   (set)

PRINTED IN THE NETHERLANDS

INTRODUCTION TO THE SERIES

The aim of the *Handbooks in Economics* series is to produce Handbooks for various branches of economics, each of which is a definitive source, reference, and teaching supplement for use by professional researchers and advanced graduate students. Each Handbook provides self-contained surveys of the current state of a branch of economics in the form of chapters prepared by leading specialists on various aspects of this branch of economics. These surveys summarize not only received results but also newer developments, from recent journal articles and discussion papers. Some orginal material is also included, but the main goal is to provide comprehensive and accessible surveys. The Handbooks are intended to provide not only useful reference volumes for professional collections but also possible supplementary readings for advanced courses for graduate students in economics.

CONTENTS OF THE HANDBOOK

LIST OF CONTRIBUTORS

Åke E. Andersson, *University of Umea, CERUM, S-90187 Umea, Sweden*

David F. Batten, *CSIRO/Division of Building Research, P.O. Box 56, Highett, Victoria 3190, Australia*

Martin J. Beckmann, *Department of Economics, Brown University, 8032 Lochamer, 36/77 Arlington, Providence, RI 02912, USA* and *Institute of Statistics, Technical University, Arcisstrasse 21, 8000 Munich 2, FRG*

Robert J. Bennett, *Department of Geography, London School of Economics, Houghton Street, London WC2A 2AE, UK*

Roger Bolton, *Williams College, Williamstown, MA 01267, USA*

David E. Boyce, *Department of Civil Engineering, University of Illinois, 208 North Romine Street, Urbana, IL 61801, USA*

Floor Brouwer, *IIASA, Schloss Laxenburg, A-2361 Laxenburg, Austria*

William A. V. Clark, *Department of Geography, University of California, Los Angeles, CA 90024, USA*

Shelby Gerking, *Department of Economics, University of Wyoming, Laramie, WY 82071, USA*

Geoffrey J. D. Hewings, *Department of Geography, University of Illinois, 220 Davenport Hall, Urbana, IL 61801, USA*

Leen Hordijk, *IIASA, Schloss Laxenburg, A-2361 Laxenburg, Austria*

Andrew Isserman, *Regional Research Institute, West Virginia University, Morgantown, WV 26506, USA*

Rodney C. Jensen, *Department of Economics, University of Queensland, St. Lucia, Queensland 4067, Australia*

Börje Johansson, *CERUM, University of Umea, S-90187 Umea, Sweden*

Robert E. Kuenne, *Department of Economics, Princeton University, Princeton, NJ 08544, USA*

Walter C. Labys, *College for Mineral and Energy Resources, West Virginia University, Morgantown, WV 26506, USA*

T. R. Lakshmanan, *Department of Geography, Boston University, 48 Cummington Street, Boston, MA 02215, USA*

Georgio Leonardi, *Piazza Piola 14, I-20131, Milano, Italy*

Wal F. J. van Lierop, *Economic and Social Research Institute, Free University, P.O. Box 7161, 1007 MC Amsterdam, The Netherlands*

Edward J. Malecki, *Department of Geography, University of Florida, Gainesville, FL 32611, USA*

Edwin S. Mills, *Department of Economics, Princeton University, Princeton, NJ 08544, USA*

Peter Nijkamp, *Department of Economics, Free University, P.O. Box 7161, 1007 MC Amsterdam, The Netherlands*

Harry W. Richardson, *Department of Economics, State University of New York, Albany, NY 12222, USA*

Piet Rietveld, *Department of Economics, Free University, P.O. Box 7161, 1007 MC Amsterdam, The Netherlands*

Uwe Schubert, *Interdisciplinary Institute for Regional and Urban Studies (IIR), Economics University, Augasse 2-6, A-1190 Wien, Austria*

Folke Snickars, *Department of Regional Planning, Royal Institute of Technology, S-1004 Stockholm, Sweden*

T. Takayama, *Japanese Studies Unit, Department of Economics, University of Western Australia, Nedlands, Western Australia 6009, Australia*

Carol Taylor, *Department of Economics, University of Florida, Gainesville, FL 32611, USA*

Jacques F. Thisse, *SPUR, Catholic University of Louvain, Louvain-la-Neuve, Belgium*

Peter M. Townroe, *School of Economic and Social Studies, University of East Anglia, Norwich NR4 7TJ, UK*

Pravin Varaiya, *University of California at Berkeley, Berkeley, CA 94720, USA*

Neil Wrigley, *Department of Geography, University of Bristol, University Road, Bristol BS8 1SS, UK*

CONTENTS OF VOLUME I

PART 2 – REGIONAL ECONOMIC MODELS AND METHODS

Chapter 7

Regional and Multiregional Economic Models: A Survey

PETER NIJKAMP, PIET RIETVELD and FOLKE SNICKARS

Chapter 8

Regional, Interregional and Multiregional Input–Ouput Analysis

Chapter 9

Spatial Interaction, Transportation, and Interregional Commodity Flow Models

Chapter 1

ADVANCES IN REGIONAL ECONOMICS

PETER NIJKAMP and EDWIN S. MILLS

1. Prologue

Regional economics analyzes the spatial dispersion and coherence of economic activities. Although it is a fairly recent discipline, the history of economics shows various early attempts to explicitly address spatial issues, e.g. in comparative cost theories and international trade theories. Furthermore, various pathfinding contributions to spatial economic analyses can be found in the work of Von Thünen, Weber, Palander, Hotelling, Predöhl, Christaller, Lösch and others. But the real take-off of regional economics as a separate discipline did not take place before World War II. In fact, it was not until the mid fifties that regional economics came into being as an accepted analytical framework for studying the implications of geographical location–allocation problems. Since then, regional economics (and later, urban economics) has made formidable progress in achieving a further understanding of the structure and evolution of spatial economic systems.

Initially, much of the field of regional economics was based on an analogy to general economics, the main difference being the explicit treatment of geographical space as a source of various location–allocation phenomena. Illustrative examples in this context are: linear programming models for transportation analysis, spatial substitution problems in neoclassical production theories, inter-regional input–output analysis, and so forth.

In a later stage, however, more emphasis was placed on the indigenous features of geographical space and its implications for the spatio-temporal evolution of complex spatial economic systems. Examples can be found inter alia in discrete choice models for spatial choice behavior, and in evolutionary theories on innovation and spatial dynamics.

At present, regional economics appears to be a rich discipline with a great many linkages to urban economic problems, transportation problems and natural resource problems. As such it is also able to generate a unifying approach to problems emerging at the cross-roads of economics and geography.

Handbook of Regional and Urban Economics, Volume I, Edited by P. Nijkamp
©Elsevier Science Publishers BV, 1986

A closer look at the history and the current achievements of regional economics teaches us that, despite the large number of diverse contributions in this area, three main fields can be identified for which regional economics may claim to have provided a real contribution to economic theorizing and analyzing, viz:

(1) locational analysis (for both industries and households),
(2) regional economic modeling and spatial interaction analysis,
(3) regional economic development and policy analysis.

These three areas which determine also the structure of the present Handbook will briefly be discussed in this introductory chapter.

2. Locational analysis

Locational analysis was originally the central question of regional economics. Based on the earlier work of Von Thünen, Weber, Lösch, Christaller and others, locational analysis has succeeded in developing an impressive series of theoretical contributions and empirical analyses in order to provide adequate answers to the question where (and why) specific economic activities are taking place in a given spatial system.

Various approaches can be distinguished in this context. First, methodological reflections on the concept of a region and the element of space have to be mentioned (based inter alia on functionality, uniformity, homogeneity or administrative principles). In recent years, interest has been directed more toward axiomatic and formal approaches to spatial systems (for instance, by using notions from systems theory, fuzzy set theory, topology, etc.). Such – often more abstract – contributions made extensive use of measurement theory and could also be observed in an analogous way in parallel disciplines (such as biology and psychology).

Second, the locational decisions of entrepreneurs and households have to be noted. Entrepreneurial locational decisions have been put into an operational framework of industrial complex analysis, growth center analysis, gravity and entropy analysis, and dynamic systems analysis. Public facility locations have been studied from an integrated spatial or network viewpoint, while residential location problems have also been fruitfully analyzed by means of operational utility models, based on a solid utility-theoretical foundation.

Furthermore, recent locational analysis is increasingly being based on disaggregate models of choice (such as logit and probit models). This gives rise to a much more refined analysis, in which various individual locational determinants (including qualitative factors) can be taken into account.

Next, the joint decisions of entrepreneurs and households lead to the problem of the existence of a spatial economic equilibrium. This is evidently a complex problem, as the allocation of scarce resources and their spatial location may involve various substitution possibilities, so that complicated trade-off questions may occur.

The latter problem is further aggravated if spatio-temporal dynamics caused by structural changes are taken into account. The occurrence of non-linear dynamic processes must be noted especially here, as such phenomena may cause unexpected perturbations in a multidimensional dynamic economic system.

In the light of the foregoing remarks, part 1 of the present Handbook is composed of five main contributions to modern location theory, viz:

- the location of production activities (Chapter 2),
- residential mobility and household location (Chapter 3),
- public facility location (Chapter 4),
- spatial equilibrium analysis (Chapter 5),
- regional economic dynamics (Chapter 6).

These five contributions will now be briefly discussed.

Chapter 2, written by Martin Beckmann and Jacques Thisse, is a comprehensive review of principles and tools developed for the prediction and analysis of the location of production activities. Though such tools may in principle be taken from the various social sciences, the authors draw especially in the microeconomics of production decisions and firm behavior in various types of markets.

In the *short run* all firms are in place, and then the question is one of the utilization of the available plant and of the transportation of goods from alternative sources of supply to the locations of demand. In the discrete space case, this question is answered by the transportation model of linear programming. In the continuous space case, transportation activities are modeled as a continuous flow field. Both approaches turn out to be open to various extensions.

As the next step in the short-run analysis, the authors examine the *pricing* and *output* decisions of firms already in place, serving markets whose extent will depend on these pricing and output decisions. Monopoly and a comparison of spatial pricing systems (mill pricing, uniform pricing, perfectly discriminatory pricing) are then the natural starting point. Duopoly is then also analyzed for all three types of pricing, while (non) existence of equilibrium is also discussed. Finally, competitive and collusive oligopolies are dealt with in the case of mill pricing, while the possibility of market area overlap is also examined for quantity-setting firms.

The heart of the chapter is the analysis of location choice, the *medium*-term problem. The classical Launhardt–Weber model has also retained its central position in modern location theory. In a one-dimensional context it gives rise to the principle of median location, which proves to be also the key to understanding location decisions within a network. Extensions of the basic model include alternative metrics for economic distance compared to the standard Euclidean metric. In the Weber–Launhardt theory, minimization of total transportation cost is regarded as the decision criterion for locational choice. But microeconomics suggests that the broader objective of maximal profits should be considered. This gives rise to the price–location problem, which is treated by the authors for spatial monopoly and spatial oligopoly under alternative pricing systems.

The authors finally examine the *long-run* problems. Here the focus is on the equilibrium patterns that emerge under entry of new firms: the spacing of firms and the resulting price patterns in a spatially homogeneous setting. These not only depend on the expectations of firms with respect to each other's reactions (their conjectural variations), but also on the dynamics of entry. It is interesting to compare the market equilibria with a planning solution that maximizes some social welfare functions. In homogeneous space this is the celebrated Christaller–Lösch problem whose solution is given by a system of hexagonal markets. In a non-homogeneous space the more complex location–allocation problem of operations research is applicable; finally, the economic implications of this issue are examined by the authors.

The third chapter is written by Bill Clark and Wal Van Lierop, and treats the locational decision problems of households and their related mobility patterns. The authors start their contribution with a general introduction to the context within which household location and residential mobility are taking place. This is followed by the definition and description of regional and local housing markets and the nature and causes of inter- and intra-urban migration. The way in which these migrations have an impact on housing markets is also discussed.

Next, the authors present an historical perspective on separate housing choice and residential mobility models, and recent developments towards linked mobility–housing choice approaches. They also examine in more detail the variety of models which together represent the current state of the art of residential mobility and household location modeling. A tabular overview of selected key-references of location and mobility modeling is used to classify these studies by their micro or macro contents and the degree to which they are statistical or behavioral.

In addition, six specific modeling strategies are described which have been (or are) used to analyze residential mobility and household location: (1) linear programming, (2) gravity and entropy analysis, (3) log-linear modeling, (4) discrete choice random utility, and elimination-by-aspects analysis, (5) behavioral and search modeling, and (6) micro-simulation modeling.

Finally, the authors deal with prospects and directions for future research: their aim is to offer researchers working in the area some sense of the potential thrust of future research. Special attention is devoted to new possibilities of analyzing (i) dynamics, (ii) systems impacts, and (iii) qualitative data, and of applying these research developments to improving the existing household location and residential mobility models.

In the fourth chapter, authored by Börje Johansson and Georgio Leonardi, the public facility location problem is dealt with. Instead of a conventional locational analysis based on programming principles applied to a network, the authors emphasize the multiregional and multiauthority decision context of public facility location.

The authors argue that the establishment and siting of public facilities is often based on decisions in the political systems of nations and regions. However, the institutional setting varies considerably between countries. A given type of (public) facility may in one country basically rely on private initiatives; in another it may largely be controlled by public authorities. In order to include such variations, this chapter outlines a multiregional and multiauthority framework with more than one decision level. The main focus is on the existence of non-cooperative equilibria, although cooperative game situations are also discussed. These decision structures with several decision-makers are contrasted with single-authority decision problems. The authors also consider consumer surplus criteria which in several analytical cases are combined with goals about income and cost flows. Moreover, they also present cases in which the objective is to generate income from tourist visitors and/or to promote technological development in regions. Finally, in the context of multiregional competition and coordination, the authors also touch upon dynamic phenomena which may have a structural impact on the output of a spatial economic system.

Chapter 5 provides an overview of advances in spatial equilibrium analysis and of related operational models developed in a multiregion framework. This chapter is produced by Tak Takayama and Walter Labys. Their contribution is focusing attention on spatial equilibrium analysis, in which optimal spatial allocation models of economic goods and activities are based on mathematical programming methods. Regions are then represented as points in space which are interconnected by various modes of transporting economic goods whose unit transport costs between any pair of regions may vary according to distance, mode of transport, type and quantity of commodity, etc. Taking the first contributions to spatial equilibrium analysis from the early 1950s as a starting point the authors show how the multiple commodity, multiple market problem can be cast within the framework of a non-linear mathematical programming formulation (e.g. the well-known quadratic assignment model). In addition to a concise theoretical review of backgrounds and contents of spatial equilibrium models, a long section is also devoted to various applications of such models to real-world spatial location and allocation problems, mainly in the field of agricultural models, energy models and mineral models. This chapter concludes with a sketch of new research areas in this field, inter alia with regard to stability analysis and regional policy analysis.

The final chapter in part 1 of this Handbook has been written by Åke Andersson and Bob Kuenne, and covers the issue of spatial dynamics. This chapter is concerned with theories and models that deal with really dynamic changes through time of phenomena marked by their location, spatial interaction, spatial availability or spatial structure. Really dynamic models internalize the laws of change within their structural definition, thus giving rise to an endogenous time process. Examples of such models are differential and difference equations, calculus of variation, optimal control theory, dynamic programming, dynamic Markov processes, and bifurcation and catastrophe theory.

This chapter provides a brief review of research in the field of the dynamics in location and transportation fields, followed by a thorough analysis of regional growth theory regarding incomes, economic activities and factor endowments. Structural change and spatial mobility are also dealt with in this context, inter alia by paying attention to the work of Isard, Liossatos and Puu on laws of motion for spatial dynamics.

In conclusion, modern location analysis is increasingly oriented towards an operational, behavioral and disaggregate approach, without being seriously hampered by the limitations inherent in the conventional macro-oriented approach to locational analysis.

3.   Regional economic models and methods

Econometric and statistical tools have exerted a dominant influence on regional economics. A basic prerequisite for a valid quantitative regional and urban analysis is the availability of data and a proper treatment of these data. In the past several statistical methods have been developed for dealing with regional and urban data, such as cluster techniques, principal component analysis, interdependence analysis, multiple regression analysis, canonical correlation analysis, spectral analysis, spatial autocorrelation analysis, etc. The "quantitative" revolution in economics has no doubt exerted a significant impact on the methodology of regional economics. This has caused much rigor and progress in analytical tools, witness the emergence of a great variety of regional and urban econometric models. Sometimes these models were based on regional variations of national models (for instance in the area of regional input–output analysis), but in other cases entirely new model concepts were introduced (for instance, in the field of disaggregate choice analysis or of non-linear spatial dynamics).

Initially, the main quantitative contribution in regional economics took place in the area of input–output analysis. Input–output analysis, developed already many decades ago by Leontief, Isard and others, provides an operational framework for integrating the sectors of a national economy by means of their mutual interactions. Given a fixed technological structure, input–output analysis allows us to calculate the direct and indirect impacts of a change in the final demand (consumption, investments, export, etc.) upon the production, value added and employment in all sectors simultaneously. Input–output analysis is still a powerful tool for assessing the consequences of external shifts and it can easily be extended to describe other spatial linkage patterns (for instance, the diffusion of information flows between different regional agencies).

Especially in a spatial context, input–output analysis has led to many useful applications. Multiregional input–output tables have played a major role in the analysis of regional economic developments in many countries such as the U.S., Canada, France, Great Britain, the Netherlands and Spain. Also the close links between spatial input–output analysis and spatial interaction analysis have to be mentioned, so that input–output analysis can be dealt in the framework of entropy and information theory.

In the last decades many stringent restrictions of input–output analysis have been relaxed. This has led to new adjustments such as the inclusion of price effects, the inclusion of substitution effects among inputs, the analysis of non-linearities in the production technology, the analysis of product-by-sector tables (leading to rectangular tables), the development of techniques for updating input–output matrices (for instance, RAS-, entropy and minimum-information principles), and the extension of input–output tables with pollution and energy sectors.

Spatial interactions (for instance, migration and transportation) can also be dealt with in the context of macro-oriented linkage models. There has been a real boom in macro spatial interaction models in the 1970s in which gravity and entropy models have played a major role. Very recently, such models have also been used in the context of the analysis of dynamic spatial systems. The general Alonso theory of movement also should be mentioned in this respect. In recent years, fortunately, much more emphasis has been placed on the theoretical framework of these models and on their micro-economic foundation.

Clearly, in addition to input–output, transportation and spatial interaction models, a wide variety of other models has been developed in the past decades. It has to be noted, however, that many of these data and modeling techniques are based on the assumption of hard and reliable information, while in practice many data are very weak (for instance, measured on an ordinal or nominal scale). Consequently, recently a whole set of new techniques has been developed focusing on so-called soft data. Examples are: multidimensional scaling techniques, ordinal regression analysis, soft econometric analysis, categorical data analysis, logit and probit analysis, PLS and LISREL models, Generalized Linear Models, etc.

This problem of "measuring the unmeasurable" is once more important, as one is often inclined to "torture the data" so as to put them on the Procrustes' bed of too rigid models and techniques, instead of flexibly adjusting conventional models and techniques to the available data. In this regard, the importance of up-to-date information systems and data-processing techniques has also to be stressed. It is surprising that, compared to other sectors of decision-making, the use and quality of urban and regional information systems is lagging far behind the potential offered by modern information technology.

In the light of the previous discussion, part 2 of this Handbook is subdivided into five major constituent chapters, viz:

- a review of regional and multiregional modeling (Chapter 7),
- regional input–output analysis including multi- and interregional dimensions (Chapter 8),
- spatial interaction models including transportation and interregional commodity flow models (Chapter 9),
- regional econometric and dynamic models (Chapter 10),
- qualitative statistical models in regional economics (Chapter 11).

Each of these chapters will be briefly reviewed.

Chapter 7 of this Handbook, produced by Peter Nijkamp, Piet Rietveld and Folke Snickars, provides a general review of regional and multiregional economic models. A historical review of the use of multiregional economic models since 1950 is given, followed by a brief presentation of a number of modeling approaches (input–output, economic base, etc.); each of these models will normally contain a combination of these approaches. The main elements of (multi)regional models are next discussed by means of a modular approach. Special attention is paid to the various ways of modeling linkages of a region with the rest of the world. Essentially, there are two ways: national–regional linkages and interregional linkages, and both approaches are frequently used. Well-known types of national–regional models are top-down and bottom-up models.

Finally, the authors discuss various ways in which (multi)regional models are used. Some bottlenecks to model use are also discussed, while special attention is paid to using these models for policy evaluation.

The next chapter on regional, interregional and multiregional input–output analysis is written by Geoff Hewings and Rod Jensen. The authors assert that the interest in interactions between various sets of actors in an economy has already a long history, but was strongly stimulated by the input–output framework designed by Leontief. In their extensive review of input–output analysis, the authors show the close links between input–output models and national accounting systems as well as economic base analysis. The inclusion of the element of space has led to the emergence of interregional input–output accounting systems, which can also be generalized to commodity–industry accounting frameworks.

Special attention is given to an evaluation of the current state of knowledge with respect to input–output tables per se, in terms of their construction, interpretation, structure and stability. Many of the arguments used hold also for the interregional (or multiregional) input–output framework.

The authors also show the correspondence between input–output approaches and general accounting schemes developed among others by Miyazawa, the demometric/demographic-economic approaches, and the general social accounting framework. Various links with linear programming analysis, labor market analysis and transportation analysis are discussed as well. The chapter concludes with an exposition of the use of input–output models for forecasting, projection, policy analysis, evaluation and monitoring.

Chapter 9 is written by Dave Batten and Dave Boyce and provides a coherent overview of spatial interaction, transportation, and interregional commodity flow models. Mathematical models describing interactive economic behavior over space, such as the transport of goods from one region to another, appear to have an analytically rigorous history as tools invented to assist the transportation planner and regional economist. Their original foundations rested on analogies with the physical world of interacting particles and gravitational force. Contemporary spatial theories have led to the emergence of two major schools of analytical thought: the macroscopic one corresponding to a statistical or probabilistic approach and the microscopic one corresponding to a behavioral or utility-theoretic approach. The solutions and conclusions often reached via these theories are more notable for their similarities than for their differences, and thus the possibility of unifying many of these hypotheses is explicitly recognized by the authors. Furthermore, transportation or commodity flow models based on such hypotheses of spatial interaction have recently been fused with models for describing and predicting economic structure. One such approach has been to apply elements of information theory to input–output analysis. Another has been to combine transportation and input–output models. In addition, transportation models have been extended to incorporate linear and non-linear programming methods.

This chapter explores these and related developments in the ongoing evolution of models describing spatial interaction, transportation and the flow of commodities between different regions. Following some excerpts from the formative years, various modern theories which have been proposed for modeling spatial interactions assuming fixed transportation costs are examined. A broad range of these hypotheses are then reconciled. Alternative formulations are presented for analyzing route choice on a transportation network where the costs are flow-dependent.

Progress with modeling of interregional commodity flows is subdivided into those with fixed and variable prices and further subdivided into those with fixed or variable service characteristics. Following the integration of the gravity and input–output models, useful generalizations have emerged based on interregional input–output formulations of regional commodity balances. Integration within transportation models of both carrier and shipper behavior are also described.

A discussion of solution procedures is followed by a brief examination of new research directions and future prospects for the development of spatial interaction models. These include (i) the possible integration of location, production and flow behavior within a single modeling framework, (ii) the possible integration of link-related transportation factors and supply or demand-related economic activity in models of international commodity trade, and (iii) the relevance of product cycle theory for the dynamic analysis of spatial interaction and the development of time–space hierarchies of production centers.

Chapter 10 is written by Bob Bennett and Leen Hordijk. It discusses econometric models of regional economies concerned with description, analysis, forecasting and policy appraisal within a set of localities and regions. First, examples of four major classes of regional econometric models are introduced concerned with regional growth, unemployment and wage inflation, dynamic spatial interaction, and spatial structure-interaction. The general linear model is then introduced and stages of regional econometric analysis are discussed. These concern specification, estimation, non-stationarity, and non-linearity.

In the next major section policy specification with regional econometric models is reviewed. Particular attention is given to optimal control solutions and to econometric estimation problems in situations in which there is policy feedback.

The final major section reviews future research priorities. These are identified as focusing on four main areas: (i) specification and estimation, particularly relating to aspects of representation and map pattern, and spatial autocorrelation, (ii) models of changing parameters and adaptive behavior, (iii) developments in catastrophe and bifurcation theory which are likely to affect regional econometric techniques, and (iv) the requirements of forecasting and control.

The final chapter in part 2 is written by Neil Wrigley and Floor Brouwer, and discusses new developments in the field of categorical data analysis. Significant methodological advances have taken place over the past twenty years in the analysis of qualitative data and these new methods have increasingly begun to penetrate the practice of statistical modeling in regional economic analysis. The authors provide a coherent overview of such methods.

The methodological advances in qualitative statistical modeling are extensively described, and their current use and future potential in regional economic analysis is illustrated with particular emphasis upon log-linear models for complete and incomplete multidimensional contingency tables, logistic/logit regression models and upon the wider class of generalized linear models. Some numerical examples are also introduced in order to illustrate the operational character of these recently developed techniques.

As a whole, one may conclude that modern regional economics has provided a great many interesting and applicable methods which lead to a fruitful treatment of many kinds of data in regional and urban analysis.

4. Regional economic development and policy

Regional development and policy issues are usually emerging at the interface of economic efficiency and socio-economic equity.

Efficiency goals have always played an important role in regional policy analysis, witness also the popularity of cost-benefit analysis. Furthermore, the rapid emergence of operations research in the postwar decades has led to the popularity of programming models for identifying efficient policy decisions. Starting from an efficiency framework for transportation problems, several optimization models have been developed during the 1960s and the 1970s, among others in the area of land use problems, regional policy problems, urban development policy, allocation problems of scarce human resources, spatial price and location equilibria, and so on. Furthermore, in the 1970s several adjustments and extensions have been made, such as: the introduction of qualitative ranking principles for policy objectives, the design of non-linear models (for instance, quadratic and geometric programming models), the development of dynamic regional models (for instance, dynamic programming and optimal control models), the inclusion of additional relevant policy criteria (for instance, spatial equity criteria, distributional conflicts, and spatial externalities), and the development of models for conflict analysis (based among others on game-theoretic, ideal point of hierarchical principles).

The issues of efficiency and equity have especially played a major role in lagging regions. The problems of lagging (often peripheral) regions are well known: low growth rates, outdated industrial structures and high unemployment figures. This, of course, has led to sharply controversial issues, such as the debate on efficiency versus equity. In this respect, regional science has offered a wide variety of contributions to regional planning problems ranging from empirical case studies, regional planning models to multiobjective multiregional planning models.

During the 1970s, however, there has also been an increasing awareness of the negative externalities of urban and regional growth. Many severe problems appeared to emerge in many regions or cities: segregation, congestion, pollution, criminality, high population density, and lack of local amenities.

In the 1970s two striking observations on urban phenomena have been made:

- many urban agglomerations in the industrialized world showed a tendency to a decrease in population (leading to suburbanization and deurbanization).
- the unemployment rate in many urban centres was extremely high, and in many cases much higher than the unemployment rates in lagging peripheral areas.

This has led to a drastic shift in the attention from lagging areas toward urban centres. Beside peripheral regions, many main centres were also regarded as "problem areas". Much emphasis has been placed in the 1970s on the analysis of agglomeration economies, optimal city size, ghetto formation, diversification of urban structures, spatial mobility and residential choices, and so on. All these studies have contributed substantially to a better understanding of the functioning of cities in a spatial context.

One of the consequences of the attention for urban developments has been the sign of urban revitalization (or urban renewal) policies in order to prevent a further urban decay and to stimulate the positive externalities of the urban climate (for instance, by providing better housing, by supplying more satisfactory urban social overhead capital, by implementing more effective migration policies, and by stimulating the labor market).

It also has to be mentioned that regional and urban planning is not only a matter of a direct use of policy tools, but also of indirect (so-called conditional) measures such as the provision of social overhead capital (or infrastructure). The empirical estimation of conditional regional economic growth models is however far from easy.

In the framework of regional policy analysis, one of the most important developments has been the construction of conflict analysis models. Such models are no longer based on the assumption of one single objective function. Instead, a whole series of welfare indicators is assumed, for instance, maximization of regional employment, minimization of transportation cost, minimization of pollution, and maximization of economic equality. Such a simultaneous optimization of many objective functions evidently requires adjusted methods, based among others on Pareto-optimality analysis. This implies that any good solution of a conflict decision problem should be located on the efficiency frontier reflecting the conflicts and trade-offs among various objectives.

Such models may adopt two different forms. The first one is a straightforward extension of traditional continuous programming models by including multiple target functions in a programming model. In this respect, many methods have recently been developed to find compromise solutions for conflicting objectives (for instance, based on multiple goal programming analysis, game-theoretic pay-off analysis, ideal point analysis etc.).

The second class of models is concerned with discrete decision models, among others for project and plan evaluation including a limited (finite) set of alternative solutions. Such models are usually called multicriteria models. There is also a great variety in multicriteria analyses (for instance, expected value analysis, goals-achievement analysis, concordance analysis, regime analysis, metagame analysis, etc.). These multicriteria models have played a dominant role in many plan and project evaluation problems in several countries (U.S., France and the Netherlands, for example).

A final remark is still in order: several multiobjective models aiming at finding compromises among conflicting issues are based on weights for the successive objectives. In order to avoid such weighting schemes it is often more convincing to employ interactive decision strategies based on an interplay between analysts and policy-makers. Such learning procedures once more emphasize the process nature of regional and urban planning. Recently, this has also led to an increased popularity of decision support systems, expert systems and computer-graphic systems in the context of urban and regional planning.

The issues of spatial dynamics are also increasingly receiving attention. We are more and more becoming aware of the fact that, by focusing attention on structural changes (e.g., in terms of technology and demography), we are touching some of the key driving forces of spatial dynamics. Much more research however is needed in the field of industrial dynamics (e.g. product cycle theory) and its relation to urban and regional cycles. Also the emergence and perturbations of agglomeration economies has to be given more satisfactory attention. Especially the incubator hypothesis deserves to be tested in a more rigorous manner. Altogether this leads to much more emphasis on micro behavioral research in regional economics. In this context, the structural changes on regional markets in both developed and developing countries (e.g., changes in segmentation, or increase in spatial discrepancies) also have to be mentioned, as the labor market is the dual side of technology development.

Given the foregoing remarks, part 3 of this Handbook has the following components:

- multiple objective decision analysis in regional economics (Chapter 12),
- regional labor market analysis (Chapter 13),
- regional energy and environmental analysis (Chapter 14),
- innovation and changes in regional structure (Chapter 15),
- regional policies in developing countries (Chapter 16).

Chapter 12, written by Peter Nijkamp and Piet Rietveld, focuses attention on the use of multiple objective decision-making in regional planning.

Multiple objectives play a role in many parts of regional and urban analysis and policy-making, at the level of individual decision-makers (choice between alternatives with multiple attributes), at the intraregional level (conflicts between actors such as consumers and firms), at the multiregional level (e.g. conflicts related to the distribution of government subsidies), and at the supraregional level (conflicts between local and central governments). The authors present in this chapter the basic concepts of multiple objective decision analysis, such as efficiency, vector maximization, etc. Various methods used in specifying priorities in the context of conflicting objectives are discussed as well. A review of multiple objective decision methods (both continuous and discrete) is also given. The chapter is concluded with an illustration of the use of multiple objective decision methods in regional economics and a discussion of the prospects in this field.

The second chapter of part 3 is written by Andy Isserman, Carol Taylor, Shelby Gerking and Uwe Schubert. It focuses on recent advances in regional labor market analysis. This analysis entails a synthesis of economic demographic modeling, in which migration, population size, labor force participation and labor supply are simultaneously considered and accompanied by an analysis of the demand side (including wages and unemployment). Given these interdependencies and the spatial context of regional growth, regional labor market analysis draws on concepts and approaches from applied econometrics, macroeconomics, labor economics, and quantitative geography, as well as regional economics and demography. The authors provide a discussion of the theoretical foundations and modeling approaches involved in studying labor force supply, labor force demand, and wage determination. The chapter concludes with a set of observations regarding the proper treatment of labor market conditions within economic models intended for policy analysis.

In Chapter 14 the authors, T. R. Lakshmanan and Roger Bolton, address the issue of regional energy and environmental analysis.

This chapter is a broad, comprehensive survey of theoretical and empirical analyses of the regional aspects of energy and environmental markets and policies. It begins with a review of the special characteristics of energy and environmental resources that require distinctive economic analysis, and the reasons why regional economics is a necessary approach to studying the issues. The special characteristics include regional and interregional externalities, and also spatial immobilities that give rise to economic rents that are unevenly distributed across space and affect the interregional distribution of income.

The chapter reviews the regional implications of varying energy intensity of production and consumption, and the regional implications of optimal policies to deal with physical externalities. It then moves on to a discussion of the regional distribution of energy and environmental rents, including the complications raised by the different locations of energy resources and their owners who receive rents, and by the uneven contributions of energy revenue rents to state, provincial, and local governments' tax bases. The chapter summarizes recent research in Canada and the United States on the effects of energy resources on "fiscal capacity" of regional governments. It then reviews extensively various approaches to modeling the regional effects of energy and environmental policies: regional and interregional input–ouput and econometric models; integrated models of economy, emissions, and natural systems; regional environmental quality models (for example, the Delaware Valley model). It concludes with lessons from past research and suggestions for future work.

Chapter 15 is written by Ed Malecki and Pravin Varaiya. These authors discuss the spatial dynamics in regional structures from the viewpoint of innovation. Their survey begins with the standard approach to technology as a residual factor in regional production functions. Models of capital investment and productivity at the regional level have mainly focused on capital-embodied technology and vintage models. The authors argue that by contrast, recent empirical research has emphasized the heterogeneity of labor and consequent impacts on regional economic specialization. These empirical findings tend to reinforce both cumulative causation models of regional growth and qualitative concerns about innovation as a major variable in regional development.

The final chapter of the Handbook, written by Harry Richardson and Peter Townroe, treats regional policy problems in developing countries. This chapter examines especially the scope for regional policies in developing countries. It starts from the premise that the developed countries' experience is of limited relevance because of differences in demographics, spatial policy objectives and the interregional economic environment. Spatially uneven development can be explained by three alternative approaches, namely, the cumulative causation, radical, and neoclassical models. Each view has different policy implications from the others. In addition, sound policy design has been impeded by both manufacturing and primate city bias. Nevertheless, the urban dimension of regional development remains important.

Four specific aspects of regional policy are then discussed: the role of regional planning agencies and the institutional framework; the impact of infrastructure investment; policies for promoting industrial development in lagging regions; and the importance of communications and human resources investments. The chapter concludes with some observations on the importance of rural planning, the current state of growth pole analysis, and the increasing emphasis in regional development on secondary city strategies.

Altogether it can be concluded that the young history of regional economics has demonstrated an admirable variety of issues and approaches, which is mainly due to its multifaceted and sometimes multidisciplinary-oriented nature. In the next section, attention will be paid to future research issues in this area.

5. Epilogue

The foregoing observations have made clear that quantitative and econometric approaches have been dominating driving forces in regional economics and related disciplines. This orientation has no doubt increased the operational relevance of regional economics, although in various cases a pure "l'art pour l'art" attitude may have been detrimental to further acceptance and advances in this field. In any case, it is plausible to assume that a formal orientation will continue to be a major characteristic of regional economics in the next decades.

The sometimes underrepresented empirical contents of regional science analyses may to a large extent be due to lack of real-world data. In this respect, two complementary directions can be chosen, viz. (i) the design of operational, up-to-date automated information systems (based on spatial referencing) and decision-aid systems (decision support, artificial intelligence, e.g.), and (ii) the development of new adjusted models and techniques which are able to encapsulate inaccurate, qualitative or soft data (based on recent advances in the area of "measuring the unmeasurable"). In this context, it is also necessary to draw more attention to the development of operational econometric and statistical tools for the estimation of non-linear dynamic models incorporating qualitative changes (singularities, bifurcations etc.).

In addition, much more attention than in the past should be paid to micro-behavioral analysis, as it is increasingly realized that the real explanation for spatial processes and spatial dynamics can only be found by means of an analysis of individual motives. In this context, a closer orientation toward spatially-oriented panel and longitudinal studies and dynamic disaggregate choice analysis is a prerequisite. Integrated human activity approaches may then be placed in a new operational framework.

Next, the policy orientation of regional economic theories and methods deserves due attention. Regional economic policy analysis is still an underdeveloped field and is often only a derivative of notions from planning theory and economic policy theory. Conflict analysis, theories on organizational behavior (including X-efficiency), and "satisficer" and "justificer" principles have to be developed in more rigorous manner and to be tested against empirical facts. In this context, various ways have to be chosen:

- the design of appropriate impact assessment methods for regional policy (e.g. the regional responses to national business cycles; the regional impacts of national policies or international trade; the regional consequences of structural changes and their impacts on policy formulation and implementation, etc.).
- the development of integrated theories and methods that are capable of explaining rural–urban dichotomies, the causes and effects of large-scale spatial mobility processes, the changing role of spatial interaction and communica-

tion costs, and the emergence of disequilibrium tendencies in dynamic spatial systems.
- the development of appropriate policy analysis tools that are able to treat efficiency and equity objectives simultaneously, to take into account the institutional barriers in regional policy-making, to clarify the risk of counterproductive actions caused by mutually conflicting competences between various policy institutions, etc.

Clearly, especially in the field of regional policy analysis, further progress is badly needed.

Finally, it may be worthwhile to call attention to certain analytical issues that may be regarded as basic areas of interest of regional economics in the next few years.

First, the drastic demographic changes in most countries will no doubt exert a profound impact on regional labor markets, housing programmes, the use of amenities and of transportation infrastructure. It is foreseeable that the role which is currently being played by technological change in spatial dynamics is likely to be taken over by demographic change in the next decade.

Second, social changes (such as emancipation, segregation etc.) will continue to exert drastic influences on mobility patterns, labor force participation, housing demand and so forth. A long-term view of such phenomena is necessary for regional economic analysis in order to ensure a balance between the new emerging trends on the one hand and the set of available methods and theories for studying them on the other hand.

Besides, the impact of new technology on spatial location and interaction patterns is likely to influence the spatial and social organization of our society in a profound way in the 1990s. This is evidently a rich research field for regional economics.

Finally, structural changes and spatial dynamics take place in an interplay between policy dynamics and individual dynamics. Recent contributions in the area of political science indicate that policy cycles (in terms of "waves" of interest from policy-makers and sometimes of drastic political shifts) are a real phenomenon in a dynamic society, witness the debate on regulation versus deregulation. The same holds true for individual attitudes and behavior. The links between spatial dynamics on the one hand and policy and individual cycles on the other hand would be a promising field of regional economic research.

In conclusion, in the past decades regional economics has rapidly evolved into a mature economic discipline with a strong research orientation and – even better – with a strong research potential.

PART 1

LOCATIONAL ANALYSIS

Chapter 2

THE LOCATION OF PRODUCTION ACTIVITIES

MARTIN J. BECKMANN and JACQUES-FRANÇOIS THISSE

1. Introduction

Among the fundamental economic problems that every society must solve are what, for whom, and how to produce. The question of how includes that of *where*. Thus, managers of firms must make decisions not only about output quantity and the technology of production but also on the locations of plants and of potential markets. The pricing decisions must include the questions of what prices to charge at various locations.

Neoclassical economics has set aside spatial aspects of production and pricing and relegated them to *location theory*. In this chapter we study how classical location theory has treated the major problems connected with the location of production activities. We also try to show how this analysis can be integrated into a more comprehensive neoclassical economic theory.

The locations of production activities are not predetermined but are subject to economic choice. Natural conditions do, however, limit the set of feasible locations for any economic activity. Thus, coal can be mined only where it is available in the ground, but not all known coal deposits are actually mined. Location theory must explain which resource deposits are used and which are not utilized.

In general, availability of resources, location of population as a source of labor and as potential markets, soil, climate and technical conditions rule out many locations for any specific economic activity. What remains is a set of feasible locations among which an economic choice is to be made. *In line with neoclassical economic theory we explain these choices as attempts to maximize profits.*

What are the main problems facing the location theorist? We may try to organize them around the conventional framework of microeconomic theory:
   (a) spatial demand and supply;
   (b) spatial pricing and output;
   (c) locational choice;

Handbook of Regional and Urban Economics, Volume I, Edited by P. Nijkamp
©Elsevier Science Publishers BV, 1986

(d) spatial resource (land) use; and

(e) spatial equilibrium of production.

Of the five themes mentioned, all but spatial resource use will be treated in this chapter. The characteristic spatial resource is of course land, and land use is a central theme of both agricultural and urban economics, to be discussed elsewhere in the companion volume on urban economics.

There is, of course, more agreement among location theorists about which topics to include than where to place them and how to solve them.

The analysis of *spatial supply and demand* revolves around the question: Which demand is satisfied through local production, which through imports, and which will not be satisfied at all? It turns out that some products are made in almost all locations for local consumption only, while some are produced in specialized locations only and shipped over certain distances. In locations beyond critical distances they are not available at all.

When supply sources and markets are given and when the activities of production and transportation can be described fairly well by means of constant technological coefficients, *linear programming models* permit a close look at the interaction of availability and transportability (Section 2.1).

Once the concentration of supply and demand in a finite set of locations is relaxed to allow production and consumption to be spatially dispersed, we have the *continuous flow models* (Section 2.2).

Spatial pricing and output of firms in given locations is at the heart of location theory since it determines the size and shape of market areas of firms, and hence the density and distribution pattern of an industry.

We begin with the analysis of *spatial monopoly* (Section 3.1). More specifically, one deals with the spatial structure of three different price policies, i.e. mill, uniform and (spatial) discriminatory pricing.

The comparison of the above price policies is pursued further in the context of two firms competing to attract customers, i.e. *spatial duopoly* (Section 3.2). The strategic interdependence between firms may generate serious difficulties regarding the existence of a (noncooperative) price equilibrium. This issue is therefore discussed in some details.

Finally, we deal with *spatial oligopoly* in a homogeneous space (Section 3.3). Only the mill pricing case is considered. Three solution concepts are compared, namely Bertrand price equilibrium (competitive oligopoly), Lösch price equilibrium (collusive oligopoly), and Cournot quantity equilibrium.

The focus now shifts to locational choice. Given the location of the markets and of the resource deposits, the problem is to locate a firm with the aim of maximizing its profits.

In the simplest case this is just a question of *transportation cost minimizing* (Section 4.1), the classical Launhardt (1882)–Weber (1909) problem. Although seemingly rather special, this model has proved to be a paradigm capable of extensions and generalizations. One direction is that of network location models in which the transportation system is represented by a topological graph. Another possible extension deals with the use of non-Euclidean metrics.

When sales revenues depend on delivered prices, the Launhardt–Weber model is inadequate. Locational choices must therefore be re-examined in the light of the interaction of profit-maximizing location and price decisions. This is done in the *price – location problem of the spatial monopolist* for the classical price policies studied in 3.1 (Section 4.2).

The issue of *price and location in spatial oligopoly* is a difficult one (Section 4.3). Consumers patronize the firm with the lowest full price, thus generating interdependence in both price and location. The mill pricing case is organized around Hotelling (1929)s paradigm. The analysis of the discriminatory pricing case is more recent and seems promising.

Like microeconomic theory, location theory culminates in the study of *spatial equilibrium*, both partial and general. As so often, general equilibrium theory is more of a pious wish than a reality, and the focus has been on the equilibrium of production for a single industry, partial equilibrium analysis: *market solution* (Section 5.1).

The classical model is that of Lösch (1940) anticipated in important ways by Palander (1935). These authors have translated the paradigm of monopolistic competition into a spatial context. This means the study of the spatial configurations that emerge as market equilibrium under free entry in the long run. The modern approach has paid closer attention to the entry processes and has thus elevated this theory from comparative statics to dynamics.

Besides the market solution, *planning* must be considered (Section 5.2). In the homogeneous space case, this is the famous Christaller (1933)–Lösch (1940) problem dealing with the optimality of the hexagonal arrangement of producers. The heterogeneous space case which is the relevant one for operations research has given rise to the location–allocation models.

We conclude this chapter by some remarks about uncovered topics.

This outline is summarized in the following schematic table of contents. In agreement with general economic theory we define time periods in location theory as follows.

Short run: All plants are in place. Prices may still be chosen, and hence output and market areas are to be determined.

Spatial supply and demand
2.1. Linear programming models of location
2.2. Continuous flow models of location
Spatial pricing and output
3.1. Spatial monopoly
3.2. Spatial duopoly
3.3. Spatial oligopoly
Medium run: Existing plants may expand or contract capacities. They may relocate. Also a single new plant may choose its location.

Locational choice
4.1. Transportation cost minimization
4.2. The price–location problem in spatial monopoly
4.3. The price–location problem in spatial oligopoly
Long run: Firms may enter or leave markets by setting up new plants or abandoning existing plants. Not only the location but also the number or density of firms is variable.
Spatial equilibrium of production
5.1. Market solution
5.2. Planning solution

Regarding further historical detail on location theory, the reader is referred to the excellent and painstaking *History of spatial economic theory* by Ponsard (1983).

2. Spatial supply and demand

2.1. Linear programming models of location

In the short run, when plants, supply sources and markets are given, one faces bottlenecks such as the capacities of plants, and limitations on the rate of supply from various resource deposits and on the quantities of product that can be disposed of in each market.

In the simplest case, the problem is to determine how the production of a given commodity is spatially distributed within given capacity limits in order to minimize costs.

Let $S = \{1, \ldots, n\}$ be a finite space. Let k_i denote short-run capacity of location $i = 1, \ldots, n$; if no capacity is available at i, then k_i equals zero. Denote q_i the actual production in location i and $\boldsymbol{q}$ the vector (q_i). Obviously we must have

$$0 \leq q_i \leq k_i, \qquad i = 1, \ldots, n. \tag{2.1}$$

The requirement (or demand) for the commodity is δ_j in location $j = 1, \ldots, n$. If no demand occurs at j, then δ_j is set equal to zero. Furthermore, these requirements are feasible if and only if the total demand does not exceed the combined production capacities, i.e.

$$\sum_{j=1}^{n} \delta_j \leq \sum_{i=1}^{n} k_i. \tag{2.2}$$

(The model does not tell us how to ration demand when (2.2) is violated.

However, one may consider a proportional reduction of each demand by an appropriate factor; or one may eliminate those demands that generate the highest transportation costs.)

The central unknown is the *shipment of commodity* from i to j, denoted q_{ij}; let $\mathbf{Q}$ be the matrix $[q_{ij}]$. All the output q_i is distributed among the locations $j = 1, \ldots, n$ (with $q_{ij} \geq 0$) so that

$$q_i = \sum_{j=1}^{n} q_{ij}, \qquad i = 1, \ldots, n. \tag{2.3}$$

In consequence, the capacity constraints imply that

$$\sum_{j=1}^{n} q_{ij} \leq k_i, \qquad i = 1, \ldots, n. \tag{2.4}$$

Furthermore, to meet the consumption requirements, one has

$$\sum_{i=1}^{n} q_{ij} \geq \delta_j, \qquad j = 1, \ldots, n. \tag{2.5}$$

Let t_{ij} denote the transportation cost per unit of the commodity shipped from i to j. Total transportation costs are then

$$T(\mathbf{Q}) = \sum_{i=1}^{n} \sum_{j=1}^{n} t_{ij} q_{ij}. \tag{2.6}$$

On the assumption that production costs are equal everywhere, that is, independent of production locations, the short-run location problem reduces to one of minimizing total transportation costs (2.6) subject to (2.4), (2.5) and the non-negativity constraints $q_{ij} \geq 0$. This is the well-known *transportation problem* [see Hitchcock (1941), Kantorovich (1942), Koopmans (1949)].

From the optimal solution, q_{ij}^*, the location of production, q_i^*, is inferred by means of (2.3). Notice that when total requirements and total capacities match exactly, the location problem becomes trivial: $q_i^* = k_i$ for $i = 1, \ldots, n$. A true location problem arises only in the presence of excess capacity.

The equilibrium conditions of Koopmans give necessary and sufficient conditions for an optimal solution to the transportation problem [see Koopmans and Reiter (1951), Dorfman et al. (1958)]. More precisely, prices λ_i and λ_j, the dual variables of the linear program, are generated such that efficient shipments are just profitable while inefficient ones incur losses:

$$q_{ij}^* \left\{ {= \atop \geq} \right\} 0 \quad \text{if and only if} \quad \lambda_j - \lambda_i \left\{ {\leq \atop =} \right\} t_{ij}, \qquad i, j = 1, \ldots, n; \qquad (2.7)$$

and such that

$$0 \leq q_i^* \left\{ {= k_i \atop {\leq k_i \atop = 0}} \right\} \quad \text{if and only if} \quad \lambda_i \left\{ {> \atop {= \atop <}} \right\} 0, \qquad i = 1, \ldots, n, \qquad (2.8)$$

which reveals "favorable" production locations as those commanding high market prices λ_i. In the excess capacity case, locations where capacities are underutilized draw commodity prices of zero, while uneconomical locations where capacities go completely unused have negatives prices; moreover, these prices are unique.

The optimal solution to the transportation problem may also be interpreted as defining sets of market and supply areas. The *market area* of a production location i is the set of demand locations j supplied from i. A demand location buying from i only is in that supplier's market area, while the presence of multiple suppliers means that this demand location lies on the "boundaries" of those suppliers' market areas. Indeed, the equilibrium conditions imply that the full prices $\lambda_i + t_{ij}$ at demand location j are equal among its active suppliers i.

Conversely, the *supply area* of a market location j is the set of production locations i from which it receives shipments. If a supply source i sells in several market locations j, then the received price $\lambda_j - t_{ij}$ is equal for all these j.

Furthermore, it is immediate that

Proposition 1

In every optimal solution to the transportation problem, the shipment of the commodity between any two different sites of S goes at most in one direction.

In other words, cross-hauling is always inefficient.

Transportation cost satisfies the triangle inequality when

$$t_{ij} \leq t_{ik} + t_{kj}, \qquad i, j, k = 1, \ldots, n. \qquad (2.9)$$

Then we easily obtain

Proposition 2

If the triangle inequality holds, then there exists an optimal solution to the transportation problem such that locations which import do not export and vice versa.

Production costs c_i are relevant only when they vary with location i. The solution to the short-run location problem is no longer purely transportation oriented but will be also production factor oriented. The object is now to minimize the sum of production and transportation costs, i.e.

$$C(\boldsymbol{q}, \boldsymbol{Q}) = \sum_{i=1}^{n} c_i q_i + \sum_{i=1}^{n} \sum_{j=1}^{n} t_{ij} q_{ij}. \tag{2.10}$$

The equilibrium conditions (2.7) still hold but conditions (2.8) are replaced by

$$0 \le q_i^* \begin{cases} = k_i \\ \le k_i \\ = 0 \end{cases} \quad \text{if and only if} \quad \lambda_i \begin{cases} > \\ = \\ < \end{cases} c_i, \quad i = 1, \dots, n \tag{2.11}$$

[see Beckmann and Marschak (1955)].

The linear programming approach to location theory is readily extended to several commodities, and to production from resources and labor with input coefficients and explicit recognition of constraints imposed by local resource availabilities [see Beckmann and Marschak (1955), Isard (1958), Stevens (1958)]. Moreover, transportation may itself be modelled as a service produced from resources and labor [see Beckmann and Marschak (1955)].

Also, nonlinear demand and cost functions can be introduced, generating a *nonlinear programming* model of spatial market equilibrium and of the location problem in the short run [see, e.g. Samuelson (1952), Takayama and Judge (1971), Mougeot (1975)]. These details are beyond the scope of this chapter and are the subject of Chapter 5 in this Handbook.

Finally, the long-run location problem requires in general the introduction of zero–one variables which change the character of the programming model to one of *integer programming* (cf. 5.2.2).

2.2. *Continuous flow models of location*

The linear programming models of Section 2.1 suppose finite sets of production and consumption places. It is natural to ask what happens when production and consumption activities are allowed to be distributed continuously in a two-dimensional space. This is the starting point of the continuous flow modelling approach in spatial economics, in particular the *continuous transportation problem* [see Kantorovich (1942), Beckmann (1952, 1953)].

Let S be a compact region of the plane, the boundary of which is formed by a finite number of smooth arcs. At location $x \in S$ the capacity of production has density of $k(x)$ units of commodity per unit area. Let $q(x)$ denote the density of production in location x. This output density is limited by local capacity:

$$0 \le q(x) \le k(x), \qquad x \in S. \tag{2.12}$$

The local demand (or requirement) for the commodity in location x has a density of $\delta(x)$. As in 2.1, we consider the case of a closed economy. In consequence, we have the feasibility constraint [cf. (2.2)]:

$$\iint_S \delta(x)\,dx \le \iint_S k(x)\,dx. \tag{2.13}$$

Consider now the *flow of commodity* through location x. Denote it by a vector $\phi(x)$ whose direction is that of the shipment and whose length is the density of the flow. The net of local production and consumption at x, i.e. $q(x) - \delta(x)$, is the surplus that must be removed when positive or absorbed when negative. The flow ϕ is therefore augmented or diminished by local surplus according to the "divergence law":

$$\operatorname{div}\phi(x) = q(x) - \delta(x), \qquad x \in S, \tag{2.14}$$

where

$$\operatorname{div}\phi(x) = \frac{\partial \phi^1}{\partial x^1} + \frac{\partial \phi^2}{\partial x^2}.$$

In other words, the net outflow from a cell of small size equals the net surplus added to the commodity stream in this cell. Since no flow can cross the boundary ∂S of S, we have the boundary conditions

$$\phi_n(x) = 0, \qquad x \in \partial S, \tag{2.15}$$

where $\phi_n(x)$ denotes the flow vector normal to ∂S at x.

The cost of moving one unit of commodity in any direction at location S is $t(x)$ per unit weight and distance. Total transportation costs are then defined as

$$T(\phi) = \iint_S t(x)|\phi(x)|\,dx. \tag{2.16}$$

The question now is how under these circumstances production will be distributed over S so as to minimize costs. In the absence of differential production costs, this amounts to determining the field of vectors $\phi(x)$ minimizing (2.16) subject to the constraints (2.12), (2.14), and (2.15).

This is a *calculus of variation problem* representing the continuous counterpart of the transportation problem in linear programming. Applying the first-order conditions, known here as the Euler–Lagrange equations, yields the following results [see Beckmann (1952), Beckmann and Puu (1985)]: There exists $\lambda(x)$, the adjoint variable associated with (2.14), such that

(i) the optimal flow $\phi^*(x)$ satisfies

$$t(x)\frac{\phi^*(x)}{|\phi^*(x)|} = \operatorname{grad}\lambda(x), \quad \text{when }\phi^*(x) \neq 0$$

$$t(x) \geq |\operatorname{grad}\lambda(x)|, \quad \text{when }\phi^*(x) = 0. \tag{2.17}$$

Interpreting $\lambda(x)$ as the price of the commodity at location x, (2.17) states that gains from interlocal trade are at best equal to transportation costs [cf. (2.7)]. When flow is positive, commodity is shipped in the direction of steepest price increase and price increases with accumulated transportation costs;

(ii) the optimal output density $q^*(x)$ satisfies

$$0 \leq q^*(x) \begin{cases} = k(x) \\ \leq k(x) \\ = 0 \end{cases} \quad \text{if } \lambda(x) \begin{cases} > \\ = \\ < \end{cases} \quad 0. \tag{2.18}$$

This means that production takes place wherever a positive price is paid and then it is realized at the maximum rate [cf. (2.11)].

More importantly, locations exist where the optimal flow has more than one direction; let us call them *singularities*. (Notice that the singularities define a zero measure set.) To give a simple interpretation of these points, we assume that freight rates $t(x)$ are independent of location. Then, there are two types of point singularity: the *sinks* where $\lambda(x)$ has a local maximum and the *sources* where $\lambda(x)$ has a local minimum. Economically, this means that a sink is the destination of inward flows and, therefore, the center of a market area; conversely, a source is the origin of outward flows and, therefore, the center of a supply area. Thus, even when production capacity and demand are continuously but irregularly distributed, the result of market forces is *a system of market and supply areas, organized around some "agglomerations"* – the atoms of the consumption and production distributions [see Beckmann and Puu (1985) for more details].

As before, when production costs $c(x)$ depend on location, the minimum of total cost yields the modified efficiency conditions:

$$0 \leq q^*(x) \begin{cases} = k(x) \\ \leq k(x) \\ = 0 \end{cases} \quad \text{when } \lambda(x) \begin{cases} > \\ = \\ < \end{cases} c(x). \tag{2.19}$$

Observe that no statement is made about the dependence of costs on location.

The continuous flow approach may be further developed to include several commodities, alternative metrics for distance, general production and utility functions, and endogenous transportation rates [see Beckmann and Puu (1985), Puu (1983) and Chapters 6 and 9 of this Handbook].

3. Spatial pricing and output

3.1. Spatial monopoly

We first consider a firm, whose market is spatially separated from markets of other firms: *spatial monopoly*. (Notice that spatial monopoly can exist even in the presence of many, but spatially isolated firms when potential market areas do not touch or overlap.)

Consider a one-dimensional economy. A single firm producing a given commodity is located at the origin. Consumers are continuously distributed over the positive half-line. The density ρ may depend on location x, i.e. distance from the firm. (Notice that the results of this section remain valid in a two-dimensional economy without any assumption of symmetry: $\rho(x)$ is then to be interpreted as the density of all consumers located in the plane at a distance x from the firm.)

When consumers ship the commodity from the supplier on their own, the resulting price policy is *mill pricing*. In this case, the full price for a consumer at a distance x, $p(x)$, is then equal to a mill price, p_M, the same for all consumers irrespective of their locations, plus transportation cost, $t(x)$: $p(x) = p_M + t(x)$.

When the firm also supplies transportation two further possibilities arise. First, *uniform pricing*, which means that consumers pay the same delivered price, p_U, regardless of distance, but ordinarily the firm may refuse to ship beyond a certain maximal range (rationing): $p(x) = p_U$. Second, (spatial) *discriminatory pricing* in which prices $p_D(x)$ are set for each location so as to maximize profits: $p(x) = p_D(x)$.

Location theory has traditionally operated with linear and identical demand curves. [See Long (1971), however, for a critique of this assumption.] This permits a straightforward analysis of the effects of price policy on prices charged, prices paid, output, market radius, profits and welfare. The demand function of a consumer may be standardized by choosing price and quantity units appropriately:

$$q(x) = 1 - p(x), \tag{3.1}$$

where $p(x)$ is the full price paid by customers at distance x.

We also suppose that transportation costs increase proportionally with distance:

$$t(x) = tx. \tag{3.2}$$

This is considered the standard case and the one usually assumed in location theory. The proportionality factor is needed to study the effect of changes in freight rates.

Finally, production of the commodity entails constant marginal cost:

$$C(q) = cq, \quad \text{with } c > 0, \tag{3.3}$$

where q denotes the monopolist's output.

3.1.1. Given market area

Let R be the market radius which we assume to be fixed at first. (In 3.1.2 we allow it to be variable and to be determined at the profit-maximizing solution.) In other words, we suppose that R is small enough for the whole market to be served at the profit-maximizing solution.

Profits G are defined as follows:

$$G = \int_0^R [p(x) - c - tx][1 - p(x)] \rho(x) \, dx. \tag{3.4}$$

To simplify notation, we set

$$A = \int_0^R \rho(x) \, dx, \tag{3.5}$$

i.e. total population served and

$$\bar{x} = \frac{\int_0^R x \rho(x) \, dx}{\int_0^R \rho(x) \, dx}, \tag{3.6}$$

i.e. average distance.

Under mill pricing, $p(x) = p_M + tx$ and profits (3.4) are given by

$$G_M = (p_M - c) q_M$$

where q_M, the output, is equal to $(1 - p_M - t\bar{x})A$.

Similarly, under uniform pricing, $p(x) = p_U$ so that (3.4) becomes

$$G_U = (p_U - c - t\bar{x})q_U,$$

where $q_U = (1 - p_U)A$.

Finally, under discriminatory pricing, $p(x) = p_D(x)$ and profits are

$$G_D = \int_0^R [p_D(x) - c - tx][1 - p_D(x)]\rho(x)\,dx.$$

The first-order conditions for the optimal mill and uniform prices, p_M^* and p_U^*, show that

$$p_M^* = \tfrac{1}{2}(1 + c - t\bar{x}), \tag{3.7}$$

$$p_U^* = \tfrac{1}{2}(1 + c + t\bar{x}). \tag{3.8}$$

The second-order conditions are trivially satisfied. Notice that

$$p_U^* - p_M^* = t\bar{x}, \tag{3.9}$$

i.e. the difference between uniform and mill prices is just equal to the average transportation cost. This implies that consumers located within (beyond) $\bar{x}$ are better off (worse off) under mill pricing than under uniform pricing.

Maximizing G_D yields the optimal discriminatory price

$$p_D^*(x) = \tfrac{1}{2}(1 + c + tx). \tag{3.10}$$

Thus the discriminatory pricer will absorb half the transportation cost [see Singer (1937)]. This implies that customers have no incentive to retrade among themselves. Notice also that

$$p_D^*(x) = \tfrac{1}{2}(p_M^* + tx + p_U^*),$$

that is, the price paid under discriminatory pricing is the average of prices paid under mill and uniform pricing. From this and (3.9), it follows that the average full price is equal under the three pricing strategies.

Introducing the optimal prices, given by (3.7), (3.8) and (3.10) into q_M, q_U and $q_D = \int_0^R [1 - p_D(x)]\rho(x)\,dx$ respectively shows that the output is the same under all prices systems:

$$q_M^* = q_U^* = q_D^* = \tfrac{1}{2}A(1 - c - t\bar{x}).$$

Furthermore, comparing G_M and G_U at the optimum, we immediately see that *mill and uniform pricing are equally profitable*, while *discriminatory pricing is more profitable* since the monopolist charges the profit-maximizing price on each local market. The amount by which profit under discriminatory pricing exceeds the profit under mill or uniform pricing depends on the density ρ and on the market size R.

Finally, it may also be shown that mill pricing is best, discriminatory pricing intermediate, and uniform pricing worst in regard to the following measures of social efficiency: total transportation cost, aggregate consumer expenditure, average full price per commodity unit, consumers' surplus and social surplus, i.e. the sum of consumers' surplus and profits [see Beckmann (1976)].

It is worth noting that the above results are independent of the form of the consumer density and remain valid for any marginal production cost increasing with output.

3.1.2. Variable market area

Let now the market radius R itself be subject to the supplier's choice.

Under mill pricing it is easy to see that the optimal radius is the maximal radius at which consumers will buy the product, when prices are calculated as before:

$$R_M = \frac{1 - p_M}{t}.$$

Under uniform pricing the firm will not ship beyond the distance at which the price covers marginal production cost plus transportation cost:

$$R_U = \frac{p_U - c}{t}.$$

Using (3.7) and (3.8) it is easily seen that the two radii are the same and equal to the smallest solution of

$$R = \frac{1}{2t} \left[1 - c + t\bar{x}(R) \right]. \tag{3.11}$$

The comparisons made in 3.1.1, therefore, can be extended to the case of variable market radius. [See Hsu (1983) for a direct argument.]

A discriminating monopolist will ship to the distance where the discriminatory price reduces quantities demanded to zero:

$$R_D = \frac{1 - c}{t}. \tag{3.12}$$

Comparing (3.10) and (3.11) shows that the optimal market radius under discriminatory pricing is larger than the common optimal market radius under mill and uniform pricing. Indeed, $R_M = R_U < R_D$ if $t\bar{x} < 1 - c$. Now $\bar{x} < (1 - c)/t$ in view of its definition (3.6), since even at prices the firm cannot sell beyond distance $(1 - c)/t$ [see also Phlips (1983)]. As an example consider the case of a uniform density in a two-dimensional market. Using polar coordinates, we thus have

$$\rho(x) = 2\pi x.$$

A straightforward calculation shows that $\bar{x}(R) = \frac{2}{3}R$. Hence, given (3.11)

$$R_M^* = R_U^* = \frac{3}{4}\frac{1-c}{t}$$

and

$$R_D^* = \frac{1-c}{t}.$$

Because of the larger market radius, output and average price per customer under discriminatory pricing are larger than under mill or uniform pricing [see also Greenhut and Ohta (1972)].

Consequently we have obtained:

Proposition 3

Assume linear demand and constant marginal costs. Then, regardless of the shape of the consumer density, the optimal market radius, output and profit under discriminatory pricing are larger than the common optimal market radius, output and profit under mill and uniform pricing.

Finally, since market areas are different, a comparison of welfare is possible only when the density of consumers is specified. For example, in the case of a uniform density, *discriminatory pricing turns out to yield a lower consumer surplus but a higher social surplus than mill pricing*, contrary to general beliefs about the social superiority of mill pricing [see Holahan (1975)]. Clearly, the reason for this difference with the results obtained in 3.1.1 is that the discriminatory pricer serves more consumers than the mill pricer.

We now briefly discuss the impact of a change in the freight rate on the monopoly solution. An important result, due originally to Launhardt (1885) and known as the neutrality of freight rate property, is as follows: The profit maximizing mill price does not depend on t provided that the market radius may be chosen and consumer density is a power function of distance. (In particular, this holds when consumers are evenly distributed.) Recently, Ohta (1984) has extended Launhardt's result to a uniform pricer and shown that it is true regardless of the demand function (which is still assumed to be the same for all customers).

Nevertheless, for other distributions of consumers, the effect of the freight rate on spatial monopoly pricing is decisive. Moreover, as shown by Hsu (1983), a change in t has opposite impacts on mill pricing and uniform pricing (see also (3.7) and (3.8)). Thus, in the case of a negative exponential density, a reduction in freight rate causes the mill price to rise and the uniform price to fall [see Heffley (1980) and Ohta and Okamura (1984)]. This means that, contrary to wide-spread opinion, *cost-reducing technical progress in transport may generate perverse effects on market price*. Notice, however, that at least in the linear demand case the rise in the mill price is more than offset by the fall in the freight paid by the average consumer so that the average full price still decreases.

Furthermore, the impact of a lower freight rate on output is ambiguous: it implies a larger output if and only if the elasticity of $\bar{x}$ with respect to t is less than unity. The effect on consumer surplus similarly depends on the elasticity of $\bar{x}$, but changes with the price policy. On the other hand, a fall in t always yields higher profits. [See Hsu (1983) for more details.]

Notice also that the optimal discriminatory price schedule is independent of the consumer density [see (3.10)]. On the other hand, it does depend on t: the lower the freight rate, the lower the price at location x. This implies that output, consumers' surplus and profit increase when the transportation rate decreases.

3.1.3. Three extensions of the basic model

Until now, the freight rate has been considered as being independent of the parties who must physically do the transport of the commodity. We now assume that the consumers and the firm have access to different transportation technologies and we allow the corresponding rates, t_C and t_F, to be different. It should be clear that the firm is no longer indifferent to mill or uniform pricing. If $t_C < t_F$, say, then the spatial monopolist will find it more profitable to follow mill pricing. Furthermore, as shown by Gronberg and Meyer (1981), *it is not necessarily optimal for the firm to price discriminate when $t_C < t_F$*. Indeed, for t_C sufficiently smaller than t_F, the profit-maximizing policy is mill pricing. Moreover, under these circumstances, the social superiority of discriminatory pricing vis-à-vis mill pricing, noted in 3.1.2, may be reversed.

Another extension of the standard model, recently considered by Furlong and Slotsve (1983), is *when customers are offered a choice between pick-up and delivery*. This implies that nearby customers will choose pick-up, while more distant customers will opt for delivery. The respective mill and uniform prices are each greater than their single price regime counterparts. Furthermore, the so-obtained market radius is larger than the common radius under mill and uniform pricing, but smaller than the market radius under discriminatory pricing. A similar ranking is obtained for profits. More surprising is the fact that consumers' surplus under pick-up or delivery is lower than consumers' surplus under discriminatory pricing.

Finally, *spatial nonlinear pricing* has been studied by Spulber (1981). Customers are endowed with a quadratic utility function $u(q)$ and choose the amount $q^*(r)$ of commodity which maximizes $u(q) - trq - qp(q)$, where $p(q)$ now denotes the marginal price schedule at the mill, i.e. the price a customer must pay to buy a $(q+1)$th unit of the commodity. (Notice that $p(q)$ constant implies mill pricing and a linear demand function.) It is first shown that the market radius under nonlinear pricing is smaller than the radius under discriminatory pricing. Furthermore, the relative levels of output, profits and customers' surplus depend on the type of customer distribution. More specifically, when the consumer density is a power function of distance, output, profits and consumer surplus under nonlinear pricing are greater than, equal to or less than the corresponding magnitudes under discriminatory pricing when the density is decreasing, constant or increasing in distance.

3.1.4. Nonlinear demands

Results for nonlinear demand functions, $q(x) = f[p(x)]$, are meager. Let the market radius be given. First, Smithies (1941a) has shown that the discriminatory pricer will never absorb freight to the extent of charging uniform or decreasing delivered prices. Second, the indifference to mill or uniform pricing does no longer hold. When demand functions are convex (concave) an argument using Jensen's inequality shows that mill pricing is more (less) profitable than uniform pricing [see Smithies (1941a), Stevens and Rydell (1966)]. Third, average transportation cost per unit sold is lower under mill pricing than under uniform pricing [see Beckmann (1985)]. Comparisons of other economic variables (such as output and welfare) have not been made. They would require additional assumptions on demands.

Of course, for special demand functions results are readily obtained. Thus, when the demand function is exponential, the optimal mill price patterns under spatial discrimination equal cost plus a fixed mark-up. In this case, it is not profitable for the firm to price discriminate. However, for demands less convex than a negative exponential function, discriminatory pricing still yields higher profits [Smithies (1941a)] and, probably, larger output.

3.2. Spatial duopoly

Let us suppose that two firms located at given points compete in price to attract customers dispersed over space. More precisely, consumers consider the possibility of buying from both sellers, which implies that the sales of a firm depend not only upon its own price but also upon the price set by its competitor. The corresponding market process is therefore modelled as a noncooperative game.

Formally, assume that two sellers $i = 1, 2$ of a homogeneous product are located on a bounded line of length l at respective distances a and b from the endpoints of this line ($a + b \leq l$; $a \geq 0$ and $b \geq 0$). The marginal production cost, c, is constant and the same for both firms. Transportation costs are linear in distance; let t be the transportation rate. Consumers are uniformly distributed along the line; without loss of generality the density is chosen equal to one. Each consumer buys exactly a single unit of the product irrespective of its price. Since the product is homogeneous, a consumer will patronize the seller with the lower full price.

The market solution of the *spatial duopoly* problem crucially depends on the price policy used by the competing firms.

3.2.1. Mill pricing

Let p_1 and p_2 be the mill prices charged by firms 1 and 2 respectively.

Given $\bar{p}_2$, the demand to firm 1, $D_1(p_1, \bar{p}_2)$, may be constructed as follows. First, if $p_1 < \bar{p}_2 - t(l - a - b)$, then the full price of firm 1 is everywhere smaller than that of firm 2 and all customers patronize seller 1:

$$D_1(p_1, \bar{p}_2) = l.$$

Second, if $\bar{p}_2 - t(l - a - b) \leq p_1 \leq \bar{p}_2 + t(l - a - b)$, then the market boundary lies at the point between the firms where the full prices are equal, i.e. at a distance $\hat{R}$ from firm 1 given by $\hat{R} = (\bar{p}_2 - p_1 + t(l - a - b))/2t$. Consequently,

$$D_1(p_1, \bar{p}_2) = a + \frac{\bar{p}_2 - p_1 + t(l - a - b)}{2t}.$$

Third, and last, if $p_1 > \bar{p}_2 + t(l - a - b)$, then the full price of firm 1 is everywhere greater than that of firm 2 so that all consumers buy from seller 2:

$$D_1(p_1, \bar{p}_2) = 0.$$

Thus the demand curve $D_1(p_1, \bar{p}_2)$, depicted in Figure 3.1, has two discontinuities which appear at the prices where a bunch of customers – those located in the hinterlands – are indifferent between the two sellers. The demand to firm 2 is similar since $D_2 = l - D_1$.

Finally, let the profit of firm i be given by $G_i = (p_i - c)D_i(p_1, p_2)$. In general G_i depends on both prices p_1 and p_2.

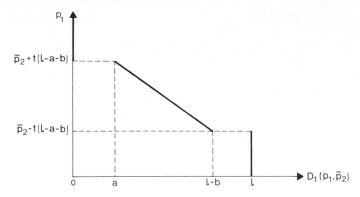

Figure 3.1. Firm 1's demand.

This is a price duopoly problem, as originally formulated by Hotelling (1929). From a modern point of view, it is a noncooperative two-person game in which players are firms 1 and 2, strategies are prices p_1 and p_2, and payoffs are profits G_1 and G_2. A *mill price equilibrium* is then a pair (p_1^*, p_2^*) such that, given the price p_j^* of firm j, firm $i \neq j$ maximizes its profits at p_i^*.

Proposition 4

Assume that firms 1 and 2 set mill prices. For $a = l - b$, the unique price equilibrium is given by $p_1^* = p_2^* = c$. For $a \neq l - b$, there is a price equilibrium if and only if

$$\left(l + \frac{a-b}{3}\right)^2 \geq \frac{4}{3}l(a + 2b) \tag{3.13}$$

and

$$\left(l + \frac{b-a}{3}\right)^2 \geq \frac{4}{3}l(b + 2a) \tag{3.14}$$

and, whenever it exists, the price equilibrium is unique and given by

$$p_1^* = c + t\left(l + \frac{a-b}{3}\right), \qquad p_2^* = c + t\left(l + \frac{b-a}{3}\right). \tag{3.15}$$

This result, due to d'Aspremont et al. (1979), provides a complete characterization of the locations for which a price equilibrium exists: firms must be located at the same point or sufficiently far apart. (In particular, when they are symmetrically located ($a = b$), the existence conditions (3.13) and (3.14) state that both firms must be established outside the quartiles.) In contrast, *when firms are close but separated, mill price competition results in indefinitely fluctuating prices.* (Notice, however, that an equilibrium in mixed strategies exists [see Dasgupta and Maskin (1986)].) This invalidates Hotelling's (1929) belief that spatial differentiation yields stability.

Notice also that existence is not restored simply by eliminating discontinuities in the demand functions. Jaskold Gabszewicz and Thisse (1986) have provided an example which has continuous demands but does not possess a price equilibrium.

Finally, as shown by MacLeod (1985), introducing more general demand functions (instead of a perfectly inelastic demand as supposed above) does not solve the existence problem.

For a more detailed discussion of Hotelling's problem, the reader is referred to Graitson (1982).

3.2.2. Uniform pricing

Let p^1 and p^2 be the uniform prices set by firms 1 and 2 respectively. Let us describe the market area $A^1(p^1, p^2)$ of firm 1 contingent to price $\bar{p}^2$ for firm 2. For simplicity in exposition, we suppose that $\bar{p}^2 > \text{Max}\{tb, t(l - b)\}$, i.e. firm 2 is able to supply all customers at price $\bar{p}^2$. First, if $p^1 < \bar{p}^2$, then all customers for which production plus transportation costs from firm 1 are covered by p^1, are served by firm 1:

$$A^1(p^1, \bar{p}^2) = \left[a - \text{Min}\left\{ \frac{p^1 - c}{t}, a \right\}, a + \text{Min}\left\{ \frac{p^1 - c}{t}, l - a \right\} \right].$$

Second, if $p^1 = \bar{p}^2$, then all consumers are indifferent between firms 1 and 2. By convention, consumers are assigned to the nearest firm. Thus

$$A^1(p^1, \bar{p}^2) = \left[0, \frac{l + a - b}{2} \right].$$

(When $b = l - a$, it is supposed that the two firms equally share the market.) Third, if $p^1 > \bar{p}^2$, then firm 1 has no customers so that

$$A^1(p^1, \bar{p}^2) = \varnothing.$$

The corresponding sales function is given by the size of the market area: $S^1(p^1, \bar{p}^2) = \mu[A^1(p^1, \bar{p}^2)]$, where μ is the Lebesgue measure on $[0, l]$. An exam-

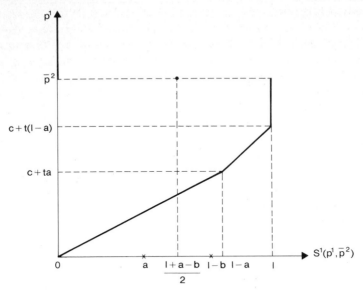

Figure 3.2. Firm 1's sales.

ple of sales function is represented in Figure 3.2 when $a < b$. We immediately notice, that over $[0, c + t(l - a)]$, $S^1(p^1, \bar{p}^2)$ *increases* in p^1. The reason for this is to be found in the fact that, for $p^1 < c + t(l - a)$, the market area expands, and therefore sales rise, when p^1 increases. Furthermore, at $p^1 = \bar{p}^2$, $S^1(p^1, \bar{p}^2)$ is discontinuous.

In the above setting, a *uniform price equilibrium* is a pair (p^{1*}, p^{2*}) such that, given the price p^{j*} of firm j, firm $i \neq j$ maximizes its profit $G^i = \int_{A^i(p^i, p^{j*})}(p^i - c - t|x_i - x|)\,\mathrm{d}x$, with $x_1 = a$ and $x_2 = l - b$, at p^{i*}.

Proposition 5

Assume that firms 1 and 2 set uniform prices. Then there exists no price equilibrium.

The proof is given in the appendix.

This is an illustration of the Bertrand–Edgeworth phenomenon, i.e. the non-existence of a price equilibrium, without assuming capacity constraints. However, when consumers have price-sensitive demands, a price equilibrium exists when firms are sufficiently distant for their market areas at the monopoly prices not to overlap. If not, we necessarily have instability. A detailed description of the corresponding price cycle, when demand is linear, is given by Schuler and Hobbs (1982).

3.2.3. Discriminatory pricing

Under mill or uniform pricing firms compete on the whole market by means of a single strategic variable. By contrast, under (spatial) discriminatory pricing, firms compete on each local market separately and, therefore, control a large number of independent strategic variables. This implies that competition between discriminatory pricers is much less constrained than competition between mill or uniform pricers. In consequence, the stability of price competition appears less problematic than above.

Let x be any location such that $0 \leq x \leq l$ and denote by $p_1(x)$ and $p_2(x)$ the delivered prices at x set by firms 1 and 2 respectively. On this specific market, both firms are in a Bertrand-like situation, i.e. they undercut each other with the aim of capturing customers at x. However, unlike Bertrand's, for $x \neq (l + a - b)/2$ this price war takes place under asymmetric cost conditions. Indeed, when $x < (l + a - b)/2$, the cost of supplying x from firm 1 is lower than the cost of supplying from firm 2, and conversely when $x > (l + a - b)/2$. This implies that the most distant firm from x must stop undercutting when its delivered price reaches the level of its marginal cost of production plus transportation cost to x. In contrast, the firm nearest to x can still undercut its competitor and, hence, can guarantee to itself the market at x. Assuming (by convention) that consumers are supplied from the nearest firm in the case of a tie, the equilibrium prices at x are therefore equal to the production and transportation costs from the most distant firm. Accordingly, we have:

Proposition 6

Assume that firms 1 and 2 set (spatial) discriminatory prices. Then, at each point x, there exists a price equilibrium schedule given by

$$p_1^*(x) = p_2^*(x) = \text{Max}\{c + t|x - a|, \, c + t|x - l + b|\} \tag{3.16}$$

and this equilibrium is unique.

This result was first suggested by Hoover (1937), and formally proved much later by Hurter and Lederer (1985) and Lederer and Hurter (1986) [see also Beckmann (1968, p. 34)]. It means two things. First, an equilibrium exists under (spatial) discriminatory pricing whatever the firms' locations. Thus, contrary to general beliefs, *spatial price discrimination is not a priori evidence of a lack of competition*. [See also Norman (1983) who reaches similar conclusions when oligopolists produce differentiated products.] Moreover, it is worth noting that the existence property can be generalized to the case of any price-sensitive demand function. Second, the equilibrium price pattern has different configura-

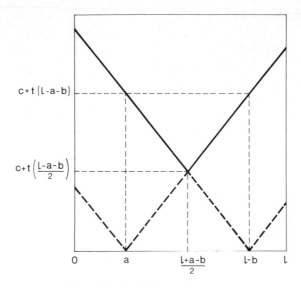

Figure 3.3. Equilibrium price pattern.

tions, depending upon firms' locations. More specifically, when they are located together ($a = l - b$), firms charge delivered prices equal to marginal cost of production plus transportation costs which are therefore increasing in distance. On the other hand, when they are separated ($a \neq l - b$), prices increase with distance in the hinterlands ($0 \leq x \leq a$ and $l - b \leq x \leq l$) while falling towards the competitor ($a \leq x \leq (l + a - b)/2$ and $(l + a - b)/2 \leq x \leq l - b$). Actually, firms do not discriminate in their hinterlands but absorb twice the freight rate in their competitive areas. An illustration is given in Figure 3.3 where the equilibrium prices are represented by the heavy lines. In addition, we see that freight absorption is greater when firms are more separated. At the limit, absorption takes place on each local market when firms are established at $x = 0$ and $x = l$ respectively.

Spatial price discrimination is often held to be economically undesirable. However, comparison of the full prices under mill and discriminatory pricing casts some doubt on this claim. To illustrate, let us assume that $a = b \leq l/4$. Then, using (3.15) and (3.16) with $a = b$, we immediately see that a customer at x will pay $c + t(l + |x - a|)$ under mill pricing and $c + t(l - (x + a))$ under discriminatory pricing. Clearly, the latter is always smaller than the former (except when $a = x = 0$ where both prices are equal). The same holds for $x \geq l/2$. In consequence it turns out that, in this example, *each consumer is better off under discriminatory pricing than under mill pricing*. Moreover, it is also economically desirable to have price stability.

3.3. Spatial oligopoly

3.3.1. Competitive spatial pricing

We now assume that "several" firms located at given points compete in price to sell to consumers spread out over space. However, as distance restricts the number of firms which effectively compete for a specific market segment, firms can hardly ignore the mutual interdependence of their price policy. We thus have *spatial oligopoly* [see Greenhut (1971)].

Let a set of firms selling a homogeneous product be equally spaced along an unbounded line market (or, equivalently, along a circular market); the distance between two firms is denoted by l. Marginal production cost, c, is constant and uniform across firms. Transportation cost per distance and per weight is equal to t. Consumers are evenly distributed over the market at a unit density. All consumers are identical and have a rectangular demand function:

$$q(x) = \begin{cases} 1 & \text{if } p(x) \leq v, \\ 0 & \text{otherwise,} \end{cases} \qquad (3.17)$$

where v is the reservation price.

Given this setting, we want to determine the mill price equilibrium (if any!) prevailing in the industry under competition.

Let us first describe the structure of demand to firm i. For simplicity, we suppose that all prices but p_i are given and equal; furthermore we have $\bar{p}_{i-1} = \bar{p}_{i+1} > v - tl$ so that consumers around firm i cannot buy from firms $i-1$ and $i+1$.

First, if $p_i > v$, then no consumer wants to buy from firm i:

$$D_i(\bar{p}_{i-1}, p_i, \bar{p}_{i+1}) = 0.$$

Second, if $2v - \bar{p}_{i-1} - tl < p_i \leq v$, then firm i can serve only the consumers who are not supplied from firms $i-1$ and $i+1$. The market radius of firm i is given by the solution R_i to $p_i + tR_i = v$ so that

$$D_i(\bar{p}_{i-1}, p_i, \bar{p}_{i+1}) = 2\frac{v - p_i}{t}. \qquad (3.18)$$

Third, if $\bar{p}_{i-1} - tl \leq p_i \leq 2v - \bar{p}_{i-1} - tl$, then firm i attracts customers from its neighbors. The market splitting between, say, firms $i-1$ and i is such that $p_i + tR_i = \bar{p}_{i-1} + t(l - R_i)$. Hence

$$D_i(\bar{p}_{i-1}, p_i, \bar{p}_{i+1}) = \frac{\bar{p}_{i-1} - 2p_i + \bar{p}_{i+1} + 2tl}{2t}. \qquad (3.19)$$

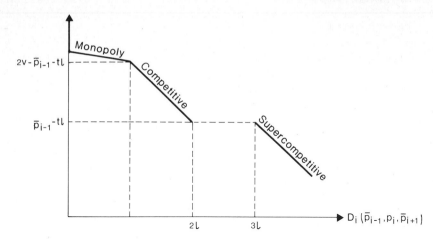

Figure 3.4. Firm i's demand.

Fourth, and last, if $p_i < \bar{p}_{i-1} - tl$, then firms $i-1$ and $i+1$ have lost their entire markets. In consequence, firm i has two new neighbors, for example firms $i-2$ and $i+2$, for which the above argument can be repeated. Notice that D_i exhibits discontinuities at prices $p_i = \bar{p}_{i-1} - ktl$, with $k = 1, 2 \dots$. Thus, the demand D_i, represented in Figure 3.4, has three different regions, corresponding to steps 2, 3 and 4 of the above description: the *monopoly*, *competitive* and *supercompetitive* regions [see Salop (1979)]. Interestingly, within the competitive and supercompetitive regions, D_i depends on the prices charged by the neighboring firms, but not on the prices set by more distant firms. This means that *demand has a chain-like structure* in which each producer competes directly with his neighbors [see Kaldor (1935)].

We define a *Bertrand price equilibrium* in the industry as a set of prices (p_i^*) such that, given p_{i-1}^* and p_{i+1}^*, firm i maximizes its profit $G_i = (p_i - c) \times D_i(p_{i-1}^*, p_i, p_{i+1}^*)$ at price p_i^*.

The following result has been shown to hold [see Beckmann (1972) and Salop (1979)].

Proposition 7

There exists a Bertrand price equilibrium. Furthermore
(i) if $v \le c + tl$, then each firm maximizes its profit at the monopoly price

$$p_i^* = \frac{v}{2} + \frac{c}{2};$$ (3.20)

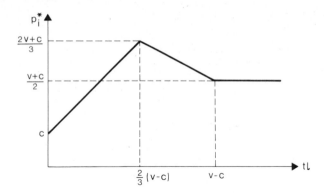

Figure 3.5. Equilibrium price as a function of *tl*.

(ii) if $c + tl < v < c + 3tl/2$, then each firm maximizes its profit at the kink of its demand function so that market areas just touch

$$p_i^* = v - \frac{tl}{2};$$
(3.21)

(iii) if $c + 3tl/2 \leq v$, then each firm maximizes its profit at a point of the competitive region which implies that potential market areas overlap

$$p_i^* = c + tl.$$
(3.22)

Several remarks are in order. First, a price equilibrium exists whatever the parameters v, c, t and l. (Remember that firms are assumed to be equidistant. In the context of 3.2.1, this corresponds to the case where firms 1 and 2 are located at the first and third quartiles of the market.) However, three different equilibrium configurations may occur, depending on the values of these parameters. Second, the equilibrium price increases with marginal production cost c in configurations (i) and (iii) but is insensitive to c in configuration (ii). Third, a decrease in tl may generate perverse effects on p_i^*. As shown in Figure 3.5, p_i^* rises when tl falls in configuration (ii). Fourth, at the equilibrium, firms earn positive profits. Nevertheless, when tl falls to zero (i.e. when one approaches the spaceless model), p_i^* converges to c, the perfectly competitive price, and profits vanish.

Thus, *when the impact of distance becomes negligible, the above model of spatial competition behaves like the perfect competition model.* However, *perverse effects may occur when the impact of distance is significant.*

3.3.2. Collusive spatial pricing

Another model of spatial pricing, which has come to be associated with the name of Lösch (1940), supposes that *firms in choosing their profit-maximizing price treat their market area as given*. In other words, firms always adjust their price by whatever amount required to prevent encroachment on their tributary area. This can be interpreted as the spatial counterpart of the Sylos–Labini postulate of consumer retention [see, e.g. Capozza and Van Order (1978)].

More precisely, because of the symmetry of locations, it is assumed that the market area of firm i cannot extend beyond the middle points of the segments between firm i and firms $i-1$ and $i+1$ respectively. As a result, the (Löschian) demand D_i^L to firm i is as follows: if $p_i > v$, then $D_i^L(p_i) = 0$; if $v - (tl/2) < p_i \leq v$, then $D_i^L(p_i) = 2(v - p_i)/t$; and, if $p_i \leq v - (tl/2)$, then $D_i^L(p_i) = l$. An example is given in Figure 3.6.

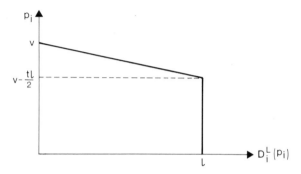

Figure 3.6. Firm i's Löschian demand.

The *Lösch price equilibrium* is then defined by the price p_i^L which maximizes the profit $G_i^L = (p_i - c)D_i^L(p_i)$, i.e.

(i) $p_i^L = \dfrac{v}{2} + \dfrac{c}{2}$ when $v \leq c + tl$, $\hspace{3em}$ (3.23)

(ii) $p_i^L = v - \dfrac{tl}{2}$ when $c + tl < v$. $\hspace{3em}$ (3.24)

Notice, first, that when $v \leq c + (3tl/2)$ (3.22) and (3.23) yield prices identical to those obtained in the model of spatial competition. Let us now suppose that $c + (3tl/2) > v$. MacLeod et al. (1987) have then shown that (3.24) corresponds to the noncooperative equilibrium of a repeated game in which each firm maximizes its discounted present value. Intuitively, this means that *Löschian pricing can be viewed as the outcome of a tacit collusion among firms.*

As observed by several authors [see, e.g. Capozza and Van Order (1978), Greenhut et al. (1975)], the Löschian price increases when the impact of distance decreases. The same holds for several other specifications of the local demand function [see for example (3.7)]. However, in the present context, this relationship ceases to be surprising. Indeed, there is no reason to expect the Löschian price to approach the perfectly competitive price since the former, unlike (3.22), is of the collusive type.

It is worth noting that the above results have been extended to deal with more general demand functions [see, e.g. the aforementioned references, but also Greenhut et al. (1977), Ohta (1980, 1981)].

Finally, notice that both the spatial competitive and collusive oligopoly models have been used by Benson and Hartigan (1983) to explore the implications of tariff restrictions in international trade. In particular, they show that the imposition of a tariff has a distributional impact among domestic customers; moreover, the domestic firm may lower its price when protected by a tariff [see Metzler (1949) for a similar result in a general equilibrium context].

3.3.3. *Spatial Cournot oligopoly*

A well-known fact in oligopoly theory is that quantity and price competition do not lead to the same results [see, e.g. Friedman (1983)]. A similar observation can be made in spatial oligopoly. Let us make it clear in the simple case of two firms.

Consider a market of length l along which consumers are distributed according to the density function $\rho(x)$. Each consumer is endowed with a linear demand function (3.1). Firms 1 and 2 are located at the extremities $x = 0$ and $x = l$ of the market. They sell a homogeneous commodity produced at constant marginal cost, supply the transportation and compete in *quantity* on each local market x.

Denote by $q_1(x)$ and $q_2(x)$ the quantities sold at x by firms 1 and 2 respectively. On market x, the two firms are in a Cournot-like situation, i.e. they set quantities in order to maximize their own profits, given the quantity sold by the other. Profits are given by

$$G_1(x) = q_1(x)\left[1 - \frac{q_1(x) + q_2(x)}{\rho(x)} - c - tx\right]$$

$$G_2(x) = q_2(x)\left[1 - \frac{q_1(x) + q_2(x)}{\rho(x)} - c - t(l - x)\right].$$

Some simple manipulations show that the profit-maximizing quantities are

(i) $\quad 0 \leq x \leq \text{Max}\left\{0, \dfrac{2l}{3} - \dfrac{1-c}{3t}\right\}: q_1^*(x) = \rho(x)\dfrac{1 - c - tx}{2}$ and

$$q_2^*(x) = 0; \tag{3.25}$$

(ii)

$$\text{Max}\left\{0, \frac{2l}{3} - \frac{1-c}{3t}\right\} < x < \text{Min}\left\{\frac{l}{3} + \frac{1-c}{3t}, l\right\}:$$

$$q_1^*(x) = \rho(x)\cdot\left(\frac{1-c+tl}{3} - tx\right)$$

$$\text{and } q_2^*(x) = \rho(x)\cdot\left(\frac{1-c-2tl}{3} + tx\right); \qquad (3.26)$$

(iii)

$$\text{Min}\left\{\frac{l}{3} + \frac{1-c}{3t}, l\right\} \le x \le l: \ q_1^*(x) = 0 \text{ and}$$

$$q_2^*(x) = \rho(x)\cdot\left(\frac{1-c-t(l-x)}{2}\right). \qquad (3.27)$$

Thus, depending on the position of the local market, three different types of equilibrium may emerge. In the first one, firm 1 acts as a monopolist; x is so far away from firm 2 that it is optimal for this firm not to supply x. In the second one, x is served by both firms; this corresponds to the typical situation in Cournot theory. In the third one, firm 2 acts as a monopolist; firm 1 chooses not to sell on market x.

Hence, provided that $tl < 2(1-c)$, some local markets are supplied by both firms 1 and 2 which means that *market areas overlap*. This is in sharp contrast with the situations observed in the above price setting models where market areas are always *exclusive*. Further, when $tl < (1-c)/2$, market areas completely overlap. This implies that markets $x = 0$ and $x = l$ are served jointly by firms 1 and 2, i.e. these places simultaneously export and import a homogeneous product. In contrast to perfect competition [cf. (2.1)], *cross-hauling is therefore consistent with spatial competition à la Cournot* [see also Benson and Hartigan (1984), Brander (1981)].

On the other hand, for $tl \ge 2(1-c)$, the two market areas turn out to be completely disjoint. Firms' strategies are then identical to those described in 3.1.2 under discriminatory pricing. In spatial monopoly, indeed, price discrimination and quantity policy yield the same outcomes. This is no longer true in spatial oligopoly where *quantity competition and discriminatory pricing give rise to very different results*. To convince him/herself, the reader can compare the results just obtained to those of 3.2.3.

Let us now turn to the price $p^*(x)$ corresponding to the equilibrium quantities $q_1^*(x)$ and $q_2^*(x)$. In regions (i) and (iii), $p^*(x)$ is equal to the monopoly price. In region (ii), it is easy to verify that $p^*(x) = (1+2c+tl)/3$, i.e. the price paid by the customers is constant, irrespective of their location (see Figure 3.7 for an illustration). In other words, spatial quantity competition implies freight absorption [see Greenhut and Greenhut (1975), Neven and Phlips (1985)].

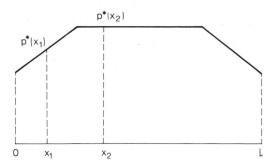

Figure 3.7. Equilibrium price pattern under spatial Cournot oligopoly.

More generally, assuming that m firms are established at $x = 0$ and $x = l$, it can be shown that $p^*(x) = (1 + m(x + tx))/(m + 1)$ when x is supplied from $x = 0$ or $x = l$ only; when x belongs to both market areas, we have $p^*(x) = (1 + 2m(x + tl/2))/(2m + 1)$. Letting $m \to \infty$, the overlapping of market areas vanishes while $p^*(x)$ approaches the marginal production and transportation costs, i.e. the perfectly competitive price. This means that, in accordance with nonspatial Cournot theory, the spatial quantity competition model behaves like the perfect competition model when the number of firms becomes large [see Dafermos and Nagurney (1985), Weskamp (1985)].

The foregoing models are very specific so that the conclusions they lead to are limited. Nevertheless, they shed some light on the large variety of situations that can arise in spatial oligopoly with respect to pricing and output. Perfect competition is not consistent with patterns of market areas as discussed here. The results of this section suggest, however, that in certain cases as the spacing of firms decreases, in the limit the price and output pattern of perfect competition is attained.

4. Locational choice

4.1. Transportation cost minimization

4.1.1. The Launhardt–Weber model

The theory of optimal location for a firm has been very much dominated by the Launhardt–Weber model [see Launhardt (1882), Weber (1909), Isard (1956)]. The essential feature of this model is that the firm's objective is sensitive to the location of both markets and resource deposits. This is achieved by assuming that the firm bears the transportation costs of its output and inputs. Since the quantities of output and inputs are taken as given in the Launhardt–Weber model, the firm will therefore elect a location which minimizes total transportation costs. In this way, we study the behavior of a firm which is not a priori oriented toward some particular location factors. Rather, one expects the cost-minimizing location to be the equilibrium position of a composite system of forces.

Formally, the model can be described as follows. The firm produces a single output and uses m inputs. They are sold to and bought from a given set $X = \{x_1, \ldots, x_n\} \subset R^2$ of markets and input sources. A point $x_i \in X$ can be simultaneously a market for the output and/or a source for one or several inputs. The quantities of output and inputs carried to and from x_i are given and denoted by $q(x_i), q_1(x_i), \ldots, q_m(x_i)$ respectively (some, but not all, quantities $q(x_i), q_k(x_i)$ may have a zero value). The transportation rates of the output and inputs are constant and denoted by $t, t_1, \ldots, t_m$. Finally, the distance between any two points is given by the crow fly distance.

Let us now define the *ideal weight* of the quantities moved from and/or to $x_i \in X$ as

$$w_i = tq(x_i) + \sum_{k=1}^{m} t_k q_k(x_i). \tag{4.1}$$

The ideal weight w_i is obtained from the quantity and transportability of the goods shipped from or to x_i. It therefore measures the force of attraction exerted by x_i on the firm.

The *Weber problem* (WP) consists of minimizing, with respect to the location $s \in S \subseteq R^2$, *the total transportation cost function $T(s)$ given by*

$$T(s) \underset{\text{def}}{=} \sum_{i=1}^{n} w_i \, d(x_i, s). \tag{4.2}$$

An equilibrium location for the firm – or an *optimal location* as it is more commonly called – is then defined by a point of S minimizing $T(s)$ over S.

In (4.2), each point x_i can be viewed as the origin of a force which, because of the advantage of proximity, attracts the firm toward x_i with an intensity proportional to the ideal weight w_i. Thus, a system of conflicting forces emerges and the optimal location is the equilibrium position of the system of forces generated by the ideal weights being pulled in their respective directions.

To begin with, let us assume that the points in X are distributed along a straight line, as with settlements in a valley or along a coast. Without loss of generality, we may suppose that points in X are indexed such that $x_1 < x_2 < \cdots < x_n$. For $s \in [x_{j-1}, x_j[$, the total transportation cost function can then be written as

$$T(s) = \sum_{i=1}^{j-1} w_i(s - x_i) + \sum_{i=j}^{n} w_i(x_i - s). \tag{4.3}$$

We say that $x_j \in X$ is a *median* for the ideal weight vector $(w_1, \ldots, w_n)$ if the following two conditions hold:

$$\sum_{i=1}^{j-1} w_i \leq \sum_{i=j}^{n} w_i \tag{4.4a}$$

and

$$\sum_{i=1}^{j} w_i \geq \sum_{i=j+1}^{n} w_i. \tag{4.4b}$$

In our terminology, this means that x_j is a median when the sums of the forces exerted at the left and at the right of x_j are both smaller than or equal to half of the sum of all forces.

Clearly, there always exists a median in X for any vector $(w_1, \ldots, w_n)$. For example, with $n = 5$, x_2 is the unique median for $(4, 3, 1, 3, 1)$ whereas x_2 and x_3 are medians for $(4, 3, 3, 3, 1)$.

Proposition 8

Given a vector $(w_1, \ldots, w_n)$ of ideal weights, x_j is an optimal solution to the WP if and only if x_j is a median for $(w_1, \ldots, w_n)$.

This result, due to Edgeworth (1883) [see Witzgall (1964) for a recent proof] and rediscovered independently by several authors [see Rosenhead (1973a) for a brief historical sketch] is known as the *principle of median location*. Among other things, it implies that, in a one-dimensional space, an optimal solution to the WP may always be found in X. Furthermore, this optimal solution does not depend on the distances between points in X. Only the ranking of these points along the line is determinant. This is comparable to the median voter principle in public choice [see, e.g. Black (1948)]. Finally, note that the principle can be extended to cover the case of the simultaneous location of several plants [see Rosenhead (1973b)].

We now suppose that the points in X are distributed over the plane. The total transportation cost function becomes

$$T(s) = \sum_{i=1}^{n} w_i \|x_i - s\|, \qquad (4.5)$$

where $\|x_i - s\| = [(x_i^1 - s^1)^2 + (x_i^2 - s^2)^2]^{1/2}$ is the Euclidean distance between x_i and s. As the points in X are not collinear, the objective function $T(s)$ can be shown to be strictly convex so that the WP with the Euclidean distance has a unique optimal solution [see Kuhn (1967)].

The convex hull of X, called hereafter *locational polygon*, is very useful for the study of the optimal solution to (4.5); it is denoted by LP.

For the WP with Euclidean distance, Kuhn (1967) has shown that the optimal location belongs to the locational polygon LP. This result is the best possible. In order to show this, it is sufficient to exhibit a particular configuration of X for which any point of LP (up to a zero-measure set) is the unique optimal location corresponding to a certain WP. Let us consider a problem with three points – the Weberian triangle. We know from Kuhn (1967) that any interior point $\bar{s}$ of the triangle is a solution to the multiobjective program defined by the simultaneous minimization of $\|x_1 - s\|, \|x_2 - s\|$ and $\|x_3 - s\|$. Consequently, w_1, w_2 and w_3 exist such that $w_i \geq 0$, $\sum_{i=1}^{3} w_i = 1$ and $\sum_{i=1}^{3} w_i \|x_i - \bar{s}\| \leq \sum_{i=1}^{3} w_i \|x_i - s\|$ for all $s \in R^2$ [see Karlin (1954), Lemma 7.4.1]. Clearly, at least one weight w_i, say w_1, is strictly positive. Assume that the other two are equal to zero. In this case, $\bar{s}$ should be identical with x_1, a contradiction. Suppose now that only one w_i, say w_3, is equal to zero. Then, $\bar{s}$ should belong to $[x_1, x_2]$, a contradiction. The three weights w_i must therefore be strictly positive. As $\sum_{i=1}^{3} w_i \|x_i - s\|$ is strictly convex, $\bar{s}$ is the unique minimizer of the function $T(s)$ defined by w_1, w_2 and w_3.

From the above it follows that *the WP with Euclidean distance is of a continuous nature*.

Two types of solution are possible. First, the optimal location is a point x_j of X. This occurs if and only if

$$w_j \geq a_j = \left\{ \left[\sum_{\substack{i=1 \\ i \neq j}}^{n} w_i \left(x_i^1 - x_j^1 \right) / \|x_i - x_j\| \right]^2 \right.$$
$$\left. + \left[\sum_{\substack{i=1 \\ i \neq j}}^{n} w_i \left(x_i^2 - x_j^2 \right) / \|x_i - x_j\| \right]^2 \right\}^{1/2} \qquad (4.6)$$

[see Kuhn (1967)]. Condition (4.6) means that the intensity of the force at x_j is greater than or equal to the intensity of the sum of the forces exerted by the other points in X, i.e. $w_i\{(x_i - x_j)/\|x_i - x_j\|\}$, $i = 1, \ldots, n$, $i \neq j$.

Second, the optimal location is the solution to the first-order conditions for the minimization of $T(s)$, viz

$$\sum_{i=1}^{n} w_i \frac{x_i - s}{\|x_i - s\|} = 0. \tag{4.7}$$

In other words, the intensity of the sum of the forces exerted by the points in X, i.e. $w_i\{(x_i - s)/\|x_i - s\|\}$, is zero at the optimal location. There exists no closed-form solution to (4.7). Accordingly, to determine the optimal location, an iterative scheme is needed. The basic scheme was devised by Weiszfeld (1936), but was rediscovered independently by several authors [see, e.g. Francis and White (1974) and the references therein]. Weiszfeld pointed out that conditions (4.7) can be reformulated as:

$$s = \frac{\left[\sum\limits_{i=1}^{n} w_i x_i / \|x_i - s\|\right]}{\left[\sum\limits_{i=1}^{n} w_i / \|x_i - s\|\right]}. \tag{4.8}$$

Then, starting from an initial point s_1 (possibly the center of gravity of $x_1, \ldots, x_n$), one computes $\|x_i - s_1\|$ for each x_i in X and from (4.8) one gets a new point s_2, replacing $\|x_i - s\|$ by $\|x_i - s_1\|$. Given s_{n-1}, $\|x_i - s_{n-1}\|$ is determined to obtain an nth point s_n in a similar way. This procedure is carried on until $T(s_n)$ is close enough to $T(s_{n-1})$. The algorithm may be summed up in the recursive relationship

$$s_n = s_{n-1} - \operatorname{grad} T(s_{n-1}) \bigg/ \left[\sum_{i=1}^{n} w_i / \|x_i - s_{n-1}\|\right] \tag{4.9}$$

where $\operatorname{grad} T(s_{n-1})$ stands for the gradient of $T(s)$ at s_{n-1}. It has been shown to converge to an optimal location provided that no point obtained during a step coincides with a point $x_j \in X$ [see Kuhn (1973)]. The reason for this restriction is that the gradient of $T(s)$ does not exist at $s = x_j$. Ostresh (1978) proposed to replace (4.9) by

$$s_n = x_j - \left(1 - \frac{w_j}{a_j}\right)\left[\sum_{\substack{i=1 \\ i \neq j}}^{n} w_i(x_i - x_j)/\|x_i - x_j\|\right] \bigg/ S\left[\sum_{\substack{i=1 \\ i \neq j}}^{n} w_i / \|x_i - x_j\|\right] \tag{4.10}$$

when $s_{n-1} = x_j$, and has shown that the algorithm (4.9)–(4.10) always converges toward an optimal location.

This algorithm applies when any point of the locational polygon is a possible location. A solution method, using (4.9)–(4.10), has been devised by Hansen et al. (1982) to deal with locational constraints defined by the union of convex polygons.

Finally, we have the following interesting comparative statics result: if an increase in an ideal weight takes place, the location will be attracted in the direction of the point which has a proportionally larger force. Consider $w'_j = w_j + \Delta w_j$ with $\Delta w_j > 0$ and let s^* and s^{**} be the optimal locations corresponding to the weight configurations with w_j and w'_j respectively. The argument is by contradiction: assume that $d_j(s^*) < d_j(s^{**})$. Then we have

$$\Delta w_j d_j(s^{**}) > \Delta_j d_j(s^*).$$

Furthermore, by definition of s^{**}

$$\sum_{i=1}^{n} w_i d_i(s^{**}) + \Delta w_j d_j(s^{**}) \le \sum_{i=1}^{n} w_i d_i(s^*) + \Delta w_j d_j(s^*).$$

Accordingly

$$\sum_{i=1}^{n} w_i d_i(s^{**}) < \sum_{i=1}^{n} w_i d_i(s^*),$$

a contradiction to the fact that s^* is an optimal location for $w_1, \ldots, w_j, \ldots, w_n$.

(Notice that this proof is independent of the Euclidean distance. In consequence, the property is true for any distance function.) For other comparative statics results, the reader is referred to Heaps (1982).

Mathematical models of a two-dimensional space abound in modern location theory. They are divided in two classes, namely the network and continuous models. The *network* models aim at taking into account the characteristics of configuration and position of the real transportation network in the (mathematical) definition of space. The distance is then constructed from that space. In contrast, the *continuous* models suppose that a distance, generally derived from a norm, is defined a priori on a subset of a two-dimensional vector space. The analytical and geometric properties of the distance express the main characteristics of the network that we intend to represent. These two classes of models are considered in the sequel.

The approach followed aims at the specification of the "smallest" subset of S – possibly a single point set – containing an optimal location: this subset is called the *candidate-solution set*. As expected, the properties of the candidate-solution set depend on the geometric arrangement of the points in X, the type of distance considered and the relative value of the ideal weights.

4.1.2. Network location theory

A *network N* is a subset of the plane which satisfies the following conditions: (i) N is the union of a finite number of rectifiable arcs, i.e. of a well-defined length; (ii) any two arcs intersect at most at their extremities; (iii) N is connected. The set of *vertices V* of the network is made of the extremities of the arcs defining the network. Without loss of generality, we may assume that any market or input source $x_i \in X$ is a vertex of the network, and that any vertex which is not a market or an input source is a *node* of the network, i.e. a point which is the extremity of at least three arcs of the network. Finally, the distance d between any two points of the network is given by the length of the shortest route linking these points in N. It is easy to see that d is a metric defined on N. [For more details, the reader is referred to Dearing and Francis (1974).]

Proposition 9

The set V of vertices contains an optimal solution to the WP on a network.

This result, due to Hakimi (1964) and Guelicher (1965) and known as the *Hakimi theorem*, has several interesting implications. First, it shows that the set of points always containing an optimal location can be reduced to a finite subset of the network. Stated differently, this means that *the WP on a network is of a finite nature*. Such a characterization has a great deal of intuitive appeal in spatial economics, insofar as locational decisions in (multi)regional spaces are often discontinuous. As Isard says "Substitution among transport inputs is not in the small but rather in the large, entailing geographic shifts over substantial distance from one focal point to another" [see Isard (1965, p. 251)]. Second, the points to be considered are remarkable in the sense that they are markets, input sources or nodes. When compared to the median principle, we thus face an enlargement of the candidate–solution set caused by the addition of the nodal points. Again, this is in accord with the nonformal discussion provided, for instance, by Hoover (1948) and Isard (1956). What kind of point will ultimately be selected hinges on the shape of the network, the spatial distribution of the points in X and the vector of ideal weights. Third, and last, in practice the search for an optimal location turns out to be easy to perform. Indeed, it suffices to compare the values of the total transportation cost function over the set of vertices and to choose the point which yields the lowest value. This is reminiscent of the comparative advantage method proposed by Isard (1956).

The Hakimi theorem has been extended in a variety of directions [see Handler and Mirchandani (1979) for references]. For our purpose, the most interesting one deals with transportation cost functions exhibiting scale economies relative to distance. Indeed, it is sometimes argued that observed transportation rates are not constant. Rather they would taper off as the distances covered increase [see, e.g. Hoover (1948) and Isard (1956)]. In such cases, transportation costs between two points should preferably be modelled by functions increasing and (strictly) concave in distance. Levy (1967) has shown that the Hakimi theorem remains valid for such functions. Furthermore, as the degree of increasing returns augments, marginal transportation costs become less and less sensitive to distance. In this case, it has been shown that it is optimal for the firm to choose a location in the set of markets and inputs sources [see Louveaux et al. (1982)]. Stated differently, the nodes of $V - X$ can be excluded from consideration when scale economies in transport are large enough. This is especially relevant for firms working in multiregional spaces, and which have access to advanced transport technologies. Other general conditions under which the Hakimi theorem holds include the multiplant, multi-output firm [Wendell and Hurter (1973a)], the multimodal transportation system [Louveaux et al. (1982)] and the risk-neutral firm facing random ideal weights [Mirchandani and Odoni (1979)].

Interestingly, properties more specific than the Hakimi theorem can be obtained for particular network configurations. For instance, in the important case of a star-shaped network, the following result has been shown to hold [see Perreur and Thisse (1974)]: the center of the network is an optimal location if and only if the sum of the ideal weights along each radial way is smaller than or equal to the sum of the ideal weights on the other points of X.

Similarly, new and meaningful results emerge when some restrictions are put on the ideal weights. We say that x_j, a market and/or an input source, is a *dominant site* if the ideal weight of x_j is greater than or equal to the sum of the ideal weights of the other points in X:

$$w_j \geq \sum_{\substack{i=1 \\ i \neq j}}^{n} w_i. \tag{4.11}$$

Intuitively, x_j is a dominant site when the force of attraction exerted by x_j is larger than or equal to the sum of the forces exerted by the other points in X. It is therefore expected that x_j is an optimal location.

Proposition 10

If x_j is a dominant site, then x_j is an optimal solution to the WP.

This result, due to Witzgall (1964), generalizes the dominant material index property stated by Weber (1909); it is called *majority theorem*.

The majority theorem is useful in the analysis of the following locational choices. It should be readily apparent that x_j is a dominant site, and therefore an optimal location, when at least one of the following conditions holds: (i) the quantities of goods carried from or to x_j are large; (ii) the goods shipped from or to x_j have a poor transportability; (iii) there are many more linkages between the firm and x_j than with any other point in X. It is then sufficient to reinterpret these conditions in concrete terms to fall back on the traditional explanations of the so-called "corner" locations: market-oriented activity, raw material-oriented activity, labor-oriented activity, etc. There is plentiful evidence that several real world activities belong to such categories [see, e.g. Hoover (1948), Isard (1956)] so that the majority theorem seems to offer a relevant and synthetic explanation of those locational decisions. It is worth noting, however, that this explanation is based on all the location factors which can be integrated into the objective function $T(s)$, and not on a single one [see Ponsard (1956)].

In some practical cases, the condition that x_j be a dominant site is not fulfilled though the firm is established at this point. We are therefore interested in determining the impact of the relaxation of the dominant site condition on the value of the total transportation cost. This leads us to introduce the following concept. Given $\theta \in \,]0,1[$, x_j is called a *θ-dominant site* when the ideal weight of x_j is equal to the fraction θ of the sum of the ideal weights corresponding to the other points in X:

$$w_j = \theta \sum_{\substack{i=1 \\ i \neq j}}^{n} w_i. \tag{4.12}$$

It is then possible to show that, given (4.12), *$T(x_j)$ is always bounded from the above by* $1/\theta \min T(s)$ [see Goldman (1972)]. Hence, we may conclude that locating a firm in a site almost dominant (i.e. θ close to one) is, in the worst cases, nearly optimal. To the extent that the firm is concerned with a "satisficing" location rather than with an optimal one [see Richardson (1969)], that property allows us to explain the decision to locate at x_j whenever the ideal weight w_j is relatively high, i.e. θ is close to 1.

In fact, x_j may be an optimal location even when w_j is negligible; x_j is then chosen because it is a central node in the transportation network. Typically, we face in this case a *purely transport-oriented* activity.

A natural generalization of the concept of a dominant site is that of a dominant region. A region $R \subset N$ is called a *dominant region* if the sum of the ideal weights in $X \cap R$ is greater than or equal to the sum of the ideal weights in $X - R$:

$$\sum_{\{i;\, x_i \in X \cap R\}} w_i \geq \sum_{\{i;\, x_i \in X - R\}} w_i. \tag{4.13}$$

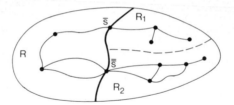

Figure 4.1. Example of a gated region.

Clearly, while a dominant site, which exists only in some WP, is always an optimal location, a dominant region, which exists in any WP, does not necessarily contain an optimal location. Additional restrictions on R must therefore be imposed.

A *region* $R \subset N$ is said to be *gated* when there exists a mapping γ from $N - R$ to R that

$$\mathrm{d}(s_1, s_2) = \mathrm{d}[s_1, \gamma(s_1)] + \mathrm{d}[\gamma(s_1), s_2] \qquad \text{for any } s_1 \in N - R \text{ and } s_2 \in R.$$
$$(4.14)$$

In words, this means that the shortest route linking $s_1 \in N - R$ and $s_2 \in R$ necessarily passes through point $\gamma(s_1)$ – the "gate" – which depends on the end-point in $N - R$ but not on the endpoint in R. Intuitively, we thus expect R to be gated when $N - R$ contains at most a few transportation closed loops. An example is given in Figure 4.1 where $\gamma(s_1) = \bar{s}$ for $s_1 \in R_1$ and $\gamma(s_1) = \bar{\bar{s}}$ for $s_1 \in R_2$.

Proposition 11

If R is a dominant and gated region, then R contains an optimal solution to the WP.

This result is due to Goldman and Witzgall (1970).

A stronger property obtains when the network possesses an isthmus. Indeed, the extremity e_i of the isthmus is the single gate to enter into region R_i, so that $\gamma_i(s) = e_i$ for $s \in N - R_i$ and $i = 1, 2$. An illustration is given in Figure 4.2. It has then been shown that, when no intermediate points of the isthmus belong to X, *the region R_i contains an optimal location if and only if R_i is a dominant region* [see Goldman (1971)]. Thus, in the presence of (natural) bottlenecks, the firm establishes itself on the side of the network with the larger ideal weights [see Lösch 1940)].

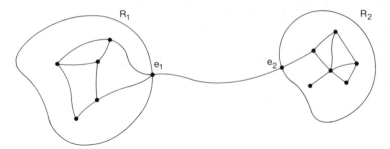

Figure 4.2. Example of a two-region economy with an isthmus.

4.1.3. Non-Euclidean continuous models

It is now assumed that the distance between two points is measured via a norm $\|\cdot\|$ defined on R^2, i.e. $d(s_1, s_2) = \|s_1 - s_2\|$. [We do not discuss here location problems on a sphere; for a review of these problems, see Wesolowsky (1982).] In this case, the total transportation cost $T(s) = \sum_{i=1}^{n} w_i \|x_i - s\|$ is a convex function defined on R^2. Our problem therefore becomes a chapter of convex mathematical programming. [In fact, it is deeply rooted in nonlinear programming, and has several times served as a motivation for some developments of that theory; see Kuhn (1976).]

In choosing a norm for the WP, we have in mind the following criteria: (i) the corresponding distance must be a good approximation of the actual distance; (ii)

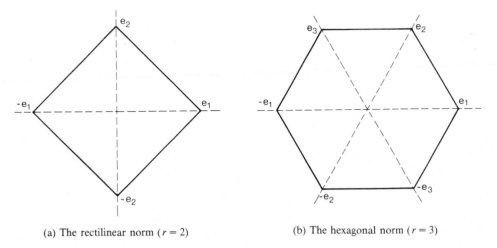

(a) The rectilinear norm ($r = 2$)   (b) The hexagonal norm ($r = 3$)

Figure 4.3. Unit contours of two block norms.

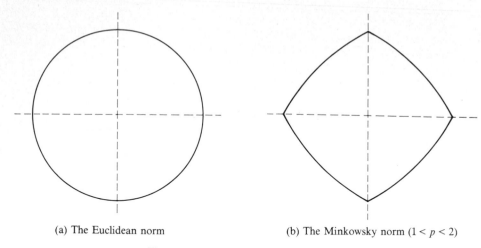

(a) The Euclidean norm   (b) The Minkowsky norm $(1 < p < 2)$

Figure 4.4. Unit contours of two round norms.

the resulting optimization problem must be easy to solve. These considerations have led some authors to distinguish between two families of norms [Witzgall (1964), Thisse et al. (1984)]: the block and round norms. Before defining these norms, let us recall that a norm in R^2 is fully characterized by the specification of a unit contour line delimiting a convex, compact set of R^2 which is symmetric around the origin [see Rockafellar (1970), Theorem 15.2]. This implies that we may define the block and round norms from the geometric description of their respective contour lines: A *block norm* is a norm whose unit contour is formed only by linear segments, while a *round norm* is a norm whose unit contour contains no linear segment. Examples of block and round norms used in location models are depicted in Figures 4.3 and 4.4.

Interestingly, the block and round norm distances can be given an intuitive interpretation in terms of feasible routes. Consider, first, a block norm $\|\cdot\|$ and denote by e_k and $-e_k$, $k = 1, \ldots, r$, the $2r$ extreme points of the polygon corresponding to the unit contour of $\|\cdot\|$. Every pair $(e_k, -e_k)$ of opposite points is associated with a *direction* L_k defined by $L_k = \{x \in R^2; \ x = \alpha e_k, \ \alpha \in R\}$. A *feasible route* for this norm is defined by a concatenation of segments parallel to the directions L_k. Examples of feasible routes for the rectilinear norm ($r = 2$: North–South and East–West directions) and the hexagonal norm [$r = 3$: see Lalanne (1863)] are given in Figure 4.5

Ward and Wendell (1985) have shown that the block norm distance $\|s_1 - s_2\|$ between $s_1 \in R^2$ and $s_2 \in R^2$ is equal to the length of the shortest feasible route

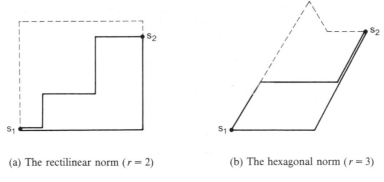

(a) The rectilinear norm ($r = 2$)   (b) The hexagonal norm ($r = 3$)

Figure 4.5. Examples of feasible routes.

between s_1 and s_2. (In the examples of Figure 4.5, the shortest routes are represented in heavy lines.) This shows how a block norm distance can approximate the shortest distance in a network organized along some major directions. By contrast, all directions are a priori feasible (though not necessarily equivalent) with a round norm distance. (This is magnified by the Euclidean distance for which the shortest route between two points is the straight line.) The purpose of a round norm is to approximate the shortest distance in a highly dense network. Empirical evidence about the abilities of some block and round norms to approximate actual highway distances can be found in Love and Morris (1979), Puu (1979) and Ward and Wendell (1985).

Let $\|\cdot\|$ be a block norm. Given the directions $L_1, \ldots, L_r$ corresponding to $\|\cdot\|$, we consider for each point $x_i \in X$ the r lines defined by $L_k^i = x_i + L_k$. A point $s \in R^2$ is then called an *intersection point* (for the problem considered) if it is the intersection of two directions $L_{k_1}^{i_1}$ and $L_{k_2}^{i_2}$ with $k_1 \neq k_2$; the set of intersection points is denoted by . *An optimal location for the WP can then be shown to belong to the set of intersection points contained in the locational polygon LP* [see Thisse et al. (1984)]. An example is given in Figure 4.6 for the rectilinear norm, where the bold dots stand for the intersection points.

In the particular case of the rectilinear norm ($r = 2$), the optimal location is easy to characterize and to obtain. Indeed, $T(s) = \sum_{i=1}^{n} w_i(|x_i^1 - s^1| + |x_i^2 - s^2|)$ and is, therefore, separable. As a result, the median principle can be applied to each subproblem separately, which means that the *optimal location is a bi-median* [see, e.g. Francis (1963) and Huriot and Perreur (1973)].

Another advantage of the rectilinear norm is that its properties can be exploited to take into account heterogeneities in the transport surface. The

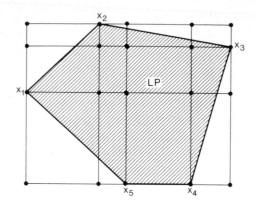

Figure 4.6. An example of candidate-solution set under the rectilinear norm.

presence of barriers to travel, when these barriers are represented by polygons, has been tackled by Larson and Sadiq (1983). They show that the set of feasible intersection points and of barrier vertices contains an optimal location. Odoni and Sadiq (1982) have similarly investigated the role of a low cost corridor parallel to one axis. It follows from their analysis that it is optimal for the firm to establish itself at the bi-median or at the nearest point along the corridor, depending upon the relative benefit provided by the corridor.

Let us come back now to the case of a general block norm. It is easy to see that the number of intersection points is at most equal to $n + n(n-1) \cdot r(r-1)/2$ – which reduces to n^2 for the rectilinear norm. Consequently, as the number r of feasible directions increases, the number of intersection points increases dramatically. At the limit, when the maximal length of a flat spot of the unit contour converges to zero, the intersection points can be shown to fill up the plane R^2 [see Thisse et al. (1984)]. As any round norm can be approached in this manner by a sequence of block norms, this implies that, *under a round norm, the optimal location is to be sought within the whole locational polygon LP*.

Note, finally, that the WP with the Minkowsky norm yields results similar to those obtained with the Euclidean norm. In particular, the Weiszfeld scheme can be amended to provide a good approximation of the optimal location [see Morris and Verdini (1979)].

It should be apparent from the above developments that the theory of metric spaces offers a wide range of relevant possibilities for modelling two-dimensional location problems. In particular, these models allow us to capture the main features of different real transportation networks.

4.2. The price–location problem in spatial monopoly

In Weber location theory, the minimization of total transportation costs is regarded as the decision criterion for firm location. Thus, this theory seems to disagree with the microeconomic theory of the firm where the decision criterion is known to be profit maximization. This apparent contradiction has led some authors to examine the conditions under which the two approaches can be reconciled. Basically, the answer is to be found in the structure of the firm production function. More specifically, Isard (1956) showed that the firm maximizes its profit by locating at the transport cost minimizing point when the production function is with fixed technical coefficients. Soon after, Moses (1958) demonstrated that the above equivalence fails to hold when substitution among production factors is permitted, a fact already known to Predöhl (1925). Consequently, a more general approach than the Weber model is required in order to place firm location in the main body of microeconomic theory.

The purpose of this new problem, called hereafter the *price–location problem of the spatial monopolist* (PLP), is to describe how the firm chooses, simultaneously, its price policy, location and input mix so as to maximize profits.

The assumptions of the PLP are as follows. The production function of the firm is given by $q = f(q_1, \ldots, q_m)$ where, as in 4.1.1, q stands for the amount of output and $(q_1, \ldots, q_m)$ for the vector of input quantities. It is assumed that f is independent of the firm location. Furthermore, the firm faces a (finite) system of demand functions $D_1(p_1), \ldots, D_l(p_l)$ for its output where p_j denotes the full price paid by the customers at x_j, $j = 1, \ldots, l$. The demand functions need not be homogeneous and may be site-specific. Input i, $i = 1, \ldots, m$, can be bought at the f.o.b. price p_i at the input source x_i. Finally, the transportation rates $t, t_1, \ldots, t_m$ are defined as in 4.1.1; the distance function is not specified and can be any one of the distances considered in 4.1.

4.2.1. Discriminatory pricing

In the case of *discriminatory pricing*, the profit function of the spatial monopolist is

$$G_D = \sum_{j=1}^{l} \left[p_j - t\,d(s, x_j) \right] D_j(p_j) - \sum_{i=1}^{m} \left[p_i + t_i\,d(x_i, s) \right] q_i. \tag{4.15}$$

The PLP under discriminatory pricing then consists in maximizing profits G_D subject to the production function constraint (as well as possible location constraints).

Clearly, in this problem, prices and quantities of output and input hauled from and to the firm are determined together with the location of the firm. Indeed, a change in firm location gives rise to new delivered prices for the inputs, and so to a new input mix; it also gives rise to a new system of mill marginal revenues, and so to a new output allocation. In consequence, a total transportation cost function cannot be constructed a priori. However, following Alonso (1967), we may define an a posteriori total transportation cost function, corresponding to the profit-maximizing quantities. Formally, this function is obtained as follows. Let $(p_1^*, \ldots, p_l^*, q_1^*, \ldots, q_m^*, s^*)$ be an optimal solution of the PLP under discriminatory pricing; then set

$$T^*(s) = \sum_{j=1}^{l} t D_j(p_j^*) \, \mathrm{d}(s, x_j) + \sum_{i=1}^{m} t_i q_i^* \, \mathrm{d}(x_i, s). \tag{4.16}$$

This function measures the cost associated with the transport of the quantities $D_j(p_j^*)$ and q_i^* when the firm is established at $s \in S$. A minimizer of $T^*(s)$ is called an *ex post transport cost minimizing point*.

The relationships between the optimal solutions to (4.15) and (4.16) have been analyzed by Nijkamp and Paelinck (1973) and Thisse and Perreur (1977). In particular, these authors showed that the location s^* is a profit-maximizing point for (4.15) if and only if s^* is an ex post transport cost minimizing point for (4.16).

This result shows that the profit-maximizing location chosen by the spatial discriminatory monopolist is socially optimal *relative to* the quantities chosen by the monopolist. Of course, this does not mean that this location is identical to the one chosen by a welfare-maximizing firm: it is well known that the quantities sold by a profit-maximizing monopolist are not socially optimal. More importantly, the above property justifies, at least for the problem under study, the Weberian approach in firm location theory, since the localization theorems proved in the context of the minimization of the total transportation cost remain valid within the present context. Accordingly, the properties mentioned in 4.1 also characterize the optimal location for the PLP under discriminatory pricing, and there is no need for specific proofs. In particular, it is still true that the spatial discriminating monopolist will choose to locate at a market for its output or an input source or a transport node. This generalizes the "endpoint property" established first by Sakashita (1967) in the case of one market and one input source located respectively at the endpoints of a linear segment [see also Eswaran et al. (1981) and Mathur (1979)].

Until now, the monopolist has been assumed to operate a single plant. Because demand is dispersed, the firm has the possibility to divide its production activities into several geographically separated plants. Roughly speaking, we may consider two polar cases of such a division of production. The first one, called *geographical* (or horizontal) *division*, supposes that each plant carries out the whole production process. In this case, the division of production is associated with a spatial segmentation of output and/or input markets, each plant being linked to a particular segment. The reason for this is to be found in the desire of the monopolist to reduce its transport expenses. The increase in the setup cost of plants is then more than compensated by the gains made on the transportation costs of output and/or inputs. The second case, called *technological* (or vertical) *division*, reflects the possibility for the firm to specialize plants in particular stages of the production process. Now the division of production corresponds to a system of (intra-firm) technological linkages. This breaking up of the production process is made with the aim to internalize the comparative advantages of particular sites. The transportation costs of the intermediate goods is then more than compensated by the gains realized on production costs. Alternately, the intermediate goods may be much easier to transport than the final product or the production inputs. [Observe that the above tradeoffs are similar to those considered in evaluating the efficiency of horizontal and vertical integration; see, e.g. Williamson (1968).]

In principle, different combinations of the above cases may occur. However, for ease in exposition, it is convenient to limit ourselves to these two cases only.

Let us first consider the case of geographical division. Since there are now several plants, the solution to the spatial monopoly problem should not only give the profit-maximizing price–location pattern, but should also specify the way in which production is allocated among the operating plants. Assume that such a solution is known. Then it should be apparent that, given the profit-maximizing prices ($p_1^*, \ldots, p_l^*$), the profit-maximizing production and location pattern must also minimize the production and transportation costs corresponding to the quantities $D_1(p_1^*), \ldots, D_l(p_l^*)$. In other words, given the quantities of output sold on the different markets, the spatial discriminatory monopolist establishes the socially optimal number of plants together with the most efficient locations and technologies. This is easy to understand since, under delivered pricing, the firm is able to internalize the whole (social) benefits generated by the choice of the efficient location–production pattern (see Kats (1980)].

This result, in turn, allows us to characterize the profit-maximizing locations in a straightforward manner. Indeed, since total costs are minimized, each plant must be located so as to minimize the transfer cost of its inputs and outputs. Accordingly, at the profit-maximizing solution, each location must be a solution of a particular Weber problem, which means again that the properties obtained in 4.1.2 also apply to the multiplant case.

Let us now turn to the case of technological division. In addition to the price and location decisions, the solution to the spatial monopoly problem must specify the input–output matrix characterizing the intra-firm system of linkages.

This matrix depends on the possible production techniques and on the geographical distribution of input prices. Assume, once again, that such a solution is given. Clearly, for $(p_1^*, \ldots, p_l^*)$ given, the firm chooses the efficient technological fragmentation of the production process. In particular, the different plants – if any – must be located in order to minimize total transportation costs, i.e. of output, inputs and intermediate goods. This is a generalized version of the Weber problem in which a set of interrelated plants, instead of a single one, is to be established. For this new problem also, the main properties of 5.1.2 can be shown to hold [see, e.g. Wendell and Hurter (1973a)].

4.2.2. Uniform pricing

Consider now the case of *uniform delivered pricing*. The profit function of the spatial monopolist is

$$G_{\mathrm{U}} = \sum_{j=1}^{l} \left[p - t \,\mathrm{d}(s, x_j) \right] \Delta_j(p) - \sum_{i=1}^{m} \left[p_i + t_i \,\mathrm{d}(x_i, s) \right] q_i \qquad (4.17)$$

where $0 \le \Delta_j(p) \le D_j(p)$ stands for the part of the demand at j which is met at a nonnegative profit margin. By introducing $\Delta_j(p)$, we recognize the possibility for the firm not to supply a particular market at price p when the corresponding profits are negative.

In view of (4.15) and (4.17), it should then be clear to the reader that the properties of the PLP under discriminatory pricing can be extended to the PLP under uniform delivered pricing. Suffice it to notice, indeed, that $(p_1^*, \ldots, p_l^*)$ can be replaced by the profit-maximizing uniform delivered price in the above developments, without affecting the results.

4.2.3. Mill pricing

Finally, we come to the case of mill pricing. The profit function can then be written as

$$G_{\mathrm{M}} = \sum_{j=1}^{l} p D_j \left[p + t \,\mathrm{d}(s, x_j) \right] - \sum_{i=1}^{m} \left[p_i + t_i \,\mathrm{d}(x_i, s) \right] q_i. \qquad (4.18)$$

The PLP under mill pricing consists in maximizing profits G_{M} subject to the production function constraint.

Comparing (4.15) and (4.18), we immediately notice the following major difference: a change in firm location directly affects the demand for the product of the monopolist. Consequently, it turns out that, under mill pricing, no total transportation cost function can be defined a posteriori since the volume of output, and therefore the quantities of inputs, necessarily vary with the firm location. As a result, the spatial monopolist would not locate at a point where total transportation costs are minimized. (This is in accordance with the general economic principle: profit-maximization implies cost-minimization if and only if revenue is independent of decisions concerning cost.) To see this, let us go back for a moment to (4.18), replacing q_i, the quantity of input i, by $\tilde{q}_i$ $(q(s), p_1(s),\ldots, p_m(s))$, namely the demand for input i expressed as a function of the quantity of output $q(s) = \sum_{j=1}^{l} D_j[p + t\,\mathrm{d}(s, x_j)]$ and of the full prices of the inputs, i.e. $p_1(s),\ldots, p_m(s)$. Assuming that all functions are differentiable and denoting the gradient in s by ∇_s, we have

$$\nabla_s G_M = \sum_{j=1}^{l} p \frac{\partial D_j}{\partial p} \nabla_s t\,\mathrm{d}(s, x_j) - \sum_{i=1}^{m} \tilde{q}_i \nabla_s t_i\,\mathrm{d}(x_i, s)$$
$$- \sum_{i=1}^{m} p_i(s) \left[\frac{\partial \tilde{q}_i}{\partial q(s)} \nabla_s q(s) + \sum_{k=1}^{m} \frac{\partial \tilde{q}_i}{\partial p_k(s)} \nabla_s t_k\,\mathrm{d}(x_k, s) \right] = 0$$

at the profit-maximizing location. As $\partial \tilde{q}_i/\partial p_k(s) = \partial \tilde{q}_k/\partial p_i(s)$, $i, k = 1,\ldots, m$, and as $\tilde{q}_i$ is homogeneous of degree zero in $p_1(s),\ldots, p_m(s)$, $i = 1,\ldots, m$ [see Intriligator (1971, p. 210)], we obtain

$$\sum_{i=1}^{m} p_i(s) \sum_{k=1}^{m} \frac{\partial \tilde{q}_i}{\partial p_k(s)} \nabla_s t_k\,\mathrm{d}(x_k, s) = \sum_{k=1}^{m} \nabla_s t_k\,\mathrm{d}(x_k, s) \sum_{i=1}^{m} p_i(s) \frac{\partial \tilde{q}_k}{\partial p_i(s)} = 0$$

by the Euler theorem. Conseqently, the above equality becomes

$$\sum_{j=1}^{l} (p - c') \frac{\partial D_j}{\partial p} \nabla_s t\,\mathrm{d}(s, x_j) - \sum_{i=1}^{m} \tilde{q}_i \nabla_s t_i\,\mathrm{d}(x_i, s) = 0$$

where $c' = \sum_{j=1}^{m} p_i(s)(\partial \tilde{q}_i/\partial q(s))$ indicates the marginal cost of producing $q(s)$ at location s. Furthermore, at the profit-maximizing price, we have $(p - c)(\partial D_j/\partial p) = -(e_j D_j/e)$ where e denotes the price-elasticity of the total demand $\sum D_j$ and e_j the price-elasticity of the local demand D_j. Substituting this in the previous equality yields

$$\sum_{j=1}^{l} D_j \frac{e_j}{e} \nabla_s t\,\mathrm{d}(s, x_j) + \sum_{i=1}^{m} \tilde{q}_i \nabla_s t_i\,\mathrm{d}(x_i, s) = 0.$$

It thus appears that, at the profit-maximizing solution, the location chosen by the monopolist minimizes a transportation cost function in which the quantities of output are weighted by the ratio of local elasticities to global elasticity. The reason for this departure from the minimization of the "true" transportation cost function is to be found in the fact that, under mill pricing, the monopolist must share with the consumers the benefits associated with the choice of a transportation cost-minimizing location. When the benefits generated by the proximity to a certain place are completely appropriated by the firm, as in the delivered pricing case, the "true" transport cost terms enter into the function which is minimized a posteriori; this ceases to be true, however, when benefits are shared.

The foregoing implies that, in the mill price case, the Weberian analysis is of no help for characterizing the profit-maximizing solution. What we therefore need here is a set of specific results obtained directly from the solution to (4.18).

Not surprisingly, the results crucially depend on the properties of the demand functions. More precisely, Hanjoul and Thisse (1984) have shown that the profit-maximizing location is a vertex of the network when the demand functions D_j are decreasing and convex and when the production function f is linear homogeneous. Note that the convexity assumption is basic for the nodal property. Indeed, using concave demand functions is sufficient to invalidate it. To illustrate this, consider the following example. There are two customers located at the extremities of the segment $[0,1]$ respectively; the demand function of a customer is given $\max\{0, a - (p + d(s, x_j))^2\}$ where a is a positive constant and t, the transportation rate of the output, is equal to 1; finally there is no production cost. Assuming that the firm location is at $\theta \in [0,1]$, the profit function P_M is $p\{a - (p + \theta)^2 + a - (p + (1 - \theta))^2\}$ for $p < \sqrt{a} - 1$. Clearly, for a sufficiently large, the only profit-maximizing location is given by the middle point $\theta = \frac{1}{2}$, a counter-example to the nodal property.

Assume now that the firm is allowed to operate several plants according to the geographical division pattern. Clearly, in this case, we notice that the whole locational configuration influences the level of demand through the way customers are allocated among plants [see also Benson (1984)]. The firm will therefore choose its profit-maximizing configuration, taking that impact into account. Hence, in general, given the quantities of output sold at the consumers at $x_1, \ldots, x_l$, the total transportation and production cost is not minimized to the profit-maximizing solution [see also Kats (1980)]. Instead, in the case of elastic demand, one would expect some "proliferation" of plants due to the fact that, here, the monopolist tries to capture as much as possible from the total demand by establishing plants close to the customers. On the contrary, when demands are inelastic, the number of plants would be smaller than the least total cost number because the monopolist now endeavours to reduce his setup costs.

A major conclusion emerges from the above analysis: *the spatial price policy of the firm strongly affects the location and production pattern chosen at the profit-maximizing solution*, thus confirming Greenhut's (1956) thesis.

The implications of the above results for policy are clear. First, under (uniform) delivered pricing, the major markets or input sources or transport nodes are expected to be the most attractive locations. In contrast, under mill pricing, the profit-maximizing location may be an "intermediate" point. Second, under (uniform) delivered pricing, the monopolist implements the socially optimal location–production pattern – relative to the quantities sold – while, under mill pricing, he does not. Again this suggests to re-evaluate some of the traditional claims about the social superiority of mill pricing over discriminatory practices (cf. also 3.1).

4.3. The price–location problem in spatial oligopoly

We now discuss how prices and locations are determined when a fixed (typically small) number of firms compete in a given market. This is a difficult problem which forces upon us a number of simplifications.

4.3.1. Mill pricing

The dominant model is that of Hotelling (1929) which has already been described in 3.2.1. However, unlike 3.2.1, not only prices but also locations can now be chosen by firms. The assumptions and notation are as follows. Two firms sell a homogeneous product to consumers spread evenly along a linear market of length l. Each consumer buys exactly one unit of the product. Production involves constant marginal cost c and transportation costs are linear in distance. The demand functions being as in 3.2.1, it is clear that the profit function G_i of firm $i = 1, 2$ depends on prices (p_1, p_2) and locations (s_1, s_2), with $s_1 = a$ and $s_2 = l - b$.

Our first task is to define the equilibrium concept(s) of the noncooperative game whose players are firms, strategies are prices and locations, and payoffs are profits. A seemingly natural approach is to assume that firms choose *simultaneously* price and location. A *price–location equilibrium* is then a quadruple $(p_1^*, s_1^*, p_2^*, s_2^*)$ such that, given the price p_j^* and the location s_j^* of firm j, firm $i \neq j$ maximizes its profits at p_i^* and s_i^*.

Unfortunately, *no price–location equilibrium exists in the Hotelling problem*. The argument is standard. Let us recall it. Assume that a price–location equilibrium exists. As each firm can always secure positive profits, this equilibrium must be such that both firms supply a positive fraction of the market and charge prices above marginal cost. Two cases may then arise. In the first one, $s_1^* \neq s_2^*$. Without loss of generality, we may assume that firm 2's profits exceed or equal firm 1's profits. Then firm 1 can increase its profits by locating at $\bar{s}_1 = s_2^*$ and by setting a price $\bar{p}_1 = p_2^* - \varepsilon$, with $\varepsilon > 0$ arbitrarily small. Indeed, $G_1(\bar{p}_1, \bar{s}_1, p_2^*, s_2^*)$

$> G_2(p_1^*, s_1^*, p_2^*, s_2^*)$ since firm 1 now serves the whole market at a price nearly equal to p_2^*. Since, by assumption, $G_2(p_1^*, s_1^*, p_2^*, s_2^*) \geq G_1(p_1^*, s_1^*, p_2^*, s_2^*)$, it follows that $G_1(\bar{p}_1, \bar{s}_1, p_2^*, s_2^*) > G_1(p_1^*, s_1^*, p_2^*, s_2^*)$, a contradiction to the equilibrium property. In the second case, $s_1^* = s_2^*$. Then a Bertrand-like argument shows that $p_1^*(>c)$ and $p_2^*(>c)$ cannot be equilibrium prices, again a contradiction. [See Schultz and Stahl (1985) for a more detailed discussion.]

In a second approach, originally developed by Hotelling (1929), the decisions on location and price are supposed to be made *sequentially*. In other words, location and price strategies are played one at a time in a two-stage process. Let us describe the two stages in detail. In the first stage, firms choose their location. Given any outcome (s_1, s_2) of the first stage, firms choose their price in the second stage. This can be modelled as a noncooperative game in which strategies are prices and payoffs are profits. The solution of this game is given by the price equilibrium defined in 3.2.1. Clearly, this equilibrium depends on the locations s_1 and s_2. This allows us, therefore, to define the location game pertaining to the first stage. Firm i's strategy is its location s_i while its payoff is given by the level of profits achieved in the second stage, i.e. G_i in which p_1 and p_2 are replaced by the equilibrium prices. The solution of this game is then a pair of locations such that, given the location of the other, no firm can find a more profitable location.

Formally, a *perfect price–location equilibrium* is defined by a pair of price functions $(p_1^*(s_1, s_2), p_2^*(s_1, s_2))$ and a pair of locations (s_1^*, s_2^*) such that, for $i = 1, 2$,

(i) $G_i\big[p_i^*(s_i, s_j), p_j^*(s_i, s_j); s_i, s_j\big] \geq G_i\big[p_i, p_j^*(s_i, s_j); s_i, s_j\big], \quad \forall p_i \geq c,$

(ii) $G_i\big[p_i^*(s_i^*, s_j^*), p_j^*(s_i^*, s_j^*); s_i^*, s_j^*\big] \geq G_i\big[p_i^*(s_i, s_j^*), p_j^*(s_i, s_j^*); s_i, s_j^*\big],$

$$\forall s_i \in [0, l].$$

The concept of perfect equilibrium captures the idea that, when firms choose their locations, they both anticipate the consequences of their choice on price competition. In particular, they should be aware that this competition will be more severe if they locate close to each other. On the other hand, if they move far apart from each other, they weaken their ability of encroaching on their competitor's market territory. The solution to this tradeoff is the perfect equilibrium pattern. Once again, it turns out that *there exists no perfect price–location equilibrium in the Hotelling model*. Indeed, this concept requires that a price equilibrium can be found for any pair of locations. Now, it follows from Proposition 4 that such an equilibrium fails to exist when firms 1 and 2 are near each other. [See, however, d'Aspremont et al. (1979) and Neven (1985) who show that a perfect equilibrium does exist when transportation costs are quadratic in distance.]

As a result, no stable price–location configuration emerges from the above process. Among other things, this implies that, contrary to Hotelling's belief, nothing can be claimed on the basis of his model about the tendency of the two sellers to cluster at the market center – the so-called principle of minimum differentiation.

Having reached these negative outcomes, it seems natural to look for solutions filling the gap. One solution, suggested by Eaton and Kierzkowski (1984), is to assume that the seller adopts a different strategy according to whether or not, when charging his profit-maximizing price, he is likely to be undercut. In the first case, he anticipates his competitor's reaction and quotes the price which maximizes his profits in a way such that his competitor has no incentive to undercut him. In the second case, he charges the Bertrand–Nash price. The resulting equilibrium, which is a kind of consistent conjectural equilibrium [see Bresnahan (1981)], can be used as a reference point in the perfect equilibrium. Eaton and Kierzkowski then show that *it is always profitable for the two firms to choose distant locations so as to avoid the damages of price competition.*

Another approach has been recently tackled by de Palma et al. (1985). These authors observe that the nonexistence of a price–location equilibrium rests on the standard assumption that consumers patronize the firm with the lowest full price. Now, empirical evidence supports the idea that consumers do not necessarily buy from the cheapest firm, since they also take variables other than full price into account. Because of the unobservability of these variables, firms can at best determine the shopping behavior of a particular consumer up to a probability distribution. More precisely, it is now assumed that firms model the utility of a consumer at x and purchasing from firm i as a random variable $u_{ix} = -p_i - t|x - s_i| + \varepsilon_i$, where ε_i is a random variable with a zero mean. As consumers maximize utility, firms evaluate the probability P_{ix} that a consumer at x will purchase from firm i as $P_{ix} = \text{Pr}[u_{ix} = \text{Max}\{u_{1x}, u_{2x}\}]$ so that the expected demand to firm i is given by $\int_0^l P_{ix} d_x$. Assuming that the variables ε_i are continuously distributed, we immediately observe that, wherever the locations s_1 and s_2, firm i's demand has always a positive and finite elasticity. In particular, no firm can price its competitor out of business. Furthermore, if the variables ε_i are identically, independently Weibull-distributed, the probabilities P_{ix} take a simple form given by the logit model [see McFadden (1973)], i.e.

$$P_{ix} = \frac{\exp\{-(p_i + t|x - s_i|)/\mu\}}{\exp\{-(p_1 + t|x - s_1|)/\mu\} + \exp\{-(p_2 + t|x - s_2|)/\mu\}}, \qquad (4.19)$$

where μ is the standard deviation of ε_i, up to a multiplicative constant. (Notice that (4.19) is consistent with spatial interaction; see Chapter 9 of this Handbook.) Then de Palma et al. show that the existence of a price–location equilibrium is guaranteed for $\mu \geq tl$. At this equilibrium, both firms are established at the market center and charge the same price given by $c + 2\mu$. This implies that *the principle of minimum differentiation holds when the transportation cost tl is smaller than or equal to the standard deviation of the random term.*

Following Lerner and Singer (1937) and Eaton and Lipsey (1975), we may also simplify the model by assuming that prices are fixed and identical for all sellers and that firms compete on location only. [It is worth noting that this model has been reinterpreted to explain the choice of political platforms in party competition; see, e.g. Downs (1957) and Enelow and Hinich (1984).] In this case, it is clear that both firms will agglomerate at the market center. Indeed, any firm away from the center can raise its profits by establishing itself close to its competitor on the larger side of the market. Consequently, the only stable configuration occurs when no firm can increase its hinterland, i.e. when they are both located at the center. This result can be extended to the case of any consumer distribution defined on $[0, l]$ in that *there is an equilibrium at which both sellers are established at the median of the consumer distribution.* This has an interesting implication from the welfare point of view: competition between two firms yields a locational pattern which does not make customers better off than in the case of a single firm minimizing total transportation costs. Indeed, we know from the median principle (see Proposition 8) that the transportation cost-minimizing location is also the median of the consumers distribution.

However, the existence property does not carry over when firms compete in a two-dimensional market [see Wendell and McKelvey (1981)] or when the number of firms increases to 3 [see Lerner and Singer (1937)]. For more than three firms competing along a linear market, the existence of a location equilibrium is restored for a uniform distribution. On the other hand, the clustering of firms at a single location does no longer hold. Instead, we obtain equilibrium configurations with some firms being pairwise located and others being single [see Eaton and Lipsey (1975)]. But the clustering emerges again when the model is reformulated to account for heterogeneity in consumers' behavior [see de Palma et al. (1985)]. More precisely, *there exists a location equilibrium with all firms agglomerated at the market center when* $\mu \geq tl(1 - 2/n)$, i.e. when transportation costs are low enough.

To conclude, let us briefly discuss the possible impact of relaxing the assumption of inelastic demands. As pointed out by Lerner and Singer (1937) and Smithies (1941b), the fact that consumers have price-sensitive demands gives rise to a centrifugal force. By moving toward its competitor a firm lowers its sales to its most distant customers, thus reducing the lure of a central location. As a result, at the equilibrium firms may be completely isolated [see Graitson (1982) for more details]. In the case of rectangular demand functions, a (perfect) price–location equilibrium *may* exist [see Economides (1984) and Graitson

(1982)]. However, such equilibria occur only when the market space is long enough for each firm to be in a monopoly situation.

4.3.2. Discriminatory pricing

We have seen in 3.2.3, Proposition 6 that there always exists a price equilibrium when firms are allowed to set (perfectly) discriminating prices. This suggests to reconsider the existence problem of perfect price–location equilibrium. (It is easy to show that no price–location equilibrium exists.)

Recently, Hurter and Lederer (1985) and Lederer and Hurter (1986) have obtained interesting and promising results. To illustrate these, consider again the Hotelling model but in which firms now charge discriminating prices. Then, the first and third quartiles of the linear market define a location equilibrium of the first-stage game. The argument is as follows. Given the equilibrium price schedule (3.16), some simple manipulations show that firm i's profit function can be rewritten as

$$G_i = \int_o^l t|s_j - x| \mathrm{d}x - T(s_1, s_2), \quad j \neq i \tag{4.20}$$

where $T(s_1, s_2) = \int_0^l t \, \mathrm{Min}\{|s_1 - x|, |s_2 - x|\} \, \mathrm{d}x$ is the sum of the transportation costs incurred by the firms at the solution of the second stage game. Clearly, firm i maximizes its profit by locating at the point that, given s_j, minimizes $T(s_1, s_2)$. In particular, $T(s_1, s_2)$ is minimized at $s_1^* = l/4$ and $s_2^* = 3l/4$. Given s_j^*, it then follows from (4.20) that firm i's profit-maximizing location is s_i^*. Thus, *there exists a perfect equilibrium such that the two firms are established at socially optimal locations*; however they do not charge socially optimal prices (cf. 4.2.1 for some comparable results in spatial monopoly). Interestingly, this property still holds for n firms, for a nonuniform consumer distribution and for a two-dimensional market. This opens the door to what seems to be a promising vein for future research.

5. Spatial equilibrium of production

5.1. Market solution

5.1.1. Spatial monopolistic competition

Our purpose is now to study the locational pattern of firms resulting from free entry and exit. This means that not only the location but also the number of firms is variable. In accordance with Chamberlin's (1933) model of monopolistic competition, it is supposed that the density of firms over space is determined at a long-run equilibrium in which profits are zero (or as close to zero as consistent with integer numbers of firms in a bounded region). The question is then to know how close the firms will locate together, i.e. how large the market area of a representative firm is in a zero-profit, long-run equilibrium. Of interest are both the *size* and the *shape* of equilibrium market areas, how they depend on the type of competition and on the demand and cost parameters of the problem. The size problem may be discussed in a one-dimensional context whenever convenient, but shape requires a two-dimensional formulation.

The analysis of the size problem presumes a model that is well-established in spatial economics. Firms produce a homogeneous product under positive fixed costs, F, and constant marginal costs, c. Transportation is under the control of the consumers and the transport rate, t, is constant. Consumers are uniformly distributed along an unbounded linear market (or, equivalently, along a circular market) with a density $\bar{\rho}$; they have identical (downward sloping) demand functions, $f[p(x)]$. Each consumer buys from the firm offering the product at the lowest full price.

Common to most approaches to spatial monopolistic competition are the following steps:

(i) Write the profit of a representative firm as a function of the mill price, p, and market radius, R:

$$G(p, R) = 2\bar{\rho} \int_0^R (p - c) f(p + tx) \, \mathrm{d}x - F. \tag{5.1}$$

(ii) Assume that the representative firm is located at a distance l from either neighbor and let $\bar{p}$ be the common price of both neighbors. Then, for $f^{-1}(0)$ large enough, the market radius is given by

$$R = \frac{\bar{p} - p + tl}{2t}. \tag{5.2}$$

(iii) Given some relationship for $\mathrm{d}\bar{p}/\mathrm{d}p$, find the solution $\tilde{p}$ of the equation

$$\frac{\mathrm{d}G}{\mathrm{d}p} = \frac{\partial G}{\partial p} + \frac{\partial G}{\partial R} \cdot \frac{\mathrm{d}R}{\mathrm{d}p} = 0 \tag{5.3}$$

so as to maximize profit. Clearly, $\tilde{p}$ is a function of the interfirm distance l.

(iv) Substitute $\tilde{p}$ for p and set $R = l/2$ in (5.1) to obtain a function solely in l: $\tilde{G}(l) = G[\tilde{p}(l), l/2]$.

(v) Choose the smallest value l^* for which $\tilde{G} = 0$: the zero-profit condition yields the equilibrium spacing.

(vi) Use the so-obtained value of l^* to determine the equilibrium mill price: $p^* = \tilde{p}(l^*)$ is the profit-maximizing price corresponding to the equilibrium configuration.

It should be clear from the above that the size of market areas in long-run, zero-profit equilibrium is influenced by the behavioral assumption made regarding $d\bar{p}/dp$. Of the many conceivable types of conjectural variation [see Capozza and Van Order (1978)], the following have been studied in the literature:

Bertrand competition: $d\bar{p}/dp = 0$. Competitors' prices are assumed given and the dependence of the firm's market radius on its own price is given by $dR/dp = -1/2t$. (See also 3.3.1.)

Löschian competition: $d\bar{p}/dp = 1$. Competitors exactly match any change in mill price so that the firm takes its market radius as an exogenous variable, i.e. $dR/dp = 0$. (See also 3.3.2.)

When individual demands are rectangular, i.e. as defined by (3.17), the long-run market equilibrium may be given in closed form [see Beckmann, (1972), Capozza and Van Order (1977), Salop (1979)]. Consider first the case of Bertrand competition. It follows from Proposition 7 in 3.3.1 that $\tilde{p}(l)$ is given by (3.20), (3.21) and (3.22) according to the value of l relative to v (the reservation price), c and t. The corresponding values of the profit gross of fixed costs are respectively $\bar{\rho}\{(v-c)^2/2t\}$, $\bar{\rho}(v-(tl/2)-c)l$ and $\bar{\rho}tl^2$. As the monopoly profits are equal to $\bar{\rho}\{(v-c)^2/2t\} - F$, it is clear that no firm will choose to enter the market when $F > \bar{\rho}\{(v-c)^2/2t\}$ since the profits of a firm are always negative. On the other hand, when $F \leq \bar{\rho}\{(v-c)^2/2t\}$, production is profitable. As F and l^* are positively related, two cases may arise depending upon the value of F. In the first one, $F > \frac{4}{9}\bar{\rho}\{(v-c)^2/t\}$ and the equilibrium market areas just touch. This implies that l^* is the smallest positive root of $-(\bar{\rho}t/2)l^2 + \bar{\rho}(v-c)l - F = 0$, i.e.

$$l^* = \frac{v-c}{t} - \sqrt{\left(\frac{v-c}{t}\right)^2 - F/t\bar{\rho}} \tag{5.4}$$

while

$$p^* = \tfrac{1}{2}\left(v + c + \sqrt{(v-c)^2 - Ft/\bar{\rho}}\right). \tag{5.5}$$

In the second case, $F \leq \frac{4}{9}\bar{\rho}\{(v-c)^2/t\}$ and the potential market areas overlap. Consequently, l^* is a solution of $\bar{\rho}tl^2 - F = 0$, i.e.

$$l^* = \sqrt{F/\bar{\rho}t} \tag{5.6}$$

Table 5.1
Summary of comparative statics.

Partial derivatives	$\dfrac{\partial l^*}{\partial F}$	$\dfrac{\partial l^*}{\partial c}$	$\dfrac{\partial l^*}{\partial t}$	$\dfrac{\partial l^*}{\partial v}$	$\dfrac{\partial l^*}{\partial \bar{\rho}}$
$\dfrac{4}{9}\bar{\rho}\dfrac{(v-c)^2}{t} < F \le \bar{\rho}\dfrac{(v-c)^2}{2t}$	+	+	+	−	−
$0 \le F < \dfrac{4}{9}\bar{\rho}\dfrac{(v-c)^2}{t}$	+	0	−	0	−

Partial derivatives	$\dfrac{\partial p^*}{\partial F}$	$\dfrac{\partial p^*}{\partial c}$	$\dfrac{\partial p^*}{\partial t}$	$\dfrac{\partial p^*}{\partial v}$	$\dfrac{\partial p^*}{\partial \bar{\rho}}$
$\dfrac{4}{9}\bar{\rho}\dfrac{(v-c)^2}{t} < F \le \bar{\rho}\dfrac{(v-c)^2}{2t}$	−	−	−	+	+
$0 \le F < \dfrac{4}{9}\bar{\rho}\dfrac{(v-c)^2}{t}$	+	+	+	0	−

and

$$p^* = c + \sqrt{Ft/\bar{\rho}}\,. \tag{5.7}$$

The *free-entry market equilibrium* is then defined by the spacing l^* and the mill price p^*.

The comparative static properties of the equilibrium are presented in Table 5.1.

A glance at Table 5.1 reveals immediately that, depending on the relative values of F, c, t, v and $\bar{\rho}$, the equilibrium solution reacts very differently to a change in cost or demand conditions. In particular, we observe that *the model does not obey the standard properties of nonspatial competitive theory*. More specifically, as costs (fixed, marginal or transport) rise, price should rise. Yet, when fixed costs and/or transport costs are large enough, price responds perversely! Even the average full price paid by consumers decreases when costs increase. Indeed, this price is given by $\bar{p} = p^* + t(l^*/4) = \{3v + c + \sqrt{(v-c)^2 - Ft/\bar{\rho}}\}/4$ which behaves like p^*. On the other hand, when fixed costs and/or transport costs are small enough, costs and price rise (or fall) together. The model thus behaves like the model of perfect competition. *The "perversities" occur only for parameter instances which are characterized by high fixed costs and/or transport costs*, i.e. when we are far away from a competitive economy. [Notice that Capozza and Van Order (1978) reach similar conclusions in the case of linear demand functions.]

Until now, no explanation has been afforded as to why firms are equally spaced in the free-entry market equilibrium. Actually, this question poses serious problems. Given the price–location pattern of its competitors, every firm in the industry can increase its profits by locating next to one of its neighbors and by charging a price slightly lower that p^* (cf. 4.3.1). Consequently, the free-entry market equilibrium is *not* a simultaneous Nash equilibrium in price and location. In order to obviate this difficulty, recourse has been made to a modification of the Nash equilibrium concept: firms treat prices and locations of their competitors as given, except in the case where one firm's actions result in its price undercutting the price of another firm at the latter firm's location. In such cases the second firm is assumed to react by cutting price to marginal cost so preventing the use of a price undercutting strategy [see Eaton (1972), Eaton and Lipsey (1978)]. Novshek (1980) has then shown that the symmetric price–location pattern (p^*, l^*) is a "modified" Nash equilibrium. However, there is a difficulty with this equilibrium concept in that it eliminates one basic ingredient of price competition since it rules out a priori any form of price war.

Let us now come to the case of Löschian competition. We know from 3.3.2 that $\tilde{p}(l)$ is given by (3.20) or (3.21). As above, production is profitable only if $F \leq \bar{\rho}\{(v - c)^2/2t\}$. Whenever this inequality is satisfied, a single market solution emerges that is given by (5.4) and (5.5): each firm in the industry sets a profit-maximizing price p^* taking as parametric its market radius $l^*/2$ which results itself from the zero-profit condition.

The comparative static properties of the Löschian solution appear in the first and third rows of Table 5.1, but they are now valid on the whole domain of the admissible values of F. Apparently, these results are therefore counter-intuitive. In fact they are not. As pointed out in 3.3.2, the Löschian model presumes a noncompetitive pricing rule so that it cannot be interpreted as a spatial competitive model.

It remains to compare the solutions obtained in the two models. First, we immediately see that the Bertrand and Löschian solutions coincide for $\frac{4}{9}\bar{\rho}\{(v - c)^2/t\} \leq F \leq \bar{\rho}\{(v - c)^2/2t\}$. On the other hand, when $F < \frac{4}{9}\bar{\rho}\{(v - c)^2/t\}$, the two solutions differ: *the market radius is smaller under Löschian competition than under Bertrand competition but the Löschian price is larger than the Bertrand price*. However, the global effect is such that the consumer surplus is higher at the Bertrand solution.

For further developments and extensions (in particular for more general demand functions), the reader is referred to Beckmann (1968, 1971), Benson (1980), Capozza and Van Order (1978), Mulligan (1981) and Ohta (1981).

Let us now briefly discuss the possible interpretations of the above two models. Clearly, the Bertrand model can be considered as a model of spatial competition with free-entry. When the conditions of perfect competition are approached, the Bertrand solution turns out to be nearly perfectly competitive. The fact that this solution can behave perversely for high fixed costs and/or transport costs does not really challenge the proposed interpretation.

On the other hand, there are several problems with the interpretation of the Löschian model. First, this model cannot be viewed as a model of spatial competition. Indeed, we would expect a reasonable model of spatial competition to behave like the perfect competition model in the limit. But we know that this property does not hold in general for the Löschian model.

An alternative interpretation, suggested by Capozza and Van Order (1978), is to consider the Löschian model as a model of tacit spatial collusion. Indeed, once market areas are determined, the Löschian price leads to maximization of profit per unit area for the whole industry. Consequently, the Löschian solution would be the solution for a spatial cartel in which profits are shared among the firms on the basis of market areas. However, as noticed by MacLeod et al. (1987), this interpretation is open to objections. In particular, there is a paradox here: why would firms collude if profits are eventually wiped out?

This has led the above authors to reformulate the Löschian model as follows. There is an initial stage in which firms enter the market under competitive conditions. The outcome of this stage is the Betrand solution. *Given* the corresponding market areas, the incumbent firms can then maximize their profits by moving to the collusive Löschian price. MacLeod et al. (1987) then show that the resulting price–location pattern has most of the properties that should be associated with a model of collusive oligopoly [see Stigler (1964)].

To the best of our knowledge, Lösch (1940) was the first to investigate the long-run spatial equilibrium of an industry in a two-dimensional (Euclidean) space. The standard case considers the following equilibrium conditions:

(i) Each firm sets marginal revenue equal marginal cost: the profit-maximization condition.

(ii) Each firm produces where its aggregate demand curve is just tangent to its average cost curve: the zero-profit condition.

(iii) The number of operating firms is maximized: the densest packing condition.

When possible market areas are restricted to the three regular polygons: equilateral triangles, squares and hexagons, it is not hard to see that hexagons represent the most profitable shape since, for many cost and demand functions, profits in a given area are a decreasing function of the average distance to customers, and for a given area this average distance is smallest in a hexagon [see Lösch (1940)]. Consequently, the equilibrium pattern of firms would be given by the *hexagonal closest packing lattice*.

But average distance is smaller still in a circle. When fixed costs are larger than the gross profits that can be achieved in a hexagon but smaller than those attainable in a circle, the question arises as to the equilibrium shape of the market area [see Mills and Lav (1964)].

One may visualize firms operating at first in the most profitable circular markets, being squeezed by new entrants, so that their market areas take the form of *rounded hexagons*. Only when fixed costs are small enough, does the squeeze continue until *hexagons* emerge. On the other hand, industries with high fixed costs cannot afford to serve all customers. Firms do not sell in those points of the plane where demand is zero because mill price plus transport cost exceeds the price intercept $f^{-1}(0)$. In such cases, it appears that not all consumers are supplied at equilibrium. Accordingly, the shape of market areas in the long run depends on the level of fixed costs.

The general shape of the equilibrium market area, determined not by individual firms but competitive forces, is thus *a hexagon with its corners rounded off* by a circle of radius $\{ f^{-1}(0) - p*/t \}$ [see Beckmann (1971), Mulligan (1981)]. As limiting cases, we have a complete hexagon (the traditional Löschian market area) and at the other extreme a complete circle (the monopoly market area).

In the above process, it is supposed that the existing firms simultaneously relocate to the new net-like arrangement in response to the entry of new firms. Recently, Holahan and Schuler (1981a,b) have questioned the validity of this assumption. It is indeed not clear why the incumbent firms, even in the absence of relocation costs, should necessarily move when entry occurs. Actually, they do so only if relocation generates more profits. Because of the intricated geometry of the problem, there may exist situations in which no new location yields larger profits than the present locations. As a result, the sequence circle–rounded hexagon–hexagon does not necessarily take place and other configurations may persist at the long-run equilibrium. Thus *it is completely consistent with long-run competitive behavior, even in the case of portable firms, to observe non-hexagonal patterns*. For instance, Holahan and Schuler have been able to identify situations with stable circular or square-like arrangements of producers.

5.1.2. *Sequential entry with immobile firms*

In contrast to the approach taken in 5.1.1, we now suppose that firms make their locational decision *once-for-all*. This assumption is made to reflect the fact that most firms do involve capital goods which once installed cannot be easily transported to new locations. When the entry process is treated explicitly as a sequential process taking place over time, this entails an asymmetry in the choices open to the existing firms and to the entrants. Whereas the former have to stick to their location, the latter are free to choose where to set up their plant.

This assumption has several important implications regarding the properties of the long-run equilibrium. First, as pointed out by Eaton (1976) and Eaton and Lipsey (1978), *free-entry is consistent with the persistence of pure profits*. The reason for this is as follows. Since the firms already established are immobile, a new entrant must expect a market substantially smaller than the market of the existing firms (and this even when there is no price competition). Hence, the market that a newcomer can capture may be too small to cover his setup costs, whereas the market of the incumbents may be large enough to allow them to earn positive profits. Somewhat surprisingly, it is the fact that the existing firms are committed to their location which essentially accounts for the existence of pure profits.

Second, *the long-run equilibrium is not unique* in that it depends on the initial conditions and on the dynamics of entry: history matters [see Capozza and Van Order (1980), Eaton (1976), Eaton and Lipsey (1976)]. In particular, the regular spacing of firms turns out to be destroyed in many cases so that firms can enjoy market areas of different sizes at equilibrium. Moreover, the hexagonal arrangement is just one of the many possible configurations which can emerge in the long run.

Third, and last, *entry can be deterred* (hence profits can be increased) *if firms are sophisticated enough to take full advantage of their position in the order of entry* [see Hay (1976), Prescott and Visscher (1977), Rothschild (1976)]. Briefly, the argument is as follows. Given the long-run nature of the locational decisions, one may expect a new firm to anticipate subsequent entry when choosing its location. More precisely, an entrant takes as given the locations of firms entered before him but treats the locations of firms entering after him as conditional on his own choice. In so doing, a firm locates so as to secure the most profitable market for itself in the long run. This, in turn, implies that the firms are fewer than under myopic behavior. [In the same vein, notice also that a monopolist with multiple plants could pre-empt the entire market by spacing its plants at the distance that maximizes his profits subject to the constraint that no additional firms can earn a profit after entry (see Eaton and Lipsey (1979), Prescott and Visscher (1977))].

5.2.   Planning solution

5.2.1.   The Christaller – Lösch problem

Even since the pioneering works of Christaller (1933) and Lösch (1940), the optimal arrangement of producers has been a major issue in location theory. The problem is to find, for a given level of demand, the distribution of firms over the plane which minimizes production and transportation costs per unit area.

More specifically, we suppose the plane uniformly covered by customers with identical requirements, δ, for a given commodity. Production of this commodity entails a fixed setup costs, F, and constant marginal costs, c, so that production costs of a firm are given by $F + cq$. Finally, the cost of transporting one unit of the commodity over a unit distance is a constant, t, and the distance between any two points x_1 and x_2 of $\mathbb{R}^2$ is given by the Euclidean distance $\| x_1 - x_2 \|$.

The existence of setup costs makes that, at the optimum, firms must be established at isolated points of $\mathbb{R}^2$. Moreover, given the homogeneity of economic space, one expects these points to form a net-like arrangement in which each point has the same environment as every other point, i.e. a lattice. The *Christaller – Lösch problem* therefore consists of finding the lattice which minimizes the production and transportation cost, per unit area, of supplying requirement δ.

It has long been argued that the solution to the above problem is obtained when each producer is equidistant from exactly six other producers. In other words, firms must be located at the vertices of an hexagonal lattice and must serve customers within a regular hexagon. In fact, it seems that the optimality of the hexagonal arrangement was often confused with another property, i.e. the densest packing property: Of all lattices having a given distance between two nearest firms, the hexagonal lattice maximizes the number of firms established within a sufficiently large area [see Alao et al. (1977) and the references therein]. Though related, these two properties are not equivalent. Consequently, a specific argument was needed to prove the optimality of the hexagonal lattice and it was only in the early 1970s that such an argument was given [see Bollobás (1973), Fejes Tóth (1972)].

In order to deal rigorously with the solution to the Christaller–Lösch problem, we start with a subproblem in which locations are limited to a plane filler, i.e. a bounded set S of $\mathbb{R}^2$ such that copies of S can cover the plane without overlapping. Let also $s_1, \ldots, s_n$ be n points of S and $M_1, \ldots, M_n$ be a decomposition of S into n disjoint subsets; denote $s = (s_1, \ldots, s_n)$ and $M = (M_1, \ldots, M_n)$. Interpreting s_i as the firm's location and M_i as its market area, we see that

$$T(s, M) = \delta \sum_{i=1}^{n} \iint_{M_i} t\|s_i - x\| dx \tag{5.8}$$

is the corresponding transportation cost. The solution to this subproblem is defined by the locations $(s_1^*, \ldots, s_n^*)$ and the market areas $M_1^*, \ldots, M_n^*$ which minimize $T(s, M)$.

Clearly, for any $s_1, \ldots, s_n$ given, the cost-minimizing decomposition of S is formed by the Dirichlet (or Voronoi, or Thiessen) regions of $s_1, \ldots, s_n$, i.e. the subsets $M_i^*(s)$ having the property that s_i is the closest of the points $s_1, \ldots, s_n$ to any $s \in M_i^*(s)$. Consequently, (5.8) can be replaced by

$$T^*(s) = \delta \iint_S t \min\|s_i - x\| dx, \tag{5.9}$$

which is now to be minimized with respect to $s_1, \ldots, s_n$ only. The basic result, due to Bollobás (1973), is the following:

Proposition 12

If S is a plane filler, then for any $s_1, \ldots, s_n$ in S we have

$$T^*(s) \geq n\delta \iint_H t\|x\| \mathrm{d}x \tag{5.10}$$

where H is a regular hexagon with a center at the origin and of area equal to one nth of that of S. Furthermore, the equality holds in (5.10) if and only if S is the union of n hexagons of an hexagonal lattice and $M_1^*, \ldots, M_n^*$ and $s_1^*, \ldots, s_n^*$ are exactly these hexagons and their centers respectively.

This result means two things. First, transportation costs over S are bounded from below by the value of the transportation costs occurring when firms are established at the centers of n regular and identical hexagons. Second, the hexagonal arrangement is the only one for which the minimum transportation cost is reached. Accordingly, given the size of a plane filler, it is optimal for the planner to distribute firms over the vertices of an hexagonal lattice whose hexagons have a size equal to that of the plane filler.

It remains to determine the size of the hexagon H^* minimizing production and transportation costs per unit area. This amounts to choosing D for which

$$\frac{F + 12\delta \int_0^{\pi/6} \int_0^{D/2\cos\theta} (c + tr) r \, \mathrm{d}r \, \mathrm{d}\theta}{12 \int_0^{\pi/6} \int_0^{D/2\cos\theta} r \, \mathrm{d}r \, \mathrm{d}\theta} \tag{5.11}$$

is minimized, D denoting the distance between two nearest firms in the hexagonal lattice. In (5.11) the numerator is the production and transportation cost corresponding to a firm supplying an hexagon of radius $D/2$ while the denominator is the area of this hexagon.

Computing the integrals, we see that (5.11) is equal to $2F/\sqrt{3} D^2 + \delta[c + (4 + 3\ln 3)tD/12\sqrt{3}]$. Solving the first-order conditions then yields

$$D^* = \left(\frac{12F}{(4 + 3\ln 3)t\delta} \right)^{1/3}. \tag{5.12}$$

To sum-up: *the optimal arrangement of producers is an hexagonal lattice whose distance between two nearest vertices is given by (5.12). Furthermore, inspection of*

(5.12) shows that the density of firms is positively related to the freight rate and demand level but negatively to the value of fixed costs. On the other hand, the marginal production cost has no impact on the optimal spacing of firms. [Notice that this problem is the spatial counterpart of the "optimal lot size" problem in inventory theory; see Hadley and Whitin (1963).]

Suppose now that the plane is uniformly covered by customers with the same demand function which is supposed to be distance-sensitive; the other assumptions are unchanged. In this case, the objective function of the planner becomes the net social surplus per unit area [see Smolensky et al. (1970)]. Bollobás (1973) and Bollobás and Stern (1972) have shown that, for this new objective, the optimal distribution of firms is still the honeycomb. Of course, the optimal spacing does no longer obey (5.12) and depends on the properties of the local demand function [see Beckmann (1971), and Stern (1972)]. In particular, contrary to general beliefs, *the equilibrium market areas are not unambiguously smaller than the optimal market areas*. [Examples can be found in Stern (1972).]

Other possible generalizations deal with nonlinear production and transportation costs. Bollobás (1973) has been able to prove the optimality of the hexagonal arrangement when variable production costs are convex and/or transportation costs are increasing in distance. On the other hand when variable production costs are not convex, there may exist a transportation cost function not necessarily linear in distance for which the regular hexagonal arrangement is not optimum.

It is also worth pointing out that *the debate about the relevance of the hexagonal arrangement rests very much on the Euclidean distance*. For example, under the rectilinear distance, one expects the locational patterns to be given by the juxtaposition of $\pi/4$-rotated squares [see Beckmann (1968, 1972), Ponsard (1974)]. Accordingly, a task for future research is to study the impact of the type of distance chosen on the shape of market areas in both market and planning solutions.

5.2.2.   *The location – allocation problem in discrete space*

A great deal of attention has been paid in the 1970s by operations researchers and management scientists to the modelling of locational decisions. There now exists a well-developed body of literature which should be of great interest to the spatial economist and the regional scientist. [See Francis et al. (1983) and Hansen et al. (1983) for recent surveys.] In particular, a model, known as the *simple plant location problem* (SPLP), has emerged as a prominent prototype. As in the Christaller–Lösch problem, the purpose is to identify the configuration of firms minimizing production and transportation costs. In contrast, however, demand is concentrated in a finite number of points in space and firms can be placed at a finite number of potential locations selected via some prior analyses [see Krarup and Pruzan (1987) for a clear and well-motivated introduction to discrete location theory].

Let $j=1,\ldots,n$ be the locations of customers with fixed requirements δ_j for a given commodity. Firms can be established at sites $i=1,\ldots,m$. The setup cost, F_i, and marginal cost, c_i, are constant and site-specific so that production costs of a firm at i are given by $F_i + c_i q$. Finally, the cost of transporting one unit of the commodity from site i to customer j is a constant t_{ij}.

The purpose of the planner is to choose the number of firms, their locations and market areas in order to serve customers at minimum costs.

To give a formal definition of the SPLP, we need the following notation: y_i is a 0-1 variable which equals 1 if a firm is established at i and 0 otherwise, and let y be the vector (y_i); q_{ij} is the shipment of commodity from a firm at i to customer j, and let Q be the matrix $[q_{ij}]$. Accordingly, production and transportation costs associated with y and Q can be written as

$$C(y,Q) = \sum_{i=1}^{m} \sum_{j=1}^{n} (c_i + t_{ij}) q_{ij} + \sum_{i=1}^{m} F_i y_i. \tag{5.13}$$

The following constraints must be taken into account. First, requirement of customer j must be satisfied:

$$\sum_{i=1}^{m} q_{ij} = \delta_j, \qquad j=1,\ldots,n. \tag{5.14}$$

Second, customer j can be supplied from a firm at i only if a firm is established there:

$$0 \le q_{ij} \le y_i \delta_j, \qquad i=1,\ldots,m, \; j=1,\ldots,n. \tag{5.15}$$

Third, and last, y_i is a $0-1$ variable:

$$y_j \in \{0,1\}, \qquad j=1,\ldots,n. \tag{5.16}$$

Formally, the SPLP consists of minimizing (5.13) subject to (5.14), (5.15) and (5.16); see Manne (1964) and Stollsteimer (1963) for the original formulations. It can be viewed as the discrete, heterogenous version of the Christaller–Lösch problem (cf. 5.2.1) in that the location and capacity of firms are determined endogenously. [Notice that a close relative of the SPLP, known as the K-median problem, has also been widely studied: given K firms the purpose is to find out the configuration minimizing total transportation costs; see Mirchandani (1987) for a recent survey.]

Let $I \subseteq \{1, \ldots, m\}$ be the configuration of firms corresponding to y. Clearly the cost-minimizing allocation is realized when customer j is supplied from the firm (or one of the firms) such that $c_i + t_{ij}$ is minimum for $i \in I$. (This is consistent with the efficiency conditions of the LP transportation problem; see 2.1.) Consequently, (5.13) can be replaced by

$$C'(I) = \sum_{j=1}^{n} \min_{i \in I} (c_i + t_{ij}) \delta_j + \sum_{i \in I} F_i. \tag{5.17}$$

Thus the SPLP is equivalent to the combinatorial problem

$$\min_{I \subseteq \{1, \ldots, m\}} C'(I). \tag{5.18}$$

An important property of function C' is a follows: Let $k \in \{1, \ldots, m\}$ and $K \subseteq I \subseteq \{1, \ldots, [k], \ldots, m\}$. Then

$$C'(I) - C'(I \cup \{k\}) \le C'(K) - C'(K \cup \{k\}). \tag{5.19}$$

Indeed, for all j, we have

$$\min_{i \in I} (c_i + t_{ij}) - \min_{i \in I \cup \{k\}} (c_i + t_{ij})$$

$$= \max\left(0, \min_{i \in I} (c_i + t_{ij}) - (c_k + t_{kj})\right)$$

$$\le \max\left(0, \min_{i \in K} (c_i + t_{ij}) - (c_k + t_{kj})\right) \quad \text{since } K \subseteq I$$

$$= \min_{i \in K} (c_i + t_{ij}) - \min_{i \in K \cup \{k\}} (c_i + t_{ij}).$$

Multiplying both sides by δ_j and summing over j, we therefore obtain the desired inequality.

This result, due to Frieze (1974), means that the additional cost reduction resulting from the setting up of a firm at k is a nondecreasing function of the configuration of firms with respect to set inclusion. In other words, the larger is I, the smaller is the cost saved by establishing a new firm.

Inequality (5.19) suggests the following greedy-like procedures for solving the SPLP: (i) Assume that a single firm has been located so as to minimize total costs. If the establishment of an additional firm brings a cost reduction, then one sets up the firm yielding the largest reduction in total costs. The procedure is iterated until the addition of any further firm necessarily increases total costs. (ii) Assume that firms are initially located at every point i. If the shutting down of a firm leads to a decrease in total costs, then one closes the firm yielding the largest cost reduction. This is carried on until the closing down of any further firm causes total costs to rise.

Unfortunately, these two procedures do not necessarily give the optimal solution. However, as shown by computational experiments, they often provide good results [see, e.g. Hansen and Kaufman (1972)].

Another possibility is to use a linear programming relaxation of the SPLP. This means that the integrality constraints $y_j \in \{0,1\}$ are replaced by $0 \le y_j \le 1$. (In fact, it is sufficient to consider $y_j \ge 0$ since the constraints $y_j \le 1$ are automatically satisfied by the optimal solution of the relaxed program.) Interestingly, the optimal solution to the linear programming relaxation is often integer and is, therefore, the optimal solution to the SPLP. This observation is very important. First, from the economic viewpoint, it implies that, *in many cases, locational indivisibilities in the SPLP do not preclude the existence of a price system sustaining the optimal configuration of firms.* [Contrast with Koopmans and Beckmann (1957).] Let us elaborate on this point. Denote by λ_j the (delivered) price of the commodity for customer j and let $\lambda = (\lambda_1, \ldots, \lambda_n)$. Then $P_i(\lambda_j) = \max\{0, (\lambda_j - c_i - t_{ij})\delta j\}$ is the profit made by firm i from supplying customer j while $P_i(\lambda) = \max\{0, \sum_{j=1}^n P_i(\lambda_j) - F_i\}$ is the total profit. Given λ, the optimal decision for firm i is to operate when $P_i(\lambda)$ is nonnegative and to supply the customers for which $\lambda_j - c_i - t_{ij}$ is nonnegative, and not to operate when $P_i(\lambda)$ is negative. The above observation therefore implies that prices $\lambda_1^*, \ldots, \lambda_n^*$ often exist such that the configuration obtained by allowing each (potential) firm to act as an independent profit-maximizer, is the optimal configuration for (5.13)–(5.16).

Second, from the computational viewpoint, it suggests to use the linear programming relaxation to compute bounds in a branch-and-bound type algorithm. In the present context, such an algorithm is expected to perform very well since very little (if any) enumeration will be required to determine the optimal solution to the SPLP. More specifically, the method DUALOC devised by Erlenkotter (1978) appears as the best existing exact algorithm. DUALOC exploits the special structure of the dual of the linear programming relaxation and uses simple and efficient heuristics to obtain a (near-) optimal solution. [The reader interested in further developments about the SPLP is referred to Cornuejols et al. (1987) and Krarup and Pruzan (1983)].

It is worth noting that several extensions of the SPLP are amenable to problems which keep the structure of the SPLP, which means that they are solvable by the above-mentioned methods. Examples are provided by situations in which customers have (site-specific) demand functions [see Erlenkotter (1977)], firms have decreasing marginal production costs [see Efroymson and Ray (1966)], the planar minimizes an intertemporal cost function [see Van Roy and Erlenkotter (1982)].

6. Conclusion

The location of man and his activities has been a subject of long-standing interest in its own right – apart from economics. The existence of regularities in spatial patterns in the face of great diversity of natural conditions has fascinated the human mind. Geography is one of the oldest of sciences.

The location of human activities has been studied through various approaches. Besides "monistic" theories, stressing the dominant role of such single factors as climate, fertility of soil, access to water, there have emerged, in our time, the theory of "social physics" bringing to bear on location analysis the concepts of mechanics: gravity and potential, and of thermodynamics: entropy. These paradigms are considered inadequate by the social science school of regional analysis which aims at theories based explicitly on an analysis of human behavior. In principle, psychology, sociology and political science are called up to present behavioral models of man capable of explaining his uses of an impediment through space.

At the risk of being one-sided, we have instead used an economic approach exclusively. In this chapter, the location of production activities has been analyzed as the result of economic choice, exercised by economic agents such as firms and households whose actions are coordinated through markets or through planning authorities. In this way, *location theory has been developed through the incorporation of spatial variables* – localized spatial resources and distances – *into microeconomic theory.*

Even this restricted program has not been carried through in all details, partly because some of these developments do not exist as yet, and partly as a result of our choice. Thus, we have not discussed

(i) models of agglomeration [see, e.g. Papageorgiou (1983)],

(ii) new industrial economics, including product differentiation and imperfect information (see Chapter 15 of this Handbook),

(iii) disaggregate discrete spatial choice models (see Chapter 3 of this Handbook),

(iv) central place theory and multipurpose shopping [see, e.g. Mulligan (1984)],

(v) uncertainty and dynamics (see Chapter 6 of this Handbook).

Perhaps most significantly (and to the greatest disappointment of some readers), we have not examined the locations of any particular industry. The reader is called upon to use the tools presented here in order to determine whether a specific industry is resource-, market-, or labor-oriented, whether it follows the principle of the median or even exhibits a Weberian triangle!

Nor have we considered the location pattern of aggregate economic activity – macroeconomic location theory, because the micro-analysis presented here does not provide the right tools for this.

A final word should be said about the relationship between location theory, as presented here, and economics. The approach of this essay has been to utilize microeconomic theory to study locations. What about the inverse relationship: can location theory be utilized beyond mere illustration, to "improve" on economic theory? We leave this question with the reader. In our opinion, the full integration of location theory into economics is one of the great challenges facing regional science today.

Appendix – Proof of Proposition 4

Suppose that a price equilibrium exists. Without loss of generality we set $p^{1*} \leq p^{2*}$.

If $p^{1*} < p^{2*}$, then the sales of firm 1 are

$$\min\left\{ a, \frac{p^{1*} - c}{t} \right\} + \min\left\{ l - a, \frac{p^{1*} - c}{t} \right\}.$$

Hence, firm 1 can raise its sales and, therefore, its profits by increasing its price by ε, with $\varepsilon > 0$ sufficiently small, which contradicts the equilibrium conditions. Let $p^{1*} = p^{2*} \overset{\text{def}}{=} p^*$. If $a = l - b$ then, by setting a price $p^* - \varepsilon$, firm 1 can have the whole market and hence increase its profits, again a contradiction. Let us now assume that $a \neq l - b$ and set $\hat{R} = (l - a - b)/2$. Three cases may arise. In the first one, we have $p^* < c + t\hat{R}$. This implies that the market areas of firms 1 and 2 do not touch each other. Accordingly, by charging $p^* + \varepsilon$ with $\epsilon > 0$ sufficiently small, firm 1 can expand its market area and, therefore, its profits, which contradicts the equilibrium conditions.

In the second case, $p^* > c + t\hat{R}$. The market is now split at distance $\hat{R}$ from firm 1. If firm 1 sets a price $p^* - \varepsilon$, with $\varepsilon < \frac{1}{2}t(a - \hat{R})$, then

$$S^1(p^* - \varepsilon, p^*) = \min\left\{ \frac{p^* - \varepsilon - c}{t}, a \right\} + \frac{p^* - \varepsilon - c}{t} > \min\left\{ \frac{p^* - c}{t}, a \right\}$$
$$+ \hat{R} = S^1(p^*, p^*)$$

since $(p^* - c)/t > \hat{R}$. Consequently, for ε small enough, the sales effect dominates the price effect so that $G^1(p^* - \varepsilon, p^*) > G^1(p^*, p^*)$, a contradiction.

In the third case, $p^* = c + t\hat{R}$. Consider now a price increase by firm 1: $p^1 = p^* + \varepsilon$. As $p^* = c + t\hat{R}$, firm 2 does not want to supply customers in $[0, a + \hat{R}]$ so that the market boundary still lies at $a + \hat{R}$. Accordingly, $S^1(p^* + \varepsilon, p^*) \geq S^1(p^*, p^*)$ and, therefore, $G^1(p^* + \varepsilon, p^*) > G^1(p^*, p^*)$, a contradiction.
Q.E.D.

References

Alao, N. et al. (1977) *Christaller central place structure: an introductory statement*. Evanston: Department of Geography, Northwestern University.

Alonso, W. (1967) 'A reformulation of classical location theory and its relation to rent theory', *Papers of the Regional Science Association*, 19:23–44.

Beckmann, M. J. (1952) 'A continuous model of transportation', *Econometrica*, 20:643–660.

Beckmann, M. J. (1953) 'The partial equilibrium of a continuous space market', *Weltwirtschaftliches Archiv*, 71:73–87.

Beckmann, M. J. (1968) *Location theory*. New York: Random House.

Beckmann, M. J. (1971) 'Equilibrium versus optimum: spacing of firms and patterns of market areas', *Northeast Regional Science Review*, 1:1–20.

Beckmann, M. J. (1972) 'Spatial Cournot oligopoly', *Papers of the Regional Science Association*, 28:37–47.

Beckmann, M. J. (1976) 'Spatial price policies revisited', *Bell Journal of Economics*, 7:619–630.

Beckmann, M. J. (1985) 'Spatial price policy and the demand for transportation', *Journal of Regional Science*, 25:367–371.

Beckmann, M. J. and T. Marschak (1955) 'An activity analysis approach to location theory', *Proceedings of the second symposium in linear programming*. Washington D. C.: National Bureau of Standards and Directorate of Management Analyses.

Beckmann, M. J. and T. Puu (1985) *Spatial economics. Density, potential and flow*. Amsterdam: North-Holland.

Benson, B. L. (1980) 'Löschian competition under alternative demand conditions', *American Economic Review*, 70:1098–1105.

Benson, B. L. (1984) 'The level of average production cost chosen by a multiplant spatial monopolist', *Regional Science and Urban Economics*, 14:37–44.

Benson, B. L. and J. C. Hartigan (1983) 'Tariffs with lower price in the restricted country', *Journal of International Economics*, 15:117–133.

Benson, B. L. and J. C. Hartigan (1984) 'An explanation of intra-industry trade in identical commodities', *International Journal of Industrial Organisation*, 2:85–97.

Bertrand, J. (1883) 'Théorie mathématique de la richesse sociale', *Journal des Savants*, 48:499–508.

Black, D. (1948) 'On the rationale of group decision making', *Journal of Political Economy*, 56:23–34.

Bollobás, B. (1973) 'The optimal arrangement of producers', *Journal of the London Mathematical Society*, 6:605–613.

Bollobás, B. and N. Stern (1972) 'The optimal structure of market areas', *Journal of Economic Theory*, 4:174–179.

Brander, J. A. (1981) 'Intra-industry trade on identical commodities', *Journal of International Economics*, 11:1–14.

Bresnahan, T. (1981) 'Duopoly models with consistent conjectures', *American Economic Review*, 71:934–945.

Capozza, D. R. and R. Van Order (1977) 'Pricing under spatial competition and spatial monopoly', *Econometrica*, 45:1329–1338.

Capozza, D. R. and R. Van Order (1978) 'A generalized model of spatial competion', *American Economic Review*, 68:896–908.

Capozza, D. R. and R. Van Order (1980) 'Unique equilibria, pure profits, and efficiency in location models', *American Economic Review*, 70:1046–1053.

Chamberlin, E. N. (1933) *The theory of monopolistic competition*. Cambridge, Mass.: Harvard University Press.

Christaller, W. (1933) *Die zentralen Orte in Süddeutschland*. Jena: Gustav Fisher, English translation: *Central places in Southern Germany*. Englewood Cliffs, N.J.: Prentice-Hall.

Cornuejols, G., M. L. Fisher, and G. L. Nemhauser (1977) 'Location of bank accounts to optimize float: an analytic study of exact and approximate algorithms', *Management Science*, 23:789–810.

Cornuejols, G., G. L. Nemhauser, and L. A. Wolsey (1987) 'The uncapacitated facility location problem', in: R. L. Francis and P. Mirchandani, eds., *Discrete location theory*. New York: Wiley-Interscience, forthcoming.

Dafermos, S. and A. Nagurney (1985) 'Oligopolistic and competitive behavior of spatially separated markets', mimeo, Leschetz Center for Dynamical Systems, Brown University.

Dasgupta, P. and E. Maskin (1986) 'The existence of equilibrium in discontinuous economic games, 1: theory', *Review of Economic Studies*, 53:1–26.

d'Aspremont, C., J. Jaskold Gabszewicz, and J.-F. Thisse (1979) 'On Hotelling's "Stability in Competition"', *Econometrica*, 47:1045–1050.

Dearing, P. M. and R. L. Francis (1974) 'A miminax-location problem on a network', *Transportation Science*, 8:333–343.

de Palma, A., V. Ginsburgh, Y. Y. Papageorgiou, and J.-F. Thisse (1985) 'The principle of minimum differentiation holds under sufficient heterogeneity', *Econometrica*, 53:767–781.

Dorfman, R., P. A. Samuelson, and R. M. Solow, (1958) *Linear programming and economic analysis*. New York: McGraw-Hill.

Downs, A. (1957) *An economic theory of democracy*. New York: Harper and Row.

Eaton, B. C. (1972) 'Spatial competition revisited', *Canadian Journal of Economics*, 5:268–278.

Eaton, B. C. (1976) 'Free entry in one-dimensional models: pure profits and multiple equilibria', *Journal of Regional Science*, 16:21–33.

Eaton, J. and H. Kierzkowski (1984) 'Oligopolistic competition, product variety, entry deterrence, and technology transfer', *Rand Journal of Economics*, 15:99–107.

Eaton, B. C. and R. G. Lipsey (1975) 'The principle of minimum differentiation reconsidered: some new developments in the theory of spatial competition', *Review of Economic Studies*, 42:27–49.

Eaton, B. C. and R. G. Lipsey (1976) 'The non-uniqueness of equilibrium in the Löschian model', *American Economic Review*, 66:77–93.

Eaton, B. C. and R. G. Lipsey (1978) 'Freedom of entry and the existence of pure profits', *Economic Journal*, 88:455–469.

Eaton, B. C. and R. G. Lipsey (1979) 'The theory of market pre-emption: the persistence of excess capacity and monopoly in growing markets', *Economica*, 46:149–158.

Economides, N. S. (1984) 'The principle of minimum differentiation revisited', *European Economic Review* 24:345–368.

Edgeworth, F. Y. (1883) 'The method of least squares', *Philosophical Magazine*, 16:360–375.

Efroymson, M. A. and T. L. Ray (1966) 'A branch-and-bound algorithm for plant location', *Operations Research*, 14:361–368.

Enelow, J. M. and M. J. Hinich (1984) *The spatial theory of voting. An introduction*. Cambridge, England: Cambridge University Press.

Erlenkotter, D. (1977) 'Facility location with price-sensitive demands: private, public and quasi-public', *Management Science*, 24:378–386.

Erlenkotter, D. (1978) 'A dual-based procedure for uncapacitated facility location', *Operations Research*, 16:992–1009.

Eswaran, M., Y. Kanemoto, and D. Ryan (1981) 'A dual approach to the locational decision of the firm', *Journal of Regional Science*, 21:469–490.

Fejes Tóth, G. (1972) 'Covering the plane by convex discs', *Acta Mathematica Academiae Scientiarum Hungaricae*, 23:263–270.

Francis, R. L. (1963) 'A note on the optimum location of new machines in existing plant layouts', *Journal of Industrial Engineering*, 14:57–59.

Francis, R. L., L. F. McGinnis and J. A. White (1983) 'Locational analysis', *European Journal of Operational Research*, 12:220–252.

Francis, R. L. and J. A. White (1974) *Facility layout and location: an analytical approach*. Englewood Cliffs, New Jersey: Prentice-Hall.

Friedman, J. W. (1983) *Oligopoly theory*. Cambridge, England: Cambridge University Press.

Frieze, A. M. (1974) 'A cost function property for plant location problems', *Mathematical Programming*, 7:245–248.

Furlong, W. H. and G. A. Slotsve (1983) '"Will that be pickup or delivery?" an alternative spatial pricing strategy', *Bell Journal of Economics*, 14:271–274.

Goldman, A. J. (1971) 'Optimal center location in simple networks', *Transportation Science*, 5:212–221.

Goldman, A. J. (1972) 'Approximate localization theorem for optimal facility placement', *Transportation Science*, 6:195–201.

Goldman, A. J. and C. J. Witzgall (1970) 'A localization theorem for optimal facility placement', *Transportation Science*, 4:406–409.

Graitson, D. (1982) 'Spatial competition à la Hotelling: a selective survey', *Journal of Industrial Economics*, 31:13–25.

Greenhut, J. and M. L. Greenhut (1975) 'Spatial price discrimination, competition and locational effects', *Economica*, 42:401–419.

Greenhut, J., M. L. Greenhut, and W. H. Kelly (1977) 'A spatial-theoretical perspective for bank merger regulation', in: *Proceedings on Bank Structure and Competition*. Chicago: Federal Reserve Bank of Chicago, 210–254.

Greenhut, M. L. (1956) *Plant location and practice*. Chapel Hill, North Carolina: University of North Carolina Press.

Greenhut, M. L. (1971) *A theory of the firm in economic space*. Austin: Lone Star Publisher.

Greenhut, M. L., M. J. Hwang and H. Ohta (1975) 'Observations on the shape and relevance of the spatial demand functions', *Econometrica*, 43:669–682.

Greenhut, M. L. and H. Ohta (1972) 'Monopoly output under alternative spatial pricing techniques', *American Economic Review*, 62:705–713.

Gronberg, T. and J. Meyer (1981) 'Transport inefficiency and the choice of spatial pricing mode', *Journal of Regional Science*, 21:541–549.

Guelicher, H. (1965) 'Einige Eigenschaften optimaler Standorte in Verkehrsnetzen', *Schriften des Vereins für Sozialpolitik* (*Neue Folge*), 42:111–137.

Hadley, G. and T. M. Whitin (1963) *Analysis of inventory systems*. Englewood Cliffs, N.J.: Prentice-Hall.

Hakimi, S. L. (1964) 'Optimum location of switching centers and the absolute centers and medians of a graph', *Operations Research*, 12:450–459.

Handler, G. J. and P. B. Mirchandani (1979) *Location on networks*. Cambridge, Mass: The MIT Press.

Hanjoul, P. and J.-F. Thisse (1984) 'The location of a firm on a network', in: A. J. Hughes Hallet, ed., *Applied decision analysis and economic behaviour*. Den Haag: Martinus Nijhoff, 289–326.

Hansen, P. and L. Kaufman (1972) 'Comparaison d'algorithmes pour le problème de la localisation des entrepôts', in: J. Brennan, ed., *Operational Research in Industrial Systems*. London: English University Press, 281–294.

Hansen, P., D. Peeters and J.-F. Thisse (1982) 'An algorithm for a constrained Weber problem', *Management Science*, 28:1285–1295.

Hansen, P., D. Peeters, and J.-F. Thisse (1983) 'Public facility location models: a selective survey', in: J.-F. Thisse and H.G. Zoller, eds., *Locational analysis of public facilities*. Amsterdam: North-Holland, 223–262.

Hay, D. A. (1976) 'Sequential entry and entry-deterring strategies', *Oxford Economic Papers*, 28:240–257.

Heaps, T. (1982) 'Location and the comparative statics of the theory of production', *Journal of Economic Theory*, 28:102–112.

Heffley, D. R. (1980) 'Pricing in an urban spatial monopoly: some welfare implications for policies which alter transport rates', *Journal of Regional Science*, 20:207–225.

Hitchcock, F. (1941) 'The distribution of a product from several sources to numerous localities', *Journal of Mathematics and Physics*, 20:224–230.

Holahan, W. L. (1975) 'The welfare effects of spatial price discrimination', *American Economic Review*, 65:498–503.

Holahan, W. L. and R. E. Schuler (1981a) 'The welfare effects of market shapes in the Löschian location model: squares vs. hexagons', *American Economic Review*, 71:738–746.

Holahan, W. L. and R. E. Schuler (1981b) 'Competitive entry in a spatial economy: market equilibrium and welfare implications', *Journal of Regional Science*, 21:341–357.

Hoover, E. M. (1937) 'Spatial price discrimination', *Review of Economic Studies*, 4:182–191.

Hoover, E. M. (1948) *The location of economic activity*. New York: McGraw-Hill.

Hotelling, H. (1929) 'Stability in competition', *Economic Journal*, 39:41–57.

Hsu, S. (1983) 'Pricing in an urban spatial monopoly: a general analysis', *Journal of Regional Science*, 23:165–175.

Huriot, J.-M. and J. Perreur (1973) 'Modèles de localisation et distance rectilinéaire', *Revue d'Economie Politique*, 83:640–662.

Hurter, A. P. and P. J. Lederer (1985) 'Spatial duopoly with discriminatory pricing', *Regional Science and Urban Economics*, 15:541–553.

Intriligator, M. D. (1971) *Mathematical optimization and economic theory*. Englewood Cliffs, N.J.: Prentice-Hall.

Isard, W. (1956) *Location and space-economy*. New York: John Wiley and Sons.

Isard, W. (1958) 'Interregional linear programming', *Journal of Regional Science*, 1:1–59.

Isard, W. et al. (1965) *Methods of regional science*. Cambridge: Mass.: The MIT Press.

Jaskold Gabszewicz, J. and J.-F. Thisse (1986) 'On the nature of competition with differentiated product', *Economic Journal*, 96:160–172.

Kaldor, N. (1935) 'Market imperfection and excess capacity', *Economica*, 2:35–50.

Kantorovitch, L. (1942) 'On the translocation of masses', *Doklady Akademii Nauk SSSR*, 37:199–201. English translation: *Management Science*, 5:1–4.

Karlin, S. (1954) *Mathematical methods and theory in games, programming and economics*, vol. 1. Reading, Mass: Addison-Wesley.

Kats, M. L. (1980) 'Multiplant monopoly in a spatial market', *Bell Journal of Economics*, 11:519–535.

Koopmans, T. C. (1949) 'Optimum utilisation of the transportation system', *Econometrica*, 17 Suppl.:136–146.

Koopmans, T. C. and M. J. Beckmann (1957) 'Assignment problems and the location of economic activities', *Econometrica*, 25:53–76.

Koopmans, T. C. and S. Reiter (1951) 'A model of transportation', in: T. C. Koopmans, ed., *Activity analysis of production and allocation*. New York: Wiley and Sons, 222–259.

Krarup, J. and P. M. Pruzan (1987) 'The simple plant location problem: survey and synthesis', *European Journal of Operational Research*, 12:36–81.

Krarup, J. and P. M. Pruzan (1985) 'Ingredients of locational analyses', in: R. L. Francis and P. Mirchandani, eds., *Discrete location theory*. New York: Wiley-Interscience, forthcoming.

Kuhn, H. W. (1967) 'On a pair of dual nonlinear programs', in: J. Abadie, ed., *Nonlinear programming*. New York: John Wiley and Sons, 37–54.

Kuhn, H. W. (1973) 'A note of Fermat's problem', *Mathematical Programming*, 4:98–107.

Kuhn, H. W. (1976) 'Nonlinear programming: a historical view', *SIAM-AMS Proceedings*, 9, 1–26.

Lalanne, L (1863) 'Essai d'une théorie des réseaux de chemin de fer, fondée sur l'observation des faits et sur les lois primordiales qui président au groupement des populations', *Compte-rendus hebdomadaires des séances de l'Academie des Sciences, Paris*, 27 juillet 1863.

Larson, R. C. and G. Sadiq (1983) 'Facility locations with the Manhattan metric in the presence of barriers to travel', *Operations Research*, 31:652–669.

Launhardt, W. (1882) 'Die Bestimmung des zweckmässigsten Standortes einer gewerblichen Anlage', *Zeitschrift des Vereins Deutscher Ingenieure*, 26:106–115.

Launhardt, W. (1885) *Mathematische Begründung der Volkswirtschaftslehre*. Leipzig: B. G. Teubner.

Lederer, P. J. and A. P. Hurter (1986) 'Competition of firms: discriminatory pricing and location', *Econometrica*, 54:623–640.

Lerner, A. and H. W. Singer (1937) 'Some notes on duopoly and spatial competition', *Journal of Political Economy*, 45:145–186.

Levy, J. (1967) 'An extended theorem for location on a network', *Operational Research Quarterly*, 18:433–443.

Long, W. H. (1971) 'Demand in space: some neglected aspects', *Papers of the Regional Science Association*, 27:45–60.

Lösch, A. (1940) *Die Räumliche Ordnung der Wirtschaft*. Jena: Gustav Fischer. English translation (1954): *The economics of location*. New Haven, Conn.: Yale University Press.

Louveaux, F., J.-F. Thisse, and H. Beguin (1982) 'Location theory and transportation costs', *Regional*

Science and Urban Economics, 12:529–545.

Love, R.F. and J. G. Morris (1979) 'Mathematical models of road travel distances', *Management Science*, 25:130–139.

MacLeod, W. B. (1985) 'On the non-existence of equilibria in differential product models', *Regional Science and Urban Economics*, 15:245–262.

MacLeod, W. B., G. Norman, and J.-F. Thisse (1987) 'Competition, collusion and free entry', *Economic Journal*, forthcoming.

Manne, A. S. (1964) 'Plant location under economies of scale: decentralization and computation', *Management Science*, 11:213–235.

Mathur, V. K. (1979) 'Some unresolved issues in the location theory of the firm', *Journal of Urban Economics*, 6:299–318.

McFadden, D. (1973) 'Conditional logit analysis of qualitative choice behavior', in: P. Zarembka, ed., *Frontiers in econometrics*. New York: Academic Press, 105–142.

Metzler, L. (1949) 'Tariffs, the terms of trade, and the distribution of national incomes', *Journal of Political Economy*, 57:1–29.

Mills, E. S. and M. R. Lav (1964) 'A model of market areas with free entry', *Journal of Political Economy*, 72:278–288.

Mirchandani, P. (1987) 'The p-median problem and generalizations', in: R. L. Francis and P. Mirchandani, eds., *Discrete location theory*. New York: Wiley-Interscience, forthcoming.

Mirchandani, P. B. and A. R. Odoni (1979) 'Locating new passenger facilities on a transportation network', *Transportation Research*, 13B:113–122.

Morris, J. G. and W. A. Verdini (1979) 'Minimum lp distance location problems solved via a perturbated and Weiszfeld's algorithm', *Operations Research*, 27:1180–1188.

Moses, L. (1958) 'Location and the theory of production', *Quarterly Journal of Economics*, 72:259–272.

Mougeot, M. (1975) *Théorie et politique économiques régionales*. Paris: Economica.

Mulligan, G. F. (1981) 'Lösch's single-good equilibrium', *Annals of the Association of American Geographers*, 71:84–94.

Mulligan, G. F. (1984) 'Agglomeration and central place theory: a review of literature', *International Regional Science Review*, 9:1–42.

Neven, D. (1985) 'Two stage (perfect) equilibrium in Hotelling's model', *Journal of Industrial Economics*, 33:317–325.

Neven, D. and L. Phlips (1985) 'Discriminating oligopolists and common markets', *Journal of Industrial Economics*, 34:133–149.

Nijkamp, P. and J. Paelinck (1973) 'A solution method for neo-classical location problems', *Regional and Urban Economics*, 3:383–410.

Norman, G. (1983) 'Spatial pricing with differentiation products', *Quarterly Journal of Economics*, 97:291–310.

Novshek, W. (1980) 'Equilibrium in simple spatial (or differentiated product) models', *Journal of Economic Theory*, 22:313–326.

Odoni, A. R. and G. Sadiq, (1982) 'Two planar facility location problems with high-speed corridors and continuous demand', *Regional Science and Urban Economics*, 12:467–484.

Ohta, H. (1980) 'Spatial competition, concentration and welfare', *Regional Science and Urban Economics*, 10:3–16.

Ohta, H. (1981) 'The price effects of spatial competition', *Review of Economic Studies*, 48:317–325.

Ohta, H. (1984) 'On the neutrality of freight in monopoly spatial pricing', *Journal of Regional Science*, 24:359–371.

Ohta, H. and M. Okamura (1984) 'Pricing in an urban spatial monopoly: a comment', *Journal of Regional Science*, 24:287–290.

Ostresh, L. M. (1978) 'On the convergence of a class of iterative methods for solving the Weber location problem', *Operations Research*, 26:597–609.

Palander, T. (1935) *Beiträge zur Standortstheorie*. Uppsala: Almqvist & Wiksells Boktryckeri A.B.

Papageorgiou, Y. Y. (1983) 'Models of agglomerations', *Sistemi Urbani*, 5:391–410.

Perreur, J. and J.-F. Thisse (1974) 'Central metrics and optimal location', *Journal of Regional Science*, 14:411–421.

Phlips, L. (1983) *The economics of price discrimination*. Cambridge, England: Cambridge University Press.

Ponsard, C. (1956) 'Note sur la localisation de la firme', *Revue Economique*, 1:101–116.

Ponsard, C. (1974) *Une révision de la théorie des aires de marché*. Paris: Sirey.

Ponsard, C. (1983) *A history of spatial economic theory*. Berlin: Springer Verlag.

Predöhl, A. (1925) 'Das Standortsproblem in der Wirtschaftstheorie', *Weltwirtschaftliches Archiv*, 21:294–331.

Prescott, E. C. and M. Visscher (1977) 'Sequential location among firms with foresight', *Bell Journal of Economics*, 8:378–393.

Puu, T. (1979) *The allocation of road capital in two-dimensional space*. Amsterdam: North-Holland.

Puu, T. (1983) 'Equilibrium in the spatial production and exchange economy—a long-run model', *Sistemi Urbani*, 3:499–534.

Richardson, H. W. (1969) *Regional economics*. London: Weidenfeld and Nicolson.

Rockafellar, R. T. (1970) *Convex analysis*. Princeton, N.J.: Princeton University Press.

Rosenhead, J. V. (1973a) 'Some comments on "A note on the location of depots" by Ralph D. Snyder', *Management Science*, 19:831–832.

Rosenhead, J. V. (1973b) 'The optimum location of transverse transport links', *Transportation Research*, 7:107–123.

Rothschild, R. (1976) 'A note on the effect of sequential entry on choice of location', *Journal of Industrial Economics*, 24:313–320.

Sakashita, N. (1967) 'Production function, demand function and the location theory of the firm', *Papers of the Regional Science Association*, 20:109–129.

Salop, S. C. (1979) 'Monopolistic competition with outside goods', *Bell Journal of Economics*, 10:141–156.

Samuelson, P. A. (1952) 'Spatial price equilibrium and linear programming', *American Economic Review*, 42:283–303.

Schuler, R. E. and B. F. Hobbs (1982) 'Spatial price duopoly under uniform delivered pricing', *Journal of Industrial Economics*, 31:175–187.

Schultz, N. and K. Stahl (1985) 'On the non-existence of oligopolistic equilibria in differentiated products spaces', *Regional Science and Urban Economics*, 15:229–243.

Singer, H. W. (1937) 'A note on spatial price discrimination', *Review of Economic Studies*, 5:75–77.

Smithies, A. (1941a) 'Monopolistic price policy in a spatial market', *Econometrica*, 9:63–73.

Smithies, A. (1941b) 'Optimum location in spatial competition', *Journal of Political Economy*, 49:423–439.

Smolensky, E., R. Burton, and N. Tideman (1970) 'The efficient provision of a local non-private good', *Geographical Analysis*, 2:330–342.

Spulber, D. F. (1981) 'Spatial nonlinear pricing', *American Economic Review*, 71:923–933.

Stern, N. (1972) 'The optimal size of market areas', *Journal of Economic Theory*, 4:154–173.

Stevens, B. H. (1958) 'An interregional linear programming model', *Journal of Regional Science*, 1:60–98.

Stevens, B. H. and C. P. Rydell (1966) 'Spatial demand theory and monopoly price policy', *Papers of the Regional Science Association*, 17:195–204.

Stigler, G. J. (1964) 'A theory of oligopoly', *Journal of Political Economy*, 72:44–61.

Stollsteimer, J. F. (1963) 'A working model for plant numbers and location', *Journal of Farm Economics*, 43:631–645.

Takayama, T. and G. G. Judge (1971) *Spatial and temporal price and allocation models*. Amsterdam: North-Holland.

Thisse, J.-F. and J. Perreur (1977) 'Relations between the point of maximum profit and the point of minimum total transportation cost: A restatement', *Journal of Regional Science*, 17:227–234.

Thisse, J.-F., J. E. Ward, and R. E. Wendell (1984) 'Some properties of location problems with block and round norms', *Operations Research*, 32:1309–1327.

Van Roy, T. J. and D. Erlenkotter (1982) 'A dual-based procedure for dynamic facility location', *Management Science*, 28:1091–1105.

Ward, J. E. and R. E. Wendell (1980) 'A new norm for measuring distance which yields linear location models', *Operations Research*, 28:836–844.

Ward, J. E. and R. E. Wendell (1985) 'Using block norms for location modeling', *Operations Research*, 33: 1074–1090.

Weber, A. (1909) *Ueber den Standort der Industrien*. Tübingen: J. C. B. Mohr. English translation

(1929): *The theory of the location of industries*. Chicago: Chicago University Press.

Weiszfeld, E. (1936) 'Sur le point pour lequel la somme des distances de *n* points donnés est minimum', *Tôhoko Mathematical Journal*, 43:355–386.

Wendell, R. E. and A. P. Hurter (1973a) 'Optimal locations on a network', *Transportation Science*, 7:18–33.

Wendell, R. E. and A. P. Hurter (1973b) 'Location theory, dominance, and convexity', *Operations Research*, 21:314–320.

Wendell, R. E. and R. D. McKelvey (1981) 'New perspectives in competitive location theory', *European Journal of Operational Research*, 6:174–182.

Weskamp, A. (1985) 'Cournot competition and the existence of spatial competition equilibria'. *Regional Science and Urban Economics*, 15:219–227.

Wesolowsky, G. O. (1982) 'Location problems on a sphere', *Regional Science and Urban Economics*, 12:495–508.

Williamson, O. E. (1968) 'Economies as an antitrust defense', *American Economic Review*, 58:18–31.

Witzgall, C. (1964) 'Optimal location of a central facility: mathematical models and concepts', National Bureau of Standards Report 8388, Washington D. C.

Chapter 3

RESIDENTIAL MOBILITY AND HOUSEHOLD LOCATION MODELLING

W. A. V. CLARK and W. F. J. VAN LIEROP

1. Introduction

Any examination or analysis of household location, either at the regional or the local level implies two things. It implies a housing market or markets and transactions in those markets. At the cross-sectional level, the discussion of household location is concerned with the distribution of residences and their occupants across regional or local space. At the dynamic level, the transactions involve both the buying (or renting) and selling (or letting) of dwellings, and by implication the movement of households through those dwellings as the transactions occur. Thus, to discuss household location we need to examine both the nature of regional and local housing markets and the nature and structure of inter- and intra-urban migration. In addition, we must be aware of the way in which housing markets change and develop as transactions in these markets vary over time, with the associated local and regional migration patterns. This chapter is focused on the nature of household location and attempts to link the two underlying components of housing markets and residential mobility and migration. As we will note in Section 3, which is largely concerned with an historical review of household location modelling, there has been a tendency to separate the investigations of housing markets and studies of migration and mobility. To some extent this separation has been artificial, and recent work, which we will examine in Section 3.3, investigates a number of the models which have been used to link markets and mobility. Several different modelling strategies have been used to examine housing markets and migration and the review of these approaches will include linear programming models, gravity and entropy models, log-linear models, discrete choice and random utility models, behavioral and search models, elimination-by-aspects models and micro-simulation models. In this way, an overview is given of the state of the art in residential mobility and household locational modelling. The chapter concludes with prospects and some suggestions for future research.

Handbook of Regional and Urban Economics, Volume I, Edited by P. Nijkamp
©*Elsevier Science Publishers BV, 1986*

Before examining the historical development of studies of household location it is important, at least briefly, to address the definition and description of regional and local housing markets, the nature and causes of inter- and intra-urban migration, and the way in which these migrations have an impact on housing markets.

2.   Housing markets and mobility

2.1.   *Contrasting views of housing markets*

Part of the difficulty of defining and describing regional housing markets relates to what Grigsby has called the two worlds of housing analysis [Grigsby (1978)]. He points out that much of the work in housing analysis has been divided into those who have used mathematically sophisticated approaches, including work by Alonso, Muth, Mills, and Wheaton, and another group, including Smith, Rapkin, Stegman, and Grebler, who have used less mathematically sophisticated methods and who are more interested in micro and submarket relationships. The latter are more policy oriented, the former more concerned with the macro and long-term changes in housing markets. While the former have contributed a great deal to understanding housing markets, especially with hedonic analyses, the latter have focused on the relationships of tenure change, of varying housing purchase behavior, and locational preference.

To contrast these approaches, we only have to refer to Smith's (1970) discussion of the housing market. Although he recognizes the role of traditional economic methods – that supply and demand approaches can be used to describe the way in which housing is produced in various quantities, and that for each quantitative output a particular price would be paid, and a particular level of costs would be incurred – the supply and demand equilibrium, he argues, is not particularly relevant to most of the problems or issues which are associated with the housing sector of the economy. Smith emphasizes the fact that supply and demand questions require a knowledge of the slopes of the demand and supply curves, and when the quantities cannot be measured in characteristics, it makes supply and demand analysis especially difficult. From these questions, Smith proceeds to a discussion of the impact of the various institutions on the housing market rather than on a detailed statistical analysis of market behavior itself.

In contrast, the analyses undertaken by Alonso, Muth and Mills, while recognizing the complexity of the housing market, use a set of simplifying assumptions to examine the pattern of housing in response to accessibility to central locations. That research on the nature of the population density function over space has led to a number of important propositions about the form of urban areas in long-run equilibrium.

A major contribution of the research by Muth, Alonso, Wingo and others, was the emphasis put on interrelationships between housing and employment, and that housing and employment accessibility are jointly purchased [Quigley (1978)]. Given the assumption of a single workplace, and additional assumptions about housing production and technology, it was possible to develop a number of propositions about the form of urban areas in the long run. These propositions, particularly related to residential density, have contributed significantly to our understanding of the structure of urban areas. Another contribution, again by economists, including that by de Leeuw, Maisel, and Kain and Quigley, introduced the notion of housing services as a measure of something that is purchased in the marketplace, rather than simply the purchase of a house. The discussion of this is beyond the scope of the present chapter, and Quigley (1978) gives an excellent overview of the relationship between price and income elasticities of demand. The point they emphasize is that households purchase housing over a long period of time and that the demand is for a composite commodity, housing services, rather than houses per se. Finally, the most recent research in housing markets has emphasized the attempt to understand the individual contributions of the components of the housing bundle to the production of satisfactions by individual consumers. To simplify much of the discussion, the question revolves around the interrelationships of physical and spatial characteristics enjoyed by the choice of a dwelling and how that bundle is reflected in that market price [Quigley (1978, p. 32)].

2.2. Defining and characterizing housing markets

Although we talk of the housing market, there are in fact, if not different markets, at least different ways of looking at the housing market. The major distinction, of course, is between the focus on the structure of the city as a whole (as a housing market) and whether that market can be segmented and how it operates in a particular economic system. There is the additional distinction of the perspective of housing as a sector of the national or local economy. When we use the term housing market, we are normally utilizing the term as a conceptual framework within which we can identify a variety of processes.

While it is not possible to give a definitive definition of a regional/local housing market, it is possible to provide some concepts which in fact inform the description of housing markets. As Van Lierop and Rima (1982) emphasize, the housing market as such does not exist. What we call the housing market is a complex phenomenon of interrelated and mutually influencing elements and submarkets. Among the factors, forces, and components which interact to form the housing market, we can include:

(i) a multitude of individual actors and groups with conflicting interests and preferences [cf. Putman (1979)];

(ii) a multitude of individual motives and attributes of residential behavior [see among others, Bird (1976)];

(iii) a multitude of choice possibilities (alternative locations, alternative dwellings, etc.);

(iv) a multitude of social and spatial spill-over effects and externalities [for instance, the fact that the quality of residential neighborhood is determined by individual housing units in that area; cf. Stahl (1980), Wilkinson (1973)];

(v) a multitude of dynamic processes associated with the economic and geographical development of a spatial system [cf. Anas (1976)];

(vi) a multitude of public regulations that constrain a free market system for the housing market.

The housing market's peculiar or particular characteristics have often been emphasized. First, housing is locationally immobile, second, it is very durable (the life expectancy of any individual dwelling place is in most cases greater than the length of life for individuals) and third, it is very expensive (housing probably represents the largest expenditure, either in rents or actual costs, for any individual). The durability, stability of occupancy, and cost, result in a situation in which the housing market, is certainly influenced if not dominated by the character of the existing stock. The character of the existing stock then is the context against which household location takes place.

Even if we can provide some general descriptive statements which characterize the housing market, when it comes to the actual definition of individual housing markets it is an empirical problem, and they may be defined in relationship to city or urban regions. In any event, the empirical delimitation of a market in space and time is not a straightforward question. What are the boundaries of the housing market, how is it measured? Is it a particular index, such as house prices and how does it change over time? Yet, in order to describe, model, and understand the processes by which households choose among dwelling units, it is critical that we at least have an understanding of the complexity of the housing market as a background or context within which those housing choices are occurring.

2.3. Migration and mobility

While the definition and description of regional and local housing markets is complicated, the nature and causes of intra-urban and inter-urban migration are somewhat more clearly understood, but their links with the housing market are no less difficult. In most of the analyses of housing markets, intra-urban mobility

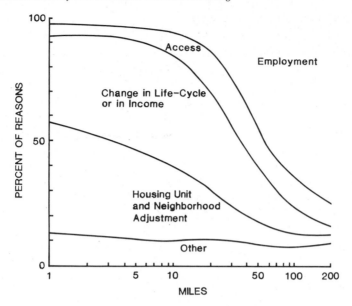

Figure 2.1. Distribution of reasons for moving by distance [adapted from Gleave and Cordey–Hayes (1977)].

or interregional mobility, which are the mechanisms by which changes in housing consumption are registered, have taken second place. (We will examine the mobility-migration mechanism in more detail in Section 3.)

A long tradition of research on migration and mobility has provided some understanding of the nature and causes of inter-urban and intra-urban migration. The relationship of long- and short-distance moves and their explanations is shown in Figure 2.1. Although there is a continuum of change in the reasons for moving, there is a reasonably clear distinction between short- and long-distance moves. Life cycle, accessibility, and housing choice reasons, that is, reasons related to the local housing market, predominate for short-distance moves, while employment reasons predominate for moves of longer distances. In other words, moves within a housing market area are very much concerned with the context and structure of that housing market, while moves between housing markets (or at least between cities) are more strictly concerned with changes and opportunities in employment.

For local or short-distance moves, the research on the dynamics of mobility has emphasized the stimulus of dissatisfaction (or relocation behavior) generated by both family circumstances and the housing environment [Wolpert (1965), Brown and Moore (1970), Speare et al. (1975)]. These dissatisfaction models were formalized in stress inertia models by Huff and Clark (1978) and Brummell

(1979), and the propensity to move was seen as a trade-off between stress or dissatisfaction and inertia. At the same time, the stress or dissatisfaction models were formalized by economists as disequilibrium models of housing expenditure, and are represented in the work by Hanushek and Quigley (1978a,b). This mobility is seen as a response to change in the demand for and supply of housing services, or to the stress created by the provision of these housing services.

The moves at an interregional level are concerned with the employment opportunities available *within* the housing markets. In understanding interregional migration, attempts to explain these changing patterns have focused on the redistribution of economic opportunities, including the locational shifts of industry and the opportunities for jobs, the increase of retirement and recreational migration, especially in advanced industrial societies with increasing numbers of elderly persons, and the changes in preferences which occur with increased affluence [Cebula (1979), Greenwood (1981)]. While the gravity model has been used as a description of the impact of distance on relocation behavior at an aggregate level, the explanatory models which have been utilized for understanding the population relocations at this regional level have emphasized the notion that individuals migrate in the expectation of being better off, and that it is the additions to human capital (considered as an income stream generated over a lifetime) that are critical components for explanations of interregional migration [DaVanzo (1981)]. The human capital notion at the interregional level parallels the life cycle housing explanation of local migration. Of course, the way in which these changes in employment are actually worked out is the subject of considerable debate. As Gordon Clark has noted in a recent review [Clark (1984)], the classic view of migration flows as an equilibrating mechanism ignores the important role of institutional impacts on the labor market.

This broad overview of the nature of housing markets and of inter-urban and intra-urban migration outlines the two important components of understanding household location. It is critical to try to understand how these two streams have developed and how they have been linked. The next section examines the relationships between the two research streams.

3.   Housing location modelling and residential mobility paradigms

3.1.   Housing market choice

The research stream which is focused on housing market choice arises out of a broad base of research in housing economics (see Figure 3.1). The initial work on the theory of consumer behavior [Lancaster (1966)] suggested that housing be viewed as a bundle of attributes, and that for utility maximizing households,

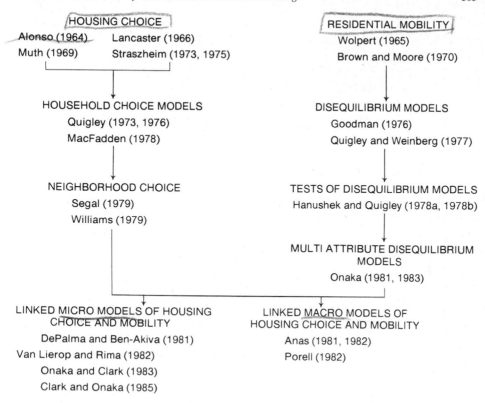

Figure 3.1. The structure of the disaggregate housing and mobility research streams.

these dwelling unit attributes will appear along with other items as arguments in its utility function. The use of hedonic analysis to evaluate the way in which elements of housing influence consumer demand stimulated both the development of hedonic theory and the consumer approach to housing. Following these suggestions, several authors, including Straszheim (1973, 1975), used a variety of dimensions of the housing bundle in an empirical analysis, which allowed the implicit prices for each of the housing dimensions to vary across locations within the metropolitan area. Straszheim in effect modified the original Alonso (1964) model and allowed (a) households to work at different locations other than the center of the city, (b) housing services to be a multi-dimensional commodity, and (c) household tastes to vary. However, his major concern is with the spatial variation in market prices, not with the analysis of residential location choice. At the same time that the development of a substantive theory of the housing market was advancing, there was a parallel technical development of models designed to analyze individual choice, especially the work on the random utility model and the logit, probit, and multinomial logit techniques [see e.g. McFadden (1973), (1978), (1984)]

The specific focus on housing choice as against the spatial distribution of prices was initiated by Quigley (1973, 1976). While he is firmly in the tradition of housing demand, he emphasizes both individual choice and the spatial structure of the housing market, and uses the technical structure of the multinomial logit model to build an individual choice model of housing choice. With a relatively restrictive set of assumptions, the paper "extends the theoretical analysis of the demand for housing to incorporate the spatial dimension, (and thus the residential location decision) as well as the choice of housing type," [Quigley (1976, p. 78)]. Three important conclusions arise from this article. First, it extends the theoretical analysis of the demand for housing to incorporate a spatial dimension. Second, the model shows how choices amongst housing types are related to systematic variations in the relative prices faced by households for the same types of residential housing. Third, choices predicted by the model are not necessarily consistent with the notion of equilibrium in the housing market as a whole. It is possible to generate excess demand or excess supply. It is clear that this model was a considerable advance on the earlier work because it involved both the distribution of the housing stock and the behavior of individuals. McFadden pointed out that the model developed by Quigley was a variant of the nested logit model in which dwelling type choice is separated from locational choice.

Subsequent research efforts used the same basic model to evaluate the relative importance of accessibility and transportation mode [Lerman (1977)] and neighborhood characteristics in housing choice [Williams (1979)]. Williams argues convincingly that most of the empirical studies of housing demand ignore the influence of neighborhood variables and often assume that household services are perfectly homogeneous. He notes that even the studies by Straszheim and Quigley do not include specific neighborhood variables. His variation of the Quigley model incorporates neighborhood measures but utilizes the same multinomial logit approach to estimate the demand for neighborhoods. He concludes that "larger households appear to place more importance on neighborhood quality, and are more likely to choose housing in better neighborhoods,...and thus that neighborhood quality is a superior good...and any exclusion from housing demand equations of neighborhood variables is likely to result in inaccurate predictions of residential location," [Williams (1979, p. 36)].

A more limited study of neighborhood choice focused specifically on the trade-off between school quality and racial mix. Segal utilized a quasi-log linear model to show that to certain household compositions (especially upper middle class white households with children), the racial characteristics of the neighborhood are important in the residential decision-making process [Segal (1979)]. The model employs a more limited set of variables than the Williams model, and examines the data in a log-linear rather than a logit formulation.

Despite the fact that much of the research on the housing choice problem has utilized information from population relocation data sets, the models themselves are essentially concerned with the static question of the choice of housing and allocation of households to houses and neighborhoods. The models do incorporate implicit behavior, the behavior of choice, but in every case, the models are concerned with the outcomes of choice, of the actual allocations rather than the trade-off aspects of leaving one location and choosing another. The notion of a dynamic trade-off is central to the notion of linking the two research paradigms.

3.2. The residential mobility paradigm

The rich tradition of studies of population relocation within the city has as antecedents studies by Wolpert (1965), who identified the notion of stress-induced residential relocations, Brown and Moore (1970) who developed a simple two-step model of the decision to move and the decision to search, and specific studies of dissatisfaction by Speare et al. (1975). The antecedent literature provided a stimulus for analytic modelling of the stress function on the one hand [Huff and Clark (1978)], and on the other, specification of the nature of stress in terms of housing dissatisfaction by economists [Goodman (1976), Hanushek and Quigley (1978a, 1978b)]. The disequilibrium approach and its variations were seen as alternatives to the more traditional sociological and geographic models of residential mobility. In fact, as has been argued recently, the basic model formulation is similar in all disciplines, it is the choice of variables and the estimating procedures used which distinguish the approaches [Clark (1983)].

The initial specification of the disequilibrium model suggested that the probability that a household will move at least once during a given time period is a linear function of the benefits and costs of moving [Goodman (1976)]. As reformulated by Hanushek and Quigley (1978a, 1978b), household mobility or the probability of a move was assumed to be a probit function of the difference between actual housing consumption at time t and the equilibrium housing demanded at time $t+1$, divided by the equilibrium consumption demanded at time t. Transaction costs, or search and moving costs are ignored in the model and housing demand is assumed to be a linear function of the household socio-economic characteristics including income, size, and race and age of the head of the household. Extensive tests of the basic disequilibrium model, and several variants, utilize data from the housing allowance demand experiments from Pittsburgh and Phoenix [Weinberg et al. (1981), Cronin (1979)].

The disequilibrium models developed by the economists are focused specifically on the housing market, on the difference between actual housing consumption and the optimal consumption of housing. Mobility is seen as a response to changes in the demand for housing services. And, in this sense, the models are quite derivative from Rossi's (1955) initial conceptualization. More recently, Onaka (1983) has developed a variation of the disequilibrium model which is designed to provide a better empirical foundation for housing disequilibrium research and which utilizes the insights of both the cumulative inertia – cumulative stress models and the housing disequilibrium models. The model proposed and tested by Onaka extends the concept of housing consumption disequilibrium to include dissatisfaction with *individual* attributes of housing instead of a single index of housing services. The Onaka approach extends the current expenditure-based disequilibrium model by utilizing the hedonic theory of housing prices. It provides a number of advantages over previous approaches. First, as mentioned above, the model represents housing consumption by a vector of housing attributes rather than by housing expenditure only; second, the model considers the heterogeneity of housing tastes among households; and third, the specification of the model permits direct comparisons with the expenditure-based disequilibrium models and the models based solely on demographic characteristics. The test of the model with the Panel Study of Income Dynamics data shows that the model provides a statistically significant improvement in fit over earlier models, and is a potentially useful method of analyzing the role of housing preferences in residential mobility [Onaka (1983)].

The residential mobility research has focused on the decision to move or stay and not on the outcome of residential selection which necessarily follows the decision to move. That is, the mobility decision is assumed to be made without reference to the alternative units to which a household may relocate, except insofar as they are represented by the price of housing services (in the expenditure disequilibrium model) or the hedonic price function (in the multiattribute disequilibrium model). The relocation models therefore are not transferable from one housing market to another, unless the hedonic price function is estimated separately for each market of interest. This limitation can be partially overcome by formulating a joint model of mobility decision and housing choice.

3.3. Linked mobility – housing choice approaches

The most recent research, either from a micro or macro perspective, has attempted to link the mobility-housing choice approaches. DePalma and Ben-Akiva (1981) developed a dynamic model of the spatial distribution of urban population based on individual choice and transaction costs. The paper postulates a decision hierarchy for an individual household which includes the decisions to search and move and conditions the expected outcomes of these decisions on the availability of alternative units in the urban area. Van Lierop and Rima (1982), Onaka and

Clark (1983), and Clark and Onaka (1985) similarly proposed a two-stage process of relocation behavior, where the probability of being willing to move from the current dwelling is equal to the probability that the utility of moving minus the transition costs exceeds the expected utility of staying. They outline the relevant utilities that can be used to estimate this probability. Given the conditional probability of the willingness to move, they then suggest that a hierarchical framework can be used to estimate the probability that a household will move to a specific location and choose a specific dwelling.

From a macro perspective, two major studies have attempted to link the housing market and the individual choice and to bridge the macro and micro perspectives. Two papers and a book by Anas (1980, 1981, 1982) and a formal statement by Porell (1982) have been concerned with the intra-urban location process within a wider aggregate framework. Porell describes his model as a short-run equilibrium model of residential relocation, but while the model builds on a base of individual choices, the model itself is more clearly one of flows between submarkets in an urban area. In fact, he describes his model as a systemic spatial interaction model of household relocation, *founded* on a short-run static equilibrium model of a housing market [Porell (1982, p. 59)]. Porell wants to move away from the assumptions of long-run equilibrium exemplified in the Muth approach, and use a more realistic view of relocation behavior, in which households face a choice of discrete submarket alternatives at any point in time. Demand is characterized as choice among submarkets constrained by the composition of the stock. Porell is firmly in the tradition of probabilistic choice theory outlined by McFadden (1978) and Quigley (1976). He uses the multinomial logit model as a micro level theoretical base, from which spatial demand functions can be derived as part of a short-run static equilibrium model of household relocation. Then, to address the problem of short-run static equilibrium, he assumes that households may be stratified into a set of internally homogeneous classes. With the important assumption that all households of a class face identical generalized commuting costs, he specifies an *aggregate* demand function for any submarket, as derived for each household class by inserting specifications for housing submarkets, relocation behavior, and commuting costs into the multinomial logit specification. The result is a set of aggregate demand equations. The final model that Porell derives bears a strong resemblance to Wilson's doubly constrained spatial interaction model, and we will consider this at a later point.

Similarly, Anas is also interested in the link between micro and macro behaviors, and he is concerned to utilize individual behavioral choice theory as the basis for aggregate parameter estimates. Unlike Porell, however, he is interested in the joint choice of housing, residential location, and mode of travel. The recent papers [Anas (1980, 1981)] and book [Anas (1982)] have focused on the problems involved in aggregate estimation of choice models. That is, given the fact that there are insufficiently detailed data to estimate probabilistic choice models on the basis of individual observations, how can estimates be derived for small aggregate units? Anas argues that the models that he develops and estimates for small area aggregated data will be far more adaptable to practical prediction, equilibration, and policy analysis than the disaggregate models, if it can be shown that the coefficients of such aggregate models have an acceptable level of behavioral validity [Anas (1981)]. Anas uses very small areas for the Chicago metropolitan region (in fact half mile by half mile square zones), and develops an aggregated logit model of joint location and mode choice for these small zones. He develops a sequential choice model (or more correctly a sequential choice structure) in which he evaluates the expected frequency of joint mode and location choice, on the conditional expected frequency of choosing a dwelling k given the choices of a mode and location. He suggests that the small area aggregate data yield highly robust predictions of the behavior for joint choices of location and mode choice and residence, and he argues that differences in model specification are much more important than differences in aggregation when the units of aggregation are small. While these papers are important contributions towards the specific linking of the macro or structural data and individual behavior, there is still much to be done in translating these models into the dynamic forms of the Van Lierop and Rima (1982) and Onaka and Clark (1983) model structures.

4. State of the art of residential mobility and household location modelling

The third component of this chapter is concerned with the variety of models – linear programming, log-linear, gravity–entropy, discrete choice, behavioral (including search models), elimination-by-aspects and micro-simulation – which have been used to analyze residential mobility and household location. There is a wide variety of approaches to understanding household location. These approaches vary by their major substantive concern, either with mobility, with location decision making, or with some interactive element of mobility and location decision making, which we call sequential or simultaneous relocation. They also vary by the level of aggregation to which the models have been applied, micro or macro, and by whether or not their concern has been with a statistical, equilibrium, or behavioral approach [see also Fischer and Nijkamp (1985)].

    While we have already discussed the *substantive* contributions of many of these models, a tabular classification of the model approaches is a good way to overview the *technical* approaches to the art of household location modelling (Table 4.1). The diagrammatic presentation which follows charts by Porell (1982) and Van Lierop and Rima (1982) indicates that the major distinctions are

Table 4.1

A classification of methods to analyze the housing market and selected references.

	Level of household aggregation					
	Macro (Aggregate)				Micro (Disaggregate)	
	Statistical	Heuristic/ entropy–gravity	Economic equilibrium	Disaggregate behavioral input	Statistical	Behavioral
Mobility	Moore, 1969 Simmons, 1974				Huff & Clark, 1978 Clark, Huff & Burt, 1978 Dieleman, 1983	Wolpert, 1965 Brown & Moore, 1970 Goodman, 1976 Hanushek & Quigley, 1978a Weibull, 1978
Location		Wilson 1970	Herbert & Stevens, 1960	Porell, 1982	Segal, 1979	Alonso, 1964 McFadden, 1978 Kain et al., 1976 Muth, 1969 Pollakowski, 1982
Sequential/ simultaneous mobility and location			Anas, 1982 Porell, 1982 Ingram et al., 1972	Wegener, 1980		Porell, 1982 Van Lierop & Rima, 1982 Smith & Clark, 1982 De Palma & Ben-Akiva, 1981 Onaka & Clark, 1983

between mobility, location, and sequential or simultaneous mobility–location analyses and between macro and micro approaches. We have already reiterated the distinction and the lack of links between the mobility and the residential location approaches. It is also worth emphasizing the distinction between micro or disaggregate methods, which focus on the individual household, and macro approaches, which are concerned with the aggregate level with a total set of households and their responses to the structure of the housing markets. The remainder of the section examines six specific modelling strategies – linear programming models, log-linear models, gravity and entropy approaches, discrete choice models, behavioral models, and micro-simulation.

4.1. A linear programming model of residential location

These models, as originally outlined by Herbert and Stevens (1960), are designed to "distribute households to residential land in an optimal configuration" [Herbert and Stevens (1960, p. 21)]. The strength of the approach was its simplicity and practicality (especially the latter), as it was used as part of the Penn Jersey Transportation study. Conceptually, a household considers its total budget, the items which constitute a market basket, and the cost of obtaining those items. For a household with a fixed total budget and for a particular market basket, the prices of the items and the "other commodities" are given. The total budget minus the cost of the other commodities yields a residual which is the residential budget. The household optimizes by selecting the market basket which will maximize the household's savings.

> ...the attempt of each household to maximize its savings will result in households being allocated to land in configuration that is optimal from the point of view of all the households that are to be located. This allocation will be optimal in a pareto sense: no household can move to increase its savings without reducing the savings of some other household and simultaneously reducing aggregate savings [Herbert and Stevens (1960, p. 26)].

Since savings in the model are equivalent to rent paying ability, maximizing aggregate rent paying ability will yield an optimal location. A linear programming solution is used to produce an optimal configuration of new households to the available land. This involves maximizing the objective function (4.1) which is the aggregate rent paying ability.

$$\text{Max } Z = \sum_{k=1}^{K} \sum_{i=1}^{I} \sum_{h=1}^{H} X_{ih}^{k}\left(b_{ih}^{k} - C_{ih}^{k}\right) \tag{4.1}$$

subject to:

$$\sum_{i=1}^{I} \sum_{h=1}^{H} s_{ih} X_{ih}^k \leq L^k \quad (k=1,2,\ldots,K)$$

$$\sum_{k=1}^{K} \sum_{h=1}^{H} - X_{ih}^k = - N_i \quad (i=1,2,\ldots,I)$$

and all

$$X_{ih}^k \geq 0 \quad (k=1,2,\ldots,K)$$
$$(i=1,2,\ldots,I)$$
$$(h=1,2,\ldots,H)$$

where
  K = areas which form an exhaustive subdivision of the region;
  I = household groups;
  H = residential bundles;
  b_{ih} = the residential budget allocated by a household group i to the purchase of residential bundle h;
  C_{ih}^k = the annual cost to a household of group i of the residential bundle h in area k, exclusive of site cost;
  s_{ih} = the number of acres in the site used by a household of group i if it uses residential bundle h;
  L^k = the number of acres of land available for residential use in area k in a particular iteration of the model;
  N_i = the number of households of group i that are to be located in the region in a particular iteration; and
  X_{ih}^k = the number of households of group i using residential bundle h located, by the model, in area k.
The importance of this seminal approach to residential allocation is Batty's (1971) comment that it is the operational formulation of the Alonso Model.

4.2. Gravity and entropy

An important alternative approach (to the linear programming models) was for a long time some form of gravity, and later, entropy model (for more technical information, see Chapter 9 in this Handbook). The traditional gravity model, which used basic information (push and pull factors or attraction indices) of the places of origin and destination and the distance between them, was an important initial attempt to understand spatial interaction, and one of the few attempts which recognized the spatial patterns of residential location. Of course, it was severely criticized, because it offered little in the way of explanatory power in terms of understanding the relocation flows of households between housing markets. With the translation of the gravity model into an entropy formulation, the usefulness of this technique, at least for understanding aggregate interaction patterns, is more clearly established in the literature.

The entropy maximizing approach to flows is designed to make the fullest possible use of all available information without making any assumptions about that which remains unknown. To translate this into terms specifically applicable to estimating migration flows, Cordey–Hayes and Wilson (1971) have argued that the best procedure, in the absence of complete information, is to define the possibilities unambiguously, define all the information available in terms of those possibilities, and find the particular distribution of moving streams (T_{ij}) that is consistent with all this information but is maximally uncommitted in relation to what is unknown.

This amounts to finding the T_{ij} distribution which maximizes entropy subject to certain constraints [Chapter 9 of this Handbook or Wilson (1970) deal with this problem extensively].

The entropy maximizing approach gives the gravity model a statistical derivation which is no longer dependent upon the analogies to Newtonian physics. Although there are difficulties in identifying the distance variable (for instance, by means of a cost function) to be used in specification and calibration, the application of the entropy formulation to population movement flows within Amsterdam yielded useful predictions of the directions of flows [Clark and Avery (1978)].

4.3.   Log-linear models

Recently, the log-linear model has been introduced to describe the interactions of household location and residential choice. The log-linear model has a natural equivalence to the gravity model, and in turn can be restructured in an entropy formulation. In addition, natural links exist between the entropy model and the multinomial logit structure [see, for example, Van Lierop and Nijkamp (1979) or Section 3.4 of Chapter 9 of this Handbook]. The principal concern in log-linear modelling has been to capture the interactions between relevant choice dimensions. For example, in housing market studies these dimensions have included housing types, tenure types, and the family cycle characteristics. In these situations, it is possible to use the cell frequencies to determine a set of underlying structures for the table as a whole. Wrigley and Brouwer discuss the more technical details of general log-linear modelling in Chapter 11 of this Handbook.

The principal application of log-linear models to household location has been in the areas of the interaction of tenure type and family cycle [Dieleman (1983)]. In that paper, the author shows that tenure and type of house are important dimensions in the choice of households in the Dutch market.

Following Willekens (1983), Scholten (1984) uses the log-linear model as a general model of the gravity formulation to represent the relationship between cell counts (m_{ij}, which is the number of movers between origin i and destination j) and the model parameters.

Taking the double-constrained gravity model

$$T_{ij} = A_i B_j O_i D_j f(d_{ij}) \tag{4.2}$$

where

T_{ij} = number of moves from area i to area j;
O_i = the number of persons leaving area i;
D_j = the number of persons arriving in area j;
$f(d_{ij})$ = the distribution or distance function; and
A_i, B_j = balancing factors.

The log-linear model for variables A (region of departure) and B (region of arrival) can be written:

$$\log m_{ij} = u + \lambda_i^A = \lambda_j^B + \lambda_{ij}^{AB} \tag{4.3a}$$

or, if written in multiplicative form:

$$m_{ij} = q \cdot w_i^A \cdot w_j^B \cdot w_{ij}^{AB}. \tag{4.3b}$$

Willekens (1983) has demonstrated that these two eqs. (4.2 and 4.3) not only look alike, but that the log-linear model is formally equivalent to the gravity model. The role of the distribution function in the gravity model is the same as that of the interaction parameters of the log-linear model. Consequently, it is possible to define the distribution function to reflect the spatial constraints that are significant to migration. Thus:

$$f(d_{ij}) = \frac{m_{ij}}{q \cdot w_i^A w_j^B} = w_{ij}^{AB}. \tag{4.4}$$

This relation is of great importance for the gravity model. It means that by using given migration matrices and the interaction parameters, the distribution function can be estimated. Snickars and Weibull successfully used this method to gain insight into the distribution of flows in 1977. Scholten applied it to estimate the parameters for the housing market region of Den Bosch in the Netherlands which has some 15 municipalities within it. Tests of comparability between actual flows and estimated flows (from the log-linear model) indicated an accurate prediction of 80–85 percent of the actual number of migrants.

4.4.   Discrete choice and random utility models

The model structures that have been discussed thus far have either examined the aggregate flows or the specific components of the mobility process, that is, tenure and life cycle characteristics. They represent in fact, two of the types of approaches that have been applied to housing markets and population reloca-tions. However, it is the discrete choice approach to consumer choice in the housing market which (i) has been emphasized most in recent work, (ii) has developed a dynamic structure for housing choice, and (iii) offers some chance of the extension of the micro models to macro behavior. Historically, the research on discrete choice models began with the work of McFadden and Quigley (see Section 3) which utilized logit models for the demand for housing. These logit models indicate the probability with which households will choose a dwelling from a limited sample (i.e. the number of affordable houses or the dwellings about which information is available). This probability depends on the utility a household expects to derive from living in a specific house. That utility, U, can be defined as a function, v, of socioeconomic aspects describing the household and elements typifying the dwelling, x, and a disturbance term, ξ, for unknown individual deviations from the average utility in the population resulting from individual taste variations, measurement errors, and so on. In formula:

$$U_{in} = v(x'_{in})\beta + \xi_{in} \tag{4.5}$$

where
$i =$ the ith dwelling alternative;
$n =$ the nth household; and
$\beta =$ the parameters belonging to the vector of attributes describing the ith choice of the nth household.

The probability that a random alternative i will be chosen by a household n, equals the probability that the utility (or attractiveness) of i exceeds or equals the utility of any other alternative i' for n:

$$P_{in} = \Pr(U_{i'n} \geq U_{i'n}; \forall i), \qquad i, i' = 1, \ldots, I; \quad i \neq i', \qquad n = 1, \ldots, N \tag{4.6}$$

with the logical condition that $\sum_{i=1}^{I} P_{in} = 1$.

Therefore, it is assumed that the choice maker will try to optimize his or her utility. The actual calculation of the choice probabilities in (4.6) depends heavily on the form chosen for the utility function. In this respect, the necessary data information is usually derived from household surveys.

Application of discrete choice and random utility models for housing market analysis has been extended from logit choices of the own/rent decision, or move/no move decision to multinomial logit choices of a variety of locational choices. In addition, researchers have utilized nested logit structures, in which choices in the housing market could be made sequentially, multinomial probit structures, and other advanced models which build on the discrete choice and random utility concept. For more extensive overviews see, for instance, Pitfield (1984), Bahrenberg et al. (1984), or Van Lierop (1986).

4.4.1. Logit models

The research area of discrete (or disaggregate) models of locational choice has developed in such a way as to provide the most coherent and integrated analysis of residential mobility and locational choice. Several investigators have pursued these issues simultaneously. The initial approaches utilized the simple logit model which was applied in some cases to the choice of the decision to move, and in other cases to the choice of housing alternatives. The use of multinomial logit models (MNL) allowed a broader range of choices to be considered (for additional technical details see also Chapter 11). This model can be defined by assuming that the error terms in (4.5) are mutually independent "Gumbel"-distributed.[1] This assumption reduces (4.6) to the multinomial logit formula [for the exact mathematical derivation, see McFadden (1973)]:

$$P_{in} = \frac{\exp(v(x'_{in}\beta))}{\sum_{i'=1}^{I} \exp(v(x'_{in}\beta))}. \tag{4.7}$$

To date, the MNL model is, without doubt, the disaggregate choice model that is most widely used for housing demand analysis.

A table adapted from Quigley (1983) indicates the structure of the work in housing market research utilizing the MNL model (Table 4.2). Reasons for the wide use of the MNL model seem to be that the model is relatively easy to

---

[1] Or "Gnedenko" or "Weibull"-distributed. These are all "skewed" distributions that can be almost normalized by using logarithms. The "Gumbel" distribution has the following form:

$$\Pr(\xi_{in} \leq \xi^*) = \exp\{-\exp(-\xi^* + \gamma)\}$$

in which $\xi^* = v(x'_{i'n}\beta) - v(x'_{in}\beta) + \xi_{i'n}$ and γ = Euler's constant, $\gamma \approx 0.577$.

Table 4.2
Multinomial logit analyses of housing choice.[a]

Author	Year of study	Number of housing alternatives	Definition of alternatives
Quigley	1976	18 rental types	Structure type by size and age classes
Kain and Apgar	1977	50 housing types	Multi/single-family by density classes, size classes and neighborhood categories
Lerman	1977 1979	145 census tracts	Average census characteristics of housing units in each tract
Williams	1979	50 rental types	Combination of lot size, structure type, and number of bedrooms, by neighborhood classes
Case	1981	9 housing types	Owner/renter occupied: by size and structure classes

[a]Adapted from Quigley (1983).

calibrate and that its properties are generally well understood. One of the most important properties of the MNL model is that the assumptions concerning the probability distribution of the error terms introduce the independence of irrelevant alternatives hypothesis (or IIa-property). That means that in the MNL model, the relative probability of choice of two alternatives depends only on their measured attractiveness. (The measurement in this respect might take place directly or indirectly by means of perception or even preference weights, which are transformed into cardinal values.) In cases where the unobserved components of alternatives (the error or residual terms) are correlated, introduction of a new alternative which is highly correlated with another (i.e. it differs only marginally from it) is assumed to have little effect on the choice probabilities of all other available alternatives. When such relationships exist, the error term assumptions of the MNL model cause obvious problems. In housing market research where there are often comparable sets of alternatives, this will be particularly troublesome. Under such circumstances, a solution may be to try to capture the interdependencies between alternatives by defining adjusted specifications for the functions $v(x'_{in}\beta)$. However, that is usually very difficult, as it may mean the introduction of a nonlinear function. A few authors have also tried to solve this problem by developing ad hoc corrections for the logit model [see Domencich and McFadden (1975), for example]. Others created new models with interdependent error terms and error terms with different variances. One of these kinds of models, the multinomial probit model, will be reviewed in Section 4.4.3 after an overview of a practical ad hoc attempt to deal with the choice axiom within the framework of the MNL model in 4.4.2 below. In Section 4.4.4 a group of different disaggregate sequential choice models, the elimination-by-aspects models, will be presented.

4.4.2. *A nested logit model of housing choice and residential mobility*

A practical way of dealing with the independence of irrelevant alternatives hypothesis, inherent in the use of the MNL model, is the introduction of sequential, multilevel or nested logit models [see McFadden (1978)]. By splitting the choice problem into several process stages, conditional choice probabilities are created. Part of the difficulty caused by the IIa problem can be solved in this way. This is because, by using a sequential approach, the number of choice situations, available alternatives and parameters in each successive stage, declines rapidly. The advantage is that the estimation results are quite comparable to direct estimation of the model.

The nested logit model consists of a set of sequential, recursive probability equations in which the choice of an alternative class at a given level of decision making is conditioned on the outcomes of prior, or higher level, decisions. The model is recursive since such choices also depend upon the composite utilities of alternatives available at later, or lower level, decisions. DePalma and Ben-Akiva (1981), Van Lierop (1981) and Onaka and Clark (1983) have adopted the nested logit structure to develop models in which individuals make a sequential set of choices of the dwelling unit, the dwelling type, the neighborhood and the decision to move or stay (Figure 4.1). Although it is not possible to fully illustrate such a model in the limited space available, the following comments sketch out the notions underlying the nested logit model.[2] We assume that a household will structure its choice among the $N+1$ alternatives according to the hierarchy represented by Figure 4.1. That is, the household first decides to stay ($l=0$) or move ($l=1$): if it moves, it chooses a particular neighborhood ($k \in K$), then the type of dwelling ($j \in J$) available in the neighborhood selected, and finally a specific dwelling unit ($i \in I$) available for the selected neighborhood and dwelling type. The decisions, however, are not sequentially independent. To reiterate, a decision at any level is conditioned on the outcomes of higher level decisions. For example, there are multiple neighborhood alternatives only if the household chooses to move. In addition, a decision at any level is affected by the alterna-

---

[2] These comments on the nested logit model are derived from Onaka and Clark (1983).

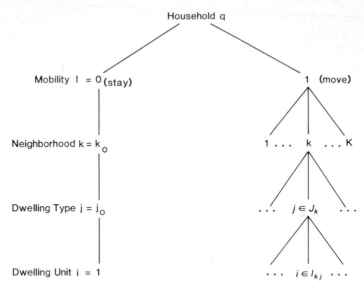

Figure 4.1. Assumed decision structure in housing choice [adapted from Onaka and Clark (1983)].

tives available at a lower level of choice. For example, choice among neighbor-hoods is affected not only by their locational characteristics, but also by the availability and characteristics of housing types in those neighborhoods. Thus, dwelling type selection $j \in J$ is conditioned on neighborhood choice k and influenced by the availability of dwelling units i of dwelling type j in that neighborhood k, and similarly for other decisions in the hierarchy. Although the aggregation of alternatives into such a decision hierarchy is somewhat arbitrary, the following observations may be made in support of this structure.

(i) The literature distinguishes the mobility decision (stay/move) from resi-dential choice.

(ii) Moving has high transaction costs and losses of psychological and social attachment to the unit and neighborhood. It may be proxied by length of stay.

(iii) Housing markets are probably stratified into submarkets, where attributes within submarkets are valued similarly by consumers.

(iv) The geographic distribution of housing units exhibits strong spatial auto-correlation. Dwelling units in a given neighborhood are likely to be similar.

Formally, let u_{lkji} be the utility associated with occupying dwelling unit i of dwelling type j in neighborhood k and following a mobility decision l, then the nested logit model which corresponds to the decision structure of Figure 4.1 is described by the inclusive value

$$\Psi = \ln \sum_{l=0}^{1} \left[\sum_{k \in K_l} \left[\sum_{j \in J_{lk}} \left[\sum_{i \in I_{lkj}} \exp\{u_{lkji}\}/\theta_{lkj}^{(I)} \right]^{\theta_{lkj}^{(I)}/\theta_{lk}^{(J)}} \right]^{\theta_{lk}^{(J)}/\theta_{l}^{(K)}} \right]^{\theta_{l}^{(I)}} \quad (4.8)$$

with

$$0 < \theta_{lkj}^{(I)} \le \theta_{lk}^{(J)} \le \theta_{l}^{(K)} \le 1, \ I_{lkj} \in \{1,\dots,I\}, \ J_{lk} \in \{1,\dots,J\}, \ K_l \in \{1,\dots,K\}$$

with the choice probability $P_{ijkl} = \partial \Psi / \partial u_{ijkl}$.

For brevity, index n of the individual household has been suppressed. However, the choice probability describes the behavior of a household belonging to some category $s \in S$. The index K_l, J_{lk}, and I_{lkj}, are conditioned on the outcomes of higher level decisions, e.g. J_{lk} on l and k. A decision to stay forces neighborhood and dwelling choices so that

$$K_0 = k_0, \quad J_{0k_0} = j_0, \quad \text{and} \ I_{0k_0j_0} = 1,$$

where the initial housing unit is located in some neighborhood $k_0 \in \{1,\dots,K\}$ and is a member of some dwelling type $j_0 \in (1,\dots,J)$, and where a household is assumed to occupy only one unit. A decision to move permits neighborhood selection among all neighborhoods in the area, $K_l = \{1,\dots,K\}$ and choice of dwelling type among those available in the neighborhood selected, $J_{lk} \in \{1,\dots,J\}$. Parameters $\theta_l^{(K)}$, $\theta_{lk}^{(J)}$, and $\theta_{lkj}^{(I)}$ measure the degrees to which alternatives in K_l, J_{lk}, and I_{lkj} respectively are perceived as dissimilar or independent. It can be shown that the probability of selecting a specific dwelling unit is the product of the following marginal and conditional probabilities.

$$P_{lkji} = P_l \cdot P_{k|l} \cdot P_{j|lk} \cdot P_{i|lkj}. \quad (4.9)$$

The nested logit model consists of separately estimating these probabilities in an ascending order, that is, beginning with $P_{i|lkj}$ and incorporating the expected utilities obtainable at a lower level in estimating the choice probabilities at a higher level.

4.4.3. Probit model[3]

The assumption that the error terms in (4.9) have a joint multivariate normal distribution with zero mean and an arbitrary variance–covariance matrix defines

---

[3] Partly derived from Van Lierop (1986).

the multinomial probit (MNP) model [see, for instance, Daganzo (1979)]. Thus, the variances of the error terms in an MNP model are allowed to be different and the error terms themselves are permitted to be correlated. This means that the IIa problem does not exist, which makes the model extremely well-suited for analyses of the housing market with its often large sets of only marginally differing alternatives. The model has the following probability function:

$$P_{in} = \int_{\xi_{in}=-\infty}^{\infty} \int_{\xi_{1n}=-\infty}^{v(x_{in}'\beta)-v(x_{1n}'\beta)+\xi_{in}} \cdots \int_{\xi_{i'n}=-\infty}^{v(x_{in}'\beta)-v(x_{i'n}'\beta)+\xi_{in}}$$

$$\cdots \int_{\xi_{In}=-\infty}^{v(x_{in}'\beta)-v(x_{In}'\beta)+\xi_{in}} \cdot N(\xi|0,\Omega)\,d\xi_{In}\ldots d\xi_{i'n}\ldots d\xi_{1n}\,d\xi_{in} \qquad (4.10)$$

in which the number of integrals equals the number of alternatives and $N(\xi,0,\Omega)$ is the multivariate normal density function with mean vector 0 and variance–covariance matrix Ω. The estimation of the coefficient-vector can be done in an iterative way, but only if specific assumptions are first made about the structure of the variance–covariance matrix Ω. Two specifications are possible in this respect.

(i) A variance–covariance matrix, which is the same for all individuals ($\Omega_n = \Omega, \forall n$). In the binomial case, this variance–covariance matrix takes the following form:

$$\Omega = \begin{bmatrix} \theta_1 & \rho \\ \rho & \theta_2 \end{bmatrix}. \qquad (4.11)$$

The values of θ_1, θ_2 (describing the variance of the alternatives) and ρ (describing the correlation between the alternatives) can be estimated (simultaneously with the influences of the specified explanatory variables of the model) by means of a numerical approximation method and a variable metric algorithm [see Daganzo and Schoenfeld (1978)].

(ii) A variance–covariance matrix of the Hausman and Wise form [Hausman and Wise (1978)]; for the binomial case, this variance–covariance matrix has the following form:

$$\Omega_n = \theta \begin{bmatrix} E(1) & \rho(E(1)E(2))^{1/2} \\ \rho(E(1)E(2))^{1/2} & E(2) \end{bmatrix} \qquad (4.12)$$

where $E(1)$ is the expectation of alternative 1 and $E(2)$ that of alternative 2.

In the case of three exogenous variables and a constant term, $E(1)$ and $E(2)$ are defined by:

$$E(1) = \beta_0 + \beta_1 X_1 + \beta_2 X_2 + \beta_3 X_3$$
$$E(2) = \gamma_0 + \gamma_1 X_1 + \gamma_2 X_2 + \gamma_3 X_3. \tag{4.13}$$

This implies that the variances of the alternatives are proportional to the means of the alternatives and that the covariances are proportional to the root of the product of the means. Also here, θ and ρ can be derived simultaneously within the framework of the entire estimation procedure of the coefficients belonging to the exogenous variables of the equations in (4.13).

From a *theoretical* point of view, the benefit of the latter specification form compared with the first one is that different variance–covariance matrices can be defined for different decision makers without a loss of degrees of freedom (caused by the introduction of additional parameters), in fact, one degree of freedom is gained. The appearance of differences of variances of alternatives and of covariances between alternatives for individuals intuitively seems realistic. It means that *taste variations* can exist concerning various choice alternatives [see Daganzo (1979)]. Altogether, the multinomial probit model has the following advantages over alternative discrete choice models [see also Sheffi et al. (1982)]:

(i) *flexibility of specification* by means of a full parameterization in terms of the covariance matrix, so that individual utility differences can be included (and consequently the independence from irrelevant alternatives property is avoided);

(ii) *introduction of taste variation* by incorporating parameters that depend on the values of specific explanatory variables;

(iii) *statistical robustness* by allowing the possibility of handling missing data and measurement errors;

(iv) *introduction of structural state dependence* by including repeated observations, so that this model is extremely useful for panel and longitudinal data; and

(v) *possibility of consistent aggregation*, so that aggregate utility for subgroups can easily be assessed.

Disadvantages of the model are:

(i) interpretation of the results cannot be done directly or easily as the choice probabilities cannot be calculated in a closed-form, but usually require special approximations; and

(ii) large numbers of alternatives are difficult to calibrate.

Van Lierop (1986) has shown that the MNP model with a variance–covariance matrix of the type of (4.12) is also to be preferred in a *practical* (empirical) housing demand analysis. He used this concept to develop a multi-level housing market model for the Netherlands focusing both on analysis and forecasting of residential mobility, dwelling preferences, and dwelling choices. In this model, the price–quality ratio of dwellings is the most important exogenous variable to explain both willingness to move and actual housing choice. The forecasting abilities of the model are remarkably good. It has, however, still to be calibrated for more than four alternatives per level of the sequential approach.

4.4.4. Elimination-by-aspects method[4]

Tversky (1972a, 1972b) has developed another discrete choice method that makes use of the random utility concept and gets around the IIa problem. The model is, however, completely different from the methods described so far. It has mainly been applied in psychology and does not deal with error terms or even assumptions about possible error terms.

The general assumption of the elimination-by-aspects (EBA) method is that the chooser selects an alternative in a sequential process based only on the known, identified, explanatory attributes or *aspects* (as they are always called in Tversky's approach). These aspects are scaled in order of importance and are to be interpreted as desirable features. The selection of a particular aspect leads to elimination of all alternatives which do not contain this desired aspect (so, trade-offs are not recognized). The process terminates with the decision based on the last relevant aspect. With that decision, the final choice is made.

In the original form of this model, the choice of aspects, which will be crucial in the successive selection steps, is made at random. The choice probabilities in the model can be defined as an increasing function of the importance of the relevant aspects. Special features of the EBA model are:

(i) Aspects which are shared by all alternatives do not affect the final choice probability. This may be a restriction in analyzing interactions, as the relative total values of alternatives cannot exert any influence. The selection process only takes into account the *presence* of aspects. This means that gradual differences of aspects do not have an influence on the choice probabilities. Only completely dissimilar aspects play a role in the EBA model. In analyzing actual spatial interactions this is usually a rigid restriction, as it may, for example, exclude relevant socioeconomic variables from the decision process. A consequence of this feature is that the choice between alternatives which are very similar cannot really be explained by this type of sequential process. Of course, this last point is a weak element in the most discrete choice methods. In the EBA model, however, there is no possibility of solving this problem even in theory.

(ii) A technical disadvantage of the method is the computational burden which is necessary to estimate the outcome of the (assumed) sequential process. The

---

[4] Partly based on Van Lierop (1986).

computational burden increases rapidly as the number of alternatives and different aspects increases.

A general limitation of hierarchical approaches is that the analyst must know the correct decision hierarchy beforehand. Without this knowledge, the analyst is reduced to fitting models by trial and error [Meyer and Eagle (1982)].

Young (1982) has developed an EBA model for urban location decisions. This model has, amongst others, been applied to the choice of residence of groups of people in Melbourne, Australia.

4.5. Behavioral models

In contrast to the purely statistical, econometric, and psychometric modelling strategies thus far, there have also been attempts to develop more pure behavioral models, in most instances based on the notions of stress and dissatisfaction, or disequilibrium. We have already noted that this research developed from initial work by geographers and sociologists [Wolpert (1965), Brown and Moore (1970), Speare et al. (1975)] and was formalized as a probability model of stress and inertia by Huff and Clark (1978) and as a disequilibrium model of residential mobility by Hanushek and Quigley (1978a, 1978b). In the Huff and Clark (1978) formulation, the level of dissatisfaction is assumed to increase at a decreasing rate over time as the household falls out of adjustment with its environment, changes its expectations, or has changes in its family composition. At the same time, there are factors that deter households from moving. This inertia also is assumed to increase over time at a decreasing rate. The balance of dissatisfaction and inertia generates a propensity to move as a function of length of stay. Thus,

$$p(t) = \begin{cases} k[S(t) - R(t)], & \text{if } S(t) > R(t) \\ 0, & \text{if } S(t) \leq R(t) \end{cases} \tag{4.14}$$

where $S(t) =$ the pressure to move at time t, and $R(t) =$ the resistance to move at time t.

Two exponential functions are utilized to provide estimates of the following probability of moving over time:

$$p(t) = k\{(\tilde{S} - \tilde{R}) - [\tilde{S} - S(0)]\exp(-\sigma t) + [\tilde{R} - R(0)]\exp(-\rho t)\} \tag{4.15}$$

where $\tilde{R} =$ the maximum resistance, and $\tilde{S} =$ the maximum stress.

Economists have been impatient with the general dissatisfaction models, because of the rather vague concepts of dissatisfaction and stress contained in these models [Weinberg et al. (1981)]. However, economists have utilized what is a very similar conceptual approach, but couched in the specific terms of housing dissatisfaction. In fact, the following housing expenditure disequilibrium model presented by Hanushek and Quigley (1978a, 1978b), and developed by a number of other economists, is focused specifically on both the housing market and the difference between the actual and optimal amounts of housing consumed:

$$P_{t,t+1} = f\left[\left(H_{t+1}^d - H_t\right)/H_t^d\right] \tag{4.16}$$

where
H_t = the actual housing consumption at time t;
H_t^d = the equilibrium housing consumption at time t; and
H_{t+1}^d = the equilibrium housing consumption at time $t+1$.
Mobility is seen as a response to the change in demands for housing and services. Brummell (1979) attempted to integrate both the consumer behavior approach, which is based on the notion that consumers attempt to obtain a combination of quantities of goods that maximizes their satisfaction or utility, subject to certain constraints, and the concepts of aspirations, needs, and stress. The model is one in which the decision to move is based upon the difference between experienced and aspiration "place utilities"

$$S = U_t^* - U_t^0 \tag{4.17}$$

where
U_t^* = the aspiration place utility at time t, and
U_t^0 = experienced place utility at time t.
In turn, U_t^0 depends upon a vector of attributes of the residential environment and a vector of attributes of other goods. Both experienced and aspiration utilities can be defined. As Brummel notes, how the household responds to stress varies with the levels and the sources of stress [Brummel (1979, p. 343)]. At low levels of stress, it is unlikely that the household would consider moving, but at higher levels there is a clear possibility of relocation. Brummel suggests that it is whether or not the value of S exceeds a household's stress threshold level that determines the probability of seeking a new residence.

These disequilibrium models or stress models have led to considerable discussion of the behavioral processes involved in residential mobility. The attempts to formalize the stress models have led to specific investigations of stress and inertia and the attempt to refine the parameters which measure stress [Phipps and Carter (1984)].

Within the area of behavior models, there has been considerable concern with the search process as distinct from the issues of deciding to move or residential choice. The search models have been particularly concerned with the decision-making processes which are involved in the process of relocation, and particularly the role that information plays in the evaluation and choice decisions in the process of residential search.

The work on search behavior and search processes can be divided into those developments related to stopping rule models, including the work of Flowerdew (1978), Weibull (1978), Phipps (1978), Smith et al. (1979), Meyer (1981), and Phipps and Laverty (1983), and the work that is more specifically related to housing markets [Maclennan and Wood (1982), Wood and Maclennan (1982)].

Flowerdew (1978) was one of the first to outline the use of stopping rule models for housing search. Although he did not carry out any empirical analysis, his study was a stimulus to further work on stopping rule models. In an important paper, Weibull (1978) suggested one of the first models that explictly incorporated space in a model of search, again without empirical tests. Similarly, Phipps (1978) adopted a stopping rule model for an experiment on student apartment selection. In this case, however, there was no specifically spatial component in the model.

Smith et al. (1979) suggest that search occurs as a result of a comparison between the expected utility of search $E_t^i(u^B)$ in region i and time t, with the best utility available (u^B). Thus,

$$\psi = E_t^i(u^B) - u^B \tag{4.18}$$

(where u^B may equal u^0). If $\psi^i > 0$ for any i, search will occur; the actual search in any period will occur in the neighborhood giving rise to the highest locational stress, $\psi = \max(\psi^1, \ldots, \psi^n)$. The criterion may be interpreted as locational stress or relative attractiveness. As we note below, whether ψ^i is greater than or smaller than zero is the condition determining if search will or will not occur in region i. It is possible to relate ψ to the probability of further search. Following Smith et al. (1979), we first write a general expression, then simplify that expression to finally obtain a form that may be cast in an operational mode.

$$E_t^i(U^B) = \rho\left[u^0 \int_{-\infty}^{u^0} \alpha q(u) + \int_{u^0}^{\infty} \hat{u}\alpha q(u)\right]$$
$$+ (1-\rho)\left[u^B \cdot \int_{-\infty}^{u^B} \alpha q(u) + \int_{u^B}^{\infty} \hat{u}\alpha q(u)\right]. \tag{4.19}$$

Equation (4.19) can be interpreted as "people search as if the present search period were to be the last period of search. At the end, they will revise their information and reconsider their decision. Search occurs at each stage in the area of highest (positive) stress. At any point, the area of search may change as beliefs are modified and as new best alternatives are found. Search continues until $\psi \le 0$ for neighborhoods" [Smith et al. (1979, p. 13)].

Meyer (1981) has outlined a much less formalized model of decision making under uncertainty, basing his approach on an argument made by Slovic et al. (1977) that normative models are difficult to test because of calibration problems. In a preliminary discussion of the model, again applied to hypothetical apartment searches, Meyer concluded that preferences change as the distribution of the utility of opportunities is learned, and that stopping is based on a process of making inferences about the distribution, the time available for search, and the quality of the alternative (the apartment unit that is being viewed).

4.6. Micro-simulation

The last approach to residential mobility and housing choice we discuss is micro-simulation. Since Forrester (1969) developed his Urban Dynamics model, this simplistic modelling approach has known periods of varying popularity. The approach lists the elements of an urban housing market and its characteristics. Each characteristic for each element is generated in relation to a known conditional probability distribution (using random numbers) in such a way as to ensure that the probability distributions and possible constraints are satisfied over all [see, for instance, Wilson (1981) and Botman (1981)]. This is normally done by means of Monte Carlo Simulation. The pattern of the conditional probability distributions that are used represents the model's causal structures. Usually the approach, however, is not based on clear behavioral underpinnings derived from surveys among real households. The causal relations are instead mostly based on assumed relations in the housing market. Although this can limit the real world value of the output from these models, they can still employ extensive disaggregate behavioral input to formulate their model relations [see, for instance, Wegener (1980)]. Micro-simulation is extremely suitable for a simple, but quick, calibration of various contrasting future scenarios of urban (housing market) planning.

An interesting example of micro-simulation by Wegener for the Dortmund region uses a system of submodels of which the housing market submodel is just one. All submodels are based on micro-simulation, and the total yields an interesting picture of interrelations between housing, labor market, services offered and so on. Since the late 1970s Wegener has tried to improve on the overall regional model by modifying various submodels, while leaving the relations between submodels intact. His original simple micro-simulation housing market model has been adapted to a multinomial logit approach.

5. Future developments in residential mobility and housing location modelling

Although the models presented in this chapter have already improved our understanding of household location and residential mobility, it is clear that several aspects of these models can still be improved in order to derive better planning instruments. Real life is likely to be much more complicated than our current models. Dynamics, levels of measurement, and systems-impacts have received only limited attention. For example:

(i) Shifts in urban systems and highly nonlinear dynamic growth patterns emphasize the need for a more problem-oriented view in housing market models.

(ii) Measures of residential location and housing choice phenomena are often qualitative in nature (for example measured by means of ordinal numbers). Qualitative information is by no means a priori inferior to quantitative information. In addition, qualitative statements may be the only available measures. How can we develop models in such situations?

(iii) Housing markets are interacting with more general regional and national systems than is shown in the models discussed here. These systems and the housing market are highly interactive entities with many intertwined factors. Demographic (stages of life cycle), economic (employment, finances), spatial (commuting flows, spatial spin-off and spill-over effects), state (management and organization, communication, technical progress), and sociopolitical (decision structures, interest groups) factors make up an important contextual background to household location and household mobility.

While it is true that ignoring system influences is partially justified in periods when the socioeconomic system is apparently in a kind of (quasi-) equilibrium, it may cause problems. In periods of drastic changes of the socioeconomic system, relocation decisions of individuals and households can be directly connected to changes in macro-variables (for instance, at the end of the 1970s and the beginning of the 1980s many housing move decisions in the Western world have been directly influenced by world-wide economic changes, especially housing price shifts). Future research can try to incorporate indicators of system developments into (existing) residential mobility and housing choice models.

To overcome shortcomings in current models, a variety of approaches to dynamic systems has been developed. At the practical level, dynamics can be taken into account by various ad hoc approaches via the introduction of:

(i) single variables that represent dynamic components, e.g., filters for first or higher order time differences of important explanatory variables;

(ii) simulated developments of variables;

(iii) the use of expectations instead of actual measured values of relevant variables – for example, expected future income instead of current income for a model analyzing housing choices at a disaggregate level; and

(iv) dummies for preferences and expert judgments.

At a more fundamental level, dynamics can be provided by longitudinal panel analysis [see, for instance, Halperin and Gale (1984), Wrigley and Dunn (1984)]. This type of research, however, is still fraught with difficulties, including:

(i) cost: longitudinal data sampling is expensive and time consuming;

(ii) robustness: no easy and robust descriptive panel methods exist as yet; and

(iii) operational methods: the in this context popular Lisrel method, for example, needs strict a priori causal assumptions, and general dynamic disaggregate methods for the analysis of longitudinal panel data are yet still in an experimental phase [see Heckman (1981) and Van Lierop (1986)].

The best way to model interrelated complex (and dynamic) systems is an open question. For each subsystem, one may identify a set of policy issues or key factors that may have a direct or indirect impact on another subsystem. For instance, a housing policy may indirectly lead to an increased attractiveness of urban districts, so that as a result, traffic problems (related to the infrastructure sector) may emerge. For the description of the developments of key factors or subsystems a variety of methods is available nowadays. Over the last couple of decades a number of scientists have tried to define models to analyze "shock-wise" oscillating development patterns in socioeconomic systems. Some of the most well-known representatives which may be of value in improving current housing market analyses (in addition to the ongoing research discussed in this chapter and in Chapter 6 of this Handbook) are:

(i) Forrester (1969) who creates simple growth models based on simulation of sets of differential equations with feedbacks;

(ii) Allen et al. (1983) and Wilson (1981) who use simple logistic differential equations with feedbacks;

(iii) Day (1981) who uses difference equations;

(iv) Dendrinos and Mullally (1981) who apply a generalized Lotka–Volterra system of "predator–prey" relationships; and

(v) Johansson and Nijkamp (1986) who employ event–history analysis for studying urban dynamics.

In recent years, significant progress has been made on the treatment of qualitative (spatial) data [see Nijkamp et al. (1985)]. New qualitative data methods and new computer software to implement these methods in practical research can broaden the scope of conventional analyses of residential mobility and housing choice. Some of these methods try to deal directly with qualitative data, others aim at designing transformation procedures from qualitative data to cardinal data. The objective of all of them is to identify a certain structure in the qualitative data, which should provide a basis for satisfactory and realistic analyses.

There is clearly a dichotomy between the increasingly sophisticated research of small subsystems (mobility, housing markets) and the aggregate approaches to overall structures. In addition, there is a number of simplified approaches that draw neither on the micro or macro approaches and that rather trade off elegance, clarity, and technical detail for rapid overviews of the whole system. The increasing use of micro-computers, accounting frameworks, computer networks, information systems, and larger data bases, emphasizes the need to draw closer links between research and practice.

References

Allen, P. M., G. Engelen and M. Sanglier (1983) 'Towards a general dynamic model of the spatial evolution of urban systems'. Paper presented at the International Symposium on New Directions in Urban Modelling, University of Waterloo, Waterloo, Canada.

Alonso, W. A. (1964) *Location and land use*. Cambridge, Mass.: Harvard University Press.

Anas, A. (1976) 'Short-run dynamics in the spatial housing market', in: S. J. Papageorgiou, ed., *Mathematical land use theory*. Lexington, Mass.: D.C. Heath, 262–275.

Anas, A. (1980) 'A probabilistic approach to the structure of rental housing markets', *Journal of Urban Economics*, 7:225–247.

Anas, A. (1981) 'The estimation of multinomial logit models of joint location and travel mode choice from aggregated data', *Journal of Regional Science*, 21:223–242.

Anas, A. (1982) *Residential location markets and urban transportation: economic theory, econometrics, and public policy analysis with discrete choice models*. New York: Academic Press.

Bahrenberg, G., M. M. Fischer and P. Nijkamp, eds. (1984) *Recent developments in spatial data analysis, methodology, measurement, models*. Aldershot, UK: Gower.

Batty, M. (1971) 'Exploratory calibration of a retail location model using search by golden section', *Environment and Planning A*3:411–432.

Ben-Akiva, M. and A. DePalma (1983) *Modelling an analysis of dynamic residential location choice*. Hamilton, Ontario: McMaster University, Working Paper 19.

Bird, H. (1976) 'Residential mobility and preference patterns in the public sector of the housing market', *Transactions of the Institutute of British Geographers* 1: no. 1, 20–33.

Botman, J. J. (1981) *Dynamics of housing and planning: a regional simulation model*. Delft/The Hague: Delft University Press/Martinus Nijhoff.

Bourne, L. S., and J. R. Hitchcock (1978) *Urban housing markets, recent directions in research and policy*. 9–19.

Brown, L. A., and E. G. Moore (1970) 'The intraurban migration process: a perspective', *Geografiska Annaler, Series B*:1–13.

Brummell, A. C. (1979) 'A model of intra-urban mobility, *k*', *Economic Geography*, 55:338–352.

Case, K. E. (1981) 'A new approach to modelling the effects of demographic change on the housing market', Wellesly Working Paper 42, Wellesly College Dept. of Economics.

Cebula, R. J. (1979) *The determinants of human migration*. Lexington, Mass.: Lexington Books.

Clark, G. L. (1984) 'Review of *Transport, location and spatial policy* edited by K. J. Button', *Environment and Planning*, A16:551–554.

Clark, W. A. V. (1981) 'On modelling search behavior', in: D. Griffiths and R. McKinnon, eds., *Dynamics spatial models*. Alphen aan de Rijn: Sijthoff and Noordhooff, 102–131.

Clark, W. A. V. (1982) *Modelling housing market search*. London: Croom Helm.

Clark, W. A. V. (1983) 'Structures for research on the dynamics of residential mobility, in: D. A. Griffith and A. C. Lea, eds., *Evolving geographical structures*. The Hague: Martinus Nijhoff, 372–397.

Clark, W. A. V. and K. Avery (1978) 'Patterns of migration: a macro-analytic case study', in: D. Herbert and R. J. Johnston, eds., *Geography in the urban environment*. London: Wiley.

Clark, W. A. V., J. O. Huff, and J. E. Burt (1978) 'Calibrating a model of the decision to move', *Environment and Planning*, A11:689–704.

Clark, W. A. V. and J. Onaka (1985) 'An empirical test of a joint model of residential mobility and housing choice', *Environment and Planning*, A17.

Clark, W. A. V., and T. Smith (1982) 'Housing market search behavior and expected utility theory II: the process of search', *Environment and Planning*, A14:17–737.

Cordey-Hayes, M. and A. G. Wilson (1971) 'Spatial interaction', *Socio-Economic Planning Sciences*, 5:73–95.

Cronin, F. (1979) *An economic analysis of intraurban search and mobility using alternative benefit measures*. Washington, D.C.: The Urban Institute.

Daganzo, C. F. (1979) *Multinomial probit, the theory and its application to demand forecasting*. New York: Academic Press.

Daganzo, C. F. and L. Schoenfeld (1978) 'CHOMP user's manual', Research report UCB-ITS-RR-78-7, Institutue of Transportation Studies, University of California, Berkeley, Calif.

DaVanzo, J. (1981) 'Microeconomic approaches to studying migration decisions', in: G. F. DeJong and R. W. Gardner, eds. *Migration decision making*. New York: Pergamon Press, 90–129.

Day, R. (1981) 'Emergence of chaos from neoclassical growth', *Geographical Analysis*, 13:315–327.

Dendrinos, D. S. and H. Mullally (1981) 'Evolutionary patterns of urban population', *Geographical Analysis*, 13:328–344.

DePalma, A. and M. Ben Akiva (1981) Interactive dynamic modelling of residential location choice, Umea, Sweden, Paper presented at the International Conference on Structural and Economic Analysis and Planning in Time and Space.

Dieleman, F. M. (1983) 'Tenure and allocation policy in the Tilburg housing market', *Tijdschrift voor Economische en Sociale Geografie*, 74:62–174.

Domencich, F. A. and D. McFadden (1975) *Urban travel demand, a behavioural analysis*. Amsterdam: North-Holland.

Fischer, M. M. and P. Nijkamp (1985) 'Developments in discrete spatial data and choice analysis', *Progress in Human Geography*, 9:515–551.

Flowerdew, R. (1978) 'Search strategies and stopping rules in residential mobility', *Institute for British Geographers, Transactions*: 47–57.

Forrester, J. W. (1969) *Urban dynamics*. Cambridge, Mass.: The MIT Press.

Gleave, D. and M. Cordey-Hayes (1977) 'Migration dynamics and labour market turnover', *Progress and Planning*, 8:1–96.

Goodman, J. (1976) 'Housing consumption disequilibrium and local residential mobility', *Environment and Planning*, A8:855–874.

Greenwood, M. J. (1981) *Migration and economic growth in the United States*. New York: Academic Press.

Grigsby, W. G. (1978) 'Response to John M. Quigley's 'Housing markets and housing demand: analytic approaches', in: L. S. Bourne and J. R. Hitchcock, eds., *Urban housing markets: recent directions in research and policy*. Toronto: University of Toronto Press, 45–49.

Halperin, W. C. and N. Gale (1984) 'Towards behavioural models of spatial choice: some recent developments', in: D. E. Pitfield, ed., *Discrete choice models in regional science*. London: Pion, 1–28.

Hanushek, E. and J. Quigley (1978a) 'An explicit model of intrametropolitan mobility', *Land Economics*, 54:411–429.

Hanushek, E. and J. Quigley (1978b) 'Housing market disequilibrium and residential mobility', in: W. A. V. Clark and E. G. Moore, eds., *Population mobility and residential change, Studies in Geography* #25. Evanston, Illinois: Northwestern Univ.

Hausman, J. A. and D. A. Wise (1978) 'A conditional probit model for quantitative choice: discrete recognizing interdependence and heterogeneous preferences', *Econometrica*, 46: no. 2, 403–426.

Heckmann, J. J. (1981) 'Statistical models for discrete panel data', in: C. F. Manski and D. McFadden, eds., *Structural analysis of discrete data with econometric applications*, Cambridge, Mass.: The MIT Press, 114–178.

Hensher, D. A. and L. W. Johnson (1981) *Applied discrete choice modelling*. London: Croom Helm.

Herbert, J. and B. Stevens (1960) 'A model for the distribution of residential activity in urban areas', *Journal of Regional Science*, 2:21–36.

Huff, J. O. and W. A. V. Clark (1978) 'Cumulative stress and cumulative inertia, a behavioral model of the decision to move', *Environment and Planning*, A10:1101–1119.

Ingram, G. K., J. F. Kain, and J. R. Ginn (1972) *The Detroit prototype of the NBER urban simulation model*. New York: Columbia University Press.

Johansson, B. and P. Nijkamp (1986) 'Analysis of episodes in urban event histories', L. Burns and L. H. Klaasser, eds., *Spatial Cycles*. Aldershot, UK: Gower, forthcoming.

Kain, J. F., W. C. Apgar, and J. R. Ginn (1976) 'Simulation of the market effects of housing allowances, Vol. 1: Description of the NBER urban simulation model', Series Urban Planning Policy Analysis and Administration, Dept. of City and Regional Planning, R 77-2, Harvard University, Cambridge, Mass.

Kain, J. F. and W. C. Apgar (1977) 'Modelling of neighborhood change', Discussion Paper D77-22, Dept. of City and Regional Planning, Harvard. Univ., Cambridge.

Lancaster, K. J. (1966) 'A new approach to consumer theory', *Journal of Political Economy*, 74:132–157.

Lerman, S. R. (1977) 'Location, housing, automobile ownership and mode to work, a joint choice model', *Transportation Research Board Record* 610, Washington D.C., 6–11.

Lerman, S. R. (1979) 'Neighborhood choice and transportation services', in: David Segal, ed., *The economics of neighborhood*. New York: Academic Press, 83–118.

MacLennan, D. and G. Wood (1982) 'Information acquisition: patterns and strategies', in: W. A. V. Clark, ed., *Modelling housing market search*. London: Croom Helm, 134–159.

McFadden, D. (1973) 'Conditional logit analysis of qualitative choice behavior', in: P. Zarembka, ed., *Frontiers in economics*. New York: Academic Press.

McFadden D. (1978) *Modelling the choice of residential location in spatial interaction theory and planning models*, in: A Karlqvist, L. Lundqvist, F. Snickars and J. W. Weibull, eds., *Spatial interaction theory and planning models*. Amsterdam: North-Holland, 75–96.

McFadden D. (1984) 'Econometric analysis of qualitative response models', in: Z. Griliches and M. Intriligator, eds., *Handbook of econometrics*, Vol. II. Amsterdam: North-Holland, 1395–1457.

Meyer, R. J. (1981) 'A descriptive model of consumer information search behaviour', Working Paper 47-80-81, College of Humanities and Social Sciences, Carnegie-Mellon University, Pittsburgh.

Meyer, R. J. and T. C. Eagle (1982) 'Context-induced parameter instability in a disaggregate-stochastic model of store choice', *Journal of Marketing Research*, 19:62–71.

Moore, E. G. (1969) 'The structure of intra-urban movement rates: an ecological model', *Urban Studies*, 6, no. 1:17–33.

Muth, R. F. (1961) 'The spatial structure of the housing market', *Papers of the Regional Science Association*, 7.

Muth, R. F. (1969) *Cities and housing*. Chicago: Univ. of Chicago Press.

Nijkamp, P., H. Leitner, and N. Wrigley, eds. (1985) *Measuring the unmeasurable*. The Hague: Martinus Nijhoff.

Onaka, J. (1981) 'A multi-attribute housing consumption disequilibrium model of intra-metropolitan residential mobility', Ph.D. Dissertation, University of California, Los Angeles.

Onaka, J. (1983) 'A multiple attribute housing disequilibrium model of residential mobility', *Environmental and Planning*, A15:751–765.

Onaka, J. and W. A. V. Clark (1983) 'A disaggregate model of residential mobility and housing choice', *Geographical Analysis*, 15:287–304.

Phipps, A. G. (1978) 'Space searching behavior: the case of apartment selection', Ph.D. Dissertation, University of Iowa.

Phipps, A. G. and J. E. Carter (1984) 'An individual-level analysis of the stress-resistance model of household mobility', *Geographical Analysis*, 16, no. 2:176–189.

Phipps, A. G. and W. H. Laverty (1983) 'Optimal stopping and residential search behavior', *Geographical Analysis*, 15, no. 3:187–204.

Pitfield, D. E., ed. (1984) *Discrete choice models in regional science*. London: Pion.

Pollakowski, H. (1982) *Urban housing markets and residential location*. Lexington, Mass.: Lexington Books.

Porell, F. W. (1982) *Models of intra-urban residential relocation*. Kluwer Nijhoff.

Putman, S. H. (1979) Urban residential location models. Boston: Martinus Nijhoff.

Quigley, J. M. (1973) 'Housing demand in the short run: analysis of polytomous choice', Econometric Society, New York, unpublished paper.

Quigley, J. M. (1976) 'Housing demand in the short run: an analysis of polytomous choice', *Explorations in Economic Research*, 3:76–102.

Quigley, J. M. (1978) 'Housing markets and housing demand, analytic approaches', in: L. S. Bourne and J. R. Hitchcock, eds., *Urban housing markets, recent directions in research and policy*. Toronto: University of Toronto Press, 23–44.

Quigley, J. M. (1983) 'Estimates of a more general model of consumer choice in the housing markets', in: R. E. Grierson, ed., *The urban economy in housing*, Lexington, Mass.: Lexington Books, 125–140.

Quigley, J. M. and D. H. Weinberg (1977) 'Intra-urban residential mobility: a review and synthesis', *International Regional Science Review*, 2:41–66.

Rossi, P. H. (1955) *Why families move: a study in the social psychology of urban residential mobility*. Glencoe, Illinois: The Free Press.

Scholten, H. J. (1984) 'Residential mobility and log-linear modelling', in: Bahrenberg, G., M. M. Fischer, and P. Nijkamp, eds., *Recent developments in spatial data analysis, methodology, measurement, models*. Aldershot, UK: Gower, 271–287.

Segal, D. (1979) 'A quasi-log linear model of neighborhood choice', in: D. Segal, ed., *The economics of neighborhood*. New York: Academic Press.

Sheffi, Y., R. Hall and C. Daganzo (1982) 'On the estimation of the multinomial probit model', *Transportation Research*, 16A(5-6):447–456.

Simmons, J. (1974) 'Patterns of residential movement in metropolitan Toronto', University of Toronto, Dept. of Geography Research Publications, Toronto.

Slovic, P., B. Fischhoff and S. Lichtenstein (1977) 'Behavioral decision theory', *Annual Review of Psychology*, 28:1–39.

Smith, T., W. A. V. Clark, J. O. Huff, and P. Shapiro (1979) 'A decision making and search model for intra-migration', *Geographical Analysis*, 11:1–22.

Smith, T. and W. A. V. Clark (1982) 'Housing market search behavior and expected utility theory I: measuring preferences for housing', *Environment and Planning*, A18:681–698.

Smith, W. (1970) *Housing*. Berkeley: University of California Press.

Snickars, F. and J. W. Weibull (1977) 'A minimum information principle: theory and practice', *Regional Science and Urban Economics*, 7:137–168.

Speare, A., S. Goldstein, and W. Frey (1975) *Residential mobility and migration and metropolitan change*. Cambridge, Mass.: Ballinger.

Stahl, K. (1980) Externalities and housing unit maintenance, Working Paper No. 8001, University of Dortmund, Dortmund.

Straszheim, M. R. (1973) 'Estimation of the demand for urban housing services from household interview data', *Review of Economics and Statistics*, 55:1–8.

Straszheim, M. R. (1975) *An econometric analysis of the urban housing market*. New York: National Bureau of Economic Research, Columbia University Press.

Tversky, A. (1972a) 'Choice by elimination', *Journal of Mathematical Psychology*, 9:341–367.

Tversky, A. (1972b) 'Elimination by aspects: a theory of choice', *Psychological Review*, 79 (4):281–299.

Van Lierop, W. F. J. (1981) 'Toward a new disaggregate model for the housing market', *Discussienota*. Amsterdam: The Free University.

Van Lierop, W. F. J. (1986) *Spatial interaction modelling and residential choice analysis*. Aldershot, UK: Gower.

Van Lierop, W. F. J. and P. Nijkamp (1979) 'A utility framework for interaction models for spatial processes', *Systemi Urbani*, 1:41–64.

Van Lierop, W. F. J. and P. Nijkamp (1982) 'Disaggregate models of choice in a spatial context', *Systemi Urbani*, 3:331–369.

Van Lierop, W. F. J. and P. Nijkamp (1984) 'Perspectives of disaggregate choice models on the housing market', in: D.E. Pitfield, ed., *Discrete choices models in regional science*. London: Pion, 141–162.

Van Lierop, W. F. J. and A. Rima (1982) 'Towards an operational disaggregate model of choice for the housing market', *Second interim report*. Amsterdam: The Free University.

Wegener, M. (1980) 'Das Dortmund Wohnungsmarktmodel', in: K. Stahl, ed., *Quantitative Wohnungsmarktmodelle*. Arbeitspapier 8006. Dortmund, BRD: Universität Dortmund.

Weibull, J. W. (1978) 'A search model for microeconomic analysis–with spatial applications', in: A. Karlqvist, L. Lundqvist, F. Snickars, J. W. Weibull, eds., *Spatial interaction theory and planning models*. Amsterdam: North-Holland, 47–73.

Weinberg, D., Friedman, J., and Mayo, S. K. (1981) 'Intraurban residential mobility: the role of transactions, costs, market imperfections, and household disequilibrium', *Journal of Urban Economics*, 9:332–348.

Wilkinson, R. K. (1973) 'House prices and the measurement of externalities', *Economic Journal*, 83:72–86.

Willekens, F. (1983) 'Specification and calibration of spatial interaction models. A contingency-table perspective and an application to intra-urban migration in Rotterdam', *Tijdschrift voor Economische en Sociale Geografie*, 74:239–252.

Williams, R. C. (1979) 'A logit model of demand for neighborhood', in: David Segal, ed., *The economics of neighborhood*. New York: Academic Press, 17–42.

Wilson, A. G. (1970) *Entropy in urban and regional modelling*. London: Pion.

Wilson, A. G. (1981) *Catastrophe and bifurcation applications to urban and regional systems*. London: Croom Helm.

Wolpert, J. (1965) 'Behavioral aspects of the decision to migrate', *Papers and Proceedings of the Regional Science Association*, 15:159–169.

Wood, G. and D. MacLennan (1982) 'Search adjustment in local housing markets', in: W. A. V. Clark, ed., *Modelling housing market search*. London: Croom Helm, 54–80.

Wrigley, N. and R. Duhn (1984) 'Diagnostics and resistant fits in logit choice models', in: D. Pitfield, ed., *London Papers in Regional Science*, Vol. 14. London: Pion, 44–66.

Young, W. (1982) 'The development of an elimination-by-aspects model of residential location choice', Ph.D. dissertation, Monash University, Clayton, Victoria, Australia.

Chapter 4

PUBLIC FACILITY LOCATION: A MULTIREGIONAL AND MULTI-AUTHORITY DECISION CONTEXT*

BÖRJE JOHANSSON and GIORGIO LEONARDI †

1. Introduction

For historical reasons the production of a large variety of services is controlled by public authorities (national, regional and local governments). The reasons for public intervention vary between the different types of services which are publicly controlled, and the degree of public control varies between societies (nations, regions, municipalities). From this one may derive a series of research problems such as (i) which type of services should according to welfare criteria be supplied publicly, (ii) given that a set of service activities are controlled publicly, how do the allocation mechanisms function, and can efficient mechanisms be identified?

Public facility location (PFL) problems have been studied within several analytical traditions, e.g. general location theory, the theories of public goods and public choice, as well as the operations research tradition. In this paper we focus on PFL-problems which are related to different aspects of these traditions. The perspective in our study is not intra-urban but regional. This is emphasized by a concentration on location problems in agendas of the following type: (i) location among municipalities in a region, and (ii) location among regions in a national (or multiregional) perspective.

Taking a region as a reference area, we identify the coordination problem of a regional authority and the simultaneous game-like competition between each municipality of the region. By municipality we mean a community with a local government. A similar two-level decision problem is also identified for settings with a national authority and independent regional authorities. With this two-level distinction it becomes important to consider spatial spillover of demand and the distribution of benefits and costs between communities and between regions. We

---

*When the work on this paper started both authors were with the International Institute for Applied Systems Analysis (IIASA), Laxenburg, Austria. The authors received helpful comments on earlier versions of this chapter from M. Fujita.

Handbook of Regional and Urban Economics, Volume I, Edited by P. Nijkamp
©Elsevier Science Publishers BV, 1986

also observe that an urban area as a whole may be thought of as a public facility. A clear example of this would be the city of Venice.

In Section 2 we present various types of PFL-problems. Section 3 deals with aggregation of demand and supply from the subregional to the regional level. In Section 4 we consider situations in which there is one upper-level coordinator, while Section 5 focuses explicitly on game-like structures. Finally, Section 6 deals with interregional migration related to the so-called Tiebout problem.

2.   Historical and conceptual remarks on the public facility location problem

2.1.   Historical background

Location theory has an important background in the classic urban economics of the nineteenth century such as von Thünen (1826) and later Weber (1909). As a continuation along this line we may also identify Christaller (1933), Palander (1935), and Lösch (1940). An ambition to analyze the location problem within the frames of a spatial economic equilibrium model can be found in Lefeber (1958) and in the works of Beckmann, starting in the early 1950s [see Beckmann (1968)]. So far, recent formulations of dynamic models of spatial allocation have not had much impact on the study of public facility location.

One may identify two main analytical traditions as regards the study of PFL. The first stems from economics and has its roots in welfare theory and the analysis of public goods. In this case the main problem concerns the existence of allocation mechanisms which may generate and safeguard a Pareto optimal solution. From a public authority's point of view this involves the problem of correctly assessing the demand for public goods. Contributions to this field relate to Tiebout's (1956) conjectures and describe competition among a set of communities which attract inhabitants with their public good policies and use land rents according to the Henry George Theorem to finance the public programmes [Stiglitz (1977, 1982), Arnott and Stiglitz (1979), Schweizer (1983)].

The second tradition focuses on facility location decisions of the Weber type: how to locate facilities which shall serve a given set of users with given locations (place of residence). The operations research literature contains a rich set of alternative ways of approaching this basic problem [see Lea (1981), Hansen et al. (1983)]. The research perspective in this second tradition is also closely associated with that of cost–benefit analysis.

The operations research tradition has its roots in works from the 1940s and 1950s. Theoretical developments during recent decades include (i) gravity-type models [Lowry, (1964), Lakshmanan and Hansen (1965), (ii) entropy models [Wilson, (1970)], and (iii) models based on random choice theory as outlined by e.g. McFadden (1974). Earlier contributions focused on how to minimize transportation costs. More recent studies may be characterized as spatial interaction models with the objective of reflecting users' empirically observed behaviour. Simultaneously, a better understanding of accessibility was developed [see, e.g. Hansen (1959), Weibull (1976)].

In a recent publication Thisse and Zoller (1983) consider a shift away from service activity analyses to problems of systems design. The latter corresponds to the problem of public facility location. In order to be classified as a PFL-problem we require in our presentation that the location decision is made by a public authority. This may be thought of as a minimum and necessary condition.

We may distinguish between three types of public facilities [compare Lea (1981), and Leonardi (1981)]:

(i) *Travel to facilities*: The consumer must travel in order to obtain the service (e.g. libraries, theatres, parks).

(ii) *Insurance service facilities*: The consumer receives benefits from the pure existence of the facility (e.g. fire and police protection).

(iii)*Delivered from facilities*: The consumer receives the (sometimes negative) benefits at his place of residence (e.g. pollutants, broadcasting).

Our presentation will mainly focus on the first two categories and will in particular consider problems in which the users' benefits are distance dependent. We consider taxation of consumer populations as well as the price-setting of service suppliers.

Our focus on two-level, multi-authority PFL decision problems and examination of non-cooperative equilibria and Pareto solutions goes beyond standard PFL-modelling. The multi-authority perspective, however, has a long tradition in Tiebout's contributions (1956, 1961). Schematically, the Tiebout problem comprises a set of municipalities. The government (authority) of each municipality imposes land (or property) taxation and uses the income to finance the provision of local public goods. An individual municipality may increase this supply and thereby attract people to migrate from other communities. It may also select a specific profile of its public goods policy to influence the socio-economic composition of in- and out-migrating households. In this way the municipality will affect the size and composition of its inhabitants, and consequently its taxation base. When several municipalities realize this mechanism, they will be involved in a non-cooperative game. Tiebout conjectured that this allocation problem has an equilibrium of Pareto type. In Section 6 we present some insights in this problem that may be gained when one recognizes that the Tiebout problem comprises dynamic processes.

2.2. The concept of public facilities

In a general study of PFL-decisions it is necessary to delineate the set of facility location problems to which the prefix "public" could and should be attached. This is not a trivial task, since many alternative criteria are available. Let us first imagine that facilities are ordered into groups or classes according to type of service provided from the facilities. The following conditions define three distinct public aspects of a facility in a given group:

(i) The service provided from the facility has a public (or semi-public) good property.

(ii) A public authority operates or controls the supply of services from the facility.

(iii) A public authority decides about the location of and investment in the facility.

The concept of public goods relates in particular to Samuelson's articles from the early 1950s (1954, 1955). In brief, a public good is such that once a certain amount is consumed by one individual, the same amount is consumed by all individuals in a given population. This requires (i) impossibility of exclusion, (ii) possibility of joint consumption, and (iii) impossibility of rejection. We may conclude that few commodities qualify as pure public goods. As shown for example by Arrow (1971) a large set of commodities belong to a category in between the two extremes of pure private and pure public goods.

In a spatial analysis of public facilities, distance effects cannot be disregarded and this motivates our concentration on "travel to facilities" and "insurance service facilities". In these two cases the associated public goods will always be impure, since a consumer's possibility to acquire the goods is affected by the distance to the supply points.

The insurance services may be classified as pure public goods with a distance decay effect. Examples from this class are fire brigades, police stations, medical emergency units with ambulances, etc. The commodity consumed by the public in these cases is an insurance service. The inhabitants in the neighbourhood acquire a joint utility as long as a facility constantly keeps a capacity available for emergencies. As soon as the capacity has to be utilized the utility falls. However, the value of the insurance is not spatially invariant but decreases with an individual's distance from the facility.

Services supplied by facilities which the consumer must visit may also have a semi-public good character. This class of facilities includes schools, hospitals, libraries, theatres, parks, etc. However, in those cases the intervention of public authorities as regards investment and operation decisions is motivated by merit good/want arguments rather than by public good considerations. Schools and libraries are for example often considered to have long-term, dynamic development effects on the society and its members, and individuals are at the same time assumed to underestimate those effects. Hence, public authorities (governments) formulate in such cases paternalistic welfare goals.

As argued by Arrow (1971), externalities, public and merit goods belong to a broader set of market failures, and this broader set defines a potential field for public interventions. We may also observe that usually public facilities are characterized by indivisibilities and decreasing marginal costs; this together with market failures provides the basic argument for public control of facility investment and operation.

For both categories of facilities discussed above we may observe that in many societies public and non-public organizations (clubs, associations and private firms) often simultaneously make investments in the same type of facilities and supply the same type of services. We will argue that descriptive as well as planning models must be outlined to cover such mixed cases.

2.3. *Partial analysis and fragmented theory*

The majority of PFL-models are formulated as partial analysis models which means that only a segment of the whole economy is depicted. Models that attempt to capture economy-wide relations achieve this by various forms of simplifications such that most aspects of market failure are assumed away. This is contrasted by frequent attempts to motivate public intervention with the existence of market failures.

One way of simplifying a regional PFL-model is to treat the set of communities as isolated islands with no spatial spillovers of benefits and costs. Simultaneously one may aggregate all public services into one single service package. For an individual community with homogeneous households we may then formulate the residential choice behaviour of each household as follows:

$$
\left.
\begin{aligned}
&\operatorname{Max} U(x, l, D(r)) \\
&x, l, r \\
&\text{subject to} \\
&x + E(r)l = Y
\end{aligned}
\right\} \tag{2.1}
$$

where U denotes the utility function of a household, x its consumption of a composite consumer (private) commodity, l the size of its residential land, r distance from the public facility, $E(r)$ the unit land rent at r, Y the household's income minus a lump sum tax, and $D(r)$ the amount of service received from the facility at distance r.

As described in Fujita (1984) this formulation assumes that all households (within the region analyzed) relocate through perfect market transactions after the introduction of the facility. With this assumption, the model allows for an examination of equilibrium land use given the facility location. We may illustrate this by the following proposition:

Proposition 1 [Fujita (1985)]

Fix a tax rate so that Y is given and assume that (i)–(v) below are satisfied. Then under each given location of the public facility in the region $G \subset R^2$, there uniquely exists a competitive equilibrium.

The assumptions in Proposition 1 are: (i) the utility function is defined for all positive combinations of x, l and D, is strictly increasing and quasi-concave in x and l for each $D > 0$, continuously differentiable, and indifference curves in the (x, l)-plane do not cut the axes, (ii) land is a normal good; (iii) $D(r)$ is continuous in r and $\partial D/\partial r < 0$ for all r; (iv) residential land and the services obtained from the facility are substitutes; (v) G is non-empty and compact.

The model introduced in (2.1) together with Proposition 1 may represent an approach to the PFL-problem in which market failure aspects are smoothed out. The alternative research tradition is instead characterized by focusing on "practical aspects" of market failures. It does so by confining itself to various forms of partial analysis. We illustrate this by outlining a framework which will be used frequently in the sequel. Consider a set of locations (i, j). By F_{ij} we denote the demand originating from the population in location i and directed towards facility services in location j:

$$F_{ij} = F_{ij}(P_i, \pi, d) \tag{2.2}$$

where P_i denotes the population in i, $\pi = \{\pi_j\}$ a vector of prices charged for the service in locations j, and $d = \{d_{ij}\}$ a matrix in which each element d_{ij} represents the total cost associated with a displacement from i to j, measured in appropriate units. This formulation basically refers to facilities which are visited by the consumers. In certain cases, like universities for example, such visits may be more of a migration than a trip making nature. We refer to a regional setting by considering one facility service capacity Q_j, in each site (community). As a consequence we stipulate that $d_{ij} > 0$ including the case $i = j$.

At the local level we introduce an income–cost function, V_j, which may also be thought of as a profit function defined for a given time period:

$$V_j = \pi_j F_j + h_j(F_j, Q_j) - f_j(\Delta Q_j) - g_j(F_j, Q_j) \tag{2.3}$$

where for an initial capacity $Q_j^0 \geq 0$
$\Delta Q_j = Q_j - Q_j^0$, and $Q_j \geq Q_j^0$;
$F_j = \sum_i F_{ij}$;
h_j = subsidy function describing the financial support from the regional authority to facility j as a function of the service level;
g_j = operation cost function with service level and capacity as arguments;
f_j = capacity increase cost function (periodized).

We may now specify a two-level problem with a regional authority at the first level and a management unit at the second. The latter may either be an agency using decision rules designed at the upper level, an independent local authority, or a private organization including a profit-making firm.

Assume that the decision criteria at the first level may be described by an objective function W which is used to assess the spatial distribution of service levels $G_i = \sum_j F_{ij}$, and cost levels $C_i = \sum_j F_{ij}(\pi_j + d_{ij})$ where d_{ij} denotes the total distance/displacement costs. In the case with only one decision level we may formulate the following optimization problem:

$$
\left.
\begin{aligned}
&\text{Max } W(G, C, b) \\
&Q, \pi \\
&\text{subject to} \\
&\text{(i) } \sum_i F_{ij} \le Q_j, \text{ all } j \\
&\text{(ii) } \sum_j V_j \ge b, \text{ or } V_j \ge b_j \text{ for each } j
\end{aligned}
\right\}
\qquad (2.4)
$$

where $G = \{G_i\}$, $C = \{C_i\}$ and b is a budget constraint. In addition, with only one decision level, the regional authority will have to decide about both Q_j and π_j for each j.

A two-level PFL-problem may be illustrated as follows:

$$
\left.
\begin{aligned}
&\text{Max } W(G, C, b : V_j = V_j^* \text{ for all } j) \\
&\sum F_{ij} \le Q_j, \text{ all } j
\end{aligned}
\right\}
\qquad (2.5)
$$

where V_j^* is the maximum of (2.3) given Q_j; the upper level selects $Q = \{Q_j\}$ and the local decision variable is π_j.

The theory which is used to formulate models as those in (2.4) and (2.5) is mostly both fragmentary and implicit. Although such models in certain respects can be thought of as comprehensive, they are indeed very partial. First, the demand function in (2.2) specifies a partial decision process of customers and cannot without ambiguity be used to assess consumers' surplus or benefits. Moreover, standard specifications of he W-function seldom incorporate the interdependency between (i) the rest of the economy and (ii) the facility variables Q_j, F_{ij} and G_i. Already within the public sector this constitutes a problem, since each community generally contains many different types of facilities which means that the sitting of all facilities should be evaluated simultaneously. We may also note that the taxation decisions have not been modeled, and we have disregarded the long-term relocation of population in response to spatial differentials in service and tax levels. In a modest way, some of these aspects will be touched upon in subsequent sections.

2.4. *Multi-authority decision problems*

In the preceding section the outline of models refers to a region–municipality interface. In principle these models also cover the national–regional interface with a national authority interacting with a set of different regional authorities.

Let us now consider insurance service facilities. In this case no prices are charged, and the demand specification in (2.2) is not appropriate. Suppose that the service capacity is shared freely between the communities in a region and that the potential benefit depends on the size of the facility and the distance to it. Then we may define for $\lambda < 0$ the welfare obtained in location i from a facility in location j as

$$U_{ij} = P_i Q_j \exp\{\lambda d_{ij}\} \tag{2.6}$$

and assign the following welfare value, W_j, to a facility in j

$$W_j = \sum_i U_{ij} = Q_j \sum P_i \exp\{\lambda d_{ij}\}. \tag{2.7}$$

The welfare of the population (customers) in location i is however equal to:

$$U_i = \sum_j U_{ij} = P_i \sum_j Q_j \exp\{\lambda d_{ij}\}. \tag{2.8}$$

We may recognize that (2.8) is a positive monotonic transformation of the welfare indicator in (3.16) from Section 3 which can be specified for a single user in location i as $u_i = \log \sum Q_j \exp\{\lambda d_{ij}\}$. The latter corresponds to a well-known demand expression for "travel to facilities" when prices are zero ($\pi_j = 0$), namely

$$F_{ij} = P_i Q_j \exp\{\lambda d_{ij}\} / \sum_j Q_j \exp\{\lambda d_{ij}\}. \tag{2.9}$$

This illustrates that it is possible to analyze "travel to" and "insurance service" facilities with models belonging to the same theoretical framework.

For a set of independent local (or regional) authorities, each may be assumed to attempt to maximize U_j in a game-like structure which also may include negotiation about reimbursement schemes. As a decision problem, this differs from an overall coordinating decision maker's objective to maximize the vector $W = \{W_j\}$ with constraints on the values of the vector $U = \{U_i\}$. This latter problem may also be formulated as a multi-criteria decision problem [see, e.g. Nijkamp and Rietveld (1982)].

Consider a long-term decision perspective in which we assume that the location of households is sensitive to the price and tax structure. Let $\tau = \{\tau_i\}$ where τ_i

denotes the tax rate in municipality (region) i. Referring to formulas (2.2) and (2.3) we may formulate an enlarged PFL-problem by writing

$$\left. \begin{aligned} V_j &= \sum_i \pi_{ij} F_{ij} + \tau_j P_j(\lambda) + \sum_i h_{ij} F_{ij} - \sum_i h_{ji} F_{ji} - g_j(F_j, Q_j) - f_j(\Delta Q_j) \\ F_{ij} &= P_j(\lambda) r_{ij}(d, \pi), \text{ and } \lambda = (\pi, \tau) \end{aligned} \right\}$$

$$(2.10)$$

where π_{ij} indicates the possibility of price differentiation with respect to a consumer's location; $\tau_j P_j(\lambda)$ denotes the tax income in j, $r_{ij} = r_{ij}(d, \pi)$ the proportion of the population in i which decides to visit the facility in j given d and π, and h_{ij} the payment from authority i to authority j per unit regional spillover from i to j.

We may observe that the payment coefficients π_{ij} and h_{ij} play different roles in the model; π_{ij} influences the behaviour of customers and does not have to be selected in a negotiation process. The opposite is true for h_{ij}. The objective function of authority j may in this case be represented by

$$\hat{W}_j = E_j(G_j, C_j) + \alpha V_j, \qquad \alpha > 0. \tag{2.11}$$

In the outlined multi-authority game structure each decision-making authority must contemplate the decisions made by all other authorities. In this context two types of solutions are relevant, viz. cooperative and non-cooperative solutions.

We have specified a relation $P_i = P_i(\lambda)$. In a long-term perspective one must in addition recognize dynamic interactions between the facility location pattern and the location of all other economic activities. In relation to this we should also observe that customers of public facilities include not only households but also firms and other producing organizations. For example, universities do not only provide education services to individuals, they also influence the local and regional supply of different categories of labour, and they produce R & D output at least partly in the form of a spatial public good. The literature on PFL decision making covers these latter aspects in a very limited way, and so far there is a lack of scientific tradition in this field.

3. Aggregation from subregional to a regional level

3.1. Structure of operational and investment costs

In (2.3) we have specified the cost structure of a facility with the help of two cost functions such that $g_j(F_j, Q_j)$ represents operation costs and $f_j(\Delta Q_j)$ investment

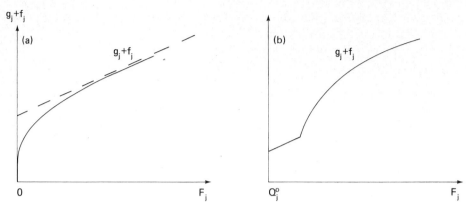

Figure 3.1. Operation plus investment costs.

costs. In most examples we assume that $g_j + f_j$ is concave in F_j when $Q_j = \Delta Q_j$ (as described in Figure 3.1a) and quasi-concave in F_j when $\Delta Q_j < Q_j$ (as described in Figure 3.1b). In case (a) $F_j = Q_j$; in case (b) $F_j \leq Q_j$ as $\Delta Q_j = 0$, while $F_j = Q_j$ as $\Delta Q_j > 0$.

In case (a) it seems reasonable to approximate the total cost function with a linear relation as indicated by the dotted line. In case (b) such an approach may also apply when decisions are made for several facilities simultaneously and when at the same time only few of them have $Q_j^\circ > 0$. If the number of facilities is given and they have equal size, Figure 3.1a may still represent the regional cost structure, only scaled up in accordance with the number of facilities.

3.2. Aggregation of a multi-facility problem at the subregional level

We shall outline a classical multi-facility PFL-problem. We consider a set of regions and assume that each region potentially may contain many small sized facilities. The decision problem has the following specification [compare Erlenkotter (1977)].

L $= \{ j : j = 1, 2, \ldots \}$ is a set of potential facility locations over a given set of regions;

$c_{ij} =$ transportation or displacement costs for customers in location i and a facility in location j;

$f_j^* = g_j + f_j$ denotes investment + operation costs per unit facility.

We assume that all facilities have equal size so that f_j^* represents the cost of an elementary facility. With this micro specification the location problem is given as

$$\underset{r,L}{\text{Min}} \sum_{j \in L} \sum_i c_{ij} r_{ij} + \sum_{j \in L} f_j^*$$

$$\sum_{j \in L} r_{ij} = 1; \ 0 \le r_{ij} \le 1. \tag{3.1}$$

Often Σf_j^* is written as $\Sigma f_j^* y_j$ where $y_j = 1$ if facility j is opened and $y_j = 0$ otherwise. We may now draw some conclusions in the form of two remarks [see e.g. Erlenkotter (1983)].

Remark 1

The minimization of (3.1) implies that customers choose the shortest distance so that

$$r_{ij} = \begin{cases} 1 \text{ if } c_{ij} = \underset{j \in L^*}{\text{Min}} \ c_{ij} \\ 0 \text{ otherwise} \end{cases} \tag{3.2}$$

where L^* denotes the set of opened facilities. This implies that customers will cross regional borders when c_{ij} gives the lowest displacement cost, and i and j belong to two different regions.

The conclusion about regional spillovers has implications for how an appropriate aggregation must be performed. We shall show that the model in (3.1) cannot be reinterpreted as a regional model where i and j denote regions instead of locations if we require that the aggregate model shall generate the same solution as the micro-level version of the model.

The regional model may be specified as follows. The set of customer locations is partitioned into sets (each representing a region) $H_i \subset I$. Similarly, the facility location points are assembled into exhaustive and mutually exclusive sets $Z_j \subset L$. Then H_i and Z_i refer to the same region. The location–allocation problem then becomes

$$\underset{r}{\text{Min}} \sum_i \sum_j c_{ij} \left(\sum_{h \in H_i} \sum_{z \in Z_j} r(h,z) \right) + \sum_j f_j^* \left(\sum_{z \in Z_j} y(z) \right)$$

subject to

(i) $\sum_j \sum_{z \in Z_j} r(h,z) = 1$

(ii) $0 \le r(h,z) \le y(z)$

(iii) $y(z) \in \{0,1\}$

$$\tag{3.3}$$

where i and j enumerate the set of regions.

Next, let us introduce the aggregate variables F_{ij}, y_j and Y_j. Consider first the following constraint:

$$\sum_i \sum_{h \in H_i} r(h, z) \le y(z) M_j, \text{ for } z \in Z_j \tag{3.4}$$

where M_j is the capacity of any facility in region j. Moreover, let

$$y_j = \sum_{z \in Z_j} y(z) \tag{3.5}$$

and

$$F_{ij} = \sum_{h \in H_i} \sum_{z \in Z_i} r(h, z). \tag{3.6}$$

Then, $\sum_i F_{ij} \le M_j y_j = Y_j$. Now an aggregate model of the following type can be formulated as an aggregate version of the micro-level model in (3.1):

$$\left.\begin{aligned}
&\underset{F}{\text{Min}} \sum_{i,j} c_{ij} F_{ij} + \sum_{i,j} f_j^* F_{ij} \\
&\sum_j F_{ij} = P_i \\
&\sum_i F_{ij} \le M_j N_j = L_j \\
&F_{ij} \ge 0 \\
&0 \le y_j \le |Z_j|;\ 0 \le Y_j \le M_j |Z_j|
\end{aligned}\right\} \tag{3.7}$$

where N_j denotes the number of available locations and $|Z_j|$ the cardinal number of Z_j. The associated Lagrangian can be written as

$$L = \sum_i \sum_j c_{ij} F_{ij} + \sum_i v_i \left(P_i - \sum_j F_{ij} \right) - \sum_j \rho_j \left(L_j - \sum_i F_{ij} \right) - \sum_i \sum_j r_{ij} F_{ij}. \tag{3.8}$$

This formulation implies that $c_{ij} + \rho_j - v_i \le 0$ and we may write

$$\left.\begin{aligned}
&\underset{v,\rho}{\text{Min}} \sum_i v_i P_i - \sum_j \rho_j L_j \\
&v_i \ge c_{ij} + \rho_j
\end{aligned}\right\}. \tag{3.9}$$

Hence, a solution is found for

$$v_i = \underset{j}{\text{Min}} \{ c_{ij} + \rho_j \}. \tag{3.10}$$

Remark 2

The conclusion in (3.10) demonstrates that the aggregate model in (3.7) generates a distorted solution as compared with the micro-level solution described in Remark 1. In (3.10) all interregional spillovers are excluded, given that $c_{ii} < c_{ij}$.

3.3. *Aggregate demand with regional spillovers*

Consider now a situation where we wish to formulate a regionally aggregated version of (3.1) such that interregional spillovers are not precluded. In other words, we want to formulate a substitute for (3.7) such that the new regional model can generate the type of spillovers that obtains with the micro model in (3.1). The most natural way to create such a model is to add a random term to travel costs, with a known probability distribution.

The following outline relates to random utility models as developed by Domencich and McFadden (1975), Williams (1977), and others. Customers are then assumed to act in accordance with a preference structure of the following kind:

$$u_{ij} = v_{ij} + y_j \tag{3.11}$$

where v_{ij} is a deterministic and y_j a random part of the total utility value u_{ij}. With these new concepts we may introduce the following model instead of the one in (3.7):

$$\underset{L}{\text{Max}} \sum_i P_i U_i(L) - \sum_{j \in L} \hat{f}_j \tag{3.12}$$

where $\hat{f}_j$ is the cost of establishing a facility in j and

$$U_i(L) = E\left\{ \underset{j \in L}{\text{Max}} \, u_{ij} \right\} \tag{3.13}$$

where E denotes expected value.

Let $v_i = \{ v_{ij} \}$ be the vector of non-random utility values, and let $\Phi(v_i)$ denote the expected utility for a rational customer in i. Following Leonardi (1983) we can use the properties of the extreme value distribution of the random variables. From this we can derive a logit-like representation of choice probabilities, which yields

$$q_j(v_i) = \frac{\exp\{v_{ij}\}\Psi_j(\exp\{v_i\})}{\Psi(\exp\{v_i\})}$$

$$\Psi_j(x) = \partial\Psi(x)/\partial x_j \qquad (3.14)$$

$$\Phi(v_i) = \log\Psi(\exp\{v_i\})$$

It should be noted that the formulation in (3.14) is equivalent to an entropy maximizing problem of the following type

$$\Phi(v_i) = \underset{q}{\mathrm{Max}}\left\{-\sum_j q_j \log q_j/\omega_j : \sum q_j = 1\right\},$$

$$\omega_j = \exp\{v_{ij}\}\Psi_j(\exp\{v_i\}) \qquad (3.15)$$

A proof is given in Leonardi (1983).

We may finally formulate $\Phi(v_i)$ in (3.14) in terms of facility size, Q_j, and distances, d_{ij}, to obtain the following expected utility expression

$$u_i = \log\sum Q_j\exp\{\lambda d_{ij}\}, \ \lambda < 0. \qquad (3.16)$$

Differentiating (3.16) we may show that the expected flow of customers between i and j becomes

$$F_{ij} = P_i\frac{Q_j\exp\{\lambda d_{ij}\}}{\sum_j Q_j\exp\{\lambda d_{ij}\}}. \qquad (3.17)$$

In this way we have derived the demand expression which was introduced in (2.9).

One should finally observe that in this section we have only considered situations in which no service price is charged, i.e. $\pi_j = 0$ for each facility j. In the next section prices are introduced, and are assumed to affect demand in a similar way as the distances (or distance costs) d_{ij}.

4. PFL-decisions with a single upper level authority

4.1. Institutional interpretation of two-level PFL-decisions

In this section we outline a set of two-level decision problems which are assumed to be relevant for decision structures of the following type:

(a) At the upper level, a national government makes coordinating decisions; the lower level consists of regional authorities which make individual decisions based on objectives which may reflect the preferences of the inhabitants in the region.

(b) A similar structure as above, but now with a regional government at the upper level and a set of individual municipalities at the lower level.

The following variations of the decision structure are elaborated in subsequent subsections:

(i) The upper-level authority determines size and location of the facilities; authorities at the lower level compete for income from customers with price as the only decision variable.

(ii) The upper-level authority decides about the location of facilities, given a predetermined price structure.

(iii) The locations of the facilities are given. The upper-level authority decides about prices and size of each facility. The welfare criterion is maximization of consumer surplus plus operation profits.

(iv) The same decision structure is assumed as above, but with the welfare criterion changed into a target for the service level of the population of customers in each region.

(v) The lower-level authorities decide about their respective prices and pay rents which are determined by the upper-level authority. The latter also selects the sizes of prelocated facilities. The upper-level objective function is a weighted measure of consumer surplus and operation profits.

In many of the selected cases the objective function combines a consumer surplus measure and operation profits. Profits are included to represent the necessity to consider budget constraints, i.e. the relation between income and cost streams. Some of the problem formulations in this analysis have been inspired by Roy et al. (1985).

4.2. Non-cooperative equilibria at the lower level

Let all locations and facility sizes be given and assume that there is a set of lower-level decision makers (manager or authority), each controlling one single facility or one group of facilities within its own regional area. We also assume that contingent on the decisions made by other local decision makers the individual facility manager tries to solve the following problem (with price as the decision variable):

$$
\left.
\begin{aligned}
& \text{Max } V_j = \pi_j F_j(\pi) - g_j\big(F_j(\pi)\big) \\
& \text{subject to} \\
& F_j \leq Q_j
\end{aligned}
\right\}.
\tag{4.1}
$$

In addition we assume that $V_j' = \partial V_j / \partial \pi_j$ is continuous and that

$$
\left.
\begin{aligned}
&\text{(i) } F_j' < 0 \text{ and that } F_j \text{ is continuous in } \pi = \{\pi_i\} \\
&\text{(ii) } F_j'(\hat{\pi}) \le F_j'(\tilde{\pi}) \text{ for } \tilde{\pi}_j < \hat{\pi}_j \text{ and } \tilde{\pi}_\kappa = \hat{\pi}_\kappa \text{ all } k \ne j \\
&\text{(iii) } g_j' = \partial g_j / \partial F_j > 0, \ g_j'\big(F_j(\hat{\pi})\big) - g_j'\big(F_j(\tilde{\pi})\big) < \hat{\pi}_j - \tilde{\pi}_j{}^1 \\
&\text{(iv) } 0 \le \pi_j \le \pi_j^{\text{Max}}; \ F_j(\pi) \text{ is finite for } \pi_j = 0
\end{aligned}
\right\}.
\tag{4.2}
$$

Proposition 2

Consider the profit function in (4.1) and let the conditions in (4.2) be given. Then there exists a non-cooperative equilibrium in prices denoted by $\pi^* = \{\pi_i^*\}$.

Proof

The proposition is true if (i) the decision set is compact, (ii) the function V_j is continuous in π, and (iii) V_j is quasi-concave in π_j.[2] The two first conditions are satisfied by assumption. Suppose initially that $F_j(\pi) \le Q_j$ for $\pi_j \ge 0$. Then we observe that

$$
V_j' = \partial V_j / \partial \pi_j = \pi_j F_j' + F_j - g_j'(F_j) F_j' \text{ is positive at } \pi_j = 0.
$$

If V_j' remains positive for all values $\pi_j > 0$, V_j is quasi-concave. Suppose therefore instead that π_j reaches a point $\bar{\pi}_j$ such that $V_j'(\bar{\pi}) = 0$ so that V_j is increasing between $\pi_j = 0$ and $\pi_j = \bar{\pi}_j$. Quasi-concavity is satisfied if V_j will decrease monotonically when π_j is increased beyond $\bar{\pi}$. This obtains if for $\hat{\pi}_j > \bar{\pi}_j$

$$
\frac{\hat{\pi}_j - g_j'\big(F_j(\hat{\pi})\big)}{\bar{\pi}_j - g_j'\big(F_j(\bar{\pi})\big)} > \frac{F_j'(\bar{\pi})}{F_j'(\hat{\pi})}
\tag{4.3}
$$

which implies that $V_j'(\hat{\pi}) < V_j'(\bar{\pi}) = 0$. Condition (4.3) is obviously satisfied since (iii) in (4.2) implies that $\hat{\pi}_j - g_j'(F_j(\hat{\pi})) > \tilde{\pi}_j - g_j'(F_j(\bar{\pi}))$ and $F_j'(\bar{\pi})/F_j'(\hat{\pi}) < 1$ from assumption (ii) in 4.2.

Our next step is to add the case $F_j(\pi) \ge Q_j$ for $0 \le \pi_j \le \tilde{\pi}$. In this range $V_j' = Q_j$ which means that initially V_j is a straight line which will cross the unconstrained V_j-function which applies when $F_j < Q_j$. This occurs at $\tilde{\pi}$ where $\tilde{\pi}_j Q_j - g_j(Q_j) = V_j(\tilde{\pi})$. After this point the function V_j has the features demonstrated above (see Figure 4.1). Hence, if $\tilde{\pi}_j < \pi_j^{\text{Max}} V_j$ is quasi-concave. If $\tilde{\pi}_j > \pi_j^{\text{Max}}$,

---

[1] In particular, this condition is satisfied when g_j' is constant.
[2] See, e.g. Berge (1957).

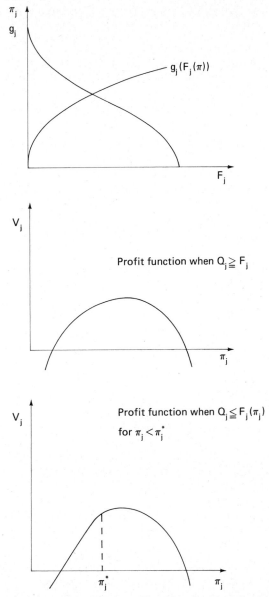

Figure 4.1. Illustration of the profit function as described in Proposition 2.

then V_j is a linear function which is also quasi-concave. This completes the proof.

Corollary 1

If V_j is concave, equilibrium prices are larger than marginal costs, since then $\pi_j^* = g_j' - F_j/F_j'$ and $F_j' < 0$.

This solution will in the sequel be contrasted by policies at the upper level such that the consumer surplus or the service level is maximized. We have started with this case, since Proposition 2 will be used in further examples. We may also observe that if the upper-level authority tries to enforce a price-setting rule $\pi_j < \pi_j^*$, this corresponds to a disequilibrium with strong incentives for individual managers (or local authorities) to deviate.

4.3. Selection of locations

The PFL-problem in this subsection corresponds to the analysis in Section 3. We shall here briefly indicate the combinatorial nature of this problem.

Let $W = W(Q, \pi, l)$ be the objective function of the upper level authority, where l denotes a selected set of locations belonging to predetermined set L of potential locations. The associated decision problem is (with Q, π, L as decision variables):

$$\left.\begin{array}{l} \text{Max } W(Q, \pi, L) \\ \text{subject to} \\ \sum f_j \Delta Q_j \le b \end{array}\right\} \tag{4.4}$$

where $\Delta Q_j = Q_j - Q_j^\circ$ and b is the budget constraint. The approach to solve this problem is to divide it into the following two steps:

(1) Select a specific subset $l \in L$, define $W_l(Q, \pi) = W(Q, \pi, l)$, and solve

$$\text{Max } W_l(Q, \pi) = W^*(l)$$
$$Q, \pi$$

(2) In the second step the following problem is solved

$$\text{Max } W^*(l)$$
$$l \subset L$$

If the price structure is not predetermined the outlined combinatorial problem may be complicated to solve.

4.4. Optimization of a welfare function based on the consumer surplus

Let S_i denote the consumer surplus in region (or subregion) i, and let V_j denote the difference between income and cost of facilities in location j. The following welfare function, $W(S, V)$, will then reflect a weighted sum of consumer and producer surplus:

$$W(S, V) = \sum_i (S_i + \alpha_i V_i) \tag{4.5}$$

where $\alpha_i \geq 0$.

Let c^i be the vector $(c_{i1}, \ldots, c_{in})$, and let $\pi^i = \pi + c^i$. Assume that $S_i = S(\pi^i)$. In order to qualify as a measure of the consumer surplus, the function S_i must satisfy four conditions:

$$\left. \begin{array}{l} \text{(i)} \ \partial S_i / \partial \pi_j^i = -F_{ij} \leq 0 \\[2mm] \text{(ii)} \ \left\{ \partial^2 S_i / \partial \pi_j^i \partial \pi_k^i \right\} \text{ is positive definite} \\[2mm] \text{(iii)} \ \partial^2 S_i / \partial \pi_j^{i\,2} = -F_{ij}' \geq 0 \\[2mm] \text{(iv)} \ \sum_j \partial S_i / \partial \pi_j^i \geq -P_i \end{array} \right\}. \tag{4.6}$$

Condition (i) implies that S_i is the integral of the demand function, (iii) implies that demand is a decreasing function, (iv) follows from $\sum_j F_{ij} \leq P_i$, and (ii) is an integrability condition. In order to be able to specify the price elasticity of demand in a transparent way, we introduce the following structure:

$$\left. \begin{array}{l} \sum_j F_{ij} = q_i(\pi^i) P_i \\[2mm] q_i(\pi^i) = -(1/P_i) \sum_j \partial S_i / \partial \pi_j^i = \sum_j F_{ij} / P_i \\[2mm] \omega_{ij}(\pi) = \left(\partial S_i / \partial \pi_j^i \right) / \left(\sum_i \partial S_i / \partial \pi_j^i \right) = F_{ij} / q_i P_i \end{array} \right\}. \tag{4.7}$$

In example I below a case with inelastic demand is presented[3]

Example I (inelastic demand):
$$S_i = (P_i / \beta) \log \sum_j f_{ij} \exp\{-\beta \pi_j\}$$
$$F_{ij} = P_i \omega_{ij}$$
$$q_i = -(1/P_i) \sum \partial S_i / \partial \pi_j = 1$$
$$\omega_{ij} = f_{ij} \exp\{-\beta \pi_j\} / \sum_j f_{ij} \exp\{-\beta \pi_j\}$$

[3] With this formulation the travel cost effects are incorporated in f_{ij}-terms.

As the reader may check, the example above satisfies the conditions in (4.6). The same conditions are also fulfilled by the second example below:

Example II (elastic demand):

$$S_i = (P_i/\beta)\log\left(\Sigma f_{ij}\, exp\{-\beta\pi_j\} + a_i\right)$$
$$F_{ij} = P_i f_{ij}\, exp\{-\beta\pi_j\}/\left(\Sigma f_{ij}\, exp\{-\beta\pi_j\} + a_i\right)$$
$$q_i(\pi) = A_i(\pi)/(A_i(\pi) + a_i)$$
$$A_i(\pi) = \Sigma f_{ij}\, exp\{-\beta\pi j\}$$
$$a_i > 0$$

We may observe that $A_i(\pi)$ is an accessibility measure where distance effects are included in the f_{ij} components.

We may use (4.5) to formulate the following optimization problem:

$$\left.\begin{array}{l} \text{Max}_{\pi}\, S(\pi) + \alpha V \\ \text{subject to} \\ \displaystyle\sum_i F_{ij} = Q_j \end{array}\right\} \qquad (4.5')$$

where $S(\pi) = \Sigma_i S_i(\pi^i)$ and $\alpha V = \Sigma \alpha_i V_i$ for $\alpha = \alpha_i$ over all i. In order to solve this the conjugate function $S^*(F)$ is introduced, and we can then consider the following "dual" problem: [4]

$$\left.\begin{array}{l} \text{Max}\, S^*(F) - \alpha \displaystyle\sum_j f_j(Q_j) \\ \text{subject to} \\ \displaystyle\sum_i F_{ij} = Q_j \end{array}\right\}. \qquad (4.5'')$$

The objective in (4.5'') may be written as $\Sigma_i S_i^*(F^i) - \alpha \Sigma_j f_j(Q_j)$, where $F^i = (F_{i1}, F_{i2}...)$, and we can formulate the Lagrangian

$$D = \sum_i S_i^*(F^i) - \alpha \sum_j f_j(Q_j) + \sum_j \mu_j\left(Q_j - \sum_i F_{ij}\right). \qquad (4.8)$$

By setting $\partial D/\partial Q_j = 0$ we obtain the optimum condition

$$\mu_j = \alpha f_j'. \qquad (4.9)$$

Observe now that for $Q_j = \Sigma_i F_{ij}$ the functional D is equivalent to

$$L^* = \sum_i \left(S_i^*(F^i) - \alpha \sum_j \pi_j F_{ij}\right) + \alpha \sum_j \left(\pi_j Q_j - f_j(Q_j)\right). \qquad (4.8')$$

---

[4] Lagrange duality related to conjugate functionals is described in Luenberger (1969, pp. 195–200 and 223–225).

From $\partial L^*/\partial Q_j = 0$ we obtain

$$\pi_j = f_j' \tag{4.9'}$$

which implies that $\mu_j = \alpha \pi_j$.

Now, returning to our original problem in (4.5) and (4.5') the associated Lagrangian is

$$L = \sum_i S_i(\pi) + \alpha \sum_i \sum_j \pi_j F_{ij} - \alpha \sum_j f_j(Q_j) + \sum_j \mu_j \left(Q_j - \sum_i F_{ij} \right). \tag{4.10}$$

It is now possible to conclude that L in (4.10) is equivalent to D in (4.8) if (i) $\alpha = 1$ and (ii) if we set

$$S_i(\pi) = \text{Max} \left\{ S_i^*(F^i) - \alpha \sum_j \pi_j F_{ij} \right\}$$

subject to

$$Q_j = \sum_i F_{ij}. \tag{4.11}$$

To show this we first insert (4.11) into (4.8). Doing this we obtain (4.10). Second, using the relation $\partial S_i/\partial \pi_j = - F_{ij}$ in (4.6) and substituting $S_i(\pi)$ for $S_i^*(F^i) + \alpha \sum \sum \pi_j F_{ij}$ in (4.8') we obtain for $\partial L^*/\partial \pi_j = 0$ the following result: $\sum_i F_{ij} = \alpha Q_j$.

This establishes the above conclusion and we can formulate the following proposition:

Proposition 3

The solution to (4.5') corresponds to a marginal cost price-setting rule if $\alpha = 1$.

Proof

The conclusion follows from (4.9') together with the result from (4.11) that $L = D$.

In view of Proposition 3 we now examine the case in which $\alpha \neq 1$. As before we assume that

$$\left. \begin{array}{l} f_j' = \partial f_j/\partial Q_j > 0 \\ \partial F_j/\partial \pi_j < 0 \\ \partial F_\kappa/\partial \pi_j \geq 0 \, \text{for} \, \kappa \neq j \end{array} \right\}. \tag{4.12}$$

In order to reflect (4.5'), we reformulate (4.10) as follows:

$$L = \sum_i S_i(\pi) + \alpha \sum_j \pi_j F_j - \alpha \sum_j f_j(F_j). \tag{4.10'}$$

Given the conditions in (4.6) and (4.12) we may conclude that when $\alpha \neq 1$, the solution to (4.10') implies that prices do not equal marginal costs.

This statement can be checked by differentiating (4.10') which yields for $x_\kappa = (\pi_\kappa - f_\kappa')$

$$- F_j(1 - \alpha) + \alpha \sum_\kappa x_\kappa \partial F_\kappa / \partial \pi_j = 0. \tag{4.13}$$

Observe that $- F_j(1 - \alpha)$ is positive when $\alpha > 1$ and negative when $\alpha < 1$. Hence,

$$\left. \begin{aligned} \alpha > 1 &\rightarrow \sum x_\kappa \partial F_\kappa / \partial \pi_j < 0 \\ \alpha < 1 &\rightarrow \sum x_\kappa \partial F_\kappa / \partial \pi_j > 0 \end{aligned} \right\}. \tag{4.14}$$

These inequalities imply that we cannot have $x_\kappa = 0$ for all κ.

4.5. The service level as welfare objective

It is possible to formulate a variant of (4.10') in which the objective is to achieve a predetermined service level $G_i = \sum_j F_{ij}$ in each subregion (municipality). However, formulating a Lagrangian of the form $L = \sum_j \pi_j F_j(\pi) - \sum_j f_j(Q_j) + \sum_i \lambda_i (G_i - \bar{G}_i)$ gives rise to similar problems in determining the solution as the ones we found with respect to (4.10').

If the authority decides to set $\pi_j = \pi_0$ for all j we obtain

$$L = \sum_j \pi_0 F_j(\pi_0) - \sum_j f_j(F_j) + \sum_i \lambda_i (G_i - \bar{G}_i). \tag{4.15}$$

An optimal solution is obtained for

$$\frac{\partial L}{\partial \pi_0} = \sum_j F_j + \pi_0 \sum_j \partial F_j / \partial \pi_0 - \sum_j f_j' \partial F_j / \partial \pi_0 + \sum_i \lambda_i \partial G_i / \partial \pi_0. \tag{4.16}$$

In this case $\partial F_{ij} / \partial \pi_0 < 0$ for all pairs (i, j), and we can assume that $\pi_0 > f_j'$ if all targets $\bar{G}_i$ are selected low enough to assure that $\lambda_i = 0$.

The described case may be compared with a PFL-problem for which the facilities produce an insurance service. Assuming that the service is proportional to the capacity, Q_j, and exponentially declining with the distance, d_{ij}, we may write

$$G_i = P_i \sum_j Q_j \exp\{-\lambda d_{ij}\} \qquad (4.17)$$

where $\lambda > 0$. Introducing welfare weights $a_i > 0$ we may formulate the following Lagrangian associated with (4.17)

$$L = \sum a_i G_i + \mu\left(b - \sum_j f_j(Q_j)\right) \qquad (4.18)$$

where b denotes the available budget. By differentiating (4.18) with respect to Q_j, we obtain the well known optimum condition for a public good [Samuelson (1954)]:

$$\sum_i a_i P_i \omega_{ij} = \mu f_j' \qquad (4.19)$$

where $\omega_{ij} = \exp\{-\lambda d_{ij}\}$.

Suppose that we allow the authority in a subregion to decide about the size of every facility with a given budget b_i and cost share parameters λ_{ij}. Then we obtain the following Lagrange function

$$L = a_i G_i + \mu_i\left(b_i - \sum_j \lambda_{ij} f_j(Q_j)\right). \qquad (4.20)$$

The optimum condition is

$$a_i P_i \omega_{ij} = \mu_i \lambda_{ij} f_j'. \qquad (4.21)$$

From (4.21) we may conclude that with a given cost share structure of λ_{ij}'s the size of the facilities should be selected in accordance with the distance measures $\omega_{ij} > 0$ such that

$$\frac{\omega_{rj}}{\omega_{r\kappa}} = \frac{\lambda_{rj} f_j'}{\lambda_{r\kappa} f_\kappa'}. \qquad (4.22)$$

Formula (4.22) implies a proportionality between ω_{rj}'s and λ_{rj}'s of the following kind

$$\left(\frac{\omega_{rj}}{\lambda_{rj}}\right)\bigg/\left(\frac{\omega_{r\kappa}}{\lambda_{r\kappa}}\right) = \left(\frac{\omega_{ij}}{\lambda_{ij}}\right)\bigg/\left(\frac{\omega_{i\kappa}}{\lambda_{i\kappa}}\right). \qquad (4.23)$$

In order to make the individual solutions in (4.21) consistent with the collective solution in (4.19) the following equalities must hold

$$\sum_i \mu_i \lambda_{ij} = \mu \text{ for all } j \tag{4.24}$$

which implies $\sum_i \mu_i(\lambda_{ij} - \lambda_{i\kappa}) = 0$, for all κ. This linear dependence between the λ_{ij}-terms is obvious from (4.24).

Let $\lambda_i \sum_j f_j(Q_j) = \sum_j \lambda_{ij} f_j(Q_j)$. Then $\lambda_i b$ represents region (or authority) i's contribution to the total cost $b = \sum f_j(Q_j)$. If we instead assume that the investments in Q_j are financed by authority j, the array $\{\lambda_{ij}\}$ corresponds to a reimbursement scheme between the set of authorities (or regions), such that $\lambda_{ij} f_j(Q_j)$ is paid from region i to region j.

4.6. Determination of rent structure by the upper-level authority

In this subsection we extend the problem described in Subsection 4.2. As described in Figure 4.2 we consider an institutional setting in which the lower-level authorities decide about their respective prices. In addition they have to pay rents to the upper-level authority. The latter determines the rent structure and selects the size of each prelocated facility. The upper-level objective function is assumed to have the following form:

$$W(F, Q) = \alpha S + \sum_j \rho_j Q_j - \sum f_j(Q_j) \tag{4.25}$$

Upper level decides about
(i)   facility size
(ii) rent level

Max $W(F, Q) =$

$\alpha S + \sum_j (\rho_j Q_j - f_j(Q_j))$

$\{F_{ij}\}$ $\{\rho_j\}$ $\{Q_j\}$

Lower-level decision makers select
(under competition)
prices in each
region j

Max $V_j =$

$\pi_j F_j(\pi) - g_j(F_j(\pi)) - \rho_j Q_j$
subject to
$V_j \geq a_j F_j$
$F_j = \sum_i F_{ij} \leq Q_j$

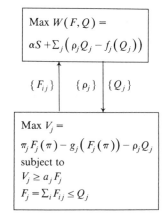

Figure 4.2. A two-level PFL-problem with selection of prices, rent levels and size of each facility.

where S denotes consumer surplus, $\alpha \geq 0$ and ρ_j is the rent per unit capacity charged to region j (and hence authority j). The function f_j is the investment cost function referring to the facility capacity in location j. The objective function related to facility j (or region j) is assumed to be the same as in (4.1), i.e.

$$V_j = \pi_j F_j(\pi) - g_j\big(F_j(\pi)\big) - \rho_j Q_j. \tag{4.26}$$

Given the assumptions in (4.2) a non-cooperative equilibrium will exist on the lower level for each given rent structure. We may just observe that the profit function in (4.26) equals the V_j-function in (4.1) minus the term $\rho_j Q_j$ which appears as a constant on the lower level.

Let us now assume that each authority on the lower level requires that

$$V_j \geq a_j F_j; \; a_j \geq 0. \tag{4.27}$$

From this we draw the following conclusion. Assume that the decision makers are maximizing their respective objective functions in (4.25) and (4.26). Moreover, let V_j be quasi-concave with a unique optimum, and assume that (4.27) applies. Then the upper level authority will select the following rent level for each region (subregion) j such that $Qj > 0$:

$$\rho_j = \big(\pi_j F_j - g_j(F_j)\big)/F_j - a_j. \tag{4.28}$$

4

Proof

The constraint in (4.27) implies that $\rho_j \leq (\pi_j F_j - g_j(F_j) - a_j)/Q_j$. Then we only need to show that $Q_j = F_j$. With the objective function in (4.25) a situation with $Q_j > F_j$ implies that S will not decrease if Q_j is lowered so that $Q_j = F_j$. At the same time we observe when Q_j is reduced ρ_j may be increased to $\rho_j^* > \rho_j$ so that the rent income is constant, i.e. $\rho_j Q_j = \rho_j^* F_j$. Finally, when Q_j is reduced $\Sigma f_j(Q_j)$ will also be reduced. Hence, by lowering Q_j so that $Q_j = F_j$ the value of W is increased. Finally, the behaviour of the lower-level decision makers ensures that $F_j \leq Q_j$.

Suppose now that operation costs is a linear function such that $g_j(F_j) = \bar{g}_j F_j$. Then we have from (4.28) that

$$\rho_j = - F_j/F_j' - a_j. \tag{4.29}$$

This follows from (i) Corollary 1 which states that $\pi_j = g_j' - F_j/F_j' = \bar{g}_j - F_j/F_j'$, together with (ii) $\rho_j = \pi_j - \bar{g}_j - a_j$ in (4.28).

It is clear that the result in (4.29) differs qualitatively from the result obtained if the upper-level authority applies a Pareto-like objective function of the following form

$$\hat{W} = W + \sum V_j \tag{4.30}$$

where W is defined in (4.25). With the function $\hat{W}$ Proposition 3 can be used to derive that $\pi_j = f_j' + g_j'$. If $g_j' = \bar{g}_j$ this implies that $\rho_j = f_j' - a_j$. With $a_j = 0$ this means that the rent level shall equal the marginal costs of investment.

5. Multi-authority, game-like decision structures

5.1. Institutional interpretation of multi-authority decision problems

In Section 5 we outline a set of one-level PFL decision problems. Hence, a distinguishing characteristic is that there is no upper-level authority who coordinates the set of decision makers. The latter may consist of all municipalities in a region or in a nation; the decision makers may also be a set of regional governments, responsible for a larger area than a municipality. The presentation aims at illuminating the competition between the set of uncoordinated regional decision makers. The following stylized cases are covered:

(i) A multi-authority game with a decision dilemma referring to a situation in which a facility may serve many regions, while at the same time no individual authority is willing to establish the facility in its own region. In one version, this decision problem has the form of a "Prisoners' dilemma".

(ii) Locations of facilities which to a large extent provide services to "foreign" visitors and which are operated mainly for the profits generated by visitors. Such facilities include museums, wild-life centres, sports facilities and other tourist attractions. As an ultimate case, a city like Venice may be thought of as a facility of this type.

(iii) PFL-decisions for which each authority uses some kind of a consumer surplus criterion to assess its decisions.

(iv) Location of facilities which affect the long-run development of the economy in the region. Such facilities may be represented by universities and research centres, and by facilities that improve the accessibility of the region in a larger spatial context.

5.2. A symmetrical decision dilemma

In this subsection we provide a sketch of a multi-authority problem of the following nature: in the interest of the population in several regions a facility must be erected, but no individual region wants it to be within its own boundaries. We may think of a facility that receives toxic materials and processes them in various ways. At the same time the operation brings about negative local effects, and these effects are clearly perceived and perhaps exaggerated by the local population. A specific example is the disposition of nuclear waste materials.

In order to bring out the essentials of the problem we consider only two regions. By W_i we denote the preference or assessment indicator used by the authority in region i. We limit the decision alternatives of each authority to only two options:

A_i = decision to locate a plant in region i

B_i = decision not to locate a plant in region i

Authority i's preference function is denoted by $W_i(X, Y)$, where $X \in \{A_1, B_1\}$ and $Y \in \{A_2, B_2\}$. We assume that the preferences are symmetric as described in Table 5.1, in which each cell consists of the pair (W_1, W_2).

The outcome pattern described in Table 5.1 means that if both authorities decide to locate a facility in its own region, the outcome is $(W_1, W_2) = (-5, -5)$; if both refrain from establishing a facility, each authority faces an even less desirable outcome, i.e. $W_i = -10$ for each of them. Finally, if authority i decides to invest in a facility, while the other authority $j \neq i$ decides to act as a free rider, the result is that $W_i = -8$ and $W_j = 0$. This asymmetrical solution has the form of a non-cooperative equilibrium, since such an equilibrium (X^*, Y^*) requires the following condition to be satisfied:

$$
\left.
\begin{aligned}
W_1(X^*, Y^*) &\geq W_1(X, Y^*) \\
&\quad X \in \{A_1, B_1\} \\
W_2(X^*, Y^*) &> W_2(X^*, Y) \\
&\quad Y \in \{A_2, B_2\}
\end{aligned}
\right\} . \tag{5.1}
$$

Obviously, both (A_1, B_2) and (B_1, A_2) satisfy the condition in (5.1).

Table 5.1
Preference outcomes of pairwise decisions.

	A_2	B_2
A_1	$(-5, -5)$	$(-8, 0)$
B_1	$(0, -8)$	$(-10, -10)$

Table 5.2
A Prisoners' dilemma structure.

	A_2	B_2
A_1	$(-5, -5)$	$(-8, 0)$
B_1	$(0, -8)$	$(-7, -7)$

We should observe, that the decision to locate a facility which is appreciated as a public harm by the inhabitants in the region with the facility, brings about a political loss. It may not be possible for the second region to compensate for this loss by means of side payments. If this is not possible, Table 5.1 illustrates a conflict between (i) the desirability of introducing an upper-level authority who manages to avoid the solution (B_1, B_2) and (ii) the desirability to allow each region to make its own, independent decisions.

If we change the preference assignments so as to correspond to Table 5.2, we obtain a problem called "Prisoners' dilemma" [see, e.g. Luce and Raiffa (1957)]. In this case (B_1, B_2) constitutes a unique non-cooperative equilibrium which is clearly less desirable than the non-viable solution (A_1, A_2).

5.3. Facilities which are operated to generate regional income flows

Suppose that region j contemplates the opening of a facility that will bring new visitors to the region. Besides the direct payment for visiting the facility, $\pi_j F_j(\pi)$, the visitors will have some additional expenditures in the region. Let the net income from these expenditures be $a_j F_j(\pi)$, where $a_j > 0$ is considered to be a constant. Let $\hat{g}_j$ be composite cost of establishing and running the facility. The following objective function, W_j, may then represent the preferences of the authority in region j:

$$W_j = \hat{V}_j + a_j F_j(\pi)   \tag{5.2}$$

where $\hat{V}_j = \pi_j F_j(\pi) - \hat{g}_j(Q_j)$ and $Q_j = (F_j(\pi))$. If a set of regional authorities has objective functions of the type described in (5.2), this constitutes a competition situation. For such a situation, the existence of a non-cooperative equilibrium can be ensured if the following conditions are satisfied [Berge (1957)]:

(i) W_j is continuous in $\pi = \{\pi_i\}$

(ii) $\pi_j^{Max} \geq \pi_j \geq \pi_j^{Min} \geq 0$ (5.3)

(iii) W_j is quasi-concave in π_j

Proposition 4

Let assumptions (i) and (ii) in (5.3) hold for each j in a given set of regions. Assume also that $\hat{V}_j$ in 5.2 has the same properties as V_j in Proposition 2. Then if $a_j = 0$, there exists a non-cooperative equilibrium π^*.

The same proof as that of Proposition 2 can be used also for Proposition 4. An essential property of $\hat{V}_j$ (as of V_j) is that $V_j' > 0$ at $\pi_j = 0$. The importance of this property is illustrated in Corollary 2 and Proposition 5.

Corollary 2

Let the assumptions in Proposition 4 be unchanged except that now we also assume that $a_j > 0$ and that W_j has the same properties as $\hat{V}_j$, including $F_j' < 0$ and $\hat{g}_j' > 0$.
  (i) In this case a non-cooperative equilibrium π^* exists;
  (ii) W_j has similar properties as $\hat{V}_j$ only if $a_j < \hat{g}_j' - F_j/F_j'$ at $\pi_j = 0$.

Proof

The first part of the corollary is self-evident from Proposition 4. The second part focuses on the property that $\hat{V}_j' = F_j - \hat{g}_j'(F_j(\pi))F_j' > 0$ at $\pi_j = 0$. Since $W_j' = \pi_j F_j' + F_j - \hat{g}_j'(F_j(\pi))F_j' + a_j F_j'$, $W_j' > 0$ at $\pi_j = 0$ only if $F_j - \hat{g}_j'(F_j(\pi))F_j' + a_j F_j' > 0$. Since $F_j' < 0$, this can only be satisfied if $a_j < \hat{g}_j' - F_j/F_j'$. This completes the proof.

The importance of Corollary 2 is that it demonstrates that the side effects, $a_j F_j(\pi)$, cannot be allowed to be too strong. If these effects become very strong, W_j will not share the same properties as $\hat{V}_j$. Very strong side effects, represented by a large a_j, will imply that authorities will settle at a zero-price policy. This is described in Proposition 5.

Proposition 5

Let there be a given set, N, of authorities who compete for visitors. Assume for all $j \in N$ that $F_j' < 0$, $\hat{g}_j' > 0$, and $a_j > \hat{g}_j' - \pi_j - F_j/F_j'$ for $\pi_j \geq 0$. Let also the assumptions (i)–(iii) in (5.3) hold. Then there exists a non-cooperative equilibrium $\pi^* = \{0\}$ if $W_j(\pi^*) = a_j F_j(\pi^*) - \hat{g}_j \ (F_j(\pi^*)) \geq 0$.

Proof

Given that $F_j' < 0$ and $\hat{g}_j' > 0$, $a_j > \hat{g}_j' - \pi_j - F_j/F_j'$ for $\pi_j \geq 0$ implies that

$$\partial W_j/\partial \pi_j = \pi_j F_j' + F_j - \hat{f}_j' F_j' + a_j F_j < 0 \qquad (5.4)$$

for all $\pi_j \geq 0$. This means that for each value of all other prices, W_j will decrease when π_j is increased from its lowest value $\pi_j^* = 0$. Hence, if there is an equilibrium, it must be $\pi^* = \{0\}$. Moreover, we know that there exists an equilibrium, since W_j is assumed quasi-concave and the decision space is compact and convex. Finally, if $W_j(\pi^*)$ is positive for each $j \in N$, the equilibrium is a meaningful solution.

The result in Proposition 5 is somewhat incomplete, since we have not allowed Q_j to be set equal to zero when $W_j < 0$. If we allow this, a new demand function $F_j(\pi, Q)$ has to be introduced, where Q is a vector $Q = \{Q_j\}$. The function F_j will then shift for each Q_i that is set equal to zero. Hence, we may enlarge the decision set of each authority to π_j and Q_j in the following way:

$$
\left.
\begin{aligned}
\pi_j^{\mathrm{Max}} &\geq \pi_j \geq 0, \text{ and } \pi_j = 0 \text{ if } Q_j = 0 \\
Q_j &= \begin{cases} 0 & \text{if } W_j < 0 \\ F_j(\pi, Q) & \text{otherwise} \end{cases}
\end{aligned}
\right\}.
\tag{5.5}
$$

With this construction the following corollary is self-evident:

Corollary 3

Let all assumptions in Proposition 5 remain unchanged except that $F_j(\pi)$ is substituted for $F_j(\pi, Q)$, that Q_j is selected according to (5.5), and that all assumptions are valid for each Q-vector such that at least one $Q_j > 0$. Then $\pi^* = \{0\}$ is an equilibrium if $W_j(\pi^*) > 0$ for at least one $j \in N$.

We will end this section by illustrating why an equilibrium of the type described in Proposition 4 (and Proposition 2) normally fails to be Pareto-optimal. First we assume that for $\kappa \neq j$

$$
\partial F_j / \partial \pi_\kappa > 0.
\tag{5.6}
$$

Proposition 6

Let π^* denote a non-cooperative equilibrium of the model in Proposition 4. Assume that (5.6) is true and that $\hat{V}_j$ in (5.2) is strictly concave. Then π^* is not Pareto-optimal.

Outline of a proof

With strict concavity in the neighbourhood of π^* we have that $\hat{V}_j' = \pi_j^* F_j' + F_j - \hat{g}_j' F_j' = 0$. From this we can conclude that $\pi_j^* > \hat{g}_j'$. Together with (5.6) this implies that

$$\partial \hat{V}_j / \partial \pi_\kappa^* = \pi_j^* \partial F_j / \partial \pi_\kappa^* - \hat{g}_j' \partial F_j / \pi_\kappa^* > 0. \tag{5.7}$$

This shows that it is possible to improve the value for each j by increasing all prices marginally to $\pi^* + \Delta$, $\Delta > \{0\}$.

The statement in Proposition 6 is directly applicable to the equilibrium in Proposition 2. The result cannot be applied to the equilibrium in Proposition 5.

5.4. *Regional distribution of consumer surplus*

In this section we describe the interregional competition that arises when regional spillovers can occur and each regional authority wants to increase the consumer surplus or welfare of its inhabitants. As a start we may return to the formulation in (4.5) and assume that each authority has an objective function of the following kind:

$$W_i = S_i + V_i \tag{5.8}$$

where S_i is a measure of the consumer surplus and where V_i denotes the difference between income and costs. From (4.6) we have that S_i is decreasing and convex with respect to π_i. If we at the same time assume that V_i is concave, we cannot ensure that (5.6) represents a quasi-concave function. Hence, we cannot establish the existence of a viable solution in the form of a non-cooperative equilibrium.

An alternative to the PFL-problem associated with (5.8) is to consider settings in which (i) the flows of the facility users are not affected by prices charged by each facility, and (ii) the regional authorities reimburse each other in accordance with the size of the different flows. We may for example think of the population, P_i, of potential university students in each region. If the individual preferences have the form $u_i = \log \sum_j Q_j f_{ij}$, the regional welfare indicator becomes $U_i = u_i P_i$; f_{ij} represents distance and attraction effects. From the form assigned to u_i we may derive the flows $F_{ij} = P_i Q_j f_{ij} / \sum_\kappa Q_\kappa f_{i\kappa}$, as in (2.9), and formulate the following regional objective function:

$$W_i = U_i - \mu_i \hat{g}_i(Q_i) + \mu_i(Y_i - X_i) \tag{5.9}$$

where μ_i associates preference values with cost values and where Y_i and X_i represent region i's income and cost flows when the reimbursement parameters

π_j are taken as predetermined:

$$Y_i = \sum_{j \neq i} F_{ji}\pi_i$$

$$X_i = \sum_{j \neq i} F_{ij}\pi_j. \tag{5.10}$$

Differentiating (5.9) with respect to Q_i we can conclude that there are no natural conditions which ensure that $\partial W_i/\partial Q_i$ is either positive or negative. Moreover, the same kind of "uncertainty" is found with regard to the second-order derivative. This negative conclusion prevails also if we set $\pi_i = \pi_j$ for all j.

5.5.   Dynamic aspects of spatial public goods

Research of PFL-problems and spatial public goods displays a strong bias towards studies of facilities and services associated with consumer satisfaction and household welfare. Much less attention has been paid to the benefits that the production system (industries) in a region may acquire from the public facility infrastructure in the region. In this section we provide an example of such an alternative focus by referring to recent studies by Andersson (1981) and Andersson and Mantsinen (1980).

   The problem analyzed by Andersson refers to facilities like universities, research centres and similar units for knowledge creation. The knowledge created in region i, G_i, is treated as a spatial public good that affects other regions, j, via a distance decay factor f_{ij}. The knowledge accessible in region j then becomes:

$$D_j = \sum_i f_{ij} G_i. \tag{5.11}$$

The accumulation of knowledge, called R & D, is represented by a differential equation

$$\dot{G}_i = H_i(g_i \tau_i Q_i) \tag{5.12}$$

where for region i, g_i denotes the productivity of the R & D sector, τ_i a taxation ratio where the tax income is used for R & D investments, and where Q_i represents the regional production. Neglecting an explicit formulation of the labour allocation, a regional growth process is formulated by combining (5.11) and (5.12) with accumulation of other capital than R & D capital, i.e.

$$\dot{K}_i = s_i(1 - \tau_i)Q_i(K_i, D_i) \tag{5.13}$$

where K denotes material, production capital, s_i an investment ratio, and where $Q_i(\ )$ represents a regional production function with K_i and D_i as inputs.

By assuming g_i, τ_i and s_i to be constant over all regions, one may demonstrate that for various versions of the growth model indicated by (5.11)–(5.13), there exists a long-run growth equilibrium. However, towards the equilibrium, disparities between regions tend to increase over long time periods as a result of time lags caused by the differences in accessibility between regions. With regional decisions about the level of τ_i and s_i such temporal conflicts will be aggravated.

The public nature of the G_i-input is reflected in the following simulation results [Andersson and Mantsinen (1980)]:

(i) A decrease of any distance (increased accessibility), speeds up the balanced rate of growth in all regions.

(ii) A reduction of the communication distances causes changes in the regional shares of total production.

6. Local public expenditures and interregional migration

In the preceding four sections we have examined PFL-problems associated with the provision of both private, semi-public and public goods. In this section we will present results that shed some light on the difference between these various cases. We also discuss local taxation and long-term relocations of individuals between local communities. In particular, this section reports on various re-examinations of the Tiebout-model (1956, 1961) which in recent years has been studied with respect to theoretical consistency and completeness [see, e.g. Bewley (1981)].

6.1. The Stahl–Varaiya test of the dynamic process

Samuelson's contribution (1954) to the theory of public goods implied that an efficient allocation would not correspond to a viable competitive equilibrium. In 1956 Tiebout suggested that in an inter-community setting each individual is able to vote with his feet in the long run and thereby guide the allocation of public investments in facilities, infrastructure and public spending in general. In other words, in migrating to the community offering the most preferred commodity bundle, consumers will properly reveal their preferences for these commodities. In a perceptive analysis, Stahl and Varaiya (1983) correctly claim that such an hypothesis must be conceived as a dynamic process and hence assessed in a dynamic setting. This means that a Tiebout solution must satisfy two simultaneous conditions: it must be (i) an efficient allocation (Pareto-optimal), and (ii) a stationary state (dynamic equilibrium).

In the Stahl–Varaiya test a model of the following form is used:

$$\left.\begin{array}{l} u^i(x^i, q) = x^i + b^i q, \ b^i > 0 \\ C(q_j) = q_j^\alpha, \ \alpha > 1 \end{array}\right\} \tag{6.1}$$

where u^i denotes the utility index of a consumer of type i, x^i his consumption of a reference good, q his consumption of a publicly provided good; $C(q_j)$ denotes the cost of producing q_j units of the publicly provided good in community j. If this latter commodity is a private good, q_j represents the per capita quantity in community j, the same interpretation is self-evident when q_j is a public good.

Let y^i denote the share of consumers type i living in community 1. When q is a pure public good, the representative authority (government) in this community solves the following problem:

$$\left.\begin{array}{l} \text{Max} \ \sum_i y^i \big(w^i(1 - t_1) + b^i q_1 \big) \\ \text{subject to} \\ q_1^\alpha = t_1 \sum_i y^i w^i \end{array}\right\} \tag{6.2}$$

where w^i is consumer i's income and t_j the tax rate. As we can see, the representative government uses the sum of all community members' welfare as decision criterion. If the authority is a majority government and i is the consumer majority, the maximum becomes

$$\text{Max} \ w^i(1 - t_1) + b^i q_1. \tag{6.3}$$

When q is a private good the decision criterion changes analogously when we shift from a representative to a majority rule government. In both cases, the constraint (with q as a private good) becomes

$$q_1^\alpha \sum_i y^1 = t_1 \sum_i y^i w^i. \tag{6.4}$$

With only two types of consumers, differentiated by $w^1/w^2 > b^1/b^2$, the dynamic test of the Tiebout process means that an efficient allocation is a viable equilibrium only if $\dot{y}^i = y^i(y^1, y^2) = 0$. The result of the Stahl–Varaiya test may be summarized as follows:

(i) With a representative government and a pure public good, the only efficient state is the one in which all people live in one community. Such a state is not stationary under reasonable conditions. The stability can be ensured only if the production of the collective good exhibits a large degree of decreasing returns to scale, i.e. if α in (6.1) is large.

(ii) With a majority rule government and a pure public good, the conclusions are similar as with a representative government. The efficient state becomes unstable when $\alpha \rightarrow 1$ or whenever the relative desire of consumer type 1 for the public good is much smaller than their relative income.

(iii) With a representative government and q as a private good, the efficient state corresponds to segregated communities, each with a homogeneous population. This state does not correspond to a stationary equilibrium if, e.g. both consumers desire the collective good to the same extent while their incomes differ substantially.

(iv) With a majority rule government and a publicly provided private good, the outcome is the same as with a representative government supplying the private good.

One may just comment that these negative results are obtained under the assumption that there are no mobility costs.

6.2. The perfect competition analogy

In earlier studies of the Tiebout model it has usually been assumed that the equilibrium is constituted by communities which are segregated in the sense that each has a homogeneous population, i.e. each type of consumer resides in an area which has copies of himself. In a recent study Stiglitz (1983) develops a Tiebout type model which to a large extent mimics the general competitive model of a market economy, and shows that within his setting communities will not be homogeneous. Stiglitz' "perfect community competition" is characterized by:

(a) Communities have the form of isolated islands between which people may migrate. However, there is no trade between communities.

(b) All public goods expenditures are paid for by pure rents.

(c) Each type of labour is distinguished by productivity and taste characteristics.

With the model sketched above, Stiglitz can conclude for communities acting competitively to attract inhabitants that

(i) In equilibrium the level of public good is uniquely determined. Such a non-cooperative equilibrium is Pareto-optimal.

(ii) If there is no active competition for migrants and majority voting is used in each community, the equilibrium will not – in general – be Pareto-optimal.

The analysis reported here is basically concerned with characterizing equilibria. It does not provide specific insights with regard to the existence of equilibria and the dynamics of migration.

6.3. *Public investments in local infrastructure*

In several recent papers Schweizer has focused on the application of the so-called Henry George Theorem [e.g. Schweizer (1983)]. This theorem also plays an important role in Stiglitz' model. It states that public expenditure should be financed by means of land rents. In this way the allocation of other resources is not disturbed. Hence, this type of property taxation is assumed to function as an ideal of lump sum taxation. Schweizer (1983) studies a case where the public authority in each community finances public investment projects. The output from these projects consists of private goods, and the investments themselves (production infrastructure) do not affect the preferences of community inhabit- ants directly. In this way the convexity of the preference structures are kept intact.

In Schweizer's setting we have: (i) there is a finite set of different communities, (ii) for every community the supply of land is fixed, (iii) a pool of workers is available for allocation among communities, (iv) the communities are driven by land-owners who wish to increase their wealth and no taxes are raised from mobile workers, (v) the production possibility set of each community is convex except for fixed costs.

The communities act so as to attract workers and each worker/consumer maximizes his utility under his budget constraint. With the help of the Henry George Principle and a type of Core analysis (Edgeworth's principle), Schweizer is able to conclude that if the entire economy is large enough, there exists at least one global equilibrium.

7. Concluding comments

In all the preceding six sections we have been forced to conclude that much work remains to be done before one may claim that there is a comprehensive theory of public facility location. There are few results with regard to the existence of multi-authority equilibrium allocations in a multi-regional world. A similar degree of incompleteness also prevails as regards the characterization of feasible solutions to multi-authority PFL-decisions under varying institutional settings. In our presentation we have implicitly alluded to the rich variety of institutional arrangements that exists among the market economies in Europe. This may be thought of as a way of enriching the contributions from the North-American tradition. The latter has its most distinguished representation in Section 6, while the two-level structure of Section 4 is an attempt to point out that many regional issues in PFL-problems are controlled by national policies.

References

Andersson, A. E. (1981) 'Structural change and technological development', *Regional Science and Urban Economics*, 11:351–361.

Andersson, A. E. and J. Mantsinen (1980) 'Mobility of resources; accessibility of knowledge, and economic growth', *Behavioral Science*, 25:353–366.

Arnott, R. J. and J. E. Stiglitz (1979) 'Aggregate land rents, expenditures on public goods and optimal city size', *Quarterly Journal of Economics*, 63:471–500.

Arrow, K. J. (1971) 'Political and economic evaluation of social effects and externalities', in: M. D. Intriligator, ed., *Frontiers of quantitative economics*, Amsterdam: North-Holland, 3–31.

Beckmann, M. J. (1968) *Location theory*. New York: Random House.

Berge, C. (1957) 'Théorie générale des jeux à *n* personnes', *Mémoriale des sciences mathématiques*, Fasc. 138. Paris: Gauthier–Villars.

Bewley, T. (1981) 'A critique of Tiebout's theory of local public expenditures', *Econometrica*, 49:713–740.

Christaller, W. (1933) *Die Zentralen Orte in Süddeutschland*. Jena: Fischer Verlag. English translation (1966) *Central places in Southern Germany*. Englewood Cliffs, N.J.: Prentice-Hall.

Domencich, T. A. and D. McFadden (1975) *Urban travel demand: a behavioral analysis*, Amsterdam: North-Holland.

Erlenkotter, D. (1977) 'Facility location with price-sensitive demands: private, public and quasi-public', *Management Science*, 24:378–386.

Erlenkotter, D. (1983) 'On the choice of models for public facility location', in J-F. Thisse and M. G. Zoller, eds., *Locational Analysis of Public Facilities*. Amsterdam: North-Holland, 385–394.

Fujita, M. (1984) 'Urban land use theory', paper prepared for Fundamentals of pure and applied economics and for Encyclopedia of Economics, manuscript, Dept. of Regional Science, University of Pennsylvania, Philadelphia (forthcoming).

Fujita, M. (1985) 'Optimal location of public facilities: area dominance approach', Regional Science and Urban Economics, (forthcoming).

Hansen, P., D. Peeters and J-F. Thisse (1983) 'Public facility location models: a selective survey', in: J-F. Thisse and H. G. Zoller, eds., *Locational analysis of public facilities*. Amsterdam: North-Holland, 223–262.

Hansen, W. G. (1985), How Accessibility Shapes Land Use, *Journal of the American Institute of Planners*, 25, 73–76.

Lakshmanan, T. R. and W. G. Hansen (1965) 'A retail market potential model', *Journal of the American Institute of Planners*, 31:134–143.

Lea, A. C. (1981) 'Public facility location models and the theory of impure public goods', *Sistemi Urbani*, 3:345–390.

Lefeber, L. (1958) *Allocation in space: production, transportation and industrial location.* Amsterdam: North-Holland.

Leonardi, G. (1981a) 'A unifying framework for public facility location problems—part 1: a critical overview and some unsolved problems', *Environment and Planning*, *A*13:1001–1028.

Leonardi, G. (1981b) 'A unifying framework for public facility location problems—part 2: some new models and extensions', *Environment and Planning*, *A*13:1085–1108.

Leonardi, G. (1983) 'The use of random–utility theory in building location–allocation models, in: J-F. Thisse and H. Zoller, eds., *Spatial analysis of public facilities*. Amsterdam: North-Holland, 357–383.

Lösch, A. (1940) *Die Räumliche Ordnung der Wirtschaft; eine Untersuchung über Standort, Wirtschaftsgebiete und Internationalen Handel*. Jena: Fischer Verlag. English translation (1954) *The economics of location*. New Haven: Yale University Press.

Lowry, I. S. (1964) 'A model of metropolis', RM-4035-RC, Rand Corporation, Santa Monica, Calif.

Luce, R. D. and H. Raiffa (1957) *Games and decisions*. New York: John Wiley and Sons.

Luenberger, D. G. (1969) *Optimization by vector space methods*. New York: John Wiley and Sons.

McFadden, D. (1974) 'The measurement of urban travel demand', *Journal of Public Economics*, 3:303–328.

Nijkamp, P. and P. Rietveld (1982) 'Multiple objectives in multilevel multiregional planning models', in: M. Albegov, A. E. Andersson and F. Snickars, eds., *Regional development modeling: theory and practice*. Amsterdam: North-Holland, 145–168.

Palander, T. (1935) *Beiträge zur Standortstheorie*. Uppsala, Sweden: Almqvist and Wiksell.

Roy, J., B. Johansson and G. Leonardi (1985) 'Some spatial equilibria in facility investment under uncertain demand', *Papers of the Regional Science Association*, 56:215–228.

Samuelson, P. A. (1954) 'The pure theory of public expenditures', *Review of Economics and Statistics*, 36:387–389.

Samuelson, P. A. (1955) 'Diagrammatic exposition of public expenditures', *Review of Economics and Statistics*, 37:350–356.

Schweizer, U. (1983) 'Edgeworth and the Henry George theorem: how to finance local public projects', in: J-F. Thisse and M. G. Zoller, eds., *Locational analysis of public facilities*. Amsterdam: North-Holland, 79–94.

Stahl, K. and P. Varaiya (1983) 'Local collective goods: a critical re-examination of the Tiebout model', in: J-F. Thisse and H. G. Zoller, eds., *Locational analysis of public facilities*. Amsterdam: North-Holland, 45–54.

Stiglitz, J. E. (1977) 'The theory of local public goods', in: M. Feldstein and R. Inman, eds., *The economics of public services*, London: McMillan Press, 48–64.

Stiglitz, J. E. (1982) 'Utilitarianism and horizontal equality: the case for random taxation', *Journal of Public Economics*: 1–33.

Stiglitz, J. E. (1983) 'Public goods in open economies with heterogenous individuals', in: J-F. Thisse and H. G. Zoller, eds., *Locational analysis of public facilities*. Amsterdam: North-Holland, 55–78.

Thisse, J-F. and H. G. Zoller (1983) 'Some notes on public facility location', in: J-F. Thisse and H. G. Zoller, eds., *Locational analysis of public facilities*. Amsterdam: North-Holland, 1–10.

Thünen, J. H., von (1926) *Der isolierte Staat in Beziehung auf Landwirtschaft und Nationalökonomie*. English translation (1966) *The isolated state*. New York: Pergamon Press.

Tiebout C. M. (1956) 'A pure theory of local expenditures', *Journal of Political Economy*, 64:416–424.

Tiebout, C. M. (1961) 'An economic theory of fiscal decentralization', in: NBER, *Public finances: needs, sources and utilization*. Princeton: Princeton University Press, 79–98.

Weber, A (1909) *Über den Standort der Industrien*. Tübingen: Verlag Mohr. English translation (1957) *The theory of the location of industries*. Chicago: University of Chicago Press.

Weibull, J. W. (1976) 'An axiomatic approach to the measurement of accessibility', *Regional Science and Urban Economics*, 6:357–379.

Williams, H. C. W. L. (1977) 'On the formation of travel demand models and economic evaluation measures of user benefit', *Environment and Planning*, A9:285–344.

Wilson, A. G. (1970) *Entropy in urban and regional modelling*. London: Pion.

Chapter 5

SPATIAL EQUILIBRIUM ANALYSIS*

T. TAKAYAMA and W. C. LABYS

1. Introduction

Location theory of von Thünen (1826), Launhardt (1885), Weber (1909) and Palander (1935) treated space as a continuum, and the economic activities on this space are considered to be related to the distance from a reference point(s) (the central city in the case of von Thünen for instance) in the space (see also Chapter 2 of this Handbook).

Based on the development of mathematical programming methods, especially the linear programming method of George Dantzig (1951a), economists began to develop optimal spatial allocation models of economic goods and activities [Dantzig (1951b), Koopmans (1949) for instance]. In these examples, demand and/or supply regions (finite in number) are represented (as an approximation to reality) by points in space which are interconnected by various modes of transporting economic goods whose unit transport costs between any pair of regions are known as constants or functions (depending on the volume of shipment, for instance). Along this line of development, emerged the "Spatial Equilibrium Theory".

"Equilibrium Among Spatially Separated Markets: Solution by Electric Analogue" by Enke (1951) marks the beginning of research in this fertile applied field, followed by Samuelson's (1952) "Spatial Price Equilibrium and Linear Programming". After a decade, "Equilibrium Among Spatially Separated Markets: A Reformulation" by Takayama and Judge (1964) showed how the multiple commodity, multiple market problem can be cast within the framework of a non-linear mathematical programming formulation. The quadratic program-

*Professor Kozo Sasaki of the University of Tsukuba, Japan, helped the first author improve the quality of this chapter, and we would like to extend our thanks to him. The first author would like to acknowledge the great assistance extended by Messrs. K. Ando and K. Kanno in the Japan Foundation in Tokyo and Canberra respectively for making the visit of Professor K. Sasaki possible. He is also grateful to the Commonwealth Tertiary Education Council (CTEC) for providing a special research grant to help finance the stay of Professor K. Sasaki at the stage of finalizing this chapter.

ming solution to this problem was shown to be especially suitable for practical
policy analysis and evaluation. Since then, this series of developments has seen a
wide range of applications in the fields of agriculture, minerals and energy.

In Section 2 of this chapter, a concise theoretical background will be described
and in Section 3 general spatial equilibrium models will be briefly discussed. In
Section 4 some applications will be selectively reviewed and appropriate conclusions derived.

2.   Spatial economic equilibrium theory

Suppose that two countries, the USA and Japan, separated by the Pacific Ocean,
produce and consume a homogeneous commodity, wheat. Both countries are
assumed to have a domestic demand function and a supply function for wheat
defined in the tradition of Alfred Marshall.

In Figure 2.1 the quantity axis of country 1, say America, is $0q_1$ and the price
axis is $0p$. On the other side of that diagram, the quantity axis of country 2, say
Japan, is drawn as $0q_2$, and the price axis is common between the two nations.

If, for some reason, the trade is completely blocked between the countries, and
for simplicity we assume that there are no other countries in the wheat trade, the

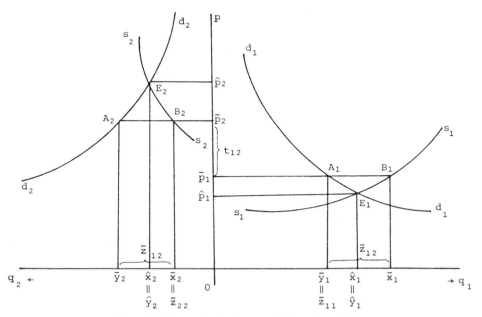

Figure 2.1. Back-to-back diagram of international trade.

domestic wheat prices in this autarkic situation will be $\hat{p}_1$ and $\hat{p}_2$ and the demand, y, and supply, x, of wheat will be $\hat{y}_1 = \hat{x}_1$ and $\hat{y}_2 = \hat{x}_2$ respectively for America and Japan. These autarky prices will prevail as long as there are no traders with shipping facilities such as ocean freighters. The existence of traders, however, provides a condition necessary, if not sufficient, for trade. If the traders see that trade is not "profitable", there will be no trade. What then is the basic criterion for "profitability"?

Since the Marshallian demand and supply functions are traditionally based on the concepts of price ($) per unit of a good consumed and cost ($) per unit of a product, and as long as the logical frame of our theoretical example is based on Marshall, the profitability criteria here should be the transportation cost ($) per unit of wheat.

Referring again to Figure 2.1, we assume simply that the unit transport cost of wheat is constant (or course, one can assume an upward sloping or U-shaped unit transport cost function if these are more realistic than the one we assumed in Figure 2.1). Under this constant unit transport cost assumption, the following three possible cases arise:

(1) $t_{12} > \hat{p}_2 - \hat{p}_1$: The transport cost is too high for the traders to engage in wheat trade.
(2) $t_{12} = \hat{p}_2 - \hat{p}_1$: There is no incentive for trade.
(3) $t_{12} < \hat{p}_2 - \hat{p}_1$: Traders will engage in trade.

If the third case persists some questions will naturally arise: How much wheat will America export (equivalently, how much wheat will Japan import) and what prices of wheat in the two countries will prevail when the traders show no further incentive to ship any more wheat from America to Japan?

By defining the quantity of wheat traded as z_{12} (quantity shipped from country 1 to country 2), the unit transport cost as t_{12}, and also the equilibrium trade quantity and prices as z_{12}, $\bar{p}_1$, and $\bar{p}_2$, we can express the equilibrium relationships among these quantities and prices as follows:

$$
\begin{cases}
\bar{p}_2 - \bar{p}_1 - t_{12} \le 0 \\
\text{and} \\
\bar{z}_{12}(\bar{p}_2 - \bar{p}_1 - t_{12}) = 0.
\end{cases}
\tag{2.1}
$$

The above equilibrium condition (2.1) contains in itself the three cases discussed above. That is, if the first case prevails, then

$$
\begin{cases}
\bar{p}_2 - \bar{p}_1 - t_{12} < 0 \\
\text{and} \\
\bar{z}_{12}(\bar{p}_2 - \bar{p}_1 - t_{12}) = 0
\end{cases}
\tag{2.2}
$$

imply $\bar{z}_{12} = 0$, a no trade case. If the second case prevails, then by identifying $\bar{p}_1 = \hat{p}_1$ and $\bar{p}_2 = \hat{p}_2$, we get

$$
\begin{cases}
\bar{p}_2 - \bar{p}_1 - t_{12} = 0 \\
\text{and} \\
\bar{z}_{12}(\bar{p}_2 - \bar{p}_1 - t_{12}) = 0
\end{cases}
\tag{2.3}
$$

leading us to conclude that at the margin of indifference $\bar{z}_{12} \geq 0$. The third case permits positive solutions of (2.1) for $\bar{z}_{12}$, $\bar{p}_1$, and $\bar{p}_2$.

The relation (2.1) is called a "complementarity" relationship and plays a crucial role, to be discussed later, in solving the classical spatial equilibrium problem.

In this simple two country and one commodity trade problem, the resulting equilibrium solution yields the following:

$$
\begin{cases}
p_1 = d_1(z_{11}) \\
d_1(z_{11}) = s_1(z_{11} + z_{12}) \\
p_2 = d_2(z_{22} + z_{12}) \\
d_2(z_{22} + z_{12}) = s_2(z_{22}) \\
p_2 - p_1 - t_{12} = 0,
\end{cases}
\tag{2.4}
$$

where z_{ij} denotes the quantity produced in i and shipped to j; $d_i(\cdot)$ and $s_i(\cdot)$ denote demand and supply functions in the ith country.[1]

In this system there are five unknowns and five equations, and presumptively the system can be solved for the unknowns, $\bar{p}_1, \bar{p}_2, \bar{z}_{11}, \bar{z}_{12}, \bar{z}_{22}$, that constitute the spatial equilibrium solutions.

This problem of solving a simultaneous equation system enables us to identify which country is the importer (exporter), by employing $\hat{p}_2 - \hat{p}_1 - t_{12} < 0$ in (2.4). If there are several countries trading a commodity with each other, developing a system which consistently identifies the importers and hence a soluble system such as (2.4) is by itself extremely difficult. In this context, replacing the simultaneous equation system approach by a mathematical (general nonlinear) programming approach such as that suggested by Samuelson was a step forward.

This process begins by writing the quantity relationships among consumption, supply, and trade in the following general (inequality) format:

$$
\begin{cases}
y_1 - z_{11} - z_{21} \leq 0 \\
y_2 - z_{12} - z_{22} \leq 0 \\
-x_1 + z_{11} + z_{12} \leq 0 \\
-x_2 + z_{21} + z_{22} \leq 0.
\end{cases}
\tag{2.5}
$$

[1] In Figure 2.1, $z_{11} = y_1$, $x_1 = z_{11} + z_{12}$, $y_2 = z_{22} + z_{12}$, $x_2 = z_{22}$ hold with a bar on all variables.

The maximand to this problem is written as the sum of the consumer satisfaction (integral of the demand function $d_i(y_i)$, $i = 1,2$, over y_i) less total cost (integral of the supply function $s_i(x_i)$, $i = 1,2$, over x_i) minus total transport costs, $\sum_i \sum_j t_{ij} z_{ij}$, $i, j = 1,2$. That is:

$$\Phi(y, x, z) = \sum_i \int_0^{y_i} d_i(\xi_i) \, d\xi_i - \sum_i \int_0^{x_i} s_i(\zeta_i) \, d\zeta_i - \sum_i \sum_j t_{ij} z_{ij} \qquad (2.6)$$

where

$$y = (y_1, y_2)', \quad x = (x_1, x_2)', \quad \text{and} \quad z = (z_{11}, z_{12}, z_{21}, z_{22})'.$$

The function $\Phi(y, x, z)$ represents the sum of the consumers' and producers' surpluses with trade, which is defined by Samuelson (1952) as "Net Social Payoff".

This can be translated to the following nonlinear programming spatial equilibrium problem (SEP): Find $(\bar{y}, \bar{x}, \bar{z})$ that maximize (2.6) subject to (2.5) and $y \geq 0$, $x \geq 0$, $z \geq 0$.

The operational implications of this SEP problem are clearly reflected in the related Kuhn–Tucker conditions as follows:

$$
\begin{cases}
w_{y_1} = -d_1(\bar{y}_1) + \bar{p}_1 \geq 0 & \text{and} \quad w_{y_1} \cdot \bar{y}_1 = 0 \\
w_{y_2} = -d_2(\bar{y}_2) + \bar{p}_2 \geq 0 & \text{and} \quad w_{y_2} \cdot \bar{y}_2 = 0 \\
w_{x_1} = s_1(\bar{x}_1) - \bar{p}^1 \geq 0 & \text{and} \quad w_{x_1} \cdot \bar{x}_1 = 0 \\
w_{x_2} = s_2(\bar{x}_2) - \bar{p}^2 \geq 0 & \text{and} \quad w_{x_2} \cdot \bar{x}_2 = 0 \\
w_{z_{11}} = -\bar{p}_1 + \bar{p}^1 + t_{11} \geq 0 & \text{and} \quad w_{z_{11}} \cdot \bar{z}_{11} = 0 \\
w_{z_{12}} = -\bar{p}_2 + \bar{p}^1 + t_{12} \geq 0 & \text{and} \quad w_{z_{12}} \cdot \bar{z}_{12} = 0 \\
w_{z_{21}} = -\bar{p}_1 + \bar{p}^2 + t_{21} \geq 0 & \text{and} \quad w_{z_{21}} \cdot \bar{z}_{21} = 0 \qquad (2.7) \\
w_{z_{22}} = -\bar{p}_2 + \bar{p}^2 + t_{22} \geq 0 & \text{and} \quad w_{z_{22}} \cdot \bar{z}_{22} = 0 \\
w_{p_1} = -\bar{y}_1 + \bar{z}_{11} + \bar{z}_{21} \geq 0 & \text{and} \quad w_{p_1} \cdot \bar{p}_1 = 0 \\
w_{p_2} = -\bar{y}_2 + \bar{z}_{12} + \bar{z}_{22} \geq 0 & \text{and} \quad w_{p_2} \cdot \bar{p}_2 = 0 \\
w_{p^1} = \bar{x}_1 - \bar{z}_{11} - \bar{z}_{12} \geq 0 & \text{and} \quad w_{p^1} \cdot \bar{p}^1 = 0 \\
w_{p^2} = \bar{x}_2 - \bar{z}_{21} - \bar{z}_{22} \geq 0 & \text{and} \quad w_{p^2} \cdot \bar{p}^2 = 0,
\end{cases}
$$

where w's are slack variables. p_i and p^i are Lagrangian shadow prices, representing demand and supply prices respectively.

Equations (2.7) are the complete description of the properties of the spatial (price) equilibrium solution.

One can easily establish that if trade takes place, then the value of (2.6) is increased over and above the sum of the consumers' and producers' surpluses of the two countries under autarkic conditions ((2.8) defined below) by the sum of the areas of the triangles of $A_1 B_1 E_1$ and $A_2 B_2 E_2$ when a spatial equilibrium is attained.[2]

$$\text{Total economic surplus before trade} = \sum_i \int_0^{\hat{y}_i} d_i(y_i)\,\mathrm{d}y_i - \sum_i \int_0^{\hat{x}_i} s_i(x_i)\,\mathrm{d}x_i$$

$$(2.8)$$

where $\hat{y}_i$ and $\hat{x}_i$ are demand and supply quantities in equilibrium before trade, respectively.

This problem can be easily generalized to include multiple countries and multiple commodities. In the next section this generalized model and its results will be discussed.

Simplex tableau for the above one commodity two region case is shown below (Table 2.1).

Table 2.1
Simplex tableau for one commodity two region case.

c		p_0	p_1	p_2	p^1	p^2	y_1	y_2	x_1	x_2	z_{11}	z_{12}	z_{21}	z_{22}	w_{p_1}	w_{p_2}	w_{p^1}	w_{p^2}
			0	0	0	0	0	0	0	0	0	0	0	0	0	0	0	0
$0\ \ w_p$		0					-1				1		1		-1			
		0						-1				1		1		-1		
		0							1		-1	-1					-1	
		0								1			-1	-1				-1
$-1\ \ u$	λ_1		1				ω_1											
	λ_2			1				ω_2										
	$-\nu_1$				-1				η_1									
	$-\nu_2$					-1				η_2								
$0\ \ w_z$	$-t_{11}$		-1		1													
	$-t_{12}$			-1	1													
	$-t_{21}$		-1			1												
	$-t_{22}$			-1		1												

u: Artificial variables introduced to give initial feasible solutions.

[2] This is a partial equilibrium counterpart of a theorem in the general equilibrium theory of international trade.

Table 2.1 continued

		p_0	w_{y_1}	w_{y_2}	w_{x_1}	w_{x_2}	$w_{z_{11}}$	$w_{z_{12}}$	$w_{z_{21}}$	$w_{z_{22}}$	u_{y_1}	u_{y_2}	u^{y^1}	u^{y^2}	u_{x_1}	u_{x_2}	u^{x^1}	u^{x^2}
c			0	0	0	0	0	0	0	0	-1	-1	-1	-1	-1	-1	-1	-1
$0\ w_p$	0																	
	0																	
	0																	
	0																	
$-1\ u$	λ_1		-1								1		-1					
	λ_2			-1								1		-1				
	$-\nu_1$				-1										1		-1	
	$-\nu_2$					-1										1		-1
	$-t_{11}$						-1											
	$-t_{12}$							-1										
$0\ w_z$	$-t_{21}$								-1									
	$-t_{22}$									-1								

3. General spatial equilibrium models

Consider a general framework suitable for determining the efficient interregional consumption y, production x, and flow (trade) z of various commodities and factors of production. The most general formulation of the mathematical programming solution to this framework can be written as follows:

Maximize:

$$\Phi(y, x, z) = \sum_{i=1}^{n} \left(R_i(y_i) - C_i(x_i) \right) - T(z) \tag{3.1}$$

where

$$R_i(y_i) = \sum_k \int_{\hat{y}_i^k}^{y_i^k} P_i^k(\xi_i^k)\, \mathrm{d}\xi_i^k,$$

$$C_i(x_i) = \sum_k \int_{\hat{x}_i^k}^{x_i^k} p^{ik}(\zeta_i^k)\, \mathrm{d}\zeta_i^k \quad \text{and}$$

$$T(z) = \sum_k \sum_i \sum_j t_{ij}^k z_{ij}^k \quad \text{(or } t'z\text{: when the unit transport cost is fixed)};$$

subject to:

$$F(y, x, z) \geq 0 \tag{3.2}$$

and

$$y \geq 0, \quad x \geq 0, \quad z \geq 0 \tag{3.3}$$

where

$$y_i = \{ y_i^1 \ldots y_i^m \}' \ (m \times 1),$$
$$x_i = \{ x_i^1 \ldots x_i^m \}' \ (m \times 1),$$
$$z_i = \{ z_{i1}^1 \ldots z_{i1}^m \ldots z_{in}^1 \ldots z_{in}^m \}' \ (m \cdot n \times 1),$$

and finally,

$$y = \{ y_1' \ldots y_n' \}' \ (m \cdot n \times 1),$$
$$x = \{ x_1' \ldots x_n' \}' \ (m \cdot n \times 1),$$
$$z = \{ z_1' \ldots z_n' \}' \ (m \cdot n \cdot n \times 1),$$
$$t = \{ t_{11}^1 \ldots t_{11}^m, t_{12}^1 \ldots t_{12}^m, \ldots, t_{nn}^1 \ldots t_{nn}^m \}' \ (m \cdot n \cdot n \times 1).^3$$

$\Phi(\cdot)$ is assumed to be quasi-concave in y, x, and z, and $F(y, x, z)$ contains (within the expression) the interregional consumption–production–shipment relationships. It is also assumed to satisfy all the regularity conditions required for regular solvability of the problem [see chapter 2 of Takayama and Judge (1971)].

$\Phi(\cdot)$ is expressed in a concrete form such as in the right-hand side of (2.6), that is, the sum of consumers' surplus and producers' surplus $\sum_i (R_i(y_i) - C_i(x_i))$, minus the total transport costs (the last term).

The necessary and sufficient Kuhn–Tucker conditions for $(\bar{y}, \bar{x}, \bar{z})$ to be the solution vector of the NLP above are:

$$
\begin{cases}
\text{(a)} \quad w_y = -\left(\dfrac{\partial \Phi}{\partial y} + \rho' \dfrac{\partial F}{\partial y} \right) \geq 0 \quad \text{and} \quad w_y' y = 0 \\[2mm]
\text{(b)} \quad w_x = -\left(\dfrac{\partial \Phi}{\partial x} + \rho' \dfrac{\partial F}{\partial x} \right) \geq 0 \quad \text{and} \quad w_x' x = 0 \\[2mm]
\text{(c)} \quad w_z = -\left(\dfrac{\partial \Phi}{\partial z} + \rho' \dfrac{\partial F}{\partial z} \right) \geq 0 \quad \text{and} \quad w_z' z = 0 \\[2mm]
\text{(d)} \quad w_\rho = F(\cdot) \geq 0 \qquad\qquad\qquad\quad \text{and} \quad w_\rho' \rho = 0,
\end{cases}
\tag{3.4}
$$

where $\rho = \{ \rho_1^1 \ldots \rho_1^m, \ldots, \rho_n^1 \ldots \rho_n^m, \rho^{11} \ldots \rho^{1m}, \ldots, \rho^{nm} \}'$ indicates Lagrangian multipliers; practically, ρ_i denotes demand price and ρ^i supply price. All of the arguments are evaluated at the optimal solution point.

When Φ is nonlinear or nonquadratic, and/or F is a vector of nonlinear functions, the required solution algorithms become extremely complicated and time-consuming. This is especially true when the variables are identified with regional indices as is usually the case in interregional (competitive) economic

---

[3]A more systematic development of hierarchical models in this category can be found in chapter 2 of Takayama and Judge (1971) where only a static model is presented.

analysis, thus expanding the dimensionality of the variables, and exponentially increasing computer time to solve a problem such as (3.1)–(3.3) above.

Because of the inherent computational difficulties,[4] Takayama has developed and advocated the use of the quadratic programming (QP) formulation or the linear complementarity programming (LCP) formulation of the SEP problem [(1971 with Judge), (1973 with Judge), (1976), (1979), and (1982 with Hashimoto)]. Since the QP solution is well known, we instead describe the relationships between QP and LCP in the framework of a *static* spatial (international and interregional) equilibrium framework, leaving the dynamic counterpart to the following sections and chapters 17 and 18 of Takayama and Judge (1971).

Let us assume that we have the following system of linear demand equations for m final consumption goods in region i. The time dimension is suppressed in the following argument:

$$
p_i = \begin{bmatrix} \lambda_i^1 \\ \lambda_i^2 \\ \vdots \\ \lambda_i^m \end{bmatrix} - \begin{bmatrix} \omega_i^{11} & \omega_i^{12} & \cdots & \omega_i^{1m} \\ \omega_i^{21} & \omega_i^{22} & \cdots & \omega_i^{2m} \\ \vdots & \vdots & \ddots & \vdots \\ \omega_i^{m1} & \omega_i^{m2} & \cdots & \omega_i^{mm} \end{bmatrix} \begin{bmatrix} y_i^1 \\ y_i^2 \\ \vdots \\ y_i^m \end{bmatrix} \tag{3.5}
$$

$$
\equiv \lambda_i - \Omega_i y_i, \quad \text{for all } i,
$$

where Ω_i, the demand coefficient matrix, can be symmetric or asymmetric and is assumed to be positive semi-definite.[5]

Supply functions are assumed to be in linear form as follows:

$$
p^i = \begin{bmatrix} \nu_i^1 \\ \nu_i^2 \\ \vdots \\ \nu_i^m \end{bmatrix} + \begin{bmatrix} \eta_i^{11} & \eta_i^{12} & \cdots & \eta_i^{1m} \\ \eta_i^{21} & \eta_i^{22} & \cdots & \eta_i^{2m} \\ \vdots & \vdots & \ddots & \vdots \\ \eta_i^{m1} & \eta_i^{m2} & \cdots & \eta_i^{mm} \end{bmatrix} \begin{bmatrix} x_i^1 \\ x_i^2 \\ \vdots \\ x_i^m \end{bmatrix} \tag{3.6}
$$

$$
\equiv \nu_i + H_i x_i, \quad \text{for all } i,
$$

where H_i, the supply coefficient matrix, can also be symmetric or asymmetric and is assumed to be positive semi-definite.[6]

When both Ω_i and H_i are symmetric the following quadratic programming problem can be meaningfully defined.

---

[4] Some practical aspects of computational difficulties will be discussed later in Section 4.

[5] There is no intrinsic rationale that Ω_i be symmetric in this linear form. This becomes especially obvious once lagged coefficients are introduced in a dynamic modeling framework.

[6] As in the use of Ω_i, H_i is usually asymmetric. This becomes especially obvious once lagged coefficients are introduced in a dynamic modeling framework.

3.1. The quadratic programming (QP) problem

Maximize:

$$\Phi(y, x, z) = \sum_{i=1}^{n} \left(\lambda_i' y_i - \tfrac{1}{2} y_i' \Omega_i y_i - v_i' x_i - \tfrac{1}{2} x_i' H_i x_i \right) - t'z, \tag{3.7}$$

subject to:[7]

$$\left\{ \begin{array}{l} -\begin{bmatrix} y_1 \\ y_2 \\ \vdots \\ y_n \end{bmatrix} + \begin{bmatrix} I_1 & I_2 & \cdots & I_n \end{bmatrix} \begin{bmatrix} z_1 \\ z_2 \\ \vdots \\ z_n \end{bmatrix} \geq 0 \\[4em] \begin{bmatrix} x_1 \\ x_2 \\ \vdots \\ x_n \end{bmatrix} + \begin{bmatrix} -E_1 & & & \\ & -E_2 & & \\ & & \ddots & \\ & & & -E_n \end{bmatrix} \begin{bmatrix} z_1 \\ z_2 \\ \vdots \\ z_n \end{bmatrix} \geq 0 \end{array} \right. \tag{3.8}$$

and

$$y \geq 0, \qquad x \geq 0, \qquad z \geq 0, \tag{3.9}$$

where the notation is the same as used before, and

$$I_m^i = \begin{bmatrix} 1 & & & \\ & 1 & & \\ & & \ddots & \\ & & & 1 \end{bmatrix}_{(m \times m)}, \qquad (i = 1, 2, \ldots, n),$$

$$I_i = \begin{bmatrix} I_m^1 & & & \\ & I_m^2 & & \\ & & \ddots & \\ & & & I_m^n \end{bmatrix}_{(m \cdot n \times m \cdot n)}, \qquad (i = 1, 2, \ldots, n),$$

$$E_i = \begin{bmatrix} I_m^1 & I_m^2 & \cdots & I_m^n \end{bmatrix} (m \times n \cdot n), \qquad (i = 1, 2, \ldots, n),$$

$$G_y = \begin{bmatrix} I_1 & I_2 & \cdots & I_n \end{bmatrix} (m \cdot n \times m \cdot n \cdot n),$$

$$G_x = \begin{bmatrix} -E_1 & & & \\ & -E_2 & & \\ & & \ddots & \\ & & & -E_n \end{bmatrix}_{(m \cdot n \times m \cdot n \cdot n)}$$

---

[7] This is a commodity-oriented formulation, and the full representation of the quadratic (Q) matrix consistent with this formulation is shown in chapter 12, p. 239, of Takayama and Judge (1971).

The Kuhn–Tucker optimality conditions (3.4) for this problem suggest the following natural market clearing and pricing mechanism:

$$
\begin{aligned}
&\text{(a)} \quad w_{y_i} = -\lambda_i + \tfrac{1}{2}(\Omega_i + \Omega_i')y_i + \rho_i \geq 0 \quad \text{and} \quad w_{y_i}' y_i = 0, \\
&\hspace{6cm} \text{for all } i; \\
&\text{(b)} \quad w_{x_i} = \nu_i + \tfrac{1}{2}(H_i + H_i')x_i - \rho^i \geq 0 \quad \text{and} \quad w_{x_i}' x_i = 0, \\
&\hspace{6cm} \text{for all } i; \\
&\text{(c)} \quad w_{z_{ij}}^k = -\rho_j^k + \rho^{ik} + t_{ij}^k \geq 0 \qquad\qquad \text{and} \quad w_{z_{ij}}^k \cdot z_{ij}^k = 0, \qquad\qquad (3.10) \\
&\hspace{6cm} \text{for all } i,\, j \text{ and } k; \\
&\text{(d)} \quad w_{\rho_j}^k = -y_j^k + \sum_{i=1}^{n} z_{ij}^k \geq 0 \qquad\qquad \text{and} \quad w_{\rho_j}^k \cdot \rho_j^k = 0, \\
&\hspace{6cm} \text{for all } j \text{ and } k; \\
&\hspace{1cm} w_{\rho_{ik}} = x_i^k - \sum_{j=1}^{n} z_{ij}^k \geq 0 \qquad\qquad \text{and} \quad w_{\rho^{ik}} \cdot \rho^{ik} = 0, \\
&\hspace{6cm} \text{for all } i \text{ and } k; \\
&\hspace{1cm} \text{and} \\
&\text{(e)} \quad y_i \geq 0,\; x_i \geq 0,\; z_{ij}^k \geq 0,\; \rho_j \geq 0,\; \rho^i \geq 0, \qquad \text{for all } i,\, j \text{ and } k.
\end{aligned}
$$

The two most important terms in expression (3.10) are:

$$
\tfrac{1}{2}(\Omega_i + \Omega_i') \quad \text{and} \quad \tfrac{1}{2}(H_i + H_i'). \tag{3.11}
$$

These terms can be said to have two properties:

$$
\text{(A)} \quad \tfrac{1}{2}(\Omega_i + \Omega_i') \quad \text{and} \quad \tfrac{1}{2}(H_i + H_i') \tag{3.12}
$$

are symmetric for any square $(n \times n)$ matrix Ω_i and H_i.
(B) If Ω_i and H_i are symmetric, then

$$
\tfrac{1}{2}(\Omega_i + \Omega_i') = \Omega_i, \qquad \tfrac{1}{2}(H_i + H_i') = H_i. \tag{3.13}
$$

The Simplex tableau for this case is shown below (see Table 3.1)

The conditions (a) and (b) given in (3.10) would thus represent the regional market demand and supply functions, only where the above property (B) holds. The symmetry condition is sometimes referred to as the "integrability condition". However, the independently estimated final goods demand and/or supply functions for each region do not have to satisfy this condition from a theoretical point of view. Also, if one superimposes this condition as an additional constraint on a particular systems estimator, the statistical fit of the equation may deteriorate. Either way, the imposition of symmetry on Ω_i's and H_i's is not generally an acceptable procedure.

Thus, we can safely argue that Ω_i's and H_i's are most likely asymmetric. Then, (3.10)(a) and (b) do not represent regional demand or supply functional relationships (generalized versions of (3.5) and (3.6)). This finding seems to deny the traditional optimization approach in this crucially important applied regional science area.

A way to overcome this impasse and allow us to use the traditional optimization approach has been suggested and expounded by various researchers. For a summary of early developments in this direction and their evolution, see Takayama and Judge (1971). A more direct method to solve this problem is to employ the LCP algorithm. It is almost intuitively clear that, if Ω_i and/or H_i are asymmetric, one just replaces $\frac{1}{2}(\Omega_i + \Omega_i')$ and $\frac{1}{2}(H_i + H_i')$ by Ω_i and H_i. By following this rule, we no longer can use the quasi-welfare maximization characterization of spatial equilibrium theory [see Dean et al. (1970)]. Instead we must pursue a new definition of an economy in spatial (international or interregional) equilibrium as follows:

Definition 1

An interregionally connected economy is said to be in a spatial equilibrium if the following conditions hold:

$$(a) \quad w_{y_i} = -\lambda_i + \Omega_i y_i + \rho_i \geq 0 \quad \text{and} \quad w'_{y_i} y_i = 0,$$

$$\text{for all } i;$$

$$(b) \quad w_{x_i} = v_i + H_i x_i - \rho^i \geq 0 \quad \text{and} \quad w'_{x_i} x_i = 0,$$

$$\text{for all } i;$$

$$(c) \quad w^k_{z_{ij}} = -\rho^k_j + \rho^{ik} + t^k_{ij} \geq \quad \text{and} \quad w^k_{z_{ij}} \cdot z^k_{ij} = 0,$$

$$\text{for all } i, j \quad \text{and} \quad k; \ (3.14)$$

$$(d) \quad w^k_{\rho^k_j} = -y^k_j + \sum_{i=1}^{n} z^k_{ij} \geq 0 \quad \text{and} \quad w^k_{\rho^k_j} \cdot \rho^k_i = 0,$$

$$\text{for all } j \text{ and } k;$$

$$w_{\rho^{ik}} = x^k_i - \sum_{j=1}^{n} z^k_{ij} \geq 0 \quad \text{and} \quad w_{\rho^{ik}} \cdot \rho^{ik} = 0,$$

$$\text{for all } i \text{ and } k;$$

and

$$(e) \quad y_i \geq 0, \ x_i \geq 0, \ z^k_{ij} \geq 0, \ \rho^k_j \geq 0, \ \rho^i_k \geq 0, \text{ for all } i, j \quad \text{and} \quad k.$$

Table 3.1
Simplex tableau for m commodity n region case.

c		0	0	0	0	0	0	0	0	0	0	-1	-1	-1	-1
		p_0	p_y	p^x	y	x	z	w_{p_y}	w_{p^x}	w_y	w_x	w_z	u_y	u^y	u_x	u^x

		p_0	p_y	p^x	y	x	z	w_{p_y}	w_{p^x}	w_y	w_x	w_z	u_y	u^y	u_x	u^x
0	w_{p_y}	0			$-I_y$	0	G_y	$-I_y$	0							
0	w_{p^x}	0			0	I_x	G_x	0	$-I_x$							
-1 or	u_y / u^y	λ	I_y	0	Ω	0				$-I_y$			I_y	$-I_y$	0	0
-1 or	u_x / u^x	$-\nu$	0	$-I_x$	0	H					$-I_x$		0	0	I_x	$-I_x$
0	w_z	$-t$	$-G'_y$	$-G'_x$								$-I_{w_z}$				

u: artificial variables introduced to give initial feasible solutions.

This formulation proves to be a direct extension of our spatial (QP) equilibrium problem in the following sense: It (1) frees the spatial equilibrium model from being normative and restrictive, and (2) leaves the model computationally as efficient as its QP counterpart. From the beginning many have recognized that the concept of net social payoff employed in QP has been a "necessary evil", despite Samuelson's teleological interpretation (1952) of it. At the same time, our new spatial (LCP) formulation yields a set of rational and efficient operational rules or conditions, which are essentially sufficient for a spatial equilibrium to hold.

We thus assert that the concept of "net social payoff" is basically academic, in the sense that the maximization of this concept has only a teleological implication (only meaningful conditions needed by researchers are (3.10) when Ω_i and H_i are symmetric). Thus in policy analyses using spatial equilibrium models the derivation of outcomes based on revenues and costs may play a more substantial role. More recent developments in this field such as those of Hashimoto (1977) and of Whitacre (1979) would seem to confirm this allegation.

Returning to the system (3.4), one should recognize that this programming model conforms exactly to that of the LCP model [see Cottle and Dantzig (1968)] defined as follows.

3.2. The linear complementarity programming (LCP) problem

Find vectors w and r that satisfy the following conditions:

$$z = w + Mr, \tag{3.15}$$

$$w'r = 0; \quad \text{and} \quad w \geq 0; \ r \geq 0; \tag{3.16}$$

where q is a real $(s \times 1)$ vector, M is a real $(s \times s)$ matrix, and w and r are $(s \times 1)$ vectors.

The following theorem [theorem 12 of Cottle and Dantzig (1968)] summarizes the finite termination property of their "principal pivoting method".

Theorem 1

The principal pivoting method (PPM) terminates in a solution of (3.15) and (3.16) if M has positive principal minors (and in particular, if M is positive definite).

It is clear that M, (3.15), has positive principal minors if $\frac{1}{2}(M + M')$ is a positive definite matrix. However, problem solvability has not progressed much beyond this since these models were developed by the early 1970s. Some exceptions with regard to this will be discussed in Section 4.

To advance the LCP model further, more general demand and supply functions could be introduced into this system. However, the computational burden of solving this type of problem increases exponentially as commodity and regional numbers increase, and this is the main reason why we have restricted the demand and supply functions to be linear.

4. Recent model developments

The 1970s have witnessed an increase in both the quantity and the quality of "market-oriented" spatial and (inter)temporal price and allocation (STPA) models. Market-oriented modeling here refers to the particular application of STPA models to commodity market analysis in agricultural, energy and mineral areas [e.g. Labys and Pollak (1984)]. These modeling activities were performed by a number of policy-making groups including national governments, international organizations, and private enterprises. The reasons underlying this unusual modeling enthusiasm have been, the increased instability in these markets, the various oil crises, and the growing international debt burden.

Because of the increased market instability, one of the greatest challenges facing modelers has been the need to forecast price and quantity swings in commodity markets. This challenge was posed by policy decision-makers who needed forecasts of specific commodity price levels as well as of price stability (cyclically convergent or divergent?). The first major price swings of interest appeared in the international grains market during 1972–73; and before the effects of this shock had worked themselves out, a second and more persistent price swing took place in the crude oil markets in late 1973. With a change in the stability (such as increases in the year-to-year deviation of the quantities supplied of various key commodities in the 1970s and 1980s), if not in the structure of these markets, questions which were considered operationally and logically relevant in the past (such as "what is the least cost allocation of commodities in the world, given the regional demands, supplies, cost of regional productions, and transport costs between any pair of the regions in the world?"), were suddenly relegated to a place of secondary concern.

Given these unusual circumstances, spatial trade analysis became important because the commodity market (trade) shares of each country become acutely subject to the law of international supply and demand. That is, how much a country is willing to pay to get a certain share in the world market is related only indirectly (due to the involvement of many countries in the world market) to the share it receives. Each country becomes a part of a total world market-clearing system, and hence cannot assume that the impact of its trade policy change(s) regarding its own internationally traded commodity(ies) will fall on the countries or trading partners intended.

A challenge of unequalled precedent was thus cast to further improve the development and application of market-oriented spatial programming models.

4.1. Agricultural models

A number of agricultural commodity market analyses were attempted by the US Department of Agriculture – Economic Research Service (USDA–ERS) to analyze the nature of multi-commodity markets and to forecast regional market prices, demands, supplies, and interregional trade flows. A comprehensive if not substantive critique of these agricultural model developments can be found in Thompson (1981), and Japan Ministry of Agriculture (JAM) (1974) study. Also see the Ford Foundation–World Bank Food Project papers published at the University of Illinois by Hashimoto (1977), Nguyen (1977) and Whitacre (1979).

The JAM strategy was to employ a market-oriented simulation model with genuinely nonlinear demand and/or supply functions in various world regions. Visions or views of the JAM concerning the future of agricultural commodity markets, however, strongly influenced the forecasts they made. The forecasts suggested that agricultural commodity prices would stabilize after the 1972–73 period, but that they would soar steadily after 1980, reflecting a relative shortage of commodity supplies in the future. It is now almost clear that there will be no such international agricultural commodity shortages during the first half of the 1980s, and that the JAM forecasts were too pessimistic concerning demand–supply balances in the 1980s. This reveals the inherent difficulty of economic forecasting not only to forecast accurately but also to implement these forecasts in a policy decision-making context. The use of general nonlinear functions in the JAM modeling system of (3.1)–(3.3) proved to be very costly, leading to the demise of this system. Other extensive studies on farm products in Japan were carried out by Sasaki (1969, 1970, 1971a, 1971b, 1974).

The USDA–ERS instead developed what has become known as the USDA–GOL (grain–oilseeds–livestock) model [1974] constructed largely through the efforts of Rojko (1978). This model, in integrating the grain–oilseeds sector with the livestock sector, combined an activity analysis formulation of the supply sector [see chapter 14 of Takayama and Judge (1971)] with an attempt to solve a set of linear equations analogous to the left-hand side of system (3.14). For example, by replacing inequality signs by equality signs and using only relevant relations in (3.14)(c), such a model can be solved for non-negative values of the variables. This assumes that the choice of the equations is correct in the sense they are identified by the LSP solution vector.

These modeling efforts subsequently led to a further development in the application of STPA models, particularly that of solving the rarely tried asymmetric Q case.[8] The model that was developed featured nine commodities and two regions (US and the rest of the world) covering the period 1970–75. The preparation of forecasts and the analysis of a stabilization policy for the ensuing period 1975–80 was completed by Hashimoto (1977). Nguyen (1977) also used the model for world trade and reserve policy evaluation by expanding the number of world regions to ten. A robustness test was conducted for 1974, and then a series of trade-related policy evaluations were pursued for 1976. Following these key developments, Whitacre (1979) studied Japanese agricultural trade policies by employing the nine-commodity and five-world region model (USA, Canada, Japan, Australia, and the rest of the world). He tested the validity of the model over the 1974–75 historical period, and then evaluated the impacts of changes in the Japanese agricultural commodity import policies ahead to the 1977–78 period. Similar spatial and intertemporal studies were also pursued by Shei and Thompson (1977) and by Puri et al. (1977) for wheat and pork respectively.

During the years 1974–79 when these agricultural commodity studies were being actively pursued on an international scale, most of the world's commodity markets experienced a return to a condition of approximately stable demand–supply similar to that of the world oil market. Throughout this period, the model back-casting or sample period validations performed by Takayama in the Ford–World Bank project proved to be reasonably good, revealing that the (basically demand-related) structure of agricultural commodity markets did not change during that period, but that sudden shocks such as climate-related supply changes or agricultural policy changes did affect the temporary conditions of these markets.

---

[8] The attempt was for a much more general solution than when only Ω_i or H_i is asymmetric. However, because of the introduction of time, the supply coefficient matrix, for instance in time t, becomes interconnected with earlier matrixes in times $t-1$, $t-2$, etc.

4.2. Energy models

Since 1974, many energy modelers have had an invaluable opportunity to gain experience through direct and indirect participation in economic policy modeling activities within as well as outside of OPEC, particularly in the United States. Among the modeling techniques they employed, Labys (1982a) has confirmed that applications of the Takayama and Judge (1971) class of STPA models did take place. These models proved effective for dealing with the spatial allocations important to international oil trade and with the noncompetitive market conditions that were induced by supply restrictions (see also Chapter 14).

Among applications of STPA models, Kennedy (1974) employed an activity analysis formulation to predict that oil prices were likely to return to their pre-1973–74 level by 1980. This proved to be a valuable modeling experience, yet the erroneous forecasts taught a bitter lesson. It was not the model, but his supply assumption that was too optimistic. Takayama (1976) later applied this model to the 1974 oil market situation with nine downstream products, fifteen crudes, and eight world regions (US–East Coast, US–Gulf Coat, US–West Coast, Japan, Europe, Caribbean Venezuela and OPEC, and the rest of the world). Using linear demand functions for the first five regions and altering the Kennedy supply assumption, the resulting quantity allocations were very close to the actual ones. This experience led Takayama (1979) to develop a design for a world energy model based on STPA which could effectively deal with the many spatial, temporal and processing complexities found in that market.

Meanwhile, the Federal Energy Administration started to build an energy model (a market-oriented energy aggregate economy model of the (3.1)–(3.5) style), to serve the purpose of the Nixon Administration – that of achieving independence from OPEC. The model christened "PIES" (Project Independence Evaluation System) was rarely used by Nixon, and was later shelved by President Ford. In retrospect it has been difficult to pinpoint the cause of the model's ineffectiveness; one of the strongest criticisms of the model was made by Commoner (1979). President Carter, nonetheless, revived the modeling effort, since he needed some numerical support for establishing the Energy Department and the then emerging National Energy Plan (NEP) I (1978).[9]

One aspect of the modeling effort which has proven useful is the "combined" energy model approach of Hogan and Weyant (1980). A theoretical as well as a simulation approach was developed for PIES and IEES which produces a market equilibrium solution by integrating over separate engineering energy supply models, econometric energy demand models, and a linear programming transportation model. While useful in further modeling efforts, such a simultaneous

---

[9] The fullest description of PIES can be found in an Energy Information Administration (1979) report. An international version of the model termed IEES (International Energy Evaluation System) was also constructed and its documentation can be found in a related Energy Information Administration (1980) report.

modeling solution can be obtained without integration in standard STPA models, e.g., the STPA energy model design of Takayama (1979).

Other aspects of the modeling effort included an expansion by the Department of Energy to produce several specialized and linked models. An example is the fully regionalized (ten US regions) model later named "MEFS" (Midterm Energy Forecasting System). This model took the form of the nonlinear programming problem of (3.1)–(3.5).[10] Although the ultimate quality of PIES was never established by those who evaluated it, the multimillion dollar a year operation came to a grinding halt in 1982, one year after the Reagan Administration took office. Examples of these model evaluations can be found in the US–ODE/EIA Model Evaluation Documentations and related reports (1979–81), the US–DOC validation reviews edited by Gass (1979), and several individual reviews such as that by Gordon (1977) and by Labys (1982b).

The OPEC energy price hikes in 1979 and 1980 were quite dramatic. But by this time, it was OPEC's concern to know how much the demand for their crudes would be reduced by this second price hike.[11] It is clear that STPA models such as that developed by Takayama (1976) or by Kennedy (1974), etc. could evaluate this price effect. The nature of the world energy market, however, seemed to have changed into a kind of gaming situation in which both producer–exporter countries and consumer–importer countries observe spot market and netback values to see which way the oil price will move. A number of energy modeling studies thus emerged which have employed noncompetitive market-oriented approaches to explain this behavior. For example, see the econometric model of Verleger (1972), the Stackelberg model of Cremer and Weitzman (1976), and the Nash–Cournot model of Salant (1981).

Among other energy applications of STPA models, the coal industry whose economic recovery has depended crucially on the oil price increases has become a focus of attention. Not surprisingly, Labys and his associates at West Virginia University have effectively applied the QP version of STPA models to domestic coal issues. Liebenthal (1978) was the first to construct a QP model to examine interstate supply competition in Appalachian steam coal markets. This work was expanded upon by Yang (1978) and by Labys and Yang (1980) who employed econometric demand and supply equations to reach QP equilibrium solution between coals originating in Appalachian coal markets and shipped to Eastern electric utility districts. This model was subsequently applied by Newcomb and

---

[10] There have been many variants of PIES ands MEFS and some other simulators. For these and other energy/economy combined modeling schemes, the reader should refer to more recent reviews in this area such as by Terrence and Goldberg (1981) and by Labys (1982b).

[11] For example, oil prices (Saudi Arabian Light–34° API) jumped from $13.34 in 1979 to $26.00 in 1980 and then to $32.00 in 1981. See the 1980 Annual Report to Congress, Volume 2, Data: US–DOE/EIA.

Fan (1980) who expanded the supply sector to include geological factors surrounding coal deposits. Independently in England, Dutton (1982) applied QP to analyze the prices and allocations of international steam coal trade.

Other studies by Yang and Labys (1981, 1982) have examined the stability and response structure of the quadratic programming STPA model using different forms of sensitivity analysis. This has included work not only with inherent model stability but also with responses to various shocks such as changes in excise taxes or transportation costs. Most recently, they (1984) examined the potential of employing linear complementarity programming solutions to expand their STPA model of the Appalachian coal industry to include natural gas. This work confirmed the STPA modeling possibility mentioned above, that of solving the asymmetric Ω_i and H_i matrix problem.

Finally, the electricity industry has also been the subject of STPA modeling, particularly in the examination of investment in generation facilities. A genuinely regionalized (nine Petroleum Allocation and Defense Districts) electricity model was constructed by Uri (1971). This model covering the period 1970–90 examined the efficient pricing and allocation of electricity as well as investment in the generating capacities of (1) hydro-electric, (2) fossil, and (3) nuclear facilities. Results of the analysis showed one way of generating investment; that is, the use of Lagrangians on the capacity constraints as their respective shadow prices. This work was later refined to accommodate a genuinely capital theoretic approach to model capital investment (1976a, b).

4.3. Mineral models

The oil crises of 1974 and 1979 together with subsequent inflation also had an impact on planners and policy-makers in the world's mineral industries. In addition to a sudden perception that world mineral supplies were becoming scarce, a fear arose of possible cartel formation in mineral markets other than petroleum. This led to a surge in the construction of mineral models. Some precedent existent for the extension of spatial price equilibrium and programming models in the minerals field. Beginning in the late 1950s the modeling of the US iron and steel industry was approached as an application of process analysis. Fabian (1958) applied static linear programming (cost minimization) to steelmaking processes and Henderson (1958) to coal allocation; Kendrick (1967) advanced linear programming to include investment analysis; and Higgins (1969) integrated a linear programming process model with a simultaneous econometric model of the US steel industry.

These various model developments together with the work of Day (1963) on recursive programming (RP) advanced the programming approach by concentrating on intertemporal market adjustments and by introducing a behavioral element (limited rationality) in the industrial decision-making mechanism. His programming algorithm represented a sequence of optimization problems in which the parameters of a linear model depend on optimal solutions of the model obtained earlier in this sequence. Nelson (1970) working with Day included regional or spatial equilibrium in developing an interregional recursive programming model of the US iron and steel industry. Abe (1973) extended this analysis to include adjustments between desired and actual steel-making capacity by including a particular system of lagged variables. As generalized by Day and Nelson (1973), this framework is useful for analyzing mineral industry development problems in a dynamic investment context. It was also applied by Tabb (1968) to analyze technological change in the growth of the coal industry.

Other mineral modelers have attempted to solve the STPA problem by using integration procedures which would appear to be less effective than quadratic programming or linear complementarity programming. Process modeling and spatial modeling were combined in a linear programming framework by Copithorne (1973) to model the world nickel industry, and by Kovisars (1975) to model the world copper industry. In constructing a model of the world zinc market, Kovisars (1976) introduced a temporal dimension by successive lagged adjustments of demand, cost, and capacity variables. Of some interest is his use of an integrating algorithm similar to that proposed above by Hogan and Weyant (1980) to integrate a demand model over time with a programming supply model and related resource requirements.

A problem in developing STPA models is providing a specific economic linkage mechansim over time. While lagged variables are important in this respect, mineral markets have in themselves two internal mechanisms for accomplishing this linkage: (1) stock adjustment in the form of materials inventories, and (2) stock adjustment in the form of reserve or productive capacity adjustments. Because of the long time lags necessary for mineral project development, mineral modelers have been more concerned with using STPA models for investment analysis. While Uri (1976), accomplished this task within the quadratic programming framework, Kendrick (1967) independently chose to modify linear programming in the direction of mixed integer programming (MIP). Like recursive programming, it represents an application of linear programming; only the integer characteristic is introduced to accommodate combinations of 0–1 variables which reflect the nonexistence or existence of a mining or production facility. Like the integrating approach of Kovisars, it employs a fixed demand specification, but suggestions have been made for endogenizing demand and price, as in the quadratic programming STPA model.

Applications and advances of the mixed integer programming approach are fully described in the work of Kendrick and Stoutjesdijk (1978) who explain its use in analyzing industrial investment programs in regional economic development. This work has stemmed from applications by the World Bank to study fertilizer sector planning [see Choksi et al. (1980)]. Other applications of this approach can be seen in the work of Dammert (1980) who employed it to study copper investment, allocation, and demands in Latin America. Dammert also showed how reserve levels and reserve limits could be coupled with depletion in the mining and processing of different ore goods. A similar approach has been taken by Brown et al. (1982) in their modeling of worldwide investment analysis in the aluminum industry. Their projections describe long-term levels of investment, production and trade needed to satisfy markets while minimizing overall costs. Finally, several of Kendrick's students at the University of Texas have applied MIP to the above energy area. Models were built for analyzing the Gulf Coast refining complex by Langston (1983), the Korean electric power industry by Kwang-Ha Kang (1981), and the Korean petrochemical industry by Jung Suh (1982).

The development of linear complementarity programming has already been mentioned as a way of dealing with energy modeling problems where multiple final product markets exhibit asymmetry in establishing demand equations and demand parameter estimates. A milestone in the application of this approach to the minerals industry can be witnessed in the world iron and steel industry model (WISE) constructed by Hashimoto (1977). This model achieved two results. First, it replaced the short-term stock adjustment mechanism of STPA models with the investment adjustment mechanism as proposed by Uri (1977). And second, it modified the concept of expectations based on backward information to include that of expectations based on forward information. The latter permitted a more complex description of investment decision making by analyzing market situations in which these decisions are based on rational expectations as compared to those based on actual industry plans.

Returning to the mentioned fear of mineral cartel formation, several regional programming models have attempted to address mineral market behavior under noncompetitive market conditions. This work has proven significant not only because of the threat of cartel formation but also because of the increased recognition of the noncompetitive nature of price and quantity adjustments in a number of mineral markets [see Labys (1980)]. In projects sponsored by the US Bureau of Mines and the National Science Foundation, Hibbard and Soyster of the Virginia Polytechnic Institute constructed highly detailed and disaggregated dynamic linear programming models of the US copper [Hibbard et al. (1980)] and US aluminum [Hibbard et al. (1979)] industries. It was Soyster and Sherali (1981), however, who investigated the structure of the copper industry and its corresponding model (MIDAS-II) under oligopolistic market conditions. Although the authors employed a linear programming framework, Takayama and Judge (1971) had already stipulated that STPA models might be redefined to deal with the problem of optimal spatial pricing and allocation for duopolists, oligopolists under collusion, market sharing arrangements, monopoly or monopsony, and bilateral monopoly.

Soyster and Sherali thus employed the results of Murphy et al. (1980) to modify their programming algorithm so as to achieve Nash–Cournot [Nash (1951)] equilibrium conditions. While traditional approaches to reaching such an equilibrium have usually relied on the complementary pivot theory of Lemke and Howson (1964) and of Scarf (1973), the modelers instead relied on solving a sequence of convex programming problems based on the underlying production conditions; e.g. Sherali et al. (1980). The results of their analysis showed that the incorporation of market structure significantly changed the spatial, temporal and process solution of the model.

4.4.   Where do we stand?

The two model developments, the Uri model and the Takayama–Hashimoto model, reveal the crucial fact that a quadratic formulation for the optimal investment determination does *not* lead to a formal quadratic programming matrix structure in which the M matrix takes the following form:

$$M = \begin{bmatrix} Q & -G \\ G' & 0 \end{bmatrix} \tag{4.1}$$

where

$$
\left\{
\begin{aligned}
& Q = \begin{bmatrix} & & -I_y & 0 \\ & & 0 & I_x \\ I_y & 0 & \Omega & 0 \\ 0 & -I_x & 0 & H \end{bmatrix} \\[2mm]
& G = \begin{bmatrix} -G_y \\ -G_x \end{bmatrix} \\[2mm]
& q = \{0' \; 0' \; \lambda' \; -\nu' \; t'\}', \\
& w = \{w'_{p_y} \; w'_{p^x} \; -w'_y \; -w'_x \; w'_z\}', \\
& r = \{p'_y \; p^{x\prime} \; y' \; x' \; z'\}', \text{ and} \\
& s = 4m \cdot n + m \cdot n \cdot n.
\end{aligned}
\right. \tag{4.2}
$$

Rather M is found to have a structure similar to (3.15). From this one can conclude that the Uri formulation and the Takayama–Hashimoto formulation are exactly the same for a single final commodity case: but the LCP formulation is the only way to deal with the investment problem if multiple final product markets exhibit an asymmetric Q matrix property. Even in shorter-term situations where investment analysis is not necessary, the LCP formulation such as that of Yang–Labys model permits multiple product analysis where asymmetry in the Q matrix is considered to be a more realistic parametric structure.

In a large number of commodity markets (agricultural, energy, and minerals as well as other natural resources), the importance of inventories (or short-term stockholding) in determining the price level(s) of the commodity(ies) is undoubtedly clear (crude oil, grains, tin, to name only a few). If the future demand situation for the commodity(ies) can be assumed known and stable, and the supply(ies) are known (in a functional form) or controllable from a firm's or society's point of view, an efficient (or optimal) inventory trajectory can be determined for each and all commodities. The schemes can be those followed by Guise and Aggrey-Mensah (1973) in the banana market who made clear the longest banana storage period on the shop counter, an by Hashimoto (1977) who developed rather ingenious modifications of the models presented in Takayama and Judge (1971) in studying the grain–oilseeds–livestock markets.

It goes without saying that the very importance of the concept of "regional" or "interregional" pricing and allocation has by now been clearly recognized. A majority of the models used for the purpose of policy evaluation and forecasting are somehow related to (or contain within themselves) the inherent spatial or interregional aspects of commodity markets.

In the case of agricultural commodities, fluctuations in supply seem to be dominated by the effects of climate on crop yields and unless these effects are accurately captured, which at this stage seems to be quite difficult, the efforts to derive an efficient storage trajectory for each (and all) agricultural commodity(ies) may prove to be unsuccessful. In the case of energy and mineral commodities, fluctuations in supply occur less often and fluctuations in demand due to changes in business conditions tend to be more dominant.

Within this industrial market environment, an inventory analysis model can be effectively formulated and solved in our STPA framework. However, interestingly enough, in this field scarcely any inventory model that uses the STPA framework exists in the literature. This does not necessarily imply that inventory or stock adjustments are not important in these industries. On the contrary, they have played an extremely important role, for example, in the recent history of the petroleum (1981–82) market and the tin market (1982). Rather, the inventory adjustment issue in these industries that requires a large sum of capital investment for their expansion is a short-term operational issue. In comparison to the short-term issue, the most important single issue among intermediate or long-term issues is that of stock adjustment in the form of changes in capacity required over, say, thirty years in the future.

Regarding the use of LP in the Day (1963) "recursive programming" framework, this can be cited as an interesting modeling exercise explicitly introducing a behavioral element (limited rationality) in the industrial decision-making mechanism [see Abe (1973), Abe et al. (1978)]. The World Bank research group has applied LP and MIP models to evaluate investment decision-making policies in the fertilizer industry (1980), the aluminum industry (1982a), and the iron and steel industry (1982b) with special consideration both to the issue of scale economy and to that of the plant indivisibility (integrality). In this framework the future demand forecasts for these commodities were given as point-estimates even though the underlying demand functions did exist in their econometric form (with price, income, and other variables as independent variables). Incorporating the existing fully nonlinear (say, double logarithmic) regional demand functions in the STPA framework leads us to a full-scale NL model which we have avoided for the specific reason of the astronomical computer time requirement in solving it.

A natural extension of a programming model with a single objective function is an approach with multiple objectives, which leads to an approach similar to that of generating a community welfare frontier in the field of modern welfare economics [for a survey of this approach, see Nijkamp (1980)]. Also, for a mind-expanding-type approach in spatial dynamics, Chapter 6 in this Handbook presents interesting alternatives.

5.   Concluding remarks

In the domain of individual firm management, the theoretical and operational modeling of inventory control and capital investment decisions has occurred routinely. However, the modeling of interregional and/or international competition of firms in a commodity market or a set of markets for interrelated commodities including noncompetitive behavior has rarely been conducted. Nonetheless, the 1972–73 grain shortage and the 1973–74 exercise of market power by OPEC have heightened the importance of such modeling efforts.

In the domain of national or regional planning and economic decision making, international and interregional commodity modeling has been employed by various private, national, or international research institutions and governmental policy decision-making agencies. Nonlinear programming and linear programming models have been widely used in this context. QP and LCP models can be looked upon as a natural extension of the LP models in the sense that the price–quantity relationship in the markets is captured in its simplest form. In this context both RP and MIP can also be considered to be variants of this approach.

In this chapter, we have briefly and selectively reviewed modeling efforts in the spatial programming modeling areas, and have introduced recent developments in LCP modeling including a world-wide bauxite–alumina–aluminum industry investment analysis model, and a regional coal and gas demand–supply alloca-tion model. It was pointed out in Section 3 that the quadratic programming model (due to the existence of substitution–complementarity relationships in demand functions and supply functions in the model) takes exactly the form of the LCP model, thus allowing the researchers to formulate this model in the LCP format [Hashimoto (1977), Yang and Labys (1984)]. Clearly the LCP formulation has a wider coverage in application than its QP counterparts. For the LCP models dealing with the *ad valorem* tariff and the investment analysis discussed in this chapter, a reasoning behind the Lemke-solvability or PPM solvability was provided at last, giving an *ex post* justification of solvability of the former model presented in chapter 13 of the Takayama and Judge (1971) book.

Possibilities for future research can be divided into two areas. The first area is the theoretical investigation of existence, uniqueness, and stability of optimal investment patterns (and capital earnings streams) leading, for example, towards the (infinite time horizon) time invariant optimal investment profile [Evers (1978)]. The second area constitutes a further application of this model formula-tion to investigate policy effectiveness of spatial commodity models in a national and an international context. The first area can be expanded to incorporate a more general commodity modeling framework such as that presented in Section 2 of this chapter. The second area offers potential benefits to many commodity researchers and hence some useful results are expected in the future.

There is one nagging point in this and other more general NL programming fields. In comparison to the LP, RP or MIP counterparts, the availability of software packages to solve QP and LCP models is rather limited. Since the development of a large-scale proprietary software package named MPXIII-QUAD in 1975, designed especially for general purpose LCP models, only a limited number of software packages designed for small to intermediate scale problems have been available. Particularly familiar to us are Tomlin's (1976) LCL and Takayama's (1979) LCRANG, the latter having been derived from RANDQP. For some future policy analysis, it is highly desirable that there exists at least one efficient LCP software comparable to that of present LP counterparts such as MPSX, MPXIII or GAMS.

References

Abe, A. M. (1973) 'Dynamic micro-economic models of production, investment and technological change in the US and Japanese iron and steel industries', in: G. G. Judge and T. Takayama eds., *Studies in economic planning over space and time*. Amsterdam: North-Holland, 345–367.

Abe, A. M., R. H. Day, J. P. Nelson, and W. K. Tabb (1978) 'Behavioral, suboptimizing models of industrial production, investment and technology', in: R. H. Day and A. Cigno, eds., *Modeling economic change: the recursive programming approach*. Amsterdam: North-Holland.

Bartilson, S., G. A. Zepp, and T. Takayama (1978) *A user's manual for the LCRAND mathematical programming system*, Economics Report 91, Food and Resources, Economics Department, Univer-sity of Florida.

Brown, M., A. Dammert, A. Meeraus, and A. Stoutjesdijk (1982a) *Worldwide investment analysis*: *the case of aluminum*, Preliminary Report, The World Bank.

Choksi, A. M., A. Meeraus, and A. J. Stoutjesdijk (1980) *The planning of investment programs in the fertilizer industry*, A World Bank Research Publication, Johns Hopkins.

Colstad, C. D. Abbey, and R. Bivins (1983) 'Modeling international steam coal trade', Paper No. LA-9661-MS, Los Alamos national Laboratory, New Mexico.

Commoner, B. (1979) *The politics of energy*. New York: Alfred Knopf.

Copithorne, L. W. (1973) *The use of linear programming in the economic analysis of a metal industry*: *the case of nickel*, Monograph. Department of Economics, University of Manitoba.

Cottle, R. W. and G. B. Dantzig (1968) 'Complementary pivot theory of mathematical programming', in: *Linear algebra and its applications*. New York: Amsterdam Elsevier Publishing Co., 103–125.

Cremer, J. and M. L. Weitzman (1976) 'OPEC and the monopoly price of oil', *European Economic Review*, 8:156–164.

Dammert, A. (1980) 'Planning investments in the copper sector in Latin America', in: W. Labys, M. Nadiri, and J. Nunez del Arco, eds, *Commodity markets and Latin American development*: *a modeling approach*. New York: National Bureau of Economic Research.

Dantzig, G. B. (1951a) 'Maximization of a linear function of variables subject to linear inequalities', in T. C. Koopmans, ed., *Activity analysis of production and allocation*, New York: John Wiley, 339–347.

Dantzig, G. B. (1951b) 'Application of the Simplex method to a transportation problem', in T. C. Koopmans, ed., *Activity Analysis of Production and Allocation*. New York: John Wiley, 359–373.

Day, R. (1963) *Recursive programming and production response*. Amsterdam: North-Holland Publishing Co.

Day, R. H. and J. P. Nelson (1973) 'A class of dynamic models for describing and projecting industrial development', *Journal of Econometrics*, 1:155–190.

Dean, R. D. et al. (1970) *Spatial economic theory*. New York: Free Press.

Dutton, C. M. (1982) 'Modelling the international steam coal trade', Paper No. EDP21, Energy Research Group, Cavendish Laboratory, Cambridge University, England.

Energy Information Administration (1979) *Documentation of the project independence evaluation system*, Vols. I–IV. Washington, D.C.: US Department of Energy.

Enke, S. (1951) 'Equilibrium among spatially separated markets: Solution by electric analogue', *Econometrica*, 19, 48–78.

Evers, J. J. M. (1978) 'More with the Lemke complementarity algorithm', *Mathematical programming*, Vol. 15, pp. 214–219.

Fabian, T. (1958) 'A linear programming model of integrated iron and steel production', *Management Science*: 415–429.

Gass, S. I. (1979) 'Validation and assessment issues of energy models', NBS Special Publication 569, National Bureau of Standards, US Department of Commerce.

Gordon, R. L. (1977) 'Economic analysis of coal supply: an assessment of existing studies', EPRI Report EIA-496, Electric Power Research Institute, Palo Alto.

Guise, J. W. B. and W. Aggrey-Mensah (1973) 'An evaluation of policy alternatives facing Australian banana producers', in G. G. Judge and T. Takayama, eds., *Studies in economic planning over space and time*. Amsterdam: North-Holland Publishing Company, 519–535.

Hashimoto, H. (1977) 'World food projection models, projections and policy evaluations', Unpublished Ph.D. Thesis, Department of Economics, University of Illinois: and Thamnu Sihsobhon (1981) 'A world iron and steel economy model: the WISE model', in: *World bank commodity models*, Vol. 1, 111–146 plus three appendices.

Henderson, J. M. (1958) *The efficiency of the coal industry*: *an application of linear programming*. Cambridge, Mass.: Harvard University Press.

Hibbard, W. R. et al. (1979) 'An engineering econometric model of the US aluminum industry', *Proceedings of the AIME*.

Hibbard, W. R., A. L. Soyster, and R. S. Gates (1980) 'A disaggregated supply model of the US copper industry operating in an aggregated world supply/demand system', *Material Society*, 4(3):261–284.

Hibbard, W. R. et al. (1982) 'Supply prospects for the US copper industry: alternative scenarios: Midas II computer model', *Materials and Society*, 6, No. 2:201–210.

Higgins, C. I. (1969) 'An econometric description of the US steel industry', in: L. R. Klein, ed., *Essays in industrial economics*, Vol. II. Philadelphia: Wharton School of Finance and Commerce.

Hogan, W. H. and J. P. Weyant (1980) 'Combined energy models', Discussion Paper E80-02, Kennedy School of Government, Harvard University.

Japan Ministry of Agriculture Contract Research Publication (March 1964) *Sekai shokuryo jukyu model ni yoru jukyu tembo* (Demand/Supply outlook by the World Food Demand/Supply Model) —Forecasts for 1980 and 1985. Kenkyu-jo: Mitsubish So-Go.

Judge, G. G. and T. Takayama, eds. (1973) *Studies in economic planning over space and time*. Amsterdam: North-Holland Publishing Co.

Jung Suh (1982) 'An investment planning model for the refining and petrochemical industry in Korea', Ph.D. Thesis, University of Texas at Austin.

Kendrick, D. (1967) *Programming investments in the processing industries*. Cambridge, MA: MIT Press.

Kendrick, D., A. Meeraus, and J. Altorre (1982) *The planning of investment programs in the steel industry*, Preliminary Report, The World Bank.

Kendrick, D. and A. Stoutjesdijk (1978) *The planning of industrial investment programs, a methodology*, A World Bank Research Publication, Johns Hopkins.

Kennedy, M. (1974) 'An economic model of the world oil market', *Bell Journal of Economics and Management Science*, 5, No. 2:540–577.

Koopmans, T. C. (1949) 'Optimal utilization of the transport system', *Econometrica*, 17:136–146.

Kovisars, L. (1975) 'Copper trade flow model', World Minerals Availability, SRI Project MED 3742-74.

Kovisars, L. (1976) 'World production consumption and trade in zinc—an LP model', US Bureau of Mines Contract Report J-0166003, Stanford Research Institute, Stanford.

Kuhn, N. W. and A. W. Tucker (1950) 'Nonlinear programming', in: J. Neyman ed., *Proceedings of the Second Berkeley Symposium on Mathematical Statistics and Probability*. Berkeley: Univ. of California Press, 481–492.

Kwang Ha Kang (1981) 'An investment programming model of the Korean electric power industry', Ph.D. Thesis, University of Texas at Austin.

Labys, W. C. (1977) *Minerals commodity modeling, the state of the art*. College of Minerals and Energy Resources, West Virginia University.

Labys, W. C. (1980) *Market structure, bargaining power and resource price formation*. Lexington, Ma: Heath Lexington Books.

Labys, W. C. (1982a) 'A critical review of international energy modeling methodologies', Energy Laboratory Working Paper, No. 82-034Wp, Massachusetts Institute of Technology.

Labys, W. C. (1982b) 'Critique of the international energy evaluation system', Contract Report, Energy Laboratory, Massachusetts Institute of Technology.

Labys, W. C. and P. K. Pollak (1984) *Commodity Models for Policy Analysis and Forecasting*. The Hague: Croom-Helm.

Labys, W. C. and C. W. Yang (1980) 'A quadratic programming model of the Appalachian steam coal market', *Journal of Energy Economics*.

Langston, V. C. (1983) 'An investment model for the US Gulf Coast refining petrochemical complex', Ph.D. Thesis, University of Texas at Austin.

Launhardt, W. (1885) *Mathematische Begründung der Volkswirtschaftslehre*. Leipzig.

Lemke, C. E. and J. T. Howson, Jr. (1964) 'Equilibrium points of bimatrix games', *Journal of Society of Industrial Application of Mathematics*, 12:413–423.

Libbin, J. D. and M. D. Boehji (1977) 'Interregional structure of the US coal industry', *American Journal of Agricultural Economics*: 456–466.

Liebenthal, A. (1978) 'Interstate supply competition in the Appalachian steam coal market', Ph.D. Thesis, West Virginia University.

Murphy, F. H., H. D. Sherali, and A. L. Soyster (1980) 'A mathematical programming approach for determining oligopolistic market equilibrium', Virginia Polytechnic Institute and State University, Blacksburg, Virginia.

Nash, J. (1951) 'Non-cooperative games', *Ann. Math.*, 54(2):286–295.

Nelson, J. P. (1970) 'An interregional recursive programming model of the US iron and steel industry: 1947–1967', Ph.D. Thesis, University of Wisconsin.

Newcomb, R. T. and J. Fan (1980) 'Coal market analysis issues', EPRI Report EA-1575, Electric Power Research Institute, Palo Alto.

Nguyen, H. D. (1977) 'World food projection models and short-run world trade and reserve policy evaluation', Unpublished Ph.D. Thesis, University of Illinois.

Nijkamp, P. (1980) *Multidimensional spatial data and decision analysis*. New York: Wiley.

Palander, T. (1935) *Beiträge zur Standortstheorie*. Uppsala: Almqvist and Wicksells Boktryckeri A-B.

Puri, R. G., K. D. Meilke, and T. G. MacAulay (1977) 'North American–Japanese pork trade: an application of quadratic planning', *Canadian Journal of Agricultural Economics*, 25:61–79.

Rojko, A. S. (1978) *Alternative futures for world food in* 1985: *vol.* 3, *world GOL model structure and equations*, FAER 151, ESCS, US Department of Agriculture.

Salant, S. W. (1981) 'Imperfect competition in the international energy market: a computerized Nash–Cournot model', *Operations Research*.

Samuelson, P. A. (1952) 'Spatial price equilibrium and linear programming', *American Economic Review*, 42:283–303.

Sasaki, K. (1969) 'Spatial equilibrium in Eastern Japan's milk market', *Journal of Rural Economics*, 41, no. 3.

Sasaki, K. (1970) 'Spatial equilibrium in Eastern Japan's pork industry', *Journal of Rural Economics*, 42, no. 1.

Sasaki, K. (1971a) 'Estimation of the optimum regional shipments of Hokkaido's milk', *Annual report on dairy planning in central Nemuro region, 1970* (in Japanese). Sapporo: Hokkaido Development Bureau.

Sasaki, K. (1971b) 'Spatial equilibrium of the broiler industry', *Journal of Rural Economics*, 43, no. 1.

Sasaki, K. (1974) *Projection of Tokyo's demands for four major vegetables produced in Hokkaido*, Research Report (in Japanese). Sapporo: Hokkaido Development Bureau.

Scarf, H. (1973) *The computation of economic equilibria*. New Haven, Connecticut: Yale University Press.

Shei, S. Y. and R. L. Thompson (1977) 'The impact of trade restrictions on price stability in the world wheat market', *American Journal of Agricultural Economics* 59:628–638.

Sherali, H. D., A. L. Soyster, and F. H. Murphy (1980). 'Mathematical analysis of the interactions between oligopolistic firms and a competitive fringe', Virginia Polytechnic Institute and State University, Blacksburg, Virginia.

Soyster, A. and H. D. Sherali (1981) 'On the influence of market structure in modeling the US copper industry', *International Journal of Management Science*: 381–388.

Tabb, W. K. (1968) 'A recursive programming model of resource allocation in technological change in the US bituminous coal industry', Ph.D. Thesis, University of Wisconsin.

Takayama, T. (1976) 'Market-oriented world petroleum modeling', Venezuela Project Report No. 9.

Takayama, T. (1979) 'An application of spatial and temporal price equilibrium model to world energy modeling', *Papers of the Regional Science Association*, 41:43–58.

Takayama, T. and H. Hashimoto (1982) 'A comparative study of linear programming model and linear complementarity programming model in multi-regional investment analysis.', Preliminary and Confidential Report, The World Bank.

Takayama, T. and G. G. Judge (1964) 'Equilibrium among spatially separated markets: Reformulation', *Econometrica*, 32, 510–524.

Takayama, T. and G. G. Judge (1971) *Spatial and temporal price and allocation models*. Amsterdam: North-Holland Publishing Company.

Terrence, E. D. and H. M. Golbert (1981) 'Dynamic equilibrium energy modeling: the Canadian BALANCE model'. *Operations Research*, 29, no. 5.

Thompson, R. L. (1981) 'A survey of recent US developments in international agricultural trade models', Bibliographies and Literature of Agriculture No. 21. USDA-ERS.

Tomlin, J. A. (1976) 'Programming guide to LCPL: a program for solving linear complementarity problems by Lemke's method', Operations Research Center, Stanford University.

Uri, N. (1971) 'The impact of environmental regulations on the allocation and pricing of electric energy', *Journal of Environmental Management*, 5:215–227.

Uri, N. (1976a) *Toward an efficient allocation of electric energy*. Lexington, Mass.: Lexington Books.

Uri, N. (1976b) 'Planning in public utilities', *Regional Science and Urban Economics*, 6:105–125.

US Department of Energy/Energy Information Administration (1979-1981). *Annual report to Con-*

gress (1979), Vol. 3. *Annual report to Congress* (1980), Vol. 3. *The integrating model of the project independence evaluation system* (in 4 volumes) (1979). *Analysis quality report series* (1981) David Freedman and Thomas Rothenberg.

Verleger, P., Jr. (1972) *Oil markets in turmoil, an economic analysis.* Ballinger Publishing Company.

von Thünen, J. H. (1826) *Der Isolierte Staat in Beziehung auf Landwirtschaft und Nationalökonomie.* Hamburg. English translation (1966) *von Thünen's Isolated State.* London: Pergamon Press Ltd.

Weber, A. (1909) *Über den Standort der Industrien.* Tübingen. English Translation Alfred Weber (1928) *Theory of Location of Industries.* Chicago: University of Chicago Press.

Whitacre, R. (1979) 'An evaluation of Japanese agricultural policies with a multiregion–multicommodity model', Unpublished Ph.D. Thesis, Department of Agricultural economics, University of Illinois.

Yang, C. W. (1978) 'A critical analysis of spatial commodity modeling: the case of coal', Ph.D. Thesis, West Virginia University.

Yang, C. W. and C. W. Labys (1981) 'Stability of Appalachian coal shipments under policy variations', *The Energy Journal*, 2, No. 3:111–128.

Yang, C. W. and W. C. Labys (1982) 'A sensitivity analysis of the stability property of the QP commodity model', *Empirical Economics*, 7:93–107.

Yang, C. W. and W. C. Labys (1983) 'Spatial taxation effects on regional coal economic activities', *Materials and Society.*

Yang, C. W. and W. C. Labys (1984) 'A sensitivity analysis of the linear complementarity programming model: the case of Appalachian steam coal and natural gas markets', in: T. Takayama, W. Labys and N. Uri, eds., *Quantitative methods for commodity market economic analysis over space and time.* JAI Press.

Chapter 6

REGIONAL ECONOMIC DYNAMICS

Å. E. ANDERSSON and R. E. KUENNE

1. The scope and methodology of spatial dynamics

Static spatial analysis is formally concerned with four reasonably distinct bodies of instantaneous spatial phenomena with their determining strategic variables;

(1) *Locations*, or the spatial coordinates of localized economic activities.

(2) *Interaction flows*, or the intensity of spatial factor, goods, and information flows among points and/or regions.

(3) *Increases or decreases in availability* of regional goods, factors, or income incident to changes in exogenous variables.

(4) *Spatial structures*, including the areal or curvilinear patterns of economic activities, such as land use patterns, urban structure, transportation networks, and market or supply areas.

By strategic variables we mean the total of relevant variables that a specific theory or model includes. They divide into endogenous and exogenous variables or parameters.

This chapter will be concerned with theories and models that deal with changes through time of phenomena in the same four categories, when such changes are the products of truly dynamic processes.

Put simply, a dynamic model or theory is one whose structural equations contain nontrivial temporal forms of the endogenous variables. Such temporal forms include intertemporally subscripted variables, time derivatives, and integrals or sums over time. By nontrivial we mean to exclude such practices as defining investment in an essentially static model to be the derivative of the capital stock with respect to time. This definition excludes models of intertemporal comparative statics which move their endogenous variables through time wholly by parametric changes administered in a predetermined time pattern (see Category 3 above). Truly dynamic models internalize their laws of change within their structural definition, giving rise to an endogenous time process.

The goals sought, problems encountered, and methods employed by regional economic dynamics are parallel to but distinct from those of its static counter-

Handbook of Regional and Urban Economics, Volume I, Edited by P. Nijkamp
©Elsevier Science Publishers BV, 1986

parts. The aims are generally to determine specific values for the endogenous variables in a numerically specified model or, less concretely, to gain qualitative insights into the structure of the solution to a model in general, nonspecified form. The methods for derivations of the structural equations from the set of assumptions and parameters include outright assumptions of form, the use of first- and second-order optimization conditions, or the use of dynamic forms of spatial interaction theory (e.g. gravity or diffusion models). Means of deriving theorems are those of comparative dynamics, in which parameters are changed singly to study the effect upon solution trajectories or structures. The best known of such parametric shocks are those administered to the initial position of the model to study the stability of the original solution.

The methodologies for performing the tasks of dynamic analysis, while generally analogous to their static counterparts, are usually more complicated. Our presentation must assume a basic familiarity with the more important of these techniques, although some of the newer forms will be explained at an elementary level. Those which are featured with suggested sources for their exposition are the following:

(1) *Differential and difference equations, stability of equilibrium solutions and of systems* [Baumol (1970), Rainville (1964), Takayama (1974), Hirsch and Smale (1974)].

(2) *Calculus of variations, optimal control theory, and dynamic programming* [Miller (1979), Intriligator (1971), Hiller and Lieberman (1980)].

(3) *Linear and nonlinear programming, Markov processes* [Hillier and Lieberman (1980), Fiacco and McCormick (1968)].

(4) *Bifurcation and especially catastrophe theory* [Poston and Stewart (1978), Haken (1983), Gilmore (1981)].

The remainder of this chapter will present the most influential work in the authors' judgment in the dynamics of the quartet of subjects discussed in the categories above: locations, flows, changes, and structures. Section 2 presents work in the location and transportation fields. Interaction analysis within dynamic contexts is presented in Section 3. Growth in regional income and economic activity is discussed in Section 4, and factor growth in Section 5. Structural change is dealt with in Sections 2 and 5, the latter section being concerned with spatial mobility. Finally, in Section 6, we discuss the current state of regional dynamic analysis and potential developments in future research.

Two major achievements in spatial analysis escape this classification. Isard et al. (1979) have sought to develop a "general" all-inclusive theory of space and temporal economics that unites these two dimensions indissolubly through the use of field theory of classical physics. Theirs is a general theory that seeks to enclose all of spatial economics in order to integrate it and give perspective to its partial components. Explicitly for a linear economy and implicitly for a two-dimensional spatial economy, they define a general function $U(x, t)$ that describes the "interactions" of point x at time t with all other points x'. Most simply for example, $U(x, t)$ is the flow of goods through x at t that summarizes the effects of all other points' x' exports to x and themselves via x. The authors believe this function provides the conceptual framework for a distinctively spatial dynamic analysis because the $\dot{U}(x, t)$ yields a differential equation of motion that brings space and time into a union in the solution to dynamic systems. $\dot{U}(x, t)$ might be energized by differences in the productivity of capital or proximity to markets of x, and in conjunction with conventional differential equations with respect to time (investment functions, etc.) it determines a solution trajectory with space integral to the solution [Isard et al. (1979, chs. 5, 6, 9, 10, 12), Liossatos (1980)].

Although it is difficult to agree with the authors that the introduction of the interaction equation of motion is the general integrating factor, or even that one such gravitational analogue is possible, the work is a unique attempt to map the boundaries of spatial dynamics, to search for a badly needed integration of the two economic dimensions, and to trace the filiations among the four bodies of analysis we review in the remainder of this chapter.

The second exception to our adopted framework is Puu's pioneering definition and exploration of the spatial stability of transportation and location structures, [see Puu, (1977, 1979a, 1979b, 1981a, 1981b, 1982)]. Spatial stability is the analogue of temporal stability that, unlike the Isard et al. work, mostly abstracts from time. Its dependence upon differential equations and its parallels with temporal dynamic stability have led us to include it in our report. A discussion of it will be found in Section 2.3.2.

2. Dynamic locational and transportation structures

We shall limit the treatment of locational dynamics somewhat arbitrarily to the motion of punctiform spatial entities through space and time under theoretical regimes. Our interest in transportation is not in these systems as such, but rather in their supporting relationship to locational structures.

2.1. Competitive repositioning of units through space and time

Most of the effort in dynamic location theory is concerned with spatial oligopoly processes with lagged reactive and conjectural variation strategies. Two questions are relevant in the analyses: (1) the locational structure of the steady state equilibria if they exist, and (2) the convergence or nonconvergence of the reactive process to such steady states.

Most work centers around the first of these questions. However, because of the complexity of the task even in relatively simple models of solving for steady states or even in establishing their existence, the second question has become important when simulation analysis is used. If, in a dynamic, sequential simulation analysis of a particular spatial oligopoly system, where each firm is given the opportunity to alter its location in a sequence while all other firms are immobile, the solution merely cycles through a series of states without converging, doubt is cast upon the existence of a steady state solution as conventionally defined. On the other hand, if the solution does converge consistently to one or more configurations, these receive some credence as optimal states of the system. "Simulative theorizing", as a newer Correspondence Principle, may yield the only insights attainable into problems whose solutions are not capable of analytic derivation.

Although the seminal articles in dynamic location theory are the analyses of Hotelling (1929), Lerner and Singer (1937), Smithies (1941), and Chamberlin (1948, Appendix C), it will be more rewarding to start with the insightful recent work of Eaton and Lipsey (1975) which unifies the earlier work and extends the analysis to two dimensions. In the interest of saving space, we generalize their results.

The economies of interest are described by the following assumptions:

(1) the spatial configuration of the market is, alternatively:
    (a) a finite line segment,
    (b) a circle,
    (c) a disc (the circle and its interior);
(2) consumers are distributed over the market, alternatively:
    (a) for the line segment and the circle either:
        (i) uniformly, or
        (ii) according to a density function that is integrable and at least once differentiable,
    (b) for the disc, uniformly;
(3) each consumer purchases one unit of product, so sales are proportionate to number of consumers in firms' market areas;
(4) transport costs are an increasing function of distance;
(5) all firms charge the same fixed price f.o.b. their locations;
(6) marginal profit for all firms is positive and constant;
(7) relocation costs of firms are zero;
(8) no more than one firm can occupy a given location;
(9) each firm chooses a location strategy on the basis of two alternative conjectures:
    (a) a Cournot conjecture that other firms will not respond to its move,
    (b) a game theoretic conjecture that some rival will react by relocation to cause the largest possible loss of the initiating firm's market;
(10) consumers purchase from the firm with the lowest delivered price;
(11) firms locate in such a manner as to maximize profits subject to their conjectures;

(12) the dynamic process of relocation occurs sequentially with each firm given the opportunity to relocate with other firms remaining fixed temporarily;

(13) the steady state is identified with a Nash equilibrium.

The Eaton–Lipsey necessary and sufficient conditions for a steady state solution to (1) linear or circular models with (2) Cournot conjectures are the following:

Condition 1

No firm's total sales are less than some firm's long-side sales, where a firm's long-side sales are the sales to customers in the longer of its market segments left and right of its site.

Condition 2

Peripheral firms, where existent, are located next to (are paired with) other firms, so that the short-sides of the paired firms are (nearly) zero.

Condition 3

Let $P(z)$ be the number of customers at point z. Then, for every unpaired firm $P(B_L) = P(B_R)$, where B_L and B_R are the left- and right-hand boundaries of the firm's market area.

Condition 4

For each paired firm, $P(B_{SS}) \geq P(B_{LS})$, where B_{SS} and B_{LS} are the boundaries of the short and long sides of the firm's market areas.

For circular market areas, peripheral firms do not exist, so Condition 2 can be eliminated. For uniformly distributed populations, Conditions 3 and 4 are met trivially and can be omitted.

For the Hotelling economy – the linear market with uniform customer distribution – his famous case for $n = 2$ firms featured a solution with pairing at the center of the line, which follows from Conditions 1 and 2. For $n = 3$, Condition 2 cannot be met and the steady state is nonexistent.[1] When $n = 4$, Condition 2

---

[1] Chamberlin (1948, p. 261) seems to accept an endless dynamic adjustment process by the firms when $n = 3$. In his work, however, Chamberlin is more interested in challenging Hotelling's assertions of an "undue" tendency of n firms to cluster than to establish exact locational criteria. As Eaton and Lipsey indicate, in his conjectures that firms would tend to avoid pairing and space out equally, Chamberlin failed to grasp Condition 2. However, his upper bounds on distances of peripheral firms to market boundaries and interior firms to neighbors are correct although that for interior firms can be reduced from $2/n$ to $2/(n+1)$.

requires pairing and Condition 1 dictates pair locations at the first and third quartiles. For $n = 5$, pairs are located at $z = 1/6$ and $z = 5/6$, and the unpaired firm is at the center. For $n > 5$, an infinite number of steady state solutions exists.

When Hotelling's economy is bent into circular form, Condition 1 alone dictates location. For $n = 2$ all configurations are steady state, and when $n > 2$ an infinite number of solutions exists.

For the linear market with nonuniform population distribution, when the market has no rectangular population distribution segments, Conditions 3 and 4 imply the important Theorem 1.

Theorem 1

A necessary condition for the existence of a steady state solution is that n be no more than twice the number of modes in the population distribution.

Hence, on a unimodal distribution, no equilibrium exists for $n > 3$, and for $n = 2$ Conditions 1,2, and 4 dictate a solution at the median of the distribution. Indeed, the latter proposition for $n = 2$ holds true whatever the form of the distribution of population (including the uniform). When the circular market with nonuniform distribution is considered, Condition 2 is eliminated, but since it does not enter into the implication of the theorem the latter continues to hold. The results, therefore are not changed from those of the linear model.

For the linear model with uniform population distribution, when firms have game-theoretic conjectures, the firms are led to a minimax solution. That is, they will maximize the short side of their market areas by locating at their centers. For all $n \neq 2$ this implies that peripheral firms will locate one-third of the distance from the end of the line to their neighbor and interior firms midway between their neighbors. When $n = 2$ firms will pair at the midpoint of the line. Each firm will have a market area of $1/n$.[2]

Since peripheral firms are not paired, when the economy is bent into circular form fewer changes in conditions occur then under Cournot conjectures. Specifically, the solutions for $n = 1$ and 2 are no longer determinate.

For both linear and circular market areas with nonuniform distributions under game-theoretic conjectures, the existence or nonexistence of a steady state depends upon the form of the population distribution. It is possible, for example,

---

[2] Teitz (1968) deals with a systematic extension of the Hotelling model in which firms can locate more than one economic entity on the line. He assumes that the firms follow a minimax strategy. For example, suppose firm A locates two branches at the first and third quartiles on the first move. Firm B then can locate anywhere between the two branches of A, but will get only 1/4 of the market, not 1/3. This is not a full minimax model, however, since firm A does not relocate in the Teitz dynamic, and his result follows. But the solution is no longer a minimax solution for firm A, and the model is not comparable with those discussed above. Were the sequence allowed to continue under minimax conjectures the equal-market-share results would emerge.

for each firm to be in a local equilibrium but not a global, so that the firm may better its position by a quantum leap. On the other hand, some forms of distribution will yield a global steady state.

Smithies (1941) broadened and deepened spatial duopoly analysis by introducing linear demand functions (instead of Assumption 3) and three alternative conjectural assumptions involving both prices and locations of rivals. His article focuses upon the interdependence of optimal pricing and location. Gannon (1972, 1973) extended the Hotelling and Smithies duopoly models in novel and imaginative ways by introducing general, well-behaved demand functions and marginal conjectural variations [see Hartwick (1972) for insightful comments on Gannon's analysis]. His central theorem is a necessary condition for a midpoint location in duopoly: both rivals must expect a locational move to lead the rival to move toward them by less than the initiating move.

However, with such conjectural variation the determinateness of the Hotelling–Smithies work disappears and the positioning of the pair of rivals becomes indeterminate. In Gannon (1973) this indeterminacy of the outcome is deepened by showing the dependence of equilibrium on the forms of the demand functions.

The early conjectures by Hotelling concerning the tendency of firms to cluster and Chamberlin's challenge to its existence, as well as the implicit assumption of determinate steady state solutions, have been replaced by the realization that multiple (or even an infinite number of) solutions are possible and also that no solutions are a possibility. The complicated dependence of the number and stability of steady state solutions upon the number of firms, conjectural assumptions, distribution of customers, and the form of the demand functions render the search for universal theorems futile in all but the simplest cases. Progress in the one-dimensional cases of the linear or circular market must be sought in the simulation of specific cases and the distillation of regularities from large bodies of computer experience.

These lessons from one-dimensional analysis are even more applicable to the analysis of oligopolistic location in two dimensions. Analyses of two-dimensional space are relatively rare, and we describe below the methodology and results of several of these studies.

Eaton and Lipsey confine their analysis to a Hotelling economy with Cournot conjectural behavior and a uniform distribution of population extended to the disc (Assumptions 1.c, 2.b, 3–8, 9.a, 10–12). When $n = 1$ the firm locates anywhere on the disc, and when $n = 2$ paired location at the center is obtained. However, when $n \geq 3$ closed analysis fails, and Eaton and Lipsey resort to an iterative sequential optimization simulation in which firms readjust locations through time as their rivals remain fixed. Results were predominantly negative. Löschian hexagons, squares, and rectangles were not sustainable as steady state market areas. For n between 3 and 17 the dynamic adjustment process failed to converge, although repeated clustering of the firms was observed. Eaton and Lipsey conjecture that no equilibrium configuration for this model exists for $n > 2$, and Shaked (1975) has provided a nonexistence proof for $n = 3$.

Kuenne (1977) has analyzed the location of n rival firms among m customers at discrete locations in the plane with linear demand functions using 0–1 nonlinear, nonconvex programming and combinatorial programming in tandem within a simulation framework. An iterative sequence was used to determine optimal prices for fixed firm locations, then with prices held constant to determine the optimal location–allocation solution for firms and customers. The square was arbitrarily chosen as a configuration with 8 customers at the corners and midpoints of the sides. The number of firms assumed was between 1 and 4. The dynamic processes converged to at least locally optimal solutions and the social cost behavior was studied as the number of firms increased.

Another line of attack to spatial oligopolistic analysis in both 1- and 2-space has been more extensive applications of game theory than the minimax conjectural variation assumption permits. Stevens (1961) modified the Hotelling problem by assuming a finite number of points on the line at which location can occur, and, to make the game zero-sum, assumed that the payoff function to firms is the difference in their sales at alternative locations. Straightforward two-person, zero-sum attack upon the spatial duopoly problem concludes that a minimax solution of pairing at the center is consistent with Hotelling. The multifirm "crippled" minimax approach of Teitz (1968) (see footnote 2) permits the importance of multi-firm bracketing of rivals and early location to emerge in a Hotelling environment.

More extensive applications of game theory were made by Isard and Smith (1967, 1968). In a Hotelling economy with linear demand curves, they used standard isoprofit contour analysis to derive a Cournot solution to the duopoly problem with each firm located one-third of the distance from the endpoints of the linear market. Of course, both firms can benefit from a collusive agreement, and the authors consider various plausible dynamic procedures to attain such agreement. They also analyze the possibility of side payments, beginning at the joint profit maximization solution (at one of the quartiles) and negotiating over the division of the spoils. The Weber agglomeration economies problem is merged with the Hotelling case by introducing the former. Most interestingly, the Weber agglomeration case is analyzed on its own, discussing various cooperative dynamic movement schemes that iteratively reduce the space within which agglomeration can occur. The later article introduces the possibility of coalition formation into this agglomeration analysis.

As in all realistic oligopoly analysis, the strength of game theory ironically coincides with its disappointing results, for it succeeds in highlighting the richness of realistic processes through the methodology's indeterminateness. It serves to reinforce the conclusions of our earlier presentation: spatial oligopoly

Figure 2.1. A linear transportation route.

presents dynamic adjustment potentialities that in the general case are essentially indeterminate in outcome. Hence, such problems must be accepted as *sui generis*; work is most profitably confined to specific cases via simulation, and the theoretical ambitions of the analyst should be constrained to the limited applicability of the solutions.

2.2. *Discontinuous breaks in location regimes through time*

One of the most difficult dynamic phenomena to model theoretically is the discontinuous movement of a state variable occurring as parameters move smoothly into critical regions that mark regime changes in environmental continuity. The anomalous nature of such events is inherent to the fact that strategic exogenous factors reveal only smooth and relatively small change, yet endogenous variables react "catastrophically" in puzzling configurations.

Catastrophe theory is one of the mathematical techniques designed to enlighten the qualitative nature of processes that reveal such behavior, and regional scientists have applied it to several dynamics problems. In this section[3] we will illustrate its use in a dynamic locational context.

Consider the decision making of a seller of goods who find it most advantageous to locate at the point of maximum population concentration (see Figure 2.1). At time $t = 0$, we suppose that the distribution of population, $P_0 = f(z; Y, T)$, is as depicted in Figure 2.2, where Y is aggregate income, and that the firm's location z_0 is optimal. We now assume a time trajectory for control points (Y_t, T_t) and reproduce four population distributions on the assumed time path in Figure 2.3. Finally, we assume that data on population distribution at any time t is fragmentary, so that the firm must relocate on the basis of local information. Its instantaneous adjustment is assumed to follow the gradient from $\dot{z} = \partial P / \partial z$, where, throughout this chapter $\dot{x} = dx/dt$.

In $t = 1$, Y rises while T remains constant, dispersing the population and leading to a local maximum in the vicinity of B (Figure 2.3a). In the flow of time the firm moves to z_1 continuously. By $t = 2$, the rise in Y continues to move

---

[3] For elementary expositions of catastrophe theory and a more exhaustive bibliography see Isnard and Zeeman (1976, pp. 44–100) to which the present application is heavily indebted; Nijkamp and van Dijk (1980); and Wilson (1976, 1980). More extensive treatments can be found in Poston and Stewart (1976) and in Gilmore (1981).

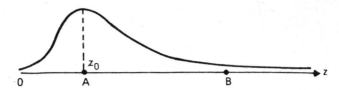

Figure 2.2. Population distribution at $t = 0$.

commuters farther from the CBD (Figure 2.3b), and the global maximum moves
to the outermost concentration. However, following its myopic reaction pattern,
the firm moves continuously to z_2, the location of the local maximum. In $t = 3$,
however, the local maximum and the minimum of $t = 2$ have converged as Y
continues to rise, leaving the firm at an unstable equilibrium (Figure 2.3c).
Following its gradient rule, the firm now "jumps" discontinuously to z_3. At this
point a sharp or "catastrophic" break in the smooth adjustments of the firm
occurs. In $t = 4$, the firm resumes its continuous adjustments (Figure 2.3d).

Catastrophe theory is designed to examine the *qualitative* characteristics of
sudden discontinuous behavioral changes and to generalize the nature of functions that move abruptly from one smooth path of adjustment to another
fundamentally or "catastrophically" different smooth path of adjustment to
control trajectories. Two characteristics of the theory must be stressed: the theory
is not designed to predict the path of the endogenous variable z_t, but merely to
describe the nature of such paths for specified exogenous variable (control point)
sequences; and the insights it yields into these paths are qualitative not quantitative. Catastrophe theory answers the question: in what manners can regimes of
smooth adjustment in state variables evolve into regimes of abrupt change, and
what governs those rules of evolution?

To illustrate these points with our example, consider the manner in which the
firm's policy relates to the control variables. For any given control point (Y, T) in
the control space, the firm chooses its location from among those points where
$\partial P/\partial z = 0$. Hence, we are interested in the function that relates these potential
equilibrium states to the control variables. Moreover, because we are interested in
qualitative results only, we may deal with any function that is *qualitatively
equivalent* to the specific function of the problem.[4] Because catastrophe theorists
have shown that the types of catastrophic changes that can occur are determined
by the number of control variables in a problem, and that these types of
catastrophes can be obtained qualitatively by simple polynomials that are qualitative equivalents of the original behavioral functions, we may deal with these
simple *canonical models*.

---

[4] In 3-space, given two surfaces G and G', qualitative equivalence will hold for them if the mapping
of G onto G' is one-to-one, is smooth, and has a smooth inverse, and if that mapping carries vertical
lines into vertical lines.

(a) $t = 1$: Y rises, T constant

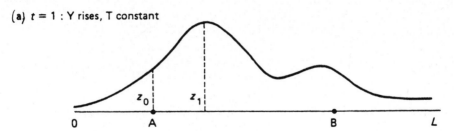

(b) $t = 2$: Y rises, T constant

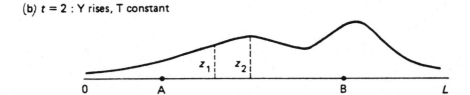

(c) $t = 3$: Y rises, T constant

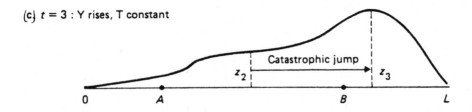

(d) $t = 4$: Y falls, T rises

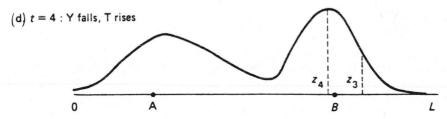

Figure 2.3. Population distributions at $t = 1, 2, 3, 4$.

For example, the canonical model for $f(z; Y, T)$ as described in our hypothesis about location behavior is

$$0.25z^4 - 0.50Tz^2 - Yz = 0, \tag{2.1}$$

whose equilibrium surface is

$$z^3 - Tz - Y = 0. \tag{2.2}$$

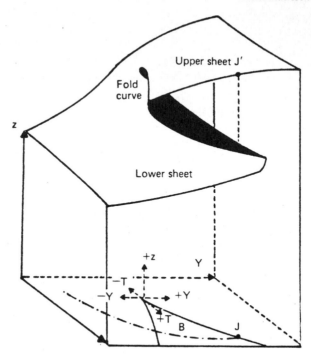

Figure 2.4. The cusp catastrophe.

This surface is graphed in Figure 2.4, but is lifted above the indicated origin at the cusp on the control space for convenience.

The surface consists of two single-sheeted sections linked by a double-sheeted (shaded) portion. The fold curve is the boundary of the single and double-sheeted portions, and is the locus of points tangent to vertical lines.[5] Its projection onto the control space yields a bifurcation set, B, with a cusp, from which the specific form of the catastrophe takes its name.[6] All controls points within B possess multiple maxima (as in Figures 2.3a or 2.3d). The folded sheet contains the minimum points and the firm therefore will never be on it.

---

[5] That is, where the derivative of the surface (2.2) is zero, or

$$3z^2 - T = 0 \Rightarrow \left[\tfrac{1}{3} T \right]^{1/2} = z.$$

[6] From (2.2) and the derivative in footnote 5, elimination of z yields the bifurcation set

$$27Y^2 = 4T^3,$$

when the origin is defined at the cusp.

Suppose the trajectory of control points is that shown by the dot–dash curve on the control set. The firm's location remains on the lower sheet (closer to A on Figure 2.1) even as the control point enters B on Figure 2.4. On the surface it travels under the folded sheet until it reaches the fold curve at J in the bifurcation set. At that critical point it jumps discontinuously to the upper sheet at J'. Hence, we can explain qualitatively how a continuous, dynamic model can yield sudden large jumps in the location of the firm.

Moreover, catastrophe theory assures us that the only manner in which a two-peaked population distribution can evolve from a one-peaked distribution is via the cusp catastrophe graphed in Figure 2.4, and that catastrophe requires two control variables. In similar fashion, a three-peaked distribution can evolve from a one-peaked distribution only by a different type of catastrophe, the *butterfly* (see Section 5.4 and Figure 5.3), which requires four control variables. It is in cataloging the qualitative forms of continuous surfaces that give rise to discontinuous jumps in endogenous variables, and in the specification of the number of control variables needed to produce them that catastrophe theory yields insights into dynamic behavior.

2.3. Optimal transportation structures

2.3.1. Discrete transportation networks

Tapiero (1971) has dynamized the "location–allocation" or "multi-source Weber" problem [see Cooper (1967) and Kuenne and Soland (1972)] and derived necessary conditions for its solution using an ingenious modification of conventional optimal control theory. The static problem is to locate n sources among m fixed sinks with given demands and to allocate sinks to sources in such a manner as to minimize total transport costs.

The dynamic problem requires treatment of product flows as rates over time. The exogenous variables are defined as follows:

1. $(0, r)$: planning period,
2. (a_j, b_j), $j = 1, 2, \ldots, m$: sink locations,
3. d_j: demand at sinks,
4. s_i, $i = 1, 2, \ldots, n$: source capacity limitations,
5. r_{ij}: transport cost per unit of product per unit of distance from sink i to sink j,
6. c_i: unit storage costs at source i,
7. $\bar{c}_j$: unit storage costs at sink j.

The endogenous variables are the following:

1. (u_i, w_i): source locations,
2. v_{ij}: shipments of source to sinks,
3. $x_i(t)$: goods in storage at sources,
4. $y_j(t)$: goods in storage at sinks.

The functional to be minimized when transport costs are proportional to units shipped and Euclidean distance is

$$\min \phi = \int_0^r \sum_{i,j} \left\{ v_{ij}(t) r_{ij} \left((a_j - u_i)^2 + (b_j - w_i)^2 \right)^{.5} + c_i x_i(t) + \bar{c}_j y_i(t) \right\} dt$$

(2.3)

subject to

$$\int_0^r y_j(t) dt = d_j, \qquad j = 1, 2, \ldots, m \tag{2.4}$$

$$\int_0^r x_i(t) dt = s_i, \qquad i = 1, 2, \ldots, n \tag{2.5}$$

$$\dot{x}_i(t) = - \sum_j v_{ij}(t) \qquad x_i(0) = s_i; \qquad x_i(r) = 0; \qquad j = 1, 2, \ldots, n \tag{2.6}$$

$$\dot{y}_j(t) = \sum_i v_{ij}(t); \qquad y_j(0) = 0, \qquad y_j(r) = d_j, \qquad j = 1, 2, \ldots, m \tag{2.7}$$

$$\dot{u}_i(t) = 0, \qquad i = 1, 2, \ldots, n \tag{2.8}$$

$$\dot{w}_i(t) = 0, \qquad i = 1, 2, \ldots, n. \tag{2.9}$$

In this formulation v_{ij}, u_i, and w_i are treated as control variables and x_i and y_j are state variables. The choice of time paths for the control variables dictates, via the equations of motion, movement of the state variables. The objective functional ϕ is minimized by optimal choices of the time paths for the control and state variables. The constraints (2.8) and (2.9) pose a problem, however, in that the sources are to be located once and for all at the first instant of time and are not to be changed over time.[7] Hence their paths cannot be altered to control the state variables.

In general assume an objective functional

$$J = \min_U \int_0^r L(X, U, t) dt \tag{2.10}$$

---

[7]It is not clear why this time invariance has to hold in a dynamic location–allocation model. It would be interesting to see how the sources would migrate under zero relocation costs. Tapiero seems to be assuming infinite relocation costs to preserve the constant source locations of the static problem.

subject to

$$\dot{X} = F(X, U, t); \qquad X(0), X(r) \text{ given,} \tag{2.11}$$

where X and U are vectors of state and control variables respectively. Form the augmented functional

$$J^* = \int_0^r \{L(X, U, t) + \lambda_1(\dot{X} - F(X, U, t))\} \, dt = H \, dt, \tag{2.12}$$

where λ_1 is a vector of costate variables. First-order conditions for a minimum of J derived from the Hamiltonian H are

$$\left. \begin{aligned} \dot{\lambda}_1 &= -H_X \\ \dot{X} &= H_{\lambda_1}, \; X(0), X(r) \text{ fixed} \\ H_U &= 0. \end{aligned} \right\} \tag{2.13}$$

When a subset of the control variables W is fixed in time, Tapiero simply converts them to state variables with constraints $\dot{W} = 0$ and introduces the constraints into J^* and H with costate variables λ_2. The resulting first-order conditions then become

$$\left. \begin{aligned} X &= H_{\lambda_1}, \; X(0), X(r) \text{ fixed} \\ \dot{\lambda}_1 &= -H_X \\ \dot{\lambda}_2 &= -H_W, \lambda_2(0) = \lambda_2(r) = 0 \\ H_V &= 0, \end{aligned} \right\} \tag{2.14}$$

where V is the subset of control variables for which $\dot{V} \neq 0$.

When these are applied to the model (2.3)–(2.9) Tapiero obtains $4n + 2m + mn$ simultaneous differential equations to be solved for the source coordinates and shipment flows. Although in general the equations must be solved by simulation, Tapiero obtains an analytic solution for quadratic transport cost functions.

Tapiero's results are not as interesting for their analytical content as for their broader methodological contribution. Indeed, it must be doubted that the dynamic location–allocation problem is of much interest to regional economists. He has, however, succeeded in confronting a peculiarly spatial analytic problem in control theory – the fixity of locations through time, when those locations are control variables – and deriving the necessary conditions for solving it. We hypothesize that the derivation will permit the solution of other dynamic optimization problems in space.

2.3.2. *Continuous transportation networks and location structures*

The purest translation of the notion of endogenously interdependent variable trajectories through the time dimension abstracting from space to such trajectories in the spatial dimension abstracting from time ("choronamics") is the continuous transportation modelling associated with Beckmann (1952) and Puu (1979a, 1982). Unlike the Liossatos–Isard work, which strives to unite the two dimensions with temporal differential equations that have spatial coordinates, Beckmann and Puu start by abstracting from time to define differential equations with respect to space.

In an interesting series of articles, Puu (1979b, 1981a, 1982) has extended Beckmann's model to include the endogenous determination of production location and has examined the "stability" of spatial structures emerging from the solutions to such models. In the space available, it is impossible to render these models formally, so we will only outline their major features as they pertain to the spatial stability issue in Puu's recent models. One interesting aspect of such theoretical constructions is that the only state variables of interest are the flow lines that form transportation paths in the space, not the quantities produced or absorbed locally in the optimal solution. Hence, little of interest is sacrificed in using simple rather than more complex economies in our presentation.

Consider a region S in Euclidean 2-space with a boundary R that is a closed curve. All fuel is imported from abroad over the boundary and is paid for from exports of the single produced good. The price of fuel, p_f, is given parametrically on R, as is the price of the good, p_g. Both commodities must be transported within S, and we may define isoprice contours for fuel by adding transport costs to p_f, and for goods by subtracting them from p_g.

The good is producible at every location in S under identical Cobb–Douglas technology with labor, fuel, capital and land, and is consumed at each location. The utility obtained from consumption is additive, and the objective function is obtained from the surface integral of the local utilities over S. Land is immobile and given at each location, but capital and labor are free to move costlessly among locations. At each point transport services needed to move units of goods and fuel through the point are produced from the same four factors by a Leontief technology whose production coefficients may vary among locations.

The flows of goods and fuel at a given point (x, y) will be characterized by (1) direction, (2) magnitude, and (3) net addition and subtractions at (x, y). The trajectories through space traced out by goods and fuel flows will connect points in patterns derived from constrained optimization, when such flow lines are completely unchanneled by any fixity of networks. What, then, will be the defining characteristics of such stream lines, and what can be said qualitatively of the stability of such spatial structures?

The solution is obtained by maximizing the integral of the utility functional subject to the constraints that:

(1) the production technology rule at each point;

(2) the integrals of capital and labor demands at each point equal supplies of these resources;

(3) demand equals supply of land at each point;

(4) net additions or subtractions to or from product flow at each point equal (positive or negative) excess supply at that point;

(5) subtraction of fuel from the flow at each point equals demand for it at that point; and,

(6) the value of product exports equals the value of fuel imports for the region.

The calculus of variations yields first-order Euler–Lagrange conditions that require (1) the marginal utility of a dollar's worth of product must be equal at each location; (2) the marginal value products of land, capital, labor, and fuel must equal their prices at each location; and (3) most importantly, the flows of goods and fuel at each point must be orthogonal to the relevant p_g and p_f isoprice contours at that point.

The two relationships containing (3) are differential equations with respect to *space* whose solutions yield the patterns of flow lines for goods and fuel in S. Most of the points on such flows lines will be "regular", i.e. with only one flow path entering and leaving. However, "singular" points on more than one flow path can arise. These will be (1) source nodes from which all flow lines in a neighborhood issue; (2) sink nodes into which all flow lines in the neighborhood empty; (3) simple saddles, in which two pairs of ingoing and outgoing flow lines serve as separatrices dividing flow lines into four sectors with hyperbolic flow lines in each sector; and (4) various unstable forms, most particularly monkey saddles into which three pairs of flow lines are incident dividing the neighborhood into six sectors with hyperbolic flow lines. Each of these flow patterns is illustrated in Figure 2.5.

Analogously to temporal stability analysis, spatial stability implies a structure of flow lines and points whose form will remain invariant to perturbations. Unstable patterns are assumed to disappear quickly in the face of continuous perturbations. Stable flows are characterized by three qualities: (1) unstable singular points like monkey saddles cannot exist; (2) all points except a finite number of isolated stable singular points will be regular; and (3) no flow line can join saddle points.

Puu demonstrates that the most basic spatial structure consistent with these stability conditions is a quadratic structure of the type illustrated in Figure 2.6. Only those flow lines incident to saddles are included to avoid clutter. Note that each sink and source is surrounded by four saddles, and each saddle by two sinks and two sources. In triangular or hexagonal tesselations of space where flow lines are the sides of triangles or diagonals of hexagons, Puu conjectures that their nonconformance to the stable quadratic pattern may make them nonexistent in real economies.

Lastly, Puu applies catastrophe theory to the analysis to study the patterns of transition from unstable to stable configurations as control variables are changed. With three control variables for a two-dimensional state space, two forms of the

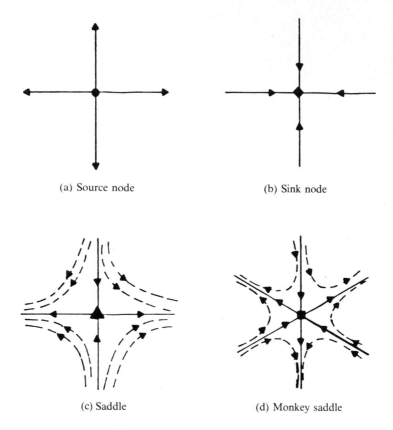

(a) Source node   (b) Sink node

(c) Saddle   (d) Monkey saddle

Figure 2.5. Types of singular points.

bifurcations set are possible. These are the elliptic umblic, with canonical equation $x^3 - 3xy^2 + a(x^2 + y^2) + bx + cy$, and the hyperbolic umblic, with canonical equation $x^3 + y^3 + axy + bx + cy$.

Puu's analysis breaks new ground in the conceptualization and analysis of a distinctively new dimension of regional economics. It uncouples the spatial dimension from the temporal to study the essential features of alternative optimal spatial structures under idealized conditions, and their survivability under parametric displacements. The results are difficult to typify. Of necessity, the method is comparative statics, and the nature of the parametric changes is not the analogue of changing the initial position of economy in time. Yet the impacts of such changes flow through differential equations, and the interest in the analysis is to see whether their new solutions yield patterns which are spatially similar to the old, as in temporal dynamics.

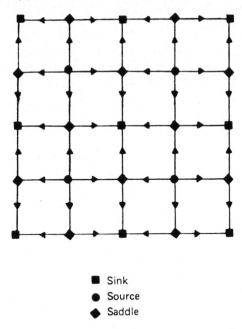

■ Sink
● Source
◆ Saddle

Figure 2.6. Basic quadratic stable spatial structure.

3.   Dynamic spatial interaction models

3.1.   An introduction

It is difficult to conceive of a regional economic model that does not feature some form of interaction or interdependence among agents and their decisions. The isolation of a body of regional economic analysis devoted to "spatial interaction" seems, therefore, an imprecise classificatory procedure. In actuality, the term has been pre-empted to describe spatial models whose interdependence is the macro cumulation of random micro-events under the regime of probability, be it in some cases (e.g. gravity models), only somewhat vaguely. Such models, therefore, lack either a basis of optimization for individuals' actions or well-defined, physically determinate bases for interaction (such as input–output relations among inputs as discussed in Section 4 or natural lines of communication among places).

3.2. Gravity entropy models

The interpretation of gravity models as entropy-based with specific analogies to the distribution of molecules in varying states of kinetic energy gave rise to the hope that such models would lend themselves to dynamic formulation in regional economic contexts. In physics, dynamic models grounded in the statistical mechanics of the Maxwell–Boltzmann theory had emerged, and the possibility of social analogues was asserted hopefully.[8]

That potentiality, however, has not materialized to any great degree, as gravity and entropy modelling has for the largest part remained static. One exception is the partial dynamization analysis by Harris and Wilson (1978) of an entropy model to determine flows of regional imports and exports as well as the distribution of export capacity among regions.

Let us define:

1. $q_{rr'}$: dollar value of exports from region r to region r',
2. d_r^I: dollar value of import demand in r, which is exogenous,
3. d_r^E: dollar value of export demand from r,
4. s_r^E: dollar value of desired supply of exports from r,
5. k_r: capacity to export from r (e.g. factory floor space),
6. $c_{rr'}$: transportation cost from r to r',
7. k_r^α: attractivity or r's capacity, $\alpha > 0$,
8. $e^{\beta c_{rr'}}$: impedance to exports from r to r', or r' to r, $\beta < 0$,
9. n: number of regions.

The logit model based on constrained entropy maximization is:

$$q_{rr'} = d_{r'}^I \left[\frac{k_r^\alpha e^{\beta c_{rr'}}}{\sum_{j=1}^n k_j^\alpha e^{\beta c_{rr'}}} \right]; (r, r' = 1, 2, \ldots, n) \tag{3.1}$$

where we define the demand function for exports from r as

$$d_r^E = \sum_{r=1}^n q_{rr'}; (r = 1, 2, \ldots, n). \tag{3.2}$$

The desire to supply exports from r is written

$$s_r^E = \lambda k_r; (r = 1, 2, \ldots, n) \tag{3.3}$$

where λ is a flow coefficient that converts the stock of capacity to export in r to a desired flow of export sales.

---

[8] See, for example, Wilson (1971). For a complete discussion of gravity and entropy models in their static setting, see Chapter 10 of this Handbook.

In equilibrium:

$$d_r^E = s_r^E; (r=1,2,\ldots,n). \tag{3.4}$$

And, finally, r's imports from all regions (including itself) must equal its given total demand for imports:

$$d_r^I = \sum_{r'=1}^{n} q_{rr'}; (r=1,2,\ldots,n). \tag{3.5}$$

Equations (3.1)–(3.5) are n^2+4n in number to determine n^2+3n variables: $q_{rr'}, d_r^E, d_r^I$, and s_r^E. But by virtue of constraint (3.5) only $n-1$ of the $q_{rr'}$ flows are independent for each r, and therefore one equation in (3.1) may be dropped for each r as nonindependent.

Consider now a dynamization of the model on a partial basis by specifying the adjustment process

$$\dot{k}_r = \vartheta(d_r^E - s_r^E), \qquad r=1,2,\ldots,n, \qquad \vartheta>0, \tag{3.6}$$

where (3.4) implies that $\dot{k}_r=0$ in equilibrium. To graph region r's demand function (3.2) as a function of k_j let us consider its alternative configurations.

First, from (3.1) to (3.2) when $k_r=0$, $d_r^E=0$, so that the export demand function passes through the origin. Next, define D to be the denominator of the expression in (3.1), and take the partial derivative of that expression with respect to k_r:

$$\frac{\partial q_{rr'}}{\partial k_r} = (d_{r'}^I - q_{rr'})\frac{ak_r^{a-1}e^{\beta c_{rr'}}}{D} = \frac{\alpha(d_{r'}^I - q_{rr'})q_{rr'}}{k_r}. \tag{3.7}$$

Since $\alpha>0$ and $q_{rr'} \le d_{r'}$, this derivative is nonnegative, and, because

$$\frac{\partial d_r^E}{\partial k_r} = \sum_{r'} \frac{\partial q_{rr'}}{\partial k_r}, \tag{3.8}$$

the slope of r's export demand as a function of k_r is nonnegative, and, if $k_r>0$ and all $d_{r'}^I>0$, can be taken as positive and declining toward zero as k_r rises. Consider next:

$$\frac{\partial^2 d_r^E}{\partial k_r^2} = \sum_{r'} \frac{\partial^2 q_{rr'}}{\partial k_r^2}$$

$$= \frac{a}{k_r} \sum_{r'} \left\{ \frac{\partial q_{rr'}}{\partial k_r}\left[d_{r'}^I - 2q_{rr'} - \frac{1}{a}\right]\right\}$$

$$= \frac{a^2}{k_r^2} \sum_{r'} q_{rr'}\left[(d_{r'}^I - q_{rr'})^2 - \left(q_{rr'} + \frac{1}{a}\right)\right]. \tag{3.9}$$

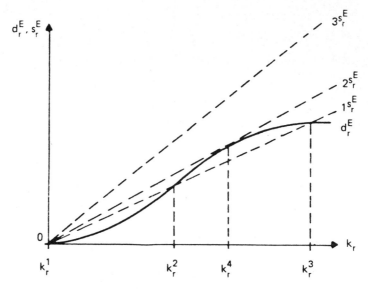

Figure 3.1. The stability of a constrained spatial interaction model.

In general, for small values of k_r (and therefore $q_{rr'}$) the second derivative should be positive but by rapidly decreasing amounts as k_r^2 rises. It should then become negative and approach zero. The expected sigmoid configuration is as depicted in Figure 3.1.[9]

From (3.6), stable equilibrium capacities are found at $k_r^1(=0)$ and k_r^3 on Figure 3.1, and an unstable equilibrium at k_r^2, when the supply function is $_1s_r^E$. When supply condition follow $_2s_r^E$, k_r^4 is unstable to the left and the origin the only stable solution. Finally, with $_3s_r^E$, only null capacity provides a solution, and it is stable.

Clarke (1981) shows that when the model is obtained as first-order necessary conditions from a maximization of consumer surplus with a constraint that $\Sigma_r k_r = \bar{k}$, where $\bar{k}$ is a parameter, λ is derived as γ/α, with γ the marginal consumer surplus value of capacity. Hence, k_r can change with α or γ. Changes in α will lead to the potential disappearance of k_r^3 in Figure 3.1, but varying γ values merely change the optimal k_r proportionately, keeping the relative structure of supply unchanged. Thus, d_r^E shifts upward as γ rises to preserve a k_r^3-type equilibrium at a small k_r value, but remains fixed as α changes.

A more ambitious dynamic model of the gravity/entropy type is typified by the externality interaction structures of Smith and Papageorgiou (1982). In a

---

[9] Harris and Wilson come to different conclusions about the shape of the function using some simplifications of the structural equations. In a later article Wilson (1980) seems to have adopted the configuration of Figure 3.1 as the general case.

region L distinct locations exist for K classes of agents, and no net migration across the boundary of the region occurs. For an agent of k class, the utility of a move from point x to point x' is a function of its after-shelter income at x' and an attraction potential, $E_{x'}^k$, exerted upon k-agents from point x'. That potential is determined essentially by the number of persons at each point and the distance of that point from x'. The probability of an agent of k class moving from point x to x' is a function of the utility of such a move and (independently, for unclear reasons) the distribution of total population among points.

The time rate of change of k-class population at point x is then expected in-migration minus expected out-migration. In the steady state these rates must be zero and the state must be a utility optimum as well: with no relocation costs, for an agent of class k at point x the utility of allocations must be equal.

In full statement the model is too difficult to analyze for stable population distributions, so that drastic dimensional reductions and simplifications are necessary. With only two classes and with the assumption that the probability of a k agent locating at x' is simply the total utility of all class k agents at x' as a ratio to their utility everywhere, Smith and Papageorgiou show that one possible equilibrium/steady state is a uniform distribution of class k agents over the L sites when uniform incomes hold for those agents over the sites. Necessary and sufficient conditions for its stability are derived. Even if small departures from equal incomes are accepted, stability is established. If those departures sum to zero, the stability conditions are the same as those for exact income equality, so that small income redistributions do not affect results.

Smith's and Papageorgiou's work has merit in being a thorough dynamization of an interaction model, but, not surprisingly, the general results are meager given the degree of effort. Results are obtained only for two-class systems with zero relocation costs, simplified probability functions, and uniform income distributions (essentially). On the other hand, it is simple enough in form to lend itself to simulation studies and econometric fitting.

3.3. Diffusion models

A form of dynamic interaction theory that has achieved substantial attention in regional science is the deterministic and stochastic process models of spatial diffusion. In such models, space is treated as an impedance factor to the flow of information or persons and consequently to the adoption of social or economic innovations. Three basic forms of diffusion theory have emerged: (a) *contagion* or *communications* theories with microsocial basis; (b) *physical* theories lifted from the wave theory of physics and wholly macro in their explanatory aims; and (c) *hierarchy* theories which seek to explain spatially discontinuous patterns of innovation by intercommunication linkages among urban areas. Some recent models incorporate or seek to unify more than one of these "pure" types, but the classification is a useful one for presentation purposes.

3.3.1. Contagion theories

The seminal work in spatial diffusion, and a pioneering application of Monte Carlo methods in the social sciences, is Hägerstrand's study of the diffusion of agricultural innovations in a Swedish rural district [Hägerstrand (1967)]. His basic theory – Model II – framed a 25 kilometer square griddled into a matrix of 5 kilometer squares each of which had a uniformly distributed population of 30 potential adopters of an innovation. At each stage of the simulation, members of the population were classified dichotomously as adopters or nonadopters, the status depending wholly on whether or not the person had or had not been contacted by an adopter in earlier stages. Hence, communication of the innovation was spread by personal contact only, and if such information was received, adoption was certain.

The probability of contact betwen individuals in two cells depended upon the distance separating cells. From data on telephone calls and migration, Hägerstrand calibrated the power function

$$I_{ij} = kd_{ij}^{-\lambda} = 0.7966d_{ij}^{-1.585} \tag{3.10}$$

to compute an interaction index between the cells i and j. The index was normalized to sum to 1 over a 25-cell region centered on a given cell of interest and yielded probabilities of contact between cells. At each stage, each adopter makes contact with a cell with probabilities based upon (3.10), and with a person (adopter or nonadopter) in that cell on the basis of a second drawing from a uniform distribution. At stage 0 only 1 adopter is assumed to exist in a central cell, and the spread of the innovation is studied by cataloging $n(t)$, the cumulative number of adopters by stage t, and the spatial pattern of adopters at stage t.

In his experiments, Hägerstrand found that $n(t)$ revealed a sigmoid (e.g. logistic) shape, which later applied and theoretical work tends to substantiate. Spatially, the typical pattern revealed "central stability", or a spread about the originating cell but merger with other centers that were seeded by outlying contacts. Hägerstrand's results are quite sensitive to the variance of his "mean information field" – the probability of contact of an adopter in the central cell with some individual in any of the relevant 25 cells. In his Model II that variance is 0.007, yielding a coefficient of variation of 2.09, which is large and leads to the expectation of frequent outlying contacts.

Various efforts to deepen the theoretical basis of the contagion model have been made. Tobler (1967) attempts to relate Hägerstrand's process to matrix systems of linear difference equations, but without notable success. Hudson (1969) challenges Hägerstrand's belief that his process generated sigmoid adoption curves over time. Casetti (1969) derives the *S*-shape by assuming that potential adopters have different degrees of resistance to change and that such resistance is overcome by repetition of contacts with adopters. Over time, average resistance of the remaining nonadopters rises faster than the proportion of adopters, slowing the rate of adoption as the upper bound of saturation is approached.

Hägerstrand's work is notable in regional dynamics for its empirical genesis and guidance. His field research is thorough with well-defined spatial and substantive phenomena. Theoretical constructions are consistently based upon explicit assumptions of human behavior, their results are checked against the real data, and they are redesigned to correct revealed explanatory deficiencies. Social analogues to physical models have not been asserted in a naive faith to have self-evident value without explicit behavioral justification in interpreting regional phenomena.

3.3.2. *Physical models*

In these regards the attempts to apply wave heat diffusion theory to social diffusion analysis are eminent examples.[10] Little attention is given to relating the physical phenomena of wave propagation and dissipation to the spread of information and adoption in a human field, nor, indeed, is there much recogni-

---

[10] The physical diffusion theory is based on the partial differential equation

$$\frac{\mathrm{d}x}{\mathrm{d}t} = \alpha \frac{\partial^2 z}{\partial x^2}$$

where x denotes one-dimensional space and t time. The general solution is given by the equations

$$Z_n(x,t) = B_n \sin\left[\frac{n\pi x}{l}\right] \exp(-\lambda_n^2 t);$$

and

$$Z(x,t) = \sum_n^\infty (x,t).$$

tion that such linkage is not self-evident. Morrill's (1968) distinction between a contagion and a wave model is not a clear one, for example, and Beckmann (1970) makes no effort to establish a rationale for the wave interpretation over a contagion model. Morrill suggests that the probability of adoption of an innovation in discrete time periods t is of Poisson form,

$$p_t = \frac{A_0 e^{-bd} d^t}{t!},$$

(3.11)

where A_0 is the initial amplitude of the wave, d is distance, and b is a coefficient of impedance to adoption. This formula yields a family of waves for varying t as a function of distance that decreases in amplitude and increases in dispersion. The envelope of such waves yields a convex curve as a function of distance displaying the expected decay of the probability of adoption with distance from an initiating center.

Beckmann's work is concerned primarily with a linear economy. His extension of wave theory to two dimensions permits the determination of the probability of adoption at a point in space at t only in the neighborhood of the frontier of the wave and for short time intervals.

3.3.3. Hierarchical models

The third type of spatial diffusion modelling seeks to explain a frequently observed phenomenon, especially in developed economies: diffusion tends to be spatially discontinuous, spreading from larger to smaller cities or towns in hierarchical fashion. This may be supplemented by contagion diffusion in the hinterlands of cities and towns. Hudson (1969) produced an early model of this type by assuming that the probability that information reached a town $t+1$ levels from the top of the size hierarchy by period t had a binomial distribution

$$p_t = \frac{(m-1)!}{t!(m-1-t)!}(1-1/q)^t(1/q)^{m-1-t},$$

(3.12)

where m is the highest ranking center and q is a spacing parameter. At every stage a given town passes the innovation to towns one level down with the same probability. The innovation spreads in rank order down the hierarchy, and, over time, the cumulative probability function reveals the desired sigmoid shape. The spread is more likely between towns with larger populations (higher up the hierarchy) and impeded by distance, so that the familiar outlines of the gravity theory are discernible in (3.12).

Pedersen (1970) argues that the hierarchical spread of an innovation must also be explained by the willingness of a given town to accept innovations, the economic/technological feasibility of an innovation in a town of given size, and the presence of entrepreneurs in the town. He defines the flow of information to a town in the hierarchy as a cumulation from *all* higher level towns. For each such earlier-adopting town, the information term is a gravity term involving the product of the receptive populations of town *i* and that town, a distance power function, and the length of time elapsed since the higher-order town adopted. The sum of these terms over all higher-order towns yields the flow of information to town *i*. When town *i* has a population level above the minimum necessary to make the innovation feasible, and when information surpasses a threshold level, town *i* adopts the innovation with a probability whose distribution is that of a cumulative negative exponential:

$$p_i(t) = 1 - e^{-P_i q}, \tag{3.13}$$

where P_i is the receptive population and q is the (Poisson-small) probability of a receptive individual being an entreprenuer.

Two more recent efforts in hierarchical diffusion are worthy of note. Alao et al. (1977) have adapted the model to Christaller central place structures, with initial adopters in all highest order places and diffusion proceeding stagewise down the hierarchy. Their modelling is notable for its formalization but is rather rigidly tied to the Christaller spatial organization.

Webber and Joseph (1978) have sought to simplify the relations of a hierarchical diffusion structure sufficiently to permit analytical solution rather than require simulation. Suppose a set of cities C exists in the plane and that $p_i(t)$ is the probability information has been received in C_i by time t. The probability of interaction between C_i and C_j, or I_{ij}, may be viewed as having a gravity structure. The probability that C_i receives information during $t + dt$, therefore, is

$$dp_i(t) = \lambda(1 - p_i(t)) \sum_{j=1}^{n} I_{ji} p_j(t) dt, \tag{3.14}$$

or the probability it has not received it by t, times the sum of the product of the probabilities it reacts with cities C_j and that C_j have received the information by t. The whole is multiplied by λ, a diffusion coefficient. By a succession of simplifications and approximations, Webber and Joseph derive an approximation to the integral of (3.14) that can be manipulated for general theorems. The propositions so derived, however, are essentially uninteresting. One is led back to the need for simulation to obtain meaningful insights into the structure.

4. Growth of regional economic activities

4.1.   *The regional growth problem*

In Section 3 the problem of regional interactions as a dynamic phenomenon is discussed without specific mention of the general economic theory of growth. Some of the results are quite reasonable, but some are not in any obvious way consistent with economic theory. It is the intention of this section to show that interactions in space can be made compatible both with dynamic economic interdependence analysis and theories of microeconomic optimization of firms. After a short introduction to Keynesian growth theory for one closed region the focus will be shifted to a pair of interconnected regions and then generalized to a finite number of interacting regions. The initial assumption of linearity is successively relaxed by introduction of substitution possibilities in a neoclassical context. The section concludes with a nonlinear growth model in which all input–output coefficients are determined by cost minimization at the plant level. The approach proposed is a generalization of Shephard's lemma, allowing for transportation costs as well as regional differences in input prices.

4.2.   *Single region growth models – an introduction to the problem*

The earliest example of a one-sector–one-region growth model goes back to the Swedish economist Gustaf Cassel but was later reformulated and fully developed by the Keynesian economist Roy Harrod (1948). The first non-spatial models of economic growth were reducible to a differential or difference equation in one variable. This theory of growth of a single region and its implied models are purely macro-oriented in the sense that there is no explicit aggregation scheme from the micro level of firms and households to the social level.

   The Keynesian assumption is made that a growth equilibrium requires market clearing at the macro level, i.e. that total supply, $Z(t)$, equals total demand, or consumer demand, $C(t)$, plus investment demand, $I(t)$.

   Furthermore, consumption demand is assumed to be determined by total income ($Z(t)$) only, because of the assumed constancy of relative prices. Investment in new capacity, which acts as the energizer of the system, is assumed to be proportional to the growth of total demand ($\dot{Z}(t)$). The simplest forms of the Harrod growth model can thus be formulated:

$$
\left.
\begin{array}{lll}
\text{a.} & Z(t) = C(t) + I(t); & \text{macro-economic equilibrium} \\[4pt]
\text{b.} & C(t) = \alpha Z(t); \quad 0 < \alpha < 1; & \text{consumption demand} \\[4pt]
\text{c.} & I(T) = \beta \dot{Z}(t) \equiv \beta \dfrac{dZ}{dt}; & \text{investment demand} \\[4pt]
\text{d.} & Z(0) = Z_0 &
\end{array}
\right\} . \quad (4.1)
$$

By substituting (4.1b) and (4.1c) into (4.1a), given (4.1d), we arrive at the first order differential equation

$$Z(t) = \alpha Z(t) + \beta \dot{Z}(t); \qquad Z(0) = Z_0. \tag{4.2}$$

This equation has the solution:

$$Z(t) = Z(0)e^{[(1-\alpha)/\beta]t}; \text{ equilibrium growth.} \tag{4.3}$$

The equation shows that increasing the propensity to consume α will decrease the rate of growth. An increased β, equivalent to a decreased capital productivity, would also decrease the rate of growth of the economy.

It should be observed that the whole analysis is valid only in a situation of *stock* equilibrium at the outset where the economy starts from a position $K(0) = \beta Z(0)$. From this it follows that $K(t) = \beta Z(t) = \beta Z(0)\exp[(1-\alpha)/\beta]t$ or that $\dot{K}/K = \dot{Z}/Z$, i.e. the rate of growth of capital equals the rate of economic growth.

It has been argued that the assumption of constant coefficients α and β in the growth process is too restrictive, because of the need to incorporate substitution phenomena. This is, however, a quite legitimate assumption as long as the analysis is performed under the Harrodian assumption of a constant relative price of capital. We will relax this assumption at a stage when it is meaningful, i.e. when we are considering a multisectoral economy.

The model presented facilitates the discussion of multiregional growth theory, which we will approach in stepwise fashion progressing via the two-region case.

4.3. Macro-economic equilibrium growth in two interdependent regions

In the case of two regions no change in the conclusions would occur if the regions coexisted in autarky. Regional growth analysis becomes meaningful only if the regions involved are connected with each other by an exchange of commodities, labor or information.

We now assume that the supply of commodities in region i is determined by production in the region, x_i, and by imports assumed to be proportional to production, $m_i x_i$. The import of one region is of course constrained to be the export of the other region.

The system can now be written in the following form:

$$
\begin{aligned}
Z_i &= x_i + m_i x_i; \quad \{i = 1, 2\} & \text{total supply in region } i \\
C_i &= \alpha_i x_i; & \text{consumption demand in region } t \\
I_i &= \beta_i \dot{x}_i; & \text{investment demand in region } i
\end{aligned}
\left.\vphantom{\begin{aligned}Z\\C\\I\end{aligned}}\right\}.
$$

$$(4.4)$$

For a two-region economy, because $m_1 x_1 =$ imports to region $1 =$ exports from region 2, we may write:

$$x_1 + m_1 x_1 = \alpha_1 x_1 + \beta_1 \dot{x}_1 + m_2 x_2$$

$$\left. \vphantom{\begin{matrix} a \\ b \end{matrix}} \right\} \text{ interregional growth equilibrium} \left. \vphantom{\begin{matrix} a \\ b \end{matrix}} \right\}.$$

$$x_2 + m_2 x_2 = \alpha_2 x_2 + \beta_2 \dot{x}_2 + m_1 x_1$$

$$(4.5)$$

Simplifying, we have:

$$\left. \begin{aligned} \dot{x}_1 &= G_{11} x_1 - G_{12} x_2 \\ \dot{x}_2 &= G_{21} x_1 - G_{22} x_2 \end{aligned} \right\} \tag{4.6}$$

where

$$G_{ii} = \left[(1 + m_i - a_i)/\beta_i \right] \text{ and } G_{ij} = \left(m_i / \beta_j \right). \tag{4.7}$$

This coupled system will now be studied from the point of view of the following question: Does there exist any balanced growth solution in the sense that the two regions will remain in constant relative economic positions indefinitely? Expressed formally: does there exist a balance growth solution such that

$$\dot{x}_i = \lambda x_i \quad \text{for } i = 1, 2? \tag{4.8}$$

Expressed in matrix form:

$$[G - I\lambda] x = 0 \tag{4.9}$$

where

$$G = \begin{bmatrix} G_{11} & G_{12} \\ G_{21} & G_{22} \end{bmatrix}. \tag{4.10}$$

This problem has a nontrivial solution (i.e. with $x_i \neq 0$ for at least one of the regions) only if $|G - I\lambda| = 0$.

The growth rate λ is an unknown to be determined by the roots of the characteristic equation:

$$\lambda^2 - (G_{11} + G_{22}) \lambda + (G_{11} G_{22} - G_{12} G_{21}) = 0 \tag{4.11}$$

or

$$\lambda = \frac{G_{11} + G_{22} \pm \left((G_{11} + G_{22})^2 - 4(G_{11} G_{22} - G_{21} G_{12}) \right)^{1/2}}{2}, \tag{4.12}$$

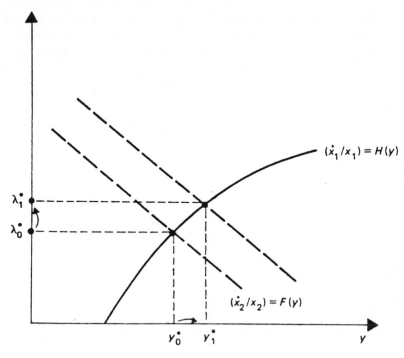

Figure 4.1. Balanced growth and income share in a two-region economy.

The solution will give exponential growth without oscillation iff $(G_{11} + G_{22})^2 > 4(G_{11}G_{22} - G_{21}G_{12})$. Assuming symmetry of behavior and size of the regions, exponential growth occurs iff $m_1/\beta_2 > 0$, which is evidently always true. Furthermore:

$$\frac{\partial \lambda}{\partial \alpha_i} < 0; \qquad \frac{\partial \lambda}{\partial \beta_i} < 0, \tag{4.13}$$

Partially increasing (decreasing) a propensity to consume or a capital–output ratio decreases (increases) the *common* rate of growth.

The determination of the rate of growth common to both regions can be illustrated with Figure 4.1. We introduce a transformation:

$$x_i \geq 0; \qquad x_1 + x_2 = 1 \quad \text{and} \quad \frac{x_1}{1 - x_1} \equiv y. \tag{4.14}$$

$$\left. \begin{array}{l} H(y) = \dfrac{\dot{x}_1}{x_1} = G_{11} - G_{12} y^{-1} \quad \text{and} \quad \dfrac{\dot{x}_2}{x_2} = G_{22} - G_{21} y = F(y) \\[2mm] \lambda^* = H(y) = F(y) \end{array} \right\} \tag{4.15}$$

Assume that α_2 decreases, with the consequence that G_{22} and $F(y)$ increase to the dotted line. The decreased propensity to consume in region 2 implies an increased *common* rate of growth but also an *increased share of region 1* in total production. Only if both regions increase their respective propensities to save (invest) could the growth rate increase with an unchanged relative production in the two regions.

4.4. Generalized multiregional growth equilibria

The Keynesian growth model easily generalizes to any finite number of regions;

$$\dot{x}_i = G_{ii}x_i - \sum_{j \neq i} G_{ij}x_j; \quad (i = 1,\ldots, n). \tag{4.16}$$

This ordinary linear differential equation system can be rewritten in matrix form:

$$\dot{x} + Gx - \hat{G}x = 0 \quad \text{where} \quad G = [G_{ij}] \quad \text{and} \quad \hat{G} = [G_{ii}]I, \tag{4.17}$$

where $\hat{G}$ is a diagonal matrix, or more compactly

$$\dot{x} = Qx \text{ with} \tag{4.18}$$
$$Q \equiv (\hat{G} - G). \tag{4.19}$$

To solve this type of differential equation we need a theorem on linear, homogeneous systems of equations.

Definitions

Let $Q = (q_{jk})$ be a given $n \times n$ matrix in the vector equation

$$\lambda x = Qx. \tag{4.20}$$

A value of $\lambda = \lambda^*$ for which this equation has a solution $x^* \neq 0$ is defined to be an *eigenvalue* or *characteristic value*. The solutions x^* corresponding to λ^* are defined to be *eigenvectors* or *characteristic vectors*. The set of eigenvalues is defined to be the *spectrum of Q*. The largest of the absolute values of the eigenvalues of Q is called *the spectral radius of Q*.

Lemma 1

Any $n \times n$ matrix Q has at least 1 and at most n distinct real or complex eigenvalues. Any $n \times n$ matrix Q has n not necessarily distinct, not necessarily real, eigenvalues.

Theorem 2

For the system $\dot{y} = Qy + h$, with $h(t)$ continuous in an interval $\alpha < t < \beta$ and starting in a point t_0 also in that interval, and with Q possessing a linearly independent set of n eigenvectors, there exists a unique solution on the specified interval.

Proof

(Proof available from the first author upon request.)

4.5. Neoclassical multiregional growth analysis

In the 1950s, Solow (1956), Swan (1956), and others insisted that the Keynesian linear models of growth, with many rigid relations built into them, were too simplistic to capture the adaptability of real economies. These authors argued that the possibilities of substitution of capital for labor as a consequence of changing relative wage rates would secure a smooth development path for the macroeconomy.

Their argument can be captured with Figure 4.2. Let $q = f(k)$ be the aggregate production function with capital, k, as input. Further, define w as wages.

As a steady state equilibrium $[\dot{k} = 0]$, with zero profits $q^* = f'(k^*) \cdot k^* + \omega$. With a sufficiently smooth linearly homogeneous macro production function $f(k)$, it is obviously possible to have a real rate of interest matching the marginal

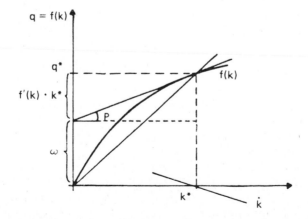

Figure 4.2. The steady state solution of a neoclassical growth model.

productivity of capital which, with wages, and when used to compensate each unit of capital, will just exhaust product q^*.

For two (or n) regions the problem becomes less trivial. For such a system we observe the basic macro equilibrium condition to be that savings equal investment (or capital accumulation), i.e. an equilibrium magnitude. Assuming no depreciation and savings to come out of total internally produced and net imported supply, we have

$$\dot{K}_r = \sigma_r(Q_r - E_r + M_r) \tag{4.21}$$

where
$\dot{K}_r$ = instantaneous rate of capital accumulation in region r,
σ_r = propensity to save (invest) in region r,
Q_r = gross regional product of region r,
E_r = exports from region r,
M_r = imports to region r.
Further, assuming a certain export share ε_r for each one of the regions, we have the following two-region application of this model:

$$\left.\begin{aligned} \dot{K}_1 &= (\sigma_1 - \varepsilon_1)Q_1 + \varepsilon_2 Q_2 \\ \dot{K}_2 &= \varepsilon_1 Q_1 + (\sigma_2 - \varepsilon_2)Q_2 \end{aligned}\right\} \tag{4.22}$$

with the assumption that

$$\sigma_r > \varepsilon_r > 0.$$

Further, assuming $Q_r = K_r^{\alpha_r} L_r^{\beta_r}$ and $L_r = L_r(0)e^{g_r t}$, a possible two-region neoclassical growth model would be:

$$\left.\begin{aligned} \dot{K}_1 &= (\sigma_1 - \varepsilon_1) K_1^{\alpha_1} L_1(0)^{\beta_1} e^{\beta_1 g_1 t} + \varepsilon_2 K_2^{\alpha_2} L_2(0)^{\beta_2} e^{\beta_2 g_2 t} \\ \dot{K}_2 &= (\varepsilon_1 K_1^{\alpha_1} L_1(0)^{\beta_1} e^{\beta_1 g_1 t} + (\sigma_2 - \varepsilon_2) K_2^{\alpha_2} L_0(0) e^{\beta_2 g_2 t} \end{aligned}\right\}. \tag{4.23}$$

A difference equation variant of this model can easily be simulated for a set of positive parameters $\sigma_r > \varepsilon_r > 0$, $g_r = 0$ and $L_r(0) = \bar{L}_{r0}$ and $K_r(0) = \bar{K}_{r0}$.

Computer simulations indicate that the two regional capital stocks develop at *converging* growth rates.

We thus could conjecture that a neoclassical multiregional growth model has some stable steady state properties, notably balanced growth of regional capital stocks.

It can be shown in a formal way that this is indeed the case. The steady state properties are covered by Theorem 3.

Theorem 3

Given a multiregional growth model, $\dot{x} = H(x)$, it is required for the model to have some balanced growth or steady state solution $\dot{x} = \lambda x$, where $x \equiv \{K_1, \ldots, K_n\}$ and $H(x)$ is a strictly positive mapping for all real valued $x > 0$. A solution $\lambda x = H(x)$ exists with $x > 0$ and $\lambda > 0$, provided that $H(x)$ is continuous.

A proof is given in Nikaido (1968). We thus know that a neoclassical system of n regional economies has got steady state properties of the kind first demonstrated in the 1950s for a one-region economy.

It should be noted that the two-region growth models of Borts and Stein (1964) and many others are *special cases* of the n-region model, whose steady state existence properties are given by Theorem 3.

The existence of steady state solutions of linear models of the kind discussed above is also covered by this theorem, although much more can be said about those models, if we use the more extensive (Frobenius–Perron) Theorem 5 given below.

We now must investigate the stability of the interregional neoclassical growth model. Iterations indicate that the discrete version of the model approaches an equilibrium structure $(x_i / \Sigma x_i)$ and a steady state growth rate if started at some suitable random point.

Let us assume that the starting point is close enough to an equilibrium to permit linearization and that the total amount of labor is given. Then $x(t+1) \approx Hx(t)$, where $H(\bar{x})$ is the first order approximation terms of the parameters of $H(x)$. Because of the strictly positive values of the parameters of the nonlinear mapping $H(x)$, it follows that $H(\bar{x})$ also contains strictly positive parameters of approximation.

Therefore, the following theorem can be used to show the *relative* stability of an equilibrium path of the growing regional capital stocks.

Theorem 4

For the solution $y(t)$ of $y(t+1) = Ay(t)$ $(t = 0, 1, 2, \ldots)$ that starts from an arbitrary $y(0) \geq 0$ and the balanced growth solution $x(t)$, there exist $\lim_{t \to \infty} y_i(t) / x_i(t)$ $(i = 1, 2, \ldots, n)$. These n limits are positive and equal to each other.

Proof

Nikaido (1970).

4.6. Interregional industrial interdependence

The models of growth of preceding sections are based on a value added representation à la Keynes. More complete interregional analysis – especially for applications – requires a full representation of the industrial structure of each region (see also Chapter 8 of this Handbook).

A convenient starting point for such an analysis is the static input–output analysis. In classical, non-spatial input–output analysis, intermediate good inter-actions between sectors, each one producing one commodity with one linear activity, are regulated by input–output coefficients $a_{ij} \equiv (x_{ij}/x_j)$, where $x_{ij} =$ flow of commodity i to sector (commodity), j, $x_j =$ gross output of commodity j, and a_{ij} is the current input coefficient. On capital account it is also possible to define b_{ij}, the investment input coefficient of sector c's product per unit of sector j output.

For an interregional development analysis, interdependence can be captured by the corresponding parameters a_{ij}^{rs} and b_{ij}^{rs}, where $a_{ij}^{rs} =$ the input of commod-ity i produced in region r for use in production of commodity j in region s per unit of production of j in s and b_{ij}^{rs} is the regional investment coefficient, defined analogously.

For each region and sector consistency requires that these assumptions allow us to describe the whole economic system by the following equations:

$$x_i^r \geq \sum_{sj} a_{ij}^{rs} x_j^s + \sum_{sj} b_{ij}^{rs} \dot{x}_j^s; \qquad (r = 1, \ldots, R; \; i = 1, \ldots, N). \tag{4.24}$$

For an equilibrium it is necessary that

$$x_i^r = \sum_{sj} a_{ij}^{rs} x_j^s + \lambda \sum_{sj} b_{ij}^{rs} x_j^s; \tag{4.25}$$

where λ is an undetermined common rate of growth for

$$\lambda x_i^r = \dot{x}_i^r; \tag{4.26}$$

and

$$x_i^r \doteq \text{gross production of commodity } i \text{ in region } r$$
$$b_{ij}^{rs} \doteq \text{the marginal capital–output ratio} = I_{ij}^{rs}/\dot{x}_j^s$$
$$a_{ij}^{rs} \doteq \text{regional input/output coefficient.}$$

At an equilibrium $x = Ax + \lambda Bx$ in matrix formulation.

We can now ask the question: what would the equilibrium *rate of capacity utilization* γ be, if the sectors instead were planned or expected to grow at a common rate λ_ω? In this case, we could formulate the problem in the following way:

$$\max_{\{x\}} \gamma$$

subject to $\gamma(\lambda_\omega)x = Ax + \lambda_\omega B_x;\ x \geq 0,\ \gamma > 0.$ \hfill (4.27)

Formulating this as a Lagrange problem we have

$$\max_{\{xy,\beta\}} H = \gamma - \sum_{i,r} \beta_i^r \left(\gamma x_i^r - \sum_{js} a_{ij}^{rs} x_j^s - \lambda_\omega \sum_{js} b_{ij}^{rs} x_j^s \right). \hfill (4.28)$$

The necessary (and in this case also sufficient) conditions of a maximum are:

$$\left.\begin{aligned}
\frac{\partial H}{\partial \gamma} &= 1 - \sum_{r,i} \beta_i^r x_i^r = 0, \\[2mm]
\frac{\partial H}{\partial x_i^r} &= \beta_i^r \gamma - \sum_{js} \beta_j^s a_{ij}^{rs} - \sum_{js} \beta_j^s b_{ji}^{rs} \lambda_\omega = 0; \qquad \left(\begin{aligned} i &= 1,\ldots, N \\ r &= 1,\ldots, R \end{aligned}\right) \\[2mm]
\frac{\partial H}{\partial \beta_i^r} &= \gamma x_i^r - \sum_{js} a_{ij}^{rs} x_j^s - \lambda_\omega \sum_{js} b_{ij}^{rs} x_j^s = 0; \qquad \left(\begin{aligned} i &= 1,\ldots, n \\ r &= 1,\ldots, R \end{aligned}\right)
\end{aligned}\right\} \hfill (4.29)$$

From this follows that

$$\lambda = \frac{1 - \sum_{js} (\beta_j^s / \beta_i^r) a_{ji}^{rs}}{\sum_{js} (\beta_j^s / \beta_i^t) b_{ji}^{rs}}; \qquad \left(\begin{aligned} i &= 1,\ldots, n \\ r &= 1,\ldots, R \end{aligned}\right) \hfill (4.39)$$

if γ is required to be at the full capacity level, i.e. equal to unity. Thus the relative shadow value of each sector product must be adjusted until the profit ratio, relative to the marginal capital–output ratio equals the common balanced growth rate.

This result is patently similar to the condition of equilibrium of a one-sector–one-region economy. The first requirement states furthermore that all shadow values should be orthogonal, so that the sum of products of shadow values and quantities are on the unit circle. This implies that if the production of commodities goes towards infinity, shadow values also go towards zero.

The problem formulated above does not rely on formal maximization for a solution. A classical mathematical theorem is available for many problems which can be expressed in the form:

$$\gamma x = Qx; \hfill (4.31)$$

Q is assumed square and indecomposable, in which

$$Q \equiv A(\bar{p}) + \hat{L}B(\bar{p});\tag{4.32}$$

i.e. a diagonal matrix of given growth rate plans or expectations.

Theorem 5 (Frobenius – Perron)

If $Q \geq 0$ and $Q^m > 0$ for some positive integer m, then there exist $\lambda^* > 0$ and $x^* > 0$ such that $Qx^* = \lambda^* x^*$; if $\lambda \neq \lambda^*$ is any other eigenvalue of Q, then $|\lambda| < \lambda^*$. If any element q_{ij} of the matrix Q is increased, λ^* increases as well.

Proofs can be found in Nikaido (1968).

Great efforts have been made to find ways of estimating the interregional input–output coefficients. In most cases data are insufficient for such a direct approach. In order to decrease the data requirements, it is sometimes suggested that the original set of coefficients (of the order $(N^*R)^2$) be approximated by the multiplicative relations $\tau^{rs}{}^* a_{ij} \approx a_{ij}^{rs}$. This means that $R^2 + N^2$ coefficients are needed, which is a smaller number for all systems with more than one region and more than one sector.

This rigid approach which in a dynamic model is inconsistent was later abandoned in favor of interaction models of the probabilistic (information theoretic) or programming type (see also Chapter 9 in this Handbook).

In these approaches all prior information in the form of supply and demand constraints by regions, transportation network capacity constraints and institutional constraints are fulfilled while optimizing a probabilistic or a transportation cost criterion.

Minimizing transportation costs subject to regional supply and demand constraints or an information criterion subject to the same constraints and additional transportation capacity constraints both lead to interregional input–output coefficients becoming *functions* of interregional distances and locations of sectoral production capacities, i.e.

$$x_i^r = \sum_{s,j} a_{ij}^{rs}(\bar{x}; d) x_j^s + f_i^r; \qquad \left\{\begin{array}{l} r, s = 1, \ldots, R \\ i = 1, \ldots, N \end{array}\right\}\tag{4.33}$$

where

$$\bar{x} \equiv \{\bar{x}_i^r\}\tag{4.34}$$

is a vector of production capacities in sectors i located in regions r. The assumption of constant a_{ij}^{rs}-coefficients is thus viable in the short run only. As soon as a longer time perspective is permitted, production capacities can and do change, and thus, nonlinearities become a necessary part of interregional economic analysis. An economically reasonable approach is to base the input–output coefficients on microeconomic optimization as proposed in Section 4.7.

4.7. *Substitution in multiregional dynamic input–output models – the neoclassical approach generalized*

In the dynamic input–output models it is usually assumed that the input–output (and investment) coefficients are constant for all prices implied by the dual version of the input–output models. Such an assumption might be tenable in a static context. In a dynamic context, it is quite untenable. The choice of techniques to be used in production of commodities is then flexible and adaptive to prices.

The substitution process is often modelled with a production function that – for convenience – is assumed to be concave and at least twice differentiable. One extremely simple example is the so-called Cobb–Douglas function:

$$\ln x_i^r = \ln a_i^r + \sum_{sj} \alpha_{ji}^{sr} \ln x_{ji}^{sr}; \qquad \sum \alpha_{ji}^{sr} \leq 1; \tag{4.35}$$

where

$$x_i^r \doteq \text{output of commodity } i,$$

$$x_{ji}^{sr} \doteq \text{input of commodity } j \text{ from region } s \text{ in the production}$$

$$\text{of commodity } i \text{ in region } r,$$

$$a_i^r, \alpha_{ji}^{sr} \doteq \text{technological parameters,}$$

A production function can be regarded as a *constraint* on some decision maker controlling a set of plants.

Based on some projected sales of the product, i, $\tilde{x}_i^r$, a reasonable objective is to minimize the *costs* of producing the planned amount $\bar{x}_i^r$ when f.o.b. input prices p_j are enhanced by unit transport costs c_j^{sr}. Formally:

$$\underset{\{x\}}{\text{minimize}}\, c_i^r = \sum_{sj} \left(p_j^s + c_j^{sr} \right) x_{ji}^{sr} \tag{4.36}$$

subject to

$$\ln \bar{x}_i^r = \ln a_i^r + \sum_{sj} a_{ji}^{sr} \ln x_{ji}^{sr} \tag{4.37}$$

with

$$x_{ji}^{sr} \geq 0.$$

This constrained minimization problem can be solved by the formulation of a Lagrange problem:

$$\text{minimize } L_i = \sum_{sj}\left(p_j^s + c_j^{sr} \right) x_{ji}^{sr} + \lambda_i'\left(-\ln \bar{x}_i^r + \sum_{sj}\alpha_{ji}^{sr}\ln x_{ji}^{sr} \right) \tag{4.38}$$

with

$$\sum_{sj}\alpha_{ji}^{sr} = 1. \tag{4.30}$$

A typical optimum condition can be written as:

$$\frac{\partial L_i^r}{\partial x_{ji}^{sr}} = \left(p_j^s + c_j^{sr} \right) - \lambda_i'\alpha_{ji}^{sr}\frac{\bar{x}_i^r}{x_{ji}^{sr}} = 0. \tag{4.40}$$

or

$$\frac{\left(p_j^s + c_j^{sr} \right) x_{ji}^{sr}}{\alpha_{jr}^{sr}} = \frac{\left(p_1^q + c_1^{qr} \right) x_{1i}^{qr}}{\alpha_{1i}^{qr}} = \cdots , \tag{4.41}$$

and

$$\ln a_i^r + \sum\alpha_{ji}^{sr}\ln x_{ji}^{sr} = \bar{x}_i^r. \tag{4.42}$$

This implies that all input demands are determined by all prices and transportation costs (given exogenously as C_j^{sr}):

$$x_{ji}^{sr} = \ln k_{ji}^{sr} + \ln \bar{x}_i^r + \sum_{ks}\alpha_i^{sr}\ln\left(p_k^s + c_k^{sr} \right)/\left(p_j^s + c_j^{sr} \right). \tag{4.43}$$

This derivation implies that

$$a_{ji}^{sr} = k_{ji}^{sr}\prod_{ks}\left[\frac{p_k^s + c_k^{sr}}{p_j^s + c_j^{sr}} \right] \tag{4.44}$$

or generally

$$\left\{ a_{ji}^{sr}(p,c) \right\} \equiv A(p,c). \tag{4.45}$$

This means that all interregional input–output coefficients are functions of prices and transportation costs.

Reformulating the interregional dynamic equilibrium problem in the dual space (the price-space), we have

$$\gamma p = pA(p,c) + \bar{\rho}pB; \tag{4.46}$$

where

$$[A(p,c) + \bar{\rho}B] = Q(p,r,\bar{c}), \tag{4.47}$$

$\gamma = 1$ implies a general, long-term equilibrium in space, because at $\gamma = 1$ revenue per unit of output exactly equals cost of production in the long run. Theorem 3 can also be used to ensure the existence of a solution to this problem for a $\bar{\rho}$ and $\bar{c}$. γ is a strictly monotonically increasing function of the rate of interest, r. Thus, there is a rate of interest ensuring a general equilibrium of all prices at any given transportation cost structure, $\bar{c} = c_j^{sr}$. At given equilibrium prices, input–output coefficients are also at an equilibrium as determined by

$$\gamma x = A(p^*,\bar{c})x + \lambda_\omega Bx, \tag{4.48}$$

which has been proved by Theorem 4 to have an equilibrium solution x^* for any positive price structure p^*, given any transportation cost structure and common growth rate λ_ω. By line search, λ_ω can be determined so as to ensure full use of production capacity, i.e. so as to make $\gamma = 1$.

The derivation of interregional inputs as functions of prices can also be achieved by the use of a spatial generalization of the so-called Shephards Lemma.

Theorem 6 [Interregional Factor Demand Theorem (IFDP)]

For twice continuously differentiable minimum cost functions, $Z(p,\bar{c},\bar{x}_i^r) = Z_i^r$, positive in p, transport costs and production scale, each input demand is determined as

$$\frac{\partial Z(p,\bar{c},\bar{x}_i^r)}{\partial p_j^s} = x_{ji}^{sr}. \tag{4.49}$$

The IFDP is obviously far more general than the approach based on any simple production function as the CD-function.

According to the IFDP there is not need to specify the technological constraints of an interregional production system by *production functions*. It is enough if cost functions can be postulated. Knowing these cost functions allows the determination of optimal factor demand and input–output functions with input prices and transport costs as arguments.

5.   Factor growth and mobility

5.1.   Capital mobility

Regional economic theory has provided some theories of capital mobility in
space. Most of these can, however, be seen either as theories of corporate
decision making on location of plants or firms – a problem already covered by
Section 2 of this chapter – or as spatial interdependence theory – already covered
in Section 4 of this chapter. In Section 4 spatial mobility of capital is captured by
the spatial accelerators b_{ij}^{rs}.

Richardson (1969) has tried to develop these essentially technological coefficients of location into behavioral parameters. These attempts have not been more
successful than the attempts at an investment theory by other non-spatial
economists. Investment decision theory at the microeconomic level remains
essentially an unexplored field of research. This is probably a consequence of the
fundamental uncertainty and speculative elements associated with investment
decisions. Adding the freedom of choice of location of the new capital goods does
not reduce the uncertainty and conjectural nature of investment decisions.

One of the few interesting attempts at a spatial investment theory is based on
the Johansen (1972) paradigm of production functions. This paradigm is essen-

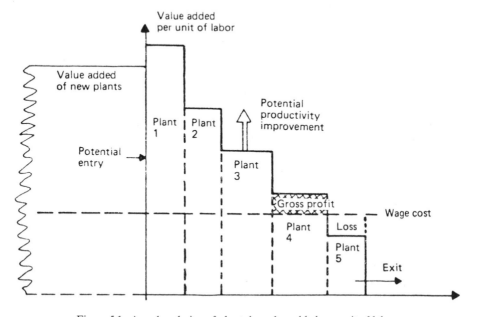

Figure 5.1. A rank ordering of plants by value added per unit of labor.

tially a generalization of the Heckscher–Salter approach [Salter (1969)]. The basic ideas can most easily be demonstrated in Figure 5.1.

In Figure 5.1 all plants of a region and a given industry are rank ordered by labor productivity. Plant 5 of the diagram faces unit wage cost above the value added per labor unit. Thus it cannot survive but must exit from the industry of the region. Entry of new plants would depend on the gross profit of those units (to the left of the origin-point of the diagram) in comparison to the unit capital cost, and of the costs of improving productivity of plants 1–4. The outcome of such a process can only be analyzed within a dynamic regional–industrial interdependency model because of the endogenous nature of wage rates and other prices. Such a model has been proposed and tested by Johansson and Strömqvist (1981).

5.2. *Innovation and diffusion of technology in regional growth models*

In Section 2.2 the diffusion of information is discussed without explicit consideration of the consequences of technological knowledge on regional economic development. The lack of such considerations in regional economic theory is surprising and distressing in view of the importance differentials in the level of knowledge have for interregional differences in the level of economic development. With the exception of a few papers [see among others Andersson and Mantsinen (1981) (hereafter, A–M)] the creation of and diffusion of knowledge as a regional development factor has not been integrated into regional growth theory. For a recent contribution see Chapter 15 in this Handbook.

The A–M model has the following structure. Each region is production characterized by a neoclassical production function. $Q_r = F_r(C_r, a_r)$, where $a_r \equiv$ accessibility to knowledge of region $r = \sum_s \exp\{-\beta d_{rs}\} K_s$, where $d_{rs} =$ distance from region r to region s, $K_s =$ stock of knowledge in region s, and $C_r =$ stock of capital in region r. Labor use in the simplest version of the model is assumed proportional to capital and is exogenously determined supply.

Capital and knowledge are assumed to grow in proportion to the propensity to save (σ_r) with an allocation between investments and R & D determined by the share of R & D, ρ_r, in total accumulation.

$$
\left.
\begin{aligned}
\dot{C}_r &= (1 - \rho_r)\sigma_r F_r\!\left(C_r, \sum_s e^{-\beta d_{rs}} K_s\right) \\[2mm]
\dot{K}_r &= H_r\!\left(K_r, \rho_r \sigma_r F_r\!\left(C_r, \sum_s e^{-\beta d_{rs}} K_s\right)\right) \\[2mm]
&(r = 1, \ldots, n)
\end{aligned}
\right\}.
\tag{5.1}
$$

The H_r-functions are assumed to be positive and smooth for positive arguments.

With the use of Theorem 3 it is possible to prove the existence of a growth equilibrium of all regions with constant capital/knowledge ratios.

Comparative dynamic analysis also shows that a decrease of any distance, d_{rs}, will increase the equilibrium rate of growth of *all* regions (after a possible reallocation of the regional relative shares of total income for the system of regions).

If increasing returns to scale is assumed, simultaneously with spatial frictions this model has shown that increasing a $\rho_r = \rho_s = \rho$ from a suboptimal level can lead to increasing regional income disparities before regional income growth rates converges to a new and higher common rate of growth.

5.3. Labor mobility

Capital allocation in space can to a large extent be handled in the framework of microeconomic location theory or as a part of dynamic interdependence analysis. This is not the case with labor mobility. The decision to migrate is taken by the household as an indirect response to decisions of firms. Thus both firm and household decision making influence immigration flows (see also Chapter 13 of this Handbook).

Classical migration analysis does not take this into proper account. Instead the growth of regionally interacting populations is built on a demographic foundation, where the purely demographic parameters regulating age specific survival and birth processes are complemented by age specific migration probabilities. In most cases the model used is a Markov chain of the following general structure:

$$\Pi(t+1) = G\Pi(t) + M\Pi(t) \tag{5.2}$$

where

$\Pi(t) \doteq$ vector of age specific population by regions

$G \doteq$ matrix of survival and birth rates specified by age and region,

$M \doteq \{m_a^{rs}\} \doteq$ matrix of migration probabilities.

The Markov-chain approach is simple in its dynamic representation [see Keyfitz (1968), Rogers (1971), Rogers and Willekens (1978)]. Others have advocated a semi-Markov model, in which "duration-of-stay-effects" can be accommodated. These models can be considered as generalization of the so-called mover stayer of migration specified by region of origin and destination by age group.

It is clear that Theorems 2 and 3 can be used to prove the existence and relative stability of this kind of growth process for given G and M.

Thus a steady state population distribution over age classes and regions can be determined as the maximal eigenvalue solution to

$$\lambda \Pi = (G + M)\Pi \tag{5.3}$$

where $(\lambda - 1)$ is often called the intrinsic rate of population growth. It is obvious that the parameters of the M-matrix are in reality not constants but (slowly) changing variables determined by the economic conditions of the regions.

For simplicity assume that the labor force is proportional to the population, i.e. $L \approx \Pi$. Furthermore assume that the migration rates m^{rs} depend on wage rates and that wage rates are determined by marginal productivity of labor. With capital preallocated, this implies that regional wage rates are functions of regional population sizes only. Thus

$$m^{rs} = f(w^s - w^r - C^{sr}) \equiv f(v^s(\Pi^2) - v^r(\Pi^r) - C^{sr}); \tag{5.4}$$

where $f(w^s - w^r - C^{sr}) \doteq$ migration rate from r to s being a function of real wage difference and moving cost between region s and region r. $v^s(\Pi^s) \doteq$ the inverse marginal productivity of labor ($\approx$ population) of region s.

$C^{rs} \doteq$ cost of migration from region r to region s.

We thus have the migration mapping

$$\begin{aligned} F(\Pi, C) &\doteq \text{a matrix of population dependent migration rates} \\ &\doteq \{m^{rs}(\Pi^r, \Pi^s, C^{rs})\}. \end{aligned} \tag{5.5}$$

One especially popular version of $m^{rs}(\Pi^r, \Pi^s, C^{rs})$ is the logit model of migration behavior (or the random utility location choice model) [see McFadden (1978) or Chapter 3 of this Handbook].

The regional population growth model can thus be reformulated as

$$\Pi(t+1) = G\Pi(t) + F(\Pi(t), \bar{c}) \tag{5.6}$$

which is a nonlinear difference equation system. The steady state problem corresponding to this system is $\lambda \Pi = H(\Pi, \bar{c})$; where $H(\Pi) = G\Pi + F(\Pi, \bar{c}) > 0$ for $\Pi > 0$. Thus Theorem 3 can be applied to prove the existence of a steady state solution at which the relative population share of each region is constant and where the absolute level of population could be growing, stagnant or declining.

It is possible to enlarge this dynamic analysis to include differences in environmental as well as accessibility differentials. An especially interesting example is the dynamic migration model by Casti and Leonardi (1986).

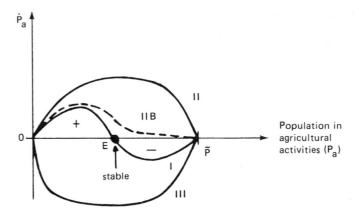

Figure 5.2. Potential movements from a stable product mix to alternative specialized labor allocations.

Smoothly increasing the capital stock or level of technology of a region would cause a smooth response in growth rate and in the regional shares of population.

5.4. Structural change of regional labor supply

The sudden and unexpected collapse or explosion of regional populations leading to ghost phenomena or explosive population growth have traditionally been explained by indivisibilities and similar large scale causalities. In a pioneering article Mees (1975) proposed the application of catastrophe theory to the problem of structural change in population and labor force. This starting point is a model compatible with Figure 5.2.

$$
\left.
\begin{aligned}
\dot{P}_a &= \alpha w(P_a) P_a (\bar{P} - P_a) \\
w(P_a) &= \beta_0 - \beta_1(\tau) P_a \\
\frac{\dot{P}_a}{P_a} &= \alpha [\beta_0 - \beta_1(\tau) P_a][(\bar{P} - P_a)]
\end{aligned}
\right\}
\tag{5.7}
$$

where
  $P_a \doteq$ population of a given region working in agriculture,
  $\bar{P} \doteq$ total working population,
$w(P_a) \doteq$ wage rate of agricultural work as a function of agricultural labor,
  $\tau \doteq$ transportation cost,

$$
\frac{\dot{P}_a}{P_a} \equiv 0 \quad \text{if} \quad P_a = \frac{\beta_0}{\beta_1} \quad \text{or if} \quad P_a = \bar{P}.
\tag{5.8}
$$

The solution shapes of the differential equation can be of three types:

I with interior solution, giving an integrated economy with *part* of the population in agriculture at the stable equilibrium;

II with the whole population in agriculture exporting agricultural commodities in exchange for city commodities at the stable equilibrium;

III with the whole population in city commodity production.

A structural change from a type I into a type II or III economy could occur if β_1 declines below a certain critical value, so that no interior solution exists but only the stable corner solution where $P_a = \bar{P}$. Mees' hypothesis is that this could happen as a consequence of declining cost. Some regions would then specialize at the zero equilibrium point, producing city commodities only. Other regions would move to opposite equilibrium producing agriculture commodities only. Declining transportation costs are thus a necessary condition for specialization and interregional trade. A smooth gradual decline of transportation costs can lead to a sudden extinction of the stable interior equilibrium E^*.

Mees then proceeds to analyze the structural change possibilities of a four parameter version of this labor allocation model. A four parameter n-dimensional

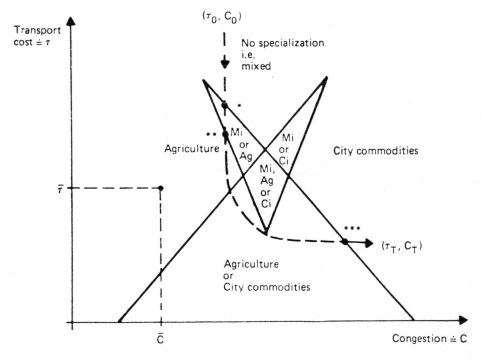

Figure 5.3. Butterfly catastrophe set for specialization patterns of regions at different transport and crowding costs.

ordinary differential equation that acts to maximize a smooth potential function with a single canonical variable has a solution set called a *butterfly*. See Figure 5.3.

The four parameters used in the model are

$\tau \doteq$ the difficulty (cost) of transportation,

$q_a \doteq$ productivity in agriculture (per unit of labor),

$q_c \doteq$ productivity in city occupations (per unit of labor),

$p \doteq$ total population to be employed;

after proper normalization the canonical parameters are:

$\tau \doteq$ difficulty of transportation,

$q \doteq$ average productivity for the occupations,

$\Delta q \doteq$ difference in productivity between the occupations,

$C \doteq P/(\text{total arable land}) \doteq$ crowding.

Assuming the starting point to be transport cost level τ_0 and congestion level C_0.

Infrastructural investments are then assumed to gradually reduce transportation costs to and from the region following the trajectory $(\tau_0, C_0 - \tau_T, C_\tau)$ vertically. At the star-marked point (*) there is *no* change. Not until the point marked by ** is there an abrupt shift from an unspecialized into agricultural production with imports of city commodities.

Further reducing the transportation costs with immigration of labor, increasing congestion C finally implies a drastic shift, from completed specialization on agriculture to a complete specialization on agriculture to a complete specialization on city commodities beyond the point marked by ***.

Based on a series of similar catastrophe theoretic arguments a powerful theorem emerges:

Theorem 7

A gradual improvement of transportation infrastructure with generally decreasing transport costs as a consequence sooner or later leads to smooth or drastic increases in regional specialization and interregional trade.

Proof

Mees (1975).

One can of course argue that the potential dynamics assumption underlying this theorem is too special. This is a valid critique if completely general economic systems are allowed for. The Darwinian character of competitive systems (as well as the overall profit maximizing character of feudal or state capitalistic systems) does, however, lend some credibility to the assumption of search in the direction of total cost minimization or profit maximization for a large class of economic systems.

6. Prospects of further progress in dynamic regional analysis

Dynamic analysis of spatial economic systems is by no accounts an old field dating back to the 1930s. Already the dynamic oligopolistic models formulated by Hotelling (1929) and his followers, indicate the intricate nature of dynamics in space. Linearization is almost always needed if closed solutions are aspired – at least if we want to address problems of a general equilibrium nature involving many producers and consumers in distinct locations. And those closed solutions are too frequently the sanitized qualities of the steady state with its questionable relevance to historical reality.

Two quasi-static paradigms have been proposed in this chapter:

(a) Eigen-equation or self-mapping [see Hirsch and Smale (1974)] reformulations of linear or weakly nonlinear dynamic models.

(b) Catastrophe theory reformulations of dynamic problems, suitable for one-dimensional optimizations.

Often these two paradigms are sufficient for a progression in understanding a specific dynamic and spatial problem, but in other cases they do not lead in the right direction, especially if the dynamics of the problem must be preserved at all stages of analysis.

We have proposed the use of large-scale computer simulation or *Simulative Theorizing* as a newer correspondence principle to provide deeper insights into some of these otherwise intractable dynamic spatial problems.

In recent years some progress has also been made in the development of truly dynamic *bifurcation analysis* (of which catastrophe theory is a special case). The classical economic model of interactions between the acceleration and the multiplier is a convenient starting point. It can be formulated as the following oscillator equation:

$$\ddot{x} + \beta \dot{x} + \gamma = 0. \tag{6.1}$$

This model can exhibit any dynamic behavior – stable approach of a node, explosive development of the x-trajectory, or even harmonic oscillations etc. – depending on the parameters. It is easy to show that, if β and γ are functions of time, the system can go through a phase transition or bifurcation zone, for instance where the system goes from a stable node into a limit cycle property.

Slightly more general is the Van der Pol oscillator

$$\ddot{x} + \varepsilon(x^2 - \gamma)\dot{x} + x = 0. \tag{6.2}$$

This system has a strong repeller at the origin and an attractive limit cycle.

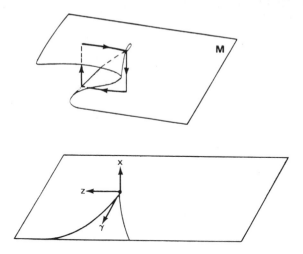

Figure 6.1. Behavior of a simple dynamic catastrophe model.

The Van der Pol oscillator can be seen as a mathematical analogue of the Schumpeter (1936) development theory according to which the general equilibrium ($x = 0$) is avoided by the entrepreneurs, who force the system into some limit cyclical behavior, with the limit of the cycle regulated by economic policy.

Recently the Van der Pol equation has been reformulated within a truly dynamic bifurcation theory framework. It is based on the reformulation:

$$\ddot{x} + K\left(x^2\dot{x} - \gamma\dot{x} - \dot{z}\right) = 0 \tag{6.3}$$

or the equivalent system of fast and slow equations.

$$\left.\begin{aligned}\dot{x} &= -K\left(1/3x^3 - \gamma x - z\right); \text{(fast equation)} \\ \dot{z} &= -K^{-1}x; \text{(slow equation)}\end{aligned}\right\}. \tag{6.4}$$

The behavior of the equation is illustrated in Figure 6.1.

Dendrinos and Mullally (1983) have also recently tried to explain the oscillatory behavior of populations and incomes in American cities. Using a dynamic equation of this type, they showed that oscillations can occur but should be expected to be of "sink and spiral type".

It is clear that further development of dynamic spatial economics requires new directions both in teaching and research. The work reported in Beckmann and Puu (1985) indicates a strong need for a firm basis in partial differential equations, while developments in other fields of applied dynamic analysis will require a better orientation in synergetics as developed by Haken (1983) and others.

References

Alao, Nurudeen, Michael F. Dacey, Omar Davies, Kenneth G. Denike, James Huff, John B. Parr, and M. J. Webber (1977) 'Christaller central place structures: An introductory statement', *Studies in geography no. 22*. Evanston, IL: Northwestern University.

Andersson, Å. E. and J. Mantsinen (1981) 'Mobility of resources, accessibility of knowledge, and economic growth', *Behavioral Science*, 25:5.

Baumol, William (1970) *Economic dynamics*, 3rd edition. New York: Macmillan.

Beckmann, Martin J. (1952) 'A continuous model of transportation', *Econometrica*, 20:643–659.

Beckmann, Martin J. (1970) 'The analysis of spatial diffusion processes', *Papers of the Regional Science Association*, 25:109–117.

Beckmann, Martin J. and T. Puu (1985) *Spatial economics: density, potential, and flow*. Amsterdam: North-Holland.

Borts, G. M. and J. L. Stein (1964) *Economic growth in a free market*. New York: Columbia.

Burmeister, E. and A. R. Dobell (1970) *Mathematical theories of economic growth*. London and New York.

Casetti, Emilio (1969) 'Why do diffusion processes conform to logistic trends?' *Geographical Analysis*, 1:101–105.

Casti, J. and G. Leonardi (1986) 'Agglomerative tendencies in the distribution of populations', *Regional Science and Urban Economics*, forthcoming.

Chamberlin, Edward H. (1948) *The theory of monopolistic competition*, 6th edition. Cambridge, MA: Harvard University Press.

Clarke, M. (1981) 'A note on the stability of equilibrium solutions of production-constrained spatial interaction models', *Environment and Planning*, A13:601–604.

Cooper, Leon (1967) 'Solutions of generalized locational equilibrium models', *Journal of Regional Science*, 7:1–18.

Dendrinos, D. and H. Mullally (1983) *Urban evolution*. New York: Academic Press.

Eaton, B. Curtis and Richard G. Lipsey (1975) 'The principle of minimum differentiation reconsidered: Some new developments in the theory of spatial competition'. *Review of Economic Studies*, 45:27–49.

Fiacco, Anthony V. and Garth McCormick (1968) Nonlinear programming: Sequential unconstrained minimization techniques. New York: Wiley.

Gannon, Colin A. (1972) 'Consumer demand, conjectural interdependence, and location equilibria in simple spatial duopoly', *Papers of the Regional Science Association*, 28:83–107.

Gannon, Colin A. (1973) 'Central concentration in simple spatial duopoly: Some behavioral and functional conditions', *Journal of Regional Science*, 13:357–375.

Gilmore, Robert (1981) *Catastrophe theory for scientists and engineers*. New York: Wiley.

Hägerstrand, Torsten (1967) (originally published 1953), *Innovation diffusion as a spatial process*. Chicago: University of Chicago Press.

Haken, Hermann (1983) *Advanced synergetics*. Berlin and New York: Springer-Verlag.

Harris, B. and A. G. Wilson (1978) 'Equilibrium values and dynamics of attractiveness terms in production-constrained spatial interaction models', *Environment and Planning*, A10:371–388.

Harrod, R. F. (1948) *Toward a dynamic economics*. London.

Hartwick, John M. (1972) 'Comments on Colin A. Gannon's paper', *Papers of the Regional Science Association*, 28:109–110.

Hiller, Frederick S. and Gerald J. Lieberman (1980) *Introduction to operations research*, 3rd edition. San Francisco: Holden-Day.

Hirsch, M. W. and Smale S. (1974) *Differential equations, dynamical systems, and linear algebra*. New York: Academic Press.

Hotelling, Harold (1929) 'Stability in competition', *Economic Journal*, 39:41–57.
Hudson, J. C. (1969) 'Diffusion in a central place system', *Geographical Analysis*, 1:45–58.
Intriligator, Michael D. (1971) *Mathematical optimization and economic theory*. Englewood Cliffs, N.J.: Prentice-Hall.
Isard, Walter, Panagis Liossatos, Yoshigeto Kanemoto, and Phyllis C. Kaniss (1979) Spatial dynamics and optimal space-time development. Amsterdam: North-Holland.
Isard, Walter and Tony E. Smith (1967) 'Location games: With applications to classic location problems', *Papers of the Regional Science Association*, 19:45–80.
Isard, Walter and Tony E. Smith (1968) 'Coalition location games: Paper 3', *Papers of the Regional Science Association*, 20:95–107.
Isnard, C. A. and E. C. Zeeman (1976) 'Some models from catastrophe theory in the social sciences', in: L. Collins, ed., *The use of models in the social sciences*. Boulder, CO: Westview Press.
Johansen, L. (1972) *Production functions*. Amsterdam: North-Holland Publishing Company.
Johansson, B., and Strömqvist, U. (1981) 'Regional rigidities in the process of economic structural development', *Regional Science and Urban Economics*, 11.
Keyfitz, N. (1968) *Introduction to the mathematics of population*. Reading, Mass.: Addison-Wesley.
Kuenne, Robert E. (1977) 'Spatial oligopoly: Price-location interdependence and social cost in a discrete market space', *Regional Science and Urban Economics*, 7:339–358.
Kuenne, Robert E. and Richard M. Soland (1972) 'Exact and approximate solutions to the multisource Weber problem', *Mathematical Programming*, 3:193–209.
Lerner, A. P. and H. W. Singer (1937) 'Some notes on duopoly and spatial competition', *Journal of Political Economy*, 45:145–160.
Liossatos, Panagis (1980) 'Spatial dynamics; some conceptual and mathematical issues', *Environment and Planning*, A12:1051–1071.
McFadden D. (1978) 'Modeling the choice of residential location', in: A. Karlqvist, L. Lundqvist, F. Snickars, and J. Weibull, eds. *Spatial interaction theory and planning models*. Amsterdam: North-Holland Publishing Company.
Mees, A. (1975) 'The revival of cities in medieval Europe', *Regional Science and Urban Economics*, 5(4).
Miller, Ronald E. (1979) *Dynamic optimization and economic applications*. New York: McGraw-Hill.
Morrill, Richard L. (1968) 'Wave of spatial diffusion', *Journal of Regional Science*, 8:1–18.
Nijkamp, Peter and Frans van Dijk (1980) 'Analyses of conflicts in dynamical environment systems via catastrophe theory', *Regional Science and Urban Economics*, 10:429–451.
Nikaido, H. (1968) *Convex structures and economic theory*. New York: Academic Press.
Nikaido, H. (1970) *Introduction to sets and mappings in modern economics*. Amsterdam: North-Holland.
Pedersen, Paul Ove (1970) 'Innovation diffusion within and between national urban systems', *Geographical Analysis*, 2:203–254.
Poston, T. and I. Steward (1978) *Catastrophe theory and its applications*. New York: Pitman.
Puu, Tönu (1977) 'On the profitability of exhausting natural resources', *Journal of Environmental Economics and Management*, 4.
Puu, Tönu (1979a) *The allocation of road capital in two-dimensional space*. Amsterdam: North-Holland.
Puu, Tönu (1979b) 'Regional modelling and structural stability', *Environment and Planning*, A11:1431–1438.
Puu, Tönu (1981a) 'Catastrophic structural change in a continuous regional model', *Regional Science and Urban Economics*, 11:317–333.
Puu, Tönu (1981b) 'Structural stability and change in geographical space', *Environment and Planning*, A13:979–989.
Puu, Tönu (1982) 'The general equilibrium of a spatially extended market economy', *Geographical Analysis*, 14:145–154.
Rainville, Earl D. (1964) *Elementary differential equations*, 3rd edition. New York: Macmillan.
Richardson, H. W. (1969) *Regional economics*. London.
Rogers, A. (1971) *Matrix methods in urban and regional analysis*. San Francisco: Holden Day.
Rogers, A. and Willekens, F. (1978) Spatial population analysis, IIASA RR-78-18.
Salter, W. (1969) *Productivity and technical change*. Cambridge, UK: Cambridge University Press.

Schumpeter, J. (1936) *Theory of economic development*. Cambridge, MA: Harvard University Press.

Shaked, A. (1975) 'Non-existence of equilibria for the two-dimensional three-firms location problem', *Review of Economic Studies*, 45:51–55.

Smith, Terence R. and George J. Papageorgiou (1982) 'Spatial externalities and the stability of interacting populations near the center of a large area', *Journal of Regional Science*, 22:1–18.

Smithies, Arthur (1941) 'Optimal location in spatial competition', *Journal of Political Economy* 49:423–439.

Solow, R. M. (1956) 'A contribution to the theory of economic growth', *Quarterly Journal of Economics*, 70.

Stevens, Benjamin H. (1961) 'An application of game theory to a problem in location strategy', *Papers of the Regional Science Association*, 7:143–157.

Swan, T. W. (1956) 'Economic growth and capital accumulation', *Economic Record*, 32, no. 63.

Takayama, Akira (1974) *Mathematical economics*. Hinsdale, IL: Dryden.

Tapiero, Charles S. (1971) 'Transportation-location-allocation problems over time', *Journal of Regional Science*, 11:377–384.

Teitz, Michael B. (1968) 'Locational strategies for competitive systems', *Journal of Regional Science*, 8:135–148.

Tobler, Waldo R. (1967) 'Of maps and matrices', *Journal of Regional Science*, 7, Supplement: 275–280.

Varayia, P. and M. Wiseman (1984) 'Bifurcation models of urban development', *Regional and Industrial Development*.

Webber, M. J. and A. E. Joseph (1978) 'Spatial diffusion processes 1: A model and an approximation method', *Environment and Planning*, A11:355–347.

Wilson, A. G. (1971) 'A family of spatial interaction models and associated developments', *Environment and Planning*, A3:1–32.

Wilson, A. G. (1976) 'Catastrophe theory and urban modelling', *Environment and Planning* A8:351–356.

Wilson, A. G. (1980) 'Aspects of catastrophe theory and bifurcation theory in regional science', *Papers of the Regional Science Association*, 44:109–118.

PART 2

REGIONAL ECONOMIC MODELS AND METHODS

Chapter 7

REGIONAL AND MULTIREGIONAL ECONOMIC MODELS: A SURVEY

PETER NIJKAMP, PIET RIETVELD and FOLKE SNICKARS

1. Introduction

The present chapter contains a concise survey and a set of reflections concerning current regional and multiregional economic models. The notation "current" refers here to the situation around the mid-1980s. A number of reviews of multiregional economic models undertaken in the first half of the 1980s forms the primary input for this survey. A major source of information on these models is found in Issaev et al. (1982) which contains a comprehensive worldwide review of operational multiregional economic models.

In the present chapter particular attention will be given to the *use* of such models. Different agencies engaged in model building have different use concepts. At the current stage, economic models marked by a great variety are developed at academic institutions as well as at national and regional governmental agencies. Also a considerable effort in modeling is made within various consultancy companies. We will confine our attention here to the use of models which relate to public or private decision making in regional planning. We exclude, therefore, models used basically for educational purposes. Models with an entire or overwhelming emphasis on one sector of the economy are also excluded. An example in question would be models for the analysis of transport sector investments, at least if the model would be partial in its treatment of regional economic factors.

Three kinds of uses are envisaged, viz. *forecasting and scenario generation*, *policy impact analysis*, and *policy generation or design*. Thus, the type of regional and multiregional economic models which we give attention to here is used for *decision-making support*. It is worth noting that issues central to regional planning have varied over the past decades. For example, problems of growth regions have not been shared by declining regions. Poor regions have tended to remain poor, even in rich nations. The openness of regional economies has led to an accentuated difficulty in preventing effects of focused policy measures from attenuating over

Handbook of Regional and Urban Economics, Volume I, Edited by P. Nijkamp
©Elsevier Science Publishers BV, 1986

space and time. The effectiveness of regional policy measures has also been questioned. The evolution of specifying and building regional economic models must be seen in the light of these diverse trends.

Regional economic models – in order to be useful – need to pass both *relevance* and *validity* tests. The *relevance* test addresses the issue of modeling for specific situations or adhering to theoretical stringency. Policy-makers are often keen on detailed, but partial and simple models. Adaption mechanisms in a model are often not appreciated. Recent developments have demonstrated [see, e.g. Lakshmanan (1982)], that theory and practice are not substitutes at the current level of applied modeling.

The *validity* issue is related to the role of regional data for economic model building. It is clear that often sacrifices in theoretical stringency need to be accepted to make regional economic models computable and operational. The provision of regional data is different in different countries [see Nijkamp and Rietveld (1984)]. Therefore, a larger diversity of approaches to applied modeling may be expected in comparison with theoretical constructs. Data problems make estimation and validation, especially of dynamic models, a problem in a regional context. This is a serious threat to the success of regional economic models for policy purposes, particularly in the current generally less stable economic environments.

The remaining part of the chapter is divided into six sections. Section 2 is devoted to a historical review of the evolution of the use of regional and multiregional economic models. The parallel processes of problem and model development will be traced since the 1950s. In the third section a number of modeling approaches are briefly discussed. Any regional economic model will contain one or more elements of these, although there is also an evolution over time in their relevance. In the fourth and the fifth sections, a presentation of different aspects of regional and multiregional economic models is given according to a modular scheme. It represents a common way of organizing applied modeling work. Modules can be introduced and replaced, as different model uses appear. Section 6 contains a brief review of the actual use of the kind of the models at hand for policy impact studies. The review goes from purposes of study via an identification of users and a discussion of major bottlenecks and barriers to an intelligent use of models for policy analysis. In the last section of the chapter we outline some perspectives for applied modeling and the use of applied models in the regional economic field.

2.   A brief historical review

Regional and multiregional models have been designed and applied under various circumstances, and with different contents. The first approaches to modeling the regional economy were essentially a natural and logical extension of modeling efforts at the national or international level. In a manner analogous to the national macro model design, models were developed for single regions (states, urban areas, counties, etc.). These models aimed at assessing the impact of regional or nationwide policies at a regional scale. By trying to replicate the national economy at a regional level, most regional economists used a so-called top-down approach, so that the national economy was assumed to be given for the regional model without allowing for a feedback influence.

Consequently, horizontal and vertical impact patterns of the regional economy with respect to other components of the spatial system at hand were left out of consideration [for surveys see Adams and Glickman (1980), Glickman (1977), Knapp et al. (1978)].

Most *single-region economic models* focused on the evolution of a limited number of variables: production output, employment, income, tax revenues, public expenditures, etc. Usually, the model structure was fairly simple, following the main structure of the national model. These models have mainly been used to provide regional forecasts of a limited number of economic indicators.

Nonetheless the single-region models have often been severely criticized. Some major flaws relating to the use of such models appear to be:

(i) The lack of horizontal (multiregional or interregional) feedback and spill-over effects. Especially in a dynamic spatial system marked by strong interregional competition, single-region forecasts tend to be unreliable.

(ii) The lack of satisfactory theoretical basis for including supply effects in the form of specific locational or infrastructural components of a region [see also Treyz and Stevens (1980)].

(iii) The lack of consistency of separate single-region models with respect to the national total system (sometimes called the additivity condition).

(iv) The lack of vertical feedback mechanisms between the national and the regional economy (top-bottom *and* bottom-up patterns).

(v) The lack of a specific orientation toward local, regional or national policy questions in various fields (employment, housing, transportation, energy, environment, etc.).

(iv) The lack of reliable data and/or accessible information systems that may serve to provide the necessary ingredients for building such models.

The criticism of single-region modeling approaches has led to various new directions in regional economic model building, originating from the end of the 1960s onwards [see also Bolton (1980), Courbis (1980), Issaev et al. (1982)].

The first direction in modern regional economic modeling may be characterized as a search for systematic and quantitative representations of spatial economic systems. Much emphasis was placed on the definition and specification of the components and interactions in these systems. At the end of the 1960s and the beginning of the 1970s, regional models were increasingly used as tools for planning and policy making in space and time; examples are urban land-use models and transportation models. In this period many crude programming models were designed to compute the most desirable state of a system according to welfare criteria given a priori. This development of models based on optimality concepts was parallelled by a strong trend towards econometrically specified regional economic models. Those econometric models were most often built on structural frameworks other than the input–output structures. Rather, direct causal relationships were sought between output and factor input, infrastructure policy, and location variables. The latter subset of models, developed in the last stage of the first generation, were in general based on assumptions of infinite resources, so that limitations emerging from environmental constraints, energy availability, land use, quality of life, and equity considerations were not explicitly taken into account.

During the 1970s the awareness of problems related to limited resources has led to a new trend in regional model building in which the impacts of various constraints and limits to growth have played a prominent role. Examples are regional environmental and energy models. This motivates the assertion of a second generation of models emerging in the regional economic field (see also Chapter 14 of this Handbook).

From the middle of the 1970s onward, efforts have been made to design integrated (and sometimes comprehensive) spatial economic models that are suitable for an evaluation of actual regional trends by means of a whole spectrum of (sometimes conflicting) regional objectives and/or side-conditions. Some of these models are multidisciplinary or even interdisciplinary in nature, incorporating also demographic, environmental, energy and social variables. They also focus attention on a multiregional rather than one a single-region system. In this third generation, the regional economic models have a clearer multiregional orientation than before. A multiregional framework has been increasingly employed by regional economic model builders both as part of the introduction of more fully fledged regional economic theory and as a response to emerging policy issues. It is evident that interactions among regions should be properly represented in applied multiregional economic models. This goes without saying for models at national–regional planning and policy levels. The treatment of such interactions is less obvious, but still warranted for cases where one region is in the focus of the analysis and the others serve as composite system exteriors.

Without a consideration of interregional and national–regional links, there is no consistency guarantee for a model of a spatial system as a whole. Only if the focus of the analysis is oriented towards a single region that forms a more or less closed system, and if the macroeconomic (national and international) development pattern is given, it may be regarded as reasonable to adopt a single-region approach at the level of states or local units.

Usually, however, there are various kinds of direct and indirect cross-regional linkages caused by spatiotemporal feedback and contiguity effects, so that regional developments may have nationwide effects. In addition, national or even international developments may significantly affect a spatial system. This is especially important because such developments may affect the competitive situation of regions in a spatial system. For instance, a nationwide innovation policy may favour especially the areas with bigger agglomerations due to their incubator potential. Thus, the diversity in a spatially open economic system requires coordination of policy handles at the national and regional level, leading to the necessity of using multiregional models in attempts to include regional welfare variables in national–regional development planning. Some countries (e.g. France) have even mandated the use of integrated multiregional economic models for setting up regional and industrial plans. In general, however, there is too little information available on the ex ante policy impacts and on the ex post performance of multiregional economic models in such use contexts [see also Folmer and Nijkamp (1985)].

3.   Modeling approaches: some examples

A considerable number of modeling approaches has been developed for understanding regional economies. Despite a wide variety, there are also some common classes which have gained much popularity in the past decades. As examples we mention: economic base methods, input–output analysis, gravity-type models, shift–share analysis, econometric models and programming models. We will briefly discuss this sample of approaches and relate them to the present state of regional economic modeling. It has to be emphasized that this set of modeling approaches is certainly not mutually exclusive. These types can be combined in several ways, giving rise to a considerable variety of (multi)regional economic model types.

3.1.   Economic base theory

Economic base theory regards essentially basic sectors as the driving forces for the economy; service sectors are just a derivative. Tiebout (1962) has placed economic base analysis in mainstream economic theory, drawing as it does from macro Keynesian analysis and the foreign trade multiplier of international trade theory. A wide variety of applications can be found in the regional economics literature, in both the USA and Europe (notably the UK). Economic base theory may be seen as a predecessor of the more elaborated theory on interregional and intersectoral linkages provided by the input–output analysis. In spite of their simplicity, economic base methods have continued to be of practical use in modern efforts to build multiregional economic models. Their essence will briefly be discussed here.

Assume that the economy of a region is subdivided into a set of basic sectors (b), and service sectors (s). Then the simplest form of input–output balance equations for the region may be written as follows:

$$\left. \begin{aligned} x_b &= A_{bb}x_b + A_{bs}x_s + f_b \\ x_s &= A_{sb}x_b + A_{ss}x_s + f_s \end{aligned} \right\} \tag{3.1}$$

where x denotes a production vector, f a final demand vector an A an input–output matrix subdivided into 4 blocks.

If we assume – in accordance with the economic base theory – that $|A_{bs}| \ll 1$, we have:

$$\left. \begin{aligned} x_b &= (I - A_{bb})^{-1} f_b \\ x_s &= (I - A_{ss})^{-1} \{ A_{sb}x_b + f_s \} \end{aligned} \right\}. \tag{3.2}$$

We see from (3.2) that the development of production in the basic sectors will be independent of the regional service sector development. The development in the service sectors will be a linear function of the basic production, and final demand for services. Some service sectors are oriented towards the production system, i.e. $|f_s| \ll 1$ (implying the standard linear basic to service sector relationship). Other sectors mainly deliver their products to final use, i.e. $|A_{sb}| \ll 1$.

Economic base theory is normally not formulated in this fashion. In most applications, the relationships are expressed directly in employment terms. Then forecasts are made for the development of the basic sectors. Our presentation is somewhat more general, as relationships (3.2) are formulated in terms of *sums* over *subsets* of basic sectors. Any such empirical specification could be brought back to the basic relationships given here.

Basic–service relationships may also be interpreted in a regional context. Then x_b and x_s may be looked upon as regional vectors of basic and service production, respectively. Under the assumption that basic sectors have inter-regional linkages and that service sectors lack such connections, (3.2) still holds. It expresses the fact that service production is an economic activity with a local market and little need for heavy basic goods input.

Clearly, a major problem inherent in economic base theory is that it does often not allow for modeling the actual working of the different product markets, though this is in principle not excluded. Although in recent years various attempts have been made to place economic base analysis on a strong theoretical foundation, it has to be admitted that empirically used economic base methods are more founded in practical considerations of data availability than in economic theory. For instance, a theoretically justified identification of basic sectors is often lacking. The main significance of economic base analysis is frequently conceptual, while the foundation of various basic assumptions is still problematic. Nevertheless, from a practical viewpoint, these models have no doubt a certain merit.

3.2. Input – output methods

Input–output methods stem from the double accounting principles of the transaction tables employed in national accounts. In principle, gross production can either be accounted for by adding up the costs of raw materials, intermediary inputs, imports, as well as labour and capital costs, or by tracing the flows of output from sectoral sources to destinations of intermediary and final use (see also Chapter 8 of this Handbook).

A major advantage of the input–output approach is its ability to analyze regional impacts of external impulses (for instance, policy measures or large-scale projects). On the other hand, some clear weaknesses are the assumptions of fixed linear coefficients over time (implying only short-term forecasts), of a homogeneous input (neglecting product diversity), and of pure quantity adjustments (instead of price adjustments).

The use of input–output techniques in a multiregional framework has become quite widespread in many countries [see Issaev et al. (1982)]. Yet the role of input–output models is not as strong in applied contexts at a regional level as it is in national economic analyses. The core of the national input–output models is the table of intermediary shipments. Intersectoral shipments of final demand elements are not normally regarded as central in the context. However, as shown by Andersson (1975) and Batten (1982), some attention has also been given to the intersectoral linkages of investments.

The central issues in regional input–output modeling relate to the theories of interregional trade and factor mobility as well as to regionally specified theories of technological choice [see Andersson (1982)]. In these theories, the production technology aspects are separated from the transport issues. Regional differentials in production techniques in a sector may then exist because of differences in the industrial composition, and varying levels of obsolescence of different capital elements. According to standard theory, technological choice is assumed to precede the choice of region of input purchases.

The classical methods of Isard (1951), Moses (1955) and Leontief and Strout (1963) have been elaborated further by different researchers. Lesuis et al. (1980) and others, have extended the interregional flows aspects to other commodities than goods and services, such as pollutants and other environmental factors. Snickars (1978) and Batten (1982) have developed the Chenery–Moses model further by statistical procedures. Karlqvist et al. (1978), and Los (1980) have integrated the Leontief–Strout model with information-theoretic concepts.

A further line of development of multiregional input–output models concerns the adaption of the interregional flows to market signals of different kind, e.g. prices of transport as well as transport network properties. Harris (1980), Los (1980), and others have contributed to this field of analysis. Recently, there have been attempts by Courbis (1982) to build multiregional, multinational input–output based models.

Multiregional input–output modeling is very data-demanding. In a framework of N sectors and R regions a full specification of an interregional model would demand N^2R^2 data items. Assuming that goods are sent from each sector to a pool, and then bought from that pool by different sectors will reduce the need for data items to $NR^2 + RN^2$. A further transformation to a goods versus product framework has recently been attempted. Let there be $M < N$ transportable products. Then a complete specification of a multiregional input–output model *without* taking recourse to the above mentioned pool concept will demand $RNM + MR^2 + RMN = 2RMN + MR^2$ data items. This calculation assumes the existence of regionally specified output matrices for goods and products as well as input matrices for products and goods. Such a model attempt would represent a step away from the standard fixed-coefficient input–output model towards a complete separation of technological and transport aspects (see for an extensive treatment of input–output analysis also Chapter 8 of this Handbook).

It may be concluded that input–output analysis has played a dominant role in regional modeling. It has been a powerful tool in the empirical description of the space economy.

3.3.   Gravity-type models

Gravity-type (sub)models have become an integrated element of several multiregional economic models. The classical model in this context is the one by Leontief and Stout (1963). It has received its most successful implementation as a part of the multiregional input–output model of Polenske (1981). This model is one of the most extensively used multiregional economic models. Gravity (and, sometimes, entropy or information-theoretic) concepts have also been used in an econometric context. In recent models like the multiregion, multi-industry model developed by Harris (1980) or the model of Milne et al. (1980b), accessibility measures are used to explain factor movements, product flows, or production increments.

Gravity relationships are most often introduced to account for the impact of industrial location on transport flows of inputs and outputs. A principal reason for adopting this framework is the empirically observed phenomenon of crosshauling of commodities belonging to a certain sector. Such shipments of the same products in both directions between pairs of regions are unlikely from a theoretical point of view and infeasible in a programming context, but an empirical fact of considerable importance.

The parameters of gravity models are often estimated by iterative methods. As shown by Snickars and Weibull (1977), and others, these calibration methods are under certain conditions equivalent to maximum likelihood techniques. They may also be inserted into a recursive framework where the information-theoretic variant of entropy methods may be utilized to weigh historical flow data against new pieces of information concerning supply–demand determinants, as new transport link structures. The strength of the methods in these contexts is that they maintain consistency among any predetermined set of exogenous variables.

Gravity models may also be used to determine the impact of location properties on factor mobility and investment patterns. This is the case in many econometric models where different accessibility indices are constructed to explain mobility and investment patterns; see for instance, the model of Ballard et al. (1980b) and the energy-oriented model of Lakshmanan (1979). There is still a need for a theoretical analysis of how these accessibility measures are to be constructed. One way at least is to make use of recursively estimated product flow data to construct dynamic distance-dependent attraction factors.

Indices of a similar type have also been applied to the labour market part of some multiregional economic models [see Treyz (1980)]. There such concepts have been used to estimate some aspects of competition between similar occupational categories. Another context in which gravity models have been applied to issues other than goods transport is the dispersion of pollutants [see (Muller (1979)], and the model of the Hessen economy developed among others by Bougikos and Erdman (1980).

3.4. Shift–share analysis

Shift–share analysis is a fairly pragmatic method to provide projections of regional economic activity with a minimum of available data. The method provides a decomposition of the difference between the growth rate in a particular region (usually in terms of employment) and the growth rate in a standard region (usually the nation). Two components are distinguished. The first component is the *proportional* shift, reflecting the influence of differences in sectoral mix of the regional economy compared with the national economy. The second component is the *differential* shift. It is defined as the employment change due to the fact that employment in each sector in the region grows at a different rate from the sector in the nation. The differential shift is meant to reflect locational advantages of a region. A good example of an interesting empirical contribution can be found in Paraskevopoulos (1974).

Shift–share analysis has been subject to considerable criticism. The outcomes are sensitive to the detail used in the sectoral classification. The differential shifts often appear to be unstable over time, so that they are not useful for forecasting purposes. Further, shift–share analysis is essentially a descriptive method. It does not explain *why* certain regions have locational advantages [see Richardson (1978)]. Therefore, the use of shift–share methods for long-term regional economic projections has to be treated with caution. An essential feature of shift–share analysis is its adoption of the national level as a frame of reference for regional developments. This is also done in top-down models, as will be discussed in Section 5. It is not surprising, therefore, that some top-down models are directly linked with shift–share analysis [see, e.g. Birg (1981)]. However, one major point of criticism of shift–share analysis does not necessarily hold for top-down models; in top-down models an analysis of regional development can be given by explaining the differential shift in terms of location factors [see, e.g. the Dutch regional labour market model, developed by Van Delft and Suyker (1982)].

3.5. Econometric models

Regional econometric models have started as further elaborations of macroeconomic models dealing with variables such as production, consumption, investments, employment [see Glickman (1977)]. In the course of time, regional models estimated by means of econometric methods have been extended into several directions, for example, by including gravity-type approaches, or by integrating spatial interactions in econometric models [see, e.g. Ballard et al. (1980a)]. In addition, input–output models have increasingly been integrated in large-scale regional economic models. This has the great advantage that the sectoral detail in econometric models has been considerably enlarged [see e.g. Stevens et al. (1982)].

The distinguishing feature of econometric models with respect to the above mentioned classes is thus not an underlying theory (as is the case with input–output or economic base models) but the way a model is specified (e.g. based on an underlying theoretical framework) and the way coefficients are estimated. The most common statistical technique is ordinary least squares, although sometimes more advanced methods are used in regional modeling, such as maximum likelihood techniques. Problems of spatial autocorrelation have often been neglected up to now in operational model building, so that it may be feared that the methods used in empirical practice are not at the frontier of econometric research (see also Chapters 10 and 11 of this Handbook for further expositions).

Econometric methods are not incompatible with the economic base approach. Neither is there an intrinsic reason why input–output coefficients cannot be estimated by means of econometric techniques [see for instance Gerking (1977)]. In recent years, there has also been an increasing interest in integrated cross-section time-series analysis (cf. also the recent emphasis on longitudinal data analysis). Further extensions of these directions in regional economic modeling would no doubt enrich this field of research.

3.6. *Programming models*

Programming models have already been used in the early history of regional economics. This cross-fertilization between regional economics and operations research has led to remarkable results [see for a large survey, Miller (1979)]. The distinguishing feature of programming models is the way in which equilibrium solutions are obtained. In the usual simulation and impact models, the number of endogenous variables is equal to the number of independent equations, so that – under these conditions – a unique solution can be obtained by means of standard solution techniques like the Gauss–Seidel method, or other suitable methods.

In programming models, the number of equations may be different from the number of variables (including slack variables), so that no unique solution, but a set of feasible solutions is obtained. In order to select one solution out of the feasible set an objective function is needed, such as to maximize regional welfare or employment or to minimize transaction costs. In most cases a linear programming formulation is specified, but sometimes more advanced methods have to be used, e.g. nonlinear programming or multiobjective programming (see also Chapter 12 of this Handbook).

Programming models are often used for normative purposes, viz. maximizing the efficiency of a spatial system, such as the determination of the optimal allocation of public investments among regions [see, e.g. Granholm (1981)]. Programming models may also serve analytical or forecasting purposes, however. For example, in the multiregion multi-industry model of Harris (1980), interregional trade is approached via a linear programming model (minimization of transport costs). The dual variables obtained are interpreted as location rents which can be used as explanatory variables for interregional location of industrial activities. In recent years, a clear trend toward a closer integration of programming theory and welfare economics (e.g. in spatial choice analysis) has been observed.

It turns out that programming models have been fairly successfully applied in the context of regional modeling (inter alia in location and spatial interaction analysis), although a major limitation of such models is the presupposed constant values of reaction coefficients, so that these models can be less meaningfully applied in case of structural changes. In such cases, singularity, bifurcation or catastrophe models may be more appropriate (see also Chapter 6 of this Handbook).

3.7. Concluding remarks

In the past decades, regional economic analysis has been dominated by a strong model orientation. The sample of modeling approaches presented above demonstrates a remarkable variety of modeling efforts, while uniformity and integration have received less attention. In the next section an attempt will be made at coherently presenting some fields in which regional economic modeling has been active.

4.   Modules in (multi)regional models

4.1.   Introduction

Multiregional economic models may be regarded as model constructs in which a set of regional economies are represented as an interlinked system. The regions should ideally be delineated according to some functional criterion. As an example we may mention labour market regions. In such a region short-term balancing of the labour market may be achieved through commuting. The short-term equilibrium in the labour market is of such general importance that a regional subdivision of this kind us usually opted for in model building. For data reasons, however, it has often been necessary for builders of multiregional economic models to adhere to administrative rather than functional regions. This has increased the need for allowing for diverse kinds of multiregional interactions in economic modeling. In this section a general "prototype" model will be presented as a frame of reference for further discussion (see Figure 4.1). The general scheme given in Figure 4.1 has often been adopted by various builders of multiregional economic models. In earlier decades these classes of models were formulated as pure multiregional or interregional input–output models. In the interregional variant direct linkages between subregions were introduced. In multiregional models also pool concepts and national–regional interactions were accommodated.

   The prototype scheme may be used to show the modeling principles for both regional and multiregional models. The scheme illustrates the fact that regional economic models tend to be built in modular form around a core consisting of a

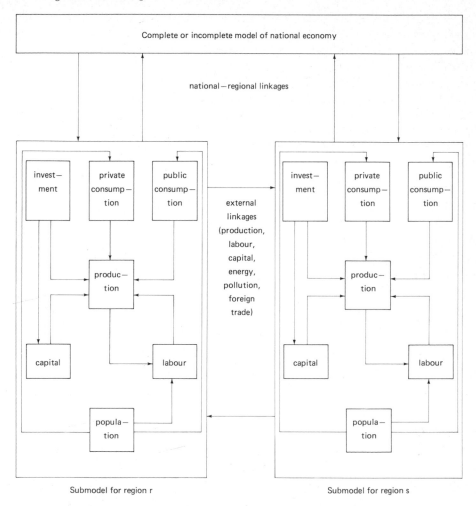

Figure 4.1. A prototype of a regional and multiregional economic model.

set of input–output balances. These regional input–output balances show how demand and supply for goods and services are cleared in each region. The modules focus on individual, or sets of, demand and supply components. Some modules treat production factors. Others represent assumptions about how production and trade flows are formed and adjusted.

Two sets of modules exist for external linkages to a region. One type deals with the connection of the regional level to the national one, often represented by some national macroeconomic model. The other type deals with interregional and international linkages of the different regions. Some examples of application-oriented specifications of a subset of modules of currently workable multiregional economic models will be given below. The prototype model sketched is not an ideal frame to be uncritically strived for. There are no models which are well-developed in all respects mentioned. Models for practical aims are simpler than models built for academic purposes. Models in policy use often place an emphasis on only two or three modules. The clearer the causal structure, the more confidence the models users are likely to attach to the results of model calculations [see Nijkamp et al. (1984b)]. In the following subsections some of these modules will briefly be discussed.

4.2.   *Regional investment, consumption and production*

Investment theory is one of the most underdeveloped areas in regional economics. There is still a fundamental lack of knowledge regarding the motives of entrepreneurial investment behaviour. In the regional economics field various interesting contributions to investment behaviour have been made by Guccione and Gillen (1972). From the literature a set of different theories can be derived that all aim at explaining investment behaviour. Four main classes of theories may be mentioned.

Acceleration theory takes for granted that the level of investments in a certain period and in a certain region is determined by the change in the level of sales. If $K(t)$, $I(t)$ and $Q(t)$ are defined respectively as the capital stock, the investments and the sales in period t and if one assumes a fixed acceleration coefficient β, one may use the following equation:

$$K(t) = \beta Q(t) \tag{4.1}$$

and

$$I(t) = K(t) - K(t-1) \tag{4.2}$$

so that substitution of (4.1) into (4.2) yields the following result:

$$I(t) = \beta \{Q(t) - Q(t-1)\}. \tag{4.3}$$

Clearly, in a *multi*regional context, the acceleration principle has to be extended by the impacts of *extra*regional sales. Some further limitations of the acceleration theory are: overcapacity is assumed away, and every increase of sales is assumed to be permanent and to lead to an extension of the capital stock, while both the supply of investment goods and of financial resources is assumed to be perfectly elastic.

Conventional neoclassical theory assumes a cost minimization based on a neoclassical production function. If we adopt a Cobb–Douglas production function:

$$Q = \alpha L^{\alpha} K^{\beta} \tag{4.4}$$

with L and K labour and capital respectively, and if we adopt a linear cost function C:

$$C = p_L L + p_K K \tag{4.5}$$

with p_L and p_K representing the respective factor prices, then the usual marginality conditions can be derived, in which capital investments are ultimately a function of factor prices and productivities. Clearly, this approach has also limitations among which the assumption of continuous substitutability without any overcapacity is the most crucial one in a regional context.

In the *marginal efficiency of capital approach* it is taken for granted that investments have to be carried out, only if the marginal efficiency of capital is higher than the normal market efficiency. Thus this theory especially points to the financial and cost–benefit aspects involved in an investment decision. A major limitation is that this theory is hardly testable empirically.

The *public intervention approach* assumes that investments are especially induced by public stimuli (taxation, subsidies, social overhead capital, regulations, etc.). It is clear that such measures are especially relevant in a multiregional context, as they may discriminate – and can be employed to discriminate – among regions. On the other hand, it has to be realized that recent findings have demonstrated the low impact of public policy on industrial investments [see, for instance, Folmer (1985)].

In regional economics, the *neoclassical* approach has played a dominant role. These models essentially take for granted that factor supply (capital, labour) determines regional output and income, while demand for output is assumed to response automatically to the growth of production factors [see, for instance, Borts and Stein (1964) and Siebert (1979)]. Dynamic versions of the neoclassical approach can be found among others in Carlberg (1981), Miyao (1981), Smith (1975) and Rabenau (1979), who have studied the stability properties of neoclassical growth theory in a regional or urban context. Such models can also be extended by including agglomeration economies and diseconomies and demand–supply feedbacks.

Despite its elegance, neoclassical investment theory has in general failed to offer an operational framework that can readily explain (structural) changes in a multiregional system, a major reason being its macro orientation. In addition, in empirical applications regional investment functions have not been based on a firmly rooted methodology, but often on ad hoc assumptions [see also Issaev et al. (1982)]. Thus, rather few macro-oriented (multi)regional investment models seem to encompass any novel viewpoints. In this regard, much more emphasis has to be placed on micro (disaggregate) behavioural approaches (see also Chapter 3 of this Handbook).

Conventional economics has devoted much attention to consumer behaviour, mainly at a macro level but also at a micro level (e.g. marketing). It is surprising that in regional economics, consumption analysis is very much underrepresented [see, however, Andersson and Lundqvist (1976)]. Clearly, consumption studies at a regional level can easily be pursued in a way analogous to macro studies, but the main question remains the specific regional implications of a given consumption pattern.

In this context, there is strikingly little empirical evidence regarding the spatial flows of origin and destination of consumption expenditures, so that the distributional pattern of consumption can hardly be traced [see also Nijkamp and Paelinck (1976)]. In this respect too, there is a basic need for more disaggregate approaches to consumer behaviour with a special emphasis on spatial dimensions of micro choice behaviour. Recent research in the area of shopping behaviour provides interesting directions which deserve more interest in future research [see, for instance, Wrigley and Dunn (1984)].

Finally, some remarks on *production theory* are in order. Conventional production theory has been applied quite extensively in (multi)regional models, either in the context of a static input–output analysis or in the context of a neoclassical growth theory. Interesting recent developments can be found in the area of economic growth, innovation, structural change and regional or urban development [see also Johansson and Strömquist (1981)]. The reader is referred to Chapters 6 and 15 of this Handbook for a more detailed discussion of these issues.

Altogether, the analysis of investments, consumption and production of regional modeling has – in the past few years – taken place along the lines of macroeconomics. Only recently the insight has grown that disaggregate choice analysis in these fields may shed new light on various intriguing (multi)regional growth problems.

4.3. Labour market

There is hardly any country in which regional (un)employment issues do not play a key role in economic planning and policy making. Consequently, the need for models enabling one to carry out policy analyses in this field is evident (see for full details also Chapter 13 of this Handbook).

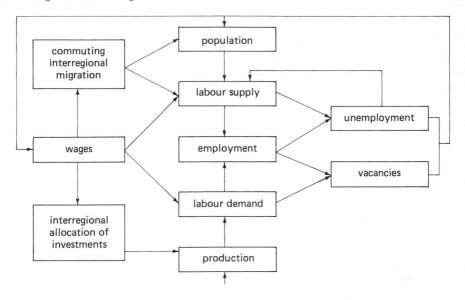

Figure 4.2. Regional labour market model.

As a starting point for the analysis of regional labour markets we use the model described by Figure 4.2. The model gives a fairly complete picture of the variables involved in regional labour markets, as well as the relationships among them [for related approaches, see Ledent (1982) and Schubert (1982a)]. Inequality of demand and supply in the labour market leads to the formation of unemployment and/or vacancies. Various adjustment mechanisms exist in the model to reduce the discrepancy between demand and supply. Unemployment exerts a negative influence on labour force participation via the so-called discouraged worker effect. Wage changes give rise to various direct and indirect responses for labour demand and supply. Commuting and interregional migration on the one hand, and interregional allocation of investment on the other hand, influence supply–demand relationships on regional labour markets. The size of the regions influences the relative importance of the various adjustment mechanisms. For example, the need to model interregional flows is larger, the smaller the regions concerned. The model is characterized by a large extent of symmetry between responses at the supply and demand side of the labour market: both unemployment and vacancies are taken into account. Further, interregional flows of both people and capital play a role. Other notable features of the model are a mixed supply–demand orientation in the determination of regional employment as well as the existence of feedback from the labour market on the production system.

As far as we know, no model exists in reality which shares all features of the model in Figure 4.2. Symmetry between demand and supply appears in the reality of model building an unattainable goal since regional data on vacancies are scarce or wholly absent in most countries [see Rietveld, 1984)]. But even if Figure 4.2 is simplified by deleting all vacancies, it is still hard to find models which satisfy the simplified structure. For example, in a comparative study of 23 regional models having a labour market submodel, Ledent (1981) found that none of these contained a feedback from the labour market system to the production system. Examples of models outside the USA which do provide such a feedback are the Dutch model developed by Van Hamel et al. (1979), and the French model developed by Courbis (1979). In these models the interregional distribution of investments depends among other things on the state of regional labour markets in terms of wages or supply–demand relationships.

Another feature of the standard model is a simultaneous determination of population, employment and unemployment, reflecting a mixed supply–demand orientation of the labour market. This property seems to be shared by a considerable number of models. Chapter 8 of this Handbook reviews also some of the labour market input–output linkages. Many models display a simpler structure, however, an exclusive demand orientation. The simplest possible form of demand-oriented models is that production determines employment.

Despite its simplicity, this form is often used. It is based on the assumption of excess supply on the labour market and the absence of possibilities of substitution between labour and other production factors as a consequence of wage changes. Models with a supply orientation on the labour market are very scarce. An example is a Japanese model, described in Fukuchi (1978) in which regional production depends on regional production capacity, determined via a production function in which labour, private capital and public capital play a role.

It cannot be denied that in some countries a pure supply or demand orientation of the labour market is an adequate representation of reality. A mixed supply–demand orientation will in many cases be more appropriate, however, since it can be used both in times of slack and of boom. Besides, such a mixed orientation is more appropriate for multiregional systems in which supply–demand relationships vary among regions.

The number of (multi)regional economic models in which a balanced attention is paid to both demographic and economic forces is very small. Usually the demographic component is underdeveloped; no attention is paid to age–sex cohorts of population. This makes many of the existing models less suitable for long-run analyses. Among the exceptions are Ledent (1981) and Olsen (1977). Another relevant aspect of the labour market is education as a means for skill improvement. This element is usually lacking. For an exception, we refer to the multiregional labour market model of Schubert (1982b).

We conclude that many (multi)regional economic models only give a partial treatment of regional labour markets. The reason for this is not a lack of theory. Unfamiliarity among economists about demographic approaches also plays a role. In some respects, lack of data plays an important role, for example on vacancies, interregional migration or occupational mobility. The most important factor seems to be that many models are built for specific purposes. Lack of funds reinforces the tendency to build models which are well developed in only a limited number of respects.

4.4. Public sector modeling

The public sector has at least three important roles to play in regional development which are reflected in regional economic model building.

(1) The public sector acts as a medium for real income transfers between individuals, firms, organizations and regions.

(2) The public sector in some economies produces infrastructures which support both household welfare and production efficiency.

(3) The public sector provides personal services to individuals and households in the form of child care, education, health care, old age care, etc.

The first kind of action by the public sector is channeled in multiregional economic models into schemes for redistributing disposable income. In a regional context some redistribution schemes are exogenous and relate to the actions of the national level, while others are based on regional policy parameters; see e.g. Dresch and Updegrove (1980). In this category of actions we will also count transfers between sectors and production units in industry. Examples are locational subsidies or employment support. To model these industrial subsidy systems recent model builders have often adopted a vintage approach; see the vintage models of d'Alcantara et al. (1980), and Johansson and Strömquist (1981).

The second role of the public sector is regarded to be of central policy importance among model builders. However, theoretical and methodological problems have hampered progress in the modeling of the productivity effects of public infrastructure provision. Infrastructure endows regions with built-up comparative advantages. Therefore, some regional economic models will contain infrastructure components also in investment functions. Among models containing elements of this type we may mention the model for the Hessen region, Bougikos and Erdman (1980), and the models of Lakshmanan (1979) and Molle (1982). Also Lakshmanan (1982) contains a discussion of the different roles of infrastructure in regional development in industrialized nations. Other researchers who have attempted to identify the infrastructure effects on regional productivity are among others Nijkamp (1984) and Wigren (1983), who have based their statistical analysis on neoclassical production functions.

In an input–output framework the public sector is treated as one of the components of final demand. The standard method of modeling this sector is to establish bridge matrices between producing sectors and consuming categories of public activities. A sample of such activities was listed above. In the modular framework used here the next step is to estimate demand functions for public services. Simple relationships of this type may be found in economic base models as the one used in Sweden's county planning system [see Guteland and Nygren (1984)]. Subgroups of the populations are often identified and related to service production via simple point estimates in ratio form. The standard method, however, is to treat the public sector as an exogenous entity in multiregional economic models [see, e.g. Dresch and Updegrove (1980) or Hoffman and Kent (1976)].

The public sector actions are major policy handles in multiregional economic models. This is one reason for the frequent exogenous treatment of the public sector. The impacts of exogenous public policy changes are then traced with the help of the model system. In these analyses the financial activities and actions of the public sector are reduced to their real-term core. Financial analyses are almost always introduced into current multiregional economic models as side models showing the financial consequences of a real-term analysis. The three-region Belgian model of Thijs-Clement and Van Rompuy (1979) is an example of a model with a well-developed financial side.

4.5. *Population, environment and energy in regional models*

This subsection will only provide a very concise presentation of respectively population, environment and energy aspects in regional models; see for more details Chapters 13 and 14 of this Handbook.

Especially in models designed for long-run planning purposes, population dynamics plays a major role caused by (a) net natural growth, and (b) inter-regional migration.

Natural growth of population can be included in two different ways. It may be seen as a generic factor (based on, e.g. uniform national fertility and death rates) and as a region-specific factor (caused inter alia by differences in local living conditions or a segmented population structure). Migration can also be included in two analogous ways, viz. as a generic factor (for instance, a uniform national mobility drift due to a welfare rise) and as a region-specific factor (related inter alia to local climatological factors, labour market conditions, technology developments, or local housing market situations).

Population dynamics exert two major influences in regional models, viz. as a supply factor that has a considerable impact on the structure and evolution of regional labour markets, and as a demand factor that influences regional consumption patterns and the use of public facilities.

The majority of (multi)regional models takes for granted the demographic development, so that from the viewpoint of demography many (multi)regional models are essentially top-down models that serve to allocate people among regions without providing an endogenous region-specific explanation for demographic developments [see also Willekens (1983)]. Various methods exist that provide the technical tools for explaining demographic developments, for instance, cohort survival methods, probabilistic (fixed transition) methods, matrix decomposition techniques, exponential or logistic growth methods, explanatory generalized linear models, contingency table and log-linear analysis, event–history analysis, or nonlinear dynamic models [see also Bahrenberg et al. (1984) and Nijkamp et al. (1985)]. A wide variety of techniques is thus available that may provide an aid to (multi)regional modeling with a particular emphasis on evolutionary approaches to regional and urban growth. Those techniques are sometimes also applied in models which have been termed sectoral in this survey and which therefore have not been treated.

Energy demand modules are another example of an important element of current regional modeling efforts. Energy supply does not only act as a constraint to regional development, but it may also act as a driving force for regional development [see, for instance, the boom-town phenomenon related to new energy services; cf. Johansson and Lakshmanan (1985)]. This issue will be further elaborated in Chapter 14 of this Handbook. The same applies to *environmental* modules in regional modeling. From an initial treatment in terms of simple linear constraints, environmental issues have increasingly become a new challenge for regional modeling. The environmental issue is further discussed in Chapter 14 of this Handbook.

5. Regional external linkages

5.1. Introduction

Regional external linkages are a main aspect of both single and multiregional models. Since in general the openness of a region decreases with its size, it is clear that external linkages deserve more attention in (multi)regional models than in macroeconomic models.

There are many reasons why external linkages may exist for regions. First, market areas may be larger than regions, giving rise to interregional flows of goods, money and production factors, including migration of people. Second, multiregional actors may exist such as central governments collecting taxes and distributing their expenditures. Of a similar type are multiregional firms. Third, information flows occur in space, giving rise to regional specific adaption rates of innovations. Fourth, physical flows of pollutants occur, influenced by the production decisions in the various regions. Fifth, institutional factors may give rise to a loss of regional independence, such as the imposition of a uniform minimum wage rate, or the linking of wages to the average price level in a system of regions, and so forth.

Traditionally, the attention in (multi)regional modeling was focused on the first aspect (interregional trade), but in the course of time some of the other factors have also received attention in (multi)regional modeling. We note that the need to model these external linkages does not only depend on the size of the regions, but also on the linkage structure. When use is made of functional interdependent regions a considerable share of the flows in the economy may occur within the regional boundaries, reducing the need to model them as external linkages. It is well known, however, that the regional concept used in the large majority of models is the administrative region [Rietveld (1982)], which is not favourable from this point of view.

Two main approaches exist for modeling external linkages: national–regional linkages (see Section 5.2) and interregional linkages (see Section 5.3). In the first approach it is assumed that the supply and demand of goods or services are cleared at the national level. Transport costs and limited information do not play an important role. A ceteris paribus increase in the supply of a good or service originating in a certain region will give rise to the same absorption pattern among the demanding regions as an increase in supply from any other region. In this approach, the interregional linkages are supposed to be transmitted via the national level so that there is no need to model them explicitly.

In the case of interregional linkages, the assumption of market clearance at the national level is replaced by the notion that transport costs and immobility of resources give rise to smaller than national market areas. Consequently, the interactions between regions will among others depend on the distances between them.

The choice of one of the two approaches will depend on several considerations. First, from the viewpoint of *theory*, a national–regional approach is most appropriate in the case of multiregional actors and of institutional factors operating at the national level (the second and fifth cases mentioned above). In addition, a national–regional approach may be used for goods and production factors with relatively low transport costs (case one above). An interregional approach is most appropriate for the modeling of flows of goods and production factors if considerable transport costs occur, and also in the case of physical flows of pollutants (cases one and four above). For information flows, the choice would depend on the communication medium.

In the practice of regional modeling, theory is not the only, and often not the most important factor affecting the specification of models. *Data availability* is often more important [see, for example, Richardson (1978)]. The number of external interactions to be taken into account in interregional models is equal to $R^2 - R$ (R being the number of regions), whereas in a national–regional approach it is only $2R$, so that clearly the interregional approach is more data demanding.

Another relevant consideration is the kind of *model use* one has in mind. For example, if a model is built to analyze the need for road infrastructure in a multiregional economy, an interregional approach is a prerequisite [see, e.g. Los (1980)].

5.2. *National–regional linkages*

Linkages betwen the national and regional economy can be specified in two ways: from the nation to the region (top-down) and from the region to the nation (bottom-up). We will deal with the top-down approach first.

The *top-down* approach has been proposed by Klein (1969) as the most promising way of building regional econometric models. This proposal "is based on the supposition that general cyclical differentials are more important and easier to deal with than are distance differentials. I would prefer to make regional predictions on the basis of careful study of local reaction to national dynamics rather than from a similarly careful analysis of distance concepts" (p. 115). Thus, in the top-down approach, the regional variables are directly linked with the corresponding national variables.

The relationship between national and regional variables can be specified in various ways. Let x_r and y_r denote variables pertaining to region r and let x and y be the corresponding national variables. Then one has:

$$y_r = f_r(y, x_r) \tag{5.1}$$

$$y_r/y = c_r \qquad \sum_r c_r = 1 \tag{5.2}$$

$$y_r/y = a_r + bx_r/x \qquad \sum_r a_r = 0 \quad b = 1 \tag{5.3}$$

$$y_r/y = f_r(x_r/x) \Big/ \left(\sum_r f_r(x_r/x) \right). \tag{5.4}$$

In (5.1), y_r depends on the corresponding national variables as well as on a regional variable. In a single regional model, there is no problem with this specification, but when it is used for a complete system of regions the adding-up problem arises, since the sum of the y_r is by definition equal to y and there is no guarantee in (5.1) that this equality holds. In some models using this specification a proportional adjustment of y_r is carried out to achieve consistency between regional and national values. From a methodological viewpoint it is better to achieve consistency beforehand by specifying (5.1) in another way [such as in (5.4) although the latter may be more difficult to estimate]. Another objection against the proportional adjustment method is that regional cycles may differ substantially, which would require that for some regions the adjustment must be more than proportional and for some regions less than proportional [see Glickman (1982)].

The problems mentioned above can be avoided by using a fixed shares assumption (5.2) or more flexible specifications in which the regional shares depend on the performance of the region compared with the nation; cf. (5.3) and (5.4).

An attractive property of top-down models is that they can easily be linked with existing national models. In many countries one or more well-tested national models exist. These models are usually based on national data with a better quality and scope than regional data so that they form an attractive starting point for regional modeling. By using an existing national model, the task of generating the necessary exogenous national variables is relatively easy. By linking a top-down model with a national one, such a model is especially suitable for analyzing regional consequences of national policies.

A major disadvantage of top-down models is that they ignore feedbacks from the regions to the national level [see, e.g. Courbis (1982)]. For example, the way in which national governmental expenditure is allocated among regions is assumed to have no impact on national employment and inflation. Such an assumption is hard to defend for an economic system in which both depressed and relatively congested regions occur. Thus, the strict top-down approach implies that a major theme is regional economics must remain untouched: the conflict between national efficiency and interregional equity. This considerably limits the value of strict top-down models for policy evaluation. Furthermore, such models require information on regional imports and exports, data which are rarely available. Examples of multiregional models using the top-down approach are: a Dutch labour market model [see Van Delft and Suyker (1982)], an English labour market model [see Keogh and Elias (1981)], and two American models; a labour market model [Olsen (1977)] and a model dealing with both production and labour market [Milne et al. (1980a)]. It is striking that all these models include the labour market. It is clear that from a theoretical viewpoint, a top-down approach is less suitable for the labour market given the strong limitations on spatial labour mobility. Especially in the short run, such mobility barriers will give rise to a spatial segmentation of labour markets. This finding reveals that theoretical considerations often do not dominate the specification of (multi)regional models. Data availability, and specific applications for which the models are built often play a more important role.

With the *bottom-up* approach the starting point of modeling is chosen in the regions. Values of national variables can be obtained by aggregation (summation or averaging) of the corresponding regional variables. A pure bottom-up structure implies that no regionally invariant variables occur in a model. Regionally invariant variables are essentially based on the top-down approach: $y_r = y$, even if the national variable y may also be determined from the regional level. The fact that in many models some regionally invariant variables occur (for example, prices, interest rates) means that in practice pure bottom-up models are rarely found.

Bottom-up models come to meet the major criterion according to which top-down models fail, namely that they should include feedbacks from the regional to the national level. Examples of multiregional models which approach a bottom-up structure to a large extent are a labour market model for Austria [Schubert (1982b)] as well as a rather comprehensive economic model for the USA [Ballard et al. (1980b)] and for Japan [Fukuchi (1978)]. Usually, these models share a rather low level of sectoral and regional detail (the US model mentioned above is an exception, incorporating 51 regions). Since bottom-up approaches are demanding as to the availability of regional data, it seems that usually regional data bases are not strong enough to allow the construction of highly detailed bottom-up models. This is a disadvantage, since a considerable level of sectoral and regional detail greatly improves the usefulness of models for policy applications.

In principle, multiregional bottom-up models can become competitors of traditional national models. A well-known result from aggregation theory [Theil (1954)] is that only under rather restrictive conditions, a linear relation specified in terms of national variables yields forecasts which are of equal quality compared with an aggregation of corresponding linear relations specified at the regional level. In general, a disaggregate approach would yield superior results.

In reality, bottom-up multiregional models have not yet become serious competitors of macro models. There are several reasons for this. First, the above-mentioned result of aggregation theory is of partial relevance, since it only holds for linear relations. A more important objection of theoretical nature [Grunfeld and Griliches (1960)] is that as soon as national variables play a role in the disaggregate relations, forecasts based on the macro relation may be more reliable than forecasts based on the disaggregate relations. The third reason is that national data are usually of better quality than regional. This topic has received little systematic attention in regional modeling and analysis. Some experiments with alternative specifications of vertical relationships of a regional model in the USA (a state–substate model for Arizona) may be found in Charney and Taylor (1983), while some Dutch regional experiments are contained in Nijkamp et al. (1984a).

It is notable that in applications of bottom-up models up to now little attention has been paid to generating national variables. This is apparently not

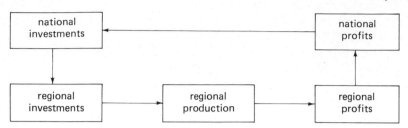

Figure 5.1. National–regional interactions in REGINA.

the prior aim of its builders and users, and weakens one of the main policy-use arguments for bottom-up models mentioned above. They include feedbacks from the regions to the nation so that they could be used to study conflicts between interregional equity and national efficiency, although this is seldom done [see Hafkamp (1984)].

Interactive national – regional models are obtained by combining top-down and bottom-up approaches so that an interdependent system of national and regional variables is formed. For example, in the French REGINA model developed by Courbis (1979), regional investments in certain sectors are obtained in a top-down fashion from national investments, taking into account locational advantages of regions. Regional investment in turn is a determinant of regional production and also of regional profits. Regional profits can be aggregated towards national profits, which are determinants of national investments (see Figure 5.1). In this way an interdependent model is formed in which regional and national variables are obtained simultaneously.

The number of models in this class is limited, however. Some examples are two Belgian models [Thijs-Clement and Van Rompuy (1979) and Glejser et al. (1973)], the French REGINA model [Courbis (1979)], and models from the USA by Lakshmanan (1979) and the USSR by Baranov and Matlin (1982). These models are all quite comprehensive.

Interactive national–regional models share the property with bottom-up models that they can be used as substitutes for macro models to generate results on national variables. The only model from the above-mentioned group which seems to have been used extensively in this respect is the REGINA model.

There are several multiregional models in which the top-down and bottom-up approaches are used without achieving full interdependence. As an example, we give some elements of a Japanese multiregional model [Mitsubishi Research Institute (1979)]. In this model some components of national final demand are exogenous (exports, investments, government expenditures). Regional values for these variables are obtained via a top-down approach. In the regional allocation of these variables input–output relationships and interregional trade patterns are

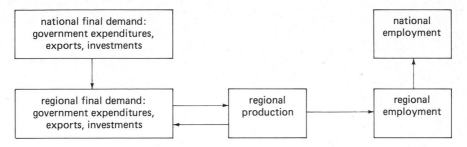

Figure 5.2. National–regional linkages in the model of Japan developed by Mitsubishi (1979).

taken into account. In the next step regional employment is determined, which yields national employment as a result (see Figure 5.2).

This structure is in accordance with the theoretical notions mentioned earlier. A top-down approach is most suitable for products for which national markets exist, whereas a regional based bottom-up approach is most suitable for markets with considerable immobility and high transport costs such as the labour market, the housing market and markets for various services.

A final example of the above-mentioned approach is to work with a top-down structure for final demand and a bottom-up structure for the labour market; it has been applied in a model for Australia [Karlqvist et al. (1978)]. The large variety of model structures used in multiregional modeling is illustrated by the fact that also models exist with the opposite approach; top-down for some production factors and bottom-up for production and final demand. An example of this approach is the Swedish model of Lundqvist (1981).

Clearly, the *non-interactive national–regional models* mentioned here are less integrated than the interactive national–regional models mentioned above. The reason for this phenomenon is their lack of complete linkages at the national level. This lack of linkages gives rise to a considerable extent of recursiveness in these models.

The same observation already made for bottom-up and interactive national–regional models can be repeated here. Model builders and users in general do not show much interest in the possibility of using the models to generate results for national variables. This means that the potential of these models has not yet been utilized to the largest possible extent.

5.3. Interregional linkages

A further dimension may be added to the classification of regional external linkages. In the earlier section top-down, bottom-up, and national–regional models have been mentioned. The latter models have been further classified as interactive or non-interactive depending on the completeness of the analysis at the national level. The individual economic models of each region are interdependent if linkages between individual or subgroups of individual subregions are treated. Otherwise they are classified as independent [see Issaev et al. (1982)].

The linking concept has much to do with the pooling concept mentioned earlier concerning input–output modeling. Then output from a certain sector is assumed to be sent to a pool in another region. Inputs are taken from that pool by different sectors in that subregion. In top-down and bottom-up modeling the national level acts as the pool to which shipments are made. Individual subregions then draw from that nationally determined pool of regions.

The modeling of commodity and service flows between individual subregions is performed by methods different from the modeling of the factor movements. One reason is that factors are mobile only in the longer run whereas commodity shipment patterns may vary, and equilibrate, even in the short term.

Interregional trade is treated in a range of various ways in current multiregional economic models. On the other hand, many of these models exhibit a very superficial treatment of international trade. Among trade modeling methods we may mention general equilibrium, linear programming and interregional input–output approaches, as well as gravity and entropy methodologies, or approaches involving econometric and potential constructs. The most common method usual in practice is the fixed coefficient input–output approach (see Subsection 3.2). This means that few models have the capability of simulating policy impacts via trade adjustments. Any model of a general equilibrium type is really an independent model in the sense defined here. The large model of Harris (1980) of the US regional economies, and the large-scale model system of Baranov and Matlin (1982) of the Soviet economy both employ linear programming techniques. As mentioned earlier, in the first model the dual variables are used as location rents. In the second model, system optimization is only performed for those products which have high specific transport costs.

Recent developments in trade modeling by Los (1980) and Boyce (1983) among others go towards a further splitting of transport markets from commodity markets. This is partly done to be able to model more appropriately the rapid technological developments in the transport sector.

The most common factor mobility represented in applied multiregional economic models is labour mobility. In the short term commuting flows act as gap closers. In the longer term occupational and geographical labour mobility complement and substitute each other as equilibrating forces. Many models assume perfect occupational mobility within each region to reduce imbalances before migration mechanisms are introduced. Some models, like the input–output model of Polenske (1981) and the policy model of Treyz (1980) have included a more theoretically refined treatment of the labour market dynamics. Several models that have a demo-economic orientation treat migration in a detailed fashion. Examples are provided by the model of the US developed by Isserman et al. (1983) and by the Austrian labour market model of Baumann and Schubert (1980).

A number of models treat capital formation exogenously. This is partly due to the fact that investments are looked upon as policy instruments. In other cases, data availability hampers the use of more refined methods. The class of programming models is less affected by these considerations than econometric models. An example of such a model is the model for Sweden of Lundqvist (1981). As stated earlier, however, capital mobility between regions is not a major phenomenon of interest to model builders in the field.

Very few multiregional economic models treat other interregional linkages than the ones we have mentioned here. In some cases issues of environmental pollution are treated by means of different distribution submodels. Many current multiregional models treat labour migration in a quite ambitious way. The costs and benefits of other types of factor mobility are not modeled in the same elaborate way. The question might be raised whether this emphasis is motivated by data availability, theoretical considerations, or search for policy relevance.

6. Model use

Regional models can be used for several purposes: pedagogical purposes, impact analysis, forecasting/projection, monitoring, policy analysis (e.g. ex ante and ex post project appraisal), and simulation. There is usually some hierarchy in the specific purposes of a model, as in many cases the construction of a model may serve multiple purposes. In the context of the present section, we will discuss models from the viewpoint of the most demanding test: their usefulness for policy analysis.

The usefulness of a model depends on various factors. We mention four such aspects of a model here, viz. its sectoral and regional detail, its scope, the recency of its data base, and its specification.

Sectoral and regional detail are important factors in determining the usefulness of a model. For example, if one wants to analyze the regional economic consequences of the stimulation of tourism in a certain area, the reliability and relevance of the outcomes strongly depend on the sectoral and regional detail of the models used. Indeed, in an international survey of multiregional models it was found that models which are frequently used are characterized by a much larger sectoral and regional detail than the average [Rietveld (1982)].

The scope of a model can be represented by the number of subsystems covered. One would expect that models with a large scope are used more extensively than are the more partial models, but this is in reality not the case [Rietveld (1982)]. An explanation may be that model users prefer partial models since they are easier to understand. The structure of comprehensive models is usually more complex. Another reason may be that there is a clear conflict between the model's scope and its level of detail. Models with a large scope are usually characterized by a low level of detail and vice versa. Model users seem to give the latter element a heavier weight than the former.

The recency of regional data bases is often problematic. It is very common that the most recent regional data used pertain to situations prevailing more than five years ago. The reason is that statistical offices attach higher priority to a fast publication for national data than for regional data. Also – as noted in Rietveld (1984) – the frequency of collecting regional data is much lower (the number of regional models based on quarterly data is very small). Producers of regional statistics are not the only cause of insufficient use of regional models, however. Often, the updating of existing regional models is not carried out on a continuous basis, so that the most recent regional data remain unused. As a consequence of these facts, many models being operational in the 1980s with their turbulent dynamics are mainly based on data from periods with a relatively stable development. Their relevance may therefore be questioned.

We will pay special attention to the usefulness of models from the viewpoint of specification. Two aspects will be covered here: national–regional interactions and demand versus supply orientation. Other aspects could be added, such as the role of the time dimension in models, but these will not be dealt with here.

The effectiveness of an instrument i on objective j (denoted as γ_{ij}) can be defined as the (relative) marginal change in objective j divided by the (relative) marginal change in instrument i. Given a set of instruments $i = 1, \ldots, I$ and of objectives $j = 1, \ldots, J$, the whole set of indicators γ_{ij} can be represented by an impact matrix Γ of size $(I \times J)$. From the viewpoint of national–regional relations, both instruments and objectives can be distinguished as national and regional ones. Thus one arrives at a partitioning of the impact matrix as represented in Table 6.1.

The matrix Γ^{rr} indicates the effects of regional policies on regional objectives. It is the traditional subject of policy studies based on regional models. The matrix Γ^{rn} indicates the (maybe) unintended effects of regional policies on national objectives. The matrix Γ^{nn} is the main interest of national policies, while Γ^{nr} describes the (perhaps unintended) effects of national policies on specific regions.

Models which have been specified in a top-down fashion, are based on the assumption of an absence of feedback from regional variables on national variables. Consequently, these models can only be used to study the impact matrices Γ^{rr} and Γ^{nr}. As indicated in Section 5.2, conflicts between national

Table 6.1
Impact matrix for region-specific and national instruments and objectives.

	Region-specific objectives	National objectives
Region-specific instruments	Γ^{rr}	Γ^{rn}
National (regionally uniform) instruments	Γ^{nr}	Γ^{nn}

efficiency and regional equity cannot be dealt with by these models. On the other hand, pure bottom-up models, in which all national variables follow as resultants of individual regional behaviour, can only be used for dealing with Γ^{rr} and Γ^{rn}. The models including a mix of bottom-up and top-down approaches can be used for the whole impact matrix. Each of the components of the Γ matrix will now briefly be discussed.

The submatrix Γ^{rr} can be dealt with in principle by all model structures (single regional, multiregional, bottom-up, top-down, national–regional) and has been covered extensively. Also the matrix Γ^{nr} received considerable attention. For example, Ballard et al. (1980a) report on the differential effects of a uniform increase of national government expenditures on regional employment in the USA. National employment is estimated to increase with 1% as a consequence of the policy. Even with relatively large regions (8 clusters of states have been distinguished), highly varying outcomes have been obtained for the regions, ranging from an increase of 0.2% to 2.8%. Similar results have been obtained by Dresch and Updegrove (1980) in an analysis of the regional effects of a cut in military exports. These results point at the importance of studying the differential regional effects of national policies, not only for government expenditures, but also for policy fields such as education, environmental standards and labour market policies.

The right upper part of the Γ matrix has received considerably less attention. Courbis (1982) reports on the national consequences of various regional invest-ment strategies in France. Due to substantial differences betwen the tightness of the regional labour markets, the national effects of the same policy applied to various regions vary widely. Stimulating one region may give rise to national inflation, whereas the same policy for another region gives rise to an increase of national employment. For an American study of the Γ^{rn} part of the impact matrix, we refer to Ballard et al. (1980b). Both studies reveal that an improve-ment of regional policies is possible, thus giving rise to a simultaneous increase of national efficiency and interregional equity. This reveals that multiregional models with bottom-up elements are useful tools to study the (potential) conflicts between the two above-mentioned policy objectives.

One might argue, that the Γ^{nn} part of the impact matrix is already covered by national models so that multiregional models do not need to be considered for this purpose. Multiregional models with some bottom-up elements are in principle suitable for this purpose, and may even be more appropriate than national models. A rare example of this approach can be found in Courbis (1980).

Another aspect of models having strong implications for policy analysis is the role attached to demand and supply factors. A considerable number of regional models is characterized by a demand orientation. In these models, policies have to be modeled via exogenous changes in final demand. Implicitly, these models assume a highly elastic supply and a large labour mobility, both between sectors and between regions. Although these assumptions may be adequate in some cases, they may in other cases be highly unrealistic. Consequently, they deserve more explicit attention than is usually the case.

An interesting illustration of the sensitivity of model outcomes for the assumption of demand orientation is given by Treyz and Duguay (1980). They analyze the regional effects of an increase of welfare payments, one approach being based on a mixed supply–demand oriented model, and another approach being based on the same model but with the assumption of completely elastic supply. Completely different impacts of this policy on regional employment were obtained: not only in size, but even in sign.

The assumption of supply versus demand orientation is especially important for investments, both private and public. In demand-oriented models, investments serve as a component of final demand, giving them only short-run relevance. In supply-oriented models, investments only add to production capacity, so that these models cannot be used to deal with short-run fluctuations.

An example of a combined treatment of these approaches is contained in Harris (1980) for the case of regional investments in road infrastructure. Short-term demand-oriented effects appeared to have a considerable positive influence, whereas long-term effects were negative, though not large. The latter fact indicates that other regions gained larger benefits from the supply effects than the region of investment itself.

From these results we conclude that the outcomes of policy analysis may strongly depend on the specification of the model used. Sensitivity analyses to check for this dependency are rarely carried out. There is consequently much reason for abandoning the common practice of using point estimates of effectiveness measures, and adopting interval estimates instead.

In conclusion, there is a variety of model structures and a versatility of model purposes. (Multi)regional models have apparently played an important role in making regional economics an operational discipline. Our critical review has, however, also pointed out various weaknesses. Hence, the final section will be devoted to a brief presentation of some caveats in (multi)regional modeling efforts.

7. Perspectives of regional modeling

In the recent past, attempts at building (multi)regional economic models have become less ambitious. Instead of designing new large-scale models for specific policy questions, there is an increasing emphasis on amendments and refinements to existing operational models.

In the past few years, several attempts have been undertaken to link sub-models in coherent overall structures rather than to try to build an entirely new master model with many subsystems [see also Isard and Anselin (1982)]. A systematic modular design of such an effort may ensure consistency and operationality. In this respect, a promising model design may be found in the so-called *satellite* concept which includes in a systematic way all main regional indicators as the core of a model, while more specific and more detailed components can then be added in a satellite form [see also Brouwer et al. (1986)].

As far as the policy relevance and use of (multi)regional models is concerned, there is an increasing tendency toward designing multiple objective *policy* simulation models (based, e.g. on scenario analyses) rather than making conditional forecasts for a spatial system. This closer orientation toward public policy and conflict analysis makes also necessary the use or design of interactive and feedback mechanisms in (multi)regional models in order to let them function as learning tools and decision support systems in policy analysis (see Chapter 12 of this Handbook).

It should also be noted that in recent years *small-scale modeling* efforts have gained increasing popularity. In many cases, however, the design of a simple model for a complex and dynamic spatial system is a formidable task. Under such circumstances it may be worthwhile to design two parallel models, viz. an integrated and large-scale model that is as accurate as possible, and a simpler version which is consistent with the elaborated one, but which includes only the core variables of the system concerned and which is used for direct policy interaction [see also Despontin et al. (1984)].

A major shortcoming in many models is their strong demand orientation. The supply side (from both a private and a public policy point of view) is usually dealt with in a less detailed way. As supply conditions (e.g. infrastructure) often provide threshold values and bottleneck conditions for regional development, the inclusion of supply factors in (multi)regional models is of utmost importance. In this context, especially the incorporation of mechanisms for the creation of new technology, the impacts of R & D investments, and of innovation deserve more attention.

It should also be mentioned that there is strikingly little evidence regarding flows of wealth in interdependent spatial systems. There are only a few models which fully incorporate public expenditure flows, tax flows, capital flows and consumption flows. This means that efficiency and equity questions can hardly be dealt with in a satisfactory manner in current (multi)regional models.

Finally, it has to be recognized that there is an increasing interest in an integrated multiple module representation of a spatial system. This means that, in addition to conventional factors and modules, also related components have to be added, such as demography and labour supply, energy supply and demand, environmental capacity limits and impacts in a region, and regional technology, innovation and R & D. Such a multiple module design has recently led to the notion of *multiple layer projection*, in which all relevant modules of a regional economies system are systematically depicted and projected on different dimensions which are constructed in such a way that a coherent and integrated representation is achieved [see Hafkamp (1984)]. In conclusion, new methodological design principles for building operational (multi)regional models are some of the most important items on a research agenda for modeling the future space economy.

References

Adams, F. J. and N. J. Glickman, eds. (1980) *Modeling the multiregional economic system*. Lexington, Mass.: D. C. Heath.

d'Alcantara, G., J. Floridor and E. Pollefilet (1980) Major features of the SERENA model for the Belgian Plan. Brussels: Planning Bureau.

Andersson, Å. E. (1975) 'A closed nonlinear growth model for international and interregional trade and location', *Regional Science and Urban Economics*, 5:422–444.

Andersson, Å. E. (1982) 'Potentials of multiregional and interregional economic modeling', in: B. Issaev, P. Nijkamp, P. Rietveld and F. Snickars, eds., *Multiregional economic modeling: practice and prospect*. Amsterdam: North-Holland, 205–216.

Andersson, Å. E. and L. Lundqvist (1976) 'Regional analysis of consumption patterns', *Papers of the Regional Science Association*, 36:117–132.

Bahrenberg, G., M. M. Fischer and P. Nijkamp, eds. (1984) *Recent developments in spatial data analysis*. Aldershot: Gower.

Ballard, K. P., N. J. Glickman and R. D. Gustely (1980a) 'A bottom-up approach to multiregional modeling: NRIES', in: F. G. Adams and N. J. Glickman, eds., *Modeling the multiregional economic system*. Lexington: Mass.: D. C. Heath, Lexington Books, 147–159.

Ballard, K. P., R. D. Gustely and R. Wendling (1980b) *NRIES: Structure, performance, and applications of a bottom-up interregional econometric model*. Washington D.C.: Bureau of Economic Analysis.

Baranov, E. F. and I. S. Matlin (1982) 'A system of models for coordinating sectoral and regional development plans', in: B. Issaev, P. Nijkamp, P. Rietveld and F. Snickars, eds., *Multiregional economic modeling: practice and prospect*. Amsterdam: North-Holland 143–156.

Batten, D. F. (1982) *Spatial analysis of interacting economies*. Boston: Kluwer–Nijhoff.

Baumann, J. and U. Schubert (1980) 'Factors of regional labor force participation rates. An econometric study of Austria', Conference of the European Regional Science Association, Munich.

Birg, H. (1981) 'An interregional population-employment model for the Federal Republic of Germany', *Papers of the Regional Science Association*, 47:97–120.

Bolton, R. (1980) 'Multiregional models in policy analysis', in: F. G. Adams and N. J. Glickman, eds., *Modeling the multiregional economic system*. Lexington, Mass.: D. C. Heath, 255–284.

Borts, G. H. and J. L. Stein (1964) *Economic growth in a free market*. New York: Columbia University Press.

Bougikos, G. and G. Erdman (1980) 'An evaluation of spatial planning objectives by means of a multiperiod, multiregional and multisectoral decision model. Presentation and discussion of certain results for the State of Hessen', Working Paper 28, Department of Regional Economics, University of Münster, Münster.

Boyce, D. (1983) 'An appraisal of the state of the art in freight transport modeling', Research Report, Department of Civil Engineering, University of Illinois, Urbana-Champaign.

Brouwer, F., W. Hafkamp, and P. Nijkamp (1986) 'Concepts of integration in integrated environmental models', *Man, Environment, Space and Time*, 4, no. 2:26–54.

Carlberg, M., (1981) 'An economic growth model of the productive city', in: P. Nijkamp and P. Rietveld, eds., *Cities in transition*. Dordrecht, The Netherlands: Martinus Nijhoff, 271–293.

Charney, A. H. and C. A. Taylor (1983) 'Consistent region-subregion econometric models: a comparison of multiarea methods', *International Regional Science Review*, 8:59–74.

Courbis, R. (1979) 'The REGINA model: a regional-national model for French planning', *Regional Science and Urban Economics*, 9:117–139.

Courbis, R. (1980) 'Multiregional modeling and the interaction between regional and national development', in: F. G. Adams and N. J. Glickman, eds., *Modeling the multiregional economic system*. Lexington, Mass.: D. C. Heath, 107–130.

Courbis, R. (1982) 'Integrated multiregional modeling in Western Europe', in: B. Issaev, P. Nijkamp, P. Rietveld and F. Snickars, eds., *Multiregional economic modeling: practice and prospect*. Amsterdam: North-Holland Publ. Co., 111–128.

Delft, A. van and W. Suyker (1982) 'Regional investment subsidies; an estimation of the labour market effects for the Dutch regions', *Papers of the Regional Science Association*, 49:151–168.

Despontin, M., P. Nijkamp, and J. Spronk, eds. (1984) *Macroeconomic policy-making with conflicting goals*. Berlin: Springer Verlag.

Dresch, S. P. and D. A. Updegrove (1980) 'IDIOM: a disaggregated policy impact model of the US economy', in: R. H. Haveman and K. Hollenbeck, eds., *Microeconomic simulation models for public policy analysis*, vol. 2. New York: Academic Press, 213–240.

Folmer, H. (1985) *Measuring the effectiveness of regional economic policy*. Dordrecht: Martinus Nijhoff.

Folmer, H. and P. Nijkamp (1985) 'Methodological aspects of impact analysis of regional economic policy', *Papers of the Regional Science Association*, 57:165–181.

Fukuchi, T. (1978) 'Analyse economico-politique d'un développement régional harmonisé', *Les Collections de l'INSEE*, C. 61, 227–253.

Gerking, S. (1977) *Estimation of stochastic input–output models*. Dordrecht: Martinus Nijhoff.

Glejser, H., G. van Daele, and M. Lambrecht (1973) 'The first experiments with an econometric regional model of the Belgian economy', *Regional Science and Urban Economics*, 3:301–314.

Glickman, N. J. (1977) *Econometric analysis of regional systems*. New York: Academic Press.

Glickman, N. J. (1982) 'Using empirical models for regional policy analysis', in: M. Albegov, A. E. Andersson and F. Snickars, eds., *Regional development modeling: theory and practice*. Amsterdam: North-Holland Publ. Co., 85–104.

Granholm, A. (1981) 'Interregional planning models for the allocation of private and public investments', Department of Economics, University of Gothenburg, Gothenburg.

Grunfeld, Y., and Z. Griliches (1960) 'Is aggregation necessarily bad?', *Review of Economics and Statistics*, 2:1–13.

Guccione, A. and W. J. Gillen (1972) 'A simple disaggregation of a neoclassical investment function', *Journal of Regional Science*, 12, no. 2:279–294.

Guteland, G. and O. Nygren (1984) 'Information systems for integrated regional planning and policy making in Sweden', in: P. Nijkamp and P. Rietveld, eds., *Information systems for integrated regional planning*. Amsterdam: North-Holland Publ. Co., 297–318.

Hafkamp, W. (1984) *Economic-environmental modelling in a national-regional system*. Amsterdam: North-Holland Publ. Co.

Hamel, B. A. van, H. Hetsen, and J. H. M. Kok, 'Un modèle economique multirégional pour les Pays-Bas', in: R. Courbis, ed., *Modèles régionaux et modèles régionaux – nationaux*. Paris: Cujas, 147–173.

Harris, C. C. (1980) 'New developments and extensions of the multiregional, multiindustry forecasting model', *Journal of Regional Science*, 20:159–171.

Hoffman, R. and J. Kent (1976) 'Design for commodity by industry interregional input–output models,' in: J. Skolka and K. Polenske, eds., *Advances in input – output analysis*. Cambridge, Mass.: Ballinger, 122–143.

Isard, W. (1951) 'Interregional and regional input–output analysis: a model of a space economy', *Review of Economics and Statistics*, 33:318–328.

Isard, W. and L. Anselin (1982) 'Integration of multiregional models for policy analysis', *Environment and Planning A*, 14:359–376.

Issaev, B., P. Nijkamp, P. Rietveld, and F. Snickars eds. (1982) *Multiregional economic modeling: practice and prospect*. Amsterdam: North-Holland Publ. Co.

Isserman, A.; P. Beaumont, D. Plane, P. Rogerson, and D. McMiller (1983) 'ECESIS: an interregional demographic-economic forecasting model of the states', Working Paper, Institute for Urban and Regional Research, University of Iowa.

Johansson, B. and T. R. Lakshmanan, eds. (1985) *Large scale energy projects: assessment of regional consequences*. Amsterdam: North-Holland Publ. Co.

Johansson, B., and U. Strömquist (1981) 'Regional rigidities in the process of economic structural development', *Regional Science and Urban Economics*, 11:363–376.

Karlqvist, A., R. Sharpe, D. F. Batten, and J. F. Brotchie (1978) 'A regional planning model and its application to South Eastern Australia', *Regional Science and Urban Economics*, 8:57–86.

Keogh, G. T. and D. P. B. Elias (1981) 'A model for projecting regional employment in the U.K.', *Regional Studies*, 13:465–482.

Klein, L. R. (1969) 'The specification of regional econometric models', *Papers of the Regional Science Association*, 23:105–115.

Knapp, J. L., T. W. Fields, and R. T. Jerome (1978) *A survey of state and regional econometric models*. Charlottesville, Va.: Taylor Murphy Institute, University of Virginia.

Lakshmanan, T. R. (1979) 'A multiregional policy model of the economy, environment and energy', Boston University, Working Paper NSF 79-1.

Lakshmanan, T. R. (1982) 'Integrated multiregional economic modeling for the USA', in: B. Issaev, P. Nijkamp, P. Rietveld and F. Snickars, eds., *Multiregional economic modeling: practice and prospect*. Amsterdam: North-Holland Publ. Co., 171–188.

Ledent, J. (1981) 'Demographic and economic interactions in statistical models of regional growth with an application to Tucson-Arizona', unpublished Ph.D. dissertation, Northwestern University, Chicago.

Ledent, J. (1982) 'Long-range regional population forecasting: specification of a minimal demoeconomic model, with a test for Tucson, Arizona', *Papers of the Regional Science Association*, 49:39–67.

Leontief, W. and A. Strout (1963) 'Multiregional input–output analysis, in: T. Barna, ed., *Structural interdependence and economic development*. London: St. Martins Press, 243–259.

Lesuis, P., F. Muller, and P. Nijkamp (1980) 'An interregional policy model for energy-economic environmental interactions', *Regional Science and Urban Economics*, 10:343–370.

Los, M. (1980) 'A transportation oriented multiregional economic model for Canada', Publication 178, Centre for Transport Studies, University of Montreal.

Lundqvist, L. (1981) 'A dynamic multiregional input–output model for analysing regional development, employment and energy use', Report TRITA-MAT 1980-20, Dept. of Mathematics, Royal Institute of Technology, Stockholm.

Miller, R. E. (1979) *Dynamic optimization and economic application*. New York: McGraw-Hill.

Milne, W., F. G. Adams and N. J. Glickman (1980a) 'A top-down multi-regional model of the US economy', in: F. G. Adams and N. J. Glickman, eds., *Modeling the multiregional economic system*. Lexington, Mass.: Lexington Books, 133–146.

Milne, W., N. Glickman, and F. G. Adams (1980b) 'A framework for analyzing regional growth and decline: a multiregional economic model of the United States', *Journal of Regional Science*, 20:173–189.

Mitsubishi Research Institute (1979) 'Regional dispersion policies and their effects on industries. Calculations based on an inter-regional input–output model (Version II)', Tokyo.

Miyao, T. (1981) *Dynamic analysis of the urban economy*. New York: Academic Press.

Molle, W. T. M. (1982) *Industrial location and regional development in the European community*. Aldershot, UK: Gower.

Moses, L. (1955) 'The stability of interregional trading patterns and input–output analysis', *American Economic Review*, 45:803–832.

Muller, F. (1979) *Energy and environment in interregional input–output models*. The Hague: Martinus Nijhoff.

Nijkamp, P. (1984) 'A multidimensional analysis of regional infrastructure and economic development', in: Å. E. Andersson, W. Isard, and T. Puu eds., *Regional and industrial development theories, models and empirical evidence*. Amsterdam: North-Holland Publ. Co., 267–293.

Nijkamp, P. and J. H. P. Paelinck (1976) *Operational theory and method in regional economics*. Aldershot, U.K.: Gower.

Nijkamp, P. and P. Rietveld, eds. (1984) *Information systems for integrated regional planning*. Amsterdam: North-Holland Publ. Co.

Nijkamp, P., H. Leitner and N. Wrigley, eds. (1985) *Measuring the unmeasurable*. Dordrecht: Martinus Nijhoff.

Nijkamp, P., P. Rietveld, and A. Rima, (1984a) 'Information context of data from different aggregation levels', in: P. Nijkamp and P. Rietveld, eds., *Information systems for integrated regional planning*. Amsterdam: North-Holland Publ. Co., 215–230.

Nijkamp, P., P. Rietveld, and F. Snickars (1984b) 'A review of multiregional economic modeling, in: G. Bahrenberg, M. M. Fischer, and P. Nijkamp, eds., *Recent developments in spatial data analysis*. Aldershot, U.K.: Gower, 93–116.

Olsen, R. J. (1977) 'MULTIREGION: a simulation forecasting model of BEA area population and employment', Oak Ridge National Laboratory, Report ORNL/RUS 25.

Paraskevopoulos, C. C. (1974) 'Patterns of regional economic growth', *Regional and Urban Economics*, 4:77–105.

Polenske, K. R., ed. (1981) *The U.S. multiregional input–output accounts and models*. Lexington, Mass.: D. C. Heath.

Rabenau, B. V. (1979) 'Urban growth with agglomeration economies and diseconomies', *Geographia Polonica*, 42:77–90.

Richardson, H. W. (1978) 'The state of regional economics, a survey article', *International Regional Science Review*, 3:1–48.

Rietveld, P. (1982) 'A general overview of multiregional economic models', in: B. Issaev, P. Nijkamp, P. Rietveld and F. Snickars, eds., *Multiregional economic modeling: practice and prospect*. Amsterdam: North-Holland Publ. Co., 15–34.

Rietveld, P. (1984) 'Information systems for regional labour markets', in: P. Nijkamp and P. Rietveld, eds., *Information systems for integrated regional planning*. Amsterdam: North-Holland Publ. Co., 163–176.

Schubert, U. (1982a) 'The development of multiregional economic models in Western Europe', in: B. Issaev, P. Nijkamp, P. Rietveld and F. Snickars, eds., *Multiregional economic modeling: practice and prospect*. Amsterdam: North-Holland, 99–110.

Schubert, U. (1982b) 'REMO, an interregional labour market study of Austria', *Environment and Planning*, 14:1233–1249.

Siebert, H. (1979) *Regional economic growth: theory and policy*. Scranton: International Textbook Company.

Smith, D. M. (1975) 'Neoclassical growth models and regional growth in the U.S.', *Journal of Regional Science*, 15:165–181.

Snickars, F. (1978) 'Construction of interregional input–output tables by efficient information adding', in: C. Bartels and R. Ketellapper, eds., *Exploratory and explanatory statistical analysis of spatial data*. The Hague: Martinus Nijhoff, 73–111.

Snickars, F. and J. Weibull (1977) 'A minimum information principle: theory and practice', *Regional Science and Urban Economics*, 7:137–168.

Stevens, B. H., G. I. Treyz and J. K. Kindahl (1982) 'Conjoining and input–output model and a policy analysis model: a case study of the regional economic effects of expanding a port facility', *Environment and Planning*, 13:1029–1038.

Theil, H. (1954) *Linear aggregation of economic relations*. Amsterdam: North-Holland Publ. Co.

Thijs-Clement, F. and P. van Rompuy (1979) 'RENA, regional model for Belgium', in: R. Courbis ed., *Modèles régionaux et modèles régionaux – nationaux*, Paris: Cujas, 103–122.

Tiebout, C. M. (1962) 'The community economic base study', supplementary paper no. 16, Committee for Economic Development, Washington.

Treyz, G. (1980) 'Design of a multiregional policy analysis model', *Journal of Regional Science*, 20:191–1206.

Treyz, G. and G. E. Duguay (1980) 'Endogenous wage determination: Its significance for state policy analysis models', Paper presented at the New Jersey State Economic conference (mineo).

Treyz, G., and B. H. Stevens (1980) 'Location analysis of multiregional modeling', in: F. J. Adams and N. J. Glickman, eds., *Modeling the multiregional economic system*. Lexington, Mass.: D. C. Heath, 75–88.

Wigren, R. (1983) 'Regional productivity differentials in Swedish manufacturing industry 1970–80', Research report, Department of Economics, University of Gothenburg.

Willekens, F. (1983) 'Log-linear modelling of spatial interaction', *Papers of the Regional Science Association*, 52:187–205.

Wrigley, N. and R. Dunn (1984) 'Stochastic panel data models of urban shopping behaviour', *Environment and Planning A*, 16:629–650.

Chapter 8

REGIONAL, INTERREGIONAL AND MULTIREGIONAL INPUT–OUTPUT ANALYSIS*

GEOFFREY J. D. HEWINGS and RODNEY C. JENSEN

1. Introduction

Interest in the interactions between the various sets of actors in an economy has not been confined to the research conducted in the latter part of this century. Brems (1986) has noted that Cantillon, even before Quesnay in the early eighteenth century, was interested in determining the relative prices of factors and goods and the associated distribution of income and employment. In his model of the economy, in which he even considered choices among alternative crops,

> Cantillon used nothing but beautiful, lucid French bristling with precise and specific quantitative estimates. He had a clear grasp of sectoral interdependence in an economy... [Brems (1986)].

However, it is usually to the work of Quesnay (1694–1774) and Walras (1834–1910) that most input–output researchers refer as their legacy, and to the brilliant interpretations and reformulations by Leontief (1953) for the development of the fundamental principles upon which the input–output model was developed. Quesnay's "Tableau Economique" provides an iterative solution to the structural interdependence in the economy: Leontief was able to move this formulation to a more general one and, in the process, expand the capabilities of the model. An interesting feature of input–output analysis has been its widespread adoption throughout the world, transcending the distinctions between developed and developing, and between centrally planned, socialist and market economies.

*The support of the National Science Foundation Grants SES 82-05961 and SES 84-10917 and a University Improvement Fund grant by the University of Queensland and the comments of David Batten, David Boyce, and Roger Bolton are gratefully acknowledged.

Handbook of Regional and Urban Economics, Volume I, Edited by P. Nijkamp
©Elsevier Science Publishers BV, 1986

Unlike many other branches of regional economics and regional science, the development of regional and interregional models occurred almost contemporaneously with the growth of interest in national-level input–output modelling. In the book edited by Leontief, *Studies in the structure of the American economy*, there are two chapters on regional models, one by Leontief on the theory of interregional models and one by Isard devoted to some of the empirical and conceptual problems with regional analysis. These developments will be discussed in more detail in the next major section of this chapter. The remaining parts of this section will be devoted to the articulation of the links between input–output analysis and national and regional accounts and the development of the mathematical structure of the various accounting schemes which have been proposed.

1.1.   Links with national accounts and economic base analysis

In the presentation of input–output analysis in many textbooks, very little attempt is made to show the relationships between this representation of the economy and the overall set of national accounts from which most of the data are derived. Consequently, input–output analysis is not seen in terms Leontief would prefer as:

> ...an empirical study of interrelations among the different parts of a national economy as revealed through covariations of prices, outputs, investments and incomes [Leontief (1951)].

At the regional level, a similar criticism could be levelled; as will be demonstrated, the input–output model can be visualized as a more extensive economic base model on the one hand and a less complex econometric model on the other hand. In the third section of this chapter, some linkages of input–output analysis with other standard modelling techniques will be presented, further reinforcing the notion that the input–output framework has a considerable degree of flexibility in its contribution to an understanding of the structure of an economy.

Kennedy (1966a, 1966b) has demonstrated the links between aggregate Keynesian analysis and input–output models. Begin with the simple identity for a closed economy:

$$Y = C + I \tag{1.1}$$

where C is gross domestic consumption and I gross investment. Including transactions on foreign account we have:

$$Y = C + I + X - M \tag{1.2}$$

Table 1.1
Two-sector macro input–output model [Kennedy (1966a)].

Producing sectors	Spending sectors Home	Foreign	Total
Home	V_{hh}	V_{hf}	Y
Foreign	V_{fh}	V_{ff}	M
Total	E	X	T

where X and M refer to exports and imports. If (1.2) is rewritten as:

$$Y + M = C + I + X. \tag{1.3}$$

Kennedy referred to this as the input–output approach to national accounts since output (supply) terms are grouped on the left-hand side of (1.3) and expenditure (demand) terms on the right-hand side. If $C + I$ are grouped into one variable, expenditure, E, then (1.3) becomes:

$$Y + M = E + X \tag{1.4}$$

and these are the row and column totals for a two-sector input–output table, shown in Table 1.1. In this model, the two sectors are a domestic and a foreign sector. The remaining entries in the table represent the traditional intersectoral flows within and between the sectors. If we disaggregate E into $C + I$ and assume that I and X are autonomous and further that there has been an autonomous change in I of δI and in X of δX, what will be the effect on Y? Define $m = \delta M / \delta T$ and $c = \delta C / \delta Y$, then we have:

$$\delta M = m \delta T.$$

Since $Y + M = T$ we have

$$\delta Y + \delta M = \delta T$$

or

$$\delta Y = (1 - m) \delta T. \tag{1.5}$$

In equilibrium,

$$\delta I + \delta X = \delta T - \delta C. \tag{1.6}$$

Substituting $\delta C = c\delta Y = c(1-m)\delta T$ into (1.6) we have:

$$\delta I + \delta X = [1 - c(1-m)]\delta T.$$

Further substitution of $\delta T = \delta Y/(1-m)$ yields:

$$\frac{\delta Y}{\delta I + \delta X} = \frac{1-m}{[1-c(1-m)]}. \tag{1.7}$$

This formulation is similar to the economic base model when import leakages are considered [see Brown (1967), Archibald (1967)]. Romanoff (1974) provided the necessary link between economic base analysis and input–output models, hence completing the link between these two systems and national accounts. Assume that the usual division of the economy has been made into basic (export) X_b and nonbasic (local) X_1, and let a represent the proportion of total activity accounted for by local, i.e. $a = X_1/X_t$. Then we have:

$$X_t = X_b + X_1 \tag{1.8}$$

$$X_t = (1-a)^{-1}X_b. \tag{1.9}$$

Now assume that the economy has been divided up into m basic and $m + n$ nonbasic sectors; following Romanoff, the system may be partitioned as follows:

$$\begin{bmatrix} X_1 \\ \cdots \\ X_2 \end{bmatrix} = \begin{bmatrix} A_{11} & \vdots & A_{12} \\ \cdots & \vdots & \cdots \\ 0 & \vdots & 0 \end{bmatrix} \begin{bmatrix} X_1 \\ \cdots \\ X_2 \end{bmatrix} + \begin{bmatrix} 0 \\ \cdots \\ f_2 \end{bmatrix}. \tag{1.10}$$

In a similar fashion to the assumption made by Weiss and Gooding (1968), this formulation assumes no interdependence among the basic sectors and, furthermore, no sales from the nonbasic sectors to final demand. The closed form solution yields:

$$X_1 = [I - A]^{-1}A_{12}f_2. \tag{1.11}$$

Since $X_2 = f_2$, we have the link between the basic and nonbasic sectors. This model of the economy is oversimplified; the strict separability of activity would appear to be the exception rather than the rule, except perhaps, for small, rural communities or for towns dominated by a major activity. Before moving on to describe the input–output model in some detail, it is worth pointing out that Gerking (1976a) has provided a link between the input–output model and econometric analysis, an issue to which we shall return in a later section.

1.2. Accounting systems

The input–output model is clearly seen as a model of the production side of an economy. Although Augustinovics (1970) and Giarratani (1976) and to some extent Tiebout (1969) have attempted to recast all or part of the system to accommodate supply-side effects, the model remains, nonetheless, a portrayal of an economic system in which demand and changes in demand create the signals for production to take place. The early regional input–output models were severely limited by the paucity of data – a complaint which appears not to have diminished in importance with time. Isard's (1953) model for a single region and subsequent interregional and multiregional prototypes were based on the accounting systems developed by Leontief at the national level.

1.2.1. The single regional accounting system

There are currently two major accounting systems in use; the early Leontief formulation has been expanded to detail flows of commodities between industries rather than composite goods referred to as "industrial output". We will begin with the standard Leontief formulation and then extend it to the commodity-by-industry framework.

Assume the existence of m commodities produced by z firms; the firms are first grouped into industrial sectors on the basis of the output of the principal product according to the conventions adopted in various Standard Industrial Classifications (SIC). Hence, some firms within an industrial sector may be producing multiple products; in addition, it is possible that some commodities may be produced in more than one industrial sector. As Rosenbluth (1968) has pointed out, further disaggregation will not solve the problem of mapping commodities on a one-to-one basis to industrial sectors. Accordingly, an alternative framework was developed. The first attempt, which we may refer to as the Cambridge model [Stone (1963)], differentiated commodities and industries (see Table 1.2a) but retained the restriction that the number of commodities and industries was the same. The UN System of National Accounts shown in the same table (Table 1.2b), removes this restriction [see Gigantes (1970)]. Hence, it is possible to detail transactions in rectangular matrices in which the number of commodities may be far greater than the number of industries.

Table 1.2
The commodity–industry model.

(a) The Cambridge Version (Stone, 1963)

(b) The Canadian/UN Version (Gigantes, 1970)

In the standard Leontief version, the accounting balances are:

$$\sum_j x_{ij} + Y_i = X_i \tag{1.12}$$

$$\sum_i x_{ij} + Z_j = X_j \tag{1.13}$$

where x_{ij} are the flows between industries, Y_i, Z_j and X_i the vectors of final demand and primary inputs and total output. Included in the vector Y would be purchases by consumers, government, by industries on investment account, and exports. Included in Z, one normally finds the various components of value added (wages and salaries, profits, undistributed dividends) and imports. The critical assumption in input–output analysis is that the inputs required to make a unit of output are invariant over all output levels and that the technological production function can be effectively portrayed by converting all flows between industries from physical units into a monetary *numeraire*. On this issue, there has been a great deal of debate, especially in the recent era of rapidly accelerating price inflation in the energy products market [see Moses (1974)]. Furthermore, it is assumed that the production function is linear and homogeneous of degree one. Given these conventions, we now define the input coefficient:

$$a_{ij} = x_{ij}/X_j. \tag{1.14}$$

Substituting in (1.12), we have:

$$\sum_j a_{ij} X_j + Y_i = X_i. \tag{1.15}$$

If matrix $A(n \times n)$ and vectors $Y(n \times 1)$ and $X(n \times 1)$ are defined to contain the elements of (1.15), then we have:

$$AX + Y = X \tag{1.16}$$

yielding the familiar solution:

$$[I - A]^{-1} Y = X. \tag{1.17}$$

This solution is the analogy to the economic base and macroeconomic solutions presented earlier. At the regional level, imports are defined to include inter-regional as well as foreign purchases. First, the matrix A is decomposed into:

$$A = R + M \tag{1.18}$$

where $r_{ij} \in R$ represent the flows from industry i to j *within* the region while $m_{ij} \in M$ are the *interregional* imports necessary to meet the total technological demand in the system. Usually, the elements of M are collapsed into a vector which is allocated to the primary inputs. Similarly, the exports are often divided into those within the country (interregional) and those on foreign account. Hence, at the regional level, the closed form solution is:

$$X = [I - R]^{-1} Y. \tag{1.19}$$

1.2.2.   The interregional input – output accounting system

There has been a strong tradition paralleling the development of regional models, namely the production of interregional models and their closely related derivatives, the multiregional models. The full interregional model proposed by Isard (1951), in which an n-sector r-region economy was portrayed by elements $^{pq}a_{ij}$, the flows of output from sector i in region p to sector j in region q, has rarely been implemented empirically. In their place, a number of modifications have been proposed. Moses (1955), for example, suggested a form:

$$^{pq}x_i = {}^{pq}t_i {}^q x_i \qquad (1.20)$$

where the left-hand side refers to the interregional flow of commodity i from region p to q and the t term reflects the proportion of i which enters region q from p per unit of output of i in q. This notion of supply and demand pools was used by Leontief and Strout (1963) in their development of a gravity version of the interregional model and has been modified and extended further recently by Broecker (1984). The Leontief–Strout version has a form:

$$^{pq}X_i = \left[{}^{p \cdot} X_i \cdot {}^q X_i / {}^{\cdot \cdot} X_i \right] {}^{pq}Q_i. \qquad (1.21)$$

Riefler and Tiebout (1970) provided a further modification of the Leontief–Strout system for the two-region case; in some senses, their model may be regarded as a compromise between the Leontief–Strout and the Isard systems. The model was implemented for the states of Washington and California where two survey-based regional input–output tables existed. Polenske (1970) has proposed two versions of the Leontief–Strout model, one a column, the other a row coefficient model. Hence, we now have a family of models; these are shown in Figure 1.1. One may note how the different formulations require varying amounts of data and assumptions concerning the nature of the interregional flows. In an empirical application with Japanese interregional input–output data, Polenske (1970) found that the column coefficient model provided much better estimates than the row or gravity model.

These interregional models have been extended and elaborated by Evans and Baxter (1980) and by Hoffman and Kent (1976) in the case of commodity–industry modelling. More recently, attempts have been made to link these models with some of the new developments in commodity flow modelling [see Batten (1982)] which are the subject of Chapter 9 in this Handbook. Their relationship with input–output modelling will be reviewed briefly in Section 3 of this chapter.

Name of modeller	Model in compact form	Conditions upon T	Structure of T
Isard	$x = (I - B)^{-1}Tf$	$t_{ij}^{rs} \geq 0$	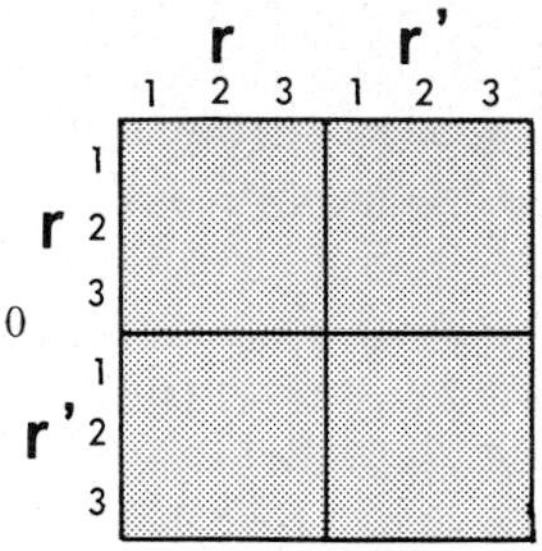
Riefler Tiebout	$x = (I - B)^{-1}Tf$ for intraregional $x = (I - TA)^{-1}Tf$ for interregional	$t_{ij}^{rs} \geq 0$ $t_{ij}^{rs} = t_i^{rs}$ when $i \neq j$ and $r \neq s$	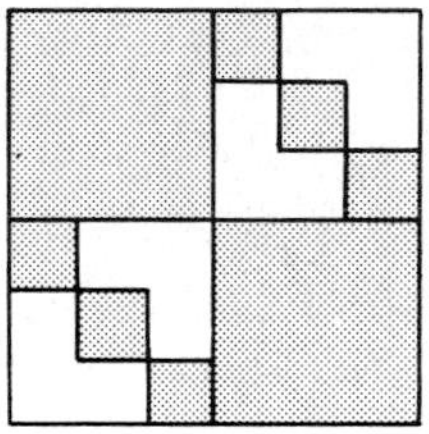
Chenery Moses	$x = (I - TA)^{-1}Tf$	$t_{ij}^{rs} \geq 0$ $t_{ij}^{rs} = t_i^{rs}$ when $i \neq j$	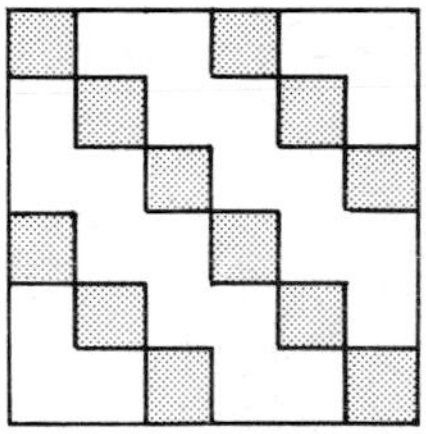
Leontief	$x = (I - VPA)^{-1}Tf$	$t_{ij}^{rs} \geq 0$ $t_{ij}^{rs} = t_i^{s}$	
Leontief and Strout	$x = (I - C^{-1}DA)^{-1}C^{-1}Df$	when $i \neq j$ or $r \neq s$	

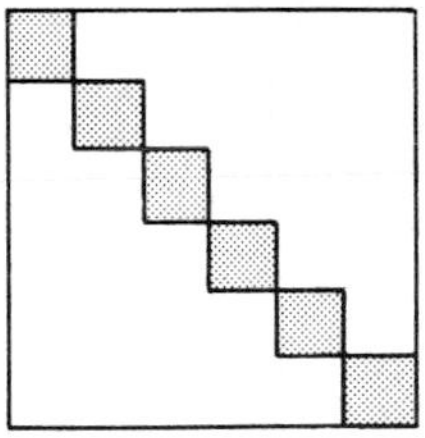

Figure 1.1. A hierarchy of classical interregional input–output models [after Batten (1982)].

1.2.3. Commodity – industry accounting frameworks

In the case of the commodity-by-industry framework, flows are shown in terms of two matrices – a make matrix displaying the production of commodities by industries and an absorption matrix showing the use of commodities in the production of output in industries (see Table 1.2). Even in this more flexible format, a number of assumptions have to be made concerning the mix of commodity output by each industry over all levels of demand and the nature of the production function within an industry [see Gigantes (1970)]. In the case of a perfect one-to-one mapping between industries and commodities, the make matrix would be diagonal and the system would reduce to a standard Leontief formulation. The presence of off-diagonal entries in the make matrix represents the production of secondary products by industries. The accounting system operates in the following fashion:

$$q = U + f \qquad (1.22)$$

which is the direct analogy, in commodity terms of the accounting balance in (1.16). If U is transformed to a matrix of coefficients multiplied by total input, we have:

$$B = UX^{-1} \qquad (1.23)$$

and hence:

$$q = BX + f. \qquad (1.24)$$

Similarly, matrix V may be represented by a matrix of coefficients multiplied by a vector of commodity outputs; this assumes that the market shares of industries are stable across all industry and commodity outputs:

$$V = Dq \qquad (1.25)$$
$$X = Dq. \qquad (1.26)$$

Substituting (1.26) into (1.24), we have:

$$q = BDq + f \qquad (1.27)$$

which yields the solution:

$$q = [I - BD]^{-1}f. \qquad (1.28)$$

By substitution, we also have:

$$X = [I - DB]^{-1} Df. \tag{1.29}$$

Even though the number of commodities may exceed the number of industries, the matrix products BD and DB not only exist but are also square – enabling matrix inversion.

Although the commodity-by-industry formulation has now been widely embraced at the national level, its development at the regional level has lagged far behind. The development of appropriate nonsurvey techniques has not advanced and since few survey-based models are now being constructed, it is unlikely that this type of accounting framework will be implemented at the regional level in the foreseeable future. Oosterhaven (1984) has provided some useful discussion of the relationships between the family of square (industry–industry) and rectangular (commodity–industry) interregional input–output tables which might be developed at the subnational level.

In the next section, the input–output model and its characteristics will be explored in greater detail. Attention will be focused on a number of problems surrounding table and multiplier development. Thereafter, several extensions of input–output analysis will be presented while, in the final section of the chapter, some new directions in input–output analysis will be reviewed.

2. Input–output tables and multipliers

The second part of this chapter summarizes and evaluates the current state of knowledge with respect to input–output tables per se, in terms of their construction, interpretation, structure and stability. The argument presented here, reflecting the current balance of the literature, is described mainly in terms of the conventional (Leontief) input–output table. It is possible, because of the properties of the input–output system generally, to extend many of these arguments to the interregional and multiregional contexts or to input–output related types of models.

2.1. Views and interpretations of the input–output table

We could, without difficulty, achieve agreement on the definition of an input–output table as a simple system of double-entry accounting for transactions between producers, and on the theoretical and empirical implications of converting the table into an economic model. Beyond this point, however, some differences in the role of the input–output table have emerged which have led to subtle differences in the view or perceptions of the table and, therefore, of the emphases in research directions. Three perceptions of the input–output table, all of which are related, can be distinguished clearly in the literature. First, the most common view of the input–output table in regional economic analysis is as a model, virtually sufficient in and of itself, for regional projections and impact analyses. This view, seen in the early work of Isard (1951, 1953), and manifest in the Miernyk tradition [Miernyk et al. (1967, 1970)], and in the Philadelphia [Isard et al. (1966–68), Isard and Langford (1971)] and Washington models [Bourque et al. (1967)], led to research on matters of table construction, multiplier definition, table accuracy and related matters concerned more with the integrity of the table per se.

A second view of the input–output table arises from its role in more complex models, ranging from simple attachments of the input–output model to other regional models to the very ambitious multimodular integrated models which have emerged in recent years [Isard and Anselin (1982)]. These developments include the cases in which the input–output model is used as the main driving device or engine of the larger model and other examples in which it is merely one component, representing interindustry production relationships, of many relationships (economic, demographic, environmental) expressed in the model. Analysts of this persuasion are interested primarily in the contribution of the input–output model to the whole socioeconomic system and less in the factors which determine the economic integrity of the input–output table. A third, closely related view sees the input–output table primarily as an integral part of a social accounting framework and, therefore, as a subset of regional and national social accounts. Although developed primarily in a national context through the System of National Accounts [United Nations (1968)] and later through the Social Accounting Matrix [see Pyatt and Roe (1977)], the regional implications are evident and will strengthen in the future [Maki (1980), Bell et al. (1982), Round (1984)]. These latter two views of the input–output model will form the focus of Section 3 of this chapter.

These perceptions of the input–output table simply reflect the differing emphases placed on it and the requirements of different areas of economic analysis. They also explain the apparent tendency for input–output researchers to demonstrate rather restricted areas of interest and thereby to forgo the benefits of similar research in related areas. The near dichotomy in research, separating interests at the national and regional levels, is an example of this tendency. At the national level, research has contributed significantly to aspects of social accounts and national policy and planning questions, but in a context which has not taken advantage of major developments in the "regional" literature. These developments have occurred in the areas of table and multiplier interpretation, nonsurvey and hybrid tables, table dynamics, stability and sensitivity. On the other hand, regional input–output researchers have not taken full advantage of developments in social accounting and more complex model extensions which have characterized research at the national level. Clearly, greater interaction would produce some substantial gains as is evident by the work of Bell et al. (1982) which is reviewed in Section 3.3.

2.2.   Construction of regional input – output tables

Governments have generally established national input–output tables as integral and permanent parts of national accounting systems. These tables are, in the main, prepared by permanently established teams of experienced professionals with access to substantial, survey-based data and, more recently, with agreement of widely accepted accounting and procedural conventions [United Nations (1968, 1973)]. Governments have relegated regional input–output analysis to a much less privileged status with the result that regional tables are usually prepared by individuals or small teams whose ephemeral existence often pre-cludes the adoption of generally accepted conventions for data collection and table construction. For these reasons, the construction of regional input–output tables, both in the development and verification of construction methodology, has been the major theme and dominant concern in the regional literature.

These difficulties have precluded comparative analysis on a scale to rival those studies undertaken at the national and international level: as a result, little is known about changes which occur in regional economies over time or how the interactions within a regional economy vary at different stages of development.

2.2.1.   Commodity-based methods

Approaches to the construction of regional input–output tables have been four-fold; these will be reviewed here briefly. First, in the very rare circumstances in which detailed data on commodity supply and usage is available at the regional level, the conventional methods used in the construction of national tables, termed here the *commodity-based* approach, has been used. This approach, outlined best by the United Nations (1973) and more recently for developing countries by Bulmer–Thomas (1982), involves the recognition of the distinction between commodities and industries outlined in Section 1. There are few exam-ples available at the regional level – for example, Parker's (1967) table for Western Australia and the interregional version for Canadian provinces by Hoffman and Kent (1976). However, this approach must constitute the ideal, with the highest level of accuracy commensurate with a macro level model of an economy. It should be noted that those involved in the assembly of commodity-based national tables often indicate low levels of confidence in many parts of the table [e.g. Bullard (1976)]. As with almost all input–output analysis, it is not uncommon for users of these tables to assume them to be error-free and to associate levels of precision which are not justified even by these "best-method" input–output tables.

2.2.2. Survey-based methods

The remaining three approaches to table construction represent efforts of input–output analysts to wrestle with inadequate regional data availability. These are discussed in the order in which they have been formally recognized in the literature and are compared and evaluated later in this section. The second and third approaches are termed respectively, *survey-based* and *nonsurvey* methods but the terms are rather loosely defined. In this review, the survey-based tables, probably the most common of all approaches, are defined as those derived in large part by the collation of primary data by a variety of methods, including formal surveys in the conventional sense. Nonsurvey tables are defined as those derived from a series of short-cut, usually one-step, techniques to produce regional tables from national tables and, occasionally, from other regional tables.

The survey-based procedure is best regarded as a two-stage process, with the stages often merging in practice. The first stage is the assembly of rows-only and columns-only matrices of industry sales and purchases patterns. These are derived from surveys (partial or complete) of firms or establishments and from other sources such as indicators, allocation methods, ad hoc judgements and the like. The second, and more contentious stage, involves the reconciliation of these two tables to derive the input–output table itself. Serious, and still unresolved problems arise at each stage. The first-stage problems are those common to the survey method, namely population identification (where the population normally includes all firms within the region), sample selection, survey design and application and interpretation [Boster and Martin (1972)] and the reliability of the less formal methods mentioned earlier.

The extent of the first-stage problems can be partially assessed by enumerating the differences between the corresponding cells of the two matrices.[1] The only available evidence on this appears to be the Central Queensland study [Jensen (1976)], which showed the difference between the two estimates to be more than 25% in 50% of the cells with two non-zero estimates, and more than 50% in about 25% of the cells, although no indication of the inverse significance of these cells was provided [along the lines proposed by Bullard and Sebald (1977)]. In view of this evidence, it is appropriate that experimental tests should show [Jensen and McGaurr (1976), Gerking (1976)] that the choice of reconciliation method used to produce a single transactions table from the purchases- and sales-based tables is a decision of some significance. The "reconciliation debate" of the mid-1970s,

---

[1] On the implied assumption that the errors in the two cells are not in the same direction.

involving the conventional "professional judgements" approach of Bourque et al. (1967), the reliability-based approach of Miernyk et al. (1970) and Jensen and McGaurr (1976) and the econometric approach initiated by Gerking (1976, 1979), has not been resolved but was probably defused by the suggestion [Jensen (1980)] that Miernyk and Gerking were pursuing different goals in table accuracy. The evidence suggests, however, that the reconciliation stage is much more than simply a matter of achieving a balance between the two first-stage matrices. In addition, problems of appropriate sampling methods, sample size and the contents of the sample have not been resolved. For example, recent research [Hewings and Romanos (1981)] has shown that the role of the households in a regional economy may be far more important than the accuracy of the majority of the interindustry coefficients. Yet, in the construction of many regional input–output tables, the entries in the consumption-by-households vector of final demand have been estimated as a residual. No matter which reconciliation technique is used, it should not be expected to produce an input–output table of higher quality than that inherent in the first-stage tables.

2.2.3. Nonsurvey methods

Despite the acknowledged sources of error in survey tables, they remain generally regarded as "preferred" tables in terms of accuracy, more so by analysts inexperienced in their construction. However, the resource and time costs of survey tables has tended to restrict the development of regional survey-based input–output tables, leading to a search for lower-cost alternatives. These came primarily in the form of nonsurvey tables, based on the use of national tables to derive regional tables, and three approaches can be identified: (1) commodity balance tables [Isard (1953)], (2) the quotient approach and (3) iterative approaches. These have been detailed and reviewed elsewhere, especially by Morrison and Smith (1974), Harrigan et al. (1980a) and Round (1978, 1983) and will not be detailed here. It is sufficient, at this stage, to examine the techniques conceptually and to review the published evaluations.

The commodity balance and quotient techniques, which have been shown to be formally related [Round (1972)], are framed in terms of coefficients but reflect continuing confusion in the distinction between trade and technical coefficients. This confusion seems to be inherent in input–output analysis in general, where the terms "technical", "technology", "direct" and "input–output" have been used interchangeably and imprecisely to describe the A matrix of input purchases of (1.18). The situation is further confused by the reluctance of most analysts to define these terms precisely.

We consider two possibilities. First, we define $a_{ij}^{(c)}$ as the technical coefficient in the sense of the production function, i.e. as expressing the technical requirements of commodity i per unit of output j at the national level, regardless of the geographical source of input supply. We can then define a national trade coefficient as ${}_{n}a_{ij}$:

$$
{}_{n}a_{ij} = {}_{n}t_{ij}a_{ij}^{(c)} \tag{2.1}
$$

where ${}_{n}t_{ij}$ is the proportion of the requirements of commodity i supplied by sector j within the nation, and the corresponding regional trade coefficient as ${}_{r}a_{ij}$:

$$
{}_{r}a_{ij} = {}_{r}t_{ij}a_{ij}^{(c)} \tag{2.2}
$$

where ${}_{r}t_{ij}$ is the proportion of similar input requirements originating in the region. It should be recognized that national input–output tables do not provide the $a_{ij}^{(c)}$ coefficients and, in the absence of back-up matrices such as the absorption matrix[2] these remain unknown and unavailable for analysis. Since intermediate inputs in the form of noncompetitive imports are recorded outside the A matrix, the national coefficients are the trade coefficients, ${}_{n}a_{ij}$'s. In this case, the nonsurvey analyst is attempting to derive regional trade coefficients, ${}_{r}a_{ij}$'s, from national trade coefficients, ${}_{n}a_{ij}$'s, without accounting for the national trade patterns, ${}_{n}t_{ij}$'s, by making the implicit assumption that the former is some function of the latter. In fact, from (2.1) and (2.2) above, this function can be shown as:

$$
{}_{r}a_{ij} = \left[{}_{r}t_{ij}/{}_{n}t_{ij} \right] {}_{n}a_{ij}. \tag{2.3}
$$

The commodity balance and quotient techniques purport to estimate ${}_{r}t_{ij}$, unintentionally applied as a proxy for ${}_{r}t_{ij}/{}_{n}t_{ij}$, illustrating a fundamental deficiency in the logic of these approaches. No quotient approach can be expected to account for the differences between regional and national import patterns, which have no necessary relationship in economic logic. The only manner in which the logic of the commodity balance and quotient techniques can be validated is to apply the techniques to the $a_{ij}^{(c)}$'s and this would require further adjustment of the national input–output table. In the GRIT procedure [Jensen et al. (1977)], the $a_{ij}^{(c)}$ were approximated by "adding back" national imports to the national input–output coefficients by distributing these over the ${}_{n}a_{ij}$'s before applying nonsurvey methods in the early stages of the procedure.[3]

A second possibility is that some analysts define the ${}_{n}a_{ij}$'s of the national input–output table erroneously as technical coefficients. In this case, the same deficiency of logic is apparent, especially in cases in which the national economy

---

[2] Or alternatively, commodity-by-industry matrices [Harrigan et al. (1980)].
[3] This is equivalent to an $A + M$ matrix, where M is an imports matrix.

itself is very open. The nonsurvey literature is silent on the question of dealing with national imports and the distinction between the $_n a_{ij}$ and $a_{ij}^{(c)}$ and indeed on the whole aspect of accounting conventions.

Perhaps the most widely accepted nonsurvey technique is the bi-proportional or RAS method even though the data requirements for its use are more extensive than other quotient methods. In summary form, the RAS system operates in the following fashion:

$$_r A = f\{_n A, _r u, _r v, _r X\} \tag{2.4}$$

where the subscripts r and n refer to the region and nation and where u, v, and X are the vectors of regional intermediate outputs and inputs and total gross outputs. As a number of authors have demonstrated [Hewings (1977)], the solution to (2.4) is very sensitive to the choice of the prior matrix, $_n A$. The general solution is of the form:

$$_r A = R _n A S \tag{2.5}$$

where R and S are diagonal matrices of quotients or multipliers which ensure that the adjusted matrix, $_r A$, is as close as possible to the prior matrix while satisfying the row and column constraints, u and v. However, there is a significant difference in the meaning of the diagonal matrix elements in the three cases shown in (2.6), (2.7) and (2.8):

$$_r a_{ij}^{(1)} = r_i^{(1)} {}_n a_{ij} s_j^{(i)} \tag{2.6}$$

$$_r a_{ij}^{(2)} = r_i^{(2)} a_{ij}^{(d)} s_j^{(2)} \tag{2.7}$$

$$_r a_{ij}^{(3)} = r_i^{(3)} a_{ij}^{(c)} s_j^{(3)}. \tag{2.8}$$

Equation (2.6) shows regional coefficients determined from national trade coefficients; this appears to have been the practice adopted in the regional applications of the RAS technique [Czamanski and Malizia (1969), Schaffer and Chu (1969), McMenamin and Haring (1974), Morrison and Smith (1974)]. In this context, the r and s elements are simply multipliers determined by the relatively unimportant relationship between national and regional trading patterns. The regional coefficients of (2.7) reflect the "pure" RAS case where $a_{ij}^{(d)}$ is some

> domestic input–output technical coefficient, including absorptions of imported amounts as well as of domestically produced amounts of good i per unit of gross output of commodity j. These imported inputs exclude "noncompetitive" imports in the sense of goods that cannot be produced in the home country [Bacharach (1970)].

The $r_i^{(2)}$ and $s_j^{(2)}$ and associated regional coefficients differ conceptually from those of (2.6) and from those based on the national technical coefficient in (2.8). It is our opinion that the $_r a_{ij}^{(1)}$ are difficult to justify as a concept, in comparison to the coefficients in (2.7 and 2.8), the former of which is preferred.

Apart from these logical flaws, the continued discussion on the theoretical and empirical applications of these nonsurvey techniques continues to point to a consensus conclusion that they have acknowledged bias and cannot be supported as single-step techniques for producing regional tables.[4] It seems that these facts have been well established such that the marginal value of proving them again by continued research is likely to be very low. New avenues of research are likely to be far more productive, such as the imaginative efforts of Stevens et al. (1983) who calculated the $_r t_{ij}$'s by regression analysis of observed trading patterns. Research of this type is more soundly grounded in logic and empirical bases than the continued tinkering with nonsurvey methods of dubious theoretical foundation.

As Round (1983) suggests, the general family of "gravity-based" models, ranging from the Leontief and Strout (1963) system, through the work of Theil and Uribe (1966), Wilson (1970), Gordon (1976) and Batten (1982) and others are, in effect, nonsurvey methods since they are applied to surrogates of coefficients or flows where these are not available. Applications have been limited so far to a system of regions, and the difficulty in obtaining survey-based or other official interregional tables for comparison has meant that these approaches have generally not been rigorously tested and evaluated. A general concensus that seems to emerge, less from the literature and more from discussion in conferences, is that these gravity-based approaches have some advantage in the calculation of gross rather than net flows. They do, however, rely, for the most part, on statistical rather than economic theory, and the concensus would probably suggest that the use of prior information should be maximized with these approaches. However, rigorous testing of these methods is necessary and can only be accomplished when reliable survey-based interregional tables become available.

2.2.4. Hybrid approaches

The fourth and most recent approach to table construction is the so-called *hybrid* or *semi-survey* method, which is defined here as incorporating explicit and formal attempts to integrate the properties of both the survey and nonsurvey approaches rather than simply the more informal and ad hoc incorporation of nonsurvey data into survey-based tables. The hybrid approaches have been, to date, multi-

---

[4] The nonsurvey tables have, in general, been "tested" by comparison with survey-based tables. This is, in effect, the comparison of two tables of unknown levels of accuracy, given the potential sources of error in survey tables. The conclusions based on such tests must therefore be interpreted with caution.

stage methods, involving the derivation of a preliminary or tentative table by a variety of methods and the incorporation into this preliminary table of survey, primary or preferred data to produce a final table. These preferred data would include the important coefficients identified using methods described in Jensen and West (1980) and Hewings and Romanos (1981). The hybrid approach seeks to capture the advantage of the presumed higher level of accuracy of the survey method and some of the economy and speed of the nonsurvey approach. It is probable that many tables have been developed from informal or unpublished hybrid approaches. Four formal approaches can be identified in the literature; these will be reviewed in turn.

The Georgia Interindustry System (GIS) was devised by Schaffer (1976) to first

> develop an input–output table wholly from secondary (published) data, and secondly, to evolve from this first estimate a table embodying as much primary data as can be obtained with available resources [Schaffer (1976, p. 20)].

The first phase is the development of a state technology matrix, i.e. a table which identifies the production technologies of industries in the state (region), $a_{ij}^{(c)}$'s, irrespective of the regional origin of inputs. This matrix is derived from several sources, including secondary data (for estimates of total purchases and sales, final expenditures and payments), primary data (for primary inputs other than imports), survey data (for manufacturing rows and columns in the A matrix) and national interindustry data for the remainder of the table. The process of creating a state technology matrix from the national (US) matrix required several steps, including (1) the distinction between direct allocation and transfer items associated with secondary products, (2) adjustment for price changes between the time of construction of the national and the proposed regional table, (3) identification of sectors as local or nonlocal, i.e. testing for the existence of sectors at the regional level, (4) accounting for transfers in the process of aggregation and (5) calculation of state technology coefficients in the usual way.

The second phase of the GIS system is the derivation of the regional transactions table from the state technology matrix. This is achieved in three steps, each moving closer to the observed trade pattern of industries in the state. First, the "supply–demand pool" technique was applied to obtain a first estimate of exports and imports. Second, these initial estimates were then compared with those derived by a variation of the supply–demand pool technique, which the author termed the "exports-only" technique, and adjusted accordingly. This procedure

> assigns exports and then applies the supply–demand pool technique to estimating the remaining regional transactions and imports [Schaffer (1976)].

Third, a technique termed a "selective-values" technique was applied, which involved the insertion of known values (prior knowledge) as a substitute for less reliable data in the transactions matrix, and rebalancing with the supply–demand pool technique.

The GIS system was aimed primarily at producing a regional table from a national table, but employing to the best effect, any prior information available to the analyst. The GIS system, although not claimed as such by Schaffer, is the first substantive attempt to combine survey and nonsurvey techniques into a formal sequence of steps to produce a regional table.

The Generation of Regional Input–Output Tables (GRIT) system, initially derived by Jensen et al. (1977) and modified by West et al. (1979, 1980) to produce either single-region tables or a set of tables, is a multiphase technique based on the calculation of preliminary tables by a combination of mechanical nonsurvey techniques, and the insertion of prior information or "superior data," where this term applies to data which is considered by the analyst as preferable to mechanically produced entries in the table. The technique is "variable inference" in that the analyst has the opportunity to insert superior data at several stages.

The GRIT technique has five phases: (1) the first phase involves the preparation of the national table by price level adjustment and updating (if necessary) and the reallocation to the intermediate sector of imports to allow the calculation of national technical coefficients, $a_{ij}^{(c)}$. (2) These coefficients are then converted to first estimates of the regional trade coefficients, $_r a_{ij}$, by the application of allocation and quotient methods. Phases (3) and (4) provide for the insertion of superior data available at high levels of disaggregation, aggregation of tables to the desired level by weighting techniques following Shen (1960) and insertion of superior data available only at the disaggregated level to produce "prototype" regional tables. (5) The final phase requires the examination and verification of the tables and the collection of further superior data, by survey methods if necessary, to ensure the professional integrity of the table.

The early GRIT procedures presumed that the larger coefficients were relatively more important in multiplier formation and that resources should be allocated primarily to ensure the accuracy of these coefficients. The empirical evidence from existing regional tables [Jensen and West (1980)] showed that over 50% of the smallest coefficients could be ignored (set to zero) before the errors in output or multipliers were significant. Later versions of GRIT [West et al. (1979, 1980)] showed that a simple listing of the coefficients in descending order of size did not necessarily reflect their relative importance in multiplier formation; position in the matrix with respect to more or less connected sectors was also important. The ability, through the establishment of the mathematical relationship between coefficients and multipliers [West et al. (1979, 1980), West (1981)] to rank coefficients according to their influence on multipliers, opens the possibility of an accuracy-maximizing approach to input–output tables by allowing cost-effective allocation of research resources among coefficients at different levels of significance. The GRIT "philosophy" is simply that the professional requirements of the input–output analyst cannot allow simple reliance on mechanically produced tables, and that sufficient superior data needs to be introduced to ensure the integrity of the input–output table. In essence, the extent and use of superior data are the main factors in influencing the accuracy of the resulting table. Earlier GRIT approaches simply claimed "freedom from significant error"; later versions attempted to achieve "holistic accuracy" [Jensen (1980)], as described in the next section. More than forty GRIT regional and interregional tables have been produced for Australian regions from the official GRIT procedure; an unknown, but large numbers of tables have been produced from unofficial "GRIT-like" procedures in several countries.

Two other techniques have been developed for use in smaller regions. The ASSET technique [Smith and Jensen (1984)] born in the GRIT philosophy, is aimed specifically at the production of input–output tables for small economies, such as small urban areas. Three phases are involved: (1) the assembly of "representative firm" data, particularly on cost structures and the conversion of these data to regional input–output coefficients and an initial transactions matrix; (2) the adjustment for regional imports and accounting prices and the preparation of a transactions table which is largely "mechanical" in nature and (3) the insertion of superior data and table verification – again in the context of holistic accuracy. The representative firm data used in this study were gathered from accounting surveys (for other purposes) of small firms over a number of regions. The approach assumes that the cost structure of firms with similar functions in rural regions (e.g. grocery retail outlets, pharmacies, etc.) are not unacceptably dissimilar and that any differences of note and any unusual features of the small local economy can be recognized by the analyst and can be incorporated through the superior data option. The further presumption is that the structure of small rural regional economies will tend, at least in the Australian context, to be more similar than different and that the significant differences will be obvious.

The final method was used to develop a truncated regional social accounting system in a short period of time for a rural region in Greece in which a major development project had been placed [Hewings and Romanos (1981)]. In the construction of the regional interindustry matrix, extensive use was made of a detailed national table. For each major industry identified at the regional level, the five largest input and sales coefficients were identified. Local firms in the region were asked to compare their sales and purchases with the industry aggregates at the national level, to adjust where appropriate and to estimate the percentage of sales and purchases made within the region. Additional survey information was obtained on payments to households and on local household consumption. The resulting survey based transactions' matrices (on purchase and sales accounts) were reconciled iteratively to ensure balance with known marginal totals. The final table was subjected to a sensitivity analysis to determine the inverse important coefficients – the set of coefficients whose estimation was deemed critical to the accurate estimation of total output, employment or some other marginal attribute. A similar analysis was conducted on a location-quotient derived nonsurvey based table (derived from the national table) and on the national table itself. There appeared to be little correspondence in the sets of coefficients identified as inverse important in all three tables. While the West and Jensen (1980) results on the importance of larger coefficients were confirmed, many of the larger coefficients observed at the national level were much smaller (or even zero) at the regional level. This finding creates some uncertainty about an analyst's ability to identify important coefficients a priori; as was noted earlier, the issue may not be difficult to resolve in small regions, but the technique might prove difficult in larger, more complex economies.

2.3. Accuracy, errors and sensitivity

The question of accuracy in input–output, and regional input–output in particular, is perhaps one of the main challenges for future research. It is one of the least researched topics, yet one which must eventually provide the ultimate framework for evaluation of present and past research.[5] We distinguish first [Jensen (1980)] A-type accuracy, or table accuracy, the extent to which any derived input–output table approximates the unknown "true" table, and B-type accuracy, or model accuracy, the degree to which the applied input–output model truly represents the operation of the economy in question. In general, we are least informed on B-type accuracy. Regional input–output tables are in daily use in planning exercises involving regional projection and impact studies and, in conjunction with other models, in a variety of circumstances some of which are inevitably inconsistent with the quite restrictive assumptions of the input–output model. We have, so far, virtually no research guidance on the possible extent of type-B error and the probable confidence levels in applied input–output analysis or ways to improve the subjective limits presently exercised by analysts. Indeed, attempts to test type-A table accuracy by the comparison of actual and surrogate vectors of gross outputs implicitly assume away type-B errors. This issue has been evaluated in a number of different contexts – the evaluation of nonsurvey techniques [Hewings (1977), Hewings and Syversen (1982)], the problems of spatial and sectoral aggregation [Miller and Blair (1981, 1985), Blair and Miller

---

[5] It is curious that input–output analysis is one branch of economics which has not been subjected to the rigorous statistical evaluations commonplace in other econometric analysis.

(1983)]–but ignored in a number of others, such as the issue of short-cut "input–output" type multipliers [see the exchange between Burford and Katz (1981) and Harrigan (1982)].

Returning to the issue of type-*A* or table accuracy, it is not a simple issue of the "degree of exactness" [Schultz (1978)] possessed by the parts or whole of the input–output table. The views and requirements of table accuracy will vary with the three perceptions (Section 2.1) of the input–output table as a self-sufficient model, as a module of a larger model or as a subset of social accounts. The variation is accommodated in a conceptual sense by the distinction between partitive and holistic accuracy, but this distinction has not been extended yet to empirical analysis. The suggestion [Jensen (1980)] that partitive accuracy is not achievable at a high level in the normal regional data context, and that holistic accuracy is a more realistic approach, has some possibly significant implications for practical perspectives on regional input–output analysis. The first implication is that the results of conventional applications of input–output models (at the regional level and to some extent at the national level) should be interpreted within the unknown but probably generous limits of accuracy and precision suggested by the concept of holistic accuracy. The second implication follows from this, namely that similar restrictions should flow on to composite models which contain input–output tables, irrespective of the level of accuracy of the remainder of the model.[6]

A third implication relates to the methods of table construction discussed in the previous section. It suggests that the most effective test of table accuracy is the extent to which a table captures the main features of the economy in question, presumably by recording with some exactness the more significant interactions (for example, the larger coefficients) rather than the analytically insignificant cells of the table. Although this would be accepted as inherent in input–output analysis, it has not been a significant part of assessing the relative value of survey, nonsurvey or hybrid tables. An instinctive evaluation would suggest that survey-based methods are best-placed to achieve high levels of holistic accuracy, along with hybrid methods which specifically seek to establish the integrity of the significant cells. It would suggest also that the nonsurvey methods are least suited for this end, in that they (particularly the gravity-related methods) have no properties which ensure that the more significant cells of the table are identified with an acceptable degree of accuracy.[7] If this line of

---

[6] No evidence has emerged to suggest that the level of accuracy of the input–output components suffers in comparison to that of other components of composite models.

[7] An early attempt to merge these two aspects of table accuracy in conjunction with a nonsurvey bi-proportional technique was made by Matuszewski et al. (1964). The cells judged, a priori, to be significant, were estimated from survey data; the remainder of the table was adjusted using a linear programming version of the RAS technique. Subsequent research has shown that the RAS, linear programming and gravity approaches may all be related [Hewings and Janson (1980)].

argument is reasonable, the conclusion follows that many of the tests which have compared nonsurvey and survey tables, based on the unweighted comparison of coefficients irrespective of their size, have not provided objective measures of the suitability of nonsurvey tables.

The question of table accuracy brings into focus the nature of error in input–output tables and the primary source of error in multipliers. Two approaches appear in the literature: the first could be termed *deterministic* in that it seeks to identify experimentally those variables which influence multiplier values (and therefore, multiplier errors) within a deterministic view of the input–output table. These experiments have produced diametrically opposed conclusions. On the one hand, Burford and Katz (1977a, b) claim evidence that the key determinants of the multipliers are the average and specific values of the individual column coefficients of the direct input table.[8] In general:

$$u_j = f\{w^*, w_j\} \tag{2.9}$$

where u is the column output multiplier, w_j the column sum of the direct input coefficients and w^* the mean of the w_j's. Phibbs and Holsman (1982) included a_{ii}, the intra-industry input coefficient, in their extension of (2.9).

The experiments reveal very accurate results – although the authors are not clear on how well the methods would work in the event that the w_j's were not known and had to be approximated.[9]

These developments highlight an important source of dissent among regional input–output analysts. There are some authors who claim that since the major uses to which the input–output model will be devoted center around the multipliers, their accurate estimation should be sufficient concern. Hence, Burford and Katz (1981) have developed multipliers for individual sectors derived from input–output models produced from random number generators and with the following characteristic:

$$a_{ij} = w_j/n \quad \text{for all columns } j \tag{2.10}$$

where w_j is the observed column sum of direct coefficients. In other words, all entries in a column are equal; Harrigan (1982) and Jensen and Hewings (1985), among others, have challenged this assumption, claiming that no known input structure approximates the one developed by Burford and Katz. Furthermore, as

[8] The interpretation of the Burford and Katz experimental evidence has been challenged by Harrigan (1982) and Jensen and Hewings (1985).

[9] This raises another issue, namely, if the w_j's are known, there may be more effective techniques which could be used to estimate not only the output multipliers but also the distribution of input coefficients.

Hewings (1977) demonstrated, techniques such as the Burford and Katz method (which may be regarded as a type of singly constrained RAS procedure) provide little indication of reliability when attention is focused on impact analyses for one or more *individual* sectors. In other words, the accurate estimation of the multiplier provides no assurance of the accuracy of the distribution of the impacts by sector within the column. These issues are closely related to the problems of errors created through aggregation; the recent work by Miller and Blair (1981) and Blair and Miller (1983) summarizes this within the context of both sectoral and spatial (across regions) interaction.

However, Stevens and Trainer (1976) would attribute the key role to regional purchase coefficients; their ideas were extended [Stevens et al. (1983)] into a nonsurvey methodology for the development of regional tables. Essentially, the method involves the estimation of the regional purchase coefficient for each sector (i.e. the proportion of regional demand which is fulfilled from local production) using econometric estimation techniques. The explanatory variables attempt to compare the relative delivered costs of intra- versus extra-regional sources. Comparison of this method with survey-based input–output tables for Washington and West Virginia yielded acceptable results. On the other hand, Jensen and West (1980) and West and Jensen (1977) would attribute the key role in the estimation of regional tables to the larger coefficients in the table, by quantifying the links between coefficient size and multiplier sensitivity. Although subject to alternative interpretation [Hamilton (1979)], West (1979) extended this argument to demonstrate that both coefficient size and location within the matrix affect multiplier sensitivity, enabling a ranking of coefficients according to their effect on multipliers and opening the way to accuracy-optimizing techniques. Page et al. (1981) have extended some ideas developed by Bullard and Sebald (1977) on the notion of inverse importance of individual coefficients to column sensitivity.

The second approach to table accuracy, termed here the *stochastic* approach has introduced a probabilistic view of both input–output tables and error. Gerking's (1976a, 1976b) attempt to place the input–output model in more traditional econometric terms in which errors are treated in a rigorous way has received increasing attention [Brown and Giarratani (1979), Hanseman (1982), Hanseman and Gustafson (1981)]. Goicoechea and Hansen (1978) and Jackson (1983) have extended this idea by examining the implied distribution of coefficients of individual firms within an industry sector and extending these probability distributions to impact analysis. West (1983), similarly, has moved in this direction, calculating density functions for output multipliers under some fairly restrictive assumptions. This allows for the calculation of confidence intervals for the multiplier estimates which provides, for the first time, an estimate of the probable size of the sampling error.

Table 2.1
Revised multiplier format.

	Output multipliers	Income multipliers	Other[a] multipliers
(i) Initial impact	1	h_j	e_j
(ii) First round effect	$\sum_i a_{ij}$	$\sum_i a_{ij} h_j$	$\sum_i a_{ij} e_j$
(iii) Industrial support effect	$\sum_i b_{ij} - 1 - \sum_i a_{ij}$	$\sum_i h_j(b_{ij} - 1 - a_{ij})$	$\sum_i e_j(b_{ij} - 1 - a_{ij})$
(iv) Consumption-induced effect	$\sum_i b_{ij}^* - b_{ij}$	$\sum_i h_j(b_{ij}^* - b_{ij})$	$\sum_i e_j(b_{ij}^* - b_{ij})$
(v) Total effect	$\sum_{i=1}^n b_{ij}^*$	$\sum_{i=1}^n h_j b_{ij}^*$	$\sum_{i=1}^n e_j b_{ij}^*$
(vi) Flow-on effect	$\sum_{i=1}^n b_{ij}^* - 1$	$\sum_{i=1}^n h_j b_{ij}^* - h_j$	$\sum_{i=1}^n e_j b_{ij}^* - e_j$
(vii) Type I Ratios			
Type IA	–	$[(i)+(ii)]/(i)$	
Type IB	–	$[(i)+(ii)+(iii)]/(i)$	
Type II Ratios			
Type IIA	–	$[(i)+(ii)+(iii)+(iv)]/(i)$	
Type IIB	–	$[(ii)+(iii)+(iv)]/(i)$	

[a]Where e_j refers to the unit requirement of some input per unit of output. For example applying e_j as an employment/output ratio provides employment multipliers. Equally e_j as energy requirements would provide energy multipliers.

2.4.   Multipliers

The notion of input–output multipliers as final demand multipliers based on the open ($b_{ij} \in [I - A]^{-1}$) and the closed, households endogenous ($b_{ij}^* \in [I - A^*]^{-1}$) inverse Leontief matrices and referring to a dollar unit of output has remained unchallenged. A set of multipliers, which have satisfied the theoretical and empirical requirements of most analysts, has emerged in an incremental manner, based on the b_{ij} as the "direct and indirect" multipliers, and the b_{ij}^* as sectoral "direct, indirect and induced" multipliers, and the addition of these over n sectors as economy-wide multipliers. Although logically sound, the conventional presentation of multipliers contains a terminological inconsistency relating to the terms "direct" and "indirect." This inconsistency led West and Jensen (1980) to suggest a slightly revised multiplier format as shown in Table 2.1 where first-round effects are defined as effects in sectors supplying direct inputs and industrial support effects refer to second, third and subsequent round input effects. Table 2.1 can be used to demonstrate the terminological consistency. The term "direct" is applied in conventional terminology in output multipliers, appropriately to describe the first-round purchases of the output of supplying firms; the same term in income (and employment) multipliers is applied to define the income (employment) occurring within the industry to which the multiplier applies, while first-round income (employment) effects are included in the indirect income (employment) multipliers. In terms of Table 2.1, the conventional system defines the effects as:

	Output Multipliers	Income and other Multipliers
Direct	(ii)	(i)
Indirect	(i) and (iii)	(ii) and (iii)
Induced	(iv)	(iv)

Clearly, the conventional "direct and indirect" system does not allow useful comparison of direct or indirect output and income (employment) effects, since these are inconsistently defined. This problem is resolved in the revised format which was extended to define "flow-on" impacts in an attempt to isolate the cause and effect components of multipliers. These flow-on effects combine the first-round, industrial support and consumption-induced effects and represent the impact on the rest of the economy of the initial dollar change of output. The fact that the logical flow of causality in input—output multipliers originates with the assumed dollar change in output is often by implication overlooked where analysts use Type I and II multipliers in a manner which implies causality between the numerator and denominator of these ratios. For the sake of consistency, the Type I and II relations are probably better described as ratios of association than multipliers suggesting causality.

The literature discloses several items of some significance in multiplier formulation. One originates with the proofs of Sandoval (1967) and Bradley and Gander (1969) showing the constant relationship between Type I and II multipliers, and the latter illustration that this relationship is equal to the common cell in the household row and column of the closed inverse. This has relevance not only for table closure, but for any additions for other purposes of new rows and columns to the intermediate matrix. A second item refers to the tendency for such closure [noted first by Moore and Petersen (1955)], using the normal assumption of a linear, homogeneous consumption function, to overstate the consumption-induced effects of multipliers. The first attempt to overcome this problem in single-region studies appears to be the relaxation of this homogeneity assumption by Moore and Petersen (1955) by the development of linear nonhomogeneous consumption functions from the national time series data. The next significant step was taken by Miernyk et al. (1967) in the Boulder study in the development of a nonlinear regional consumption function from consumption functions for different income groups, enabling the use of marginal rather than average propensities in multiplier calculation. Miernyk also distinguished between the spending patterns of new households and established residents, in the form of an income multiplier termed Type III. Drawing on these notions, Tiebout (1969) developed a projection model for the state of Washington in which the contributions of extensive income growth (through in-migration) were differentiated from intensive income growth (additions to the income of existing residents). Miyazawa's (1968, 1976) extensions along these lines will be reviewed in Section 3; Batey (1985) has developed an interesting typology of multipliers based on these notions of the role of different actors in the regional consumption system. However, two points should be noted here; first, many survey-based regional input–output models have estimated consumption expenditures as a residual after all other interindustry and final demands have been estimated. The second point is that the reason for this procedure often stems from the scarcity of reliable data on regional consumption patterns. Given the dominance of the household row and column in connectedness and multiplier formation, it is of some concern that these rows are frequently derived from the least reliable data.

A third item relates to input–output multiplier definition and use. A common and appropriate justification for the derivation of input–output tables lies in the detailed representation of economic interaction and interdependence at a disaggregate level. It is somewhat surprising, therefore, to note that the majority of applications of input–output multipliers appears to be in the aggregate or whole-economy form, in which they can be seen as analogous to the economic base and Keynesian multipliers described earlier. Polenske (1970) has been one of the few regional analysts to demonstrate best the use of the disaggregated multipliers in the multiregional context. An alternate approach, multiplier decomposition has been developed in the context of social accounting matrices and is reviewed in Section 3. Both these approaches appear to offer opportunities to explore the inherent *matrix* formation of input–output multipliers in a more explicit fashion.

2.5. Table connectedness and structure

The representation of economic structure is the *raison d'être* of the input–output table. It is therefore disappointing to note the limited amount of research effort devoted to using these tables in formal studies of the important questions of economic structure at the regional level.[10] It is possible to identify three general directions of research of relevance to economic structure, namely those of economic connectedness, the ordering of tables and linkage structures. These are addressed in turn.

---

[10]At the national level, there have been some limited attempts; the work of Simpson and Tsukui (1965) and Harrigan et al. (1980a, 1980b) are probably the best known.

Connectedness, interconnectedness and interrelatedness are terms used to describe the strength of interindustry linkages or complexity of an economy, the amount of "churning" or the number of transactions required to achieve a given level of output [Robinson and Markandya (1973), Hewings et al. (1984)]. Connectedness measures vary from the more naive to more complex along a scale which includes (1) the percentage of non-zero A coefficients, used by Peacock and Dosser (1957) and termed an index of diversification by Yan and Ames (1965), (2) the percentage of transactions which are intermediate, used by Chenery and Watanabe (1958), (3) coefficient sums and means [Jensen and West (1980)], (4) average output multipliers [Jensen and West (1980)], (5) determinants [Wong (1954)], (6) the order-matrix and (7) the entropy approach. Yan and Ames (1965) defined an order matrix as one recording for each cell the number of rounds of transactions necessary for non-zero cells to occur in the A matrix. The Robinson and Markandya (1973) rounds of transactions matrix is a variation of the order matrix. The first five measures, together with the Yan and Ames order matrix, were compared by Hamilton and Jensen (1983). Their study pointed to the weakness of the more naive methods and the importance of accounting procedures and aggregation levels in determining interconnectedness. The order matrix approaches have the common pattern of their failure to distinguish sufficiently the analytically significant transactions. Erlander's (1980) interpretation of entropy as a measure of dispersion has been shown [Jensen and Hewings (1985), Hewings (1983)] as an alternative view of connectedness but shares the common weakness with other approaches that a given degree of connectedness can be calculated from tables representing economies which are substantially different in structure. More recently, Jackson and Hewings (1984) have used the entropy approach to measure changes in structure over time and found the results to be more encouraging.

Since research so far concludes that single-dimension measures of connectedness have limited value, we examine attempts to express the structural characteristics of input–output tables, through the concepts of triangulation, fundamental structure and entropy decomposition. Triangulation essentially expresses one characteristic, namely linear dependence, or the extent to which flows are uni-directional in the economy. The expositional triangulation work of Chenery and Watanabe (1958) and Helmstädter (1969) led to the triangulation of eighteen standardized tables by Lamel et al. (1970) which illustrated some value of triangulation in structural analysis. The study showed the tendency of some sectors to be stable in their position in the hierarchy of sectors and to have a tendency towards clustering. Both Lamel et al. and Helmstädter used triangulation to take some tentative steps in seeking concepts of economic structure by recognizing "blocks" of similar hierarchical structure. Lamel et al. identified several "blocks", concluding that the level of economic development was the significant factor in block identification. Simpson and Tsukui (1965) had earlier used triangulation in an imaginative attempt to discover a "fundamental structure of production" in a common pattern of industries, or a "skeleton" of the production of the productive system. They recognized four "blocks", each with recognizable technical qualities, and a tendency to block-independence. Somewhat surprisingly, the promising lines of research by these authors have not attracted attention in the last decade. Some tentative steps in the direction of entropy decomposition [Jensen and Hewings (1985), Jackson and Hewings (1984)] based on Theil's formulae (1972) is a further area for productive research on economic structure.

The third and most recent approach to structural analysis lies in comparative analysis of economic structure and linkages with compatible sets of tables, both in the temporal and spatial dimension. Several tests, including entropy decomposition, interdependence measures, triangulation and banded matrices have been applied to the three survey-based models for the Washington economy [Hewings (1985), Hewings et al. (1985)] in an attempt to identify temporal changes in regional economic structure. Jensen et al. (1985) have examined the ten GRIT tables for the Queensland regions to determine any broad regularities in table construction over a variety of regions which range from metropolitan regions to remote rural regions, both in terms of the size and connectedness of the tables. The results suggest that the primary sectors tend to be more spatially variable and region specific, with significant and more stable patterns shown by secondary and tertiary sectors. This research provides preliminary evidence that, once the nature of a regional system is known, it could be possible to predict many coefficients at various levels of regional size and connectness, and that the development of a taxonomic system for the objective description of economies may not be an unrealistic goal. A similar venture, by Defourny and Thorbecke (1984), has cast the input–output model in terms of a network in the hopes of extracting some important dimensions of the economy in concert with multiplier decomposition.

In the next section, some of the extensions to input–output analysis will be explored; many of the issues raised in this section will be addressed in the context of the integration of the input–output model in a broader context.

3. Extensions to regional input–output analysis

One of the most promising developments in regional and interregional input–output analysis in recent years has been the extension of the modelling framework in two important ways:

> the extension of the input–output model per se;
> the linkage of input–output analysis within much more extensive modelling systems.

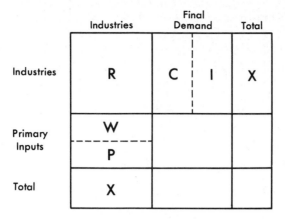

Figure 3.1. The Miyazawa framework.

In Section 1 of this chapter, the link between economic base, Keynesian macro accounting analysis and input–output systems was demonstrated. This section will begin by developing a link with another useful framework, the Kalecki system as interpreted in input–output terms by Miyazawa (1976). This extension was used as the basis for the development of much of the demometric/demographic–economic analysis associated with the work of Schinnar (1976) and Batey and Madden (1982) and is consistent with a parallel development in what may be referred to as social accounting matrices (SAMs). Miyazawa was interested in the incorporation of the distribution of income received and the expenditure into the input–output framework. The idea will be developed first with a simple one sector model and thereafter it will be extended to the more general case.

3.1. Miyazawa's framework

Figure 3.1 shows the standard framework: there is one intermediate sector, R; two components to final demand, consumption C and investment, I; and two primary inputs, W (wages) and P (profits). Hence, the accounting system is:

$$R + C + I = X \tag{3.1}$$

$$R + W + P = X. \tag{3.2}$$

If the usual conventions are followed then we have:

$r = R/X$ and $f = C + I$ then

$$X = (1-r)^{-1}f. \tag{3.3}$$

Assume that $C = cY$ and hence $= c(W + P)$, then we have the Keynesian solution:

$$Y = (1-c)^{-1}I. \tag{3.4}$$

Since $C + I = W + P$ (i.e. $f = Y$), by substitution of (3.4) into (3.3):

$$X = (1-r)^{-1}f = (1-r)^{-1}(1-c)^{-1}I. \tag{3.5}$$

This holds only for a particular income distribution; if the shares of wages and profits are:

$$d_1 = W/Y; \qquad d_e = P/Y \tag{3.6}$$

and consumption (C) is similarly disaggregated into the share by wage-earners (C_1) and the share by those receiving profits (C_e):

$$C = C_1 + C_e = c_w/W + c_p/P. \tag{3.7}$$

The generalized income multiplier may now be written as:

$$(1-c)^{-1} = \left[1 - (c_1 d_1 + c_e d_e)\right]^{-1}. \tag{3.8}$$

If the value-added ratio, $v = Y/X = (1-r)$ is further subdivided into: $v_1 = W/X$ and $v_e = P/X$, we have:

$$X = (1-r)^{-1}\left[1 - (c_1 v_1 + c_e v_e)(1-r)^{-1}\right]I. \tag{3.9}$$

This scalar system may now be expanded by dividing the input–output part into n sectors and k income groups. Hence, we now have:

$R =$ an $n \times n$ matrix of regional input coefficients;
$V =$ a $k \times n$ matrix of value added ratios (for wages and salaries);
$C =$ an $n \times k$ matrix of consumption coefficients (out of wages and salaries);
$f_c =$ an $n \times 1$ vector of consumption demand;
$f^\sim =$ an $n \times 1$ vector of the rest of final demand.

The accounting balance is now:

$$X = RX + f_c + f^{\sim} \tag{3.10}$$

for which the normal solution would be of the form:

$$X = [I - R]^{-1}[f_c + f^{\sim}]. \tag{3.11}$$

Instead, the consumption effect will be made endogenous in a way that will enable the analyst to measure the effects of changes in consumption without repeated matrix inversion. The matrix f_c may be defined as CVX since VX represents the income accruing to consumers from wages and salaries and C represents the expenditure pattern per unit of income (i.e. average propensities to consume). Hence, (3.10) may be written:

$$X = RX + CVX + f^{\sim} \tag{3.12}$$

which yields the closed form solution:

$$X = [I - R - CV]^{-1}f^{\sim}. \tag{3.13}$$

If B is defined as the usual Leontief Inverse matrix (i.e. $[I - A]^{-1}$), then we may write:

$$X = B[I - CVB]^{-1}f^{\sim} \tag{3.14}$$
$$= B[I + CKVB]f^{\sim} \tag{3.15}$$

where $K = [I - L]^{-1}$ and $L = VBC$. L is the macroeconomic propensity to consume; with only one income group, K would reduce to a scalar. KVB may be regarded as the multisector income multiplier. With this formulation, we are now ready to explore the structure of the propagation process:

$$\begin{bmatrix} X \\ \cdots \\ Y \end{bmatrix} = \begin{bmatrix} R & \vdots & C \\ \cdots & \cdots & \cdots \\ V & \vdots & 0 \end{bmatrix} \begin{bmatrix} X \\ \cdots \\ Y \end{bmatrix} + \begin{bmatrix} f^{\sim} \\ \cdots \\ g \end{bmatrix} \tag{3.16}$$

where g is exogenous income. Further manipulation reveals:

$$\begin{bmatrix} X \\ \cdots \\ Y \end{bmatrix} = \begin{bmatrix} I - R & \vdots & -C \\ \cdots & \cdots & \cdots \\ -V & \vdots & I \end{bmatrix}^{-1} \begin{bmatrix} f^{\sim} \\ \cdots \\ g \end{bmatrix} \tag{3.17}$$

$$= \begin{bmatrix} B[I + CKVB] & \vdots & BCK \\ \cdots & \cdots & \cdots \\ KVB & \vdots & K \end{bmatrix} \begin{bmatrix} f^{\sim} \\ \cdots \\ g \end{bmatrix} \tag{3.18}$$

In an analysis of this modelling framework applied to a three-region case study for Japan, Miyazawa (1968) expanded the interpretation of L such that a typical element 1^{pq} shows how much income in region p is generated by an additional unit of income in region q. He was able to show the degree to which the middle region of Japan (including the Tokyo region) had a 83.5% self-sufficiency ratio for income whereas the Northeast and Western regions were dependent on the middle for 40% and 35% respectively of their incomes. This formulation presented by Miyazawa anticipates a great deal of the conceptual development of social accounting matrices, a topic to be discussed below.

3.2.   The Batey–Madden activity analysis framework

Two important extensions of this formulation at the regional level have been developed by Schinnar (1976) and in various papers by Batey and Madden [see (1982) for references to earlier work]. In parallel with the attempts by Ledent to link demographic and economic base models, these authors have linked demographic components with the interindustry model. The work by Batey and Madden has been developed the most extensively to date; drawing on some earlier notions by Tiebout (1969) about the role of different labor groups (inmigrants and local residents) in the generation of expenditure effects and some empirical work by Blackwell (1978) who suggested the incorporation of the impacts of previously unemployed residents on local income generation, Batey and Madden have produced some extensions to the Miyazawa framework. Figure 3.2 shows one such extension; in this case, an activity analysis framework is employed in which consumption effects are differentiated by status (employed or unemployed) in the work force. In matrix form, this yields:

$$
\begin{bmatrix} I - R & \vdots & -Q \\ \cdots & \vdots & \cdots \\ -L & \vdots & I - Z \end{bmatrix} \begin{bmatrix} X_I \\ \cdots \\ h \end{bmatrix} = \begin{bmatrix} f_1 \\ \cdots \\ f_2 \end{bmatrix} \tag{3.19}
$$

where h refers to different types of workers, Q their associated consumption patterns, Z a matrix for allocating workers between active and inactive status and f_1 and f_2 are the components of final demand and active population constraints. The solution for h is:

$$
h = \left[I - Z - L(I - R)^{-1}Q \right]^{-1} \left[f_2 + L(I - R)^{-1}f_1 \right]. \tag{3.20}
$$

In this formulation, it is possible to trace the impacts of changes in final demand on the labor supply. In an empirical analysis of the model in the Merseyside

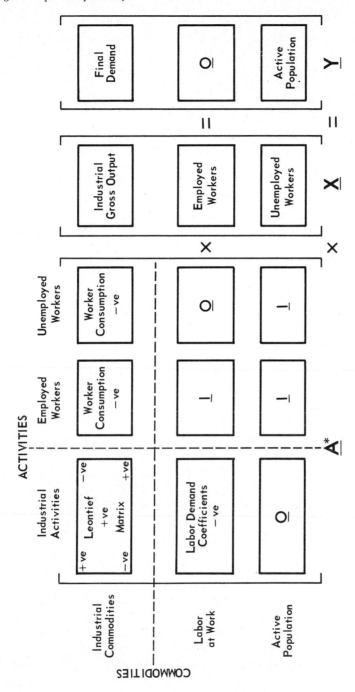

Figure 3.2. The Merseyside model.

region of the UK, they were able to show that, ceteris paribus, the overall unemployment rate would have been 43% higher were it not for the expenditure effects generated by unemployment compensation.

3.3. The general social accounting framework

The inclusion of an exogenous income term, g, in the Miyazawa framework has been further modified in the social accounting system. Originally pioneered by Nobel Laureate Sir Richard Stone (1961), these systems have been extended by Pyatt and Roe (1977) and applied at the regional and interregional level by Round (1984) and Bell et al. (1982). Table 3.1 shows a typical social accounting system for a single region. The analytical solution may be derived in several ways; first, a generalized inverse may be obtained and the solution vector found in the usual way:

$$X = [I - R^*]^{-1} f^{~} \qquad (3.21)$$

where R^* is the matrix of coefficients derived from Table 3.1. Second, the partitioned matrix may be employed separately and the use of permutation matrices will yield a solution of the form:

$$X = M_1 M_2 M_3 f^{~}. \qquad (3.22)$$

In this case, $f^{~}$ represents final demand outside the region since consumption and government activities are now endogenous. The separate effect of the components of multiplier matrices may be described briefly as follows. (i) M_1 captures the separate effects of multipliers *within* a group of accounts, e.g. the intraregional multiplier matrix in an interregional context; (ii) the *feedback* effect of an exogenous injection, via other parts of the system, e.g. the feedback on output of an initial increase in output part of which was translated into factor income, thence to household income, to consumption and finally back to output effects; (iii) M_3 captures the effects that an increase in income or output in one group of accounts might have on that of the other accounts or, as an interregional context, on accounts in other regions. The reader is referred to Pyatt and Roe (1977) for an explanation of the decomposed solution system. Round (1984) has recently proposed a methodology for developing interregional solutions of this type, although the procedures are not quite as tractable once the number of regions exceeds two. These multiplier decomposition approaches appear to offer some potential also for structural analysis of interindustry transactions in the input–output table and therefore for more systematic study of economic structure.

Table 3.1
Single region social accounting scheme.[a]

	Factors of production	Institutions current account	Production activity	Interregional & foreign accounts
Factors of production Labour : : Capital			(Value added in production)	(Net factor incomes from other regions and rest of the world)
Institutions Firms Households Government	(Gross profits) (Wages, salaries)	(Transfers and taxes)		(Transfers from outside regions)
Production activity Agriculture : : Manufacturing : Services		(Consumer expenditures on regional goods)	(Interindustry transactions)	(Exports of goods outside the region)
Interregional & foreign accounts	(Consumer expenditures on imports)	(Imports of intermediate goods)		

[a] Entries in the matrix provide examples of some of the transactions between accounts.
Source: After Pyatt and Roe (1977).

Perhaps one of the most creative extensions of this system has been the work of Bell et al. (1982). They applied the system to the Muda region of Malaysia to evaluate the effects of a large-scale irrigation project. In so doing, they adopted a variation of Tinbergen's semi-input–output method and linked the system to a cost–benefit framework [see also Kuyvenhoven (1978) for a similar exercise]. Tinbergen (1966) adopted a distinction that Isard (1953) made in the development of a regional interindustry model for New England, namely that the sectors in an economy could be divided according to the degree to which they engaged in local, interregional (national) or international trade. In the version to be described here, as modified by Karunaratne (1976), it is assumed that the economic sectors are characterized by tradeables (t) and nontradeables (n), the former entering interregional trade while the latter serve only the local (regional) market. Clearly, the distinction is reminiscent of the bifurcation in the economic base models. To illustrate the use of the model in conjunction with cost–benefit analysis, it will be assumed that the final demand for nontradeables, f_n, is zero. Then, the level of output in the nontradeable sectors is given by:

$$X_n = [I - R_{nn}]^{-1} R_{nt} X_t. \tag{3.23}$$

Assume that a project, for which appraisal is desired, is located in sector j ($j \in T$), the cost–benefit criterion is

$$T_j = \frac{K_j + K_n [I - R_{nn}]^{-1} R_{nj}}{v_j + V_n [I - R_{nn}]^{-1} R_{nj}} \tag{3.24}$$

where K_j and v_j are the direct capital and value added coefficients for sector j, V_n and K_n are the nontradeable value-added and capital coefficient vectors and A_{nj} the vector of inputs from the nontradeable sector to sector j. Since all elements in the ratio are multiplied by X_j, the term drops out of the final expression. Note that it is assumed that there are no interactions among the tradeable sectors at the regional level, i.e. $R_{11} = R_{12} = 0$.

Bell et al. (1982) adopted a more extensive analysis in the case of the Muda region irrigation project. The standard balance equation was given as:

$$X_i = \sum_j r_{ij} X_j + \sum_k b_{ik} + V_i + E_i \tag{3.25}$$

where the second term on the right-hand side refers to consumption by the set of household sectors and V and E refer to investment and exports. The income of each household is assumed to be comprised of wages and salaries and distributed profits and net transfers:

$$Y_k = \sum_j w_{kj} X_j + \mathrm{Tr}_k.$$ (3.26)

Taxes and savings are similarly defined as linear functions of income and, in the case of taxes, an exogenous component, T^*:

$$Tx_k = t_k Y_k + T_k^*$$ (3.27)

$$S_k = s_k (Y_k - T_k).$$ (3.28)

Finally, a linear consumption function is defined as:

$$b_{ik} = \alpha_{ik} + \beta_{ik} B_k$$ (3.29)

where B_k represent total outlays on consumption. In matrix form the system may be written:

$$\begin{bmatrix} I-R & : & -BC \\ \cdots & \cdots & \cdots \\ -\Omega & : & I \end{bmatrix} \begin{bmatrix} X \\ Y \end{bmatrix} = \begin{bmatrix} \Gamma e & : & B[I-S]T^* \\ \cdots & \cdots & \cdots \\ 0 & : & \mathrm{Tr}_k \end{bmatrix} + \begin{bmatrix} V \\ \cdots \\ 0 \end{bmatrix} + \begin{bmatrix} E \\ \cdots \\ 0 \end{bmatrix}$$

(3.30)

where B is an $n \times h$ matrix of β_{ik}'s
C an $h \times h$ diagonal matrix of c_k's $= (1-s_k)(1-t_k)$
Γ an $n \times h$ matrix of α_{ik}'s
E an $n \times 1$ vector of E_i's
e an $h \times 1$ vector of 1's
V an $n \times 1$ vector of V_i's
T^* an $n \times 1$ vector of T_k^*'s and
Ω an $h \times n$ matrix of w_{kj}'s.
In this form, (3.30) represents the standard regional version of the Leontief model; as with the Miyazawa version described earlier, given the levels of exogenous demand, the model may be solved for outputs and incomes. In their application to the Muda region in Malaysia, Bell et al. (1982) adopted a modified version of the semi-input–output approach proposed by Tinbergen (1966) and further elaborated in Kuyvenhoven (1978). Sectors were classified into tradeable and nontradeable (in a spatial sense), the latter being restricted to transactions within the region. Thence, the output of traded goods was assumed to be given, while their associated exports were determined endogenously, whereas the output of the nontraded sectors was assumed to be determined endogenously. This

model, and variations on it, was used to measure the impact of a large irrigation scheme on the region through comparison of regional growth and income distributions with and without the project.

One major difficulty, of course, was that the analysts were confined to the measurement of direct and indirect effects within the region. Round (1972, 1978a, 1978b, 1979, 1983) has argued persuasively for the development of at least two-region models (the region in question and the rest of the country of which it is a part) on the basis of a number of factors – especially, the provision of consistency in estimation of the original parameters. Recently, Round (1984), has provided some guidance to the development of two- and larger region social accounting systems, incorporating the multiplier decomposition ideas noted in (3.22). In the Muda region case, the need for consideration of the extra-regional effects became more pressing when rural incomes began to rise above a sub-sistence level, creating the opportunities for rural households to engage in consumption of additional goods and services. Since many of these would be produced outside the region, the effects of increasing rural incomes might not continue to narrow disparities between rural and urban incomes. Clearly, the changes in rural marginal propensities to consume in total and the changes in consumption of local versus nonlocal goods would play a very important role.

3.4.   Links with the labor market

The role of differences in consumption patterns by different groups within a region has been addressed by Van Dijk and Oosterhaven (1985) and in the spirit of the Bell et al. (1982) work noted earlier by Oosterhaven (1981). The latter work is notable for the fact that it linked an interregional input–output model to traditional cost–benefit appraisal to measure the effect of alternative land re-clamation schemes in a small part of Holland. If an accurate attempt to link the role of households to the economic system is to be made, then some careful consideration is needed of labor market behavior. While Batey and Madden (1982) accounted for movements into and out of the employed ranks, Van Dijk et al. (1984) examined the regional impact of inmigration and linked it with both the input–output model and a labor force vacancy chain model. The consump-tion effects of different households in-migrating into the region were considered. In the analysis which follows, it will be assumed that the regional system experiences five changes in demand, only one of which is exogenously de-termined, namely the consumption demand of inmigrants. The other changes in demand are the changes in regional intermediate demand and consumption induced effects. These are shown in (3.31):

$$\delta x = A\delta x + q^1 \delta c^1 + q^u \delta c^u + q^n \delta c^n + \delta f \tilde{\ } \tag{3.31}$$

where δx is the change in production levels, q^1 the regional consumption vector associated with people with high labor incomes, q^u the consumption of those receiving unemployment benefits and q^n the consumption of those with non labor-force active benefits. The δc terms are the associated changes in consumption and $\delta f^{\sim}$ are the inmigrants consumption.

The vacancy chain model provides a link between employment creation and changes in output (which are created by the expenditures of the inmigrants) and increases in labor productivity:

$$\delta e = l \delta x - p^1 e_{t-1} \tag{3.32}$$

where δe is the vector of employment changes by industry, l is the vector of marginal employment coefficients, p^1 is a diagonal matrix of labor productivity increases and e_{t-1} the base year employment levels by industry. The total number of vacancies is shown below:

$$v = Tv + \delta e + v^{\sim} \tag{3.33}$$

where v is the total number of vacancies, T the interindustry transition probability matrix of people leaving industry i to take up jobs in industry j. $v^{\sim}$ is a miscellaneous category comprising movements out of the region, out of the labor force because of retirement and as a result of frictional vacancies. In addition, to transfers among industries by those already employed, other vacancies are filled by unemployed who enjoyed benefits (3.34), nonactives who enjoyed nonactive benefits (3.35) or no benefits (3.36) and inmigrants from other regions (3.37):

$$\delta u = t^u v \tag{3.34}$$
$$\delta n = (t^n)'v \tag{3.35}$$
$$\delta r = (r^r)'v \tag{3.36}$$
$$m = t^m v \tag{3.37}$$

where the t's refer to transition probabilities for unemployed, nonactives with and without benefits and migrants. In the case study, it was assumed that there was no exogenous change in the number of vacancies. Since the number of vacancies being filled with equal the change in the number of jobs, the following will be true:

$$\delta u = t^u (I - T)^{-1} \delta e \tag{3.38}$$
$$\delta n = (t^n)'(I - T)^{-1} \delta e \tag{3.39}$$
$$\delta r = (t^r)'(I - T)^{-1} \delta e \tag{3.40}$$
$$m = t^m (I - T)^{-1} \delta e. \tag{3.41}$$

The vacancy chain model is tied to the input–output system through the income–consumption model. The change in consumption of employed people is:

$$\delta c^1 = (c^q)' w \delta e + \delta c_{\tilde{1}} \tag{3.42}$$

where c^q is the consumption vector by industry, w the average labor incomes per industry and the last term is the change in consumption which derives from changes in the exogenous incomes of workers. In the application to the northern provinces of the Netherlands, it was assumed that the latter term was zero. In addition, the part of labor income accruing to migrants has to be deducted from (3.42) to avoid double counting (since these migrants have already been included as part of the exogenous final demand). Hence, (3.42) becomes:

$$\delta c^1 = (c^q)' w (\delta e - m). \tag{3.43}$$

The decrease in consumption expenditures of the unemployed are derived in (3.44); the 0.80 coefficient is the product of an assumption that their unemployment benefits are approximately 90% of their former labor incomes and that they fill vacancies with incomes that are 90% of the corresponding sectoral average:

$$\delta c^u = -0.80 (c^{qu})' w \delta u + \delta c_{\tilde{u}} \tag{3.44}$$

where c^{qu} are the consumption vector of coefficients for the unemployed and $\delta c_{\tilde{u}}$ the consumption changes from exogenous income changes of the unemployed (also assumed to be zero in the case study). The final decrease in consumption that will occur is associated with those who move from the status of nonactive with benefits to employment:

$$\delta c^n = -12{,}227 \delta n + \delta c_{\tilde{n}} \tag{3.45}$$

where $\delta c_{\tilde{n}}$ is the consumption from exogenous income (again assumed to be zero); the value $-12{,}227$ is the average nonactive benefits, assumed to apply to all nonactives who get a job. The solution of the integrated model is shown in Figure 3.3. The model solution works in the following way; the exogenously induced effects (inmigrant expenditures) create industry demands which, through the operation of the interindustry multiplier, create jobs. The vacancy chain model operates to fill these jobs and thereby to create income. These consumption-induced expenditures again create demands on industry and so the process continues until convergence. From the empirical model, the authors were able to show that from the 6,700 families who entered the northern regions, 5,000 persons gained employment in the region; the effect of this employment creation was the further creation of 2,421 additional person years of employment.

	Dimensions of the symbols:					Endogenous variables:	Exogenous and lagged endogenous variables:
	28	28	1	1	1		
28	$(I-A)$	0	$-\underline{q}^1$	$-\underline{q}^u$	$-\underline{q}^n$	Δx	Δf^{ex}
28	$-\hat{I}$	$(I-T)$	$\underline{0}$	$\underline{0}$	$\underline{0}$	$\underline{v}$	$\underline{v}^{ex}-\hat{p}^1\underline{e}_{t-1}$
1	$-(\underline{c}^q)'\hat{w}\hat{I}$	$\underline{0}'$	1	0	0	Δc^1	$= \quad \Delta c_1^{ex}-(\underline{c}^q)'\hat{w}\hat{p}^1\underline{e}_{t-1}$
1	$\underline{0}'$	$0.80(\underline{c}^{qu})'\hat{w}\hat{t}^u$	0	1	0	Δc^u	Δc_u^{ex}
1	$\underline{0}'$	$12{,}227\,(\underline{t}^n)'$	0	0	1	Δc^n	Δc_n^{ex}

Figure 3.3. The integrated I–O labor model for the Dutch northern provinces.

3.5. Linear programming input – output links

Two major limitations have curtailed the more widespread use of input–output models. The first relates to the problem of coefficient stability over time and the second to the problem of the absence of limitations on capacity in the regional economy. A number of authors have provided some creative ways of dealing with these problems, either through the linkage of the input–output model with a linear program or the respecification of the input–output model per se as a linear program. In the latter category, the work of Bargur (1969) and Mathur (1972) should be noted; Bargur developed a formulation in which a linear programming form of the input–output model was used to examine the effect of water capacity problems on output in Californian industries. Mathur's model examined inter-regional investment allocation – very much in the spirit of some of Ghosh's (1973) work. However, the MORSE model [Lundqvist (1981)] is probably the most advanced since it employs a dynamic formulation; it was used for a variety of impact analyses, the substitution of nuclear power in conjunction with increased oil prices and the case of increased regional self-sufficiency (see Table 3.2).

A similar concern for energy issues prompted the application of a linked input–output and linear programming model to part of a six state region in the US [Page et al. (1981)]. The ORBES model structure is shown in Figure 3.4; note that the A matrix is divided into three major components, energy supplies, energy products (nontradeable items such as space heating, air conditioning) and non-energy sectors. The *numeraire* varies by submatrix; essentially, final demands generate demand for energy products. These products are supplied from the set of available energy supplies through a linear programming model which seeks to minimize the cost of production subject to energy conversion, energy supply, capacity and pollution constraints. Changes in relative prices of energy supplies are thus incorporated in the linear programming model and then, in turn, into the input coefficients (A_{ss} and A_{sp}) matrices. Thus, some degree of endogenous price substitution is incorporated into the system, if only in a limited number of sectors. Liew and Liew (1984) have approached this problem using production

Table 3.2
The Morse model.

$$
\underset{\substack{X_{it}, X_{irt},\\ XC_{rt}, l_{irt},\\ EX_t}}{\text{Maximize}} \sum_{t=1}^{NT} \left\{ V1 \cdot d_t \sum_{r=1}^{NR} XC_{rt} + V2 \cdot \sum_{i=1}^{NS} \sum_{r=1}^{NR} l_{irt} X_{irt} + V3 \right.
$$

$$
\left. \cdot \sum_{r=1}^{NR} \sum_{k=1}^{NK} u_k \left[\sum_{i=1}^{NS} e_{irt}^k X_{irt} + ec_{rt}^k XC_{rt} \right] \right\}
$$

subject to:

$$
X_{irt} + m_{irt} \cdot X_{irt} \geq \beta_{ir} \sum_{j=1}^{NS} a_{ij}^r X_{jrt} + \gamma_{ir} \left\{ a_{iC}^{rt} XC_{rt} + \sum_{j=1}^{NS} B_{ij} I_{jrt} \right\} + ex_{irt} EX_t + dx_{irt}
$$

$$
dx_{irt} = \sum_{s=1}^{NR} \omega_{ir}^s \left[(1 - \beta_{is}) \sum_{j=1}^{NS} a_{ij}^s X_{jst} + (1 - \gamma_{is}) \left\{ a_{iC}^{st} XC_{st} + \sum_{j=1}^{NS} B_{ij} I_{jst} \right\} \right]
$$

$X_{irt} = \alpha_{ir} X_{it}$ (type 1 sectors)

$$
XC_{rt} \geq g_{rt} \sum_{i=1}^{NS} f_{ir} X_{irt}
$$

$$
- \sum_{i=1}^{NS} \sum_{r=1}^{NR} m_{irt} \epsilon_i X_{irt} + EX_t \geq_1 \overline{BOP}_t
$$

$c_{irt} X_{irt} \leq C_{ir}^0 (1 - \delta_i)^t + (1 - \delta_i)^{t-1} I_{ir1} + \cdots + I_{irt}$

$$
\overline{L}_{rt} \leq \sum_{i=1}^{NS} l_{irt} X_{irt} \leq \overline{\overline{L}}_{rt}
$$

$$
\sum_{r=1}^{NR} \left[\sum_{i=1}^{NS} e_{irt}^k X_{irt} + ec_{rt}^k XC_{rt} \right] \leq \overline{\overline{E}}_t^k
$$

$$
\sum_{i=1}^{NS} \sum_{r=1}^{NR} \{ C_{ir}^0 (1 - \delta_i)^t + (1 - \delta_i)^{t-1} I_{ir1} + \cdots + I_{irt} \} \geq \overline{CT}_t
$$

$X_{it} \geq 0$ (type 1 sectors), $X_{irt} \geq 0$ (type 2–3 sectors), $XC_{rt} \geq 0$, $I_{irt} \geq 0$,
$EX_t \geq 0$

Notation:
Variables:

X_{it} = National production levels (sector i, time t; sector type 1) to be determined by the model,

X_{irt} = Production levels (sector i, region r, time t; sector type 2–3) to be determined by the model,

XC_{rt} = Total consumption levels to be determined by the model,

I_{irt} = Investment levels to be determined by the model,

EX_t = Export levels to be determined by the model.

Table 3.2 continued

Parameters:

NT, NR, NS, NK	= Number of time periods, regions, production sectors and energy kinds,
$V1, V2, V3$	= Weights on consumption, employment and energy goals,
d_t	= Discounting factor,
l_{irt}	= Labour coefficients,
e_{irt}^k	= Energy coefficients, energy type k,
ec_{rt}^k	= Energy coefficients for consumption, energy type k,
u_k	= Weight on energy type k,
m_{irt}	= Import coefficients,
ex_{irt}	= Export coefficients,
a_{ij}^r	= Input–output coefficients,
a_{iC}^{rt}	= Consumption coefficients,
B_{ij}	= Composition of investment goods,
β_{ir}	= Regional self-sufficiency in provision of intermediary goods,
γ_{ir}	= Regional self-sufficiency in provision of consumption and investment goods,
dx_{irt}	= Exports to other regions,
ω_{ir}^s	= Proportion of regional imports (sector i, region s) coming from region r ($\omega_{ir}^r = 0$),
α_{ir}	= Exogenous regional distribution of sector type 1,
g_{rt}	= Minimum proportion of gross regional product to be consumed,
f_{ir}	= Value added coefficients,
ϵ_i	= Net share of import value after deduction of customs,
$\overline{BOP}_t$	= Lower bound of balance of payments in constant prices,
c_{irt}	= Capital coefficients,
C_{ir}^0	= Initial capital shock,
δ_i	= Rate of depreciation,
$\underline{L}_{rt}, \overline{\overline{L}}_{rt}$	= Lower and upper bounds on regional employment
$\overline{\overline{E}}_t^k$	= Upper bound on national energy use
$\overline{CT}_t$	= Lower bound of total capital stock

---

frontiers from which price frontiers are derived; regional technical coefficients, trade coefficients and modal choice are determined by price and cost variables.

This link with the transportation system, especially with the latter mapped into a network, provides one important linkage which is currently the subject of some promising developments [Batten (1982)]. Many of these developments are discussed in the Chapter 9 by Batten and Boyce in this Handbook.

A further set of linkages involving an input–output model, centers on the role of the input–output model as a module of a larger, integrated set of models. Two examples will be described briefly here; the Isard and Anselin (1982) model is the precursor of an ambitious attempt to link national and regional econometric, demographic, investment, industrial location, input–output and commodity flow

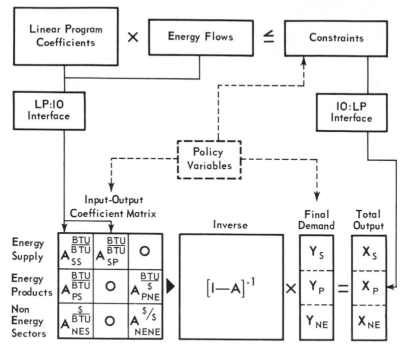

Figure 3.4. Generalized solution for the combined Input–Output Linear Programming Model.

models in what has been termed "integrated modelling" (see Figure 3.5). While many of the components have been developed, the linkages have not been made and hence, the empirical implementation may reveal some substantial problems as well as providing some new insights into the operation of the space economy. ORANI [Dixon et al. (1982)] is a disaggregated model of the Australian economy, built in the tradition of the multisectoral models associated with Johansen (1960). These general equilibrium models have proved popular at the national level [see Adelman and Robinson (1978) for a Korean version] but ORANI is one of the few national models which has a regional component. To use Bolton's (1980) distinction, the model may be characterized as "top-down" since the Australia-wide data are apportioned to the six constituent states. The model for the regional disaggregation derived its rationale from the work of Leontief and Strout (1963); national level commodities created by an exogenous shock are allocated to the regions; a set of commodity–balance equations are used to solve for the production of regional outputs of local goods. While the allocation rule for national commodities (tradeables in the social accounting nomenclature) ensures that the regional aggregates sum to the national totals, consistency is not

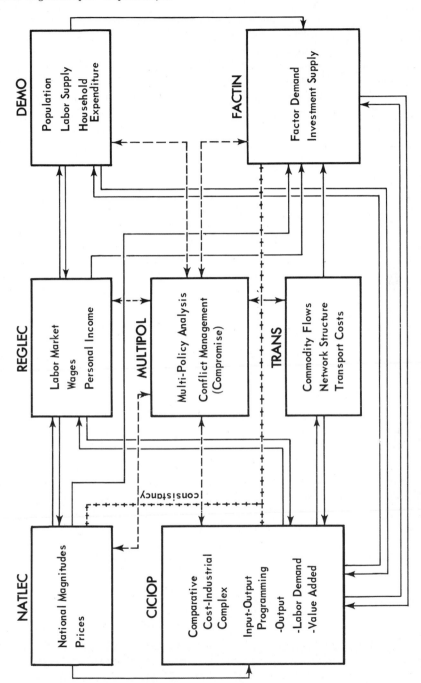

Figure 3.5. Outline of an integrated multi-region model: its components and linkages.

assured for nontradeables. A separate set of equations ensures that the national and regional sums balance. The ORANI model enables a link to be made between international trade and regional economic activity, a feature which has not been common in many regional models [see Hewings (1982) for a review]. Cavalieri et al. (1983) have provided a strong regional–interregional link; their model of Tuscany is cast in a two-region framework but contains the possibility of substitution between interregional and international trade. The reason for this is the fact that foreign exports drive about 25% of regional product.

Two final sets of links will be described; the first integrates input–output and econometric models, not in the sense alluded to earlier [e.g. Gerking (1976)] but in the context of state/regional econometric models [L'Esperance (1977), Conway (1975)]. The final set of links focuses on input–output ecologic models [Isard and Langford (1971), Cumberland (1966), Miernyk and Sears (1974), Thoss (1976)].

The developments described in this section provide a representative sample of the directions in which input–output models have been moving in the last decade. The needs for more accurate impact assessment of policy options have created an attendant need for more complex, yet tractable models in which an input–output component is often seen as a major component.

In the final section of this chapter, some attention will be devoted to some more modest, yet potentially important, new developments in input–output modelling. These initiatives focus on the development of more flexible forms of the input–output model and the more rigorous specification of structure of the model itself.

4.   Some remaining problems in application of input–output models

The application of input–output models has ranged from simple impact studies of the effects of new firms, new enterprises (including the impacts of sports franchises on metropolitan areas) to more complex studies involving projections of future levels of activity in a regional economy. While the former category of uses requires little additional commentary, the use of input–output models in forecasting and projection of regional economies has created some additional difficulties and an associated set of research issues.

4.1.   Forecasting and projection with input – output models

Immediately one begins to contemplate the use of input–output models in this context, a whole battery of objections can be raised, ranging from the usual issues of coefficient change, price changes, measurement of capacity, dynamic versus comparative static to more fundamental issues of what is to be forecast or projected. The former set of issues has been addressed rather extensively in the literature: approaches to coefficient change have been many and, in some cases rather imaginative. Tiebout (1969) introduced the notion of coefficient borrowing – adopting, as a first approximation, the coefficients from another region about the size of the one to which the region in question was expected to grow by the time of the forecast year. Miernyk et al. (1970) adopted a variation of the "best-practice" technique: in this case, a small subset of firms was identified whose technology was assumed to be such that over some time span (say, 10 to 15 years) it would become the average technology for the industries of which these firms were a part. In a sense, the assumption was made that technological change, and its manifestation on coefficient change, could best be described by a moving average process [Carter (1970)]. In any one year, the degree of change would tend to be rather small, but over time, as new firms entered and older firms either ceased production or converted to new techniques, the coefficients would be expected to change. In his comparative static model for West Virginia, Miernyk et al. (1970) was thus able to develop a forecast year coefficient matrix from the best-practice firms. By assuming a linear extrapolation of technological change, he was also able to generate an expected time series of coefficient matrices for use in a dynamic forecasting model of the same economy. A comparison of the comparative static and dynamic forecasts yielded only a small difference in aggregate estimates of total gross output in the state: however, the sector-by-sector differences were rather large in some of the cases. Miernyk also assumed that the regional purchase patterns of the best-practice firms would also become the average by the forecast year. This assumption may be questioned on a number of grounds: Beyers' (1972) work with the 1963 and 1967 Washington State models suggested that the regional purchases coefficients were not necessarily the most stable. In addition, there was a suggestion from Beyers' work that they were very dependent upon the phase of the business cycle. Returning to the Miernyk suggestion, one might counter by commenting that local suppliers might not be able to meet the demands of a small subset of best-practice firms – the volume of demand might be too small or they might not have the capacity or new technology which might be necessary to produce the necessary components.

Lawson (1980) has suggested a "rational modelling" procedure to the estimation of input–output coefficients, particularly in the context of updating for use in forecasts or projections. He suggests four models to be considered:

$$a_t = a_{t-1} \tag{4.1}$$

$$a_t = a_{t-1} + u_t \tag{4.2}$$

$$a_t = k + gt \tag{4.3}$$

$$a_t = a_{t-1} + g_t + u_t. \tag{4.4}$$

In the first case (4.1), it is assumed that there is coefficient stability over time: the second possibility is that change will take place but it will be, on the average, zero (i.e. u_t is assumed to be a normally distributed random variable with mean zero). The third alternative, (4.3), assumes that the direction of change is known but that the process generating change is, itself, stable (i.e. g is constant over time). The final possibility, (4.4), provides for the case in which g itself can change. Lawson provides guidance in the use of these models (all of which can be generated from 4.4) under different conditions of information – about individual coefficient change or in cases where new information may be restricted to column or row totals. A similar concern with a more rigorous approach to coefficient change and estimation may be found in Park et al. (1981) and Sasaki and Shibata (1984). The former paper attempts to derive analytical errors for all parts of the matrix and while final demand was not considered, the authors claimed that their procedure could be generalized to include these elements. Sasaki and Shibata have provided some interesting extensions to nonsurvey methods for use in projecting the input–output coefficients at a small-region level. Their model, a modified export determination method, provides for ways in which limited information can be incorporated in a far more efficient manner.

However, few authors involved in forecasting or coefficient change have addressed the issue about the accuracy of the forecasts of final demand which might be necessary to implement the forecasting system. In some cases, these estimates may be derived from hypothetical vectors of proposed government expenditures. In the more general cases, it is unlikely that simple extrapolative techniques will suffice. For this reason, there has been some interest in linking input–output models with econometric models: Figure 4.1 shows one such attempt, developed by Joun and Conway (1983) for the Washington and Hawaii state economies. The model is clearly top-down, with two major sources of exogenously induced change: (1) coefficient change and (2) national econometrically estimated parameters affecting the major components of state final demand. The latter linkage is provided using standard econometric analysis. Note, however, that some components of state final demand are influenced by local activity levels. Employment, population, and income influence investment and the latter, of course, influences consumption. Research on the nature of the links between the final demand components and exogenous influences presents a major challenge for input–output analysts if these models are to continue to occupy an important role in policy analysis.

4.2. Policy links

While the preceding section alluded to the uses to which input–output models have been applied, some general comments need to be made here about the

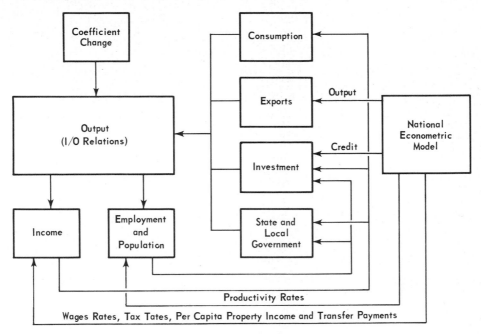

Figure 4.1. Logical structure of Washington and Hawaii models.

possible role of input–output analysis in policy formation. In the context of project selection, monitoring and evaluation, input–output analysis has been used extensively for evaluation. Its uses in monitoring have been few and some of the early promise for use in project selection has not been fulfilled. There was some early expectation that input–output models could be used to assist policy makers identify key linkages or sectors in the context of industrial development strategies in regional economies in both developed and developing countries. The possibility of linking input–output analysis with concepts such as growth center strategies was never fulfilled. The debate on the role of linkages and key sectors has attracted some attention at the regional level [see Hewings (1983) for a review]: the methods of analysis used on the input–output tables have not yielded the kinds of insights deemed useful. Czamanski (1971), Czamanski and Ablas, (1979), Czamanski and Czamanski (1976), Campbell (1972, 1974, 1975), Slater (1974, 1977) and, most recently, O'Huallachain (1984) have attempted to use input–output models for the purposes of identifying clusters of industries: the analogy here with the work on the fundamental structure of an economy reported in Section 2 should be apparent. Somewhat more ambitious policy analyses has been conducted with an integrated model, in which the input–

output system plays an important role, developed for Massachusetts [Treyz et al. (1980)]. Their Massachusetts Economic Policy Analysis (MEPA) model has been widely used by legislative committees and executive agencies in the state. Among other interesting features of their model is its ability to handle comparative costs changes in the state vis-à-vis the rest of the country. This location effect provides a major addition in the integrated modelling literature and avoids the assumption of "business as usual" which seems to dominate many of the early attempts to develop more general equilibrium frameworks at the regional level.

4.3.   Links with the non-economic system

Most of the linkages described in Section 3 involved the integration of the input–output model with sets of other economic or demographic models. While some early attempts were made [Cumberland (1966), Cumberland and Korback (1973)] to link the input–output model with the ecologic system, these have not been developed as extensively as other linkages. The [Isard et al. (1972)] framework provided the specification for a two-region version: in this case, linkages within the economic and ecologic systems were specified as well as linkages between them. Hence, the increase in output in the economic system consequent upon an increase in final demand could be extended to a consideration of its effect on the ecologic community. Cumberland's (1966) model provided an intriguing link between input–output analysis and project appraisal in the presence of environmental degradation. Laurent and Hite (1972), Miernyk and Sears (1974) and Thoss (1976) have all approached aspects of this problem. However, the advent of the energy concerns of the early 1970s shifted research away from general ecologic linkages to the issues of energy supply–demand interactions.

5.   New directions

It is clear from the preceding discussion that some of the major developments in regional input–output analysis are in the direction of linking such models with other models of the socioeconomic and environmental systems. However, research is also being directed towards a number of other problems. Some of these will be highlighted here.

One of the major advantages of an input–output model is its ability to portray the structure of an economy. Unfortunately, at the regional level, little attempt has been made to undertake significant comparative analyses and thereby to develop some important conceptual understandings of the relationship between regional structure, regional growth and development stage. Part of the reason for the absence of these items in the literature may be traced to the absence of a generally accepted system of regional accounts' definitions and conventions. Accordingly, it becomes difficult, if not impossible, to undertake the sort of work illustrated by scholars at the national level. However, the need for some theoretical understanding of the space–time development of regional interindustry systems remains. To this end, some of the work of Hewings et al. (1985) provides a beginning; they have explored a number of what may be termed "holistic" matrix descriptors of regional systems. The objective here is to try to find measures which will be able to describe the structure (i.e. the internal arrangement) of flows in a regional input–output table at various spatial scales and at various stages of economic development. Some preliminary results of evaluation of a number of these techniques with reference to the Queensland regional input–output tables has been reported in Jensen et al. (1985). This research should yield significant insights into the linkages between development, spatial scale and economic structure. In addition, it would provide some useful inputs into the selection of an appropriate input–output model for use as an a priori estimator in the development of a nonsurvey model for another region using the RAS technique. Since this technique guarantees holistic or system-wide accuracy, little attention has been focused on the problems of partitive accuracy. While the usual form of the RAS technique may be shown as:

$$R = f[R^*, u, v, X] \tag{5.1}$$

where u, v, and X are the vectors of intermediate demand, supply and total output and R^*, the prior matrix, there are many possible candidates for R^* which would satisfy the marginal constraints. The careful choice of a prior would seem to be important especially if the nonsurvey model is to be used for individual sector impact analyses.

The application of regional and interregional input–output analyses for project selection, monitoring and evaluation has been reviewed in an earlier section. With few exceptions, many of these applications have been rather mundane with little consideration taken of the peculiar dynamics of regional economies in developing countries. In fact, the use of input–output models for development planning issues has not proven to be very satisfactory. Industrial complex analysis, key sector identification and growth center theory have all, to some degree, made use of input–output analyses. However, the static models employed could not capture the essentially dynamic character of the theory being evaluated. The input–output framework is still an empirical model of an economy: far too often, development or growth connotations are extrapolated on the basis of a single model. A major future need would appear to be some creative way to identify the most important components of the regional economic system such that these can be surveyed and used to continuously update the model. While many regional econometric and time series models remain limited as a result of the paucity of time series data, the same is really true of the input–output models.

A final area in which some significant work has begun is in the relaxation of some of the assumptions about stability of coefficients, economies of scale and substitution. The work of Hudson and Jorgensen (1974) and the application of the combined input–output/linear programming model described in Page et al. (1981) provide some useful insights into the way in which partial substitution could be handled. Lahiri (1976, 1980) in a number of papers has begun work on the problem of scale economies, introducing a choice mechanism for the size of input coefficients based on the level of demand placed on the industry. While the model has been demonstrated theoretically, no one has yet considered the issues of data collection! The work of West (1983) and Jackson (1983, 1986) in exploring various aspects of the distribution properties of multipliers and individual coefficients respectively, may see the input–output model cast more firmly in standard statistical frameworks than has been the case to date.

There is one area in which there has been very little development at the regional and interregional levels and that is in the direction of what may be referred to as price models [see Miller and Blair (1985) for a review]. The work of Hudson and Jorgensen (1974) provides an example of an input–output system in which coefficients are endogenously determined by relative prices of commodity inputs but this work has not been extended to the regional level. Moses (1974) made a very strong case for a return to price-based input–output models but, thus far, there has been no response to his request. The only way in which prices have been incorporated into the models has been through the processes of updating coefficients to account for changes in relative prices.

Notwithstanding all these developments, the growth of research in regional and interregional input–output analysis is unlikely to be divorced from research in many other parts of regional science and regional economics. The recognition of the importance of linking models may begin to blur the distinctions between commodity flow analysis, input–output analysis, land-use modelling, demographic modelling and so forth. The results achieved thus far from linking many of these models have been so favorable as to suggest that this development will prove to be the major growth area in the forseeable future.

References

Adelman, I. and S. Robinson (1978) *Income distribution policy in developing countries*. Palo Alto: Stanford.
Archibald, G. C. (1967) 'Regional multiplier effects in the U.K.' *Oxford Economic Papers New Series*, 19:22–45.

Augustinovics, M. (1970) 'Methods of international and intertemporal comparisons of structure', in: A. P. Carter and A. Brody, eds., *Contributions to input–output analysis*. Amsterdam: North-Holland, 249–269.

Bacharach, M. (1970) *Biproportional matrices and input–output change*. Cambridge University Press.

Bargur, J. (1969) *A dynamic interregional input–output programming model of the California and Western States water economy*. Berkeley: University of California.

Batey, P. W. J. (1985) 'Input–output models for regional demographic–economic analysis: some structural comparisons', *Environment and Planning, A* 17:73–99.

Batey, P. W. J. and M. Madden (1982) 'An activity analysis approach to the integration of demographic–economic forecasts', in: H. Voogd, ed., *Strategic planning in a dynamic society*. Delft: Delftsche Uitgevers Maatschappij BV.

Batten, D. F. (1982) 'The interregional linkages between national and regional input–output models', *International Regional Science Review*, 7:53–68.

Bell, C., P. Hazell and R. Slade (1982) *Project evaluation in regional perspective*. Baltimore: Johns Hopkins.

Beyers, W. B. (1972) 'On the stability of regional interindustry models: the Washington economy data for 1963 and 1967', *Journal of Regional Science*, 12:363–374.

Blackwell, J. (1978) 'Disaggregation of the household sector in regional input–output analysis: some models specifying previous residence of workers', *Regional Studies*, 12(3):367–377.

Blair, P. D. and R. E. Miller (1983) 'Spatial aggregation of multiregional input–output models', *Environment and Planning*, A15:187–206.

Bolton, R. (1980) 'Multiregion models: an introduction to a symposium', *Journal of Regional Science*, 20:131–142.

Boster, R. S. and W. E. Martin (1972) 'The value of primary vs secondary data in interindustry analysis: a study of the economic models', *Annals of Regional Science*, 6(2):35–43.

Bourque, P. J. et al. (1967) *The Washington economy: an input–output study*. University of Washington.

Bradley, I. E. and J. Gander (1969) 'Input–output multipliers: some theoretical comments', *Journal of Regional Science*.

Brems, H. (1986) *Pioneering economic theory 1630–1980*. University Press: Johns Hopkins.

Broecker, J. (1984) 'A generalization of the Chenery–Moses model', Second World Regional Science Conference, Rotterdam, The Netherlands.

Brown, A. J. (1967) 'The "Green paper" on the development areas', *National Institute Economic Review*, 40:26–33.

Brown, D. M. and F. Giarratani (1979) 'Input–output as a simple econometric model: a comment', *Review of Economics and Statistics*, 61:621–623.

Bullard, C. W. (1976) *Uncertainty in the 1967 U.S. input–output data*, Document No. 191, Center for Advanced Computations, University of Illinois.

Bullard, C. W. and A. V. Sebald (1977) 'Effects of parametric uncertainty and technological change on input–output models', *Review of Economics and Statistics*, 59(1):75–81.

Bulmer-Thomas, V. (1982) *Input–output analysis in developing countries*. Chichester: John Wiley and Sons.

Burford, R. L. and J. L. Katz (1977a) 'An estimator of regional interindustry multipliers without an I–0 matrix', Business and Economic Statistics Section, Proceedings of the American Statistical Association.

Burford, R. L. and J. L. Katz (1977b) 'Regional input–output multipliers without a full I/0 table', *Annals of Regional Science*, 11(3):21–36.

Burford, R. L. and J. L. Katz (1981) 'A method for the estimation of input–output–type output multipliers when no I–0 model exists', *Journal of Regional Science*, 21:151–161.

Campbell, J. (1972) 'Growth pole theory, digraphy analysis and interindustry relationships', *Tijdschrift voor Economische Sociale Geografie*, 63:79–87.

Campbell, J. (1974) 'Selected aspects of the interindustry structure of the state of Washington, 1967', *Economic Geography*, 50:91–106.

Campbell, J. (1975) 'Application of graph theoretic analysis to interindustry relationships', *Regional Science and Urban Economics*, 5:91–106.

Carter, A. P. (1970) *Structural change in the American economy*. Cambridge: Harvard University Press.

Cavalieri A., D. Martellado and F. Snickars (1983) 'A model system for policy impact analysis in the tuscany region', *Papers of the Regional Science Association*, 52:105–120.

Chenery, H. B. and T. Watanabe (1958) 'International comparisons of the structure of production', *Econometrica*, 26:487–510.

Conway, R. S. (1975) 'A note on the stability of regional interindustry models', *Journal of Regional Science*, 15:67–72.

Conway, R. S. (1979) 'The simulation properties of a regional interindustry econometric model', *Papers of the Regional Science Association*, 43:45–57.

Cumberland, J. H. (1966) 'A regional interindustry model for analysis of development objectives', *Papers of the Regional Science Association*, 17:65–94.

Cumberland, J. H. and R. J. Korbach (1973) 'A regional inter-industry environmental model', *Papers of the Regional Science Association*, 30:61–75.

Czamanski, S. (1971) 'Some empirical evidence of the strengths of linkages between groups of related industries in urban–regional complexes', *Papers of the Regional Science Association*, 27:137–150.

Czamanski, S. and L. A. de Q. Ablas (1979) 'Identification of industrial clusters and complexes: a comparison of methods and findings', *Urban Studies*, 16:61–80.

Czamanski, S. and D. Z. Czamanski (1976) *Study of formation of spatial complexes*. Halifax, Canada: Dalhousie University Press.

Czamanski, S. and E. Malizia (1969) 'Applicability and limitations in the use of input–output tables for regional studies', *Papers and Proceedings of the Regional Science Association*, 23:65–77.

Davis, H. C., E. M. Lofting and J. A. Sathaye (1977) 'A comparison of alternative methods of updating input–output coefficients', *Technological Forecasting and Social Change*, 10:79–87.

Defourny, J. and E. Thorbecke (1984) 'Structural path analysis and multiplier decomposition within a social accounting framework', *The Economic Journal*, 94:111–136.

Dixon, P. B. et al. (1982) *ORANI: a multisectoral model of the Australian economy*. Amsterdam: North-Holland.

Erlander, S. (1980) *Optimal spatial interaction and the gravity model*. Berlin: Springer-Verlag.

Evans, M. and J. Baxter (1980) 'Regionalizing national projections with a multiregional input–output model linked to a demographic model', *Annals of Regional Science*, 14(1):57–71.

Folmer, H. and P. Nijkamp (1985) 'Some methodological aspects of impact analysis of regional economic policy', *Papers of the Regional Science Association*: forthcoming.

Gerking, S. D. (1976a) 'Input–output as a simple econometric model', *Review of Economics and Statistics*, 58(3):274–282.

Gerking, S. D. (1976b) 'Reconciling "rows only" and "columns only" coefficients in an input–output model', *International Regional Science Review*, 1:30–46.

Gerking, S. D. (1979) 'Reconciling reconciliation procedures in regional input–output analysis', *International Regional Science Review*, 4:23–36.

Ghosh, A. (1973) *Programming and interregional input–output analysis: an application to the problem of industrial location in India*. Cambridge University Press.

Giarrantani, F. (1976) 'Application of an interindustry supply model to energy issues', *Environment and Planning*, A8:447–454.

Gigantes, T. (1970) 'The representation of technology in input–output systems', in: A. P. Carter and A. Brody, eds., *Applications of input–output analysis*. Amsterdam: North-Holland.

Goicoechea, A. and D. R. Hansen (1978) 'An input–output model with stochastic parameters for economic analysis', *AIIE Transactions*, 10:291–295.

Gordon, I. R. (1976) 'Gravity demand functions, accessibility and regional trade', *Regional Studies*, 10:25–37.

Hamilton, J. R. (1979) 'Sensitivity of multipliers to errors in the estimation of input–output coefficients', *Proceedings of the input–output workshop*, Fourth Meeting of the Australian and New Zealand Section, Regional Science Association.

Hamilton, J. R. and R. C. Jensen (1983) 'Summary measures of interconnectedness for input–output models', *Environment and Planning*, A15:55–65.

Hanseman, D. J. (1982) 'Stochastic input–output analysis: a simulation study', *Environment and Planning*, A14(11):1425–1435.

Hanseman, D. J. and E. F. Gustafson (1981) 'Stochastic input–output analysis: a comment', *Review of Economics and Statistics*, 63:468–470.

Harrigan, F. J. (1982a) 'The estimation of input–output-type output multipliers where no input–output model exists: a comment', *Journal of Regional Science*, 22:375–381.

Harrigan, F. J. (1982b) 'The relationship between industrial and geographical linkages: a case study of the United Kingdom', *Journal of Regional Science*, 22:19–31.

Harrigan, F. J., J. W. McGilvray and I. H. McNicoll (1980a) 'A comparison of regional and national technical structures', *Economic Journal*, 90:795–810.

Harrigan, F. J., J. W. McGilvray and I. H. McNicoll (1980b) 'Simulating the structure of a regional economy', *Environment and Planning*, A12:927–936.

Harrigan, F. J. and I. H. McNicoll (1984) 'Data use and simulation of regional input–output matrices', Fraser of Allander Institute, Glasgow, Scotland.

Helmstädter, E. (1969) 'The hierarchical structure of interindustrial transactions', in: United Nations Industrial Development Organisation Report, *International comparisons of interindustry data*, Industrial Planning and Programming Series No. 2. New York: United Nations.

Hewings, G. J. D. (1977) 'Evaluating the possibilities for exchanging regional input–output coefficients', *Environment and Planning*, A9: 927–944.

Hewings, G. J. D. (1982) 'The empirical identification of key sectors in an economy: a regional perspective', *The Developing Economies*, 20(2):173–195.

Hewings, G. J. D. (1983) 'Design of appropriate accounting systems for regional development in developing countries', *Papers of the Regional Science Association*, 51:179–195.

Hewings, G. J. D. (1985) 'The role of prior information in updating regional input–output models', *Socio-Economic Planning Sciences*, 18:319–336.

Hewings, G. J. D. and B. N. Janson (1980) 'Exchanging regional input–output coefficients: a reply and further comments', *Environment and Planning* A12:843–854.

Hewings, G. J. D., R. C. Jensen and G. R. West (1985) 'Holistic matrix descriptors of regional input–output systems', Mimeo, Department of Economics, University of Queensland.

Hewings, G. J. D., J. Merrifield and J. Schneider (1984) 'Regional tests of the linkage hypothesis', *Revue d'Economie et Urbane*, 25.

Hewings, G. J. D. and M. C. Romanos (1981) 'Simulating less developed regional economies under conditions of limited information', *Geographical Analysis*, 13(4):373–390.

Hewings, G. J. D. and W. M. Syversen (1982) 'A modified bi-proportional method for updating regional input–output matrices: holistic accuracy revaluation', *Modeling and Simulation*, 13:115–120.

Hoffman, R. B. and J. N. Kent (1976) 'Design of a commodity-by-industry interregional input–output model', in: K. R. Polenske, ed., *Advances in input–output analysis*. Ballinger, 251–262.

Hudson, E. A. and D. W. Jorgensen (1974) 'U.S. energy policy and economic growth, 1975–2000', *Bell Journal of Economics and Management*, 5(2):461–513.

Isard, W. (1951) 'Interregional input–output analysis: a model of a space economy', *Review of Economics and Statistics*, 33:318–328.

Isard, W. (1953a) 'Regional commodity balances and interregional commodity flows', *American Economic Review*, 43:167–180.

Isard, W. (1953b) 'Some empirical results and problems of regional input–output analysis', in: W. Leontief, et al., eds., *Studies in the structure of the American economy*. Oxford University Press.

Isard, W. and L. Anselin (1982) 'Integration of multiregional models for policy analysis', *Environment and Planning*, A14:359–376.

Isard, W. and T. W. Langford (1971) *Regional input–output study: recollections, reflections and diverse notes on the Philadelphia experience*. Cambridge, Mass.: MIT Press.

Isard, W., T. M. Langford and E. Romanoff (1966–68) 'Philadelphia region input–output study', Working Papers, Regional Science Research Institute, Philadelphia.

Isard, W., C. Chougill, J. Kissin, R. H. Seyfarth and R. Tatlock (1972) *Ecological economic analysis for regional development*. New York: Free Press.

Jackson, R. W. (1983) 'A distributional approach to the modelling and simulation of industrial systems', unpublished Ph.D. dissertation, Department of Geography, University of Illinois at Urbana-Champaign, Urbana, IL.

Jackson, R. W. (1986) "The 'full distribution' approach to aggregate representation in the input–output modeling framework", *Journal of Regional Science*: forthcoming.

Jackson, R. W. and G. J. D. Hewings (1984) 'Structural change in a regional economy: an entropy decomposition approach', *Modeling and Simulatuon*, 15.

Jensen, R. C. (1976) 'The Central Queensland study: some supplementary notes and tables', Working Paper No. 13, Department of Economics, University of Queensland.

Jensen, R. C. (1980) 'The concept of accuracy in input–output', *International Regional Science Review*, 5:139–154.

Jensen, R. C. and G. J. D. Hewings (1985) 'Short-cut "input–output" multipliers: a requiem', *Environment and Planning*, A17:747–759.

Jensen, R. C., T. Mandeville and N. D. Karunaratne (1977) 'Generation of input–output tables for Queensland', Report to the Co-ordinator-General's Department and the Department of Commercial and Industrial Development, Department of Economics, University of Queensland.

Jensen, R. C. and D. McGaurr (1976) 'Reconciliation of purchases and sales estimates: an input–output table', *Urban Studies*, 13:59–65.

Jensen, R. C. and G. R. West (1980) 'The effect of relative coefficient size on input–output multipliers', *Environment and Planning*, 12:65–70.

Jensen, R. C., G. R. West and G. J. D. Hewings (1985) 'Connectedness in regional input–output tables: further explorations with the Queensland data', Paper Presented to Ninth Pacific Regional Science Conference, Molokai, Hawaii.

Johansen, L. (1960) *A multi sectoral study of economic growth*. Amsterdam: North-Holland.

Joun, R. Y. P. and R. S. Conway Jr. (1983) 'Regional economic demographic models: a case study of the Washington and Hawaii models', *Socio-Economic Planning*, 17(5–6):345–353.

Karunaratne, N. D. (1976) 'Quantification of sectoral development prospects in Papua New Guinea using Tinbergen and Rasmussen criteria', *The Developing Economies*, 14:280–305.

Katz, J. L. and R. L. Burford (1982) 'The estimation of input–output type multipliers where no input–output model exists: a reply', *Journal of Regional Science*, 22:383–387.

Kennedy, C. M. (1966a) 'Keynesian theory in an open economy', *Social and Economic Studies*, 15:1–21.

Kennedy, C. M. (1966b) 'Domar-type theory in an open economy', *Social and Economic Studies*, 15:22–45.

Kuyvenhoven, A. (1978) *Planning with the semi-input–output method with empirical applications to Nigeria*. Leiden: Martinus Nijhoff.

Lahiri, S. (1976) 'Inout–output analysis with scale dependent coefficients', *Econometrica*, 44:947–962.

Lahiri, S. (1980) 'Capacity constraints, alternative technologies and input–output models', Discussion Paper No. 163, Department of Economics, University of Essex.

Lamel, J., J. Richter, and W. Teufelsbauer (1971) 'Triangulation of input–output tables for EEC countries', annex iii to R. Gentile, R. Messy and J. Skolka, 'Preparation of the set of the EEC standardized input–output tables and first results of comparative analysis; Paper presented at the Fifth International Input–Output Conference, Geneva, Switzerland.

Laurent, E. A. and J. C. Hite (1972) *Environmental planning: an economic analysis: applications for the coastal zone*. New York: Praeger.

Lawson, T. (1980) 'A "rational modelling" procedure', *Economics of planning*, 16:105–117.

Leontief, W. (1951) *The structure of the American economy*. New York: Oxford University Press.

Leontief, W., ed. (1953) *Studies in the structure of the American economy*. New York: Oxford University Press.

Leontief, W. and A. Strout (1963) 'Multiregional input–output Analysis', in T. Barna, ed., *Structural interdependence and economic development*. London: St. Martin's Press.

L'Esperance, W. (1977) 'Conjoining an Ohio input–output model with an econometric model of Ohio', *Regional Science Perspectives*, 7:54–77.

Liew, C. K. and C. J. Liew (1984) 'Multi-model, multi-output, multi-regional variable input–output model', *Regional Science and Urban Economics*, 14:265–281.

Lundqvist, L. (1981) 'Applications of a dynamic multiregional input–output model of the Swedish economy', *Papers of the Regional Science Association*, 47:77–95.

Madden, M. and P. W. J. Batey (1980) 'Achieving consistency in demographic–economic forecasting', *Papers of the Regional Science Association*, 44:91–106.

Maki, W. R. (1980) 'Regional input–output and accounting systems for agricultural and rural development planning in Thailand', paper delivered to the First World Regional Science Congress, Cambridge, Massachusetts.

Mathur, P. N. (1972) 'Multiregional analysis in a dynamic input–output framework', in: A. P. Carter and A. Brody, eds., *Input–output techniques*. Amsterdam: North-Holland.

Matuszewski, T. I., P. R. Pitts and J. A. Sawyer (1964) 'Linear programming estimates of change in input–output coefficients', *Canadian Journal of Economics and Political Science*, 30:203–210.

McMenamin, R. G. and J. E. Haring (1974) 'An appraisal of nonsurvey techniques for estimating regional input–output models', *Journal of Regional Science*, 14:191–205.

Miernyk, W. H., et al. (1967) *Impact of the space program on a local economy*. West Virginia University Press.

Miernyk, W. H. (1970) *Simulating regional economic development: an interindustry analysis of the West Virginia economy*. Lexington, Mass.: Lexington Books, D. C. Heath.

Miernyk, W. H. and J. T. Sears (1974) *Air pollution abatement and regional economic development: an input–output analysis*. Lexington, Mass.: Lexington Books.

Miller, R. E. and P. D. Blair (1981) 'Spatial aggregation in interrelational input–output models', *Papers of the Regional Science Association*, 48:150–64.

Miller, R. E. and P. D. Blair (1985) *Input–output analysis: foundations and extensions*. Englewood Cliffs, N.J.: Prentice Hall.

Miyazawa, K. (1976) *Input–output analysis and the structure of income distribution*. Berlin: Springer-Verlag.

Miyazawa, K. (1968) 'Input–output analysis and interrelational income multipliers as matrix', *Hitotsubashi Journal of Economics*, 8:39–58.

Moore, F. J. and J. W. Petersen (1955) 'Regional analysis: an interindustry model of Utah', *Review of Economics and Statistics*, 37:368–383.

Morrison, W. I. and P. Smith (1974) 'Non-survey input–output techniques at the small-area level: an evaluation', *Journal of Regional Science*, 14(1):1–14.

Moses, L. M. (1955) 'On the stability of interregional trading patterns and input–output analysis', *American Economic Review*, 45:802–803.

Moses, L. M. (1974) 'Output and prices in interindustry models', *Papers of the Regional Science Association*, 32:7–18.

O'Huallachain, B. (1984) 'The identification of industrial complexes', *Annals of the Association of American Geographers*, 74(3):420–436.

Oosterhaven, J. (1981) 'Some comments on the regional attraction model', Research Memorandum No. 88, International Conference on Structural Economic Analysis and Planning in Time and Space, University of Umea, Sweden.

Oosterhaven, J. (1984) 'A family of square and rectangular interregional input–output models', *Regional Science and Urban Economics*.

Page, W. P., D. Gilmore and G. J. D. Hewings (1981) *An energy and fuel demand model for the Ohio River Basin energy region, phase II*, Office of Research and Development, U.S. Environmental Protection Agency.

Park, S. H., M. Mohtadi and A. Kubursi (1981) 'Errors in regional non-survey input–output models: analytical simulation results', *Journal of Regional Science*, 21(3):321–337.

Parker, M. L. (1967) *A interindustry study of the Western Australian economy*, Agricultural Economics Research Report No. 6. University of Western Australia Press.

Peacock, A. T. and D. G. M. Dosser (1957) 'Regional input–output analysis and government spending', *Scottish Journal of Political Economy*, 6:229–236.

Phibbs, P. J. and A. J. Holsman (1982) 'An evaluation of the Burford–Katz short-cut technique for deriving input–output multipliers', *Annals of Regional Science*, 15:11–19.

Polenske, K. R. (1970) *A multiregional input–output model of the United States*, Economic Development Administration Report, Harvard University Economic Research Project.

Pyatt, G. and A. R. Roe (1977) *Social accounting for developing countries*. Cambridge: Cambridge University Press.

Quesnay, F. (1972) *Tableau economique*, edited with new materials, translation and notes, by M. Kucznyski and R. L. Meek. London: Macmillan.

Riefler, R. and C. M. Tiebout (1970) 'Interregional input–output: an empirical California–Washington model', *Journal of Regional Science*, 10:135–52.

Robinson, S. and A. Markandya (1973) 'Complexity and adjustment in input–output systems', *Oxford Bulletin of Economics and Statistics*, 35:119–134.

Romanoff, E. (1974) 'The economic base model: a very special case of input–output analysis', *Journal of Regional Science*, 14(1):121–129.

Rosenbluth, G. (1968) 'Input–output analysis', paper presented at the AUTE Conference, York, England.

Round, J. I. (1972) 'Regional input–output models in the U.K. a reappraisal of some techniques', *Regional Studies*, 6:1–9.

Round, J. I. (1978a) 'An interindustry input–output approach to the evaluation of nonsurvey methods', *Journal of Regional Science*, 18:179–194.

Round, J. I. (1978b) 'An interregional input–output approach to the evaluation of nonsurvey methods', *Journal of Regional Science*, 18:179–194.

Round, J. I. (1979) 'Compensating feedback effects in interregional input–output models', *Journal of Regional Science*, 19:145–155.

Round, J. I. (1983) 'Nonsurvey techniques: a critical review of the theory and the evidence', *International Regional Science Review*, 8:189–212.

Round, J. I. (1984) 'Decomposing multipliers for economic systems involving regional and world trade', Conference of the British Section of the Regional Science Association, Canterbury, Kent.

Sandoval, E. (1967) 'Constant relationship between input–output income multipliers', *Review of Economics and Statistics*, 49:599–602.

Sasaki, K. and H. Shibata (1984) 'Nonsurvey methods for projecting the input–output system at a small-region level: two alternative approaches', *Journal of Regional Science*, 24:35–50.

Schaffer, W., ed. (1976) *On the use of input–output models for regional planning, studies in applied regional science*, Vol. 1. Leiden: Martinus Nijhoff.

Schaffer, W. and K. Chu (1969) 'Non-survey techniques for constructing regional interindustry models', *Papers and Proceedings of the Regional Science Association*, 23:83–101.

Schinnar, A. P. (1976) 'A multidimensional accounting model for demographic and economic planning interactions', *Environment and Planning*, A8:455–475.

Schultz, W. M. (1978) 'On accuracy and precision in statistical estimates', *Canadian Journal of Agricultural Economics*, 25:15–26.

Shen, T. Y. (1960) 'An input–output table with regional weights', *Papers of the Regional Science Association*, 6:113–119.

Simpson, D. and J. Tsukui (1965) 'The fundamental structure of input–output tables: an international comparison', *Review of Economics and Statistics*, 47:434–446.

Slater, P. B. (1974) 'Graph-theoretic clustering of transaction flows: an application to the 1967 United States interindustrial transactions table', Mimeo, Regional Research Institute, West Virginia University, Morgantown.

Slater, P. B. (1977) 'The determination of functionally integrated industries in the United States using a 1967 interindustry flow table', *Empirical Economics*, 2:1–19.

Smith, C. A. and R. C. Jensen (1984) 'A system for the generation of small-economy input–output tables', *Papers of the Eighth Meeting of the Australian and New Zealand Section of the Regional Science Association*.

Stevens, B. H. and G. A. Trainer (1976) *The generation of errors in regional input–output impact models*, Regional Science Research Institute Working Paper A1–46.

Stevens, B. H., G. I. Treyz, D. H. J. Ehrlich and J. R. Power (1983) 'A new technique for the construction of non-survey regional input–output models and comparisons with two survey-based models', *International Regional Science Review*, 8:271–86.

Stone, J. R. N. (1961) 'Social accounts at the regional level: a survey', in: W. Isard and J. Cumberland, eds., *Economic planning: techniques of analysis for less developed areas*. Paris: OECD.

Stone, J. R. N. (1963) *A programme for growth: input–output relationships 1954–1966*, vol. 3. Cambridge: Chapman and Hall.

Theil, H. (1972) *Statistical decomposition analysis*. Amsterdam: North-Holland.

Theil, H. and P. Uribe (1966) 'The information approach to the aggregation of input–output tables', *Review of Economics and Statistics*, :451–462.

Thoss, R. (1976) 'A generalized input–output model for residuels management', in: K. R. Polenske and J. V. Skolka, eds., *Advances in input – output analysis*. Cambridge, Mass.: Ballinger, 411–32.

Tiebout, C. M. (1969) 'An empirical regional input–output projection model: the State of Washington, 1980', *Review of Economics and Statistics*, 51:334–340.

Tinbergen, J. (1966) 'Some refinements of the semi-input–output method', *Pakistan Development Review*, 6:243–247.

Treyz, G. I., A. F. Friedlaender and B. H. Stevens (1980) 'The employment sector of a regional policy simulation model', *Review of Economics and Statistics* 62:63–73.

United Nations (1968) *A system of national accounts*, Studies in Methods, Series F, No. 2, Rev. 3, New York.

United Nations (1973) *Input – output tables and analysis*, Studies in Methods, Series F, No. 14, Rev. 1.

Van Dijk, J. and J. Oosterhaven (1985) 'Regional impacts of migrants expenditures—an input–output vacancy chain approach', *London Papers of Regional Science* 15, *Integrated Analysis of Regional Systems*. London: Pion.

Walras, L. (1954) *Elements of pure economics: or the theory of social wealth* (trans. W. Jaffe) published for the American Economic Association and the Royal Economic Society. London: Allen & Unwin.

Weiss, S. J. and E. C. Gooding (1968) 'Estimation of differencial employment multipliers in a small regional economy', *Land Economics*, 44:235–244.

West, G. R. (1979) 'A procedure for the accurate optimization of input–output multipliers', *Proceedings of the Input – Output Workshop*, Fourth Meeting of the Australian and New Zealand Section, Regional Science Association.

West, G. R. (1981) 'An efficient approach to the estimation of regional input–output multipliers', *Environment and Planning*, A13:857–867.

West, G. R. (1983) 'Approximating the moments and distributions of input–output multipliers', Paper to the Input–Output Workshop, Eighth Meeting of the Australian and New Zealand Section, Regional Science Association.

West, G. R. and R. C. Jensen (1977) 'Some effects of errors in coefficients on input–output multipliers', *Proceedings of the input – output workshop*, Second Meeting of the Australian and New Zealand Section, Regional Science Association.

West, G. R. and R. C. Jensen (1980) 'Some reflections on input–output multipliers', *Annals of Regional Science*, 14(2):77–89.

West, G. R., J. T. Wilkinson and R. C. Jensen (1979) *Generation of regional input – output tables for the state and regions of South Australia*, Department of Economics, University of Queensland.

West, G. R., J. T. Wilkinson and R. C. Jensen (1980) *Generation of regional input – output tables for the Northern Territory*, Report to the Department of the Chief Minister of the Northern Territory, Department of Economics, University of Queensland.

Wilson, A. G. (1970) *Entropy in urban and regional modelling*. London: Pion.

Wong, Y. K. (1954) 'Mathematical concepts of linear economic models', in: O. Morgenstern, ed., *Economic Activity and Analysis*. New York: Wilson.

Yan, C. and E. Ames (1965) 'Economic interrelatedness', *Review of Economic Studies*, 32(4):299–310.

Chapter 9

SPATIAL INTERACTION, TRANSPORTATION, AND INTERREGIONAL COMMODITY FLOW MODELS

DAVID F. BATTEN and DAVID E. BOYCE

1. Introduction

Spatial interaction and transportation models are used to facilitate the explanation and prediction of patterns of human and economic interaction over geographic space. Theoretical methods for studying these phenomena have been modified considerably during the last 30 years in order to provide operational assistance to the transportation planner and, more recently, the regional economist. The original foundations for modelling interactions over space were based on the analogous world of interacting particles and gravitational force, as well as potential effects and notions of market area for retail trade. Since that time, the gravity model has been extensively employed, with important refinements relating to appropriate weights, functional forms, definitions of economic distance and transportation costs, and with disaggregations by route choice, trip type, trip destination conditions, trip origin conditions, transport mode, and so forth.

More recently, various theories have been advanced in support of particular statistical and behavioural relationships found in spatial interaction models. The conclusions of these theories are more notable for their similarities than for their differences [Smith (1975)], and the possibility of unifying many of these hypotheses has been recognized. Furthermore, transportation models based on such hypotheses of spatial interaction have become increasingly fused with models for describing and predicting economic structure. One typical approach has been to combine transportation and input–output models. Since the input–output approach does not provide an optimizing framework, transportation models have also been extended to incorporate linear and nonlinear programming methods.

This chapter explores these and related developments in the ongoing evolution of models describing spatial interaction, transportation and the flow of commodities between different regions. In the following section, some brief historical excerpts from the formative years are given. Section 3 examines various modern

Handbook of Regional and Urban Economics, Volume I, Edited by P. Nijkamp
©Elsevier Science Publishers BV, 1986

theories and formulations which have been proposed for modelling spatial interactions assuming transportation costs are fixed, and demonstrates how a broad range of hypotheses may be reconciled within a single unifying framework. Alternative formulations are presented in Section 4 for analyzing route choice on a transportation network where the costs are flow-dependent. Sections 5 and 6 deal with interregional commodity flow models in which the prices and service characteristics are, respectively, fixed and variable. A discussion of solution procedures (in Section 7) is followed by a brief examination of new research directions and future prospects for the development of spatial interaction and transportation models.

Throughout the chapter, a synthesizing framework is developed within which most of the notable advances may be classified and compared. The scope of the discussion is broadened considerably beyond the traditional bounds of spatial interaction modelling, namely intraurban trip and commodity flow distributions, to the analysis of flows between cities, towns and regions. The reader is referred to the companion volume on urban economics for further insights from an intraurban viewpoint, and to Chapters 3, 6, 7 and 8 of this Handbook for additional insights into particular aspects of the family of models discussed in this chapter.

2. Historical review

2.1. *Gravity and potential models*

The explanation and prediction of patterns of social and economic interaction over geographic space has always been one of the central problems of interest to regional scientists. Since the late 1940s, geographers and economists have actively promulgated theoretical and empirical research in which concepts drawn from Newtonian physics have been applied to the analysis of socioeconomic interactions in space. The resulting paradigm, known as the *Gravity Hypothesis*, is not so much a legacy of spatial economic theory but more a product of cross-disciplinary fertilization.

The use of gravitation to explain human spatial interactions was first suggested in the last century. Carrothers (1956) noted the formulation by H. C. Carey (1858) in his work, *The principles of social science*. Carey's work was directly inspired by Newton's law of universal gravitation, which states that the force of attraction, F_{ij}, between two bodies i and j is directly proportional to their respective masses, m_i and m_j, and inversely proportional to the square of the distance, d_{ij}, between them, i.e.

$$F_{ij} = k \frac{m_i m_j}{(d_{ij})^2}. \tag{2.1}$$

This formula has generally been modified when it has been applied to human and economic interactions. Gravitation is presented as an increasing function of mass and a decreasing function of distance. More precisely, two types of models have been used. On the one hand, *gravity models* allow one to estimate the absolute number of interactions between two elements of space (generally represented by points). The number varies directly according to a certain function of the masses (or sizes) of the points and varies inversely with a certain function of the distance separating the two points. On the other hand, *potential models* aim at measuring the influence exerted by a set of masses on a unit of mass located at a given point in space. The total potential at the point i, designated V_i, is given by

$$V_i = k \sum_j \frac{m_j}{d_{ij}}. \tag{2.2}$$

The history of gravity and potential models as applied to socioeconomic interactions largely hinges on discussions about the nature of these masses, the choice of a definition for distance, the numeric value of its exponent, and the evaluation of constants like the parameter k.[1]

2.2. Market area and retail trade models

Although the first major impetus in the development of socioeconomic gravity models is generally credited to Stewart, Zipf and Dodd, who simultaneously worked on gravitational formulae from independent angles,[2] it is actually an earlier study of retail trade which serves as the reference model and point of departure for the modern economic analysis of spatial interactions. Reilly (1931)

---

[1] Discussions concerning the development and application of gravity models for socioeconomic behaviour may be found, among others, in the references cited at the end of this chapter, especially Carrothers (1956), Schneider (1959), Isard and Bramhall (1960), Styles (1969), Batty (1978) and Ponsard (1983).

[2] Stewart (1948) formulated his hypothesis in terms of social physics, defining *demographic force* using formula (2.1). In this instance, the population of cities i and j were taken as the relevant masses. He also introduced the concepts of *demographic energy* and *demographic potential*. Zipf (1949) associated his empirical findings with a *principle of least effort* which pervades all human behaviour. He implicitly linked the gravity model to the rank-size rule which holds for various socioeconomic phenomena and embraces Pareto's law of income distribution. Dodd (1950) suggested a linkage between the gravity model and an optimization process using crude probabilistic arguments.

presented his law for the first time in 1929, and then later in a revised version which has since become well known:

> Two cities attract trade from an intermediate town in the vicinity of the breaking point, approximately in direct proportion to the population of the two cities, and in inverse proportion to the squares of the distances of the intermediate town [Reilly (1931, p. 9)].

Reilly derived this law from more general considerations, however, beginning with no preconception as to the way in which population and distance formed specific direct and inverse proportions like those suggested by social physics as in (2.1) and (2.2). Our brief historical discussion begins with this more general form.[3]

Let places or regional centres be classified according to whether they are the origin of consumer demand for particular goods, or whether they are points of supply or exchange, such as market centres. Assume that there are N places of consumer demand, denoted by the subscript i, and M market centres given by the subscripts j and k. Then the general equation which Reilly adopted is given by

$$\frac{p_{ij}}{p_{ik}} = \left(\frac{p_j}{p_k}\right)^\alpha \left(\frac{d_{ik}}{d_{ij}}\right)^\beta \tag{2.3}$$

where p_{ij} and p_{ik} are the proportions of all the demand or trade attracted from some place of consumer demand i to centres j and k respectively, p_j and p_k are the populations of j and k, and d_{ij} and d_{ik} are the distances from i to the centres j and k (see Figure 2.1); α and β are empirical constants.

The equilibrium condition proposed by Reilly to define the "breakpoint" between centres j and k, that is, to define the market hinterlands around j and k, is the condition which gives the point at which the proportions of sales accruing to j and k are equal, namely

$$p_{ij} = p_{ik}. \tag{2.4}$$

Equation (2.4) implies that (2.3) equals one, and thus it is clear that the boundary

---

[3] Much of the discussion which follows in this section is taken from Batty (1978). The reader is referred to this source for a complete reformulation and generalization of Reilly's law, as well as a critique of its relationship to the hierarchical theory of central places.

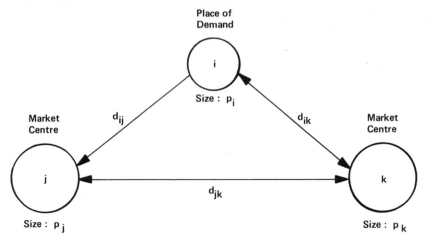

Figure 2.1. Market centres and places of consumer demand.

condition between market areas can be specified as

$$\frac{d_{ik}}{d_{ij}} = \left(\frac{p_k}{p_j}\right)^{\alpha/\beta}.$$ (2.5)

By using the identity $d_{jk} \equiv d_{ij} + d_{ik}$, we can reach an explicit breakpoint equation (which Reilly did not appear to derive), namely

$$d_{ij} = d_{jk} \bigg/ \left[1 + \left(\frac{p_k}{p_j}\right)^{\alpha/\beta}\right].$$ (2.6)

A more common way of deriving (2.6) is to postulate a model of retail trade to calculate the proportions of trade from any place i to another place j.

A classical form of the unconstrained gravity model[4] suggested by Anderson (1955), in which the influence of mass (in terms of population) on retail trade is raised to some power different from unity, is convenient from the viewpoint of later discussions:

$$T_{ij} = K P_i^\gamma P_j^\alpha d_{ij}^{-\beta}$$ (2.7)

where T_{ij} is the trade flowing from i to j, K is a scaling constant needed for

---

[4] The term *unconstrained* implies that there is no explicit limit on the total supply of or demand for goods.

normalization, and γ, α and β are parameters. The proportions of trade, p_{ij} and p_{ik}, can be calculated as

$$p_{ij} = \frac{T_{ij}}{\sum_j T_{ij}} \quad \text{and} \quad p_{ik} = \frac{T_{ik}}{\sum_k T_{ik}} \tag{2.8}$$

and the ratio of these proportions yields the same result as (2.3). This illustrates that Reilly's law is essentially a condition *derived* from an unconstrained gravity model which must first be defined, calibrated and tested.[5]

Reilly's law corresponds to a model of spatial competition reflecting duopoly between pairs of central places. As we shall see later, by using more recent gravitational theory in which wider competitive effects are handled through constraints on movement, it is possible to take account of system-wide interaction when predicting the breakpoint between any two places. Moreover, his law may also be regarded as a special case of the economic market area analysis originating from Fetter (1924) and Hotelling (1929), in which specific spatial price–cost indifference functions are implied. We shall explore some of these more generalized gravity models in Section 3.

2.3. Supply – demand potentials and spatial price variations

To study price variations over space, Warntz (1957, 1959) argued that demand and supply should each be formulated as spatially continuous variables. In accordance with the concept of potential introduced by Stewart, shown as (2.2), Warntz derived a *product supply space potential* for a commodity by setting $k = 1$ and defining as mass, m_j, the production of this commodity in region j. Thus,

---

[5] The estimation of α and β must be treated as part of the model calibration process, although it is possible to estimate α and β from the derived condition. Reilly appeared to guess α as unity and then compute β using very detailed data on the flow proportions of trade between a series of market centres. He obtained values for β of between 1.5 and 2.5, hence he approximated β as 2. Of marginal interest here is the fact that his guess for α appears to have been borne out in more recent applications of retail trade models [for example, Batty (1978), Coelho and Wilson (1976)]. For $\alpha = 1$ and $\beta = 2$, the breakpoint equation becomes

$$d_{ij} = d_{jk} \bigg/ \left[1 + \left(\frac{p_k}{p_j} \right)^{1/2} \right]$$

which may have been used by Converse as early as 1930 [according to Styles (1969)]. However, the earliest known (to us) statement of the above equation is by Strohkarck and Phelps (1948), and their article seems to have prompted Converse (1949) into publishing the fact that he had been using the same equation for many years.

region j's contribution to the supply potential in region i is m_j/d_{ij}, and the total contribution of all other regions to the supply potential at i is $\sum_j(m_j/d_{ij})$.

Warntz did not develop direct measures of demand space potential, instead utilizing *income potential* as a substitute. His initial hypothesis, advanced as a refinement of the traditional view of supply and demand, may be stated as follows:

> In any local area, the price of a commodity varies inversely with the area's supply space potential and directly with the area's demand space potential for which the area's income potential may be substituted [Isard and Bramhall (1960, p. 534)].

Further refinement was necessary to recognize that the local price is also affected by the timing of peaks in the supply potential in relation to peaks in the demand (income) potential.[6] Warntz constructed for each commodity a *product supply time potential*. His full hypothesis was:

> that in any local area the price of a commodity not only varies inversely with the area's supply space potential and directly with the area's income potential, but also varies inversely with the area's supply time potential.[7]

The specific terms of this hypothesis have been confirmed statistically by the resulting signs of the separate net regression coefficients. To this extent, the extension of the potential concept to embrace both supply and demand aspects yielded an early insight into the spatial characteristics of important economic and social phenomena.

2.4. Spatial interactions on a transportation network

Although much of the early literature of spatial interaction models employs geographic distance as a measure of the separation of centres, the consideration of other measures of separation was not ignored. Pigou (1918, p. 194) discussed the issue of alternative routes between places and the effect of route choice on the cost of each route. Knight (1924) addressed this issue more explicitly as an

---

[6] The related notion of *intervening opportunities* is discussed in Stouffer (1940), Strodtbeck (1949) and Anderson (1955); the probabilistic notion of *relative potential*, and demand-constrained shopping models for evaluating the potential area of a sales outlet, are discussed in Huff (1963) and Lakshmanan and Hansen (1965).

[7] If Warntz had been able to construct a measure of *product demand time potential*, his hypothesis would have been modified further so that in any local area the price of the commodity varies directly with the area's demand time potential.

example of public or social vs private costs. He stated, in effect, the principle of equilibrium for a transportation network connecting pairs of places that users "will tend to distribute themselves among" the routes connecting each pair of places "in such proportions that the cost per unit of transportation will be the same" for every user on each route. Although the solution of the route choices and the corresponding costs for a transportation network of more than a few routes connecting two places was not possible in the 1920s, the correct route choice criterion had been devised. This *user-equilibrium* or *user-optimal* criterion, as it is now widely known, was independently restated by Wardrop (1952, p. 345) in terms of journey times and is generally associated with his name.

The first mathematical formulation of equilibrium in a transportation network was accomplished by Beckmann et al. (1956). They showed that a mathematical statement of the above route choice criterion, and an origin–destination travel demand function defined on the equilibrium route costs for each pair of places, were the optimality conditions of an equivalent convex optimization problem if the routes consisted of sequences of links in which the travel costs were increasing with flow. The authors proved that the solution to this problem exists and is unique. They also studied the stability of the solution, but did not devise an algorithm to compute the solution. Although these results extend to any invertible travel demand function, they have been studied in great depth for spatial interaction models. Further details of these developments are discussed in Section 4.

3. Modelling spatial interactions assuming transportation costs are fixed

Many attempts have been made to develop a satisfactory theoretical foundation for the classical gravity model which does not necessarily rely on any physical analogy. A similar search has also eventuated for other related interaction models which have been used to estimate the distribution of trips or flows on a transportation network. In very general terms, two currents of thought have emerged: the first one adopts a probabilistic or statistical approach; the second one a behavioural or utility approach. In this section, we discuss the relationships of these two schools of thought to the classical gravity model, and later demonstrate that the two approaches may be reconciled because they can lead to an identical or equivalent solution given the same problem.

3.1.   The gravity model of spatial interaction

The simplest gravity model used in spatial interaction models, and based on Newton's specification (2.1), is usually written as

$$x_{rr'} = kO_rD_rf(d_{rr'})$$
(3.1)

where $x_{rr'}$ is the flow from place r to place r', k is a constant of proportionality, O_r is the flow originating from place r, $D_{r'}$ is the flow terminating at place r', and $f(d_{rr'})$ is a distance deterrence function between places r and r', assumed to be a decreasing function of the intervening distance $d_{rr'}$. Such a gravity model is frequently used in analysing trip origin–destination flows, commodity flows, migration flows and other forms of spatial interaction. More general specifications have been proposed, such as

$$x_{rr'} = kO_r^\alpha D_{r'}^\gamma f(d_{rr'}). \tag{3.2}$$

Relationships (3.1) and (3.2) can be considered as functions which determine $x_{rr'}$ as an unweighted *arithmetic* and a weighted *geometric* average of O_r and $D_{r'}$, respectively [see Andersson and Marksjö (1972), Nijkamp (1975)].

One weakness of the gravity model in its classical form is that the aggregate flows do not necessarily sum to the total flows in the system. This methodological requirement is called the *additivity* condition. In the framework of spatial interaction models, this condition can be formalized as

$$\sum_{r'=1}^{R'} x_{rr'} = O_r, \qquad r = 1, \ldots, R \tag{3.3}$$

$$\sum_{r=1}^{R} x_{rr'} = D_{r'}, \qquad r' = 1, \ldots, R'. \tag{3.4}$$

Suppose, for example, that (3.1) is used to forecast future flows between all places r and r' of a spatial system. Next, suppose that each O_r and each $D_{r'}$ double. For the classical gravity model, doubling each O_r and each $D_{r'}'$ would quadruple the flows between all places r and r'. Such an absurd result is obviously codetermined by the multiplicative structure of a gravity model, but is essentially caused by the fact that the additivity conditions are not fulfilled. This implies that forecasting spatial interactions will be unreliable whenever the additivity conditions are not satisfied.

The additivity conditions can always be satisfied if the gravity model is rewritten as

$$x_{rr'} = A_r B_{r'} O_r D_{r'} f(d_{rr'}) \tag{3.5}$$

where the parameters A_r and $B_{r'}$ are defined, respectively, as

$$A_r = \left\{ \sum_{r'=1}^{R'} B_{r'} D_{r'} f(d_{rr'}) \right\}^{-1}, \tag{3.6}$$

and

$$B_{r'} = \left\{ \sum_{r=1}^{R} A_r O_r f(d_{rr'}) \right\}^{-1}. \tag{3.7}$$

Parameters A_r and $B_{r'}$ are balancing factors which guarantee the fulfilment of the additivity conditions. In empirical work, these unknown parameters can be readily estimated by means of iterative techniques.

More general specifications of (3.5) have also been proposed, such as Alonso's (1978) formulation:

$$x_{rr'} = A_r^{\alpha-1} O_r B_{r'}^{\gamma-1} D_{r'} f(d_{rr'}). \tag{3.8}$$

The generality of (3.8) is evident from the number of gravity models subsumed in its structure with predetermined values of α and γ:

(i) $\alpha = 1$, $\gamma = 1$ entails traditional gravity models [e.g. (3.1) or Lowry (1966)];
(ii) $\alpha = 0$, $\gamma = 0$ entails two-way distribution models [e.g. Wilson (1967)];
(iii) $\alpha = 1$, $\gamma = 0$ or $\alpha = 0$, $\gamma = 1$ entails one-way distribution models [e.g. Lakshmanan and Hansen (1965)].

One may contend that α and γ should be empirically estimated rather than predetermined. We shall elaborate on these aspects later in this section.

3.2. The statistical family of spatial interaction models

3.2.1. Early probabilistic approaches

It was the various attempts to find a theoretical justification for Stouffer's (1940) intervening opportunities model which prompted the first probabilistic approach to spatial interaction modelling. Schneider (1959) and Isard and Bramhall (1960) provided simple probabilistic interpretations of the gravity model.

3.2.2. The maximum entropy approach

Although Cohen (1959) may have been earliest to recognize the potential applicability of concepts from statistical mechanics, Wilson (1967, 1970) provided the first theoretically convincing derivation of the gravity model using entropy-maximizing principles, among others such as Tomlin and Tomlin (1968). Murchland (1966) formulated an equivalent problem but ignored the underlying rationale.

Entropy is a concept that stems originally from thermodynamics [see Fast (1970)]. We can characterize the entropy function in its traditional form as a measure of the probability of a system being in a particular state. The entropy of such a system is proportional to the number of possible assignments which correspond, or give rise to, each particular state. In elementary statistical mechanics, this view typecasts the entropy-maximizing procedure as the process of determining the most probable distribution (macrostate) which corresponds to the largest number of possible assignments (microstates).

Suppose we wish to find the most probable distribution of flows, $x = (x_{11}, x_{12}, \ldots, x_{RR'})$. Further suppose that the total of all flows

$$X = \sum_{r=1}^{R} \sum_{r'=1}^{R'} x_{rr'} \tag{3.9}$$

is known; then, assuming that (i) all permissible microstates are equally probable, and (ii) each unit being transported (person, commodity) is clearly distinguishable, the probability of $\hat{x}$ is proportional to the number of ways in which X units can be distributed into $R \times R'$ groups with values $(x_{11}, x_{12}, \ldots, x_{rr'}, \ldots, x_{RR'})$. The number of ways is given by the combinatorial formula

$$W = X! \left/ \prod_{r=1}^{R} \prod_{r'=1}^{R'} x_{rr'}! \right. \tag{3.10}$$

If we also know the total transportation cost, T, and the unit transportation cost between each pair of places, $t_{rr'}$, such that

$$\sum_{r=1}^{R} \sum_{r'=1}^{R'} t_{rr'} x_{rr'} = T \tag{3.11}$$

then the most probable distribution of flows is found by maximizing W subject to (3.11) and the additivity constraints (3.3) and (3.4).

So far, we have neither invoked an entropy-maximizing principle nor even any physical analogy. In practice, however, it turns out to be more convenient to maximize $\ln W$ rather than W itself. Once we apply this logarithmic transformation, the similarity to Boltzmann's famous entropy formula becomes obvious.[8]

For large $x_{rr'}$ $(r = 1, \ldots, R: r' = 1, \ldots, R')$, we may use Stirling's approximation for factorials [see Wilson (1970)] to obtain the following entropy function:

$$\ln W \approx - \sum_{r=1}^{R} \sum_{r'=1}^{R'} (x_{rr'} \ln x_{rr'} - x_{rr'}). \tag{3.12}$$

---

[8] Boltzmann (1872) formulated the original definition of entropy, S, as a measure of disorder, namely

$$S = k \log W$$

where k is a physical constant known as Boltzmann's constant.

It may be readily demonstrated that the maximization of (3.12) subject to (3.3), (3.4) and (3.11) leads to the following result:

$$\hat{x}_{rr'} = \exp(-\alpha_r - \beta_{r'} - \gamma t_{rr'}) \qquad (3.13)$$

where α_r, $\beta_{r'}$ and γ are the Lagrange multipliers or shadow prices associated with (3.3), (3.4) and (3.11), respectively. For a discussion of solution techniques, see Section 7. By defining the balancing factors as

$$A_r = \exp(-\alpha_r)/O_r \qquad (3.14)$$

and

$$B_{r'} = \exp(-\beta_{r'})/D_{r'}, \qquad (3.15)$$

one can specify the most probable flow distribution as

$$x_{rr'} = A_r B_{r'} O_r D_{r'} \exp(-\gamma t_{rr'}). \qquad (3.16)$$

This result is equivalent to the above mentioned gravity model (3.5), in which the additivity conditions are satisfied. Thus we reach the important conclusion that the entropy-maximizing method may provide a theoretical framework for deriving the gravity model.

Since the initial appearance of Wilson's derivation, many extensions or refinements to the basic methodology have been suggested. Some have been prompted by different combinatorial definitions of W that may apply under different circumstances, others by the a priori assumption of equi-probable microstates being sensitive to the choice of microstate space. Papers discussing alternative microstate descriptions based on Maxwell–Boltzmann, Fermi–Dirac and Bose–Einstein statistics include Fisk and Brown (1975), Dacey and Norcliffe (1977), Snickars and Weibull (1977), Lesse et al. (1978), Roy and Lesse (1981, 1985), and Batten (1983, ch. 3). Fotheringham (1983) has also demonstrated that the use of these traditional microstate formulations for, say, origin-constrained models can result in mis-specification, as they fail to separate spatial deterrence effects from competition or agglomeration effects between destinations [Roy and Batten (1985, p. 705)].

Furthermore, a wide variety of entropy-maximizing models have been derived under different sets of constraints. In the terminology of Wilson (1970), one can identify four types of trip distribution model: (i) the unconstrained model; (ii) the production-constrained model; (iii) the attraction-constrained model; and (iv) the doubly-constrained model. These differ according to the inclusion of one or both of the additivity conditions. Batten (1983) has developed a similar family of commodity flow models.

The second and more recent interpretation of the entropy function is one of a measure of the amount of *uncertainty* or *lack of information* associated with a probability distribution. In theory, this approach necessitates the transformation of variables such as $x_{rr'}$ into probabilities, wherein the elementary event is a shipment from region r to region r'; $p_{rr'}$ is the probability of such an event, and is defined by

$$p_{rr'} = \frac{x_{rr'}}{X},$$

(3.17)

where $\sum_{r=1}^{R}\sum_{r'=1}^{R'} p_{rr'} = 1$. The most probable flow distribution is then determined by maximizing the function

$$S = -\sum_{r}\sum_{r'} p_{rr'}\ln p_{rr'}$$

(3.18)

subject to a set of constraints containing whatever flow information is available [see Shannon (1948)].

This information-theoretic approach provides a constructive criterion for estimating probability distributions on the basis of partial knowledge, and characterizes the maximum-entropy estimate as a type of *statistical inference*. It is simply the least-biased estimate possible with the given information, and is therefore maximally non-committal with regard to missing information [Jaynes (1957)].

If we consider statistical mechanics to be a form of statistical inference, these two seemingly different views of entropy can generally be reconciled. It has consequently been argued that the perspective which should be adopted may simply be a matter of taste [see, for example, Williams and Wilson (1980)]. Nevertheless, in order to alleviate possible doubts regarding the ability of approaches based on information theory to take into account all the known information characterizing a spatial system [see Fisk (1985)], it may be both useful and important to maintain a clear distinction between the *enumerative* and the *statistical* aspects of entropy modelling. The former consists of the correct enumeration of the feasible microstates of the system, whereas the latter is a straightforward example of statistical inference.

One of the strengths of the information-theoretic concept of entropy is that because it is actually a measure of uncertainty, it does not imply any physical analogy. But two weaknesses are also apparent. First, the a priori assumption that the flows between regions are equally probable often seems unrealistic owing, for example, to different production and consumption levels in each region. Second, entropy-maximizing is generally regarded as a statistical approach which apparently ignores the underlying principles of individual human behaviour. We shall deal with the first of these problems immediately and take up the latter in Sections 3.3 and 3.4.

3.2.3. *The minimum information principle*

In information theory, the versatile measure of *information gain* introduced by Kullback (1959) rests on the assumption that information is a relative quantity; it compares probabilities before and after an observation. Information gain is defined by comparing the posterior flow distribution $\{p_{rr'}\}$ with a prior distribution $\{q_{rr'}\}$. The gain, $I(P:Q)$, is given by

$$I(P;Q) = \sum_r \sum_{r'} p_{rr'} \ln(p_{rr'}/q_{rr'}). \tag{3.19}$$

The minimum information principle asserts that the particular distribution $\{\hat{p}_{rr'}\}$ should be chosen that minimizes $I(P;Q)$ subject to related facts about P treated as constraints. It is equivalent to finding the most probable distribution given that the prior probabilities are non-uniform and that the underlying relative frequencies behave like independent random samples from this prior distribution.

Various arguments have been invoked to justify the use of this principle [see, for example, Jaynes (1968), Snickars and Weibull (1977), Webber (1979) or Batten (1983)]. Equation (3.19) is perhaps the most general of all information measures, in so much as it represents a relative measure which

(i) is independent of the total flow or number of observations;
(ii) is always positive;
(iii) has more reasonable additive properties than Shannon's measure (3.18);
(iv) can be extended to continuous sample spaces; and
(v) allows for non-uniform prior probabilities.

At its first approximation, application of this principle is equivalent to the minimization of the chi-square statistic [Kadas and Klafsky, (1976)]:

$$\sum_r \sum_{r'} (p_{rr'} - q_{rr'})^2 / p_{rr'} \tag{3.20}$$

and it therefore resembles a measure of deviation or goodness of fit. However, it is not a pure goodness-of-fit measure since it also relates to the prior information.

Since the early suggested extensions towards using prior information, Snickars and Weibull (1977) have demonstrated that the classical gravity model is considerably less powerful as a tool for describing historical changes in metropolitan commuting patterns than models based on a priori trip patterns. Similar results have been found to hold for flow patterns of international trade [see Anderstig (1982) and Batten and Johansson (1985)]. The close mathematical relation between the Kullback measure (3.19) and the asymptotic behaviour of indepen-dent random samples lies at the core of all applications in which this measure has demonstrated *predictive* capabilities [Smith (1985)]. Apart from the applications discussed in this chapter, the chosen assignment of prior probabilities $\{q_{rr'}\}$ may also serve as (i) a candidate probabilistic theory of interactive behaviour, (ii) an ideal point in the context of multiobjective optimization, and (iii) a target flow pattern in prescriptive modelling. For a summary of these applications, see Batten (1984b). Nevertheless, it may not necessarily provide a sound methodol-ogy for the derivation of all (e.g. *dynamic*) models of spatial interaction.

3.2.4. *The entropy-constrained approach*

As an alternative to the entropy-maximizing model formulated in Section 3.2.2, Erlander (1977, 1980) has examined the entropy-constrained version of the same model. The entropy of the flow matrix may be interpreted as a broad measure of "interactivity" or dispersion within the transportation system. Erlander's formu-lation minimizes average generalized transportation cost subject to the additivity conditions (3.6) and (3.7) and the following constraint on the dispersion of flows:

$$- \sum_{r} \sum_{r'} p_{rr'} \ln p_{rr'} \geq S_o. \tag{3.21}$$

Not surprisingly, this formulation yields an identical solution to (3.16) because the optimality conditions are equivalent for both. The transportation problem of linear programming may be obtained as a limiting case of Erlander's formulation (see Section 5.1), and generalizations have been derived to consider a hierarchy of travel choices by defining two or more dispersion constraints on marginal values of the choice variable [Boyce et al. (1983)].

3.2.5. *Other statistical approaches*

It should be noted that the specification of flows in (3.16) does not necessarily rest upon entropy-maximizing approaches or principles of information theory. A similar result may be obtained using Bayes' theorem for conditional probabilities [see Hyman (1969) or Sheppard (1976)], using contingency table analysis [see Willekens (1980) or Batten (1983)], or by means of maximum likelihood estima-tors of the spatial interaction model [see Evans (1971)]. All these methods, however, are based on similar statistical foundations, and might therefore be unified in the future by perceiving them all as the most-probable-state (MPS) approach to macrostatistical analysis [see Smith (1985)]. In the absence of any disaggregate information explaining the microeconomic choice behaviour that underlies a flow pattern, the problem *is* purely a macrostatistical one. In the following section, we shall explore some alternative behavioural models which are based on utility theory.

3.3.   The behavioural family of spatial interaction models

In contrast to the statistical family of spatial interaction models, which have usually been regarded as macroscopic (aggregate) approaches to the problem, the microeconomic behavioural approaches base an individual or group's travel decision on his/their utility or preference function. Within this disaggregate framework, the neoclassical approach refers explicitly to the utility function and deterministically derives a function of continuous demand for spatial interactions, while the stochastic (or choice-theoretic) approach includes a random term as part of the utility function and derives a probabilistic statement based on the decision maker's discrete likelihood of choosing a particular alternative.

3.3.1.   Neoclassical utility theories

The neoclassical approach is exemplified in the work of Niedercorn and Bechdolt (1969), Golob and Beckmann (1971), Choukroun (1975) and Williams (1977). Variations in their derivations, which stem from different basic assumptions, cause certain difficulties in presenting a representative summary. Furthermore, their results are given in terms of person trips. In the following, we shall modify Niedercorn and Bechdolt (1969) in such a way as to develop a complementary commodity flow model, drawing heavily on Nijkamp (1975).

  Let us assume that each place of origin (or shipper) can be conceived of as a *collective decision-unit*, which allocates a certain transportation budget among a series of shipments to alternative destinations. The situation is similar to the well-known theory of consumer behaviour, where a given income is to be divided among alternative uses. An "optimal" allocation is here obtained by postulating a utility function which reflects the relative preferences of the shipper for each combination of deliveries.[9] Analogously, the assumption will be made here that each origin r has a collective preference function ω_r with arguments $x_{rr'}$ ($r' = 1, \ldots, R'$). This preference function has to be maximized subject to a certain transportation budget, which is assumed to be a known linear function of the flow from place r. Therefore, the utility-maximizing problem for place r is

$$\text{Maximize } \omega_r = \omega_r(x_{r1}, x_{r2}, \ldots, x_{rR'}) \tag{3.22}$$

---

[9] This utility function may be replaced by a revenue function for a group of firms engaged in distributing commodities [see Niedercorn and Moorehead (1974)].

subject to

$$\sum_{r'=1}^{R'} t_{rr'} x_{rr'} = \mu O_r \qquad (3.23)$$

where μO_r denotes the total available transportation budget of place r. In other words, $\mu = T_r / O_r$ where $\sum_{r=1}^{R} T_r = T$.

The first-order conditions for the maximization of (3.22) are

$$\dot{\omega}_{rr'} = \lambda t_{rr'}, \quad r' = 1, \ldots, R' \qquad (3.24)$$

where λ is the Lagrange multiplier associated with the budget constraint, and $\dot{\omega}_{rr'}$ denotes the first derivative of $\omega_{rr'}$ with respect to $x_{rr'}$. The unknown $x_{rr'}$ $(r' = 1, \ldots, R')$ can be solved for a given origin r on the basis of the following system of $(R'-1)$ equations:

$$\frac{\dot{\omega}_{rr'}}{t_{rr'}} = \frac{\dot{\omega}_{rR'}}{t_{rR'}} \qquad (r' = 1, 2, \ldots, R'-1) \qquad (3.25)$$

together with the budget constraint (3.23).

To clarify the relationship between the above solution and our basic gravity model, we must rewrite the latter's classical specification (3.1) for a flow between r and a certain place of destination R', namely

$$x_{rR'} / k D_{R'} f(d_{rR'}) = O_r \qquad (3.26)$$

or

$$x_{rR'} \mu / k D_{R'} f(d_{rR'}) = \sum_{r'=1}^{R'} t_{rr'} x_{rr'} \qquad (3.27)$$

where use is made of (3.23). Defining γ_r as

$$\gamma_r = \sum_{r'=1}^{R'} D_{r'} f(d_{rr'}) \qquad (3.28)$$

we may rewrite (3.27) as

$$x_{rR'} \mu k^{-1} D_{R'}^{-1} f^{-1}(d_{rR'}) \gamma_r^{-1} \sum_{r'=1}^{R'} D_{r'} f(d_{rr'}) = \sum_{r'=1}^{R'} t_{rr'} x_{rr'}. \qquad (3.29)$$

A sufficient but very strong condition for the fulfilment of (3.29) is that

$$x_{rR'}\mu k^{-1}D_{R'}^{-1}f^{-1}(d_{rR'})\gamma_r^{-1}D_r f(d_{rr'}) = t_{rr'}x_{rr'} \qquad (r'=1,2,\dots,R') \qquad (3.30)$$

or by dividing the first $(R'-1)$ equations by the last one,

$$\frac{D_r f(d_{rr'})}{t_{rr'}x_{rr'}} = \frac{D_{R'} f(d_{rR'})}{t_{rR'}x_{rR'}} \qquad (r'=1,2,\dots,R'-1). \qquad (3.31)$$

Now it is evident that (3.25) and (3.31) are similar whenever the collective preference function ω_r of place r takes the following additive logarithmic form:

$$\omega_r = \sum_{r'=1}^{R'} D_r f(d_{rr'})\ln x_{rr'}. \qquad (3.32)$$

We may therefore conclude that, under certain conditions, the classical gravity model of spatial interaction may be derived from the economic principles of utility maximization. In this case, the underlying utility function is based on collective behaviour and the preference weights are formed by multiplying the aggregate volume of flows to place r', $D_{r'}$, by the corresponding deterrence function of distance, $f(d_{rr'})$.

Furthermore, if instead of (3.1) use is made of (3.5), a similar result will be obtained. The reader can easily check this result by applying the foregoing procedure to (3.5) instead of (3.1). The underlying utility function has a shape similar to that of (3.32), apart from the preference parameters. Ultimately, if a more general gravity model like (3.2) is employed, a similar procedure may be adopted to identify the underlying preference function. In this general case, the preference function turns out to be a separable power function.

3.3.2. Discrete choice theories

The above derivation helps to explain an individual's or group's behaviour on a continuous basis (i.e. the number of spatial interactions per unit of time). However, there are many situations in which decision making involves discrete choices. For example, the problems of travel mode or route, household or industry location, and shopping destination are problems in which consumers or producers must choose from a finite number of discrete alternatives; for a discussion of the use of discrete choice theories in household location models, see Chapter 3 of this Handbook.

Although Luce (1959) may have set this field of individual choice theory in motion, and Warner (1962) developed a binary choice model for the travel mode problem, it was McFadden (1973) who provided a general theoretical grounding for these behavioural methods with his derivation of the multinomial logit model from random utility maximization. The resulting family of discrete choice theories and disaggregate demand models has been extended into the context of spatial interaction [see, for example, Smith (1975)]. We shall briefly review the theoretical derivation of the multinomial logit model in the spatial context of the doubly-constrained model of joint origin–destination choice discussed previously (see Sections 3.1 and 3.2), drawing heavily on Anas (1981a, b).

Consider a group of $h = 1, \ldots, H$ individual decision makers – the shippers or suppliers in a system of regions – who have homogeneous preferences up to an additive term. Each supplier faces a choice set involving $s = 1, \ldots, R$ potential locations for production and $s' = 1, \ldots, R'$ potential customers (or delivery points). For simplicity, we shall presently assume that each supplier chooses just one place in which to produce and one place as his main customer.[10] Thus each supplier faces a choice among $n = 1, \ldots, N$ alternatives, where $N = RR'$.

The utility of each origin–destination pair (s, s') is assumed to be a linear function of the observed attributes of each alternative, or a predetermined nonlinear transformation of these attributes. Hence,

$$U_{ss'}^h = \alpha_s + \beta_{s'} + \sum_{k=1}^{K} \gamma_k z_{ss'k}^h + \varepsilon_{ss'}^h \tag{3.33}$$

where $U_{ss'}^h$ is the perceived utility to supplier h of choosing the origin–destination pair (s, s'), α_s and $\beta_{s'}$ are origin and destination-specific utility coefficients common to all suppliers, $z_{ss'k}^h$ is the value of attribute k for the origin–destination alternative (s, s') and supplier h, γ_k are taste parameters which can be interpreted as weights associated with particular components of the attributive vector of alternatives, and $\varepsilon_{ss'}^h$ is an unobserved vector containing all the attributes of the alternatives and characteristics of the supplier which we are unable to measure. Provided we sample randomly from a set of suppliers with common socioeconomic characteristics and the same alternatives (s, s'), the vector $\varepsilon_{ss'}^h$ will be random and therefore the values of $U_{ss'}^h$ will be stochastic. An individual supplier will choose option (r, r') if this alternative maximizes his utility, i.e. if

$$U_{rr'}^h > U_{ss'}^h \quad \text{for} \quad \forall r \neq s, \forall r' \neq s'. \tag{3.34}$$

Since these utility values are random, the event that supplier h chooses alterna-

---

[10] Generalization to m_h regions for production and n_h customers is possible.

tive (r, r') will occur with some probability, which we can denote by $p^h_{rr'}$ where

$$p^h_{rr'} = \text{Prob}\left(U^h_{rr'} > U^h_{ss'}; \forall r \neq s; \forall r' \neq s'\right). \tag{3.35}$$

The multinomial logit model is derived by assuming that each $\varepsilon^h_{rr'}$ is independently and identically distributed over the population and for each supplier according to a Weibull distribution, i.e.

$$\text{Prob}\left(\varepsilon^h_{rr'} \leq \varepsilon\right) = \exp\left\{\exp - (\phi\varepsilon)\right\} \tag{3.36}$$

where ϕ is a parameter which determines the mode of the distribution. If, for example, we select the Gumbel distribution for which $\phi = (\pi^2/6\sigma^2)^{1/2}$ with variance σ^2, then the mode is zero and the multinomial logit model takes the form

$$p^h_{rr'} = \frac{\exp\left\{\tilde{\alpha}_r + \tilde{\beta}_{r'} + \sum_k \tilde{\gamma}_k z^h_{rr'k}\right\}}{\sum_s \sum_{s'} \exp\left\{\tilde{\alpha}_s + \tilde{\beta}_{s'} + \sum_k \tilde{\gamma}_k z^h_{ss'k}\right\}} \tag{3.37}$$

where $\tilde{\alpha}_s = \phi\alpha_s$, $\tilde{\beta}_{s'} = \phi\beta_{s'}$ and $\tilde{\gamma}_k = \phi\gamma_k$. Although the original utility coefficients $(\alpha_s, \beta_{s'}, \gamma_k)$ cannot be identified, the scaled coefficients $(\tilde{\alpha}_s, \tilde{\beta}_{s'}, \tilde{\gamma}_k)$ can be estimated uniquely, with the exception of one alternative-specific constant; see Anas (1981a). The method of maximum likelihood estimation is usually preferred for this purpose; see Hensher and Johnson (1981, p. 43).

3.4. Reconciliation and equivalence

In order to reconcile the above derivation with our earlier models, it is necessary to recognize that random utility-maximizing models are traditionally estimated from disaggregate (chooser-specific) data, whereas entropy-maximizing models are generally estimated from aggregate data. However, it is perfectly reasonable and computationally feasible to recast the maximum entropy model into a disaggregate format. Likewise, it is also feasible and realistic (in terms of data availability) to recast the maximum utility model into an aggregate format. The two approaches can then be recognized as complementary views which may lead to identical parameter estimation equations and solutions for the same problem.

For example, suppose that each origin, s, is not a distinct place of production but a region (spatial aggregation) of alternatives; and each destination, s', is likewise a spatial aggregation of customer alternatives. Then only the mean value of each attribute k for each origin–destination alternative (s, s'), i.e. $\bar{z}_{ss'k} = \sum_h \delta^h_{ss'} z^h_{ss'k} / \sum_h \delta^h_{ss'}$ is observed. The above model of joint origin–destination choice now becomes a model of joint origin–destination *region-pair* choice, and may be written in the aggregate form as

$$p_{rr'} = \frac{\exp\left\{\alpha_r^A + \beta_{r'}^A + \sum_k \gamma_k^A \bar{z}_{rr'k}\right\}}{\sum_s \sum_{s'} \exp\left\{\alpha_s^A + \beta_{s'}^A + \sum_k \gamma_k^A \bar{z}_{ss'k}\right\}} \tag{3.38}$$

where α_r^A, $\beta_{r'}^A$ and γ_k^A are the coefficients to be estimated with aggregation error, and $p_{rr'}$ is the predicted relative frequency or expected choice probability for alternative (r, r').

The entropy-maximization problem whose optimality condition corresponds exactly to the multinomial logit model specified in (3.38) is as follows:

$$\text{Maximize } S = -\sum_r \sum_{r'} p_{rr'} \ln p_{rr'} \tag{3.39}$$

subject to

$$\sum_{r'} p_{rr'} = O_r / X, \qquad r = 1, \ldots, R \tag{3.40}$$

$$\sum_r p_{rr'} = D_{r'} / X, \qquad r' = 1, \ldots, R' \tag{3.41}$$

$$\sum_r \sum_{r'} p_{rr'} \bar{z}_{rr'k} = \bar{Z} / X. \tag{3.42}$$

Using the method of Lagrangian minimization, it can be shown that the parameter estimation equations for this problem have an identical form to (3.38), but with α_r^A, $\beta_{r'}^A$ and γ_k^A denoting the Lagrange multipliers of (3.40), (3.41) and (3.42) respectively. Furthermore, the first order optimality conditions for maximizing the likelihood of (3.38) are identical to those needed to maximize (3.39) subject to (3.40)–(3.42). It thus follows that each Lagrange multiplier takes on an identical value to each scaled utility coefficient.

Because disaggregate attribute information is not observed, the estimated coefficients in (3.38) will naturally differ from those estimated using the underlying disaggregate data in (3.37). The difference corresponds to aggregation bias. Empirical studies have shown that meaningful estimates can be obtained when the aggregation units (regions) are reasonably small [see Anas (1981b)].

The relationship between the multinomial logit model (3.38) and the conventional gravity model follows if first we define the following:

$$\exp(\alpha_r^A) = O_r \left/ \sum_{r'} \exp\left(\beta_{r'}^A + \sum_k \gamma_k^A \bar{z}_{rr'k}\right) \right. \tag{3.43}$$

$$\exp(\beta_{r'}^A) = D_{r'} \left/ \sum_r \exp\left(\alpha_r^A + \sum_k \gamma_k^A \bar{z}_{rr'k}\right) \right. \tag{3.44}$$

and then rewrite (3.14) and (3.15) in the form

$$A_r = \exp(\alpha_r^A)/O_r \tag{3.45}$$

$$B_{r'} = \exp(\beta_{r'}^A)/D_{r'}. \tag{3.46}$$

Recalling from (3.17) that $x_{rr'} = X \cdot p_{rr'}$, we can now write

$$x_{rr'} = A_r B_{r'} O_r D_{r'} \exp\left(\sum_k \gamma_k^A \bar{z}_{rr'k}\right). \tag{3.47}$$

This result is similar to the gravity model (3.5), but with several attributes in the exponential term. It is identical to (3.5) if we replace this term with a generalized function of distance, $f(d_{rr'})$.

We have thus come the full circle by demonstrating that under the conditions of equivalent information, a doubly-constrained gravity or entropy model can yield identical estimates to a multinomial logit model of joint origin–destination choice consistent with random utility maximization up to some aggregation error in the estimated coefficients. Furthermore, the same model without any aggregation error may be derived in disaggregate form from both entropy and utility maximization and can therefore be estimated.[11] The gravity model has also been shown to be equivalent to two interlocking logit models – one for destination choice given the origin and the other for origin choice given the destination [see Smith (1984)]. The fact that models estimated using one approach have yielded different results from similar models estimated via another approach is not necessarily due to any fundamental difference in principle, but may simply be attributable to differences in (i) the use of data, (ii) its aggregation, and (iii) value judgments used in specifying explanatory attributes.

Historically, the different uses of available information within the two paradigms have obscured the close relationship of these two schools of spatial interaction modelling. The pioneering work on entropy-maximization took aggregate gravity models as the focus, and overlooked the applicability of information theory at the disaggregate level. It is evident that the enumerative flexibility of the most-probable-states approach (including alternative microstate descriptions and/or additional constraints) may be capable of replicating many of the behavioural postulates of the utility approach, suggesting that a unified view may be preferable.

---

[11] For further information concerning the reconciliation and unification of these approaches, see Beckmann (1974), Choukroun (1975), Williams (1977), Lesse et al. (1978), Anas (1981a) and Smith (1984).

4. Modelling spatial interaction assuming transportation costs depend on flows

The specification and solution of spatial interaction models with flow-dependent costs originated quite independently of spatial interaction modelling with the formulation of Beckman et al. (1956). Subsequently, this formulation was specialized to the spatial interaction formulation by Evans (1973a), who also devised an efficient algorithm. A reformulation by Erlander (1977, 1980) has provided the basis for an economic interpretation of the model and a reconciliation with the random utility theory formulation. In this section these developments are presented and their relationships examined.

4.1. *General network equilibrium problem*

The general formulation of the network equilibrium problem proceeds from two assumptions concerning travel behaviour. First, the number of trips from place r to place r', $x_{rr'}$, is assumed to be a decreasing function of the unit travel cost, $t_{rr'}$, separating the two places. Travel cost is considered to be defined as a generalized cost, namely a function of two or more deterrence variables including travel time as well as monetary cost,

$$x_{rr'} = f(t_{rr'}). \tag{4.1}$$

For the following formulation, (4.1) is assumed to be invertible, although this is not strictly necessary in all cases.

$$t_{rr'} = g(x_{rr'}). \tag{4.2}$$

Second, travellers are assumed to choose routes between each pair of places such that the cost of travel on all used routes is equal, and no unused route has a lower cost. These route costs, C_p, are defined as the sum of the costs, $c_l(f)$, of the sequence of links comprising the route, where $c_l(f)$ is an increasing function of the vector of link flows, $f = (f_l,\ l=1,\ldots, L)$. Route costs may be formally related to link costs by defining a link-route incidence matrix $A = (a_{lp})_{L \times P}$ where a_{lp} equals one if link l belongs to route p, or equals zero otherwise. Then,

$$C_p = \sum_{l=1}^{L} a_{lp} c_l(f), \qquad p=1,\ldots, P. \tag{4.3}$$

Furthermore,

$$f_l = \sum_{p=1}^{P} a_{lp} h_p, \qquad l=1,\ldots, L \tag{4.4}$$

where h_p is the number of persons travelling on route p, P is the total number of routes and $P_{rr'}$ is the number of routes from place r to r'. L is the total number of links.

The two assumptions given above are the optimality conditions of the following optimization problem:

$$\underset{(x_{rr'},h_p)}{\text{Minimize}} \sum_{l=1}^{L} \int_0^{f_l} c_l(y)\,\mathrm{d}y - \sum_{r=1}^{R} \sum_{r'=1}^{R'} \int_0^{x_{rr'}} g(z)\,\mathrm{d}z \qquad (4.5)$$

$$\text{subject to:} \quad \sum_{p=1}^{P_{rr'}} h_p = x_{rr'} \qquad r=1,\ldots,R;\ r'=1,\ldots,R' \qquad (4.6)$$

$$h_p \geq 0, \qquad\qquad p=1,\ldots,P \qquad (4.7)$$

$$\text{where} \qquad f_l = \sum_{p=1}^{P} a_{lp} h_p, \qquad l=1,\ldots,L. \qquad (4.8)$$

This optimization problem is convex, and therefore has a unique solution if the Hessian of the objective function is positive semidefinite. This condition is often satisfied by restricting $c_l(f)$ to the simpler function $c_l(f_l)$, meaning that flows on intersecting links have no effect on the cost of link l. Likewise, the travel demand function $f(t_{rr'})$ may be restricted to the travel cost $t_{rr'}$.

The optimality conditions corresponding to the convex optimization case are:

$$h_p \left(\sum_{l=1}^{L} c_l(f_l)a_{lp} - u_{rr'} \right) = 0, \qquad p=1,\ldots,P_{rr'} \qquad (4.9a)$$

$$x_{rr'}(-g(x_{rr'}) + u_{rr'}) = 0 \qquad r=1,\ldots,R;\ r'=1,\ldots,R' \qquad (4.9b)$$

where $u_{rr'}$ is the Lagrange multiplier associated with the conservation of flow constraints (4.6). For all $h_p > 0$,

$$C_p = \sum_{l=1}^{L} c_l(f_l)a_{lp} = u_{rr'}, \qquad p=1,\ldots,P_{rr'}.$$

Hence, $u_{rr'}$ is the equilibrium travel cost from place r to r'. If $h_{p'} = 0$, then $C_{p'} \geq u_{rr'}$; moreover, $C_{p''} > u_{rr'}$ implies $h_{p''} = 0$. Thus, condition (4.9a) is the formal statement of the route choice equilibrium condition.

For all $x_{rr'} > 0$,

$$g(x_{rr'}) = u_{rr'}, \quad \text{or } x_{rr'} = f(u_{rr'}), \qquad r=1,\ldots,R;\ r'=1,\ldots,R'.$$

Thus, the assumption that the number of trips is a function of the equilibrium place-to-place travel cost is satisfied. For many specific demand functions, it is necessary to assume that $x_{rr'}$ is strictly positive; hence, the demand function is always an equality.

Following the formulation by Beckmann et al. (1956), the network equilibrium problem received little attention until the late 1960s. Dafermos and Sparrow (1969) analysed the fixed demand case and proposed two algorithms. In a related group of papers Gibert (1968), Bruynooghe (1969) and Murchland (1970) proposed convergent algorithms for solving the above problem based on linearization of the objective function. Evans (1973a) studied the problem in great depth, and described a partial linearization algorithm. Although her Ph.D. dissertation considers the general problem stated above, the emphasis was on the specific case of the spatial interaction model described in Section 3. This case is now examined in more detail.

4.2. Network equilibrium problem and the gravity model

Suppose it is assumed that

$$t_{rr'} = g(x_{rr'}) = -\frac{1}{\gamma}(\ln x_{rr'} + 1).$$

Then

$$\int_0^{x_{rr'}} g(z)\,dz = -\frac{1}{\gamma}\int_0^{x_{rr'}}(\ln(z)+1)\,dz = -\frac{1}{\gamma}x_{rr'}\ln x_{rr'}$$

yielding the following specific version of objective function (4.5):

$$\underset{(x_{rr'},\,h_p)}{\text{Minimize}} \sum_{l=1}^{L}\int_0^{f_l}c_l(y)\,dy + \frac{1}{\gamma}\sum_{r=1}^{R}\sum_{r'=1}^{R'} x_{rr'}\ln x_{rr'}. \tag{4.10}$$

If this function is minimized subject to constraints defined on $x_{rr'}$, then the gravity model (3.14–3.16) is obtained as the optimality condition for $x_{rr'}$. Hence the entropy function may be interpreted as the integral of the inverse demand function, if the demand function is proportional to the negative exponential function:

$$x_{rr'} \approx e^{-\gamma t_{rr'}}.$$

The above formulation was considered somewhat earlier by Tomlin (1971) with constant link costs and strict capacity constraints. With increasing cost functions in the manner of Beckmann et al. (1956), Evan's formulation provided a more tractable and realistic model. Evans' algorithm for solving the above problem consists of linearizing only the first term of the objective function. Similar algorithms for the fixed demand network equilibrium problem were proposed independently by LeBlanc et al. (1975) and Nguyen (1974).

The entropy-constrained formulation

Instead of writing the entropy function in the objective function as in (4.10), suppose this term is written as a constraint as follows:

$$\text{Minimize} \sum_{l=1}^{L} \int_{0}^{f_l} c_l(y)\,dy \tag{4.11}$$
$$_{(x_{rr'}, h_p)}$$

$$\text{subject to:} \sum_{r=1}^{R} \sum_{r'=1}^{R'} x_{rr'}\ln x_{rr'} \geq S \tag{4.12}$$

and constraints (3.3), (3.4), (4.6), (4.7), where S is the assumed value of the entropy function for the system of places under consideration, and $1/\gamma$ is the Lagrange multiplier associated with constraint (4.12). The value of S determines the extent of the dispersion of place-to-place flows in the system, a low value corresponding to less dispersion than a high value. The properties of this solution for extreme values of S are examined again in Section 6.1.

It is also useful to consider the related entropy-maximizing formulation in which (4.12) is maximized subject to constraints (3.3), (3.4), (4.6), (4.7) and

$$\sum_{l=1}^{L} \int_{0}^{f_l} c_l(y)\,dy \leq C \tag{4.13}$$

where C is the observed or assumed value of the left-hand side for the network under consideration. Here, constraint (4.13) plays the same role as constraint (3.11) in the fixed cost model. The value of C could be based on observed link flows, eliminating the need for observed place-to-place flows to determine the value of S. This model can be used to estimate place-to-place flows corresponding to observed link flows and place origins and destinations O_r and $D_{r'}$. For a review of related literature, see Fisk and Boyce (1983).

4.3. Extensions to mode and location choice

The user-optimal problem described above is one example of a family of location and travel choice problems that can be derived by choosing various constraint sets and by generalizing the concept of the entropy function as a measure of dispersion. Such models have been explored by Florian and Nguyen (1978), Boyce (1980) and Boyce et al. (1983).

The extension to choice of mode can be readily made by defining mode-specific link cost functions and summing the objective function over this subscript, as follows:

$$\underset{(x_{rr'm}, h_p)}{\text{minimize}} \sum_{m=1}^{M} \sum_{l=1}^{L_m} \int_0^{f_l^m} c_l^m(y)\, dy \tag{4.14}$$

$$\text{subject to} \quad \sum_{p=1}^{P_{rr'm}} h_p = x_{rr'm}, \qquad r=1,\ldots, R;\ r'=1,\ldots, R'; \tag{4.15}$$

$$m=1,\ldots, M$$

$$\sum_{r'=1}^{R'} \sum_{m=1}^{M} x_{rr'm} = O_r, \qquad r=1,\ldots, R \tag{4.16}$$

$$\sum_{r=1}^{R} \sum_{m=1}^{M} x_{rr'm} = D_{r'}, \qquad r'=1,\ldots, R' \tag{4.17}$$

$$-\sum_{r=1}^{R} \sum_{r'=1}^{R'} \sum_{m=1}^{M} x_{rr'm} \ln x_{rr'm} \geq S \tag{4.18}$$

$$h_p \geq 0, \qquad p=1,\ldots, P_m,\ m=1,\ldots, M \tag{4.19}$$

where

$$f_l^m = \sum_{p=1}^{P_m} a_{lp} h_p, \qquad l=1,\ldots, L_m,\ m=1,\ldots, M \tag{4.20}$$

and M is the number of modes and L_m is the number of links in the network of mode m. Modal networks are regarded as independent. The resulting spatial interaction model is:

$$x_{rr'm} = A_r B_{r'} O_r D_{r'} \exp(-\gamma t_{rr'm}) \tag{4.21}$$

where

$$t_{rr'm} = \underset{p=1}{\overset{P_{rr'm}}{\min}} \left(\sum_{l=1}^{L_m} c_l^m(f_l^m) a_{lp} \right)$$

and A_r and $B_{r'}$, are determined so that constraints (4.16 and 4.17) are satisfied.

If the destination constraint is omitted, the above model may be interpreted as a destination and mode choice model. In this case, it is appropriate to define prior probabilities (see Section 3.2.3) of choosing destination r' which could be proportional to $D_{r'}$ now taken to be a measure of the activity at place r'. Redefining the entropy constraint as

$$-\sum_{r=1}^{R} \sum_{r'=1}^{R'} \sum_{m=1}^{M} x_{rr'm} \ln\left(\frac{x_{rr'm}}{D_{r'}/R'M} \right) \geq S \tag{4.22}$$

and omitting constraint (4.17) yields

$$x_{rr'm} = \frac{O_r D_{r'} \exp(-\gamma t_{rr'm})}{\sum_{r'=1}^{R'} D_{r'} \exp(-\gamma t_{rr'm})}. \tag{4.23}$$

Many other particular models can be specified including models with two or more hierarchical dispersion constraints yielding hierarchical logit functions [see Boyce et al. (1983)].

5. Modelling interregional commodity flows with fixed prices and service characteristics

5.1. The transportation model of linear programming

There is a very close relationship between the family of gravity models discussed in Section 3 and the transportation model of linear programming [Evans (1973b)]. The latter may be formulated as the following commodity flow problem:

$$\underset{x_{rr'}}{\text{Minimize}} \sum_{r=1}^{R} \sum_{r'=1}^{R'} t_{rr'} x_{rr'} \tag{5.1}$$

subject to

$$\sum_{r'=1}^{R'} x_{rr'} = x_{r*} \qquad r = 1, \ldots, R \tag{5.2}$$

$$\sum_{r=1}^{R} x_{rr'} = x_{*r'} \qquad r' = 1, \ldots, R' \tag{5.3}$$

$$x_{rr'} \geq 0, \qquad r = 1, \ldots, R; \ r' = 1, \ldots, R' \tag{5.4}$$

where x_{r*} is the total amount of the commodity produced in region r and $x_{*r'}$ is the total amount consumed in region r'. Note the identical form of (5.2) and (5.3) to the earlier additivity conditions (3.3) and (3.4), respectively. As in (3.13), the Lagrangian multipliers can be interpreted as shadow prices or location rents.

The solution to the above transportation problem is equivalent to the doubly-constrained gravity model in the limiting case where $\gamma \to \infty$ [Evans (1973b),

Bröcker (1980)].[12] In the gravity model, heterogeneity is formally represented by the parameter γ in the distance function. The transportation model of linear programming as an explicative approach depends heavily on the assumption of perfect competition [Peschel (1981)]. Because distance affects the economy as a monopolistic territorial influence, imperfect behaviour and agglomeration economies designed to overcome distance deterrence result in practice, thereby rendering the assumption of perfect competition to be unrealistic. Crosshauling is also excluded from the transportation model. This drawback has been emphasized by those regional economists who advocate gravity or entropy approaches to interregional flow modelling [Batten (1983)].

Tobler (1982) and others have suggested quadratic variants of the original linear transportation and transshipment problems. For example, in a version of the quadratic transshipment problem, the objective is to minimize

$$\sum_{r=1}^{R} \sum_{r'=1}^{R'} x_{rr'}^2 / b_{rr'} \tag{5.5}$$

subject to (5.2)–(5.4), where $b_{rr'}$ is the length of the border between regions r and r'. Then (5.5) corresponds to a situation in which the square of the flux across these borders is minimized. The solution to this problem is $x_{rr'} = b_{rr'}(\alpha_r + \beta_{r'})/2$, a simpler additive form which may have stronger appeal for certain contexts than the multiplicative form of traditional gravity models.

General functional forms have also been suggested which may subsume these two particular forms [see, for example, Ledent (1985)]. On other occasions, linear and quadratic terms have appeared additively in the objective function to represent different elements of total cost [see, for example, Brotchie et al. (1980)].

5.2. Multiregional gravity trade models

The gravity model was first discussed for use with regional input–output models by Isard and Bramhall (1960) as a possible means of estimating commodity shipments. Soon thereafter, Leontief and Strout (1963) presented a form of the gravity trade model which can be readily implemented for multiregional trade analysis. Compared with the more extensive data on transportation costs required for a linear programming transportation model, only a limited amount of data is needed to implement the Leontief–Strout gravity trade model (hereafter referred to as the LSG model). The basic data include: technical input–output coefficients, preferably for each region; final demands for each region; and trade

---

[12] Bröcker (1980) has shown that both approaches depend on the same behavioural assumptions, the gravity model having the special characteristic that although the individual does not necessarily choose the supplier with the lowest inclusive price, it is still assumed that the probability of the product being chosen increases with decreasing price.

coefficients which reflect the costs of shipping a commodity from one region to another. The summary presented here is taken mostly from Polenske (1970) and Batten (1983); a more complete description may be found in Leontief and Strout (1963).

The notation used in the equations includes:

$a_{ii'}^r$ the amount of commodity i required by industry i' located in region r to produce one unit of output of commodity i';

x_i^{r*} the total amount of commodity i produced in region r;

x_i^{*r} the total amount of commodity i consumed by all intermediate and final users in region r;

x_i^{**} the total amount of commodity i produced (consumed) in all regions;

y_i^r the total amount of commodity i consumed by final users in region r;

$x_i^{rr'}$ the amount of commodity i produced in region r which is shipped to region r';

$q_i^{rr'}$ a trade parameter which is a function of the cost of transferring commodity i from region r to region r' (where the transfer costs can reflect various factors which determine interregional trade, including transportation costs).

The superscripts in this section always refer to regions, while the subscripts always designate commodities.

The Leontief–Strout gravity trade model is fully specified by the following set of equations:

$$x_i^{*r} = \sum_{i'=1}^{I'} a_{ii'}^r x_i^{r*} + y_i^r \tag{5.6}$$

$$x_i^{r*} = \sum_{r'=1}^{R'} x_i^{rr'} \tag{5.7}$$

$$x_i^{*r} = \sum_{r'=1}^{R'} x_i^{r'r} \tag{5.8}$$

$$x^{rr'} = \frac{x_i^{r*} x_i^{*r'}}{x_i^{**}} q_i^{rr'}. \tag{5.9}$$

The nonlinear interregional equation (5.9) permits crosshauling to occur between any two regions, which is a useful feature since data describing commodity shipments are rarely assembled for strictly homogeneous products. The multi-regional system is completed by substituting (5.9) into (5.7) and (5.8). Assuming that the final demands, the technical coefficients and the trade parameters are known, a simplified solution to the model can be obtained to determine x_i^{r*}, $x_i^{*r'}$ and x_i^{**}. One can then obtain estimates of each interregional shipment, $x_i^{rr'}$, from (5.9).

Theil (1967) formulated a similar gravity model for interregional shipments using (5.9) and known values of x_i^{r*} and $x_i^{*r'}$. He postulated that the trade parameter was a function of historical patterns, namely

$$q_i^{rr'} = \frac{\hat{x}_i^{rr'} \hat{x}_i^{**}}{\hat{x}_i^{r*} \hat{x}_i^{*r'}} \tag{5.10}$$

where the symbol $\wedge$ refers to known values from the recent past. Theil minimized a measure of information inaccuracy:

$$\sum_{r=1}^{R} \sum_{r'=1}^{R'} \bar{x}_i^{rr'} \ln\left(x_i^{rr'}/\bar{x}_i^{rr'}\right) \tag{5.11}$$

to obtain commodity flow estimates, $\bar{x}_i^{rr'}$, which satisfied (5.7) and (5.8). His approach corresponds to the inverse of the standard information minimization procedure (see Section 3.2.3).

Wilson (1970) later recognized the similarity of these two models and chose to integrate them using entropy-maximizing methods. He replaced the trade parameter equation (5.9) with the transportation cost constraint

$$\sum_{r=1}^{R} \sum_{r'=1}^{R'} t_i^{rr'} x_i^{rr'} = T_i, \qquad i = 1, \ldots, I \tag{5.12}$$

where $t_i^{rr'}$ is the unit cost of delivering commodity i from region r to region r' and T_i is the total freight bill for commodity i. By maximizing entropy S defined as

$$S = -\sum_{i=1}^{I} \sum_{r=1}^{R} \sum_{r'=1}^{R'} x_i^{rr'} \ln x_i^{rr'} \tag{5.13}$$

subject to (5.6), (5.12) and all possible joint assignments of (5.7) and (5.8), he formulated four model versions: (i) unconstrained, (ii) production-constrained, (iii) attraction-constrained, and (iv) doubly-constrained.

The conceptual elegance of Wilson's derivation partly obscures some methodological weaknesses. In reality, it is more likely that historical values of x_i^{r*} and even $x_i^{*r'}$ can be ascertained for each region than reliable input–output coefficients $a_{ii'}^{r}$. Consequently, there have been significant attempts during the last three decades to compile nonsurvey and semisurvey regional tables (see Chapter 8 in this Handbook).

A simple bi-regional input–output model can be derived given the availability of one accurate regional input–output table and another for the same time period which describes the remaining aggregate (e.g. an "almost" national table). While this type of model makes small demands for data, it inevitably understates the true nature of interregional trade and the extent of crosshauling, feedbacks and spillovers. In a genuine interregional input–output system, the basic requirement is that each significant pair of industries trading between different locations should be recognized, leading normally to consideration of a larger number of regions [Batten (1982)]. In the following section, we shall summarize progress with interregional input–output specifications of commodity flows and explore unifying links with the aid of information theory.

5.3. Interregional input – output models

As was mentioned near the outset of Chapter 8, the oldest interregional input–output formulation is the model proposed by Isard (1951). It is a straightforward extension of the classic Leontief national model under the assumption that not only the sectoral but also the geographical origin of each delivery can be specified. Analytically, this implies the following set of balance equations between production in each sector of each region and total demand:

$$x_i^r = \sum_{r'} \sum_{i'} a_{ii'}^{rr'} x_{i'}^{r'} + \sum_{r'} y_i^{rr'} \tag{5.14}$$

where $a_{ii'}^{rr'}$ is the input of commodities produced by sector i in region r to the production of sector i' in region r', and $y_i^{rr'}$ is the final demand in region r' satisfied by the production of sector i in region r.

The assumption of stability in the pattern of interindustry shipments between production units located in different places is of course much stronger than the classical one of stability only of technical coefficients. For example, each interregional input coefficient, $a_{ii'}^{rr'}$, may be split into a regional technical coefficient, $a_{ii'}^{r'}$, and an interregional trade coefficient, $t_{ii'}^{rr'}$, as follows:

$$x_i^r = \sum_{r'} \sum_{i'} a_{ii'}^{r'} t_{ii'}^{rr'} x_{i'}^{r'} + \sum_{r'} y_i^{rr'}. \tag{5.15}$$

This makes it clear that the stability of the technical coefficient does not necessarily imply stability of the trade coefficient. In reality, however, the delivery pattern between a system of regions depends not only on trade preferences and technical structure, but also on conditions of excess demand or supply (one for each commodity) inside each region [see Batten (1983, ch. 5)].

The above model has been called "ideal" by Riefler (1973) because the trade pattern is perfectly specified at both origin and destination by the set of trade coefficients. However, the implementation of Isard's model has been severely restricted, even with survey or nonsurvey-based regional tables at hand. Only recently has the use of information theory and related statistical techniques made its general implementation more feasible.

The above problem has not impeded empirical applications of interregional input–output analysis because, as Riefler (1973) and Miernyk (1973) have noted, subsequent applications have circumvented the basic difficulty of Isard's model in different ways.[13] It should be noted, however, that these simplifications are not only attempts to overcome a statistical difficulty, but are also expressions of different (theoretical) assumptions concerning interregional trade. In Figure 5.1, we employ a compact notation and graphical representations to compare these different assumptions pertaining to the trade coefficients $\{t_{ii'}^{rr'}\}$ and to establish a hierarchical relationship between these models.

The key to the successful calibration of any interregional model is the extent to which information on the trading relationships and interindustry flows *between* regions is available, together with the accuracy and consistency of these inter-regional data. More recent approaches to interregional trade modelling attempt to combine survey and nonsurvey methods in order to overcome the limited availability of pertinent trade information.

In Section 3, we introduced the principle of minimum information gain. This methodological principle may be used for the estimation of interregional input–output systems when the availability of specific information on the inter-regional trade flows is limited [see Snickars (1979), Batten (1983)]. However, in addition to statistical data in the form of accounting constraints, the inherent flexibility of this approach also allows a broad range of behavioural constraints to be considered, and a diverse collection of theoretically different interregional models to be tested and compared [see Batten and Martellato (1985)]. In this respect, the principle may be regarded as a modern methodological counterpart to the family of classical interregional models.

The basic equation system normally associated with this statistical methodology yields a pattern of interregional trade which is consistent with Isard's original model. However, by simply expressing additional or alternative theoretically-based assumptions in the form of different prior flow probabilities or linear constraints, one can actually test the complete family of classical interregional models. In summary, the versatility of this modern methodology enables a variety of survey information and/or theoretical hypotheses which can be expressed as linear constraint equations or inequations to be tested, combined or contrasted.[14]

---

[13] There have been at least four distinct approaches to an empirically workable simplification of the ideal interregional model. These have been pioneered by Leontief (1953). Chenery et al. (1953), Moses (1955), Leontief and Strout (1963), and Riefler and Tiebout (1970). Each of these approaches corresponds to an application of either (i) the theory of demand distinguished by place of production [Armington (1969)], or (ii) trade pool theory.

[14] A computer program known as INTEREG has been developed in order to put the principle of information gain into practice in an interregional context. INTEREG has been tested on some multiregional systems in Australia, and has subsequently been adopted in Sweden, Italy and Canada for ongoing studies of interregional trade. Additional information on the INTEREG package is available from the first author.

Modeller	Model in compact form	Conditions upon T	Structure of T (3-sector example)
Isard	$x = (I - B)^{-1} Tf$	$t_{ii'}^{rr'} \geq 0$	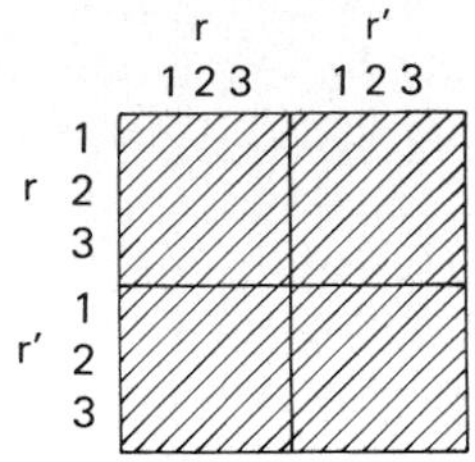
Riefler Tiebout	$x = (I - B)^{-1} Tf$ for intraregional flows $x = (I - TA)^{-1} Tf$ for interregional flows	$t_{ii'}^{rr'} \geq 0$ $t_{ii'}^{rr'} = t_i^{rr'}$ when $i \neq i'$ and $r \neq r'$	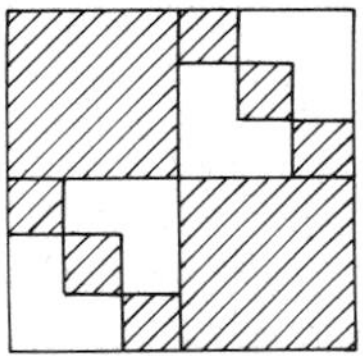
Chenery Moses	$x = (I - TA)^{-1} Tf$	$t_{ii'}^{rr'} \geq 0$ $t_{ii'}^{rr'} = t_i^{r'}$ when $i \neq i'$	
Leontief	$x = (I - VPA)^{-1} Tf$	$t_{ii'}^{rr'} \geq 0$ $t_{ii'}^{rr'} = t_i^{r'}$ when $i \neq i'$ or $r \neq r'$	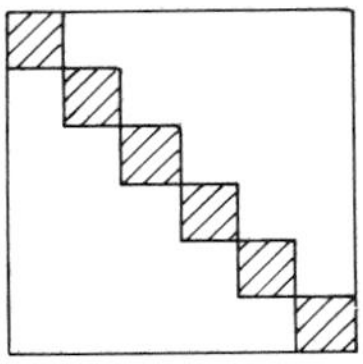
Leontief Strout	$x = (I - C^{-1} DA)^{-1} C^{-1} Df$		

Notes: The compact notation is as follows:

     B is the matrix of interregional input–output coefficients;
     T is the matrix of trade share coefficients;
     f is the vector of final regional demands;
     A is the matrix of regional technical coefficients;
     V is the share vector denoting proportions of total production from each region;
     P is the pooling strategy of regional demand shares;
     C is the share of regional production not pooled;
     D is the share of total regional demand not imported from the pool.

In general, if I is the number of sectors and R the number of regions, then the maximum number of different entries assumed in the T matrix is as follows:

     Isard model   : $I^2 R^2$
     Riefler–Tiebout model   : $IR(I + R - 1)$
     Chenery–Moses model   : IR^2
     Leontief pool models   : IR

Figure 5.1. A hierarchy of classical interregional input–output models.

6. Modelling interregional commodity flows with flow-dependent transportation costs

6.1. A generalized transportation model

The classical transportation model of linear programming may be readily generalized to include route flows and flow-dependent costs by replacing objective function (5.1) with an equivalent function defined on links:

$$\underset{(x_{rr'}, h_p)}{\text{Minimize}} \sum_{l=1}^{L} c_l(f_l) \cdot f_l \tag{6.1}$$

subject to: production and consumption constraints (5.2) and (5.3), and

$$\sum_{p=1}^{Prr'} h_p = x_{rr'}, \qquad r = 1,\ldots, R; \; r' = 1,\ldots, R' \tag{6.2}$$

$$h_p \geq 0, \qquad p = 1,\ldots, P \tag{6.3}$$

where

$$f_l = \sum_{p=1}^{P} h_p a_{lp}, \qquad l = 1,\ldots, L. \tag{6.4}$$

The optimality conditions of this formulation, however, are fundamentally different from the network equilibrium models described in Section 4.

$$h_p \left(\sum_{l=1}^{L} (c_l(f_l) + f_l \cdot \partial c_l(f_l)/\partial f_l) a_{lp} - v_{rr'} \right) = 0, \quad p = 1,\ldots, P_{rr'} \tag{6.5}$$

$$x_{rr'}(v_{rr'} - \alpha_r + \beta_{r'}) = 0, \quad r = 1,\ldots, R; \; r' = 1,\ldots, R' \tag{6.6}$$

where $v_{rr'}$ is the Lagrange multiplier associated with constraint (6.2) and α_r and $\beta_{r'}$ are the Lagrange multipliers of constraints (5.2) and (5.3).

Condition (6.5) states that for all $h_p > 0$, $p = 1,\ldots, P_{rr'}$ the *marginal* cost of travel on route p equals $v_{rr'}$, the *system-optimal* transportation cost from place r

to r', since the marginal cost of transportation on link l is by definition,

$$m_l(f_l) = \frac{\partial(c_l(f_l) \cdot f_l)}{\partial f_l} = c_l(f_l) + f_l \cdot \frac{\partial c_l(f_l)}{\partial f_l}.$$

Condition (6.6) states that if $x_{rr'} > 0$, then $\alpha_r - \beta_{r'} = v_{rr'}$; if $x_{rr'} = 0$, then $\alpha_r - \beta_{r'}$ $\leq v_{rr'}$. Thus, the difference in shadow prices (location rents) at r and r' just equals the marginal cost of transportation if the place-to-place flows are postive, and is less than or equal to the marginal cost if the flow is zero. The signs of α_r and $\beta_{r'}$ can be derived by formulating constraints (5.2) and (5.3) as inequalities requiring that no more than x_{r*} is shipped and no less than $x_{*r'}$ is received.

Unlike model (5.1–5.3), model (6.1–6.4, 5.2, 5.3) is not the limiting form of the doubly-constrained gravity model with $1/\gamma \to 0$ since the transportation costs are marginal costs, not unit costs [Evans (1973b)]. To obtain the form analogous to the spatial interaction model, (6.1) must be replaced by

$$\sum_{l=1}^{L} \int_0^{f_l} c_l(y) \, dy \tag{6.7}$$

resulting in condition (6.5) changing to

$$h_p \left(\sum_{l=1}^{L} c_l(f_l) a_{lp} - u_{rr'} \right) = 0, \qquad p = 1, \ldots, p_{rr'}.$$

Minimizing (6.7) subject to (6.2)–(6.4), (5.2), (5.3) and a dispersion constraint defined on the entropy function (4.12) yields the gravity model. The interpretation of the limiting form of this model for $1/\gamma = 0$ is that place-to-place flows follow the minimum *unit cost* routes rather than the minimum *marginal cost* routes. This solution corresponds to a behavioural assumption that the transportation costs are minimized for each pair of places, rather than for the entire system of places, and hence is termed a *user-optimal* solution.

6.2. Multiregional commodity flow models

The interregional commodity flow model described in Section 5.2 can be generalized to the case of flow-dependent costs in the same manner as the models of Section 4. In this case, however, it is necessary to reconsider whether the commodity transportation costs can indeed be represented by cost functions that increase with flow, and thus that economies of scale are not present in the freight transportation system. Such an assumption does not seem tenable for truckload or trainload shipments over a congested transportation system. More complex formulations are required if the unit shipment size is less than one vehicle load.

The following formulation applies to a multimodal, multicommodity transportation system operating under congestion:

$$\text{Minimize} \sum_{(x_{rr'm}, h_p)}^{M} \sum_{m=1}^{L_m} \int_0^{f_l^m} c_l^m(y)\,dy \tag{6.8}$$

$$\text{subject to: } \sum_{p=1}^{P_i^{rr'm}} h_p = x_i^{rr'm}, \qquad r=1,\ldots,R;\ r'=1,\ldots,R'; \tag{6.9}$$

$$m=1,\ldots,M;\ i=1,\ldots,I$$

$$\sum_{r'=1}^{R'} \sum_{m=1}^{M} x_i^{r'rm} = \sum_{i'=1}^{I} a_{ii'}^r \sum_{i'=1}^{R'} \sum_{m=1}^{M} x_{ii'}^{rr'm} + y_i^r, \qquad i=1,\ldots,I;\ r=1,\ldots,R \tag{6.10}$$

$$-\sum_{r=1}^{R} \sum_{r'=1}^{R'} \sum_{m=1}^{M} x_i^{rr'm} \ln x_i^{rr'm} \geq S_i, \qquad i=1,\ldots,I \tag{6.11}$$

$$h_p \geq 0, \qquad p=1,\ldots,P \tag{6.12}$$

$$x_i^{rr'm} > 0, \qquad r=1,\ldots,R;\ r'=1,\ldots,R';\ m=1,\ldots,M;\ i=1,\ldots,I \tag{6.13}$$

where

$$f_l^m = \sum_{i=1}^{I} \sum_{p=1}^{P_i^m} h_p a_{lp} \qquad l=1,\ldots,L_m;\ m=1,\ldots,M. \tag{6.14}$$

The optimality conditions for this model are:

$$h_p \left(\sum_{l=1}^{L_m} c_l^m(f_l^m) a_{lp} - u_i^{rr'm} \right) = 0, \qquad p=1,\ldots,P_i^{rr'm} \tag{6.15}$$

$$x_i^{rr'm} \left\{ u_i^{rr'm} + \frac{1}{\gamma_i} \left(\ln x_i^{rr'm} + 1 \right) + \sum_{i'=1}^{I} \alpha_{i'}^r a_{i'i}^r - \alpha_i^{r'} \right\} = 0, \tag{6.16}$$

$$r=1,\ldots,R;\ r'=1,\ldots,R';$$
$$m=1,\ldots,M;\ i=1,\ldots,I.$$

Condition (6.15) states that the route costs for all used routes are equal to $u_i^{rr'm}$ and no unused route has a lower cost. Condition (6.16) may be restated for

$x_i^{rr'm} > 0$ as

$$x_i^{rr'm} = \exp\left\{ \gamma_i \left(\alpha_i^{r'} - \sum_{i'=1}^{I} \alpha_{i'}^r a_{i'i}^r - u_i^{rr'm} - 1 \right) \right\}$$

where (γ_i) are the reciprocals of the Lagrange multipliers associated with the entropy constraints and (α_r^i) are the Lagrange multipliers associated with the materials balance constraints (6.10) defined by the input–output system. Notice that in this model there are no origin and destination constraints. These constraints could also be added, however, to obtain the four versions of Wilson's (1970) model described in Section 5.2.

The above model synthesizes elements of network equilibrium theory with input–output and spatial interaction theory. Because freight transportation services are produced by one or more firms, the cost functions defined in objective function (6.8) are a rather unrealistic representation of the commodity transportation system. An alternative formulation proposed by Friesz et al. (1985) considers carriers and shippers of commodities as interacting agents by making use of the system-optimal and user-optimal principles.

7. Solution procedures

The principal models presented in this chapter can be formulated as linear or nonlinear programming problems. These formulations in turn suggest solution procedures of a general or specialized nature. Standard mathematical programming methods given in operations research textbooks may be consulted for solving general linear programs or the transportation model of linear programming [see, for example, Wagner (1975)].

Special purpose algorithms have been devised to solve most of the nonlinear optimization problems formulated earlier. Spatial interaction models of the maximum entropy type are generally solved iteratively using linear approximation methods. One of the most effective algorithms devised for large-scale entropy problems is the iterative technique pioneered by Eriksson (1980), which transforms the original formulation into a system of nonlinear equations that can be solved using Newton's linear approximation method. In each step of Newton's method, the resulting linear system is solved using a scaled version of the conjugate gradients method. Eriksson's algorithm is computationally efficient and has been modified to handle inequality constraints [Eriksson (1981)]. Problems consisting of 40,000 elements and 850 constraints have been solved within 90 seconds on a DEC-10 computer.

A package has been developed to compute least-biased estimates of interregional input–output coefficients under conditions of limited information [see

Batten (1983, Appendix E)]. This package contains Eriksson's algorithm and has recently been tested on some simple interregional systems in Australia, Italy and Sweden. Further testing on large-scale problems will be needed before the usefulness of this package can be properly evaluated.

Special purpose algorithms have also been devised to solve the nonlinear optimization formulation of the network equilibrium problem. The most effective algorithm devised to date appears to be the partial linearization procedure of Evans (1976) which has been tested by Frank (1978) and LeBlanc and Farhangian (1981). A statement of the algorithm and a discussion of methods for choosing Lagrange multipliers may be found in Boyce et al. (1983).

Models of the type described in Section 4 have been solved for urban and regional systems with over 300 zones and 2500 links by Chon (1982); see also Boyce (1984). Fixed demand route choice problems are now solved in transportation planning practice using a simplified version of Evans' algorithm [cf. LeBlanc et al. (1975)] for networks with hundreds of zones and tens of thousands of links. The multicommodity flow model described in Section 6, however, has not been solved. A single commodity flow model for the United States formulated as a network equilibrium problem has been solved by Friesz et al. (1981).

8. New developments and future prospects

In reflecting on the achievements of transportation research over ten years ago, Walter Isard (1975) pointed to a number of seminal advances in gravity modelling and transportation analysis. He emphasized the importance of synthesizing economic thinking with geographical approaches and planning techniques. This unification has been favourably realized in the case of utility-maximizing and entropy-maximizing spatial interaction models and, to a lesser extent, in the case of transportation models which have been fused with input–output models for describing and projecting economic structure.

He also identified two particular shortcomings at that time. The first was a concern that transportation should never be divorced from the problems of location, whether industrial, commercial or residential. This was a plea for retaining an integrated or comprehensive type of analytical system. Our limited success in this regard can be assessed by perusing the contents of Chapters 2, 3 and 4 of this Handbook as well as the discussion in this chapter.

But Isard's chief concern was that we had failed to embed our various subsystems in a proper *dynamic* framework:

> Witness the drastic changes in the last 20 years. Yet our research sorely
> neglects this dynamic aspect of transport system development – its relation

to changing hierarchical organization of society which in turn imparts to the world transportation subsystems, and the transportation subsystem of various parts of the world, an hierarchical structure. [Isard (1975, p. 135)]

In the few pages left to us in this chapter, we shall focus on some of these issues as we look at a small sample of new research efforts and cross-disciplinary prospects.

8.1.   *Integration of location, production and interaction behaviour*

Recent attempts to unify a broad class of location–interaction and production–interaction models have identified various structural similarities between different classes of spatial behaviour. The conceptual foundation for location–production–interaction (LPI) modelling, laid by Williams and Wilson (1980) and Batten and Roy (1982), can be generalized by considering all three phenomena in a simultaneous formulation. For example, we can relate Ohlin's (1933) unified theory of location and trade to Wilson's (1970) input–output version of the production–interaction model. The following summary of progress towards this type of unifying effort is taken from Batten (1984a).

In LPI modelling, we are concerned jointly with the following three phenomena:
(1) location of physical capital stock;
(2) productive activities occurring within this stock; and
(3) flows generated by these activities.
Typical examples of the first subproblem include the location of residential housing, business firms, shopping centres, public facilities or service centres. The activities undertaken within these subsystems produce goods, services and employees, which in turn generate flows of commodities, people and money.

The spatial system of interest is defined by a set of origin and destination regions within which various productive activities occur and between which interaction takes place. Within each origin region r, the activities occurring at facility i are responsible for the production (or reproduction) of factor k. Inside each destination region s, factor k is used (or may just be serviced) by facility j. In such a model, the elementary event is the movement of any mobile factor of production k from facility i in region r to facility j in region s; let p_{ijk}^{rs} be the probability of such an event. This interaction can be regarded as a measure of the covariation between random variables defining each set of regional activities, and as such it is fully described by the probability distribution $\{ p_{ijk}^{rs} \}$.

Each of the steps in the general procedure can be summarized diagrammatically (see Figure 8.1). By distinguishing the model's purpose (forecasting or theoretical model), the first stage of problem selection also quantifies our a priori

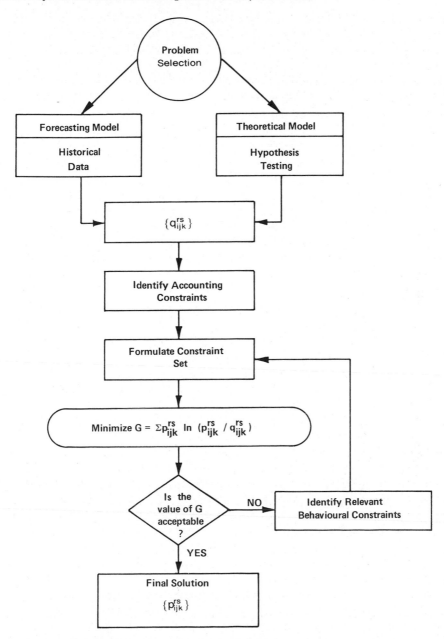

Figure 8.1. Procedural sequence for location–production–interaction modelling.

knowledge concerning the model's parameters $\{q_{ijk}^{rs}\}$. The full matrix of inter-regional movements might be related, for example, to the rectangular structure of the economy in terms of commodities and industries; also to regional imbalances between production and demand. In this instance, we have resorted once again to the use of the minimum information principle (see Section 3.2.3). Should such a model fail to achieve a satisfactory level of information content, it may be deemed statistically unacceptable.

It is interesting to note that other authors have recently identified certain structural similarities and equivalences between multiactivity location models (such as the Lowry model) and spatial input–output models [see, for example, Macgill (1978) or Macgill and Wilson (1979)]. There are clearly a number of recognizable circumstances under which seemingly different spatial phenomena may be analysed using a representative methodology. To this extent, the example discussed here simply demonstrates the potential for linking industrial location theory with production analysis and spatial interaction models.

8.2. Integration of transportation and economic activity in models of international commodity trade

In this section, we examine some recent modelling efforts involving the spatial analysis of international trade flows. The potential contribution which could be made by regional scientists to complement the monetary approaches of classical trade theorists in this field is quite substantial.

Since his own critical remarks in 1975, Isard has pioneered attempts to unify transportation behaviour and economic activity more extensively within a multi-regional modelling context; see Isard and Anselin (1982). More recently, he has discussed the preliminary construction of an integrated multinational model; see Isard and Smith (1983). Unfortunately, the state of the art in global modelling is such that we cannot yet go as far at the multinational level as we can within a nation on a multiregional basis (see Chapter 11 of this Handbook). The linking of models at an international level – such as Isard's proposal to bring together an econometric model of the LINK type [Klein (1977)], a global input–output model of the Leontief et al. (1977) type, a world programming model of the Novosibirsk type [Granberg and Rubinshtein (1979)], and an industrial location–trade model [Isard and Anselin (1982)] – is an interesting but challenging task. To complement this effort, a number of less ambitious projects are underway.

Initial attempts by Boyce and Hewings (1980) to include transportation behaviour, interregional commodity flows and input–output analysis within a single composite formulation have stimulated further research into the integration of international commodity flows and the world transportation system [e.g. Griffin et al. (1983)]. The latter model represents transportation shippers and carriers as decision-making agents optimizing their own system, with international production and demand specified in the Leontief–Strout gravity input–output form (see Section 5.2). Tariffs, exchange rates and other trade barriers are included to depict trade between countries in a more realistic manner.

Link-specific considerations (i.e. trade barriers and trade agreements) have also motivated other new research. It is well known that many bilateral patterns of international commodity trade are relatively stable over time (see Section 3.2.3). It appears that the impact of distance may be of lesser importance compared to the influence of cultural and linguistic affinity of spatial association and political relationship. This realization has prompted recent attempts to develop a modelling framework which is capable of combining price-formation mechanisms with factors which contribute to trade inertia and barriers to change [see Batten (1984b), Batten and Johansson (1985)].

In some respects, this ambition is closely related to the earlier work of Takayama and Judge (1971), which combines various spatial frictions and trade barriers within a neoclassical price equilibrium framework (see Chapter 5 of this Handbook). In other respects, the two differ since the information-theoretical approach represents a probabilistic framework which generates solutions that are not perfectly competitive equilibria. Whereas the Takayama–Judge approach adheres to the Marshallian tradition, the approach outlined in Batten and Johansson (1985) is Walrasian in nature.

8.3. *Product cycles and time–space hierarchies of spatial interaction*

When we turn to the crucial question of embedding various theories of spatial interaction within a dynamic framework, the cupboard is almost bare. Two notable exceptions are the work of Harris and Wilson (1978) and Bennett et al. (1985). Nevertheless, the building blocks are emerging slowly (see Chapters 5 and 6 of this Handbook). In this final section, we shall briefly summarize one promising line of inquiry: the theory of product cycles. Much of the following is taken from Andersson and Johansson (1984).

Two different paradigms can be helpful in understanding the development of interregional and international trade patterns, the location and relocation of production centres, and corresponding differences in economic specialization. These two approaches are (i) the theory of comparative advantages, and (ii) the theory of product cycles. The former is traditionally presented in the guise of comparative statics while the latter concentrates on the dynamic processes of change.

The theory of comparative advantages asserts that each region (or nation) tends to specialize in the production and export of those commodities in which its cost level is seen as most competitive relative to other regions. A special version of this theory is the factor proportions theory [Ohlin (1933)], which predicts specialization in the production of goods which require factors of production that are relatively abundant inside the region. In this case the relevant criterion is the comparative position of the region. It is now evident that the relevance of the factor proportions explanation of specialization and trade depends crucially on the types of input factors considered in the analysis.

To analyse changes in productive activities over time, a subdivision of factors of production into the classic trio of land, labour and capital is inadequate. Leontief's (1953) pioneering work made it clear that the concept of capital must be broadened to include education and other characteristics of the labour force in order to shed light on changes to the spatial division of labour. This means that knowledge and its expansion through research and development are fundamental factors in determining future patterns of location and market specialization.

The consequences of knowledge development on patterns of location, interaction and specialization may be discussed qualitatively in the medium term using the theory of product cycles. This theory can be understood most fruitfully in a spatial context, where it prescribes the location of birthplaces for new products or processes and the successive relocation of existing production [Vernon (1966)]. Vernon's basic position can be explained by reference to Figure 8.2. Each new product undergoes an initial development cycle during which it enters the most advanced regions of the world after a period of research, development and testing. The product is then produced primarily in the region with a comparative advantage in terms of high R & D capability and access to employment categories with the required profile of competence (leader).

The product is exported from this region to other regions (followers). When the product has matured in terms of process development (design of production techniques) and market penetration, the region where it was originally introduced loses its comparative advantage and production decentralizes.

This development cycle portrays a time–space hierarchy of comparative advantages for a give technological solution. What is an advantage in an initial phase later becomes a disadvantage, while initially less favourable locations become more competitive as alternatives for production once the product matures. The ramifications of this leader–follower behaviour for the analysis of interregional and international trade patterns are quite profound. We are just beginning to see these important elements of an integrated dynamic theory of location, relocation and spatial interaction being addressed in a modelling context.

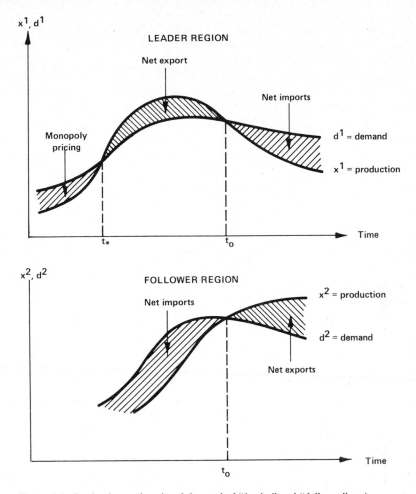

Figure 8.2. Production and notional demand of "leader" and "follower" regions.

References

Alonso, W. (1978) 'A theory of movement' in: N. M. Hansen, ed., *Human settlement systems*. Cambridge, Mass: Ballinger, 195–212.

Anas, A. (1981) 'The estimation of multinomial logit models of joint location and mode choice from aggregated data', *Journal of Regional Science*, 21:223–242.

Anas, A. (1983) 'Discrete choice theory, information theory and the multinomial logit and gravity models', *Transportation Research*, 17B:13–23.

Anderson, T. R. (1955) 'Intermetropolitan migration: a comparison of the hypotheses of Zipf and Stouffer', *American Sociological Review*, 20:287–291.

Andersson, Å. E. and B. Johansson (1984) 'Industrial dynamics, product cycles and employment structure', Working Paper WP-84-09, International Institute for Applied Systems Analysis Laxenburg.

Andersson, Å. E. and B. Marksjö (1972) 'General equilibrium models for allocation in space under interdependency and increasing returns to scale', *Regional and Urban Economics*, 2:133–158.

Anderstig, C. (1982) *Actual and predicted trade flows of forest products*. Umeå: Department of Economics, University of Umeå.

Armington, P. S. (1969), 'A theory of demand for products distinguished by place of production', *International Monetary Fund, Staff Papers*, 16:159–176.

Batten, D. F. (1982) 'The interregional linkages between national and regional input–output models', *International Regional Science Review*, 7:53–67.

Batten, D. F. (1983) *Spatial analysis of interacting economies*. Boston: Kluwer–Nijhoff.

Batten, D. F. (1984a) 'A unifying framework for location–production–interaction modelling', *Geoforum*, 15:231–242.

Batten, D. F. (1984b) 'Modelling interregional and international trade using information theory', *Chiikigaku-Kenkyu* (Japanese Papers in Regional Science), 13:171–182.

Batten, D. F. and B. Johansson (1985) 'Price adjustments and multiregional rigidities in the analysis of world trade', *Papers, Regional Science Association*, 56:145–166.

Batten, D. F. and D. Martellato (1985) 'Classical versus modern approaches to interregional input–output analysis', *The Annals of Regional Science*, 19: 1–16.

Batten, D. F. and J. R. Roy (1982) 'Entropy and economic modelling', *Environment and Planning*, A14:1047–1061.

Batty M. (1978) 'Reilly's challenge: new laws of retail gravitation which define systems of central places', *Environment and Planning*, A10:185–219.

Beckmann, M. (1974) 'Entropy, gravity and utility in transportation modelling', in: G. Menges, ed., *Information, Inference and Decision*. Dordrecht, Holland: D. Reidel, 155–163.

Beckmann, M., C. B. McGuire, and C. B. Winsten (1956) *Studies in the economics of transportation*. New Haven: Yale University Press.

Bennett, J. R., R. P. Haining and A. G. Wilson (1985) 'Spatial structure, spatial interaction, and their integration: a review of alternative models', *Environment and Planning*, A17:625–645.

Boltzmann, L. (1872) 'Weitere Studien über das Warmgleichgewicht unter Gasmolekulen', *K. Akad. (Wien) Sitzb., II. Abt.*, 66:275.

Boyce, D. E. (1980) 'A framework for constructing network equilibrium models of urban location', *Transportation Science*, 14:77–96.

Boyce, D. E. (1984) 'Network models in transportation/land use planning', in: M. Florian, ed., *Transportation planning models*. Amsterdam: North-Holland, 221–243.

Boyce, D. E., K. S. Chon, Y. J. Lee, K. T. Lin and L. J. LeBlanc (1983) 'Implementation and computational issues for combined models of location, destination, mode and route choice', *Environment and Planning*, A15:1219–1230.

Boyce, D. E. and G. J. D. Hewings (1980) 'Interregional commodity-flow, input–output and transportation modelling: an entropy formulation', Paper presented at the First World Regional Science Congress, Cambridge, Massachusetts.

Bröcker, J. (1980) 'An application of economic interaction models to the analysis of spatial effects of economic integration', *Environment and Planning*, A12:321–338.

Brotchie, J. F., J. W. Dickey and R. Sharpe (1980) *TOPAZ: general planning technique and its applications at the regional, urban and facility planning levels*. Berlin: Springer-Verlag.

Bruynooghe, M. (1969) 'Une modèle intégré de distribution et d'affectation du trafic sur un réseau', Institut de Recherches sur des Transports, Département de Recherche Opérationnelle et Informatique, Paris.

Carey, H. P. (1858–1859) *Principles of social science*. Philadelphia: Lippincott.

Carrothers, G. A. P. (1956) 'An historical review of the gravity and potential concepts of human interaction', *Journal of the American Institute of Planners*, 22:94–102.

Chenery, H., P. G. Clarke and V. Cao Pinna (1953) *The structure and growth of the Italian economy*. Rome: US Mutual Security Agency.

Chon, K. S. (1982) 'Testing of combined urban location and travel choice models', Ph.D. dissertation, University of Illinois, Urbana.

Choukroun, J. M. (1975) 'A general framework for the development of gravity-type distribution models', *Regional Science and Urban Economics*, 5:177–202.

Coelho, J. D. and A. G. Wilson (1976) 'The optimum location and size of shopping centres', *Regional Studies*, 10:413–421.

Cohen, M. H. (1959) 'The relative distribution of households and places of work: a discussion of the paper by J. G. Wardrop', in: R. Herman, ed., *Theory of traffic flow*. Amsterdam: Elsevier.

Converse, P. D. (1949) 'New laws of retail gravitation', *Journal of Marketing*, 14:379–384.

Dacey, M. P. and A. Norcliffe (1977) 'A flexible doubly-constrained trip distribution model', *Transportation Research*, 11:203–204.

Dafermos, S. C. and F. T. Sparrow (1969) 'The traffic assignment problem for a general network', *Journal of Research of the National Bureau of Standards*, 72B:91–118.

Dodd, S. C. (1950) 'The interactance hypothesis: a gravity model fitting physical masses and human groups', *American Sociological Review*, 15:245–256.

Domencich, T. and D. McFadden (1975) *Urban travel demand: a behavioural analysis*. Amsterdam: North-Holland.

Eriksson, J. (1980) 'A note on the solution of large sparse maximum entropy problems with linear equality constraints', *Mathematical Programming*, 18:146–154.

Eriksson, J. (1981) 'Algorithms for entropy and mathematical programming', Ph.D. dissertation, Department of Mathematics, University of Linköping, Linköping.

Erlander, S. (1977) 'Accessibility, entropy and the distribution and assignment of traffic', *Transportation Research*, 11:149–153.

Erlander, S. (1980) *Optimal spatial interaction and the gravity model*. Berlin: Springer-Verlag.

Evans, A. W. (1971) 'The calibration of trip distribution models with exponential or similar cost functions', *Transportation Research*, 5:15–38.

Evans, S. P. (1973a) 'Some applications of mathematical optimization theory in transport planning', Ph.D. thesis, University of London, London.

Evans, S. P. (1973b) 'A relationship between the gravity model for trip distribution and the transportation problem in linear programming', *Transportation Research*, 7:39–61.

Evans, S. P. (1976) 'Derivation and analysis of some models for combining trip distribution and assignment', *Transportation Research*, 10:37–57.

Fast, J. D. (1970) *Entropy*. London: MacMillan.

Fetter, F. A. (1924) 'The economic law of market areas', *Quarterly Journal of Economics*, 28:520–529.

Fisk, C. (1985) 'Entropy and information theory: are we missing something?', *Environment and Planning*, A17:679–687.

Fisk, C. S. and D. E. Boyce (1983) 'A note on trip matrix estimation from link traffic count data', *Transportation Research*, 17B:245–250.

Fisk, C. S. and G. R. Brown (1975) 'A note on the entropy formulation of distribution models', *Operational Research Quarterly*, 9:143–148.

Florian, M. and S. Nguyen (1978) 'A combined trip distribution, modal split and trip assignment model', *Transportation Research*, 12:241–246.

Fotheringham, A. S. (1983) 'A new set of spatial-interaction models: the theory of competing destinations', *Environment and Planning*, A15:15–36.

Frank, C. (1978) 'A study of alternative approaches to combined trip distribution-assignment modelling', Ph.D. dissertation, University of Pennsylvania, Philadelphia.

Friesz, T. L., J. Gottfried, R. E. Brooks, A. J. Zielen, R. Tobin and S. A. Meleski (1981) *The Northeast regional environment impact study*, ANL/ES-120, Argonne National Laboratory, Argonne, Illinois.

Friesz, T. L., P. A. Viton and R. L. Tobin (1985) 'Economic and computational aspects of freight network equilibrium models: a synthesis', *Journal of Regional Science*, 25:29–49.

Gibert, A. (1968) 'A method for the traffic assignment problem when demand is elastic', LBS-TNT-85, Transport Network Theory Unit, London Business School, London.

Golob, T. F. and M. J. Beckmann (1971) 'A utility model for travel forecasting', *Transportation Science*, 5:79–90.

Granberg, A. and A. G. Rubinshtein (1979) 'Some lines in the development of the United Nations global input–output model', Institute of Economics and Organization of Industrial Production, Novosibirsk, USSR.

Griffin, C., D. E. Boyce and T. J. Kim (1983) 'Integrated model of international commodity flows and the world transportation system', Department of Civil Engineering, University of Illinois, Urbana.

Harris, B. and A. G. Wilson (1978) Equilibrium values and dynamics of attractiveness terms in production-constrained spatial–interaction models, *Environment and Planning*, A10:371–388.

Hensher, D. A. and L. W. Johnson (1981) *Applied discrete choice modelling*. London: Croom Helm/New York: Wiley.

Hotelling, H. (1929) 'Stability in competition', *Economic Journal*, 39:41–57.

Huff, D. L. (1963) 'A probabilistic analysis of shopping centre trade areas', *Land Economics*, 39:81–90.

Hyman, G. M. (1969) 'The calibration of trip distribution models', *Environment and Planning*, 1:105–112.

Isard, W. (1951) 'Interregional and regional input–output analysis: a model of a space economy', *The Review of Economics and Statistics*, 33:318–328.

Isard, W. (1975) 'Transportation research: some reflections on its development', *Regional Science and Urban Economics*, 5:133–135.

Isard, W. and L. Anselin (1982) 'Integration of multiregional models for policy analysis', *Environment and Planning*, A14:359–376.

Isard, W. and D. F. Bramhall (1960) 'Gravity, potential and spatial interaction models', in: W. Isard, *Methods of regional analysis*. Cambridge, Mass: MIT Press, 493–568.

Isard, W. and C. Smith (1983) 'Linked integrated multiregional models at the international level', *Papers, Regional Science Association*, 51:3–19.

Jaynes, E. T. (1957) 'Information theory and statistical mechanics', *Physical Review*, 106:620–630.

Jaynes, E. T. (1968) 'Prior probabilities', *IEEE Transactions on System Science and Cybernetics*, SSC-4:227–248.

Kadas, S. A. and E. Klafsky (1976) 'Estimation of the parameters in the gravity model for trip distribution: a new method and solution algorithm', *Regional Science and Urban Economics*, 6:439–457.

Klein, L. R. (1977) *Project LINK*. Athens: Centre of Planning and Economic Research.

Knight, F. H. (1924) 'Some fallacies in the interpretation of social cost', *Quarterly Journal of Economics*, 38:582–606.

Kullback, S. (1959) *Information theory and statistics*. New York: Wiley.

Lakshmanan, T. R. and W. G. Hansen (1965) 'A retail market potential model', *Journal of American Institute of Planners*, 31:131–143.

LeBlanc, L. J. and K. Farhangian (1981) 'Efficient algorithms for solving elastic demand traffic assignment problems and mode-split-assignment problems', *Transportation Science*, 15:306–317.

LeBlanc, L. J., E. K. Morlok and W. P. Pierskalla (1975) 'An efficient approach to solving the road network equilibrium traffic assignment problem', *Transportation Research*, 9:309–318.

Ledent, J. (1985) 'The doubly constrained model of spatial interaction: a more general formulation', *Environment and Planning*, A17:253–262.

Leontief, W. (1953) 'Interregional theory', in: W. Leontief, ed., *Studies in the structure of the American economy*. New York: Oxford University Press.

Leontief, W., A. Carter and P. Petri (1977) *The future of the world economy*. New York: Oxford University Press.

Leontief, W. and A. Strout (1963) 'Multiregional input–output analysis', in: T. Barna, ed., *Structural interdependence and economic development*. London: MacMillan, 119–150.

Lesse, P. et al. (1978) 'A new philosophy for regional modelling', *Papers, Regional Science Association (Australia – New Zealand Section)*, 3:165–178.

Lowry, I. (1966) *Migration and metropolitan growth: two analytical models*. San Francisco: Chandler.

Luce, R. D. (1959) *Individual choice behaviour: a theoretical analysis*. New York: Wiley.

Macgill, S. M. (1978) 'Rectangular input–output tables, multiplier analysis and entropy-maximizing principles', *Regional Science and Urban Economics*, 8:355–370.

Macgill, S. M. and A. G. Wilson (1979) 'Equivalence and similarities between some alternative urban and regional models', *Sistemi Urbani*, 1:9–40.

McFadden, D. (1973) Conditional logit analysis of qualitative choice behaviour', in: P. Zarembka, ed., *Frontiers in econometrics*. New York: Academic Press, pp. 105–142.

Miernyk, W. H. (1973) 'Regional and interregional input–output models: a reappraisal', in: M. Perlman, C. Leven and B. Chinitz, eds., *Spatial, regional and population economics*. London: Gordon and Breach, 263–292.

Moses, L. N. (1955) 'The stability of interregional trading patterns and input–output analysis', *American Economic Review*, 45:803–832.

Murchland, J. D. (1966) 'Some remarks on the gravity model of traffic distribution and an equivalent maximization formulation', LSE-TNT-38, Transport Network Theory Unit, London Graduate School of Business Studies, London.

Murchland, J. D. (1970) 'Road network traffic distribution in equilibrium', *Operations Research – Verfahren*, 8:145–183.

Nguyen, S. (1974) 'Une approche unifiée des méthodes d'équilibre pour l'affectation du trafic', Ph.D. thesis, Département d'Informatique, Université de Montreal, Montreal.

Niedercorn, J. H. and B. V. Bechdolt, Jr. (1969) "An economic derivation of the 'gravity law' of spatial interaction", *Journal of Regional Science*, 9:273–282.

Niedercorn, J. H. and Moorehead, J. D. (1974) 'The commodity flow gravity model: a theoretical reassessment', *Regional and Urban Economics*, 4:69–75.

Nijkamp, P. (1975) 'Reflections on gravity and entropy models', *Regional Science and Urban Economics*, 5:203–225.

Ohlin, B. G. (1933) *Interregional and international trade*. Cambridge, Mass.: Harvard University Press.

Peschel, K. (1981) 'On the impact of geographic distance on the interregional patterns of production and trade', *Environment and Planning*, A13:605–622.

Pigou, A. C. (1918) *The economics of welfare*. London: MacMillan.

Polenske, K. R. (1970) 'Empirical implementation of a multiregional input–output gravity trade model', in: A. P. Carter and A. Brody, eds., *Contributions to input–output analysis*. Amsterdam: North-Holland, 143–163.

Ponsard, C. (1983) *A history of regional economics*. Berlin: Springer-Verlag.

Reilly, W. J. (1931) *The law of retail gravitation*. New York: Pilsbury, republished in 1953.

Riefler, R. F. (1973) 'Interregional input–output: a state of the arts survey', in: G. G. Judge and T. Takayama, eds., *Studies in economic planning over space and time*. Amsterdam: North-Holland, 133–162.

Riefler, R. F. and C. M. Tiebout (1970) 'Interregional input–output: an empirical California–Washington model', *Journal of Regional Science*, 10:135–152.

Round, J. I. (1978) On estimating trade flows in interregional input–output models', *Regional Science and Urban Economics*, 8:289–302.

Roy, J. R. and D. F. Batten (1985) "Invited comment on 'Entropy and information theory: are we missing something?'" *Environment and Planning*, A17:704–706.

Roy, J. R. and P. F. Lesse (1981) 'On appropriate microstate descriptions in entropy modelling', *Transportation Research*, B15:85–96.

Roy, J. R. and P. F. Lesse (1985) 'Modelling commodity flows under uncertainty', *Environment and Planning*, A17:1271–1274.

Schneider, M. (1959) 'Gravity model and trip distribution theory', *Papers, Regional Science Association*, 5:137–176.

Shannon, C. E. (1948) 'A mathematical theory of communication', *Bell System Technical Journal*, 27: 379–423, 623–656.

Sheffi, Y. (1984) *Urban transportation networks*. Englewood Cliffs, N.J.: Prentice-Hall.

Sheppard, E. S. (1976) 'Entropy, theory construction and spatial analysis', *Environment and Planning*, 8:741–752.

Smith, T. E. (1975) 'A choice theory of spatial interaction', *Regional Science and Urban Economics*, 5:137–176.

Smith, T. E. (1984) 'Testable characterizations of gravity models', *Geographical Analysis*, 16:74–94.

Smith, T. E. (1985) 'Remarks on the most-probable-state approach to analyzing probabilistic theories of behaviour', *Environment and Planning*, A17:688–695.

Snickars, F. (1979) 'Construction of interregional input–output tables by efficient information adding', in: C. P. A. Bartels and R. H. Ketellapper, eds., *Explanatory statistical analysis of spatial data*. Leiden: Martinus Nijhoff, 73–112.

Snickars, F. and J. W. Weibull (1977) 'A minimum information principle: theory and practice', *Regional Science and Urban Economics*, 7:137–168.

Stewart, J. Q. (1948) 'Demographic gravitation: evidence and applications', *Sociometry*, 11:31–58.

Stouffer, S. A. (1940) 'Intervening opportunities: a theory relating mobility and distance', *American Sociological Review*, 5:845–867.

Strodtbeck, F. (1949) 'Equal opportunity intervals: a contribution to the method of intervening opportunity analysis', *American Sociological Review*, 14:490–497.

Strohkarck, F. and K. Phelps (1948) 'The mechanics of constructing a market area map', *Journal of Marketing*, 13:493–496.

Styles, B. J. (1969) 'Principles and historical development of the gravity model', in: R. L. Davis and B. J. Styles, eds., *Gravity models in town planning*. Coventry: Lancaster Polytechnic.

Takayama, T. and G. G. Judge (1971) *Spatial and temporal price and allocation models*. Amsterdam: North-Holland.

Theil, H. (1967) *Economics and information theory*. Amsterdam: North-Holland.

Tobler, W. (1982) 'The quadratic transportation problem as a model of interregional migration patterns', CP-82-84, International Institute for Applied Systems Analysis, Laxenburg.

Tomlin, J. A. (1971) 'A mathematical programming model for the combined distribution-assignment of traffic', *Transportation Science*, 5:122–140.

Tomlin, J. A. and G. S. Tomlin (1968) 'Traffic distribution and entropy', *Nature*, 220:974–976.

Vernon, R. (1966) 'International investment and international trade in the product cycle', *Quarterly Journal of Economics*, 80:190–207.

Wagner, H. (1975) *Principles of operations research*, 2nd edition. Englewood Cliffs, N.J.: Prentice-Hall.

Wardrop, J. G. (1952) 'Some theoretical aspects of road traffic research', *Proceedings of the Institution of Civil Engineers, Part II*, 1:325–378.

Warner, S. L. (1962) *Stochastic choice of mode in urban travel: a study in binary choice*. Evanston, Ill.: Northwestern University Press.

Warntz, W. (1957) 'Geography of prices and spatial interaction', *Papers, Regional Science Association*, 3:118–129.

Warntz, W. (1959) *Towards a geography of price*. Philadelphia: University of Pennsylvania Press.

Webber, M. J. (1979) *Information theory and urban spatial structure*. London: Croom Helm.

Willekens, F. (1980) 'Entropy, multiproportional adjustment and analysis of contingency tables', *Sistemi Urbani*, 2/3:171–201.

Williams, H. C. W. L. (1977) 'On the formulation of travel demand models and economic evaluation measures of user benefit', *Environment and Planning*, A9:285–344.

Williams, H. C. W. L. and A. G. Wilson (1980) 'Some comments on the theoretical and analytical structure of urban and regional models', School of Geography, University of Leeds.

Wilson, A. G. (1967) 'A statistical theory of spatial distribution models', *Transportation Research*, 1:253–269.

Wilson, A. G. (1970) *Entropy in urban and regional modelling*. London: Pion.

Zipf, G. K. (1949) *Human behaviour and the principle of least effort*. Reading, Mass.: Addison-Wesley.

Chapter 10

REGIONAL ECONOMETRIC AND DYNAMIC MODELS

ROBERT J. BENNETT and LEEN HORDIJK

1. Introduction

Regional econometric models are concerned with the description, analysis, forecasting and policy appraisal of economic development within a set of localities or regions. Such models concern not only internal structures and relationships, but also interregional interrelationships. A wide class of models has been developed for the purposes of regional economic analysis and many are concerned with the dynamics of income, demand, supply and investment determination; others are concerned with more slowly changing structural properties relating to the layout of facilities and infrastructure (such as retail centres, employment location, roads); yet other models concern the extremely rapid adjustments in the flows of people, commodities and resources between regions (journey-to-work, journey-to-shop, migration, capital flows, etc). Clearly it is not possible here to develop a comprehensive description of all such models (see also Chapter 7 of this Handbook). Rather an approach is pursued in which regional phenomena are related to models and methods of analysis. The chapter falls into five main sections. In the first of these major examples of dynamic regional models are introduced. In the next section methods of approach are reviewed and the general linear model is introduced. This section also reviews specification and estimation methods for a wide class of problems including nonlinear and nonstationary structures. The chapter then discusses briefly the application of regional models to policy specification, and finally the chapter concludes with a summary of research priority areas.

2. Examples of dynamic regional economic models

In order to initiate the subsequent discussion, this section outlines four major areas of examples which have been important as core areas for the development of dynamic analysis in regional economics. A wide-ranging review of multire-

Handbook of Regional and Urban Economics, Volume I, Edited by P. Nijkamp
©*Elsevier Science Publishers BV, 1986*

gional models is provided by Rietveld (1982) and the examples used here are not intended to be exclusive of all species of models, but instead to highlight the nature of the modelling problems that result and which form the basis of subsequent sections and chapters on specification, estimation and policy appraisal. Four main examples are employed:

(i) Regional growth models;
(ii) Models of unemployment and wage inflation;
(iii) Dynamic spatial interaction models; and
(iv) Models of spatial structure-interaction.

2.1. Regional growth models

The macroeconomic models of economic dynamics, developed originally by Hicks (1950), Harrod (1949) and Domar (1957), have provided an important basis for regional growth analysis. The classic specifications of this development are by Airov (1963) and Hartman and Seckler (1967). The basic model can be specified in simplest terms as:

$$Y_{tr} = C_{tr} + I_{tr} + E_{tr} - M_{tr}^c - M_{tr}^k \tag{2.1}$$

$$C_{tr} = bY_{t-1,r} \tag{2.2}$$

$$I_{tr} = c(Y_{t-1,r} - Y_{t-2,r}) \tag{2.3}$$

where Y, C and I refer respectively to income, consumption and investment in region r at time t; M^k and M^c are respectively imports of consumption and capital goods; and E is the net export of production goods. In the simplest version of the model, E, M^c and M^k are combined to give A_{tr}, a measure of regional autonomous expenditures. Equation (2.2) defines the multiplier, and (2.3) the accelerator of the overall multiplier–accelerator model. Two special forms result, as follows:

(i) *inventory accelerator* [Metzler (1941)]:

$$\left. \begin{array}{l} Y_{tr} = U_{tr} + S_{tr} + A_{tr} \\ U_{tr} = b'C_{t-1,r} \\ S_{tr} = c'(Y_{t-1,r} - Y_{t-2,r}) \end{array} \right\} \tag{2.4}$$

where U_{tr} are consumer goods for sale, and S_{tr} consumer goods for inventory.

(ii) *flexible accelerator* [Goodwin (1948)]:

$$\left.\begin{array}{l} Z_{tr} = C_{tr} + I_{tr} + A_{tr} \\ \Delta Y_{tr} = \mu(Z_{tr} - Y_{tr}) \\ C_{tr} = b' Y_{t-1,r} \\ I_{tr} = c' X_{tr} - c'' K_{tr} \\ \Delta K_{tr} = I_{tr} \end{array}\right\} \tag{2.5}$$

where Z_{tr} is aggregrate demand, X_{tr} aggregate supply, and K_{tr} capital stock.

There are other special forms; for a more recent review see Van Duijn (1972). However, these equations capture the main forms. It can be seen that substitution of (2.2) and (2.3) into (2.1) yields a distributed lag structure in which income growth in any one region is dependent on past changes in income plus changes in imports and exports. The nature of the model depends on the eigenvalue structure, so that oscillations and/or explosive movements may take place. The result is, therefore, a typical time series structure to which a wide variety of econometric estimation methods can be applied. These models can be generalised to multiregional dynamic input–output models [see, e.g. Hewings (1977) as well as Chapter 8 of this Handbook].

2.2. Models of unemployment and wage inflation

The developments of regional economic models in this field derive from generalising Phillips' (1958) relationship of increase in money wage rates ($\dot{w}/w$) to the rate of unemployment (u) and rate of change in unemployment ($\dot{u}/u$). Lipsey (1960) developed this work further, and the regional version was specified by Albrecht (1966), and Weissbrod (1976). Estimates have been developed by Martin (1979, 1981). The usual model assumed is:

$$\left.\begin{array}{l} \dot{w}/w = f(u) \\ f'(u) < 0, \text{ and} \\ f''(u) > 0 \end{array}\right\}. \tag{2.6}$$

Within submarkets this becomes:

$$(\dot{w}/w)_i = \sum_{j=1}^{n} g_{ij}(X_j) \tag{2.7}$$

where $g_{ij}(X_j)$ is the adjustment function of submarket i to changes in submarket j, and X_j is the excess demand for labour in submarket j. Albrecht uses i as an index of regional submarkets, but other analysts have used i as an index of different sector/product markets. Various developments of (2.6) are as follows:

(i) *Albrecht (1966)*: linear-in-parameters model:

$$(\dot{w}/w)_{rt} = a_0 + a_1 u_{rt}^{-1} + a_2 \bar{u}_t^{-1} \tag{2.8}$$

where u is unemployment in region r, and $\bar{u}_t$ is the national average rate.

(ii) *King and Forster (1973)*: quadratic in parameters model:

$$(\dot{w}/w)_{rt} = a_0 + a_1 u_{rt}^{-b} + a_2 (u_{rt} - \bar{u}_t), \tag{2.9}$$

(iii) *Thomas and Stoney (1971)*: adjustment model:

$$(\dot{w}/w) = a + kP + (b/\bar{u}) + b(S^2/\bar{u}^3) \tag{2.10}$$

where P is the macro price level, and S is a Taylor Series expansion term of the parameters. This allows combinations of local employment rates to "spillover" into other labour markets.

(iv) *Brechling (1972), Weissbrod (1976), Treble (1972)*: leading submarket model:

A particular submarket k is specified as a "leading" submarket and the adjustment function is specified as:

$$(\dot{w}/w)_{kt} = a_0 + a_1 u_{kt}^{-b}. \tag{2.11}$$

Introducing this into the adjustment of other submarkets gives:

$$(\dot{w}/w)_{rt} = \beta_0 + \beta_1 u_{rt} + \beta_2 [(\dot{w}/w)_{kt} - \alpha_0 - au_{kt}^{-b}]. \tag{2.12}$$

(v) *King and Forster (1973)*: distance weighted adjustment model:

$$(\dot{w}/w)_{rt} = a_0 + a_1 u_{rj}^{-2} + a_2 \sum_{j=1} (\dot{w}/w)_{jt}/d_{rj} \tag{2.13}$$

for areas r and j. This is generalised by Weissbrod (1976) to the case where hierarchies of central places provide a strong structure to the interdependence of the adjustment process.

Each of these models presents a spatially structured set of time series relationships based on difference equation distributed lag dependence and, as with interregional growth models, have been the subject of estimation by standard econometric methods.

2.3. Dynamic spatial interaction models

These generally derive from attempts to introduce explicit modelling of the adjustment mechanism in the Lowry (1964) location–allocation model. The initial recasting of the Lowry model into dynamic form is due to Batty (1971) who specified the following model:

$$\left.\begin{aligned}
P_{ti} &= aE_{ti}^{B} \\
E_{t+1i}^{R} &= bP_{ti} \\
E_{ti}^{T} &= E_{ti}^{B} + E_{ti}^{R}
\end{aligned}\right\} \tag{2.14}$$

and

$$E_{ti}^{B} = b_1 E_{t-1i}^{B} + b_2 E_{t-2i}^{B} + \cdots + b_n E_{t-ni}^{B} \tag{2.15}$$

and on substitution yields

$$P_{ti} = a\left(b_1 E_{t-1i}^{B} + \cdots + b_n E_{t-ni}^{B}\right) \tag{2.16}$$

where P_{ti} is population, E_{ti}^{B} basic employment, E_{ti}^{R} nonbasic retail employment, a and b are coefficients all for zones i, at time t. This gives a disequilibrium model of adjustment dynamics of population to lagged changes in basic employment. Bennett (1975a) extended this to give a dynamic version of Wilson's (1970, 1974) entropy maximising model. This yields

$$S_{tij} = A_{ti} B_{tj} O_{ti} D_{tj} f(c_{ij}) \tag{2.17}$$

with balancing factors:

$$\left.\begin{aligned}
A_{ti} &= \sum_{i=1} B_{tj} D_{tj} f(c_{ij}) \\
\text{and} \quad & \\
B_{tj} &= \sum_{i=1} A_{ti} O_{ti} f(c_{ij}),
\end{aligned}\right\} \tag{2.18}$$

subject to

$$\left.\begin{aligned}
\sum_{j} S_{tij} &= O_{ti} \\
\sum_{i} S_{tij} &= D_{tj} \\
\sum_{i} \sum_{j} S_{tij} c_{tij} &= C_t
\end{aligned}\right\}. \tag{2.19}$$

In the singly, or unconstrained case, this translates to a distributed lag model as follows:

$$D_{tj} \approx \sum_{L=0}^{q} W_{t-Lj}\theta_{Lj}$$

$$O_{tj} \approx \sum_{L=0}^{q} W_{t-Li}\theta_{Li}.$$

(2.20)

The Batty distributed lag model is then a special case of (2.20) with particular constraints on origins and destinations. In each case above S_{tij} are the interactions (e.g. journey to work) between i and j at time t. O_{ti} and D_{tj} are respective trip origins and destinations and $f(c_{ij})$ is a cost function with total system cost C_t. A_{ti} and B_{tj} are determined iteratively, and W_{t-Lj}, W_{t-Li} are origin and destination surrogates with coefficients θ_L.

2.4.   Models of spatial structure-interaction

Although originally derived for cross-sectional static situations there has recently been considerable development of models of spatial fields for description of rapid-adjustment processes characterised by successive, but changing, equilibrium fields. The basic model will be described for a price surface p_t between retail sites i $(i = 1, 2, \ldots, n)$, with demand D_t and supply S_t, all at time t:

$$\left. \begin{aligned} D_t &= Ap_t + c + u \\ S_t &= Bp_{t-1} + e \end{aligned} \right\}$$

(2.21)

where c and e are constants, $A = \{a_{ij}\}$ and $B = \{b_{ij}\}$ are $n \times n$ matrices with

$$\left. \begin{aligned} a_{ij} &\begin{cases} < 0, & i = j \\ > 0, & i = j \text{ and } j \in N(i) \\ = 0, & i = j \text{ and } j \notin N(i) \end{cases} \\ b_{ij} &\begin{cases} > 0, & i = j \\ = 0, & \text{otherwise} \end{cases} \end{aligned} \right\}$$

(2.22)

where $N(i)$ is the set of "neighbours" of site i, and u is an independent random error term with zero mean and variance σ^2. Assuming market equilibrium and market clearance, then the equilibrium price is given by:

$$p_{i,e} = \sum_{j \in N(i)} \frac{a_{ij}}{b_{ii} - a_{ii}} p_{j,e} + \frac{c_i - e_i}{b_{ii} - a_{ii}} + \frac{u_i}{b_{ii} - a_{ii}} \qquad (i = 1, \ldots, n). \qquad (2.23)$$

In each case $N(i)$ denotes the "neighbours" of site i. Various specifications of this structure are possible and the definition is quite general. The price model given above is derived from Haining (1983) and employs estimation procedures based on pseudo-likelihood methods deriving from the literature on Markov-random fields developed by Besag (1972, 1974). This integration of purely-spatial and time series adjustment models is identified by Bennett and Haining (1985) as a major area of future research development. One particular model which they specify is the nonstationary model, for random variable X defined at sites x_i on a spatial surface:

$$\left. \begin{aligned} X &= a_1 W_1 X + e \\ a &= c\mathbf{1} + b \\ b &= \rho W_2 b + u \end{aligned} \right\} \qquad (2.24)$$

where e and u are vectors of i.i.d. random variables, c is an unknown constant, the vector b obeys a spatial autoregressive scheme with coefficient ρ, and W_1 and W_2 are spatial connectivity (weights) matrices [Cliff and Ord (1973)].

3. Methods of approach and the general linear model

3.1. General linear model

For presentational purposes most aspects of the preceding examples can be reduced to various forms of the general linear model. In its simplest form this is stated as:

$$Y_i = \alpha + \beta x_i + e_i \qquad (3.1)$$

for observation $i = 1, \ldots, N$, response variable Y, independent variable X and independent error sequence e. For dynamic modelling a wide class of time series models can be developed from the general linear model above. The traditional approach to time series analysis using these models, is to split the components of the variables (Y_t) and (X_t) under study into three parts: trend, seasonal, and stochastic. A more recent approach, popularised by Box and Jenkins, is to model discrete dynamics as either transfer function processes in the bivariate case, where both (Y_t) and (X_t) are available, or as autoregressive moving-average processes in the univariate case when only a single variable (Y_t) is available [Box and Jenkins (1970), Jenkins and Watts (1968), Johnston (1972), Chatfield (1975)]. Note that the specific problems associated with discrete choice models are treated in Chapter 3 of this Handbook, while the problems of log-linear models are discussed in Chapter 11.

3.2. *Stages of analysis of spatial and temporal systems*

In most practical applications of the models discussed in Section 3.1 a series of stages of analysis are followed as shown in Figure 3.1. Whatever prior knowledge

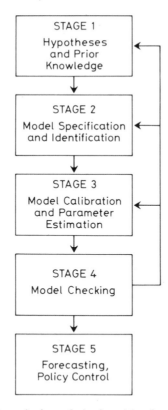

Figure 3.1. Stages in the analysis of spatial and temporal systems.

is available can be used to pre-specify the important variables and directions of linkage in the overall model which it is desired to create. Stage 2 of the analysis of space time processes is concerned with specifying and identifying the nature of the equation for the transfer function governing the system of input–output relations. Stage 3 is an estimation stage which develops estimates, for example by least-squares, of the magnitude of the parameters making up the transfer function structure specified in Stage 2. Stage 4 of the analysis is a "checking" stage in which the efficiency and fit properties of the resulting parameter estimates of the transfer function structure are tested in order to determine if the model is indeed a useful and successful explanatory device. If it is found that the parameter estimates are inefficient, or suboptimal in some fashion (for example, low significance levels, poor simulation properties, residual autocorrelation), then recourse must be made to previous stages of analysis to determine if the initial hypotheses, and the resulting model specifications and parameter estimates were correct. If the model is acceptable, then the final stage of analysis is to use the estimated model to generate forecasts and simulations of the regional economic system under study.

Early examples of the use of these time series models are Bell (1967) who considered their relation to neoclassical economic growth theory; and Czamanski (1965, 1969) who estimated a model of the Nova Scotia regional economy. Paelinck (1970) has extended the economic basis and has made links with comparative static models, whilst Glickman (1972, 1977) has given a simple two-zone disaggregation (city and suburbs) for Philadelphia which links closely to input–output formulations. Bennett (1974) has applied Box–Jenkins specification techniques to determination of local labour markets and migration. Most attention in regional economic research, however, has been directed towards the interregional dynamics to time series processes. For example, King et al. (1969), Jeffrey et al. (1969) and King et al. (1972) have applied such methods to defining interrelations between unemployment levels in a set of North American cities. This has been combined with a factor analysis of the time series components by Casetti et al. (1971) in order to determine spatial and nonspatial groups of US cities based on similarities in unemployment dynamics. Unemployment data has also been analysed by Bassett and Tinline (1970), Bassett and Haggett (1971), and Haggett (1971) for determining the feedback structure of labour market areas in South-West England. Spectral and cross-spectral techniques have been applied to unemployment data by Hepple (1975) in North-East England, and by Bartels (1977) in eleven Netherlands provinces. The interactions between unemployment and wage inflation has been examined by King and Forster (1973) and Weissbrod (1976) in the United States. Bennett (1975b) has constructed a five-equation model describing interzonal transfer function relations of unemployment, migration, employment, industrial movement, and population in North-West England. Other such studies are reviewed by Haggett et al. (1977), Bennett (1979) and

Bennett and Chorley (1978). Wider classes of approach to specification and causality analysis are reviewed by Blommestein and Nijkamp (1983).

3.3. Estimation

Most work in regional economics has proceeded by generalising the general linear model to spatial situations which allow joint estimation of the autoregressive and distributed lag characteristics for each region. For this purpose the general linear model is respecified as a matrix reformulation of (3.1) as:

$$y = X\beta + e \tag{3.2}$$

where y is an $R \times 1$ vector of dependent variables, X is an $R \times k$ matrix of independent variables (which may include lagged endogenous variables), β is a $k \times 1$ vector of parameters, and e is a $R \times 1$ vector of error terms, for R regions in space. Rewriting this linear model in this form, it is already clear that spatial econometrics bears a close resemblance with nonspatial econometrics. As a consequence many of the properties of traditional econometric estimation techniques can be employed in the spatial case. However, complications arise from the fact that in spatial econometrics the unilateral dependence of variables in nonspatial econometrics (a point in time has only two nearest neighbours) is replaced by multilateral dependence (a point in space may have more than two nearest neighbours). Complication is further increased by the observation that whereas in the nonspatial case variables are related unidirectionally (variables at time t influence variables at time $t, t+1, \ldots$ and generally not at time $t-1, t-2, \ldots$), in spatial econometrics this relationship is multidirectional.

In his very instructive monograph Anselin (1980) distinguishes four different spatial variants of the general linear model:

(a) a pure spatial first order autoregressive structure

$$y = \rho W y + \varepsilon, \quad \text{with } \varepsilon \sim N(0, \sigma^2 I) \tag{3.3}$$

where W is a matrix of weights w_{rj} which describes the intensity of dependence between regions.

(b) a first order spatial autoregressive structure with exogenous variables

$$y = \rho W y + X\beta + \varepsilon \quad \text{with } \varepsilon \sim N(0, \sigma^2 I) \tag{3.4}$$

(c) the linear model with spatial autocorrelation in the disturbance

$$\left. \begin{aligned} & y = X\beta + \varepsilon \\ & \text{with } \varepsilon = \rho W \varepsilon + \mu, \quad \mu \sim N(0, \sigma^2 I) \end{aligned} \right\} \tag{3.5}$$

(d) a spatial autoregressive model with exogenous variables and spatial autoregression in the disturbance

$$y = \lambda Wy + X\beta + \varepsilon \tag{3.6}$$

$$\varepsilon = \rho w\varepsilon + \mu, \quad \mu \sim N(O, \sigma^2 I). \tag{3.7}$$

Already from this brief sketch of different types of linear models in spatial econometrics one may conclude that straightforward application of nonspatial econometric techniques should be considered with caution. In general three major conditions of the widely applied techniques of Ordinarily Least Squares (OLS) do not hold in regional applications. These are:

(i) the error terms are not independent of each other (autocorrelation),

(ii) the error terms differ in their variance (heteroscedasticity),

(iii) the matrix X is not generally independent of e because of lagged endogenous variables in time or space (multicollinearity), i.e.

$$E(X'e) \neq 0. \tag{3.8}$$

The effect of each of these components is briefly reviewed before a general estimation approach is introduced.

3.3.1. Autocorrelation

In this case instead of e being distributed as identical and independent variates we have

$$E(e'e) = \sigma^2 V, \tag{3.9}$$

where V is an $R \times R$ variance–covariance matrix. Most frequently this is specified as a first order Markov scheme.

$$e_r = \rho \sum_j w_{rj} e_j + u_r, \quad r = 1, \ldots, R \tag{3.10}$$

or

$$e = \rho We + u \tag{3.11}$$

for u mean zero and variance $E(u'u) = \sigma_u I$; W is a matrix of weights w_{rj} which describes the intensity of dependence between regions (e.g. adjoining, distance decay structures, etc). A generalised equivalent of the first order scheme is the m-order Markov process which describes higher order dependencies [see, inter alia, Lebart (1969), Hordijk (1974)]

$$e = \rho_1 W_1 C + \rho_2 W_2 e + \cdots + \rho_m W_m e + u \qquad (3.12)$$

If such processes of autocorrelation do govern the residuals e, then OLS estimates will be unbiased but inconsistent, they will be inefficient and the variance estimates of e and standard errors will be biased (hence invalidating significance tests) [Theil (1971), Cliff and Ord (1981), Bennett (1979), Hordijk (1979), Anselin (1980)]. Hence in most cases alternatives to OLS must be sought.

3.3.2. Heteroscedasticity

When the error terms differ in their variances between regions, estimates of coefficient by OLS will be unbiased but, as with autocorrelated residuals, estimates will be inconsistent and inefficient, and significance texts biased. Again alternatives to OLS must be sought.

3.3.3. Lagged endogenous variables

In this case OLS estimation of the linear model is biased, consistent and inefficient, and cannot be employed. It should be noted that lagged endogenous variables occur very frequently in regional economics since dependence between regions is rarely limited to dependence solely on the exogenous variables. For example in the inflation–wage rate models, wage rates are likely to have strong spatial influences upon each other as well as upon unemployment rates. In this case also, therefore, alternatives to OLS must be sought.

3.3.4. Alternative estimators

The simplest case of alternative estimators arises where ρ is known in (3.4). In this case OLS can be replaced by the generalised Aitken estimator [Theil (1971)]. However, normally ρ is not known. In this situation estimates can be made iteratively for spatial problems in the same way as suggested for time series by Durbin (1960) [see, e.g. Cliff and Ord (1973), Hordijk (1974)]. Maximum likelihood provides an alternative [Hepple (1976), Hordijk and Paelinck (1976), Anselin (1980)].

For the general estimation problem, however, estimation of ρ alone is inadequate and Arora and Brown (1978), Bennett (1979), Hordijk (1979) and Tan

(1979) suggest use of the methods of standard econometrics applied to simultaneous equation systems. The starting point is Zellner's (1962) method of "seemingly unrelated regressions". This allows dependencies to be taken account of between relationships over time and over space.

Now write the general linear model as:

$$y = X\beta + u \tag{3.13}$$

with y an $R \times T \times 1$ vector of dependent variables, X an $RT \times K'$ matrix and independent variables, β an $K' \times 1$ vector of parameters, and u is an $RT \times 1$ vector of errors, for K' equal to the sum of the number of independent variable effects over all time periods T and regions R. Writing the variance–covariance matrix of the errors as:

$$\Sigma = \begin{bmatrix} \sigma_{11}I & \cdots & \sigma_{1R}I \\ \vdots & & \vdots \\ \sigma_{R1}I & \cdots & \sigma_{RR}I \end{bmatrix} = \Sigma_c \otimes I \tag{3.14}$$

for I identity matrices for order T and $\otimes$ the Kronecker product, then the Zellner estimator is given by the GLS estimate:

$$\bar{\beta} = (X'\Sigma^{-1}X)^{-1}X^1\Sigma^{-1}Y. \tag{3.15}$$

If there are no lagged endogenous variables Σ can be estimated from the OLS residuals and then placed in (3.6) as a two-step procedure. This estimator is unbiased where there is no residual autocorrelation or lagged endogenous variables [Kakwani (1967)]. However, in regional economics these features are normally present and hence Zellner's procedure has to be extended.

The most commonly used extensions are based on the econometric methods derived by Parks (1967) and Kmenta and Gilbert (1970) using various special forms of Aitken estimator. However, the most satisfactory approach, where there are lagged endogenous variables as well as residual autocorrelation, must be based on Instrumental Variable (IV), Maximum Likelihood Estimation (MLE), and related techniques [see Johnston (1972), Cliff and Ord (1973), Bennett (1979), Hordijk and Nijkamp (1977)]. Given these results Hordijk (1979) has suggested the best practical procedure is as follows:

(i) Regress all y on all exogenous variables,

(ii) Use estimates $y_{r,t-1}$ as the lagged dependent variable,

(iii) Apply OLS to all regions to provide a consistent estimation of β_r,

(iv) Transform y and X using this estimate [this uses Kadiyala's (1968) approach and is given in detail by Hordijk (1979)],

(v) Apply the Zellner seemingly "unrelated regressions method".
In recent literature the use of maximum likelihood estimators is advocated.
Bennett (1979), Cliff and Ord (1981), Ord (1975) and Anselin (1980) present more
detail about this estimation technique.

Extensive Monte Carlo simulations for different model specifications and
different estimation techniques are reported in Anselin (1980, 1981). One of his
major conclusions is that in cases with a small degree of autocorrelation OLS
performs best in small samples. For higher values of autocorrelation ($|p| > 0.8$)
maximum likelihood and iterative procedures are better.

3.4. Nonstationary and nonlinear problems

The estimators discussed above represent fairly direct extensions of the methods
of econometric analysis to spatial problems. In each case, it has been suggested
that multivariate parameter estimators transform the R-region system to an
R-variate estimation problem. More recently the need to expand these models to
take account of nonlinear and nonstationary structures has been recognised.

First re-express the general linear model (3.2) in vector-matrix form for one
time point t:

$$Y_t = X_t \beta_t + e_t, \qquad e_t \sim N(O, R). \tag{3.16}$$

Here X_t is a matrix of explanatory variables, Y_t is the system vector output
variable, and (e_t) is an independent error sequence. The parameter vector β_t is
now defined with subscript t as a time dependent vector sequence (β_t). Changes
to the parameter sequence are described by a second equation or *parameter
submodel* which is given by the expression

$$\beta_{t+1} = F\beta_t + GV_t + \Gamma n_t, \qquad n_t \sim N(O, Q). \tag{3.17}$$

In this equation, the evolution of the parameter vector is described by a function
of previous values of the parameters up to maximum lag L, system endogenous
variables X_t, exogenous variables V_t, noise disturbances n_t, and time t itself.

Most instances in the practical analysis of regional systems involve the handling of uncertainty in which only partial information on structure is available.
This is due to five main factors. First, the presence or absence of explanatory
variables V_t which allow exogenous prediction of parameter changes. Second, the

presence or absence of parameter noise (n_t), which makes the parameter sub-model stochastic or deterministic. Third, the presence or absence of system noise (e_t), which makes the overall system stochastic or deterministic. Fourth, the availability of explanatory variables X_t, which determines whether the system model is a transfer function or (Autoregressive-Moving-Average) ARMA structure. Finally, the state of knowledge available on the matrices F, G and Γ, which determines whether modelling of evolutionary parameters is undertaken in an environment of certainty or uncertainty. The interplay between these five elements gives rise to a wide variety of parameter evolution models. To simplify this range of discussion, Table 3.1 places continuous parameter evolution models into seven broad classes.

The most important classes of problems arising with the regional economic models discussed earlier are those in class 6 and 7. These arise when only input–output information (the data sequences (X_t) and (Y_t) on system behaviour) is available. Not only is it necessary to apply estimation methods to determine the parameter vector at each point in time, but also an estimator is required for the determination of the parameter evolution matrices at each point in time. For stochastic systems this is further complicated by the need to estimate the covariance matrices R and Q.

All estimators of this class of problems derive in some form from the Kalman filter. This is a generic term for a species of methods which make estimates of a system equation by incorporating estimation of the changing parameters deriving from a parameter equation. A wide variety of such filters is available depending upon our degree of knowledge of each of these terms. The general Kalman filter structure provides estimates of the system outputs and parameters at each point in time by recursive calculation of a set of extrapolation equations. The importance of this approach is that regional models need no longer be held in a straightjacket of unchanging structure; evolutionary and nonlinear dynamics can be estimated. Despite the potentialities of this approach, there have, as yet, been only a small number of applications in regional economics. The first of these appears to be Bennett (1975d) who estimated a series of models of parameter change in a distributed lag, transfer function model of the regional economy of North-West England. Shifts in parameter terms were traced over a 20-year period and were found to affect especially the parameters controlling policy feedback. Subsequent developments by Bennett (1977, 1979) have refined the statistical properties of the Kalman filter for the short series cases characteristic of planning problems [see also Martin (1978), Hepple (1978), Bennett (1979) and Müller (1980)]. In many cases it is feasible to employ recursive least squares or the Kalman filter directly to the parameter estimation problem. However two difficulties may arise. First, since the system noise covariance matrix R is unknown, some initial guess must be inserted into the Kalman gain equation. Second, if an

Table 3.1
Categories of parameter change models defined by pattern of knowns and unknowns.

Model class	Deterministic or stochastic	Knowns	Unknowns	Category of problem
1 $\Gamma = O$	deterministic system	Y, X, V, β, F, G	—	recursive simulation
2 $\Gamma = O$	deterministic with mean $(e_t) = $ var$(e_t) = 0$	Y, X, V, F, G	β	Luenberger observer
3 var$(n_t) = Q$	stochastic system	Y, X, V, F, G, Γ, Q	β	Kalman observer
4 $\Gamma = O$ var$(e_t) = R$	stochastic system	Y, X, V, F, G, R	β	Kalman stochastic observer
	var$(e_t) = R$	$Y, X, V, F, G, \Gamma, Q, R$	β	Kalman filter
5 $\Gamma = O$ var$(n_t) = Q$	stochastic system	Y, X, F, R	β, V, G	Kalman filter
	var$(e_t) = R$	Y, X, F, Γ, Q, R	β, V, G	Kalman filter
6 $\Gamma = O$ var$(n_t) = Q$	stochastic system	Y, X	β, V, G, F, R	transfer-function estimation with Kalman filter
	var$(e_t) = R$	Y, X	$\beta, V, G, F, \Gamma, R, Q$	Kalman filter
7 $\Gamma = O$ var$(e_t) = R$	stochastic system	Y	β, V, G, F, X, R	ARMA estimation
	var$(e_t) = R$	Y	$\beta, V, G, F, \Gamma, X, R, Q$	with Kalman filter

arbitrary guess of R is not employed, and instead it is assumed that $R = I$, then the Kalman filter algorithm provides poor tracking capacity: the updating equations in the algorithm tend to zero in finite time (usually fairly rapidly) with the consequence that no new information on the parameter vector is allowed to enter the update equations. The parameter estimates then exhibit increasing error from the true parameters with time: a phenomenon termed *divergence*. To prevent this it is necessary to formulate some rule to keep the algorithms open to new information, or to provide optimal estimates of the error R and Q.

For simplicity here we give an example only of adaptive estimation [other methods are discussed at length in Bennett (1979, ch. 5)]. Adaptive estimation seeks to determine the covariance matrices Q and R. There are a wide range of models for estimating Q and R [Mehra (1971)] but the Jazwinski filter has proved the most successful covariance estimator in many practical applications [Bennett (1977)]. This filter [Jazwinski (1969)] depends upon a sequential test of the residual sequence. If the system is evolutionary then the residual series will begin to diverge with time and exhibit autocorrelation. Hence by testing the autocorrelation of the residuals at each step, a measure of possible divergence is possible which can be fed back to improve the estimates of the variances R_t and Q_t.

The Jazwinski filter can be summarised as follows:

System model	$Y_t = X_t \boldsymbol{\beta}_t + e_t, \quad e_t \sim N(O, R\delta(t - \tau))$
Parameter model	$\boldsymbol{\beta}_t = F\boldsymbol{\beta}_{t-1} + GV_t + \Gamma n_t, \ n_t \sim N(O, Q\delta(t - \tau))$
Parameter extrapolation	$\hat{\boldsymbol{\beta}}_{t/t-1} = F\hat{\boldsymbol{\beta}}_{t-1} + GV_t$
Parameter covariance extrapolation	$P_{t/t-1} = FP_{t-1}F' + \Gamma Q \Gamma'$
System noise covariance extrapolation	$R_{t/t-1} = e_t e_t' - X_t P_{t/t-1} X_t' - X_t Q_{t/t-1} X_t'$
Parameter noise covariance extrapolation	$Q_{t/t-1} = \begin{cases} \dfrac{e_{t+1}^2 - X_{t+1} P_{t/t-1} X_{t+1}' - R_{t/t-1}}{X_{t+1} X_{t+1}'}, & \text{if positive} \\ 0, & \text{otherwise} \end{cases}$
Parameter update	$\hat{\boldsymbol{\beta}} = \hat{\boldsymbol{\beta}}_{t/t-1} - K_t(X_t \hat{\boldsymbol{\beta}}_{t/t-1} - Y_t)$
Parameter covariance update	$P_t = P_{t/t-1} - K_t X_t' P_{t/t-1}$
Kalman gain	$K_t = P_{t/t-1} X_t [R + X_t' P_{t/t-1} X_t]^{-1}$

$$(3.18)$$

The significant portion of this algorithm is the error setting on e_t^2. If this is set at less than this value, then the predicted residuals are within one-standard-error limits, and are small and consistent with their statistics, and no value for Q need enter the prediction equation. A correction is only made when the prediction error exceeds the limit of one standard error. This provides a condition whereby the prediction equations are opened and closed to noise depending upon the magnitude of the L-step-ahead predicted residuals. L is usually taken equal to one to reduce the lag in estimation [Jazwinski (1969, 1970)].

4. Policy specification

Most research in regional economics which has been concerned with policy specification has adopted a simulation approach; e.g. once an econometric model has been estimated in a supposedly "free system", simulations are developed for changes in independent variables which are manipulable as policy instruments. This approach is direct and can be very useful. However, it suffers from two drawbacks: first, it cannot yield optimal results, except by chance; second, it ignores the feedback between policy and free systems.

4.1. Optimal control

Whereas simulation methods applied to policy appraisal tell us "what happens if", optimal control seeks an answer to the alternative question "to achieve a given policy target, how should policy instruments be set". This approach has now been widely employed in regional economics and the following are major sources:

(i) *Planning national settlement systems*: MacKinnon (1975), Mehra (1971), Evtuskenko and MacKinnon (1976), Propoi and Willekens (1978), and Tan (1980) for irrigation control, and Nijkamp (1980) for environmental regulation.

(ii) *Environmental problems*: Nijkamp (1975, 1980), Nijkamp and Verhage (1976), Sakawa and Ueda (1978) and Bennett and Chorley (1978).

(iii) *Urban and regional planning*: Domanski (1973), Lee (1982), Coelho and Wilson (1976), Williams and Wilson (1978), Phiri (1979), Karlqvist et al. (1978), Nijkamp (1980), Wilson (1981), Wilson and Bennett (1985), and Tan and Bennett (1984).

(iv) *Intergovernmental resource allocation*: Bennett and Tan (1979), and Tan (1979).

The translation of the econometric model, discussed earlier as a specification and estimation problem, into a control problem for regional economies has recently been synoptically reviewed by Nijkamp (1980) and Tan and Bennett (1984). First transform the general linear model into an equivalent first-order system:

$$Y_t = A_t Y_{t-1} + B_t x_t + b_t \tag{4.1}$$

where,

$$
Y_t = \begin{bmatrix} Y_t \\ \vdots \\ Y_{t-p+1} \\ \hline X_t \\ \vdots \\ X_{t-q+1} \end{bmatrix}, \quad
B_t = \begin{bmatrix} B_{0t} \\ 0 \\ \vdots \\ 0 \\ \hline I \\ 0 \\ \vdots \\ 0 \end{bmatrix}, \quad
b_t = \begin{bmatrix} b_t \\ 0 \\ \vdots \\ 0 \\ \hline 0 \\ 0 \\ \vdots \\ 0 \end{bmatrix}
\tag{4.2}
$$

$$
A_t = \left[\begin{array}{ccccc|ccc}
A_{1t} & A_{2t} & \cdots & A_{pt} & B_{1t} & \cdots & B_{qt} \\
I & 0 & \cdots & 0 & 0 & \cdots & 0 \\
\vdots & & \vdots & & & & \\
0 & \cdots & I & 0 & 0 & \cdots & 0 \\
\hline
& & & 0 & \cdots & 0 & \\
& & & I & \cdots & 0 & \\
0 & & & \vdots & & & \\
& & & 0 & \cdots & I & 0
\end{array}\right]
\tag{4.3}
$$

and the matrices A_{it} and B_{it} contain the respective autoregressive and distributed lag parameters (a_{ijt}) and (b_{ijt}) for regional interaction between i and j at time t ($i, j = 1, \ldots, R$). The optimal control solution is given for a specified initial condition Y_0 by determining that setting of the control variable $x_1, \ldots, x_T$ which minimises a specified objective function. It is assumed that the exogenous variables X are amenable to manipulation and that there are T time periods over which control is exercised. The most frequently used objective function is the quadratic:

$$
W_t = (Y_t - a_t)' M_t (Y_t - a_t) = Y_t' H_t Y_t - 2 Y_t' h_t + d_t
\tag{4.4}
$$

where a_t are targets, M_t is a weight function, and

$$
H_t = M_t; \qquad h_t = M_t a_t; \qquad d_t = a_t' M_t a_t.
\tag{4.5}
$$

The quadratic form is not without difficulties, but does yield a wide class of practical solutions. The optimal control solution for the quadratic case is found by Bellman's (1957) principle of dynamic programming or related techniques [e.g. the Pontryagin method, see Pontryagin et al. (1962)]. This yields the optimal value x_t^* of the exogenous variables as:

$$x_t^* = G_t Y_{t-1} + g_t, \qquad t = 1, \ldots, T \tag{4.6}$$

where

$$G_T = -(B_T' H_T B_T)^{-1} B_T H_T A_T \tag{4.7}$$

and

$$g_T = (B_T' H_T B_T)^{-1} B_T'(h_T - H_T b_T) \tag{4.8}$$

and this can be solved at the initial conditions Y_0, setting $H_T = M_T$, then moving to Y_1, and so on, until we reach Y_T.

The wide potential of the optimal control approach is surveyed by Tan and Bennnett (1984) who show that the optimal control solution (4.6) can be extended to situations in which there are constraints on the control variables, system state variables, or both, where parameters are unknown, are varying over time or space, and where each of these features is combined. The optimal control solution under constraints is particularly important, not only because it frequently arises in economic situations where limitless setting of policy instruments is rarely possible, but because it allows most of the problems of the quadratic objective function to be overcome. Most important of the criticisms of the quadratic function is that it treats both positive and negative deviations from a target with equal weight. The control solution with constraints on both state and control variables allows this criticism to be overcome [Tan and Bennett (1984, ch. 6)].

4.2. Estimation in situations with policy feedback

Almost all econometric work in regional economics has ignored the fact that the system has been operating with various levels of policy intervention. Hence it is usually assumed that regional systems are operating in a so-called open-loop, i.e. the system is responding to the natural and free interplay of relationships between variables and indicators. Since, however, past policy decisions affect most economic systems, models should be developed which explicitly recognise the effects of policy determination, i.e. models must be constructed in the so-called *closed loop*. Closed-loop regional models cannot be constructed merely by explicit recognition of the role of policy goals and instruments, however. Instead, a different approach to identification and estimation of space–time models is required. Take as an example the forecasting model:

$$\hat{Y}_{t+L} = MX_t. \tag{4.9}$$

In this equation X_t is an explanatory variable or leading indicator, Y_t is the variable it is sought to forecast, the $\hat{Y}_{t+L}$ is the forecast or estimate of Y_t at lead time L, and M is used to express a general model structure. In this case policy targets are identified as predetermined levels of the forecast variable Y_t which it is desired should be achieved. The policy question then is: at what level must we set the instrument X_t to achieve the goal set for Y_t. This requirement may be specified in the following form:

$$X_t = KY_{t+L}. \tag{4.10}$$

The policy problem is to determine the values of K, termed the control model, which give the appropriate settings of the instrument X_t to yield the prespecified value of Y_t. If (3.18) and (4.1) are compared, it may be seen that they are identical in structure, but differ in both the form of the model, and the direction of dependence specified. The use of the leading indicator as a setting for policy targets using a control model therefore gives a closed-loop in which the directions of dependence are reversed, as shown in Figure 4.1 In this figure the solid line shows the natural or free structure of dependence (3.18), and the dashed line shows the control settings. We may reduce this system to a single structure by use of the feedback policy settings derived from continuous planning and monitoring as discussed in the previous section. This is given simply by substituting (4.10) into (4.9) to give:

$$\hat{Y}_{t+L} = MKY_{t+L}. \tag{4.11}$$

It should be apparent that the best policy will be that which renders the deviation of the forecast $\hat{Y}_{t+L}$ from the desired settings Y_{t+L} a minimum. This can be achieved by choosing the control model to have the inverse structure to the system model, i.e. $K = M^{-1}$. Substituting this result into (4.11) we have:

$$\hat{Y}_{t+L} = MM^{-1}Y_{t+L} \tag{4.12}$$

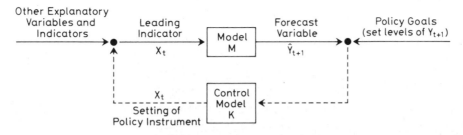

Figure 4.1. Closed-loop effects produced by feedback and feed-forward policy strategies. The solid line shows the pattern of free system response, and the dashed line the pattern of control effects.

or

$$\hat{Y}_{t+L} = Y_{t+L} \tag{4.13}$$

and the forecast should then equal the preset goals. A major consequence of implementation of a completely effective policy based on feedback is that the operation of the system becomes cancelled out, i.e. the observations of the forecast variable exactly equal the specified goals. As a result the effect of the free system becomes unobservable. Even in the case of imperfect and uncertain policy effects, the consequences for statistical models of regional economies are thus considerable. Four conditions, depending upon our knowledge of the system model and the control model, can be distinguished. The consequences of each of these for model building, statistical analysis, and policy determination can be summarised as follows [Bennett (1978)].

4.2.1. Control model (K) and system model (M) known perfectly

In this case the substitution $K = M^{-1}$ allows the definition of the perfect policy model in (4.3) and we have no statistical modelling problem to determine M. This is usually a trivial case since seldom, if ever, are either policies or regional systems understood with sufficient accuracy.

4.2.2. Control model (K) known and perfect, system model (M) unknown

This is again a fairly trivial case since K is seldom known with a high degree of accuracy, but it is important as a special case in order to show the effects of policy feedback. In this case $K = M^{-1}$ and (4.4) is satisfied. Hence any attempt to determine the model M will result merely in identifying the present goals for the forecast variable Y_t. However, since K is known, M can be determined from K.

4.2.3. Control model (K) is unknown and perfect, system model (M) is unknown

This case is similar to (4.2.2) in that the forecast variable will equal preset goals, but there is now an opportunity to determine either K or M since both are unknown. The system operations are completely cancelled out by the policy, and future attempts to identify a forecasting relationship between Y_t and X_t will find no relation between the sample data for the two variables. No statistical method will allow this problem to be overcome. Instead, either we require additional a priori information, or we may estimate a "reduced form" equation. The reduced form structure recognises the stochastic nature of (3.18), i.e.

$$\hat{Y}_{t+L} = MX_t + Ce_{t+1} \tag{4.14}$$

where (e_t) is a normally distributed independent random variable sequence. On substituting (4.1) and rearranging we obtain:

$$\hat{Y}_{t+L} = (1 - MK)^{-1} Ce_{t+L}. \tag{4.15}$$

Since we cannot separately determine M, K, or C, forecasts must now be generated merely from past values of the forecast variable Y_t as an extrapolation or autoprojective autoregressive, moving-average structure.

4.2.4. *Imperfect control model (K) and system model (M) both unknown*

This is the most frequent case to occur in practice. The policy equation is imperfect and exact achievement of goals is impossible. Moreover policy is sufficiently intuitive and imprecise in definition that it is not possible to define as a simple mathematical structure such as (4.1). In addition, our knowledge of the model (3.18) is also imperfect and imprecise. Thus we have the normal statistical estimation and calibration problem of determining the structure of an unknown model, and an unknown policy model, in a situation in which both the policy mechanism and the regional model coefficients are unknown. Complete cancellation of the free pattern of dynamics does not occur if the policy is imperfect, but the consequences are no less severe. It is only possible to obtain estimates of $M = 1/K$, i.e. from substitution of (4.1) into (3.18) with imperfect K we can determine, from data records of Y_t and X_t alone, only the rule K by which past policy has been chosen [Bohlin (1971)]. Under specific conditions it is possible to identify the model, e.g. if the control is nonlinear or nonstationary while the system is linear and stationary, or vice versa [Ljung et al. (1974), Soderstrom et al. (1975)]. But when these conditions do not apply, a special approach to statistical estimation and calibration of the model must be adopted.

The statistical problem is that under feedback or feed-forward policies, an infinite number of space–time models can represent (3.18): the model is statistically underidentified. When only one of a series of leading indicators is used as an instrument of policy feedback, this element is cancelled and each independent variable affected by feedback will be collinear with each other independent variable affected by feedback. In addition such independent variables become correlated with the errors [Bennett (1978)]. Hence, least-squares estimates are biased, and most other parameter estimators are inefficient.

Three methods for overcoming these problems are available. First, the so-called direct method [Gustavsson (1975)] involves the use of special estimators such as maximum likelihood estimates or stochastic approximation. Second, the indirect method [Lindberger (1972)] reduces the model to an autoregressive, moving-average or reduced form structure as in (4.7). Third, a joint method (Caines and Chan (1975)] applies a simultaneous equation estimator approach to a reduced form equation for both the model and the policy elements. Each method will give the same results asymptotically, but the joint method has the advantage that it yields estimates of the policy component as well as the system model.

These various effects discussed above can be summarised very simply: if a regional system has been operating under even a fairly small degree of policy influence, statistical approaches to identification and parameter estimation of space–time models will yields unstable, inefficient, and biased results. If the regional system has been subject to a high degree of policy influence, it may not be possible to construct space–time models at all. Instead it will only be possible to model policy itself.

5.   Future research priorities

The discussion of this chapter has reviewed a series of approaches to dynamic modelling of regional economies and then examined the way in which these models interface with a number of issues of policy. It is now appropriate to ask where the research priorities should lie in future developments of these models.

5.1 Specification and estimation

First, the techniques for specifying and estimating regional models require development. A far wider range of specification techniques can be employed, for example, those discussed by Blommestein and Nijkamp (1983). In addition, although the statistical theory of single series problems (autoregressive moving-average models) has been extensively researched by statisticians, there is as yet, little information on the small sample properties of many of these statistical specification and estimation techniques. For regional economics this presents a special range of particular difficulties. The major of these are as follows:

5.1.1.   Representation and map pattern

A major hurdle in the way of practical application and interpretation of regional models is the specificity of each practical situation: the spatial arrangement, size, shape and organisation of the spatial cells or lattice for which data is derived affects the spatial processes which can be identified and the parameters which can be estimated, i.e. model structure is not independent of the spatial data base adopted: the so-called "Curry effect" [see Curry (1972), Sheppard (1979)].

There are several separate but interacting issues involved in these effects to which considerable attention has been directed. First there is *map pattern*: that the results of any finite sample analysis depends on the specifics of the sample structure of the data set [Curry (1972), Johnston (1973)]. The second issue is *spatial autocorrelation*: discussed further below. The third issue is that of *areal units*. Where aggregated data, such as that from censuses, is employed the individual objects of study cannot be accessed directly. For any set of individuals there is a wide range of possible ways of aggregating and each will produce different results when statistical methods are applied to the resulting aggregated data. This problem, which has been extensively recognised in statistics [Gehlke and Biehl (1934), Kendall and Yule (1950)], has only recently been approached by regional economists [see Openshaw and Taylor (1981)], but there are now extensive simulation results available which demonstrate the effects of different zoning systems [Openshaw (1977, 1983), Openshaw and Taylor (1979, 1981)]. However, there is still no general theory available.

5.1.2. Spatial autocorrelation

The theory of test statistics for the presence of a particular pattern of spatial autocorrelation has been one of the main areas for developments in regional economics in the past, especially deriving from the work of Cliff and Ord (1973, 1981) generalising the Moran and Geary statistics [see also Curry (1972), Cliff and Ord (1973, 1981), Cliff et al. (1974, 1975, 1976), Curry et al. (1975), Bennett (1979), Sheppard (1979)]. More recently, concern with spatial autocorrelation has shifted from one mainly of detection to one of model calibration and estimation with respect to underlying spatial process. This shift in attention is well-illustrated by Haining (1981b) who distinguishes two levels of conception of spatial realisations. At a first level is *spatial process* which requires mathematical statements about variables and their parameters, defining a system state with all possible values of variables spanning a state space. Spatial process is then conceived as the rule governing the temporal trajectory of the system as a chain of changes in state through time. *Spatial pattern* is the second level of information: the map of a single realisation of the underlying spatial process. It is this second level which constitutes the data available for empirical analysis. For stochastic systems this two-level conception is extended to a three-level one in which the underlying process is stochastic giving a second level of the spatial probability distribution (random field) which is then observed as one map surface at a third level. Considerable developments need to be made with statistical methods which seek to infer the structure of the underlying spatial processes from outcome data based on deductive theory of the underlying spatial process. Early work in statistics by Whittle (1954, 1963) extended by Besag (1972, 1974) has now been extensively developed by Haining for purely spatial cases. This work includes the development of significance tests for the Whittle r statistic and determination of whether underlying processes are autoregressive or moving-average [Haining (1977a, 1977b, 1978a)]; whether processes are unilateral or multilateral [Haining (1977b)]; and estimating parameters in spatial process models [Haining (1978a)]. These methods have been extended to central place systems [Haining (1980)], interaction models [Haining (1978b, 1978c)], and population distribution [Haining (1981a, 1981b)]. Other recent work on this problem is that by Getis and Boots (1978) and Getis (1982) which extends Ripley's (1977) work on spatial models and point pattern evolution. Burridge (1981) has sought a common factor approach to asymptotic tests for spatial autoregressive processes which define conditions where models can be reduced to nonspatial processes with spatially autocorrelated disturbances. Developments are also required in the spatial autocorrelation test statistics of Cliff and Ord. Recent contributions have been Hubert et al. (1981), Besag and Diggle (1977), Brandsma and Ketellapper (1979), Anselin (1980), Cliff and Ord (1981), Hubert (1978), Sen (1976), Sen and Soot (1977), Shapiro and Hubert (1979), Sokal (1979) and Guptill (1975). However, for small sample situations considerable research is still required.

5.1.3. Identification and estimation techniques

As impressive as the developments with spatial autocorrelation are, few of these consider the relation of spatial pattern to spatial process and the way in which spatial time series can be used to reveal the latter. Major developments in the understanding of the properties of space–time correlation functions have been given by Griffith (1976, 1980, 1981) and by Hewings [see White and Hewings (1980), Hooper and Hewings (1981)]. These now allow a wider description of the properties, sample size characteristics, and wider applications of spatial autocorrelation and partial autocorrelation statistics applied as diagnostics of space–time processes.

Considerable developments in both identification and estimation theory have been made by extending multivariate statistical estimation theory to space–time processes. The main generalisations of multivariate estimation theory were those by Hepple (1976), Hordijk and Nijkamp (1977), Arora and Brown (1978), Paelinck and Klaassen (1979), Bennett [(1979, chs. 6 and 7)], Hordijk (1979), Otter (1978a) and Hepple (1979). These now include most major examples of the general linear model for regional econometric (e.g. 2SLS, 3SLS, FIML) and Bayesian inference. However, despite early suggestions for Bayesian work [e.g. Curry (1968)], this is an area which still requires development.

5.1.4. Boundaries and missing data

Despite their rather specific characteristics, these two issues raise considerable difficulties in the way of analysis of spatial time series which, like the map pattern problem, have often been conveniently ignored and this has led to considerable inadequacy in results. Most finite models are relatively sensitive to boundary conditions. Ripley (1981) and Haggett (1980, 1981) summarise the effect of internal and external boundary effects on models of trend surfaces, point patterns and distance distributions. More recently simulation methods have been applied by Haining et al. (1984a) and Bennett et al. (1984) to the assessment of the effect of missing data at the boundary of the system of interest. Using the results of the statistical theory of Orchard and Woodbury (1972), Haining et al. demonstrate that missing data have considerable effects on model estimates. Alternatively, turning the problem around, they demonstrate that missing data (either internal or at the boundary) can be estimated optimally using the spatial process models discussed earlier. However, considerable research is still required on this problem.

5.2. Models of changing parameters

Ten years ago the notion of adaptation and change over time in the structure of models estimated for spatial data was barely perceived and little discussed. Since the mid-1970s, however, various evolving parameter structures have been hypothesised for regional economics and considerable advances have been made in both statistical technique and mathematical theory. Some of the earliest developments of changing-parameter models for regional economics are those by Bennett (1977, 1979) and Martin (1978), using Kalman filtering and related methods. Much of the spirit of thinking of these developments has been applied to the developments by Cliff et al. (1980) who have combined Kalman filtering with the weights matrix model. This has been employed extensively for forecasting and simulating the spatial passage of an epidemic with the main area of application being measles in Iceland. Subsequent work by Martin (1979, 1981) has extended the Kalman structure to applications with reduced form estimation of spatial patterns of wage inflation linked to developments of the Phillips-curve model. One of the perennial problems with this area of work has been that of determining if patterns of parameter change which have been detected reflect significant and real shifts or are a purely random pattern arising from misspecification or corruption from data errors or other influences of noise. Early applications use the Quandt likelihood ratio test to assess significance of shifts between two parameter regimes and this has been subsequently extended to the use of cumulative sum tests on the residuals [Bennett (1979)]. This approach has now been extensively applied to unemployment time series by Dunn (1981, 1982) who has also developed a number of both ad hoc diagnostics of parameter changes and tests based on serial correlation or heteroscedasticity of the residuals. These tests derive from the statistical theory developed by Garbade (1976), Harvey and Collier (1977), Harvey and Phillips (1974, 1977), Phillips and Harvey (1974), Otter (1978a, 1978b) and Hepple (1979). Results with each of these developments are extremely encouraging and should stimulate a wide range of further applications and developments of these methods in the future.

A further development of changing-parameter models has been by use of two groups of techniques developed at the Department of Statistics, UMIST: evolutionary spectral analysis, the threshold autoregression. Evolutionary spectral analysis, due originally to Priestley (1965) has now been applied successfully to a number of regional economic phenomena. Threshold autoregression and more general threshold models is the result of the work mainly of Tong [see Tong and Lim (1980), Tong (1980c)] who has extended the theory to a wide class of phenomena and transformations. Particularly stimulating of future research and application in regional economics is the suggestion of the close link of nonstationary parameter models with catastrophe theory.

5.3.   Catastrophe theory

Important early work with catastrophe theory by Amson (1972a, 1972b) has been developed by Wilson (1978) and his coworkers, and Adelman (1984) to include developments also of more general dynamical systems in which bifurcation theory provides the main focus. This is discussed at length in Chapter 6 of this Handbook. Depending as it does on analysis of points of singularity in systems of related differential or difference equations, it is likely that bifurcation theory will prove to be an important stimulus to regional economics. For example, following the ideas speculated by Bennett and Chorley (1978), Tong (1980a, 1980b) has developed the formal theory linking the canonical cusp catastrophe and threshold autoregressive models. It is now becoming clear that catastrophe and bifurcation theory is likely to provide increasing stimulus to the development of adaptive regional models over the next few years. For example, it is in such problems that the complex coupling of regional and dynamic behaviour in highly interdependent systems occurs, and many complex singularities in manifolds of coefficient and control spaces arise [see Wilson and Bennett (1985)]. Early developments of this work are encouraging for model choice models [Wilson (1976, 1978)], speed flow curves [Dendrinos (1978a)], central place studies [Casti and Swain (1975)], Mees (1975)], housing stock location models [Dendrinos (1977, 1978b)], and retailing location [e.g. Wilson (1981), Harris and Wilson (1978), Wilson and Clark (1979)].

5.4.   Forecasting and control

Regional econometric models have been highly stimulative of development of both forecasting and control. Major development of the spatial location aspects of control work has derived from the interfacing of traditional location–allocation models with dynamic equations of spatial evolution. Important theoretical and practical development of this work has been made by Williams and Wilson (1978), Coelho and Wilson (1976), Otter (1979a, 1979b) and Phiri (1979), with the main practical application being the allocation of retail and other stock in urban systems. Two major research problems in applications of regional models to forecasting and control concern the relation of control to the underlying statistics of the system under study. A first difficulty is that the system model is not usually known with certainty but is identified and estimated from time series data. This has important implications since it is usually not the case that a separation principle holds between attempts at estimation and control. Separate treatment of the two problems usually does not lead to attainment of a global minimum for control or an unbiased estimate for estimation [Åstrom and Wittenmark (1971)]. The properties of solutions to this difficulty using either the self-tuning regulator, suggested by Åstrom and Wittenmark, or the learning algorithm suggested by Chow (1975), are not known for spatial time series, and experience needs to be accumulated with both methods of approach. The second research problem concerns the difficulty of identifying and estimating spatial systems which have been operating under policy feedback; so-called identification in the closed-loop which has been discussed earlier.

References

Adelman, I. and J. M. Hihn (1984) 'The estimation and modelling of discontinuous change', in: L. Chatterjee and P. Nijkamp, eds., *Urban and regional policy analysis in developing countries*. Aldershot: Gower, 251–263.

Airov, J. (1963) 'The constitution of inter-regional business cycle models', *Journal of Regional Science*, 5:1–19.

Albrecht, W. P. (1966) 'The relationship between wage change and unemployment in metropolitan and industrial labour markets', *Yale Economic Essays*, 6:279–341.

Amson, J. C. (1972a) 'Equilibrium models of cities: An axiomatic theory', *Environment and Planning Series*, A4:429–444.

Amson, J. C. (1972b) 'Equilibrium models of cities: Single species cities', *Environment and Planning Series*, A5:295–338.

Anselin, L. (1980) *Estimation methods for spatial autoregressive structures*, Regional Science Dissertation and Monograph Series No. 8, PURS, Ithaca, NY.

Anselin, L. (1981) 'Small sample properties of estimators for the linear model with a spatial autoregressive structure in the disturbance', in: W. Vogt and M. Mickle, eds., *Modelling and Simulation*, 12:899–904.

Arora, S. S. and M. Brown (1978) 'Alternative approaches to spatial autocorrelation: an improvement over current practice', *International Regional Science Review*, 2:67–78.

Åstrom, K. J. and B. Wittenmark (1971) 'Problems of identification and control', *Journal of Mathematics and its Applications*, 34:90–113.

Bartels, C. P. (1977) *Economic aspects of regional welfare, income distribution and unemployment*. Dordrecht: Martinus Nijhoff.

Bassett, K. and P. Haggett (1971) 'Towards short-term forecasting for cyclic behaviour in a regional system of cities', in: M. Chisholm, A. Frey and P. Haggett, eds, *Regional forecasting*. London: Butterworths, 389–413.

Bassett, K. and R. Tinline (1970) 'Cross spectral analysis of time series and geographical research', *Area*, 2:19–24.

Batty, M. (1971) 'Modelling cities as dynamic systems', *Nature*, 231:425–428.

Bell, F. W. (1967) 'An econometric forecasting model for a region', *Journal of Regional Science*, 7:109–128.

Bellman, R. E. (1957) *Dynamic programming*. Princeton, N. J.: Princeton University Press.

Bennett, R. J. (1974) 'Process identification for time series modelling in urban and regional planning', *Regional Studies*, 8:157–174.

Benett, R. J. (1975a) 'Dynamic systems modelling of the North West Regions: 1. Spatio–temporal representation and identification', *Environment and Planning*, A7:525–538.

Bennett, R. J. (1975b) 'Dynamic systems modelling of the North West Region: 3. Adaptive-parameter policy model', *Environment and Planning*, A:617–636.

Bennett, R. J. (1977) 'Consistent estimation of nonstationary parameters for small sample situations – A Monte Carlo study', *International Economic Review*, 18:489–502.

Bennett, R. J. (1978) 'Forecasting in urban and regional planning closed loops: the example of road and air traffic forecasts', *Environment and Planning*, A10:145–162.

Bennett, R. J. (1979) *Spatial time series: analysis, forecasting and control*. London: Pion.

Bennett, R. J. and R. J. Chorley (1978) *Environmental systems: philosophy analysis and control*. London: Methuen.

Bennett, R. J. and R. P. Haining (1985) 'Spatial structure and spatial interaction: modelling approaches to the statistical analysis of geographical data', *Journal Royal Statistical Society* A148:1–36.

Bennett, R. J., R. P. Haining and D. A. Griffith (1984) 'The problem of missing data on spatial surfaces', *Annals of the Association of American Geographers*, 74:138–156.

Bennett, R. J. and K. C. Tan (1979) 'Allocation of the U.K. rate support grant by use of the methods of optimal control', *Environmental and Planning*, A11:1011–1027.

Besag, J. E. (1972) 'On the correlation structure of two-dimensional stationary processes', *Biometrika*, 59:43–48.

Besag, J. E. (1974) 'Spatial interaction and the statistical analysis of lattice systems', *Journal Royal Statistical Society B*, 36:192–235.

Besag, J. E. and P. J. Diggle (1977) 'Simple Monte Carlo tests for spatial pattern', *Applied Statistics*, 26:327–333.

Blommestein, H. and P. Nijkamp (1983) 'Causality analysis in soft spatial econometric models', *Papers of the Regional Science Association*, 51:65–77.

Bohlin, T. (1971) 'On the problem of ambiguities in maximum likelihood estimation', *Automatica*, 7:199–210.

Box, G. E. P. and G. M. Jenkins (1970) *Time series analysis, forecasting analysis and control*. San Francisco: Holden-Day.

Brandsma, A. S. and R. H. Ketellapper (1979) 'A biparametric approach to spatial autocorrelation', *Environment and Planning*, A11:51–58.

Brechling, F. (1972) *Wage inflation and the structure of regional unemployment*, Discussion paper No. 40, Department of Economics, University of Essex.

Burridge, P. (1981), 'Testing for a common factor in a spatial autoregression model', *Environment and Planning*, A123:795–800.

Caines, P. E. and C. W. Chan (1975) 'Feedback between stationary stochastic processes', *IEEE Transactions on Automatic Control*, AC-20:498–508.

Casetti, E., L. King and D. Jeffrey (1971) 'Structural imbalance in the U.S. urban-economic system, 1960–1965', *Geographical Analysis*, 3:239–255.

Casti, J. and H. Swain (1975) 'Catastrophic theory and urban processes', IIASA Report RM-75-14 Laxenburg, Austria.

Chatfield, C. (1975) *The analysis of time series: theory and practice*. London: Chapman and Hall.

Chow, K. C. (1975) *Analysis and control of dynamic economic systems*. New York: Wiley.

Cliff, A. D., P. Haggett, J. K. Ord, K. Bassett and R. Davies (1975) *Elements of spatial structure*. Cambridge: Cambridge University Press.

Cliff, A. D., P. Haggett, J. K. Ord and G. R. Versey (1980) *Spatial diffusion: an historical geography of epidemics in an island community*. Cambridge: Cambridge University Press.

Cliff, A. D., R. L. Martin and J. K. Ord (1974) 'Evaluating the friction of distance parameters in gravity models', *Regional Studies*, 8:281–286.

Cliff, A. D., R. L. Martin and J. K. Ord (1975) 'Map pattern and friction of distance parameters: reply to comments by R. J. Johnston and by L. Curry, D. A. Griffith and E. S. Sheppard', *Regional Studies*, 9:285–288.

Cliff, A. D., R. L. Martin and J. K. Ord (1976) 'A reply to the final comment', *Regional Studies*, 10:341–342.

Cliff, A. D. and J. K. Ord (1973) *Spatial autocorrelation*. London: Pion.

Cliff, A. D. and J. K. Ord (1981) *Spatial processes: theory and applications*. London: Pion.

Coelho, J. D. and A. G. Wilson (1976) 'The optimum location and size of shopping centres', *Regional Studies*, 10:413–421.

Curry, L. (1968) 'Seasonal programming and Bayesian assessment of atmospheric resources', in: W. R. D. Swell, ed., *Human dimensions of weather modification*, Dept. of Geography, Research Paper 105, University of Chicago, 127–138.

Curry, L. (1972) 'A spatial analysis of gravity flows', *Regional Studies*, 6:131–147.

Curry, L., D. A. Griffith and E. S. Sheppard (1975) 'Those gravity parameters again', *Regional Studies*, 9:289–296.

Czamanski, S. (1965) 'A method of forecasting metropolitan growth by means of distributed lags analysis', *Journal of Regional Science*, 6:33–49.

Czamanski, S. (1969) 'Regional econometric models: A case study of Nova Scotia', in: A. J. Scott, ed., *London Papers in Regional Science 1, Studies in Regional Science*. London: Pion, 143–180.

Dendrinos, D. S. (1977) 'Slums in capitalist urban setting: some insights from catastrophe theory', *Geographica Polonica*, 42:63–75.

Dendrinos, D. S. (1978a) 'Operating speeds and volume to capacity ratios: the observed relationship and the fold catastrophe', *Transportation Research*, 12:191–194.

Dendrinos, D. S. (1978b) 'Urban dynamics and urban cycles', *Environment and planning*, A10:43–49.

Domanski, R. (1973) 'A general model of optimal growth in a system of regions', *Papers of the Regional Science Association*, 31:73–82.

Domar, E. (1957) *Essays in the theory of economic growth*. Oxford: Oxford University Press.

Dunn, R. (1981) 'Time series analysis in a spatial context', unpublished Ph.D., University of Bristol.

Dunn, R. (1982) 'Parameter instability in models of local unemployment responses', *Environment and Planning* A:75–94.

Durbin, J. (1960) 'The fitting of time series models', *Revue de l'Institut International de Statistique*, 28:233–243.

Evtushenko, Y. and R. D. MacKinnon (1976) 'Nonlinear programming approach to optimal settlement system planning', *Environment and Planning*, A8:637–654.

Garbade, K. (1976) 'Two methods for examining the stability of regression coefficients', *Journal of the American Statistical Association*, 72:54–63.

Gehlke, C. E. and K. Biehl (1934) 'Certain effects of grouping upon the size of the correlation coefficient in census tract material', *Journal of the American Statistical Association*, 29:169–170.

Getis, A. and B. Boots (1978) *Models of spatial processes: an approach to the study point, line and area patterns*. Cambridge: Cambridge University Press.

Getis A. (1982) 'Pattern change and distance variation in the square', *Geographical Analysis*, 14:72–78.

Glickman, N. J. (1972) *An area-stratified regional econometric model*. Discussion Paper No. 58, Regional Science Research Institute, University of Pennsylvania.

Glickman, N. J. (1977) *Econometric analysis of regional systems: explorations in model building and policy analysis*. New York: Academic Press.

Goodwin, R. M. (1948) 'Secular and cyclical aspects of the multiplier and accelerator', in: *Income, employment and public-policy: essays in honour of A. H. Hansen*. New York: W. W. Norton, 108–132.

Griffith, D. A. (1976) 'Spatial structure and spatial interaction: a review', *Environment and Planning*, A8:731–740.

Griffith, D. A. (1980) 'Towards a theory of spatial statistics', *Geographical Analysis*, 12:325–339.

Griffith, D. A. (1981) 'Interdependence in space and time; numerical and interpretative considera-
    tions', in: D. A. Griffith and R. D. Mackinnon, eds., *Dynamic spatial models*. Alphen aan de Rijn:
    Sijthoff Noordhoff, 258–287.
Guptill, S. C. (1975) 'Spatial filtering of nominal data: an explanation', Unpublished Ph.D.,
    University of Michigan, Ann Arbor.
Gustavsson, I. (1975) 'Survey of applications of identification in chemical and physical processes',
    Automatica, 11:2–24.
Haggett, P. (1971) 'Leads and lags in inter-regional systems: A study of cyclic fluctuations in the
    South West economy', in: M. Chisholm and G. Manners, eds., *Spatial policy problems of the British
    economy*. Cambridge: Cambridge University Press, 69–95.
Haggett, P. (1980) 'Boundary problems in quantitative geography', in: H. Kishimoto, ed., *Die
    Bedeutung von Grenzen in der Geographie*. Zurich: Kimmerley and Frey, 64–84.
Haggett, P. (1981) 'The edge of space', in: R. J. Bennett, ed. *European progress in spatial analysis*.
    London: Pion.
Haggett, P., A. D. Cliff and A. Frey (1977) *Location analysis in human geography*. London: Arnold.
Haining, R. P. (1977a) 'Model specification in stationary random fields', *Geographical Analysis*,
    9:107–129.
Haining, R. P. (1977b) 'The moving average model of dependences for a rectangular plane lattice',
    Transactions of the Institute of British Geographers N.S., 3:202–225.
Haining, R. P. (1978a) *Specification and estimation problems in models of spatial dependence*,
    Northwestern Studies in Geography No. 12. Evanston, Ill.: Northwestern University Press.
Haining, R. P. (1978b) 'Interaction modeling of central place lattices', *Journal of Regional Science*,
    18:217–228.
Haining, R. P. (1978c) 'Estimating spatial interaction models', *Environment and Planning*,
    A10:305–320.
Haining, R. P. (1980) 'Intraregional estimation of central place population parameters', *Journal of
    Regional Science*: 365–375.
Haining, R. P. (1981a) 'Spatial interdependencies in population distributions: a study of univariate
    map analysis. 1. Rural population densities; 2. Urban population densities', *Environment and
    Planning*, A13:65–84, 85–96.
Haining, R. P. (1981b) 'Analysing univariate maps', *Progress in Human Geography*, 5:58–78.
Haining, R. P. (1983) 'Modelling intra-urban price competition: an example of gasoline pricing',
    Journal of Regional Science, 23:517–528.
Haining, R. P., D. A. Griffith and R. J. Bennett (1984a) 'A statistical approach to the problem of
    missing spatial data using a first-order Markov model', *Professional Geographer*, 36:338–345.
Haining, R. P., D. A. Griffith and R. J. Bennett (1984b) 'Simulating two-dimensional autocorrelated
    surfaces', *Geographical Analysis*, 16:247–255.
Harris, B. and A. G. Wilson (1978) 'Equilibrium values and dynamics of attractiveness terms in
    production–constrained spatial interaction models', *Environment and Planning*, A10:371–398.
Harrod, R. F. (1949) *Towards a dynamic economics*. New York: Wiley.
Hartman, L. M. and D. Seckler (1967) 'Towards the application of dynamic growth theory of
    regions', *Journal of Regional Science*, 7:167–174.
Harvey, A. C. and P. Collier (1977) 'Testing for functional misspecification in regression analysis',
    Journal of Econometrics, 6:103–119.
Harvey, A. C. and G. D. S. Phillips (1974) 'A comparison of the power of some tests for
    heteroscedasticity in the general linear model', *Journal of Econometrics*, 2:307–316.
Harvey, A. C. and G. D. S. Phillips (1977) 'Testing for stochastic parameters in regression models',
    Dept. of Quantitative Social Science, University of Kent.
Hepple , L. W. (1975) 'Spectral techniques and the study of interregional economic cycles', in: R.
    Peel, M. Chisholm and P. Haggett eds., *Processes in physical and human geography*, *Bristol Essays*,
    London: Heinemann, 94–106.
Hepple, L. W. (1976) 'A maximum likelihood model for econometric estimation with spatial series',
    in: I. Masser, ed., *Theory and practice in regional science*. London: Pion, 90–104.
Hepple, L. W. (1978) 'Forecasting the economic recession in Britain's depressed regions', in: R. L.
    Martin, N. Thrift, and R. J. Bennett, eds., *Towards the dynamic analysis of spatial systems*. London:
    Pion, 172–190.

Hepple, L. W. (1979) 'Bayesian analysis of the linear model with spatial dependence', in: C. A. P. Bartels and R. H. Ketellapper, eds., *Exploratory and explanatory statistical analysis of spatial data.* Leiden: Nijhoff, 179–198.

Hewings, G. J. D. (1977) *Regional industrial analysis and development.* London: Methuen.

Hicks, J. R. (1950) *A contribution to the theory of the trade cycle.* Oxford: Clarendon Press.

Hooper, P. M. and A. J. D. Hewings (1981) 'Some properties of space–time processes', *Geographical Analysis*, 13:203–223.

Hordijk, L. (1974) 'Spatial correlation in the disturbances of a linear interregional model', *Regional and Urban Economics*, 4:117–140.

Hordijk, L. (1979) 'Problems in estimating econometric relations in space', *Papers of the Regional Science Association*, 42:99–115.

Hordijk, L. and P. Nijkamp (1977) 'Dynamic models of spatial autocorrelation', *Environment and Planning*, A9:505–519.

Hordijk, L. and J. H. P. Paelinck (1976) 'Some principles and results in spatial econometrics', *Recherches Economiques de Louvain*, 42(3):175–197.

Hubert, L. J. (1978) 'Nonparametric tests for patterns in geographic variation: possible generalizations', *Geographical Analysis*, 10:86–88.

Hubert, L. J., R. G. Colledge and C. M. Costanzo (1981) 'Generalized procedures for evaluating spatial autocorrelation', *Geographical Analysis*, 13:224–233.

Jazwinski, A. H. (1969) 'Adaptive filtering', *Automatica*, 5:475–485.

Jazwinski, A. H. (1970) *Stochastic processes and filtering theory.* New York: Academic Press.

Jeffrey, D., E. Casetti and L. King (1969) 'Economic fluctuations in a multi-region setting: A bifactor analytic approach', *Journal of Regional Science*, 9:397–404.

Jenkins, G. M. and D. G. Watts, (1968) *Spectral analysis and its application.* New York: Holden-Day.

Johnston, J. (1972) *Econometric methods, second edition.* New York: McGraw-Hill.

Johnston, R. J. (1973) 'On frictions of distance and regression coefficients', *Area* 5:187–191.

Kadiyala, K. R. (1968) 'A transformation used to circumvent the problem of autocorrelation', *Econometrica*, 36:93–96.

Kakwani, N. C. (1967) 'The unbiasedness of Zellner's seemingly unrelated regression equations estimators', *Journal American Statistical Association*, 62:141–142.

Karlqvist, A. R., L. Lindquist and F. Snickars eds. (1978) *Dynamic allocation of urban space.* Farnborough: Saxon House.

Kendall, M. G. and G. U. Yule (1950) *An introduction to the theory of statistics.* London: Griffin.

King, L., E. Casetti and D. Jeffrey (1969) 'Economic impulses in a regional system of cities: a study of spatial interactions', *Regional Studies*, 3:213–218.

King, L., E. Casetti and D. Jeffrey (1972) 'Cyclical fluctuations in unemployment levels in U.S. metropolitan areas', *Tijdschrift voor Economische en Sociale Geographie*, 63:345–352.

King, L. J. and J. J. H. Forster (1973) 'Wage-rate change in urban labor markets and intermarket linkages', *Papers of the Regional Science Association*, 30:183–196.

Kmenta, J. and R. F. Gilbert (1970) 'Estimation of seemingly unrelated regressions with autoregressive disturbances', *Journal of the American Statistical Association*, 65:186–197.

Lebart, L. (1969) 'Analyse statistique de la contiguïté', *Publications de l'Institut de statistique de l'Université de Paris*, 18:81–112.

Lee, R. (1982) 'Optimal government intervention in regional development', *Geographical Analysis*, 14:124–134.

Lindberger, N. A. (1972) 'Stochastic modelling of computer-regulated linear plants in noisy environments', *International Journal of Control*, 16:1009–1019.

Lipsey, R. G. (1960) 'The relation between unemployment and the rate of change of money wage rates in the United Kingdom, 1862–1957: a further analysis', *Economica*, 27:1–31.

Ljung, L., I. Gustavsson and T. Soderstrom (1974) 'Identification of linear multivariable systems operating under linear feedback control', *IEEE Transactions of Automatic Control*, AC-19:836–840.

Lowry, I. S. (1964) *A model of metropolis.* Santa Monica: Rand Corporation.

MacKinnon, R. D. (1975) 'Controlling interregional migration processes of a Markovian type', *Environment and Planning*, A7:781–792.

Martin, R. L. (1978) 'Kalman filter modelling of time varying processes in urban and regional planning', in: R. L. Martin, N. Thrift and R. J. Bennett, eds., *Towards the dynamic analysis of spatial systems.* London: Pion, 104–126.

Martin, R. L. (1979) 'Subregional Phillips curves, inflationary expectations, and the intermarket relative wage structure: substance and methodology', in: N. Wrigley, ed., *Statistical application in the spatial sciences*. London: Pion, 64–110.

Martin, R. L., ed. (1981) *Regional wage inflation and unemployment*. London: Pion.

Mees, A. I. (1975) 'The renewal of cities in medieval Europe–an application of catastrophe theory', *Regional Science and Urban Economics*, 5:403–426.

Mehra, R. K. (1971) 'On-line identification of linear dynamic systems with applications to Kalman filtering', *IEEE Transactions on Automatic Control*, AC16:12–21.

Metzler, L. A. (1941) 'The nature and stability of inventory cycles', *Review of Economics and Statistics*, 23:113–129.

Müller, R. A. (1980) Matrizenmodelle und Zustandsschätzung zur Bevölkerungsprognose, Schriftenreihe Heft No. 17, Institut für Regionalwissenschaft, University of Karlsruhe.

Nijkamp, P. (1975) 'Spatial interdependencies and environmental effects', in: A. Karlqvist, L. Lundqvist and F. Snickars, eds., *Dynamic allocation of urban space*. Farnborough: Saxon House, 175–210.

Nijkamp, P. (1980) *Environmental policy analysis*. New York: Wiley.

Nijkamp, P. and C. Verhage (1976) 'Cost benefit analysis and optimal control theory for environmental decisions: a case study of the Dollard estuary', in: M. Chatterji and P. von Rompuy, eds., *Environment, regional science and interregional modelling*. Berlin: Springer, 74–110.

Openshaw, S. (1977) 'Optimal zoning systems for spatial interaction models', *Environment and Planning*, A9:169–184.

Openshaw, S. (1983) *The modifiable areal unit problem*, CATMOG 3B, Geobooks, University of East Anglia.

Openshaw, S. and P. J. Taylor (1979) 'A million or so correlation coefficients: three experiments on the modifiable areal unit problem', in: N. Wrigley, ed., *Statistical applications in the spatial sciences*. London: Pion, 127–145.

Openshaw, S. and P. J. Taylor (1981) 'The modifiable areal unit problem', in: N. Wrigley and R. J. Bennett, eds., *Quantitative geography: a British view*. London: Routledge, 60–69.

Orchard, T. and M. A.. Woodbury (1972) 'A missing information principle: theory and applications', *Proceedings of 6th Berkeley Symposium*, *Mathematical Statistics and Probability*, 1:697–715.

Ord, J. K. (1975) 'Estimation methods for models of spatial interaction', *Journal of the American Statistical Association*, 70:120–126.

Otter, P. W. (1978a) 'The discrete Kalman filter applied to linear regression models: statistical considerations and an application', *Statistica Neerlandica*, 32:41–56.

Otter, P. W. (1978b) *Kalman filtering in time-series analysis compared with the Box–Jenkins approach and exponential smoothing*, Econometric Institute, University of Groningen.

Otter, P. W. (1979) *Identification and estimation of linear (economic) systems, operating under linear closed-loop control*, Econometric Institute, University of Groningen.

Paelinck, J. (1970) 'Dynamic urban models', *Papers of the Regional Science Association*, 14:25–37.

Paelinck, J. H. P. and L. H. Klaassen (1979) *Spatial econometrics*. Farnborough: Saxon House.

Parks, R. W. (1967) 'Efficient estimation of a system of regression equations when disturbances are both serially and contemporaneously correlated', *Journal American Statistical Association*, 62:500–509.

Phillips, A. W. (1958) 'The relation between unemployment and the rate of change of money wage rates in the United Kingdom', *Economica*, 25:283–299.

Phillips, D. A. and A. C. Harvey (1974) 'A simple test for serial correlation in regression analysis', *Journal of the American Statistical Association*, 69:935–939.

Phiri, P. A. (1979) 'Equilibrium points and control problems in dynamic urban modelling', unpublished Ph.D. thesis, University of Leeds.

Pontryagin, L. S., R. V. Boltyanski, R. V. Gamekrelidge and E. F. Mischchenko (1962) *The mathematical theory of optimal processes*. New York: Wiley.

Priestley, M. B. (1965) 'Evolutionary spectra and nonstationary processes', *Journal Royal Statistical Society B*, 27:204–237.

Propoi, A. and F. Willekens (1978) 'A dynamic linear programming approach to the planning of national settlement systems', *Environment and Planning*, A10:561–576.

Rietveld, P. (1982) 'Causality structures in multiregional economic models', in: B. Issaev et al., eds., *Multiregional economic modelling*. Amsterdam: North-Holland, 15–34.

Ripley, B. D. (1977) 'Modelling spatial patterns', *Journal of the Royal Statistical Society B*', 39:172–212.

Ripley, B. (1981) *Spatial statistics*. New York: Wiley.

Sakawa, Y. and Y. Ueda (1978) 'The optimal investment for the control of environmental pollution and economic growth', *International Journal of Systems Science*, 9:193–203.

Sen, A. K. (1976) 'Large sample-size distribution of statistics used in testing for spatial autocorrelation', *Geographical Analysis*, 8:175–184.

Sen, A. K. and J. K. Soot (1977) 'Some tests for spatial correlation', *Environment and Planning*, A9:897–903.

Shapiro, C. P. and L. Hubert (1979) 'Asymptotic normality of permutation statistics derived from weighted sums of univariate functions', *The Annals of Statistics*, 4:788–794.

Sheppard, E. S. (1979) 'Gravity parameter estimation', *Geographical Analysis*, 11:120–132.

Soderstrom, T., L. Gustavsson and L. Ljung (1975) 'Identifiability conditions for linear systems operating in closed loop', *International Journal of Control*, 21:243–255.

Sokal, R. R. (1979) 'Testing statistical significances of geographical variation patterns', *Systematic Zoology*, 28:227–232.

Tan, K. C. (1980) 'Solution strategies for national settlement system planning models', *Geographical Analysis*, 12:68–79.

Tan, K. C. (1979) 'Optimal control of linear econometric systems with linear equality constraints on the control variables', *International Economic Review*, 20:253–258.

Tan, K. C. and R. J. Bennett (1984) *Optimal control of spatial systems*. London: Allen and Unwin.

Theil, H. (1971) *Principles of econometrics*. New York: Wiley.

Thomas, R. L. and P. J. M. Stoney (1971) 'Unemployment dispersion as a determinant of wage inflation in the UK, 1925–1966', *The Manchester School*, 39:83–116.

Tong, H. (1980a) 'On the structure of threshold time series models', Technical Report No. 134 University of Manchester Institute of Science and Technology.

Tong, H. (1980b) 'Catastrophe theory and threshold autoregressive modelling', Technical Report No. 125, University of Manchester Institute of Science and Technology.

Tong, H. (1980c) 'A note on the connection between threshold autoregressive models and catastrophe theory', Technical Report No. 129, University of Manchester Institute of Science and Technology.

Tong, H. and K. S. Lim (1980) 'Threshold autoregression, limit cycles and cyclical data', *Journal of the Royal Statistical Society B*, 42:244–254.

Treble, J. G. (1972) 'Multisectoral models of labor markets: some empirical results', unpublished, quoted in Weissbrod (1976).

Van Duijn, J. J. (1972) *Interregional models of economic fluctuation*. Lexington, Mass.: D. C. Heath.

Weissbrod, R. S. P. (1976) *Spatial diffusion of relative wage inflation*, Northwestern University Studies in Geography.

White, E. N. and G. J. D. Hewings (1980) 'Space–time employment modelling: some results using seemingly unrelated regression estimates', mimeo, University of Illinois.

Whittle, P. (1954) 'On stationary processes in the plane', *Biometrika*, 41:434–449.

Whittle, P. (1963) 'Stochastic processes in several dimensions', *Bulletin of the International Statistical Institute*, 34:974–933.

Williams, H. C. W. L. and A. G. Wilson (1978) 'Dynamic models for urban and regional analysis', in: T. Carlstein, D. N. Parkes and N. Thrift, eds., *Timing space and spacing time*. London: Arnold, 81–95.

Wilson, A. G. (1970) *Entropy in urban and regional modelling*. London: Pion.

Wilson, A. G. (1974) *Urban and regional models in geography and planning*. London: Wiley.

Wilson, A. G. (1976) 'Catastrophe theory and urban modelling: an application to model choice', *Environment and Planning*, A8:351–356.

Wilson, A. G. (1978) Towards models of the evolution and genesis of urban structure', in: R. L. Martin, N. Thrift and R. J. Bennett, eds., *Towards the dynamic analysis of spatial systems*. London: Pion, 79–90.

Wilson, A. (1981) *Catastrophe theory and bifurcation*. London: Croom Helm.

Wilson, A. G. and R. J. Bennett (1985) *Human geography and planning: a guidebook to mathematical theory*. London: Wiley.

Wilson, A. G. and M. Clark (1979) 'Some illustrations of catastrophe theory applied to urban retailing structure', in: M. Breheny, ed., *London papers in regional science*. London: Pion, 64–77.

Zellner, A. (1962) 'An efficient method of estimating seemingly unrelated regression and tests of aggregation bias', *Journal American Statistical Association*, 57:348–368.

Chapter 11

QUALITATIVE STATISTICAL MODELS FOR REGIONAL ECONOMIC ANALYSIS

NEIL WRIGLEY and FLOOR BROUWER

1. Introduction

Traditionally, the statistical modelling conducted in regional economic research has focused on the analysis of high-level, metric or quantitative data measured at the ratio or interval scales. The tradition has its roots in natural science where high-quality data can be obtained under experimental conditions. Unfortunately, this tradition too often ignores the realities of regional economic research where the information available for statistical modelling purposes will frequently have been obtained from official government statistics or from a wide range of sample surveys, and will frequently be non-metric (qualitative, discrete or categorical) in nature. As a result, many analyses are forced through a narrow, and often inappropriate, filter of methods and models which demand high-quality information on high-level, quantitative scales of measurement.

Fortunately, this situation has in recent years begun to change. Significant methodological advances in the analysis of qualitative data have taken place over the past twenty years and these new methods have increasingly begun to penetrate the practice of statistical modelling in regional economic analysis. The aim of this chapter is to describe these methodological advances and to illustrate the current use and future potential of qualitative statistical models in regional economic analysis. Particular attention will be placed upon log-linear models for complete and incomplete multidimensional contingency tables, logistic/logit and probit regression models, and upon the wider class of qualitative statistical models which can be specified within Nelder and Wedderburn's family of "generalized linear models" (GLMs).

The chapter begins with a review of the state of the art in qualitative statistical modelling. This focuses upon: (a) basic model types and their integration; (b) alternative estimation procedures; (c) model assessment and selection procedures; (d) extended and hybrid forms of the basic models. It is followed by

Handbook of Regional and Urban Economics, Volume I, Edited by P. Nijkamp
©*Elsevier Science Publishers BV, 1986*

Table 2.1
A classification of statistical problems.

		Explanatory variables			
		Continuous	Mixed	Categorical	None
Response variables	Continuous	(a)	(b)	(c)	
	Categorical	(d)	(e)	(f)	(g)

discussion of a range of empirical examples to illustrate the current use of qualitative data models in regional economic analysis. These examples focus upon regional variations in rates of industrial innovation in the U.K., regional quality-of-life and residential preferences in the Netherlands, and a regional industrial accessibility survey conducted in Northern Ireland. The chapter concludes with a review of several topics which are of central importance to the future potential of qualitative statistical models in regional economic analysis.

2.   State of the art in qualitative statistical modelling

2.1.   Model types and their integration

One possible framework for understanding the range and interrelationships of the new methods for analysing qualitative data is that shown in Table 2.1 [see also Wrigley (1979, 1981, 1985)]. What this table shows is a classification of statistical problems on the basis of the type of response (or dependent) and explanatory (or independent) variables involved. Categorical variables are those measured at the low level, nominal or ordinal scales, and mixed variables are a mixture of continuous and categorical. Qualitative/categorical variables can be of three different types:

(i) dichotomous (e.g. presence or absence, yes or no);
(ii) unordered polytomous (e.g. region A, region B, region C);
(iii) ordered polytomous (high income, middle income, low income).

Variable types (i) and (ii) can only be distinguished by their names or attributes and are measured at a nominal scale. A natural ordering from low to high exists for the third type which is measured at an ordinal scale.

Table 2.1 has two important pedagogic features. First, it is organized in such a way that the qualitative data problem becomes progressively more important in the movement from cell (a) to cells (f) and (g). Second, the structure of the table serves to link together the traditional metric-data models of regional economic analysis (classical regression models, dummy variable regression models, and so on) which are appropriate for cells (a), (b) and (c), with the newer methods of qualitative data analysis (log-linear models, logistic/logit and probit regression models, and so on) which provide appropriate methods for handling the problems in cells (d) to (g).

Within the class of statistical problems in the lower row of Table 2.1, a distinction can be drawn between those problems (cells (d) to (f)) in which a division of variables into response and explanatory is possible, and those problems (cell (g)) in which no division is possible or in which the researcher chooses not to make use of any response/explanatory distinction which might exist. In cells (d) to (f) the aim of the researcher is to assess the effects of explanatory variables (continuous, mixed or solely categorical) on a qualitative/categorical response variable and the models which are now widely used for such purposes are logistic/logit and probit regression models. In contrast, in cell (g) problems all variables are treated as response variables. Here, the aims of the researcher are simply to describe and decompose the structural relationships between the response variables, and the models now widely used for such purposes are log-linear models.

Stated in this simple way, it may appear that qualitative data models for cells (d) to (f) and those for cell (g) have no connection. This is certainly not the case. The most suitable way to perceive the models appropriate for problems in the lower row of Table 2.1 is to imagine the influence of logistic/logit and probit regression models pushing towards the right from cells (d) and (e) and the influence of log-linear models pushing towards the left from cell (g). As a result, cell (f) becomes a zone of transition in which both logit models and a special form of log-linear model (an "asymmetric" form in which a division of variables into explanatory and response is recognized) represent appropriate and widely used techniques. Furthermore, it is possible to demonstrate [see Wrigley (1985, pp. 223–230)] that, despite superficially different appearances, log-linear and logit models for cell (f) problems are mathematically related. The implication of this is that there is a formal linkage between all the models in the lower row of Table 2.1, and it justifies the treatment of qualitative data models as an *integrated* family of statistical techniques.

Implicit in the structure of Table 2.1 is the fact that the family of statistical models now used for qualitative data analysis form part of a much broader unified family of linear models. Indeed, the linkage of qualitative/categorical data models and conventional quantitative/continuous data linear models which underpins Table 2.1 can be formalized by regarding all models appropriate for the statistical problems in Table 2.1 as members of Nelder and Wedderburn's (1972) unified family of "generalized linear models" (GLMs).

A "generalized linear model" can be expressed [see McCullagh and Nelder (1983), Nelder (1985), Wrigley (1985)] in the form:

$$Y_i = \mu_i + \varepsilon_i \qquad i = 1, \ldots, N \tag{2.1}$$

where: Y_i is a response variable which is assumed to come from the exponential family of probability distributions; μ_i is the expected value (mean) of Y_i, i.e. $\mu_i = E(Y_i)$; ε_i is a randomly distributed error term.

The explanatory variables, X_{ik}, which are thought to influence the variation in the response variable, Y_i, in the model can be summarized in the structure of the so-called "linear predictor" (η_i) which takes the form:

$$\eta_i = \sum_k \beta_k X_{ik} \tag{2.2}$$

where β_k are parameters which require estimation. The linear predictor can then be related to the expected value of Y_i by the so-called "link function" g,

$$\eta_i = g(\mu_i) \tag{2.3}$$

or, alternatively, by g^{-1}, the inverse of the link function

$$\mu_i = g^{-1}(\eta_i). \tag{2.4}$$

The link function g is a monotonic twice differentiable function.

Substituting the linear predictor and the inverse link function into (2.1) implies, therefore, that a generalized linear model can be written in the form:

$$Y_i = g^{-1}(\eta_i) + \varepsilon_i \tag{2.5}$$

or, alternatively,

$$Y_i \simeq F\left(g^{-1}\left[\sum_k \beta_k X_{ik} \right] \right) \tag{2.6}$$

where F represents the assumed exponential family of probability distributions. Any particular member of the class of generalized linear models can then be specified from a particular combination of the three modules of a GLM; i.e. from link function, linear predictor, and probability ("error") distribution.

As Table 2.2 shows, all models appropriate for the statistical problems in Table 2.1 can be specified in this way. It can be seen that the exponential family of probability distributions includes both the normal distribution which underlies conventional continuous data linear models, and also the important distributions for qualitative data analysis: Poisson, binomial and multinomial. In addition, it includes many other distributions (e.g. the gamma, Weibull, chi-squared and so on) which have played important roles in economic research and, in practice, the exponential family will normally prove sufficiently broad to handle a majority of

Table 2.2
Examples of generalized linear models.

Model	Link function	Error distribution
Linear regression	Identity	Normal
ANOVA (fixed effects)	Identity	Normal
ANOVA (random effects)	Identity	Gamma
Logistic/logit regression	Logit	Binomial or multinomial
Binary probit regression	Probit	Binomial
Linear logit model for cell (f) problems	Logit	Binomial or multinomial
General log-linear model for cell (g) problems	Logarithmic	Poisson
Log-linear model for cell (f) problems	Logarithmic	Poisson

the statistical analysis requirements of most researchers. In addition, the exponential family has several attractive theoretical properties [see O'Brien and Wrigley (1984)] not least those which enable parameters of exponential distribution models to be estimated with ease using straightforward computational methods.

2.2. Log-linear and logistic/logit models: the workhorses of qualitative statistical modelling

Having placed qualitative models into the wider context of the statistical methods used in regional economic research, it is now appropriate to consider in greater detail the primary workhorses of qualitative data analysis: logistic/logit regression models, and log-linear models for two-dimensional and multidimensional contingency tables.

2.2.1. Logistic/logit regression models

It is now well known by regional economists that if the conventional regression models adopted in cells (a), (b) and (c) of Table 2.1 are extended to the problems in cells (d), (e) and (f), a number of difficulties are encountered which necessitate an alternative form of model. First, a conventional regression model with a categorical response variable will violate the constant error variance or homoscedasticity assumption of the classical linear regression model and thus the problem of heteroscedasticity will be present. Whilst heteroscedasticity does not result in biased or inconsistent parameter estimates, it does result in a loss of efficiency. In addition, it can give rise to biased estimates of the variances of the coefficients which, in turn, may result in serious problems if conventional inferential tests are used. Second, a conventional regression model with a categorical response variable may generate predictions which are seriously deficient. It can be shown that the predicted values of the response variable in such a model are best interpreted as predicted probabilities. Unfortunately, whereas probability is defined to lie within the range 0 to 1, the predictions generated from such a model are unbounded and may take values from $-\infty$ to $+\infty$. Consequently, the predictions may lie outside the meaningful range of probabilities and may thus be inconsistent with the probability interpretation advanced. [See Pindyck and Rubinfeld (1980) and Wrigley (1985) for further discussion of these problems.]

The solution to this latter problem is to replace the conventional regression model with an alternative regression model whose predictions are automatically constrained to lie within the range 0 to 1. There are several potential models which satisfy this requirement but perhaps the most convenient of them, and the one which has become most widely used in the past decade, is based upon the cumulative logistic probability function and is referred to as the *logistic regression model*. (The only other model which has been used to any extent is based upon the cumulative normal probability function and is referred to as the *probit regression model*.) In the case of a dichotomous (i.e. 2-category) response variable, the logistic regression model takes the form:

$$p_i = \frac{e^{x_i'\beta}}{1+e^{x_i'\beta}} \qquad i=1,\ldots,N \tag{2.7}$$

where, in the simplest case:

$$x_i'\beta = \beta_0 + \sum_{k=1}^{K} \beta_k X_{ik}. \tag{2.8}$$

p_i (sometimes written $p_{1|i}$) represents the probability that the first category will be selected by the ith individual, or at the ith locality, given the values of the K explanatory variables. As the value of $x_i'\beta$ ranges from $-\infty$ to $+\infty$, p_i ranges in value from 0 to 1.

The logistic model (2.7) can be rewritten [see Pindyck and Rubinfeld (1980) and Wrigley (1985)] and shown to be equivalent to a linear model of the form:

$$\log_e \frac{p_i}{1-p_i} = x_i'\beta. \tag{2.9}$$

The left-hand side of this model is a transformation of p_i known as the *logit transformation* (logarithm of the odds ratio) and its value increases from $-\infty$ to $+\infty$ as p_i increases from 0 to 1. As a result, the model is normally referred to as the *linear logit model*. In both models (2.7) and (2.9) categorical explanatory variables can be included in the function (2.8) by adopting the well-known principles used in the extension of the conventional regression models of cell (a) of Table 2.1 to the "dummy" variable regression models of cell (b).

In the case of polytomous (i.e. more than 2-category) response variables, the dichotomous models (2.7) and (2.9) generalize in a straightforward manner [see Mantel (1966), Cox (1970, p. 105), Cragg and Uhler (1970, p. 396), Mantel and Brown (1973, p. 651), Wrigley (1975, p. 191), Schmidt and Strauss (1975a, p. 485)]. In the case of an R-category response variable, the logistic regression model takes the form:

$$p_{r|i} = \frac{e^{x_i' \beta_r}}{\sum_{s=1}^{R} e^{x_i' \beta_s}} \qquad \begin{array}{l} r = 1, \ldots, R \\ i = 1, \ldots, N \end{array} \tag{2.10}$$

where in the simplest case,

$$x_i' \beta_r = \beta_{0r} + \sum_{k=1}^{K} \beta_{kr} X_{ik}. \tag{2.11}$$

(More complex forms of (2.11) are possible where (2.11) also includes what in the transportation science literature are termed "generic" variables [see Wrigley (1985, pp. 72–76 and Appendix 2.1) for further details].) In (2.10) $p_{r|i}$ represents the probability that the rth category will be selected by the ith individual, or at the ith locality, given the values of the K explanatory variables. The linear logit regression model for the same case generalizes [for details see Theil (1970), Wrigley (1976, 1985), Pindyck and Rubinfeld (1980)] to the form:

$$\log_e \frac{p_{r|i}}{p_{R|i}} = x_i' \beta_r \qquad \begin{array}{l} r = 1, \ldots, R-1 \\ i = 1, \ldots, N \end{array}. \tag{2.12}$$

Once again, in both models (2.10) and (2.12), categorical explanatory variables can be included in the function (2.11). When such variables are mixed with continuous variables, models appropriate for the problems in cell (e) of Table 2.1 are produced; when categorical explanatory variables are the only variables included in the function (2.11), the logistic/logit models take a form suitable for the problems of cell (f).

The generalized models (2.10) and (2.11) are those appropriate for unordered polytomous response variables. In the situation where the categories of the response variable have a natural ordering, logistic/logit models which preserve the ordinal nature of the response without imposing an arbitrary scoring system are required. Cox (1970, p. 104) suggested that one way to achieve this is to appeal to the existence of an underlying continuous and perhaps unobservable random (latent) variable. In this way, the ordered response categories can be thought of as contiguous intervals on a continuous scale. McCullagh (1980) utilized this concept and suggested ordered response category logit models of the form:

$$\log_e \left(\frac{p_{r|i}^*}{1 - p_{r|i}^*} \right) = \theta_r - \sum_{k=1}^{K} \beta_k X_{ik} \qquad (1 \le r < R). \tag{2.13}$$

In this model it is assumed that there are R ordered categories of the response variable (Y_i) with probabilities $p_{1|i}, p_{2|i}, \ldots p_{R|i}$ respectively. Letting $p_{r|i}^*$ represent the cumulative summation $p_{1|i} + p_{2|i} + \ldots p_{r|i}$ (where $r < R$), the odds of a response category r or less in the ordering is the ratio $p_{r|i}^* / (1 - p_{r|i}^*)$. In this model, response categories are envisaged as contiguous intervals on a continuous scale separated by unknown points of division ("cut points") denoted $\theta_1, \ldots, \theta_r, \ldots, \theta_R$.

An alternative class of logit models can also be derived for response categories with a natural ordering. These models are based upon what are termed "continuation ratios" [see Fienberg (1980, p. 110), Fienberg and Mason (1978, p. 35)] and one simple form [see Wrigley (1985, p. 255)] considers logits based upon the conditional probabilities of selecting the rth response category given that the category is greater than $r - 1$ in the order. In this case,

$$p_{r|i}^{**} = \text{Prob}(Y_i = r | Y_i > r - 1) \tag{2.14}$$

and

$$\log_e \frac{p_{r|i}^{**}}{1 - p_{r|i}^{**}} = \theta_r + \sum_{k=1}^{K} \beta_k X_{ik}. \tag{2.15}$$

Pregibon (1982) points out that this amounts to factoring the multinomial response Y_i into conditionally independent binomials, and that this conditional independence can usefully be exploited in the estimation of the models.

2.2.2.   *Log-linear models for two-dimensional and multidimensional contingency tables*

In cells (f) and (g) of Table 2.1, all variables are categorical and sample data are most logically displayed in the form of the two-dimensional or multidimensional contingency tables which result from the cross-classification of the categorical

Table 2.3
An $I \times J$ two-dimensional contingency table.

		Variable B			
		$j = 1$	$2 \cdots$	J	Total
	$i = 1$	n_{11}	$n_{12} \cdots$	n_{1J}	n_{1+}
	$i = 2$	n_{21}	$n_{22} \cdots$	n_{2J}	n_{2+}
Variable A	$\vdots$				
	$i = I$	n_{I1}	$n_{I2} \cdots$	n_{IJ}	n_{I+}
	Total	n_{+1}	$n_{+2} \cdots$	n_{+J}	$n_{++} = N$

variables. For the statistical problems in both cells, log-linear models provide a powerful, and now widely adopted, tool of analysis.

In the case of cell (g) problems, no division of variables into explanatory and response is recognized, and in the simplest situation a two-dimensional $I \times J$ table takes the form shown in Table 2.3, where n_{ij} denotes the observed cell frequency (or count) in the typical cell ij. The most general linear model which can be used to represent the data in Table 2.3 (i.e. to represent the structural relationship between the variables which form the table) is linear in the logarithms of the frequencies, m_{ij}, to be expected in the cells and takes the form:

$$\log_e m_{ij} = \log_e E(n_{ij}) = \lambda + \lambda_i^A + \lambda_j^B + \lambda_{ij}^{AB} \quad \begin{matrix} i = 1, \ldots, I \\ j = 1, \ldots, J \end{matrix} \tag{2.16}$$

(where n_{ij} is in this case being viewed as a random variable). The parameters λ_i^A and λ_j^B are the main effects of variables A and B and λ_{ij}^{AB} is the first-order interaction effect between variables A and B [see also Birch (1963)]. The number of parameters in (2.16) is equal to $IJ + I + J + 1$ which is larger than the number of cell elements. Therefore, in order to identify the parameters of this model, constraints must be imposed. The two most common systems of parameter constraints are:
(a) the "centred effect" system

$$\sum_{i=1}^{I} \lambda_i^A = \sum_{j=1}^{J} \lambda_j^B = \sum_{i=1}^{I} \lambda_{ij}^{AB} = \sum_{j=1}^{J} \lambda_{ij}^{AB} = 0 \tag{2.17}$$

in which the first parameter, λ, is analogous to the overall mean term in an analysis-of-variance model, and the "main effect" parameters λ_i^A, λ_j^B, and "interaction" parameters, λ_{ij}^{AB}, represent deviations from the overall mean;
(b) the "cornered effect" system

$$\lambda_1^A = \lambda_1^B = \lambda_{1j}^{AB} = \lambda_{i1}^{AB} = 0 \tag{2.18}$$

in which the first parameter, λ, is analogous to the overall mean term in an analysis-of-variance model, and the "main effect" parameters λ_i^A, λ_j^B, and "inter-action" parameters, λ_{ij}^{AB}, represent deviations from the overall mean;
(b) the "cornered effect" system

The linear model (2.16) is referred to as the *saturated log-linear model* for a two-dimensional contingency table. The reason for this is that it is linear in the logarithms of the expected cell-frequencies and, because of (2.17) or (2.18), it has as many independent parameters as there are cells in the contingency table. The model will fit the observed cell-frequencies perfectly and there are no degrees of freedom.

By setting different parameters in (2.16) to zero, it is possible to specify a family of log-linear models. Each member of this family has a totally different interpretation, and is associated with a particular hypothesis about the nature of the structural relationships between the variables, A and B, in the two-dimensional contingency table. For example, if the interaction parameters λ_{ij}^{AB} are set to zero the resulting model takes the form

$$\log_e m_{ij} = \lambda + \lambda_i^A + \lambda_j^B \tag{2.19}$$

and this is a representation of the hypothesis of independence between variables A and B. Similarly, by setting λ_{ij}^{AB} and λ_j^B (or λ_{ij}^{AB} and λ_i^A) to zero the resulting models take the form

$$\log_e m_{ij} = \lambda + \lambda_i^A \tag{2.20}$$

$$\log_e m_{ij} = \lambda + \lambda_j^B \tag{2.21}$$

and these are representations of the hypotheses that the categories of the B (or A) variables are equally probable. Finally, by setting the interaction parameters and all the main effect parameters to zero, the model

$$\log_e m_{ij} = \lambda \tag{2.22}$$

is derived, and this model is a representation of the hypothesis that all categories of both variables are equally probable.

Taken together, models (2.16), (2.19), (2.20), (2.21) and (2.22) define what is termed the *hierarchical* set of log-linear models for a two-dimensional contingency table. This set of models has the property that higher-order parameters are only included in a model if all related lower-order parameters are also included (e.g. the λ_{ij}^{AB} parameters are only included if both the λ_i^A and λ_j^B parameters are also included). For both technical and interpretative reasons, non-hierarchical models such as

$$\log_e m_{ij} = \lambda + \lambda_{ij}^{AB} \tag{2.23}$$

or

$$\log_e m_{ij} = \lambda + \lambda_j^B + \lambda_{ij}^{AB} \tag{2.24}$$

which break this principle of parameter inclusion are only rarely considered.

Stated in somewhat crude terms, the log-linear modelling approach to the analysis of contingency tables involves the elimination, in a hierarchical fashion, of the parameters of the saturated model which are *not* essential to a description of the structural relationships between the variables in the table. By reducing the number of parameters in this fashion, an attempt is made to reduce the model to the most parsimonious form consistent with the relationships between the variables revealed in the contingency table data. As a result, log-linear modelling of a contingency table such as Table 2.3 involves the fitting of a hierarchical set of models, and the selection of one of these models as the most "acceptable" representation of the structural relationships between the variables in the table on the basis of its goodness-of-fit, parsimony, and substantive meaning.

Although log-linear models represent a valuable alternative to traditional tests for independence and measures of association in two-dimensional tables, their real advantages are to be seen most clearly in the case of *multidimensional* contingency tables. Such tables have traditionally been treated in a rather inadequate fashion by regional economists, yet multidimensional tables are the rule rather than the exception in research work in the social sciences [see also Fienberg and Meyer (1983)]. The simplest type of a multidimensional table is a three-dimensional table such as that shown in Table 2.4. In this case the two-dimensional saturated log-linear model extends to the form

$$\log_e m_{ijk} = \lambda + \lambda_i^A + \lambda_j^B + \lambda_k^C + \lambda_{ij}^{AB} + \lambda_{ik}^{AC} + \lambda_{jk}^{BC} + \lambda_{ijk}^{ABC} \quad \begin{matrix} i = 1, \dots, I \\ j = 1, \dots, J \\ k = 1, \dots, K \end{matrix} \tag{2.25}$$

Table 2.4
An $I \times J \times K$ three-dimensional contingency table.

		Variable C 1			Variable C 2			$\cdots$	Variable C K		
		Variable B 1	2 $\cdots$ J		Variable B 1	2 $\cdots$ J		$\cdots$	Variable B 1	2 $\cdots$ J	
Variable A	$i=1$	n_{111}	$n_{121} \cdots n_{1J1}$		n_{112}	$n_{122} \cdots n_{1J2}$		$\cdots$	n_{11K}	$n_{12K} \cdots n_{1JK}$	
	$i=2$	n_{211}	$n_{221} \cdots n_{2J1}$		n_{212}	$n_{222} \cdots n_{2J2}$		$\cdots$	n_{21K}	$n_{22K} \cdots n_{2JK}$	
	$\vdots$	$\vdots$	$\vdots \qquad \vdots$		$\vdots$	$\vdots \qquad \vdots$			$\vdots$	$\vdots \qquad \vdots$	
	$i=I$	n_{I11}	$n_{I21} \cdots n_{IJ1}$		n_{I12}	$n_{I22} \cdots n_{IJ2}$		$\cdots$	n_{I1K}	$n_{I2K} \cdots n_{IJK}$	
Total		n_{+11}	$n_{+21} \cdots n_{+J1}$		n_{+12}	$n_{+22} \cdots n_{+J2}$		$\cdots$	n_{+1K}	$n_{+2K} \cdots n_{+JK}$	

Table 2.5
Hierarchical set of log-linear models for a three-dimensional contingency table.

Model type	Number of models of such type	λ terms set to zero	Model specification
1	1	None	$\log_e m_{ijk} = \lambda + \lambda_i^A + \lambda_j^B + \lambda_k^C + \lambda_{ij}^{AB} + \lambda_{ik}^{AC} + \lambda_{jk}^{BC} + \lambda_{ijk}^{ABC}$
2	1	λ^{ABC}	$\log_e m_{ijk} = \lambda + \lambda_i^A + \lambda_j^B + \lambda_k^C + \lambda_{ij}^{AB} + \lambda_{ik}^{AC} + \lambda_{jk}^{BC}$
3	3	$\lambda^{ABC}, \lambda^{AB}$	$\log_e m_{ijk} = \lambda + \lambda_i^A + \lambda_j^B + \lambda_k^C + \lambda_{ik}^{AC} + \lambda_{jk}^{BC}$
4	3	$\lambda^{ABC}, \lambda^{AB}, \lambda^{BC}$	$\log_e m_{ijk} = \lambda + \lambda_i^A + \lambda_j^B + \lambda_k^C + \lambda_{ik}^{AC}$
5	1	$\lambda^{ABC}, \lambda^{AB}, \lambda^{AC}, \lambda^{BC}$	$\log_e m_{ijk} = \lambda + \lambda_i^A + \lambda_j^B + \lambda_k^C$
6	3	$\lambda^{ABC}, \lambda^{AB}, \lambda^{BC}, \lambda^{B}$	$\log_e m_{ijk} = \lambda + \lambda_i^A + \lambda_k^C + \lambda_{ik}^{AC}$
7	3	$\lambda^{ABC}, \lambda^{AB}, \lambda^{AC}, \lambda^{BC}, \lambda^{A}$	$\log_e m_{ijk} = \lambda + \lambda_j^B + \lambda_k^C$
8	3	$\lambda^{ABC}, \lambda^{AB}, \lambda^{AC}, \lambda^{BC}, \lambda^{A}, \lambda^{C}$	$\log_e m_{ijk} = \lambda + \lambda_j^B$
9	1	$\lambda^{ABC}, \lambda^{AB}, \lambda^{AC}, \lambda^{BC}, \lambda^{A}, \lambda^{B}, \lambda^{C}$	$\log_e m_{ijk} = \lambda$

and the additional parameter constraints

$$\sum_{i=1}^{I} \lambda_{ijk}^{ABC} = \sum_{j=1}^{J} \lambda_{ijk}^{ABC} = \sum_{k=1}^{K} \lambda_{ijk}^{ABC} = 0 \tag{2.26}$$

or

$$\lambda_{1jk}^{ABC} = \lambda_{i1k}^{ABC} = \lambda_{ij1}^{ABC} = 0 \tag{2.27}$$

are added to (2.17) and (2.18) respectively.

By setting different parameters in the saturated model (2.25) to zero, a hierarchical family of log-linear models for the three-dimensional table can be specified. This is shown in Table 2.5.

Once again, each member of the family implies a particular hypothesis about the relationships between the three variables. These hypotheses are discussed in detail by Bishop et al. (1975, p. 37), Payne (1977, p. 119), Haberman (1978, p. 197) and Wrigley (1985, pp. 171–172) and can be summarized as follows.

(a) *Type 1 hypothesis – saturated model.* This implies that the association between every pair of variables varies with the level of the third.

(b) *Type 2 hypothesis – pairwise association or "no three-variable interaction"* *model.* This implies that each pair of variables is associated but each two-variable effect is unaffected by the level of the third variable.

(c) *Type 3 hypothesis – conditional independence model.* This implies that a pair of variables is independent given the third, e.g. variable B may be independent of C given A.

(d) *Type 4 hypothesis – multiple independence model.* This implies that two variables considered as a joint variable are independent of the third, e.g. the joint variable *AB* may be independent of variable *C*.

(e) *Type 5 hypothesis – mutual independence model.* This is the three-dimensional equivalent of the model of independence (2.19) for two-dimensional tables.

(f) *Type 6 – 9 – "non-comprehensive" models.* These models involve the exclusion of one or more of the "main effect" terms. They indicate that the categories of one or more variables are equally probable given the other variables and, therefore, that one or more of the variables in the table is redundant. The implication is that the dimensionality of the table can be reduced accordingly.

As in the case of two-dimensional tables, the aim in log-linear modelling of a three-dimensional table such as Table 2.4 is to achieve a parsimonious representation of the structural relationships between the variables in the table. In practice, this involves the fitting of the hierarchical family of models shown in Table 2.5, and the selection of the most parsimonious member of this family which has a good fit to the observed data, and which provides a meaningful representation of the structural relationships between the variables in the table.

Extension of log-linear models from three-dimensional to four-dimensional and higher-dimensional tables is straightforward. For example, in the case of a four-dimensional $I \times J \times K \times L$ table, the saturated log-linear model becomes

$$\log_e m_{ijkl} = \lambda + \lambda_i^A + \lambda_j^B + \lambda_k^C + \lambda_l^D + \lambda_{ij}^{AB} + \lambda_{ik}^{AC} + \lambda_{il}^{AD} + \lambda_{jk}^{BC}$$

$$+ \lambda_{jl}^{BD} + \lambda_{kl}^{CD} + \lambda_{ijk}^{ABC} + \lambda_{ijl}^{ABD} + \lambda_{jkl}^{BCD} + \lambda_{ijkl}^{ABCD} \qquad (2.28)$$

and there are straightforward extensions to the parameter constraints systems (2.17) and (2.26) or (2.18) and (2.27).

Once again, by setting different parameters in (2.28) to zero, a hierarchical family of log-linear models for the four-dimensional table can be specified, each member of which implies a particular hypothesis about the structural relationships between the variables in the table [see Wrigley (1985, p. 174) for a description of the 167 models (28 model types) in this hierarchical family].

Log-linear models for multidimensional contingency tables can be seen, therefore, to be relatively simple extensions of log-linear models for two-dimensional tables. The advantages of using such models, and analysing multidimensional tables directly, rather than by splitting or collapsing such tables into a series of two-dimensional tables, are considerable. For example, it is now well known that sequential analysis of a series of two-dimensional tables formed by collapsing an essentially multidimensional underlying table can give rise to fallacious or paradoxical results [some extreme possibilities of this type were demonstrated by Simpson (1951) and have subsequently been referred to as *Simpson's paradox*].

Table 2.6

The hierarchical set of log-linear models fitted to Table 2.4 assuming variable A is the response variable and variables B and C are explanatory variables.

$$\log_e m_{ijk} = \lambda + \lambda_j^B + \lambda_k^C + \lambda_{jk}^{BC} + \lambda_i^A + \lambda_{ij}^{AB} + \lambda_{ik}^{AC} + \lambda_{ijk}^{ABC}$$

$$\log_e m_{ijk} = \lambda + \lambda_j^B + \lambda_k^C + \lambda_{jk}^{BC} + \lambda_i^A + \lambda_{ij}^{AB} + \lambda_{ik}^{AC}$$

$$\log_e m_{ijk} = \lambda + \lambda_j^B + \lambda_k^C + \lambda_{jk}^{BC} + \lambda_i^A + \lambda_{ij}^{AB}$$

$$\log_e m_{ijk} = \lambda + \lambda_j^B + \lambda_k^C + \lambda_{jk}^{BC} + \lambda_i^A \qquad + \lambda_{ik}^{AC}$$

$$\log_e m_{ijk} = \lambda + \lambda_j^B + \lambda_k^C + \lambda_{jk}^{BC} + \lambda_i^A$$

$$\log_e m_{ijk} = \lambda + \lambda_j^B + \lambda_k^C + \lambda_{jk}^{BC}$$

In the case of the statistical problems in cell (f) of Table 2.1, a division of variables into explanatory and response can be recognized. In this case a special ("asymmetric") form of the general class of log-linear models is utilized and attention centres upon assessing the effects of the explanatory variables on the response variable(s). These "asymmetric" log-linear models have essentially the same general form as those discussed above, and the same principles of hierarchical structuring, reduction to a parsimonious form, and so on, apply. The difference is that now the structural relationships between the explanatory variables are treated as fixed or given "facts of life". This implies that the marginal totals of the contingency tables corresponding to the explanatory variables are treated as fixed, and the *only* models considered are those in which all interactions between the explanatory variables (and the lower-order relatives of these interactions) are automatically included. For example, if in Table 2.4, variable A is regarded as a response variable and variables B and C as explanatory variables, all the log-linear models considered must automatically include the interaction between B and C and the lower-order relatives of this interaction. Table 2.6 shows all possible members of a hierarchical set of log-linear models formed in this way. The parameters which must be included have been written as the first terms in each model, and reduction of the models to a parsimonious form concentrates upon the latter terms in the models, i.e. upon the parameters which concern the relationships between the response and explanatory variables.

Although log-linear models for problems in cell (f) have an appearance which differs considerably from the logit models (2.9) and (2.12) which can also be used to analyse cell (f) problems, it is a simple matter to demonstrate that they are mathematically equivalent. Assuming, for example, a three-dimensional $2 \times J \times K$ contingency table in which variable A is the response variable and variables B and C are explanatory variables, we can focus on the log-odds ($\log_e(m_{1jk}/m_{2jk})$) of being in each category of variable A given the particular combination of categories of the explanatory variables. An expression for the log-odds can be obtained from the saturated log-linear model by noting that

$$\log_e m_{1jk} = \lambda + \lambda_j^B + \lambda_k^C + \lambda_{jk}^{BC} + \lambda_1^A + \lambda_{1j}^{AB} + \lambda_{1k}^{AC} + \lambda_{1jk}^{ABC} \tag{2.29}$$

and

$$\log_e m_{2jk} = \lambda + \lambda_j^B + \lambda_k^C + \lambda_{jk}^{BC} + \lambda_2^A + \lambda_{2j}^{AB} + \lambda_{2k}^{AC} + \lambda_{2jk}^{ABC} \tag{2.30}$$

and that

$$\log_e \frac{m_{1jk}}{m_{2jk}} = \log_e m_{1jk} - \log_e m_{2jk}$$

$$= \left(\lambda_1^A - \lambda_2^A\right) + \left(\lambda_{1j}^{AB} - \lambda_{2j}^{AB}\right) + \left(\lambda_{1k}^{AC} - \lambda_{2k}^{AC}\right) + \left(\lambda_{1jk}^{ABC} - \lambda_{2jk}^{ABC}\right). \tag{2.31}$$

Assuming a "centred effect" parameter constraint system, it follows that $\lambda_1^A = -\lambda_2^A$, $\lambda_{1j}^{AB} = -\lambda_{2j}^{AB}$, and so on. Consequently, the terms in brackets in (2.31) can be seen to be $(\lambda_1^A - \lambda_2^A) = (\lambda_1^A + \lambda_1^A) = 2\lambda_1^A$, and so on [see Payne (1977, p. 137), Fienberg (1980, p. 78), Wrigley (1985, p. 224)]. This implies that (2.31) can be written as

$$\log_e \frac{m_{1jk}}{m_{2jk}} = 2\lambda_1^A + 2\lambda_{1j}^{AB} + 2\lambda_{1k}^{AC} + 2\lambda_{1jk}^{ABC}$$

$$= \omega + \omega_j^B + \omega_k^C + \omega_{jk}^{BC} \tag{2.32}$$

which is, clearly, a logit model of the type discussed in Section 2.2.1. It represents an *equivalent* way of expressing the saturated log-linear model for the $2 \times J \times K$ table, and illustrates the mathematical relationship between log-linear and logit models for cell (f) problems.

In deriving this equivalence, it should be noted that the terms in (2.29) and (2.30) which involve only the explanatory variables cancel out (e.g. $\lambda_{jk}^{BC} - \lambda_{jk}^{BC}$), and that the logit model (2.32) can also be derived using the "cornered effect" parameter constraints. [See Wrigley (1985, pp. 227–230) for further details, including the equivalence of log-linear models for multidimensional cell (f)-problem contingency tables and polytomous logit models.]

2.3. Estimation procedures

The parameter estimation procedures which are appropriate for qualitative statistical models can be divided into three main classes [see also Imrey et al. (1981)].

(1) Iterative proportional fitting methods.

(2) Weighted least squares (WLS) methods, both iterative and non-iterative.

(3) Function maximization techniques, e.g. Newton–Raphson, Davidon–Powell.

However, the distinction between the classes is not, in practice, as clear as it might first appear. For example, in the context of log-linear models, Haberman (1978, pp. 64, 128, 170, 207) shows that the Newton–Raphson procedure reduces to a series of weighted least squares problems and, as such, the procedure is very similar to Nelder and Wedderburn's iterative weighted least squares method which can be used to estimate the parameters of any member of the family of "generalized linear models". An alternative approach to the classification of the estimation procedures, involves, therefore, a consideration of which methods are appropriate for the logistic/logit models of cells (d) to (f) of Table 2.1, and which are appropriate for the log-linear models of cells (g) and (f).

In the case of logistic/logit models, both function maximization techniques and weighted least squares procedures can, theoretically, be used. However, in practice, the *non-iterative* WLS procedure is confined to the problems in cell (f) of Table 2.1 in which *all* explanatory variables are categorical. For problems of this type, WLS parameter estimates can be obtained by minimizing the quadratic form

$$(\bar{L} - X\beta)' V_{\bar{L}}^{-1}(\bar{L} - X\beta) \tag{2.33}$$

where $\bar{L}$ is a vector of observed logit values, and V^{-1} is a matrix of weights [see Grizzle et al. (1969), Theil (1970), Koch et al. (1977), Parks (1980), Wrigley (1985, pp. 121–125) for details]. The WLS estimator of the parameters β, in the logit models (2.9) or (2.12) then takes the form

$$\hat{\beta} = \left(X' V_{\bar{L}}^{-1} X \right)^{-1} X' V_{\bar{L}}^{-1} \bar{L} \tag{2.34}$$

The non-iterative WLS procedure provides a computationally convenient method of estimating the parameters of cell (f) logit models, and WLS estimates can be shown to have desirable asymptotic properties; even though they are not, in general, MLEs – maximum likelihood estimators. [Examples of logit models for regional economic analysis estimated using this procedure are to be found in

Brouwer and Nijkamp (1984), Imrey et al. (1982) and Wrigley (1980a)]. However, it is a procedure which assumes that the data to be modelled have arisen from an underlying product multinomial sampling model [see Wrigley (1985, pp. 14, 125)] and most importantly, it is a procedure which depends upon the availability of moderate- and large-size samples in each combination of categories of the explanatory variables. For problems in cells (d) and (e) of Table 2.1, where explanatory variables are continuous or a mixture of categorical and continuous, this latter condition is rarely satisfied [see Wrigley (1985, p. 34)]. For this reason, the non-iterative WLS procedure is rarely used for such problems and direct function maximization (numerical optimization) techniques [see Wrigley (1985, pp. 33–38, pp. 67–69)], or Nelder and Wedderburn's iterative weighted least squares method, become the universally adopted procedures. Both procedures produce MLEs and these have the usual very desirable properties.

In the case of log-linear models, iterative proportional fitting, iterative weighted least squares, or Newton–Raphson estimation procedures can be adopted, and all three procedures produce MLEs. However, as noted above, the Newton–Raphson procedure reduces to a series of weighted least squares problems and can therefore be subsumed in the discussion of Nelder and Wedderburn's iterative weighted least squares procedure.

The iterative proportional fitting (Deming–Stephan) procedure is the most commonly employed method for the estimation of log-linear models. Its name derives from the fact that each iteration in the procedure involves a proportional adjustment of a row or column of the table of estimated values of the expected cell frequencies. For example, in fitting the model

$$\log_e m_{ijk} = \lambda + \lambda_i^A + \lambda_j^B + \lambda_k^C + \lambda_{ij}^{AB} + \lambda_{ik}^{AC} + \lambda_{jk}^{BC} \tag{2.35}$$

the initial estimates of the expected cell frequencies are adjusted to fit the observed AB marginal totals, then the observed AC marginal totals, and finally the BC observed marginal totals [see also Fienberg (1970)]. With each new fit, however, the previous adjustments are lost. Hence, it is necessary to begin a new cycle of the iteration process, starting with the final estimates of the previous cycle. The process continues until only an arbitrarily small difference between the estimated marginal totals and the specified observed marginal totals remains, and at this stage the procedure is concluded. Generally, convergence is very rapid, and it seldom takes more than ten cycles. Once the expected cell frequencies have been estimated in this way, the parameter estimates can be computed in a straightforward manner, and approximations to the asymptotic variances of the parameter estimates can be obtained [see Wrigley (1985, pp. 184–188)].

Nelder and Wedderburn's iterative weighted least squares procedure is a general method which can be used to obtain maximum likelihood estimates for any member of the family of "generalized linear models". In the case of log-linear models, the iterative WLS estimator of the vector of parameters, λ, takes the form

$$\hat{\lambda} = \left(X'V_z^{-1}X \right)^{-1} X'V_z^{-1}z \qquad (2.36)$$

where V_z^{-1} is a matrix of weights which has terms of the form $\hat{m}_{ijk}$ (or alternatively $\hat{m}_{ij}$, $\hat{m}_{ijkl}$, etc.) down its principal diagonal and zeros elsewhere, and where z is a vector of modified or "working" values of the logarithms of the expected cell frequencies which take the form

$$z_{ijk} = \log_e \hat{m}_{ijk} + \frac{n_{ijk} - \hat{m}_{ijk}}{\hat{m}_{ijk}}. \qquad (2.37)$$

A direct solution of (2.36) is not possible for it depends upon the m_{ijk} values and, initially, these are unknown. An iterative solution is, therefore, necessary and this begins by taking the observed frequencies, n_{ijk}, as a first approximation to the $\hat{m}_{ijk}$ and setting $z_{ijk} = \log_e n_{ijk}$. From this a first approximation of the weights and of the elements of $\hat{\lambda}$ can be obtained. This allows a second approximation to the $\hat{m}_{ijk}$ to be computed and the iterative process continues until convergence. Standard errors can then be obtained directly from the square roots of the elements along the principal diagonal of the matrix

$$V_{\hat{\lambda}} = \left(X'V_z^{-1}X \right)^{-1}. \qquad (2.38)$$

Each of the estimation procedures discussed above is now operationalized by a standard computer program. In the case of log-linear models, the GLIM (Generalized Linear Interactive Modelling) package developed by The Royal Statistical Society and NAG (Numerical Algorithms Group) utilizes the iterative WLS estimation procedure [see Baker and Nelder (1978)], and the BMDP (Biomedical Computer Programs, P-Series) package uses the iterative proportional fitting method [see Brown (1981)]. Both packages are very widely available, and are regularly updated. In the case of logistic/logit models: the GENCAT package [Landis et al. (1976)] provides non-iterative WLS estimation of the logit models appropriate for the problems in cell (f) of Table 2.1; the GLIM package currently provides iterative WLS estimation of binomial logistic/logit models for problems in cells (d), (e) and (f) of Table 2.1 (and is likely to be extended to polytomous models); and econometric packages such as BLOGIT [Hensher and Johnson (1981)] and QUAIL [Berkman et al. (1979)] use function maximization techniques to derive maximum likelihood estimates of the parameters of both dichotomous and polytomous logistic/logit models [see Wrigley (1985, pp. 233–238) for further discussion].

2.4.   Model assessment and selection procedures

2.4.1.   Goodness-of-fit measures

The goodness-of-fit of any model within Nelder and Wedderburn's family of "generalized linear models" can be assessed using a generalized measure known as the "deviance". The value of this statistic is produced automatically for any model fitted within the GLIM computer package, and it takes the form:

$$D = -2\left[\log_e \Lambda(\hat{\boldsymbol{\beta}}) - \log_e \Lambda_{\max}\right] \tag{2.39}$$

where $\log_e \Lambda(\hat{\boldsymbol{\beta}})$ denotes the maximized log-likelihood of the fitted model, and $\log_e \Lambda_{\max}$ denotes the maximized log-likelihood of the so-called "complete" model which fits a parameter for every observation and so explains everything, reducing the residual variation to zero [see Nelder (1974)]. In the case of logistic/logit models, the general expression for the "deviance" specializes to the form $-2\log_e \Lambda(\hat{\boldsymbol{\beta}})$ (i.e. -2 times the maximized log likelihood value of the fitted model) or more fully, for dichotomous models (2.7), to the form:

$$D = -2 \sum_{i=1}^{N} \left[Y_i \log_e \hat{p}_i + (1 - Y_i)\log_e(1 - \hat{p}_i)\right] \tag{2.40}$$

[see Landwehr et al. (1984, p. 62)]. Similarly, in the case of log-linear models, the general expression (2.39) specializes [see Nelder (1974)] to the form

$$\begin{aligned}
D &= -2 \sum_{i=1}^{I} \sum_{j=1}^{J} \sum_{k=1}^{K} n_{ijk}\left[\log_e(\hat{m}_{ijk}/n_{ijk})\right] \\
&= 2 \sum_i \sum_j \sum_k n_{ijk}\left[\log_e(n_{ijk}/\hat{m}_{ijk})\right]
\end{aligned} \tag{2.41}$$

for three-dimensional tables, or equivalent expressions for two-dimensional or higher-dimensional tables. (In the literature of log-linear modelling, expression (2.41) is usually referred to as G^2 – the likelihood ratio statistic [see Bishop et al. (1975, p. 125), Everitt (1977, p. 79)].)

An alternative type of goodness-of-fit measure for both logistic/logit and log-linear models is the standard Pearson chi-squared statistic, X^2. This takes the form

$$X^2 = \sum_{i=1}^{I} \sum_{j=1}^{J} \sum_{k=1}^{K} \frac{(n_{ijk} - \hat{m}_{ijk})^2}{\hat{m}_{ijk}} \tag{2.42}$$

(or equivalent expressions) for log-linear models, and the form

$$X^2 = \sum_{i=1}^{N} \frac{(Y_i - \hat{p}_i)^2}{\hat{p}_i(1 - \hat{p}_i)} \tag{2.43}$$

for the logistic/logit models of expressions (2.7) and (2.9). However, although asymptotic arguments suggest that both the deviance and Pearson's chi-squared measures have the same approximate χ^2 distributions with degrees of freedom equal to the number of cells in the table minus the number of model parameters that require estimating, and are asymptotically equivalent, it can be shown that the deviance measures have several important and useful features [e.g. divisibility into additive portions (Bishop et al. 1975, p. 125)] which the chi-squared measures do not possess. Another disadvantage of Pearson's chi-squared statistic is its proportionality to the sample size. For these reasons the deviance statistics are the most widely adopted goodness-of-fit measures.

2.4.2.   Model selection procedures

Model selection procedures for both log-linear and logistic/logit models are based, essentially, upon the goodness-of-fit measures described above. In log-linear modelling, for example, the G^2 statistics for various members of a hierarchical set of log-linear models are compared, and the most parsimonious member of the set which has a satisfactory fit to the observed data (as measured by the G^2 statistic) is the model selected as the "acceptable" representation of the structural relationships between the variables in the contingency table. In the case of two-dimensional or three-dimensional tables, selection of the "acceptable" model can be achieved by fitting all possible models in the hierarchical set. However, in the case of higher-dimensional tables, where there are many hundreds of possible models, this naive selection strategy is no longer satisfactory. In such cases, systematic, efficient and, if possible, statistically elegant model selection strategies are required. Many possibilities have been suggested, but of these, the three following methods are the most widely adopted [see Fingleton (1981, 1984), Wrigley (1985, pp. 190–211)].

(a) *Abbreviated stepwise selection* [Goodman (1971), Upton (1978)]. In this procedure standardized values ($\hat{\lambda}/\sqrt{\text{var}\,\hat{\lambda}}$) of the parameter estimates in the saturated log-linear model are used to determine an initial approximation to the final "acceptable" model, and this initial approximation is then refined using a forward selection or backward elimination process based on the G^2 values of alternative models. The forward selection procedure adds significant effects to the basic model and the backward elimination procedure eliminates insignificant effects from the saturated model. It should be noted that both approaches will not necessarily give the same model specification.

(b) *Screening* [Brown (1976)]. In this procedure, each term in the saturated log-linear model is evaluated using two test statistics; one of partial association and the other of marginal association. These tests assess each term in two extreme situations; the first conditional on all terms of the same order, and the second conditional on only the lower-order relatives of the term in question. The two tests are representative of the range (they can be thought of as approximate lower and upper bounds to the range) of the conditional G^2 values that would be obtained by adding that particular term to a previous specification of the log-linear model. As such, the two tests enable each term in the saturated model to be screened, and placed into one of three alternative categories:

(i) significant and necessary in the final "acceptable" model;

(ii) insignificant and unnecessary in the final model;

(iii) of questionable significance and in need of further investigation.

Screening the parameters of the saturated log-linear model in this way guides the selection of an initial approximation to the final "acceptable" model, and this initial model is then refined using forward selection or backward elimination methods. (Screening tests for the parameters of saturated log-linear models are a standard feature of the widely available BMDP computer program.)

(c) *Simultaneous test procedure* [Aitkin (1979, 1980)]. A common characteristic of all selection strategies for log-linear models is that they involve multiple tests of the data. Theoretically, some allowance should be made for this and, to avoid attributing significance to what is merely random variation, significance levels of the tests should be adjusted to compensate for the multiple testing. In this procedure, significance levels are adjusted in this way, and a systematic, internally consistent, and efficient approach to model selection is provided. The method is statistically elegant and is well suited to use with the GLIM computer problem. However it is more complex to use than procedures (a) or (b).

2.4.3. Diagnostics

Whichever of the possible model selection strategies is adopted (similar selection procedures are applicable to logistic/logit models) it is important that selection should not be allowed to become a mechanical process, and that it should be supplemented by as wide a range of diagnostic measures and tests as possible. In this context, the most commonly used diagnostic is, of course, the *residual* which measures the difference between the observed and fitted values and which is used to detect anomalous/ill-fitted data points ("outliers"), or unmodelled systematic patterning in the data. In the case of qualitative statistical models, residuals can be defined in several different ways, but two of the most useful definitions are the so-called "components of chi-squared" and the "components of deviance". For logistic/logit and log-linear models these can readily be obtained from expressions (2.42) and (2.43) and (2.41) and (2.40) respectively. For example, in the case of log-linear models, the "components of chi-squared" residual takes the form

$$e_{ijk} = (n_{ijk} - \hat{m}_{ijk})/\sqrt{\hat{m}_{ijk}} \tag{2.44}$$

and is often referred to as the "standardized residual" [see Haberman (1974, 1978, p. 230)]. Similarly, for the logistic/logit models of expressions (2.7 and 2.9) the "components of chi-squared" residual takes the form

$$\chi_i = (Y_i - \hat{p}_i)/\sqrt{\hat{p}_i(1 - \hat{p}_i)} \tag{2.45}$$

and the "components of deviance" residual takes the form

$$d_i = -2[Y_i \log_e \hat{p}_i + (1 - Y_i)\log_e(1 - \hat{p}_i)] \tag{2.46}$$

[see Wrigley (1984)]. Both types of residual can be used to focus attention on observations where the qualitative statistical model fits poorly. As in conventional continuous-data linear models, it can then be asked whether these ill-fitting observations reveal any systematic patterning or have any common characteristic which might suggest that the model is not fully specified.

In the case of logistic/logit models, it will often be useful to supplement the inspection of residuals with a second diagnostic measure which considers extreme points in the "design space" (the so-called "high leverage" points which may be inordinately influential in the model fitting process). The *leverage* of the ith data point is defined as the ith diagonal element, h_{ii}, of the projection or "hat" matrix

$$H = V^{1/2}X(X'VX)^{-1}X'V^{1/2} \tag{2.47}$$

where X is a $N \times K$ (N observations, K parameters) matrix of explanatory variables, and V is a diagonal matrix with elements

$$v_{ii} = \hat{p}_i(1 - \hat{p}_i).$$

Large h_{ii} values represent extreme points in the "design space" (high leverage points). Large leverage values are usually taken to be those exceeding $2K/N$ or $3K/N$ [Hoaglin and Welsch (1978), Belsley et al. (1980)] and these data points should be the subject of further investigation. For example, are they *so* different from the rest of the sample that they may have been incorrectly coded or mispunched and should they be excluded from the analysis?

By plotting χ_i against i, d_i against i, and h_{ii} against i in logistic/logit models, it is usually a simple matter to identify which data points are "troublesome" in the two senses of: (a) being poorly explained by the model, or (b) having the

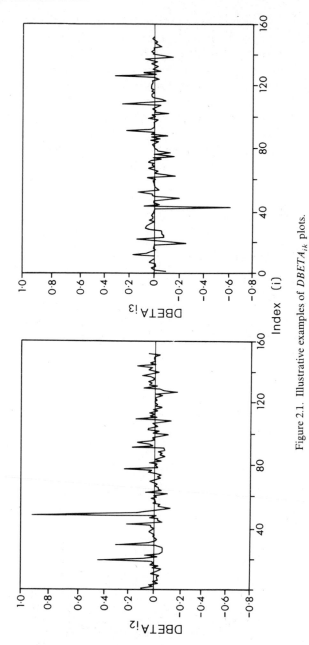

Figure 2.1. Illustrative examples of $DBETA_{ik}$ plots.

potential to exert an unduly large influence on some aspect of the fit. However, such plots are not suited to an assessment of the *impact* of such data points on the parameter estimates obtained, or on the fitted values predicted by the logistic/logit model. To answer these questions, two further diagnostic measures have recently been suggested [see Pregibon (1981, 1982), Wrigley and Dunn (1984)].

The first of these considers the effect which deletion of a single data point will have on the stability of individual parameter estimates. Across all K parameter estimates in the logistic/logit model, the overall change resulting from the deletion of data point i can be expressed as

$$DBETA_i = \hat{\boldsymbol{\beta}} \text{ (all obs.)} - \hat{\boldsymbol{\beta}} \text{ (all obs. except } i) = \frac{(X'VX)^{-1}x_i s_i}{1 - h_{ii}} \qquad (2.48)$$

where x_i is a $(K \times 1)$ vector of explanatory variables for data point i, $s_i = Y_i - \hat{p}_i$, and $DBETA_i$ can be seen to be a $(K \times 1)$ vector. The usual procedure is then to focus on each parameter estimate, $\hat{\beta}_k$, in turn (i.e. each element of the $DBETA_i$ vector) and to plot the standardized values obtained by dividing element k of $DBETA_i$ by the estimated standard error of $\hat{\beta}_k$. The standardized diagnostics obtained are referred to as $DBETA_{ik}$. Plots of $DBETA_{ik}$ against i (as shown in

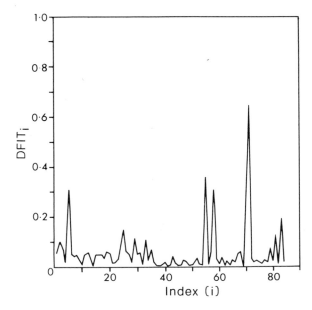

Figure 2.2. Illustrative example of a $DFIT_i$ plot.

Figure 2.1) for each of the K parameters in the model show clearly which observations are causing instability, and how great an effect deletion of a particular data point will have on a particular parameter estimate. A positive value of $DBETA_{ik}$ indicates that removing observation i would decrease the value of $\hat{\beta}_k$: a negative value the reverse.

The second of the diagnostics, $DFIT_i$, takes the form

$$DFIT_i = \frac{\chi_i^2 h_{ii}}{(1 - h_{ii})^2} \qquad (2.49)$$

and measures the effect which deletion of the single data point i has on the fitted values obtained from the model. $DFIT_i$ can also be viewed as providing a useful summary measure of the *overall* effect of the changes in the parameter estimates shown in the individual $DBETA_{ik}$ plots. (This second interpretation results from the fact that changes in individual parameter estimates shown in the $DBETA_{ik}$ plots can be offset by changes in other parameter estimates in such a way that the fitted values change very little.) Once again, it is valuable to plot $DFIT_i$ against i as shown in Figure 2.2.

2.5. *Some extended forms of the basic model*

The log-linear and logistic/logit models derived in Section 2.2 are merely the simplest forms of such models, and a wide range of important extensions are available to the researcher. To illustrate this range of extensions, two examples will now be considered.

The first extension concerns models for *incomplete* contingency tables. The need for such models arises when empty cells (i.e. zero observed frequencies) in a contingency table represent logically impossible combinations. Empty cells of this type are referred to as *structural* or "fixed" zeros, and must be distinguished from *sampling* zeros which result from the difficulty of obtaining a sufficiently large and well structured sample to avoid certain cells having no recorded observations. Sampling zeros should, theoretically, disappear as sample size increases, but structural zeros will not. The analysis of incomplete tables will therefore be necessitated "when some categories are a priori impossible given the way in which data are collected and restructured" [see also Fienberg and Mason (1978, p. 12)].

Appropriate forms of both log-linear and logit models have been proposed for the analysis of incomplete contingency tables. Logit models for such tables are discussed by Koch et al. (1972, 1977), Imrey et al. (1976, 1981, 1982) and can be estimated using the non-iterative WLS procedure and the GENCAT package. Particularly important in this context is the fact that a number of seemingly unrelated statistical techniques (e.g. paired comparison experiment methods) can be reformulated as logit models for incomplete tables and incorporated within a unified approach to the analysis of qualitative data [see Wrigley (1980b, 1985, pp. 264–271)].

Log-linear models for incomplete tables are more widely known than the equivalent logit models, and they are discussed in most of the standard texts [e.g. Bishop et al. (1975), Everitt (1977), Upton (1978), Fienberg (1980), Fingleton (1984), Wrigley (1985)]. In these circumstances, the appropriate forms of the models are referred to as *quasi* log-linear models, and they are applied to only the subset of non-structural-zero cells. In the case of a two-dimensional incomplete table, for example, the most general log-linear model takes the form:

$$\log_e m_{ij} = \lambda + \lambda_i^A + \lambda_j^B + \lambda_{ij}^{AB} \quad \text{for all cells which are not structural zeros.} \tag{2.50}$$

Assuming a "centred effect" system, the parameter constraints associated with this model take the form:

$$\sum_{i=1}^{I} \delta_i^{(2)} \lambda_i^A = \sum_{j=1}^{J} \delta_j^{(1)} \lambda_j^B = 0 \tag{2.51}$$

$$\sum_{i=1}^{I} \delta_{ij} \lambda_{ij}^{AB} = \sum_{j=1}^{J} \delta_{ij} \lambda_{ij}^{AB} = 0 \tag{2.52}$$

$\delta_{ij} = 1$ for all ij cells which are not structural zeros

$\quad = 0$ otherwise $\tag{2.53}$

$\delta_i^{(2)} = 1$ if $\delta_{ij} = 1$ for some j

$\quad = 0$ otherwise $\tag{2.54}$

$\delta_j^{(1)} = 1$ if $\delta_{ij} = 1$ for some i

$\quad = 0$ otherwise. $\tag{2.55}$

By setting different parameters in (2.50) to zero, a hierarchical set of quasi log-linear models can be specified. For example, by setting the λ_{ij}^{AB} parameters to zero for all ij cells which are not structural zeros, a model of quasi-independence can be obtained. The parameters and expected cell frequencies of such quasi log-linear models can be estimated without difficulty using the iterative WLS or proportional fitting procedures described in Section 2.3. The only requirement is to ensure that the initial cell estimates are set to zero for the structural zero cells. However, when the goodness-of-fit of a quasi log-linear model is assessed, the degrees of freedom must be adjusted to take account of the structural zero cells via the expression

$$\text{d.f.} = \frac{\text{number of cells in table–number of structural}}{\text{zero cells–number of parameters that require estimation.}} \quad (2.56)$$

The use of quasi log-linear models is especially relevant in spatial interaction analysis. Consider for example a spatial interaction matrix with cell-frequencies which denote interregional migration flows. In this case, the principal diagonal of the matrix (the intraregional flows) will be a set of structural zeros.

Finally, it should be noted that quasi log-linear models can be regarded as forerunners of a wider class of models which Willekens and Baydar (1985) have termed *hybrid* log-linear models. Hybrid models occur when a set of restrictions (other than independence-related restrictions or the conventional parameter constraints) are imposed on the interaction parameters associated with a subset of the cells in a contingency table, and they will often include extra parameters which are not found in conventional log-linear models [e.g. Fienberg and Mason (1978) discuss the age–period–cohort analysis of social mobility tables, especially the underidentified models corresponding to such tables, and show that restrictions on parameters are necessary to be able to identify and estimate the parameters of such models]. Some special forms of hybrid log-linear models, including the diagonals parameter model, the triangles parameter model, and the crossings parameter model, were proposed by Goodman (1972) and are potentially useful in regional economic analysis. These models are discussed and utilized by Haberman (1974, pp. 215–227, 1979, pp. 500–503), Bishop et al. (1975, pp. 320–324), Upton (1978, pp. 126–129), Fienberg and Mason (1978), Upton and Sarlvik (1981), and Fingleton (1984).

The hybrid nature of log-linear models can be used for spatial interaction analysis by means of an entropy function for the off-diagonal cell elements. Brouwer et al. (1985), for example, make use of the hybrid log-linear model:

$$
\begin{aligned}
m_{ij} &= w w_i^A w_j^B w_{ij}^{AB} & \text{if } i = j \\
m_{ij} &= w w_i^A w_j^B \exp\left[-\beta(d_{ij})\right] & \text{if } i \neq j
\end{aligned}
\quad (2.57)
$$

Formula (2.57) is the multiplicative formulation of the log-linear model for a two-way contingency table with overall mean effect w, the main effects w_i^A and w_j^B and w_{ij}^{AB} the first-order interaction effect between variables A and B. The well-known interaction effects arise in formula (2.57) when i equals j, and an entropy function is included for the off-diagonal elements.

A second extension of the basic models of Section 2.2 concerns forms of log-linear and logistic/logit models which are appropriate for *systems* of equations; both recursive equation systems and simultaneous equation systems.

Recursive systems of logit models are considered by Fienberg (1977, pp. 94–104) and shown to "mimic" recursive systems of conventional regression models. That is to say, the parameters in each of the logit equations in the recursive system should be estimated by the usual methods and the MLEs for the parameters in the system are just the MLEs of the parameters for each equation in the system when viewed separately. Recursive models of this type underlie attempts by Goodman (1973a, 1973b, 1978) to provide a log-linear model/categorical-data analogue to conventional path analysis. Like conventional path analysis, Goodman's analogue has two key features. First, the models in the system make explicit the assumed order of priority (causal ordering) of the categorical variables. Second, the relationships between the variables are described in terms of path diagrams [see also Knoke and Burke (1980, p. 47), Wermuth and Lauritzen (1982)]. However, unlike conventional path analysis, there is no simple method of assigning numerical values (path coefficients) to the paths and arrows which connect together the causal structure (path) diagram. Goodman suggests using the parameter estimates of cell (f)-type log-linear models or their logit-model equivalents, but Fienberg (1977, p. 92) suggests a more cautious approach limited to an indication of the sign of the causal relationships.

Systems of logistic/logit models for simultaneous equation systems have generated a considerable literature [e.g. Nerlove and Press (1973), Amemiya (1975), Schmidt and Strauss (1975b, 1976), Olsen (1978), Schmidt (1978), Heckman (1977, 1978, 1981), Maddala (1983)]. In early work on this topic, Schmidt and Strauss (1975b) considered simple simultaneous systems of logit models of the form

$$\left.\begin{aligned}\log_e\left[\frac{\text{Prob }(Y_i=1|Q_i)}{\text{Prob }(Y_i=0|Q_i)}\right] &= x_i'\beta + \alpha Q_i \\[2ex] \log_e\left[\frac{\text{Prob }(Q_i=1|Y_i)}{\text{Prob }(Q_i=0|Y_i)}\right] &= x_i^{*\prime}\beta^* + \delta Y_i\end{aligned}\right\} \tag{2.58}$$

in which there are two dichotomous response variables, Y_i and Q_i, a set of exogenous variables x_i affecting Y_i and a set of exogenous variables x_i^* affecting Q_i, and a "symmetry" condition which implies that $\alpha = \delta$. They then went on to consider the polytomous response variable extension of (2.58), and also "mixed" systems of models [Schmidt and Strauss (1976)] in which one of the response variables (say Y_i) is categorical but the other (Q_i) is continuous. The structure of their simultaneous logit models has been subject to considerable debate [e.g. Olsen (1978), Schmidt (1978), Maddala (1983, pp. 349–362)] and Heckman (1977, 1978, 1981) has adopted a rather different approach to the "mixed" model system problem. In this, he assumes that there is an unobservable (latent) continuous variable, S_i, which reflects "sentiment" for or against choice of a particular response category, and that actual response category choices ($Y_i = 1$ or 0) are generated by the latent variable crossing particular thresholds. Using the same definition of terms as in (2.58) his model takes the form

$$
\left.
\begin{aligned}
S_i &= x_i'\beta + \alpha Q_i + \gamma_1 Y_i + \varepsilon_{1i} \\
Q_i &= x_i^*{}'\beta^* + \delta S_i + \gamma_2 Y_i + \varepsilon_{2i} \\
Y_i &= \begin{array}{l} 1 \text{ if } S_i > 0 \\ 0 \text{ if } S_i \le 0 \end{array}
\end{aligned}
\right\}
\tag{2.59}
$$

where ε_{1i} and ε_{2i} are error terms. The parameters γ_1, γ_2 and α of (2.59) obey certain constraints and, as a result, the model can be written in reduced form. [Full details of this approach and of the current state-of-the-art in the modelling of qualitative simultaneous-equation systems is to be found in Maddala (1983).]

3. Empirical examples

Some of the qualitative statistical models and methods discussed in the previous sections will now be illustrated using three examples from recent regional economic studies. The examples focus on:
(1) regional variation in rates of industrial innovation in the U.K.;
(2) regional quality-of-life and residential preferences in the Netherlands; and
(3) a regional industrial accessibility survey in Northern Ireland.

3.1. Example 1: Regional variations in rates of industrial innovation

As part of a wider research programme on interregional differences in rates of technological change in British manufacturing industry, a survey of 807 enterprises in three leading-edge industries (scientific and industrial instruments, electronic components, metalworking machine tools) was conducted [Thwaites et al. (1981)]. Logit models were then used [Alderman et al. (1982)] to explain three dichotomous measures of innovative activity: (a) process innovation – whether any new process was introduced at the plant between 1973 and 1977; (b) product innovation – whether any new product was introduced at the plant between 1973 and 1977, and (c) research and development – whether carried out on site at the plant or not.

In the case of product innovation, some of the potential determinants of variation in rates of industrial innovation were believed to be plant size (P), enterprise type (E), industrial sector (I), regional location (L), and importance of on-site research and development (R). Each of these potential explanatory variables was categorical in nature. Plant size and research and development were dichotomies representing plants in terms of total number of employees (greater than 100 or less than 100) and importance of on-site R & D effort (more than 5 full-time R & D employees, or less than 5). Enterprise type and industrial sector were trichotomies representing size of enterprise (single-plant-independent, multi-plant enterprise with less than 10 plants, multiplant enterprise with more than 10 plants) and sector (scientific instruments, electronic components, metalworking machine tools). Regional location was a variable with four categories representing the degree of assistance from regional policy measures (non-assisted South-East England, other non-assisted regions, regions with "intermediate area" status and assistance, and regions with "development area" status and assistance). As a result, the data used to calibrate the logit model of product innovation could be represented as a contingency table, and the simplest "main-effects" logit model of product innovation took the cell (f) form shown in equation (2.32) above: that is to say,

$$\log_e \frac{m_{1jklmn}}{m_{2jklmn}} = \omega + \omega_j^P + \omega_k^E + \omega_l^I + \omega_m^L + \omega_n^R \qquad \begin{aligned} & j = n = 1,2 \\ & k = l = 1,\ldots,3 \\ & m = 1,\ldots,4. \end{aligned} \qquad (3.1)$$

Initial fitting of model (3.1) showed that, in the presence of the R & D variable, the plant size variable was redundant (the larger the plant the more able it was to support a large R & D effort). As a result, plant size was removed from the model and the contingency table collapsed over that variable. A revised model was then fitted using the GLIM computer program which uses a "cornered effect" system of parameter constraints [see (2.18)]. The fit of this model as measured by its "deviance" statistic was satisfactory and the parameter estimates obtained are shown in Table 3.1. These indicate that the odds of product innovation at a plant are increased if: (a) the plant has a sizable on-site R & D capacity; (b) if it belongs to a large multiplant enterprise, and (c) if it is in the scientific instrument sector. However, the odds of product innovation are significantly reduced if plants are located in regions with "development area" status, or to a lesser extent in regions with "intermediate area" status. The latter finding was of particular importance for it confirmed the view that innovative performance (particularly that of independent single-plant enterprises with low or zero on-site R & D) was much poorer in the assisted regions of Britain than elsewhere, and that there was a need to develop an innovation dimension to regional policy in the U.K. and to target innovation policy at indigenous enterprise in the peripheral regions.

Inspection and analysis of the standardized residuals from the revised model (i.e. the deviant cells of the contingency table) was then conducted [Alderman

Table 3.1
Product innovation model – parameter estimates.

Parameter	Interpretation	Estimate	Standard error
ω	anchor cell parameter – single plant independent with low or zero R & D in metalworking machine tools located in non-assisted South-East England	1.23	0.29
ω_2^E	multiplant enterprises with less than 10 plants	0.16	0.24
ω_3^E	multiplant enterprises with more than 10 plants	1.55	0.41
ω_2^I	scientific instruments sector	0.57	0.29
ω_3^I	electronic components sector	-0.34	0.28
ω_2^L	other non-assisted areas	-0.47	0.28
ω_3^L	intermediate areas	-0.47	0.33
ω_4^L	development areas	-1.01	0.30
ω_2^R	larger on-site R & D effort	1.47	0.29

et al. (1982, pp. 20–22)]. This indicated that, of the independent single-plant enterprises with low or zero R & D located in development areas, it was particularly those in the scientific instruments sector which performed less well than predicted in terms of product innovation. This sector is, in general, a highly innovative one in the U.K., and single-plant independent enterprises without R & D will be highly dependent on the local environment for technological inputs, not having access to corporate R & D and technical knowledge. This finding suggests, therefore, that the environment for independent enterprise in a highly innovative sector is much poorer in the development status regions of the U.K. than in other industrial sectors or elsewhere.

3.2. *Example 2: Regional quality-of-life and residential preference surveys*

Table 3.2 shows information on regional quality-of-life characteristics and residential preferences obtained in the Netherlands [see also Heida and Gordijn (1978)]. The contingency table is a four-dimensional $3 \times 2 \times 2 \times 3$ table with variables:

$M = $
1 if the probability of staying in the region is larger than the probability of moving to another region within the next five years;
2 if there is no difference in preference whether to move or to stay in the region one lives in;
3 if the probability of moving to another region is larger than the probability of staying in the region for the next five years.

Table 3.2
$3\times2\times2\times3$ table of regional quality-of-life and residential preference.

	O = 1				O = 2				O = 3			
	E = 1		E = 2		E = 1		E = 2		E = 1		E = 2	
M	P = 1	P = 2	P = 1	P = 2	P = 1	P = 2	P = 1	P = 2	P = 1	P = 2	P = 1	P = 2
1	843	253	22	6	579	143	29	4	161	66	8	3
2	54	89	2	3	29	49	1	7	17	22	1	2
3	20	62	1	11	14	38	1	7	3	20	1	1

$P = 1$ if the region one lives in corresponds with the region one prefers;
    2 if the region one lives in does not correspond with the preferred region.
$E = 1$ if a good quality of environment (especially air quality) in the region one
    lives in is very important;
    2 if a good quality of environment (especially air quality) in the region one
    lives in is less important.
$O = 1$ if one prefers to buy a house;
    2 if one prefers to rent a house;

Description of the structural relationships between the variables in Table 3.2 can be achieved by fitting all possible members of the hierarchical set of log-linear models and by selecting the most parsimonious member of that set which has a satisfactory fit to the observed data. Alternatively, and preferably, a formal model selection strategy of the type discussed in Section 2.4.2 can be utilized.

Table 3.3 shows some of the simplest members of the hierarchical set of log-linear models fitted to Table 3.2. On the basis solely of parsimony and

Table 3.3
Some members of the hierarchical set of log-linear models fitted to Table 3.2.

Model	G^2	d.f.	Critical value
$M + P + E + O + M \times P + M \times E + P \times O + M \times O + P \times E + E \times O$	15.42	16	26.30
$M + P + E + O + M \times P + M \times E + P \times O + M \times O + P \times E$	22.44	18	28.87
$M + P + E + O + M \times P + M \times E + P \times O + M \times O$	22.47	19	30.14
$M + P + E + O + M \times P + M \times E + P \times O$	24.29	23	35.17
$M + P + E + O + M \times P + M \times E$	34.87	25	37.65
$M + P + E + O + M \times P$	59.53	27	40.11
$M + P + E + O + M \times E$	391.2	27	40.11
$M + P + E + O + M \times O$	410.5	25	37.65
$M + P + E + O + P \times E$	411.2	28	41.34
$M + P + E + O + P \times O$	405.2	27	40.11
$M + P + E + O + E \times O$	408.9	27	40.11
$M + P + E + O$	415.8	29	42.56

goodness-of-fit, the most acceptable representation of the structural relationships between the variables in Table 3.2 is provided by the model

$$\log_e m_{ijkl} = \lambda + \lambda_i^M + \lambda_j^P + \lambda_k^E + \lambda_l^O + \lambda_{ij}^{MP} + \lambda_{ik}^{ME} + \lambda_{jl}^{PO} \tag{3.2}$$

with a G^2 value of 24.29 which is smaller than its associated critical value. The more parsimonious model

$$\log_e m_{ijkl} = \lambda + \lambda_i^M + \lambda_j^P + \lambda_k^E + \lambda_1^O + \lambda_{ij}^{MP} + \lambda_{ik}^{ME} \tag{3.3}$$

which also has an acceptable fit based upon its G^2 value (34.87) can be rejected as the "acceptable representation" on the basis of a "conditional-G^2" test [see Wrigley (1985, p. 178)] which can be used to compare the difference between the G^2 values of the two models. The difference $(34.87 - 24.29) = 10.58$ with $(25 - 23)$ $= 2$ degrees of freedom is well above the tabulated χ^2 of 5.99 at the conventional 5 percent significance level. Thus the null hypothesis that the $P \times O$ interaction is zero can be rejected, and model (3.2) which suggests interactions between movement expectation and regional preferences ($M \times P$), between movement expectations and environmental quality ($M \times E$) and between regional preferences and housing tenure preference ($P \times O$) can be chosen as the most acceptable representation of the structural relationships between the variables in Table 3.2.

3.3. *Example 3: A regional industrial accessibility survey*

Table 3.4 contains information from an industrial accessibility survey of manufacturing firms in Northern Ireland. As part of this survey, each firm was asked to evaluate the importance to its operations of access to four so-called "freight gateways" – Aldergrove airport (A); Belfast docks (B); Larne docks (L) and Warrenpoint docks (W). Each firm classified each gateway as "important" (I) or "unimportant" (U), and a firm could make one of 2^4 possible types of response – ranging from an evaluation of all four gateways as being important to an evaluation of all four as being unimportant. The firms themselves were grouped into eight types according to the cross-classification of three explanatory variables – (O): ownership of the firm (Irish or non-Irish, determined by the location of the head office); (S): size (large: more than 100 employees; small: less than 100 employees); (M): market orientation (export oriented: more than 10% exported to the markets outside Northern Ireland and the Irish republic, or non-export oriented: less than 10% exported).

In any analysis of Table 3.4, two important issues must be considered.

(a) First, a response variable/explanatory variable distinction exists and can usefully be taken into account in the modelling procedure. As a result, two types

Table 3.4
Response to freight gateway questions [Wrigley (1980)].

				Response profiles															
Subpopulations			Ald	I	I	I	I	I	I	I	I	U	U	U	U	U	U	U	U
			Bel	I	I	I	I	U	U	U	U	I	I	I	I	U	U	U	U
			Lar	I	I	U	U	I	I	U	U	I	I	U	U	I	I	U	U
Ownership	Size	Market	War	I	U	I	U	I	U	I	U	I	U	I	U	I	U	I	U
j=1 Non-Irish	Larger	Exporter		16	30	1	6	0	5	1	2	0	3	0	3	0	4	1	4
j=2 Non-Irish	Larger	Non-exporter		2	8	0	2	1	0	0	0	0	0	0	1	0	0	0	3
j=3 Non-Irish	Smaller	Exporter		5	4	1	2	0	1	0	0	1	0	0	2	0	1	0	2
j=4 Non-Irish	Smaller	Non-exporter		5	5	0	0	1	1	0	0	0	5	0	0	0	0	0	1
j=5 Irish	Larger	Exporter		8	19	0	4	1	4	0	1	0	5	1	1	0	1	1	7
j=6 Irish	Larger	Non-exporter		2	4	1	0	0	0	0	1	0	2	0	6	0	0	0	3
j=7 Irish	Smaller	Exporter		9	28	1	9	1	4	1	2	1	10	0	6	2	2	3	8
j=8 Irish	Smaller	Non-exporter		19	19	0	16	0	1	1	3	1	5	1	11	2	7	0	25

Ald U
Bel I
Lar I = { Access to freight services of Belfast and Larne Docks an important advantage of location, access to freight services
War U   of Aldergrove Airport and Warrenpoint Docks an unimportant advantage of location.

of models can be adopted. The first of these are hierarchical log-linear models with a form suitable for the problems of cell (f) of Table 2.1. In such models, the interactions between the explanatory variables O, S and M (and possibly also those between the response variables A, B, L and W), together with the lower-order relatives of these interactions, are treated as fixed or given "facts of life". These terms, which are of relatively minor interest, are automatically included in all members of the hierarchical set of log-linear models considered, and attention centres upon the other parameters which concern the relationships between the response and explanatory variables. The second type of models are logit models which attempt to exploit the "repeated measurement research design" structure of Table 3.4 and which can be estimated with non-iterative WLS procedures [see Koch et al. (1977), Lehnen and Koch (1974)]. In this example, consideration will be confined to just the first of these possibilities, i.e. to hierarchical log-linear models, and the results of an analysis performed by Upton (1981) will be discussed. However, logit models with complex non-hierarchical and nested structures have also been fitted to the same data by Wrigley (1980).

(b) Second, it is clear that Table 3.4 is both large and sparse, and contains many zero cell frequencies. This feature must be borne in mind in any analysis and in any interpretation of models fitted to the data.

In his analysis of Table 3.4, Upton (1981) used the screening procedure suggested by Brown (1976) as his basic model selection technique (see Section 2.4.2). As a result, each term in the saturated log-linear model fitted to the data of Table 3.4 was evaluated using the partial association and marginal association test statistics and could be placed in one of three alternative categories: (i)

Table 3.5
Some results of screening the freight gateway data

Interaction	Marginal association G^2	Partial association G^2
Probably important:		
OML	4.5	6.8
AB	77.0	44.2
AL	68.0	22.7
BL	48.4	16.1
LW	21.6	10.1
AW	20.1	8.7
Questionable significance:		
OA	10.8	1.5
OL	10.7	2.5
ML	10.1	3.7
MA	9.2	2.1
MLW	7.6	2.9
SA	6.8	0.9
MAW	4.4	2.3
SL	4.0	0.0
SML	3.9	1.3
BW	4.5	0.2
Insignificant:		
MW	0.1	0.2
SW	0.1	1.4
⋮	⋮	⋮
OMB	0.3	0.8

significant and necessary in the final "acceptable" model; (ii) insignificant and unnecessary in the final model; (iii) of questionable significance and in need of further investigation. Table 3.5 shows some results of this screening. From these it can be concluded that (apart from the automatically included interactions between the explanatory variables O, S and M, the fixed "facts of life") there are 6 interactions which are probably significant and necessary in the final "acceptable" model, and a further 10 which are of questionable significance and in need of further study.

The 16 interactions (and their lower-order relatives whether individually insignificant or not) were then used by Upton to form an initial approximation to the final "acceptable" model. This initial model was then refined using backward elimination methods to produce a final model with a satisfactory overall fit which included the terms, $O \times S \times M$, $A \times B$, $A \times L$, $B \times L$, $A \times W$, $O \times M \times L$, $O \times A$, $M \times L \times W$, $S \times M \times L$ (and the lower-order relatives of these terms).

As noted above, attention in this case centres upon the parameters which concern the relationships between the response and explanatory variables ($O \times M \times L$, $O \times A$, $M \times L \times W$ and $S \times M \times L$). These indicate the following:

(i) $O \times A$ – non-Irish owned firms are more likely than Irish owned firms to consider access to the freight services of Aldergrove airport to be an important location factor;

(ii) $O \times M \times L$ and $S \times M \times L$ – the perceived importance of access to the freight services of Larne docks is related to the firm's market orientation ownership and size (70% of export-oriented firms, regardless of size or ownership type, and 70% of non-Irish non-export-oriented firms consider such access to be an important location factor, but only 50% of Irish non-export-oriented ("insular") firms consider access to the freight services of Larne docks to be important).

(iii) $M \times L \times W$ – the attitude of export-oriented firms towards the freight services of Warrenpoint docks is virtually independent of their attitude towards the freight services of Larne docks. (However, it should be noted that Upton believes that this term is likely to be of doubtful substantive (as opposed to statistical) importance.)

4. Other issues and future developments

The analysis of qualitative data continues to be a major focus for advances in statistical methodology and this chapter has provided little more than the briefest possible introduction to the field. Several topics which are of central importance to the future potential of qualitative statistical models remain unconsidered. In particular, no consideration has yet been given to:

(a) the interlinkage of developments in microeconomic theory, psychological choice theory and the statistical analysis of qualitative data;

(b) the integration of classical spatial analysis techniques into qualitative statistical models for regional analysis;

(c) the members of the wider class of qualitative statistical methods which lie outside the core family of models (log-linear, logistic/logit and probit, etc.) discussed above;

(d) the likely developments in computer software for qualitative data analysis.

A brief, and necessarily partial, guide to several of these issues will now be given, and this will highlight some of the developments in qualitative statistical modelling which can be expected over the next decade.

4.1. *Choice models and qualitative data analysis*

Over the past ten years, there has been widespread recognition that microeconomic theory needs modifying to allow the focusing of attention on choices at the *extensive* margin (i.e. discrete choices) rather than the *intensive* margin which is treated in traditional analysis. In the work of McFadden, Manski, Heckman, Hensher and others [see Manski and McFadden (1981), Manski (1981), McFadden (1982), Hensher and Johnson (1981)] significant progress has been made in this direction and it has been shown that a logically consistent discrete choice theory can be developed based upon an interpersonal interpretation of the hypothesis of random utility maximization. Moreover, it has been shown that computationally tractable forms of probabilistic discrete choice models can be developed which, in practice, take the logistic/logit and probit forms discussed above.

Although it is not appropriate in this short section to attempt any extensive discussion of the research field (discrete choice modelling) which has developed out of this interlinkage of developments in microeconomic theory, psychological choice theory and the statistical analysis of qualitative data [see instead Chapter 3 of this Handbook; Hensher and Johnson (1981), McFadden (1982), Wrigley (1985, pp. 310–357)] there are, however, three themes in this research which must be picked out as potentially important to the future development of qualitative models for regional economic analysis.

4.1.1. *IIA and the search for less restrictive qualitative choice models*

Multiple choice-alternative logit models (referred to as multinomial logit or MNL models) have a property known as "independence from irrelevant alternatives" (IIA) and assume independent and identically distributed error components. In many cases, this property and these assumptions impose no unrealistic restriction on the structure of the choice probabilities. However, this is not always the case and, in certain situations when the error components are correlated [see Wrigley (1985, pp. 324–326) for examples], MNL models will produce counter-intuitive predictions. As a result there has been a search for alternative qualitative/discrete choice models based upon less restrictive assumptions.

In recent years, a wide spectrum of such models has been considered, and several of these are likely to find application in regional economic analysis. The most general, least restrictive, of the alternative discrete choice models is the multinomial probit (MNP) model [Daganzo (1979)]. The MNP allows error components to be correlated and to have unequal variances, and it also permits random taste variation. By restricting the form of the variance–covariance error structure of the MNP model, a family of special cases of the MNP can be specified, and these have already been shown to be capable of providing insight into problems of economic location [see Miller and Lerman (1981)]. Unfortunately, the MNP model is conceptually complex and computationally unwieldy, and the most popular estimation procedure (which uses the Clark approximation to reduce the estimation problem to one of sequential univariate integration) remains controversial [Sheffi et al. (1982)]. As a result, there has been a search for what might be termed "half-way house" models which lie somewhere between the generality and complexity of the MNP model and the restrictiveness but tractability of the MNL model.

The two most popular "half-way house" models are the *dogit* [Gaudry and Dagenais (1979)] and the *nested logit* model [see Sobel (1980), Wrigley (1985, pp. 329–332)]. In particular, the nested logit, which is a special case of the so-called *generalized extreme value* (GEV) model has recently held a prominant theoretical and empirical position. The work of Williams (1977) and McFadden (1979) established the consistency of nested logit models with random utility maximization and the correct form and significance of the so-called "composite utility or inclusive value" terms within such models. Nested models can readily handle correlated error components, and they can thus embody more general properties of cross-substitution than the MNL without sacrifice of computational tractability. (Traditionally, a sequential form of parameter estimation has been used but, more recently, full information maximum likelihood (FIML) estimation techniques have been adopted.) Nested logit models have already been widely used in the context of regional transport planning and applications in many fields of regional economic analysis can be expected.

4.1.2. Choice experiment data and decompositional multiattribute preference models

Discrete choice models are usually calibrated using survey data on observed choice behaviour. Such data can be subject to many sources of confoundment, and are often available for only a limited range of attribute levels: a range which may be insufficient to permit extrapolation of choice predictions to the unobserved attribute mixes which are likely to define any "new" alternatives which might enter the choice set. In these circumstances, preference data obtained from controlled choice experiments involving hypothetical alternatives may have a particularly valuable role to play (e.g. in the context of regional industrial preference surveys). Such experiments allow the separation out of error components which become confounded in normal sample survey data and allow decision makers to formulate preferences over new or unattainable alternatives.

In practice, choice experiments of this kind form the basis of a class of choice models known as "decompositional multiattribute preference models" [see Timmermans (1984)]. Such models are sometimes regarded as competitive alternatives to discrete choice models; the issue being closely related to the relative merits of revealed versus expressed preferences. However, there is a growing concensus [e.g. Timmermans (1984), Hensher and Louviere (1983), Louviere and Hensher (1983)] that the two types of models may be used in a complementary way depending on the type of choice problem.

4.1.3. Longitudinal data and dynamic models

Discrete choice models have traditionally been estimated using cross-sectional sample survey data. However, in certain situations, the researcher will have access to much richer longitudinal data which can be exploited to develop dynamic models of individual choice behaviour and to identify the influences on economic, social and environmental change. Identifying such influences is by no means a simple task. It requires an understanding of a number of interrelated sources of variation; in particular, heterogeneity (variation between individuals due to both observed and unobserved exogenous influences), non-stationarity (variation over time of individual event probabilities), and intertemporal state-dependence (the dependence of current behaviour on past behaviour and future behaviour on current behaviour). When some influences on change are unobserved, in the sense of being omitted or unmeasurable, with the further possibility that they are temporally invariant and hence correlated with any time-invariant observable variables, it becomes a very difficult task indeed to disentangle the influences of intertemporal state-dependence and heterogeneity. Yet such a separation is vital if "spurious" state-dependence is not to be confused with "true" state-dependence [see Davies and Crouchley (1985)].

Fortunately, in recent years, there have been major advances in the statistical analysis of longitudinal data [see Wrigley (1986) for a wider review] and techniques have now been developed which permit identification of the structural parameters of exogenous determinants of choice behaviour whilst controlling for other influences on behaviour (i.e. state-dependence, initial conditions, non-stationarity, and the heterogeneity caused by omitted and unobservable variables). In the latter case, for example, both parametric and non-parametric methods have been developed to represent heterogeneity and to identify the exogenous determinants of choice behaviour. The parametric methods give rise to the so-called *beta-logistic* [Heckman and Willis (1977)] and *Dirichlet-logistic* [Dunn and Wrigley (1985)] models which are essentially longitudinal data extensions of the conventional dichotomous and polytomous cross-sectional logistic models of Section 2.2.1. The non-parametric methods, on the other hand, produce what are referred to as *mass point* models: models which have proved to be both theoretically and computationally attractive in many recent applications [see Davies and Crouchley (1984), Pickles and Davies (1985), Dunn et al. (1986)].

4.2. Integration of spatial analysis techniques into qualitative statistical models

A pivotal concept in spatial analysis is that of spatial dependence or spatial autocorrelation, and over the past twenty years considerable attention has been paid to the problems which derive from applying classical statistical models and inferential procedures (which assume independent observations) to geo-graphical/regional data which typically exhibit systematic ordering over space (see also Chapter 10 of the present Handbook). During this period, the analysis of spatial data has developed from a stage of relatively uncritical application of standard inferential tests and statistical models to a stage of wide appreciation of the effects of spatially dependent data. Tests for spatial autocorrelation have been developed, classical statistical models and tests have been modified to handle spatially dependent data, and extensive research on spatial process modelling and spatial time-series analysis has been conducted [see Cliff and Ord (1973, 1981), Hepple (1974), Bennett (1979), Griffith (1980), Haining (1980), Bennett and Haining (1985)].

To some extent, it is possible to view qualitative data methods in regional economic analysis as being in an analogous position to the classical continuous data methods used in spatial analysis a decade or more ago. As a result, integration of spatial dependence concepts into the analysis of qualitative data is likely to proceed along the same path as described above, but at a much accelerated rate. Indeed, the first steps along this path have already been taken. For example, Fingleton (1983, 1984) has shown that considerable care is neces-sary when attempting to apply log-linear models to spatially dependent data. In these circumstances the standard model selection procedures (see Section 2.4.2) may erroneously detect interaction effects between variables (or even main effects) which are, in fact, spurious and a consequence of the spatially dependent observations. Fingleton's solution to this problem involves modifying Pearson's chi-square statistic by means of a correction for positive spatial dependence. Similarly, Odland and Barff (1982) have attempted to combine the logic of existing space–time interaction tests with qualitative statistical models in order to model the space–time patterns of housing deterioration in an American city, and there have also been several useful extensions of the traditional family of spatial interaction models proposed which build upon qualitative statistical methods [see Smith and Slater (1981), Brouwer et al. (1985)].

Further integration of spatial dependence concepts and spatial analysis tech-niques into qualitative statistical models is of vital importance [see Fischer and Nijkamp (1985), Nijkamp et al. (1985) for a wider discussion of this issue]. To some extent this integration is likely to follow an accelerated version of the path established in the late 1960s and 1970s for continuous spatial data. However, its nature is likely to be different as any integration will be influenced by the prevailing trends in statistical methodology: for example, the adoption of a more interactive and exploratory approach to statistical modelling and the use of a much wider range of diagnostic tools [see Wrigley (1983)], and the growing interest in the effects of complex survey designs on classical statistcal models and methods [see Holt et al. (1980a, 1980b)].

4.3. The wider class of qualitative statistical methods

Beyond the core family of log-linear, logistic/logit and probit models discussed in this chapter, there is a wider class of qualitative statistical methods which ranges from path analysis and linear structural models to correspondence analysis and scaling techniques [see Nijkamp et al. (1985)]. Some of these methods have already been found to be useful in areas such as the analysis of regional economic policy [Folmer (1983)], whilst others are still rarely applied in regional economics. As illustrations of this wider class of methods, two techniques will be picked out for further discussion: linear structural equation (LISREL) models and partial least squares (PLS) techniques.

4.3.1. Linear structural equation models

Linear structural equation (LISREL) models are based on latent variable methods which allow handling of both latent (or non-observable) and observable variables simultaneously. They may be regarded as a synthesis of path analysis, covariance structure models, recursive and non-recursive models for cross-sectional and longitudinal data, factor analysis and simultaneous equation models. The relationships between the latent variables and their observable indicators are denoted in a latent variables measurement model. The relationships between the latent variables are given in a structural model. This model approach allows the simultaneous estimation of parameters to describe the relationships between theoretical variables, and parameters to represent the relationships between observable and theoretical variables. A LISREL model can be estimated by the LISREL-5 computer program which will give consistent maximum likelihood estimators.

Folmer (1983) dealt with spatial auto- and cross-correlation in the framework of LISREL models. He demonstrated that the LISREL approach could measure regional effects of instruments of the control type and of instruments of the influencing type under various conditions. This research issue is highly relevant for spatial analysis because recently categorical data have been included in conventional LISREL models.

4.3.2. Partial least squares

The mainstream of qualitative statistical models is based on the maximum likelihood principle, with observations which correspond to a joint probability distribution function (e.g. product multinomial distribution). Partial least squares (PLS) is now a well established method in quantitative research and systems analysis because it tries to bridge the gap between theory and statistical techniques by providing a general and flexible scope for causal predictive analysis in causal chain models [Wold (1985)]. The analysis of causal relations by means of the PLS-approach may be relevant when the theoretical knowledge concerning model specification is scarce and the availability of information is incomplete or inadequate. The PLS approach was originally developed for the analysis of causal relationships with cardinal information. However, recent developments in the form of the PLS approach deal with contingency table analysis with categorical data, qualitative canonical correlation analysis, nested qualitative causal models and mixed (quantitative and qualitative) path analysis [Bertholet and Wold (1985)]. Very little attention has been given to spatial dependent variables in PLS models [Nijkamp et al. (1985)]. In conclusion, qualitative spatial analysis with PLS models is still in a premature stage of development but offers much promise in the near future.

4.4.   Developments in computer software for qualitative data analysis

As noted in Section 2.3 standard computer programs now exist to fit all members of the core family of qualitative statistical models. Indeed, a feature of the past ten years has been the gradual incorporation of such programs into the major statistical packages used by social scientists (SPSS, BMDP, SAS and so on). These programs now form key elements of these worldwide distributed packages and, with the recent release of the programs LOGLINEAR and HILOGLINEAR in SPSS[x] [User Guide (1984)] and the annotated description provided in the SPSS[x] Advanced Statistics Guide [Norusis (1985, pp. 295–365)] it is certain that log-linear, logistic/logit models, etc. will be used with even increasing frequency in regional analysis.

Inevitably, however, it is to specialized econometric software rather than the standard packages that we must look for the most recent developments. Particularly noteworthy in this context are: (a) programs for longitudinal data versions of logistic/logit models estimated using either parametric or non-parametric (mass point) representations of heterogeneity [see Section 4.1, Davies and Crouchley (1984), Dunn and Wrigley (1985), Dunn et al. (1986), Pickles and Davies (1985)]; (b) programs for full information maximum likelihood (FIML) estimation rather than sequential estimation of nested logit models [Hensher (1984)]; (c) improved software for the estimation of multinomial probit (MNP) models [Sheffi et al. (1982)]; (d) subroutines for graphical diagnostic testing of logistic/logit, probit models [Wrigley and Dunn (1984, 1986)], and so on. However, there is at least one major package, GLIM [see Baker and Nelder (1978)], which has the capacity to incorporate the most recent software developments in qualitative statistical modelling. GLIM not only allows the fitting of any member of the wide family of "generalized linear models" (GLMs) which can be specified from the exponential family of probability distributions, but also allows the fitting of extensions of conventional GLMs derived using composite link functions [Thompson and Baker (1981)], quasi-likelihood estimation procedures [Nelder (1985)], and user-supplied subroutines which are referred to as GLIM "macros". The regular *GLIM Newsletter* contains many topical and valuable macros and, in the context of the software developments picked out above, it is worthwhile to note that GLIM macros have already been used to fit longitudinal-data logistic models by mass point techniques [Hinde and Wood (1985)] and to perform resistant fitting of logistic models [Wrigley and Dunn (1984)]. The major limitation of GLIM as it is currently configured is the lack of a multinomial error distribution as a default option. However, it is hoped that this limitation will soon be rectified [see Clarke (1982)].

This study is partly supported by the Netherlands Organization for the Advancement of Pure Research (ZWO), project-number 46–125.

References

Aitkin, M. (1979) 'A simultaneous test procedure for contingency table models', *Applied Statistics*, 28:233–242.
Aitkin, M. (1980) 'A note on the selection of log-linear models', *Biometrics*, 36:173–178.
Alderman, N., J. B. Goddard, A. T. Thwaites and P. A. Nash (1982) 'Regional and urban perspectives on industrial innovation: applications of logit and cluster analysis to industrial survey data', Discussion Paper No. 42, Centre for Urban and Regional Development Studies, University of Newcastle upon Tyne, U.K.
Amemiya, T. (1975) 'Qualitative response models', *Annals of Economic and Social Measurement*, 4:263–272.
Amemiya, T. (1981) 'Qualitative response models: a survey', *Journal of Economic Literature*, 19:1483–1536.
Baker, R. J. and J. A. Nelder (1978) *The GLIM System, Release 3*. Oxford: Numerical Algorithms Group.
Belsley, D. A., E. Kuh and R. E. Welsh (1980) *Regression diagnostics: identifying influential data and sources of collinearity*. New York: Wiley.
Bennett, R. J. (1979) *Spatial time series: analysis, forecasting and control*. London: Pion.
Bennett, R. J. and R. P. Haining (1985) 'Spatial structure and spatial interaction: modelling approaches to the statistical analysis of geographical data', *Journal of the Royal Statistical Society, Series A*, 148:1–36.
Berkman, J., D. Brownstone et al. (1979) 'QUAIL 4.0 users and programmers manuel (Berkeley)'. Available from D. Brownstone, Dept. of Economics, Princeton Univ., Princeton, New Jersey 08540, USA.
Bertholet, J.-L. and H. Wold (1985) 'Recent developments in categorical data analysis by PLS', in: P. Nijkamp, H. Leitner, N. Wrigley, eds., *Measuring the unmeasurable*. Dordrecht: Martinus Nijhoff, 253–286.
Birch, M. W. (1963) 'Maximum likelihood in three-way contingency tables', *Journal of the Royal Statistical Society B*, 25:220–233.
Bishop, Y. M. M., S. E. Fienberg and P. W. Holland (1975) *Discrete multivariate analysis: theory and practice*. Cambridge, Mass.: MIT Press.
Brouwer, F. and P. Nijkamp (1984) 'Linear logit models for categorical data in spatial mobility analysis', *Economic Geography*, 60:102–110.

Brouwer, F., P. Nijkamp and H. Scholten (1985) 'Hybrid log-linear models for spatial interaction and stability analysis', Department of Economics, Free University, Amsterdam.

Brown, M. B. (1976) 'Screening effects in multidimensional contingency tables', *Applied Statistics*, 25:37–46.

Brown, M. B. (1981) 'Frequency tables. P4f', in: W. J. Dixon et al., eds., *BMDP. Statistical software, 1981*. Berkeley: University of California Press, 143–206.

Clarke, M. R. B. (1982) 'GLIM 4—the new facilities', in: R. Gilchrist, ed., *GLIM 82: proceedings of the international conference on generalized linear models*. New York: Springer, 25–35.

Cliff, A. D. and J. K. Ord (1973) *Spatial autocorrelation*. London: Pion.

Cliff, A. D. and J. K. Ord (1981) *Spatial processes: models and applications*. London: Pion.

Cox, D. R. (1970) *The analysis of binary data*. London: Methuen.

Cragg, J. G. and R. S. Uhler (1970) 'The demand for automobiles', *Canadian Journal of Economics*, 3:386–406.

Daganzo, C. F. (1979) *Multinomial probit: the theory and its application to demand forecasting*. New York: Academic Press.

Davies, R. B. and R. Crouchley (1984) 'Calibrating longitudinal models of residential mobility and migration: an assessment of a non-parametric likelihood approach', *Regional Science and Urban Economics*, 14:231–247.

Davies, R. B. and R. Crouchley (1985) 'Control for omitted variables in the analysis of panel and other longitudinal data', *Geographical Analysis*, 17:1–15.

Dempster, A. P., N. M. Laird and D. B. Rubin (1977) 'Maximum likelihood from incomplete data via the EM algorithm', *Journal of the Royal Statistical Society B*, 39:1–38.

Dunn, R., S. Reader and N. Wrigley (1986) 'A non-parametric approach to the incorporation of heterogeneity into repeated polytomous choice models of urban shopping behaviour', *Transportation Research*.

Dunn, R. and N. Wrigley (1985) 'Beta-logistic models of urban shopping centre choice', *Geographical Analysis*, 17:95–113.

Everitt, B. S. (1977) *The analysis of contingency tables*. London: Chapman and Hall.

Fienberg, S. E. (1970) 'An iterative procedure for estimation in contingency tables', *Annals of Mathematical Statistics*, 41:907–917.

Fienberg, S. E. (1977) *The analysis of cross-classified categorical data*, 1st edition. Cambridge, Mass.: MIT Press.

Fienberg, S. E. (1980) *The analysis of cross-classified categorical data*, 2nd edition. Cambridge, Mass.: MIT Press.

Fienberg, S. E. and W. M. Mason (1978) 'Identification and estimation of age–period–cohort models in the analysis of discrete archival data', in: K. F. Schuessler, ed., *Sociological methodology 1979*. San Francisco: Jossey-Bass, 1–67.

Fienberg, S. E. and M. M. Meyer (1983) 'Log-linear models and categorical data analysis with psychometric and econometric applications', *Journal of Econometrics*, 22:191–214.

Fingleton, B. (1981) 'Log-linear modelling of geographical contingency tables', *Environment and Planning A*, 13:1539–1551.

Fingleton, B. (1983) 'Log-linear models with dependent spatial data', *Environment and Planning* A, 15:801–813.

Fingleton, B. (1984) *Models of category counts*. Cambridge: Cambridge University Press.

Fischer, M. M. and P. Nijkamp (1985) 'Developments in explanatory discrete spatial data and choice analysis', *Progress in Human Geography*, 9:515–551.

Folmer, H. (1983) 'Measurement of effects of regional economic policy', Ph.D. Dissertation, Department of Economics, University of Groningen, The Netherlands.

Gaudry, M. J. I. and M. G. Dagenais (1979) 'The dogit model', *Transportation Research* 13*B*:105–111.

Goodman, L. (1971) 'The analysis of multidimensional contingency tables, stepwise procedures and discrete estimation methods for building models for multiple classifications', *Technometrics*, 13:33–61.

Goodman, L. (1972) 'Some multiplicative models for the analysis of cross classified data', in: L. le Cam et al., eds., *Proceedings of the sixth Berkeley symposium on mathematical statistics and probability*, vol. 1. Berkeley: University of California Press, 649–696.

Goodman, L. (1973a) 'The analysis of multidimensional contingency tables when some variables are posterior to others: a modified path analysis approach', *Biometrika*, 60:179–192.

Goodman, L. (1973b) 'Causal analysis of data from panel studies and other kinds of surveys', *The American Journal of Sociology*, 78:1135–1191.

Goodman, L. (1978) *Analyzing qualitative-categorical data: log-linear models and latent-structure analysis*. Cambridge, Mass.: Abt Books.

Griffith, D. A. (1980) 'Towards a theory of spatial statistics', *Geographical Analysis*, 12:325–339.

Grizzle, J. E., C. F. Starmer and G. G. Koch (1969) 'Analysis of categorical data by linear models', *Biometrics*, 25:489–504.

Haberman, S. J. (1974) *The analysis of frequency data* (2 volumes). Chicago: University of Chicago Press.

Haberman, S. J. (1978) *The analysis of qualitative data* (vol. 1: Introductory topics). New York: Academic Press.

Haberman, S. J. (1979) *The analysis of qualitative data* (vol. 2: New developments). New York: Academic Press.

Haining, R. P. (1980) 'Spatial autocorrelation problems', in: D. T. Herbert and R. J. Johnson, eds., *Geography and the urban environment*, vol. 3. Chichester: John Wiley, 1–44.

Heckman, J. J. (1977) 'Simultaneous equations models with both continuous and discrete endogenous variables with and without structural shift in the equation', in: S. M. Goldfeld and R. E. Quandt, eds., *Studies in nonlinear estimation*. Cambridge, Mass.: Ballinger.

Heckman, J. J. (1978) 'Dummy endogenous variables in a simultaneous equation system', *Econometrica*, 46:931–959.

Heckman, J. J. (1981) 'Statistical models for discrete panel data', in: C. F. Manski and D. McFadden, eds., *Structural analysis of discrete data: with econometric applications*. Cambridge, Mass.: MIT Press, 114–178.

Heckman, J. J. and R. Willis (1977) 'A beta-logistic model for the analysis of sequential labour force participation by married women', *Journal of Political Economy*, 85:27–58.

Heida, H. and H. Gordijn (1978) 'Regionale woonvoorkeuren' (Regional living preferences), Research Centre Physical Planning TNO, Delft (in Dutch).

Hensher, D. A. (1984) 'Full information maximum likelihood estimation of a nested logit mode-choice model', Dimensions of Automobile Demand Project, Working Paper No. 13, School of Economic and Financial Studies, Macquarie University, Sydney, Australia.

Hensher, D. A. and L. W. Johnson (1981) *Applied discrete-choice modelling*. Beckenham, Kent: Croom Helm/New York: Halstead Press.

Hensher, D. A. and J. J. Louviere (1983) 'Individual preferences for international air forces', *Journal of Transport Economics and Policy*, 17:225–245.

Hepple, L. W. (1974) 'The impact of stochastic process theory upon spatial analysis in human geography', in: C. Board, R. J. Chorley, P. Haggett and D. R. Stoddart, eds., *Progress in geography* 6. London: Edward Arnold.

Hinde, J. and A. Wood (1985) 'Fitting mass points in GLIM', Paper presented at ESRC Conference on Longitudinal data and life histories, University of Surrey, February 1985.

Hoaglin, D. C. and R. E. Welsch (1978) 'The hat matrix in regression and ANOVA', *American Statistician*, 32:17–22.

Holt, D., A. J. Scott and P. D. Ewings (1980a) 'Chi-squared tests with survey data', *Journal of the Royal Statistical Society, Series A*, 143:303–360.

Holt, D., T. M. F. Smith and P. D. Winter (1980b) 'Regression analysis of data from complex surveys', *Journal of the Royal Statistical Society, Series A*, 143:474–487.

Imrey, P. B., W. D. Johnson and G. G. Koch (1976) 'An incomplete contingency table approach to paired-comparison experiments', *Journal of the American Statistical Association*, 71:614–623.

Imrey, P. B., G. G. Koch and M. E. Stokes (1981) 'Categorical data analysis: some reflections on the log-linear model and logistic regression. Part 1: historical and methodological overview', *International Statistical Review*, 49:265–283.

Imrey, P. B., G. G. Koch and M. E. Stokes (1982) 'Categorical data analysis: some reflections on the log-linear model and logistic regression. Part 2: data analysis', *International Statistical Review*, 50:35–63.

Knoke, D. and P. J. Burke (1980) 'Log-linear models', *Series: Quantitative applications in the social sciences*, No. 20. Beverley Hills: Sage Publications.

Koch, G. G., P. B. Imrey and D. W. Reinfurt (1972) 'Linear model analysis of categorical data with incomplete response vectors', *Biometrics*, 28:663–692.

Koch, G. G., J. R. Landis, J. W. Freeman, D. H. Freeman and R. G. Lehman (1977) 'A general methodology for the analysis of experiments with repeated measurements of categorical data', *Biometrics*, 33:133–158.

Landis, J. R., W. M. Stanish, J. L. Freeman and G. G. Koch (1976) 'A computer program for the generalized chi-square analysis of categorical data using weighted least squares (GENCAT)', *Computer Programs in Biomedicine*, 6:196–231.

Landwehr, J. M., D. Pregibon and A. C. Shoemaker (1984) 'Graphical methods for assessing logistic regression models', *Journal of the American Statistical Association*, 79:61–71.

Lehnen, R. G. and G. G. Koch (1974) 'The analysis of categorical data from repeated measurement research designs', *Political Methodology*, 1:103–123.

Louviere, J. J. and D. A. Hensher (1983) 'Using discrete choice models with experimental design data to forecast consumer demand for a unique cultural event', *Journal of Consumer Research*, 10:348–361.

Maddala, G. S. (1983) *Limited-dependent and qualitative variables in econometrics*. Cambridge: Cambridge University Press.

Manski, C. F. (1981) 'Structural models for discrete data: the analysis of discrete choice', in: S. Leinhardt, ed., *Sociological methodology 1981*. San Francisco: Jossey-Bass, 58–109.

Manski, C. F. and D. McFadden, eds. (1981) *Structural analysis of discrete data with econometric applications*. Cambridge, Mass.: MIT Press.

Mantel, N. (1966) 'Models for complex contingency tables and polychotomous dosage response curves', *Biometrics*, 22:83–95.

Mantel, N. and C. Brown (1973) 'A logistic re-analysis of Ashford and Sowden's data on respiratory symptoms in British coal mines', *Biometrics*, 29:649–665.

McCullagh, P. (1980) 'Regression models for ordinal data', *Journal of the Royal Statistical Society*, 42:109–142.

McCullagh, P. and J. A. Nelder (1983) *Generalized linear models*. London: Chapman and Hall.

McFadden, D. (1979) 'Quantitative methods for analysing travel behaviour of individuals: some recent developments', in: D. A. Hensher and P. R. Stopher, eds., *Behavioural travel modelling*. London: Croom Helm.

McFadden, D. (1982) 'Qualitative response models', in: W. Hildebrand, ed., *Advances in econometrics*. Cambridge: Cambridge University Press.

Miller, E. J. and S. R. Lerman (1981) 'Disaggregate modelling and decisions of retail firms: a case of study of clothing retailers', *Environment and Planning* A, 13:729–746.

Nelder, J. A. (1974) 'Log-linear models for contingency tables: a generalisation of classical least-squares', *Applied Statistics*, 23:323–329.

Nelder, J. A. (1985) 'Statistical models for qualitative data', in: P. Nijkamp, H. Leitner and N. Wrigley, eds., *Measuring the unmeasurable*. Dordrecht: Martinus Nijhoff, 31–38.

Nelder, J. A. and R. W. M. Wedderburn (1972) 'Generalized linear models', *Journal of the Royal Statistical Society* A, 135:370–384.

Nerlove, M. and S. J. Press (1973) 'Univariate and multivariate log-linear and logistic models', RAND Corporation R-1306-EDA/NIH, RAND Corporation, Santa Monica, California.

Nijkamp, P., H. Leitner and N. Wrigley, eds. (1985) *Measuring the unmeasurable*. Dordrecht: Martinus Nijhoff.

Norusis, M. J. (1985) *SPSS^x advanced statistics guide*. New York: McGraw-Hill.

O'Brien, L. G. and N. Wrigley (1984) 'A generalised linear models approach to categorical data analysis: theory and applications in geography and regional science', in: G. Bahrenberg, M. M. Fischer and P. Nijkamp, eds., *Recent developments in spatial data analysis, methodology, measurement, models*. Aldershot, U.K.: Gower Publishing Company, 231–251.

Odland, J. and R. Barff (1982) 'A statistical model for the development of spatial patterns: applications to the spread of housing deterioration', *Geographical Analysis*, 14:327–339.

Olsen, R. J. (1978) "Comment on 'The effect of unions on earnings and earnings on unions: a mixed logit approach'", *International Economic Review*, 19:259–261.

Parks, R. W. (1980) 'On the estimation of multinomial logit models from relative frequency data', *Journal of Econometrics*, 13:293–303.

Payne, C. (1977) 'The log-linear model for contingency tables', in: C. Payne and C. A. O'Muircheartaigh, eds., *The analysis of survey data: model fitting*, vol. 2. London: John Wiley and Sons, 105–144.

Pickles, A. R. and R. B. Davies (1985) 'The longitudinal analysis of housing careers', *Journal of Regional Science*, 25:85–101.

Pindyck, R. S. and D. L. Rubinfeld (1980) *Econometric models and economic forecasts*. New York: McGraw-Hill.

Pregibon, D. (1981) 'Logistic regression diagnostics', *The Annals of Statistics*, 9:705–724.

Pregibon, D. (1982) 'Resistant fits for some commonly used logistic models with medical applications', *Biometrics*, 38:485–498.

Schmidt, P. (1978) 'Estimation of a simultaneous equations model with jointly dependent continuous and qualitative variables: the union-earnings question revisited', *International Economic Review*, 19:453–465.

Schmidt, P. and R. P. Strauss (1975a) 'The prediction of occupation using multiple logit models', *International Economic Review*, 16:471–486.

Schmidt, P. and R. P. Strauss (1975b) 'Estimation of models with jointly dependent qualitative variables: a simultaneous logit approach', *Econometrica*, 43:745–755.

Schmidt, P. and R. P. Strauss (1976) 'The effect of unions on earnings and earnings on unions: a mixed logit approach', *International Economic Review*, 17:204–212.

Sheffi, Y., R. Hall and C. F. Daganzo (1982) 'On the estimation of the multinomial probit model', *Transportation Research A*, 16A:447–456.

Simpson, E. H. (1951) 'The interpretation of interaction in contingency tables', *Journal of the Royal Statistical Society B*, 13:238–241.

Smith, T. R. and P. B. Slater (1981) 'A family of spatial interaction models incorporating information flows and choice set constraints applied to the U.S. interstate labour flows', *International Regional Science Review*, 6:15–31.

Sobel, K. (1980) 'Travel demand forecasting with the nested logit model', *Transportation Research Record*, 775:48–55.

Theil, H. (1970) 'On the estimation of relationships involving qualitative variables', *American Journal of Sociology*, 76:103–154.

Thompson, R. and R. J. Baker (1981) 'Composite link functions in generalized linear models', *Applied Statistics*, 30:125–131.

Thwaites, A. T., R. Oakey and P. Nash (1981) 'Industrial innovation and regional economic development', A final report to the Department of the Environment, Centre for Urban and Regional Development Studies, University of Newcastle upon Tyne, U.K.

Timmermans, H. J. P. (1984) 'Decompositional multiattribute preference models in spatial choice analysis', *Progress in Human Geography*, 8:189–221.

Upton, G. J. G. (1978) *The analysis of cross-tabulated data*. Chichester: John Wiley.

Upton, G. J. G. (1981) 'Log-linear models, screening and regional industrial surveys', *Regional Studies*, 15:33–45.

Upton, G. J. G. and B. Sarlvik (1981) 'A loyalty-distance model for voting change', *Journal of the Royal Statistical Society, Series A*, 144:247–259.

Wermuth, N. and S. L. Lauritzen (1982) 'Graphical and recursive models for contingency tables', Institute for Electronic Systems, Aalborg University Centre, Aalborg.

Willekens, F. and N. Baydar (1985) 'Hybrid log-linear models', in: P. Nijkamp, H. Leitner and N. Wrigley, eds., *Measuring the unmeasurable*. Dordrecht: Martinus Nijhoff, 141–176.

Williams, H. W. C. L. (1977) 'On the formation of travel demand models and economic evaluation measures of user benefit', *Environment and Planning*, A9:285–344.

Wold, H. (1985) 'Systems analysis by partial least squares', in: P. Nijkamp, H. Leitner and N. Wrigley, eds., *Measuring the unmeasurable*. Dordrecht: Martinus Nijhoff, 221–252.

Wrigley, N. (1975) 'Analysing multiple alternative dependent variables', *Geographical Analysis*, 7:187–195.

Wrigley, N. (1976) 'An introduction to the use of logit models in geography', *Series: Concepts and techniques in modern geography*, vol. 10. Norwich: Geo Abstracts.

Wrigley, N. (1979) 'Developments in the statistical analysis of categorical data', *Progress in Human Geography*, 3:315–355.

Wrigley, N. (1980a) 'Categorical data, repeated measurement research designs, and regional industrial surveys', *Regional Studies*, 14:455–471.

Wrigley, N. (1980b) 'Paired-comparison experiments and logit models: a review and illustration of some recent developments', *Environment and Planning* A, 12:21–40.

Wrigley, N. (1981) 'Categorical data analysis', in: N. Wrigley and R. J. Bennett, eds., *Quantitative geography: a British view*. London: Routledge and Kegan Paul, 111–122.

Wrigley, N. (1983) 'Quantitative methods: on data and diagnostics', *Progress in Human Geography*, 7:565–575.

Wrigley, N. (1984) 'Quantitative methods: diagnostics revisited', *Progress in Human Geography*, 8:525–535.

Wrigley, N. (1985) *Categorical data analysis for geographers and environmental scientists*. London: Longman.

Wrigley, N. (1986) 'Quantitative methods: the era of longitudinal data analysis', *Progress in Human Geography*, 10:84–102.

Wrigley, N. and R. Dunn (1984) 'Diagnostics and resistant fits in logit choice models', in: D. E. Pitfield, ed., *Discrete choice models in regional science*. London: Pion, 44–66.

Wrigley, N. and R. Dunn (1986) 'Graphical diagnostics for logistic oil exploration models', *Mathematical Geology*, 18:355–374.

PART 3

REGIONAL ECONOMIC DEVELOPMENT
AND POLICY

Chapter 12

MULTIPLE OBJECTIVE DECISION ANALYSIS IN REGIONAL ECONOMICS

PETER NIJKAMP and PIET RIETVELD

1. General orientation

Regional and urban economic theory and empirical analysis have always had strong roots in conventional economic utility and choice theory. Examples of prevailing paradigms in this context are:

(i) maximization of economic surplus in cost–benefit analysis;

(ii) minimization of transportation costs in travel behaviour analysis; and

(iii) maximization of locational rent in location analysis, etc.

The underlying hypotheses of these paradigms took for granted rational choice behaviour based on a one-dimensional well-defined performance indicator (net social benefit, transportation costs, profit).

The use of such conventional optimization models has been criticized by many authors [see for a review Brill (1979)]. Such models are often hampered by many limitations: tradeoff analysis in sometimes hard to understand for a decision maker (indifference curves of decision makers may involve local optima, and the complete set of policy objectives is hard to specify), the use of incomplete or partial models may lead to inferior solutions, various objectives may be mutually conflicting, the level of measurement of one or more objectives may be imprecise, and so forth.

Until the end of the 1960s, decision analysis was still dominated by simple optimization methods such as single objective programming, cost–benefit analysis and fixed target approaches. As a result, a systematic analysis of conflicts involved in economic decision problems with multiple goals and multiple actors did not receive sufficient attention. This situation has changed for several reasons, particularly due to the increasing awareness of negative external effects of economic growth and the emerging concern for distributional issues in (regional) economic development. These developments led to a need for appropriate analytical tools for analyzing conflicts between policy objectives. Multiple objective decision analysis aims at providing such a set of tools.

Handbook of Regional and Urban Economics, Volume I, Edited by P. Nijkamp
©Elsevier Science Publishers BV, 1986

Multiple objective decision analysis has in the past decade become one of the most powerful methodologies in programming theory. It serves to enhance the quality of decision making by providing both a sound methodological platform for decision analysis and an operational framework for actual decision making. A wide variety of theoretical and empirical contributions can be found in the literature, and in the field of regional economic analysis many multiple objective programming analyses have been employed.

The major strength of multiple objective decision analysis is that it addresses – in an operational sense – evaluation and choice problems marked by various conflicting interests. The aim of multiple objective decision analysis is to provide systematic information on the nature of these conflicts so as to make the tradeoffs in a complex choice situation more transparent to decision makers. In this way, multiple objective decision analysis may lead to a rationalization of (regional) economic choice problems.

Multiple objective decision analysis has played an important role in many regional and urban economic optimization problems for various reasons:

(i) at the level of *individual decision makers* (consumers, e.g.) multiple objective conflicts may arise because of multiple attributes or multiple criteria playing a role in the preference ranking of alternatives (e.g. search problems in transportation behaviour);

(ii) at an *intraregional* level many conflicting objectives may exist between different actors (consumers, firms, institutions, etc.), which can formally be represented as multiple objective problems and which have a clear impact on the spatial organization of a certain area (e.g. industrialization, housing construction, road infrastructure construction);

(iii) at a *multiregional* level various spatial linkages do exist which affect through spatial interaction and spillover effects a whole spatial system (e.g. diffusion of environmental pollution, spatial price discrimination) and which in a formal sense can be described by means of a multiple objective programming framework;

(iv) at a *supraregional* level various hierarchical conflicts may emerge between regional government institutions and the central government or between regional branches and the central office of a firm, which implies again a multiple objective decision situation.

This chapter will provide a presentation and discussion of the theoretical framework of multiple objective decision analysis and its use in regional economics. First, some basic concepts in multiple objective decision analysis will be presented (Section 2), while also its links to choice theory will be clarified (Section 3). Then the attention will be directed toward the specification of preferences in conflicting choice problems (Section 4). In a subsequent section (Section 5) a brief review of some multiple objective decision methods (both continuous and discrete) will be provided, while next interactive decision analyses will be discussed (Section 6). The chapter concludes with an illustration of the use of multiple objective methods in regional economics and a discussion of the prospects in this field.

2. Multiple objective decision analysis: introduction

2.1. Conventional approaches to multiple objective decision analysis

It was usual to describe a multiple objective decision problem by formulating it as a *general optimization* problem by transforming different objectives into one decision criterion. Assume that J evaluation criteria have been formulated: $z_1, \ldots, z_J$. Then a utility function is assumed to exist, which measures the performance of each alternative in terms of a single utility index: $U = U(z_1, \ldots, z_J)$. Alternatives are formulated in terms of a number of decision variables $x_1, \ldots, x_I$. These decision variables have to satisfy certain constraints, for example due to the limited availability of various resources. Then the optimization problem reads:

$$\left.\begin{aligned} \max_{x_1, \ldots, x_I}: \quad & U(z_1, \ldots, z_J) \\ \text{subject to } \ & z_j = z_j(x_1, \ldots, x_I), && j = 1, \ldots, J \\ & f_n = (x_1, \ldots, x_I) \le a_n, && n = 1, \ldots, N \end{aligned}\right\} \tag{2.1}$$

where $f_n(x_1, \ldots, x_1) \le a_n$ represent the constraints on the decision variables for $n = 1, \ldots, N$.

Depending on the specification of (2.1), a solution method can be chosen. For example, if the inequality signs in (2.1) are replaced by equality signs, the Lagrange method is applicable [see, e.g. Lancaster (1968)]. If all functions in (2.1) are linear, linear programming may be used [see, e.g. Zionts (1974)]. If no such simplifications can be made, (2.1) can be solved by studying the Kuhn–Tucker conditions [Kuhn and Tucker (1951)], or by using some nonlinear programming algorithm [e.g. Fiacco and McCormick (1968)]. In all cases, more or less intricate analytical problems have to be solved, which usually cannot be easily handled by decision makers; this is a typical job for computer-equipped analysts.

The dominating concept in this approach is *optimality*. The optimal solution is the one made by the best utility score, given the relevant constraints. The optimal solution is (almost) always unique.

Another major contribution of economics to multiple objective decision making is social cost–benefit analysis [see Mishan (1971), Layard (1972)]. Social cost–benefit analysis has been developed to evaluate projects in terms of economic welfare of all parties involved. Projects are described in terms of positive and negative effects on groups of persons. Social cost–benefit analysis aims at translating these effects in terms of one indicator: economic welfare. This is not an easy task, since some effects may occur completely outside the range of market forces (for example, in case of environmental damage or public goods). In this case, special valuation methods are needed [see, e.g. Sinden and Worrell (1979)]. However, also when market prices are available, difficulties may arise, related among others to market distortions (such as monopoly and taxes) and to market disequilibria (such as unemployment).

The performance of each project can be measured in terms of usual indicators such as net present value, benefit–cost ratio or internal rate of return. The project with the best performance is then regarded as the optimal one.

Both conventional approaches to multiple objective decision making described above share some important features. First, they have a normative orientation: they lead to unambiguous statements on the best alternative to be chosen. Second, these methods involve many technical and analytical problems. Therefore, they cannot be carried out without analytical assistance. To put it even stronger, once the decision problem has been adequately formulated, it is the analyst who plays the main role. And finally, the methods are outcome-oriented: it is the outcome of the decision-making process which matters, not so much the procedures used to reach it.

A major feature of modern multiple objective decision analysis is the close cooperation between analysts and decision makers. The decision maker is formally responsible for the decision. The analyst, taking care of the analytical aspects of decision making, is the partner of the decision maker, and – given the complexity of multiple objective decision problems – his main task will usually be the development and operation of computerized information systems [see also Nijkamp and Rietveld (1984)]. The next subsection will provide a concise overview of some important elements and backgrounds of the history of multiple objective decision analysis.

2.2. A brief historical review

A first major contribution to the development of multiple objective decision analysis was given by Pareto in 1896 by introducing the concept of Pareto-optimality. Pareto was looking for a criterion to judge a certain distribution of goods among people. In his opinion, interpersonal utility comparisons were not possible, so that a social welfare function concept could not be used [see Tarascio (1968)]. Thus, he ended up with the much weaker concept of Pareto-optimality: a distribution of goods among people is Pareto-optimal, when it is impossible to improve a given person's utility performance without making other people worse off. Clearly, the Pareto-optimality concept is closely related to the efficiency concept which plays a major role in multiple objective decision analysis (see Section 2.3).

Approximately half a century later, Koopmans (1951) introduced a similar concept in activity analysis. The problem addressed was, whether it is possible to make a certain selection of a production process without any information about the prices of inputs and outputs. The conclusion was that indeed a distinction can be made between efficient and inefficient processes. The latter will never be chosen, whatever the prices of inputs and outputs may be. In the same year, Kuhn and Tucker (1951) introduced the concept of vector maximization, which is also related to the efficiency concept (see Section 2.3).

After the formulation of these basic concepts, multiple objective decision analysis did not immediately take off, however. Almost all efforts in decision analysis in the 1950s were devoted to the development of methods for single criteria decision making, especially linear programming. The fact that in decision making usually more than one objective plays a role was not really recognized in the mainstream of research. Additional constraints served mainly to count for the existence of multiple objectives. This situation continued until the late 1960s, when suddenly an expansion of multiple objective-oriented decision analysis started.

This new interest in adjusted decision techniques was accompanied by substantial changes that took place in the field of planning and policy making. Planners and politicians became increasingly aware of the need for integrated planning [see, e.g. McLoughlin (1969)]. Especially the negative effects of post-war economic development on environmental quality made it clear that economic policies no longer could be pursued without paying explicit attention to external effects (e.g. on the environment). Thus, in many countries a tendency arose towards integration of economic, environmental, energy and physical planning. This integration did not only call for the development of models that were capable of indicating the mutual impacts among the various planning fields, but also for methods for generating and/or selecting alternatives which had to be judged from multiple viewpoints. The latter is exactly the aim of multiple objective decision methods. A related factor is that post-war welfare society reached a new stage in this period. Instead of one or a limited set of unambiguous policy objectives (such as the maximization of growth), a wide variety of interest groups called for more attention to neglected aspects of the economy (e.g. distributional problems, the new scarcity). This led to a multi-actor conflict, which could not be covered by means of conventional decision analysis and called for a multidimensional policy analysis.

An influential book in this period was Johnsen (1968), in which a strong plea is made for decision analysis in terms of multiple criteria. The development of multiple criteria decision analysis gained momentum in the 1970s. From 1972 onwards several conferences were held on multicriteria decision making at one or two years' intervals [see Gal (1983)]. The proceedings of these conferences strongly stimulated the development of this field. This holds especially true for the first one, edited by Cochrane and Zeleny (1973). In the 1970s an explosive growth of literature on multicriteria decision analysis took place, and the bibliographies on this topic became longer and longer. Surveys on the subject can be found among others in Chankong and Haimes (1983), Hwang and Yoon (1981), Nijkamp (1979, 1980), Rietveld (1980), Sinden and Worrell (1979), Voogd (1983) and Zeleny (1982). Furthermore, a very interesting sketch of almost 100 multiple objective analyses can be found in Despontin et al. (1983).

In addition to contributions from economics and operations research, in other disciplines too (psychology, e.g.) various interesting contributions to multiple objective decision analysis have been made. For instance, analyses of search behaviour in case of conflicting options and multiple alternatives have been made among others by Skull et al. (1970), Dawes (1980), Hansen (1972), Hollnagel (1977), Kornai (1971), May (1954), Meehl (1954), Pitz (1977), Reitman (1964), Shepard (1964) and Tversky (1972).

After this concise presentation, one of the key concepts of multiple objective decision analysis, viz. the efficiency concept, will be discussed in Section 2.3.

2.3. The efficiency concept in multiple objective decision analysis

In the preceding section it was mentioned that the efficiency concept plays a central role in multiple objective decision analysis. This concept can be illustrated with the following example (see Figure 2.1). Let us assume four alternatives A, B, C and D, evaluated according to two criteria. Assume that the only information available on the priorities is that for each criterion "more is preferred to less", and that nothing is known on the relative importance of the criteria.

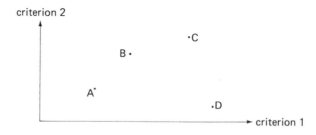

Figure 2.1. Efficiency in the two-dimensional case.

A look at Figure 2.1 makes it clear that, however incomplete this priority information may be, it is already sufficient to exclude two of the four alternatives. Alternative C performs better than B in all respects and hence C is preferred above B. The same holds for B compared with A. Thus, only C and D are serious alternatives to be examined. Clearly, the larger the number of criteria, the smaller the probability that an alternative can be found which is non-efficient.

In a formal sense, an *efficient* alternative can now be defined as follows:

Definition 1

Let $X \subseteq R^J$ be the set of feasible alternatives. An alternative x in X is called an efficient alternative if there does not exist another alternative $\hat{x}$ in X, where $\hat{x}$ is different from x, with the property that the performance of $\hat{x}$ is equal or better according to all criteria.

Some other usual, but equivalent terms for the concept of an efficient alternative are: non-dominated alternative, non-inferior alternative or Pareto-optimal alternative.

An important difference between optimality and efficiency is, that there are usually many efficient alternatives, whereas the optimal alternative is almost always unique. Thus, the efficiency concept is much less demanding than the optimality concept.

Note that efficiency does not imply that every efficient solution is necessarily to be preferred above every non-efficient solution. For example, in Figure 2.1, the non-efficient alternatives A and B are preferable above the efficient alternative D if the second criterion would receive a high priority compared with the first criterion.

The relationship between optimality and efficiency has been discussed by Geoffrion (1968). In this theory, the concept of proper efficiency is used, which is slightly more restrictive than the efficiency concept defined above. The author assumes a convex set of feasible solutions X with elements x. The relationships between the policy variables represented in x and the criteria j are assumed to be concave functions $z_j = z_j(x)$ for $j = 1, \ldots, J$. He formulates then the following theorem: x^p is properly efficient with respect to X (convex) and $z_1, \ldots, z_J$ (concave), if and only if there exists a vector of positive weights $\lambda_1, \ldots, \lambda_J$, so that x^p is the optimal solution of the mathematical programming problem:

$$\left. \begin{array}{l} \displaystyle \max_{x}! \ \sum_{j=1}^{J} \lambda_j z_j(x) \\[2ex] \text{subject to } x \in X. \end{array} \right\} \tag{2.2}$$

For a review of the related theorems we refer to Gal (1983).

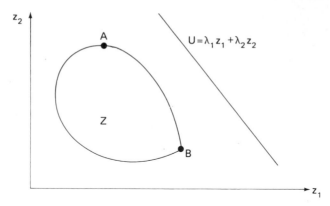

Figure 2.2. Illustration of Geoffrion's theorem with two criteria.

The meaning of Geoffrion's theorem can easily be illustrated by means of Figure 2.2. The set Z in this figure represents the set of feasible solutions in the criteria space under the simplifying assumption that only two criteria are considered. The set of (properly) efficient solutions is found on the curve between A and B. The theorem says that every (properly) efficient solution can be found as an optimal solution by specifying certain positive weights λ_1 and λ_2 in a linear utility function $U = \lambda_1 z_1 + \lambda_2 z_2$. The set of (properly) efficient solutions can be generated by repeatedly solving the mathematical programming problem (2.2) for various combinations of positive weights.

According to the theorem there is a close relationship between the set of (properly) efficient solutions and the set of positive weight vectors. Every positive weight vector $(\lambda_1, \ldots, \lambda_J)$ in (2.2) yields a (properly) efficient solution. On the other hand, for every (properly) efficient solution there is a corresponding weight vector yielding this solution as an optimal one by means of (2.2).

This does not mean, however, that there is a one-to-one relationship between the two above-mentioned sets. Figure 2.3, which is an example of a linear multiple objective decision problem may help to illuminate this point.

The corner point B, which is properly efficient corresponds to a large number of weight vectors. On the other hand, if the weights of the utility function $U = \lambda_1 z_1 + \lambda_2 z_2$ are chosen such that it runs parallel to the segment BC, all points on this segment (all of them being efficient), correspond to only one weight vector. For a more detailed study of these properties, see Rietveld (1980).

The efficiency theorem only holds for a convex set X and concave functions z_j. Figure 2.4 gives two examples of situations which may arise when these conditions are not satisfied. In Figure 2.4a, the points on the curve between A and B are (properly) efficient. They will not be found as optimal solutions to problem

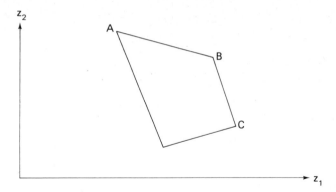

Figure 2.3. Example of a linear multiple objective problem.

(2.2), however. Similarly, alternative D in the discrete problem represented in Figure 2.4b is certainly efficient, but no positive weight vector exists that ensures D to be an optimal solution. Various methods have been developed to enable one to generate efficient solutions under these less favourable conditions [see, e.g. Bowman (1976), Cohon (1978), Zionts (1981), Gal (1983)].

Parallel to the distinction between optimality and efficiency runs the distinction between scalar maximization and vector maximization. Formulation (2.2) is an example of a *scalar maximization* problem: the variable to be maximized is a scalar. The solution of a scalar maximization problem is called an optimal solution.

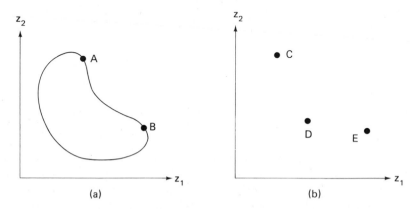

Figure 2.4. Non-convex cases in multiple objective analysis.

In a *vector maximization* problem, the variable to be maximized is a vector. Such a problem is formulated as [see Kuhn and Tucker (1951)]:

$$\left.\begin{array}{ll} \text{max:} & z_1(x), z_2(x), \ldots, z_J(x) \\ \text{subject to} & x \in X \end{array}\right\} \tag{2.3}$$

The solution of (2.3) is called the set of efficient solutions. After discussion of the efficiency concept, Section 2.4 will now provide some classification of multiple objective decision methods.

2.4.   *Classification of multiple objective decision methods*

Multiple objective decision analysis aims at improving the quality of understanding and decision making in case of choice problems in which several mutually contrasting judgement criteria play a role. The difficulties inherent in dealing with structural choice conflicts should not be underestimated. Although many problems faced by decision makers in large organizations such as governments and firms are of a more or less routine nature, the more strategic choice problems are usually very difficult to tackle. Rittel and Webber (1973) call such problems "wicked".

If one looks upon decision problems from the viewpoint of uncertainty, one arrives at three main sources of uncertainty:

(1) *Uncertainty on priorities*. In strategic problems always a multiplicity of criteria plays a role owing to the involvement of various policy fields, interest groups, regions, time periods, etc. Given this multiplicity of interests, decision makers are in general unwilling to formulate their preferences in an explicit way, even after serious deliberations.

(2) *Uncertainty on impacts*. Predicting the impacts of policies is a difficult task. Economic impacts, for example, usually depend strongly on the development of the world economy and on the development in some relevant markets. Also, short-term and long-term effects of policies may differ substantially. Regional policy impact analysis is a field that is still fraught with many problems.

(3) *Uncertainty on decisions of other actors*. Decision makers in firms or government agencies will find that their decision environment is strongly affected by decisions of actors in related firms or agencies. For example, changes in safety standards for nuclear reactors may have far-reaching consequences for physical planning.

Various kinds of analyses have been developed to tackle these problems. Uncertainty on priorities is especially the subject covered by multiple objective decision analysis, while uncertainty on impacts receives special attention in impact assessment and "decision making under uncertainty" [see Winkler (1982)].

Finally, game theory in particular addresses uncertainty problems of the third type: uncertainty on decisions of other actors [see, e.g. Luce and Raiffa (1957)].

The type and degree of uncertainty forms a major classification principle for multiple objective decision methods, so that *quantitative, qualitative, mixed quantitative – qualitative* and *fuzzy* methods can be distinguished. Another major typology of such methods is based on the number of alternatives to be considered, as this may vary between 2 (zero–one) and infinity. Depending on the question whether a finite or an infinite number of alternatives may be discerned, one may classify multiple objective decision methods into *discrete* and *continuous* methods.

Another way of classifying methods is to consider the *aims* they are addressed to. Four main aims can be distinguished:

(1) generating (efficient) solutions;

(2) formulating priorities;

(3) generation of (efficient) solutions and formulation of priorities in an interactive way; and

(4) detailed analysis of pros and cons of alternatives.

The first group of methods aims at generating the set of efficient solutions, or a representative subset thereof. Sometimes, also non-efficient alternatives are taken into account. The main developments in this field started after the paper by Geoffrion (1968) on efficiency. Special attention has been paid to generating the efficient alternatives in the linear case [see, e.g. Steuer (1976)]. These methods are usually related to continuous problems (see Section 2.3).

The second group of methods is addressed to formulating priorities on a multiplicity of objectives. In this context, an important branch is multiattribute utility theory [see, e.g. Keeney (1968)], although also methods outside the realm of utility theory deserve attention. These methods are useful for both continuous and discrete problems. They are discussed in Section 4.

The third group of methods aims at designing interactive decision structures in which decision maker and analyst can cooperate. These methods use elements of both preceding groups. Developments in this group started in the early 1970s [see Benayoun et al. (1971)]. Interactive methods are usually related to continuous problems. They are discussed in Section 6.

The last group (which will be presented in Section 5) has especially been designed for problems with a *small* number of alternatives. In this case, a detailed analysis of the pros and cons of alternatives, for example via pairwise comparisons, will produce useful information for the decision maker. A well-known branch of methods in this group is based on concordance analysis, the development of which was initiated by Roy (1968). Two branches of methods can be distinguished in this group: one dealing with quantitative data, and one with qualitative data. It is only recently that the latter group of methods started to develop. In terms of the sources of uncertainty faced in decision problems mentioned before, the latter group combines a treatment of uncertainties on priorities and on impacts, which is rather unusual in multiple objective decision analysis.

As mentioned briefly before, two main classes of problems have been studied in multiple objective decision analysis: discrete and continuous ones.

In discrete choice problems, normally called multiple criteria decision problems, usually a very limited number of alternatives is considered. Here an explicit description of the alternatives in terms of the evaluation criteria is usually available. In continuous problems, the number of alternatives is infinite. Then the alternatives are defined in a implicit way by means of the vector maximum problem (2.3). An important function of the methods addressed to the aims 1 and 3 is that they describe the performance of some of the alternatives in an explicit way. By so doing, these alternatives become better understandable to the decision maker. This is also an important way of helping to improve the decision maker's understanding of the structure of the decision problem.

3.   Multiple objective decision analysis and choice theory

3.1.   Introduction

A main reason why multiple objective decision analysis came into being was the need to extend traditional decision methods to adequately deal with priorities in the face of multiple judgement criteria. In the present section the relationship between multiple objective decision analysis and utility theory will be further investigated. A relaxation of the assumptions underlying conventional utility theory appears to be a necessary condition to make utility theory more relevant for situations in which information on priorities is incomplete.

3.2.   Preference relations and utility theory

Our point of departure is the set of feasible alternatives X. Opinions on the relative attractiveness of alternatives in X can be represented by preference relations. An example of a preference relation is: "is preferred to". The statement "x is preferred to y" will be denoted by $x \geq y$, where x and y are elements of X. There are two other preference relations which are closely related to $\geq$. The first is the *indifference* relation $=$. This relation can be defined as follows:

$$x = y \quad \text{if} \quad \left\{ x \geq y \text{ and } y \geq x \right\} \qquad \text{for all } x \text{ and } y \text{ in } x.$$

The second relation concerns *strict preference* $>$. The relation "is strictly preferred to" can be defined as follows:

$$x > y \quad \text{if} \quad \left\{ x \geq y \text{ and not } y \geq x \right\} \qquad \text{for all } x \text{ and } y \text{ in } X.$$

A conclusion which can immediately be drawn after these statements is that when $x \,(\geq)\, y$, either $x \,(=)\, y$, or $x \,(>)\, Y$.

In the literature on choice theory several properties of preference relations have been proposed for $(\geq)$, notably reflexivity, transitivity and completeness.

Reflexivity means: $x \,(\geq)\, x$ for all x in X. It is not difficult to check that when $(\geq)$ is reflexive, also $(=)$ is reflexive, whereas it is impossible that both $(\geq)$ and $(>)$ are reflexive.

Transitivity means that for all x, y and z in X, $x \,(\geq)\, y$ and $y \,(\geq)\, z$ imply $x \,(\geq)\, z$.

If a preference relation does not satisfy the transitivity property, serious problems may arise. For example, when $x \,(\geq)\, y$, $y \,(\geq)\, z$ and $z \,(\geq)\, x$, the alternative which will be chosen depends on the order in which the alternatives are compared (except in case of an indifference relationship). This is usually regarded as an undesirable property, particularly because it gives rise to a possibility to manipulate the outcome of decision processes. A well-known example of an intransitivity arises in Arrow's voting paradox. Arrow (1951) has shown how a pairwise majority voting procedure may produce an intransitivity in the preference relation of the pertaining collective. It is not difficult to show that when $(\geq)$ is transitive, also $(>)$ and $(=)$ are transitive.

Completeness means that for all x and y in X, where x and y are different, either $x \,(\geq)\, y$ or $y \,(\geq)\, x$.

The completeness property means that for each pair of alternatives it can be said unambiguously whether the first is preferred to the second, or whether the reverse is true. Thus, when a preference relation is complete, no incomparable pairs of alternatives occur. In the next subsection it will be shown that completeness plays an essential role in multiple objective decision analysis.

Next the concept of utility can be defined as follows: a utility function is a function $U: X \rightarrow R$, where R denotes the set of real numbers. Therefore, by means of a utility function, each alternative x in X is assigned a real number. It is useful to introduce an additional requirement on a utility function, such that it reveals something of the preference relations on X. This can be formulated as follows:

$x \,(\geq)\, y$,   if and only if $U(x) \geq U(y)$

$x \,(>)\, y$,   if and only if $U(x) > U(y)$

$x \,(=)\, y$,   if and only if $U(x) = U(y)$.

A utility function defined in the above way is said to give a "faithful representation" of a preference relation on X [cf. Aumann (1964)]. When x is preferred to y, the utility function indicates a higher value for x than for y. Inversely, when the utility function shows a higher value for x than for y, alternative x is preferred to y. Thus, a utility function is simply a very concise way of representing a preference relation on a certain set of alternatives X.

Since utility functions are a very efficient way to describe a preference relation, one may wonder whether each preference relation can be represented by means of a utility function. A short examination teaches that preference relations have to satisfy certain requirements to allow their representation by a utility function. For example, the lexicographic ordering (see Section 4.6) is a total quasi-ordering, but a utility indicator does not exist for it. It appears that an additional property has to be stated for a preference relation before representability can be proved: continuity. Roughly speaking, continuity means that any alternative x which is very close to an alternative y that is preferred to some given alternative x' must be preferred to x' [for a formal definition, see Quirk and Saposnik (1968) and Takayama (1974)].

Debreu (1959) has shown the following theorem for a very general class of spaces of feasible alternatives: if the preference relation $\geq$ is reflexive, transitive, complete and continuous, then there exists a continuous utility function giving a faithful representation of the preferences.

If U gives a faithful representation of a preference relation, any function Z satisfying the following condition represents the same preference relation:

$$Z(x) > Z(y), \quad \text{if and only if} \quad U(x) > U(y)$$
$$Z(x) = Z(y), \quad \text{if and only if} \quad U(x) = U(y).$$

Thus, any monotone increasing transformation of U can be used to represent the preference relation. For example, $Z = a - b/U (b > 0)$ represents the same preference relation as U does. This makes clear that utility as defined above is measured on an ordinal scale [see Torgerson (1958)]. As a consequence, no specific meaning may be attached to a positive or negative value of the utility index. Also, if the difference between the utility values of two alternatives is larger than the difference for two other alternatives, one may not conclude that the difference in attractiveness for the first pair is larger than for the second pair. By using a monotone transformation of U, one may easily reverse the outcome.

3.3.   Completeness of preference

The completeness property of the preference relation implies that all alternatives in X are comparable: for all x and y in X, either x is preferred to y, or y to x.

It seems a very trivial property, but it certainly is not. The completeness property would imply that decision makers do not experience difficulties when they are comparing the attractiveness of various alternatives. In the light of Section 2 this assumption is unrealistic for many fields of decision making, because incomplete preference relations are a common ingredient of multiple objective methods. A complete preference relation would imply the absence of incomparability of alternatives due to conflicting multiple objectives.

Consequently, it is important to know for multiple objective methods whether a theory of choice can be retained when the completeness property is abandoned. Is it possible to maintain a utility concept after such a reduction of conditions has been imposed on preference relations? It will be shown that even when the completeness assumption is abandoned a meaningful utility concept can be maintained. One should realize that the removal of the completeness property does not imply that all alternatives are necessarily incomparable. It only means that one is no longer sure that *all* alternatives are necessarily pairwise comparable. Many pairs of alternatives may simply remain comparable, as a utility function is a function $U: X \rightarrow R$ with an "if and only if" condition: for all x and y in X, $x \mathbin{\textcircled{>}} y$ or $x \mathbin{\textcircled{=}} y$ imply $U(x) > U(y)$ or $U(x) = U(y)$, respectively, while $U(x) > U(y)$ or $U(x) = U(y)$ imply $x \mathbin{\textcircled{>}} y$ or $x \mathbin{\textcircled{=}} y$, respectively. The first part of the definition is not affected by an omission of the completeness condition. However, this is not the case for the second part. In the set of real numbers R, one knows that either $U(x) \geq U(y)$ or $U(y) \geq U(x)$. This property does not hold true for the space X, because it is not certain that for each x and y either $x \mathbin{\textcircled{\geq}} y$ or $y \mathbin{\textcircled{\geq}} x$.

These remarks lead to the conclusion that for incomplete preference relations an adapted utility concept has to be defined. Therefore, the term *partially representing utility function* is introduced. It is defined as follows [cf. Aumann (1964)]:

Definition 2

A partially representing utility function U_{pr} is a function $U_{pr}: X \rightarrow R$ so that for all x, y and X:

$$x \mathbin{\textcircled{>}} y \quad \text{implies} \quad U_{pr}(x) > U_{pr}(y)$$

$$x \mathbin{\textcircled{=}} y \quad \text{implies} \quad U_{pr}(x) = U_{pr}(y).$$

Partially representing utility functions should be treated carefully. One may never conclude that if $U_{pr}(x) \geq U_{pr}(y)$, then $x \mathbin{\textcircled{\geq}} y$. The reverse may be equally true.

Concerning the relationship between faithfully and partially representing utility functions, it is clear that every utility function faithfully representing a preference relation is also partially representing the same preference relation. Therefore, the set of utility functions faithfully representing $\geq$ is a subset of the set of partially representing functions. A computational example may clarify this statement. Let X contain four discrete alternatives (w, x, y, z):

$$\begin{pmatrix} w & x & y & z \\ 0 & 110 & 50 & 25 \\ 100 & 0 & 75 & 100 \end{pmatrix}$$

A transitive and complete set of preference statements is:

$$y \geq x \geq z \geq w. \tag{3.1}$$

Let us restrict the set of utility functions to a linear form:

$$U(v) = \lambda_1 v_1 + \lambda_2 v_2 \tag{3.2}$$

where v_1 and v_2 denote the values obtained by the first and the second attribute of any alternative $v(w, x, y, z)$ respectively, and where $\lambda_1 \geq 0$ and $\lambda_2 \geq 0$ are the corresponding weights. Then (3.1) implies:

$$\frac{2}{3} \leq \frac{\lambda_2}{\lambda_1} \leq \frac{3}{4}. \tag{3.3}$$

Consider now a case for which the preference statements are not complete, so assume that we only know:

$$y \geq w. \tag{3.4}$$

This implies:

$$0 \leq \frac{\lambda_2}{\lambda_1} \leq 2. \tag{3.5}$$

Comparing (3.3) and (3.5), we conclude that the set of linear utility functions representing the complete ordering is a subset of the set of utility functions representing the incomplete ordering. Statement (3.5) leaves room for no less than five complete orderings, (3.1) being one of them:

$$
\left.
\begin{array}{l}
z \;\geq\; y \;\geq\; w \;\geq\; x \\[4pt]
z \;>\; y \;>\; x \;>\; w \\[4pt]
y \;\geq\; z \;\geq\; x \;\geq\; w \\[4pt]
y \;\geq\; x \;\geq\; z \;\geq\; w \\[4pt]
x \;\geq\; y \;\geq\; z \;\geq\; w
\end{array}
\right\} .
\tag{3.6}
$$

Statement (3.3) only allows preference ordering (3.1).

This example shows that the less we know about the ordering of alternatives, the more scope there is for utility functions to give a partial representation of the preference relation. An extreme case arises when all pairs of alternatives are incomparable. Then every function $U\colon X \to R$ is partially representing the preference relation on X.

3.4. Degrees of incompleteness

In multiple objective decision problems, one often starts with a situation of an incomplete preference relation. The information available on the preferences is then not sufficient to determine the most preferred alternative. The information contents of a specific preference statement implying a reduction of the degree of incompleteness, can be conceptualized in various ways.

First, it can be approached from the viewpoint of the utility function. New information on preferences reduces the set of relevant values for the parameters of the utility function. This information content is denoted by s_1.

Second, the statement will affect the set of alternatives being candidate for the final choice. Some alternatives may be removed from this set by a certain preference statement. This information content is indicated by means of s_2.

Third, the information will affect the probability that a certain alternative is optimal. To explain this, consider as an example Figure 3.1. Figure 3.1a represents the set of feasible alternatives in the space of objectives. It is a convex polyhedron with efficient solutions on the faces AC and BC. Figure 3.1c represents the set of weights of the linear utility function $U = \lambda_1 z_1 + \lambda_2 z_2$, under the assumption that $\lambda_1 + \lambda_2 = 1$. It is not difficult to see that when $0 \leq \lambda_1 \leq 0.2$, the optimal solution will be A; when $0.2 \leq \lambda_1 \leq 0.8$, the optimal solution is C, etc. For Figures 3.1b and 3.1d, a similar relationship between weights and optimal alternatives has been presented. The latter information content is represented by means of the symbol s_3.

The probability that a certain alternative is optimal can be defined as the share of the weights set which leads to the outcome that the pertaining alternative is

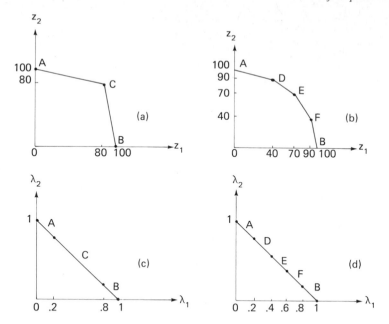

Figure 3.1. Corner points and corresponding weights of a linear multiple objective problem.

optimal [see Rietveld (1980)]. For example, when no information is available on the weights of the linear utility function, the probability that alternative C is optimal is equal to 0.6, since, as shown by Figure 3.1c, for all values of λ_1 between 0.2 and 0.8, alternative C appears to be optimal.

The above suggestions will be made more precise by means of the following example. Assume that at the beginning no information on preferences is available. Then, consider the consequences of the information that $\lambda_1 \geq 0.3$. Let s again denote the information content in this statement.

Then s_1, the information content according to the first mentioned concept, is equal to 0.30, since 30% of the line in Figures 3.1c and 3.1d can be left out of consideration. It is characteristic for s_1 that it only depends on the information about the weights, and not on the structure of the set of feasible solutions. This is the reason why Figures 3.1c and 3.1d yield the same value for s_1.

In addition, one may also focus attention on the effects of the priority information on the set of relevant solutions. When $\lambda_1 \geq 0.3$, the line segment AC no longer contains candidates for the optimal solution. Only the segment BC is maintained, so that one may conclude that 50% of the original set of efficient alternatives is ruled out by the preference statement. Therefore one may say that s_2 is equal to 0.50. In Figure 3.1b only the piece AD of the set of efficient

Table 3.1
Probabilities that efficient points are optimal.

	Efficient points				
(a)	A	C	B		
Probability before message (p)	0.200	0.600	0.200		
Probability after message (q)	0.000	0.714	0.286		
(b)	A	D	E	F	B
Probability before message (p)	0.200	0.200	0.200	0.200	0.200
Probability after message (q)	0.000	0.143	0.286	0.286	0.286

alternatives is ruled out, so that s_2 will attain a smaller value in this case (i.e. 0.27).

To measure the information content of the preference statement in terms of the probabilities that certain efficient solutions are optimal, one can make use of information theory [see Theil (1967)]. The following notation will be used. Let $p_1, \ldots, p_N$ be the probabilities that the efficient solutions $1, \ldots, N$ are optimal before the message, and $q_1, \ldots, q_N$ be the corresponding probabilities after the message. Then the information content of the message can be measured by means of the following entropy expression:

$$s_3 = \sum_{n=1}^{N} \left(q_n \ln(q_n/p_n) \right) / \ln N. \tag{3.7}$$

Note that when the message contains no information (i.e. when $q_n = p_n$), $s_3 = 0$.

The values for q_n and p_n have been represented in Table 3.1. Application of (2.10) on these data yields: $s_3 = 0.206$ for case (a) and $s_3 = 0.160$ for case (b).

Thus, various ways exist to measure the reduction in the degree of incompleteness owing to a certain preference statement. Each measure focuses on another aspect, so that it is no surprise that for the three measures different values are obtained.

It is interesting to play around with alternative assumptions on the available priority information. For example, when $0.65 \leq \lambda_1 \leq 0.75$, one obtains for case (a): $s_1 = 0.90$, $s_2 = 1.00$ and $s_3 = 0.46$. Thus, although according to s_1 there is still some uncertainty on the parameters of the utility function, s_2 shows that the information is sufficient to determine the optimal solution in an unambiguous way.

The conclusion can be drawn that multiple objective decision analysis is not in contrast with conventional economic choice theory, but only offers a more general framework. The next sections (4 and 5) will now be devoted to two major aspects in multiple objective decision analysis, viz. the possibility of assessing preference statements and a presentation of a typology of different multiple objective decision methods.

4.   Preference statements in multiple objective policy methods

4.1.   Introduction

In the present section we will focus on the ways in which a decision maker can express his priorities. In psychological research it has been found that people have limited capacities concerning the number of conceptual units that can be handled at a certain point in time [Shepard (1964)]. Thus, in complex decision problems, decision makers often experience serious difficulties in expressing their priorities. From this viewpoint it is favourable that a considerable variety of ways of expressing priorities has been developed, so that a method can be chosen which is in agreement with the features of the decision situation. In this section we will discuss the following ways of formulating priorities: weights, aspiration levels, minimum requirements and lexicographic orders.

4.2.   Direct estimation of weights

Weights, reflecting the relative importance of the objectives concerned, are in economics a very common way of dealing with priorities. By direct estimation of weights we mean that the priority statements of a decision maker are directly expressed in terms of weights. As we will discuss in Section 4.3, there are also other ways of estimating weights, viz. based on preference or indifference statements concerning alternatives.

Although weights can be used outside the realm of utility functions (for example, in concordance analysis; see Section 4.6 of this chapter), they are usually in this realm aligned to tradeoffs in a utility context. The most simple (linear) form of a utility function is

$$U = \lambda_1 \omega_1 + \lambda_2 \omega_2 + \cdots + \lambda_J \omega_J \qquad (4.1)$$

The vast majority of weighting methods is addressed to this linear specification.

We will subsequently present a series of methods for directly estimating the weights $\lambda_j (j = 1, \ldots, J)$.

4.2.1. Tradeoff method

In the tradeoff method, the decision maker is directly asked to indicate values for weights (or relative weights) by answering questions of the type Q: "how large should c_{12} be in order to guarantee that an improvement of one unit of ω_1 is equally attractive as an improvement of c_{12} units of ω_2?". Given the utility function as specified in (4.1), one finds for the relative weight:

$$\lambda_2/\lambda_1 = 1/c_{12}. \tag{4.2}$$

By repeating this question for all pairwise combinations of objective 1 with respect to all other objectives ($j = 2,\ldots, J$), the entire weight vector $\lambda = (\lambda_1,\ldots,\lambda_J)$ can be determined (apart from a scaling factor). If desired, consistency checks [see Kendall (1955)] can be carried out by adding similar questions regarding other pairs of objectives and checking whether the following consistency requirement holds:

$$c_{jm} = c_{jk} \cdot c_{km} \qquad (j, k, m = 1,\ldots, J). \tag{4.3}$$

The tradeoff method has some serious limitations in empirical practice. It appears that decision makers usually have great difficulties in providing point estimates of weights in the above-mentioned way. Feelings about priorities are usually characterized by a lack of precision or fuzziness.

Another problem is that the linear form in (4.1) often only serves as an approximation of a more complex utility function so that it only is of local relevance. Thus, non-linear utility functions such as

$$U = \lambda_1 f_1(\omega_1) + \cdots + \lambda_J f_J(\omega_J) \tag{4.4}$$

or even non-additive structures may give better representations of the decision maker's preferences, but are obviously more difficult to estimate. In the case of (4.4), the answer to question Q will depend on the values of ω_1 and ω_2 (and in the case of a non-additive function also on the values attained by the other objectives). Here we are in the realm of the so-called *multiattribute utility theory* [see Keeney and Raiffa (1976), Farquhar (1983)]. This theory addresses the problem of formulating composite utility expressions from partial ones pertaining to attributes (or characteristics) of alternatives in a given choice situation.

Finally, decision makers usually do not like to express their priorities without knowing the implications in terms of outcomes in the objectives space.

A remedy to overcome these problems to a certain extent is to drop the requirement that a point estimate of the tradeoffs has to be given, by allowing interval statements such as $\lambda_2/\lambda_1 \leq 0.40$. This type of response is discussed by Steuer (1976) in the context of linear multiple objective decision models.

4.2.2. Rating method

In the rating method the decision maker is asked to allocate a fixed number of points (say 100) among the objectives distinguished in such a way that the number of points allocated on an objective reflects its relative importance. This method is used rather frequently in spatial planning [see, e.g. Miller (1980) and Voogd (1983)].

An important difference between this method and the tradeoff method is that the rating method assumes that the objectives have been normalized, whereas for the tradeoff method such an assumption is not necessary. There exist several ways of normalizing objectives [see Rietveld (1980)]. Here we present two ways which are frequently used:

$$\alpha_j = \omega_j / \max \omega_j \qquad (4.5)$$

and

$$\beta_j = (\omega_j - \min \omega_j)/(\max \omega_j - \min \omega_j). \qquad (4.6)$$

For both normalizations we find a maximum attainable level equal to 1. The minimum attainable level for α_j is equal to 0, whereas for β_j its value depends on $\min \omega_j$. There is no general reason to prefer one of these normalizations to the other on methodological grounds.

4.2.3. Ranking method

Here the decision maker is asked to rank the objectives in order of importance. If, for example, for three objectives the order of importance is 1, 2, 3, then the set of feasible weights can be formulated as [cf. Eckenrode (1965)]:

$$S = \left\{ \lambda | \lambda_1 \geq \lambda_2 \geq \lambda_3 \geq 0, \sum_j \lambda_j = 1 \right\}. \qquad (4.7)$$

Figure 4.1 shows that the information implied by a complete ranking of objectives is substantial. From the original set of weights only 1/6 appears to remain feasible; this area is indicated by S.

On the basis of S one may proceed in various directions. Paelinck (1976) proposes to focus on the extreme points of S, i.e. $(1,0,0)$, $(\frac{1}{2},\frac{1}{2},0)$ and $(\frac{1}{3},\frac{1}{3},\frac{1}{3})$. Another way is to use the centre of gravity of $S(11/18, 5/18, 2/18)$ as the most

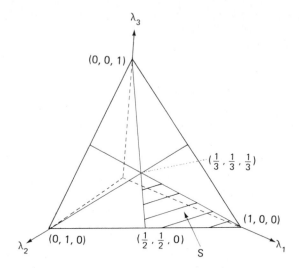

Figure 4.1. Set of feasible weights given a ranking of objectives.

typical representative of S. It can be shown that this point is equivalent to selecting the mean value of λ assuming that λ is uniformly distributed in S [see Rietveld (1984)].

Achieving a complete ranking will be difficult when a large number of objectives has to be ranked. In such a case one will usually end up with an incomplete ranking in which several objectives are in the same class of importance. A stepwise approach may also be helpful [see Eckenrode (1965)]. First, two distinct sets of objectives are distinguished: the important ones and the less important ones. Then for each of the subsets a ranking of objectives in terms of importance can be carried out.

4.2.4. *Verbal statements on weights*

Some methods have been devised to transform verbal statements into quantitative outcomes. A well-known approach is the seven-points scale proposed by Osgood et al. (1957). For each of the objectives the importance is indicated on a scale as illustrated in Figure 4.2. After some standardization the outcomes obtained for the various objectives can be transformed into weights.

A more sophisticated way of dealing with verbal statements is fuzzy set theory. This theory deals with assigning numerical values – based on so-called membership functions – to expressions such as "objective 1 is far more important than objective 2". See for example Blin (1977) and Leung (1983).

Figure 4.2. An illustration of a seven-points scale.

4.2.5. *Paired comparisons*

The paired-comparisons method shares with the preceding method the property that it is based on verbal statements. The difference between both methods is that in the paired-comparisons method the verbal statements are aligned to *pairs* of objectives. The method has been developed by Saaty (1977). For all pairs of objectives j, j', where objective j is more important than objective j', he proposes to ask the decision maker the degree of difference in importance (denoted as $b_{jj'}$) on a nine-points scale, ranging from 1 (equal importance) to 9 (absolutely more important). By assuming that $b_{j'j} = 1/b_{jj'}$ and $b_{jj} = 1$, a paired-comparison matrix B can be achieved consisting of J^2 elements. Saaty proposes to interpret the $b_{jj'}$ as relative weights: $b_{jj'} = \lambda_j / \lambda_{j'}$.

In principle, each row of the matrix B can be used to estimate the vector of relative weights. Since, in general, the decision maker will not reach complete consistency, a different weight vector will be found for each row of B [cf. the consistency test in (4.3)]. It can easily be shown that when the decision maker is completely consistent, then

$$B \cdot \lambda = J \cdot \lambda, \tag{4.8}$$

where J is the number of objectives. Therefore, Saaty proposes to approximate the weights vector as the largest eigenvector of the matrix B. For an application and evaluation of the method, we refer to Blair (1979) and Johnson (1980), respectively.

In a comparison of some of these methods, Voogd (1983) reports that the ranking method and the seven-points scale perform relatively well according to the criteria: time needed for an operational application, and degree of difficulty as reported by the decision maker. The rating method and the paired-comparisons method were reported as less favourable in these respects. This does not mean, of course, that the last mentioned methods have to be discarded, however. They may enable the decision maker to express his priorities in a more refined way.

All methods presented above lead to difficulties when the number of objectives becomes large (say larger than 8). In this case it is advisable to impose a hierarchical structure of objectives. For example, if in a planning problem 18 objectives have been distinguished aligned to 3 economic and 6 environmental objectives for two regions, a hierarchical structure may be discerned as illustrated

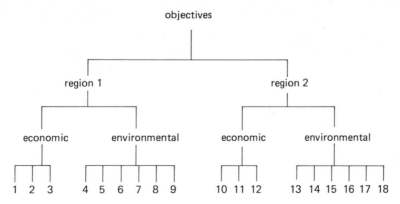

Figure 4.3. Hierarchical structure of objectives according to region and type (environmental versus economic).

by Figure 4.3. By using the methods for each group in the hierarchy separately, the number of objectives to be dealt with one at a time is never larger than 6 in this example.

A side-benefit of this approach is that a bias can be avoided towards aspects for which data are abundantly available. This is important, since one often finds in decision problems that the number of indicators used for a certain type of objective depends heavily on the available information. Without an hierarchical approach it may be difficult to avoid a bias against objectives which are underrepresented due to data reasons.

4.3. Indirect estimation of weights

In this section we will discuss methods for estimating weights in an indirect way, viz. based on preference or indifference statements concerning weights. Three types of methods will be distinguished here. First, weights may be estimated on the basis of actual choices in the past. Second, weights may be derived from a ranking of some given alternatives. Third, weights may be derived from a ranking of alternatives in an interactive way.

4.3.1. Weights based on previous choices

As indicated in Section 2, for every non-dominated solution of a convex constraint set there exists at least one vector of weights λ so that this solution is the optimal one according to the utility function $U = \Sigma_j \lambda_j \omega_j$. Thus, it is in principle possible to translate information on a previous choice into the weights of a linear utility function. Depending on the structure of the set of feasible solutions a unique value of λ or a feasible set for λ will be found. The main problem inherent in this approach is of course that one needs not only information on a previous choice, but also on the previous set of feasible solutions as well as on all objectives which played a role at that time. Further explorations into this area of revealed preference methods can be found among others in Nijkamp and Somermeyer (1973). It should be added that not so much the actual set of feasible solutions at a previous point in time, but especially the set of feasible solutions perceived at the time of the decision plays a crucial role here. Clearly, reliable information of this type is usually not available, so that this approach is not frequently used [see also Rietveld (1980)].

4.3.2.   *Weights based on a ranking of alternatives*

In this approach the decision maker is provided with a set of say N alternatives and is asked to rank them in order of attractiveness. The alternatives can be represented in terms of related objectives as a series of N vectors: $\omega_1, \omega_2, \ldots, \omega_N$. Assume the ranking is determined as follows: alternative 1 is preferred to alternative 2, alternative 2 to alternative 3, etc. Let $U_1, \ldots, U_N$ be the unknown values of the utility function underlying the ranking. If we assume that the utility function is linear as in (4.1), the weights λ can be found by solving the following quadratic programming problem [see Nievergelt (1971)]:

$$
\left.
\begin{aligned}
\min_{(U_1,\ldots,U_N;\lambda_1,\ldots,\lambda_J)} \quad & \varphi = \sum_n (U_n - \lambda'\omega_n)^2 \\
\text{subject to} \quad U_1 \;&\geq U_2 \\
U_2 \;&\geq U_3 \\
&\vdots \\
U_{N-1} \;&\geq U_N \\
\sum_j \lambda_j \;&= 1 \\
\lambda \;&\geq O
\end{aligned}
\right\}
\qquad (4.9)
$$

This method has close links with multidimensional scaling techniques which can be used to transform ordinal information (a ranking of alternatives) into cardinal information in the form of a weights vector [see Nijkamp (1979)]. For a method taking into account the possibility of intransitivities in preference statements we refer to Pekelman and Sen (1974).

4.3.3. Interactive estimation of weights

A common characteristic of the interview methods discussed above is that all questions have been devised beforehand. Frisch (1976) has proposed to introduce an interactive element in the interviews so that a certain question depends on the answers to the preceding questions. This approach can be delineated as follows. First, the decision maker is asked to indicate the most preferred and most deferred values of each objective. These values will be denoted as ω_j^p and ω_j^d, respectively. In the second stage, the decision maker is confronted for each pair of objectives j and j' with a series of questions in an interactive way in order to arrive at two alternatives which are equally attractive in his view. This information can then be used to determine the relative weight $\lambda_j/\lambda_{j'}$.

The interactive procedure in the second stage runs as follows. First, the decision maker is asked which of two alternatives he prefers: $(\omega_j^p, \omega_{j'}^d)$ or $(\omega_j^d, \omega_{j'}^p)$. If the decision maker selects the first alternative, ask him to choose between $(\frac{1}{2}\omega_j^p + \frac{1}{2}\omega_j^d, \omega_{j'}^d)$ and $(\omega_j^d, \omega_{j'}^p)$. If in this case the decision maker selects the second alternative, present him with a choice between $(\omega_j^p, \omega_{j'}^d)$ and $(\omega_j^d, \frac{1}{2}\omega_{j'}^p + \frac{1}{2}\omega_{j'}^d)$. Suppose that in the first choice the decision maker prefers alternative 1, and in the second choice alternative 2, then the third choice is between $(\frac{3}{4}\omega_j^p + \frac{1}{4}\omega_j^d, \omega_{j'}^d)$ and $(\omega_j^d, \omega_{j'}^p)$. By proceeding in this way one will finally end up with a pair of alternatives between which the decision maker is indifferent so that the relative weight $\lambda_j/\lambda_{j'}$ can be determined.

In principle, a series of $J-1$ interviews is sufficient to determine all relative weights. Additional interviews may be carried out to check consistency (as with the tradeoff method). Clearly, this method can only be used if the number of objectives is small, since otherwise it becomes too time-consuming for the decision maker.

4.4. Aspiration levels

Aspiration levels express the decision maker's ideas about the desired outcomes of the decision in terms of a certain level to be aimed at for each objective. Aspiration levels play an important role in psychological theories on decision-making behaviour [cf. Hansen (1972)]. They have been introduced in various branches of economic theory, e.g. consumer choice [Katona (1951)], theory of the firm [Simon (1957)] and economic planning [Kornai (1971)]. There is a close link between the concept of aspiration level and the theory of satisficing behaviour.

Aspiration levels (goals) usually have a somewhat hybrid character. On the one hand they depend on wishes, whereas on the other hand also constraints play a role since they depend on the decision maker's internal expectations concerning the set of feasible solutions. When provided with more accurate information on the set of feasible solutions, decision makers may feel inclined to adjust their aspirations. This makes aspiration levels suitable for use in interactive methods (see also Section 6 of this chapter).

The usual way in which aspiration levels are treated is by means of goal programming [see, e.g. Spronk (1981)]. Let ω_j^g denote the aspiration level for objective j. Further, let ω_j^+ denote the level of overattainment for objective j, whereas ω_j^- denotes the level of underattainment for objective j. Then we know that $\omega_j^+ \cdot \omega_j^- = 0$. A rather general formulation of a utility function on the basis of the aspiration levels is:

$$f\left(\omega_1^+, \ldots, \omega_j^+ ; \omega_1^-, \ldots, \omega_J^-\right) = \sum_j \lambda_j^- \left(\frac{\omega_j^-}{\omega_j^g}\right)^p + \lambda_j^+ \left(\frac{\omega_j^+}{\omega_j^g}\right)^p. \tag{4.10}$$

This formula has the advantage of flexibility in that it can be specified in several ways. For example, it allows one to assume that decision makers are indifferent with respect to overattainments ($\lambda_j^+ = 0$). The other side of the coin is of course that it may often be difficult to fix the parameters λ_j^-, λ_j^+ and p on firm grounds. The analyst may use default values such as $\lambda_j^- = 1$ for all j, $\lambda_j^+ = 0$ for all j, and $p = 2$, but one must be aware that often the choice of a preferred alternative depends strongly on these default values [see Rietveld (1980)]. Hence a sensitivity analysis is advisable in these circumstances.

4.5. Minimum requirements

A straightforward way of expressing priorities among objectives is to state minimum requirements. These minimum standards express necessary conditions for acceptability of alternatives and can be used to eliminate irrelevant alternatives [see also Tversky (1972) on sequential elimination of alternatives].

In a sense, minimum requirements are the antipode of aspiration levels. There is usually no feasible alternative which satisfies all aspiration levels simultaneously, whereas on the other hand usually more than one alternative satisfies the minimum requirements.

In a mathematical programming problem the imposition of minimum requirements means that side-conditions are added to the original set of feasible solutions. The dual variables related to these constraints can be interpreted as weights to be attached to the various objectives.

A feature shared with aspiration levels is that minimum requirements depend on some prior knowledge of the set of feasible solutions. As a consequence both approaches are suitable for use in interactive methods, as will be shown in Section 6 of the present chapter.

4.6.   Lexicographic orders

By expressing a lexicographic order of objectives a decision maker indicates that the objective ranked as most important is of overriding importance for the decision problem. The objective mentioned in the second place is only taken into account when two alternatives attain equal scores for the most important objective. Thus, the choice between two alternatives is only determined by the most important objective for which they are unequal.

Lexicographic orders usually lead to a straightforward selection of the most preferred alternative. Most of the information collected on alternatives will not play a role in the selection process. A distinguishing feature of lexicographic orders is that they cannot be represented by utility functions [see Fishburn (1974)].

More flexible versions of lexicographic orders can be achieved in two ways. First, by introducing satiation levels. In this case, the first objective is only of overriding importance as long as the alternatives do not reach the satiation level for this objective. When the satiation level of the most important objective is reached by two alternatives, the choice among the two will depend on the first unsatisfactory objective for which the alternatives are unequal.

Another refinement which is often used is that objectives are ranked in a limited number of priority classes such that objectives in a certain class have pre-emptive priority above the objectives in the subsequent classes. Then the problem must still be considered as to how to deal with the objectives in the same priority class. In principle, all methods mentioned above can be used for this purpose. In practice, mainly goal-programming methods are used for this purpose [see Ignizio (1976) and Spronk (1981)].

4.7.   Conclusion

This section has shown that a considerable variety of methods exists for estimating and modelling preferences. The usefulness of the methods depends among others on the time needed, the degree of difficulty to understand, the precision of the outcomes and the range of problems it can be used for. No method has been found that dominates the other ones according to all aspects.

Several times we found in this section that it will be too demanding for a decision maker to give such a precise indication of his preferences that it enables the analyst to determine a most preferred solution in an unambiguous way [cf. Vickrey (1960)].

Expression of preferences in decision-making processes is an activity which is greatly facilitated if it is done with some background knowledge concerning the set of feasible solutions. On the other hand, the provision of information on feasible solutions can be carried out most properly if the analyst has some information about the decision maker's knowledge. Therefore, more recently developed interactive methods may be helpful in integrating both processes. This will be further treated in Section 6.

The empirical applications in the field of preference assessments have demonstrated a wide range of methodologies, varying from ad hoc specifications of preference rankings to policy scenarios, from simulation experiments to econometric estimation procedures, and from historically based event analysis to prospective preference assessments. The same variety is also reflected in regional economic applications, where no uniform methodology has been developed but where – analogous to general policy analysis – a great diversity of methods for inferring preference statements co-exist.

5. A typology of multiple objective decision methods

In the present section, a brief presentation of some major classes of multiple objective decision methods will be given. By no means is this section meant to be an exhaustive description of all methods developed in the past decade [see for more details, among others, Rietveld (1980) and Voogd (1983)]. Two main categories will be distinguished here, viz. discrete multiple criteria methods dealing with a distinct number of alternatives and continuous multiple objective programming methods dealing with an infinite set of alternatives (see also Section 2).

5.1.   Discrete methods

The main aim of discrete multiple criteria methods is to provide a rational basis for classifying a number of choice possibilities (for instance, alternative policies, plans, neighbourhoods, regions, etc), on the basis of multiple criteria. There are many different discrete multiple objective evaluation methods currently in use [see Kmietowicz and Pearman (1981), Nijkamp (1979), Rietveld (1980), Voogd (1983)]. A major step in all these methods is the construction of an impact (or evaluation) matrix representing the effect of a certain alternative on a decision criterion. In order to aggregate the information of the evaluation matrix usually a weighting scheme is necessary which expresses the relative importance of the various scores. This was already discussed in Sections 4.2 and 4.3. The impact matrix (sometimes also called evaluation matrix or project-effect matrix) will be denoted by the symbol P. This matrix has elements P_{ij}, which represent the impact of alternative i ($i = 1, \ldots, I$) on the value of criterion j ($j = 1, \ldots, J$). In the case of a qualitative evaluation problem, p_{ij} may be measured on an ordinal, binary or nominal scale. However, it is not unusual that a part of the p_{ij} elements are quantitative in nature, i.e. some of the criterion effects are determined on a cardinal scale, whereas other effects are represented in a qualitative way. This is called a *mixed data* problem.

The set of weights provides information on the relative importance attached to the outcomes of the successive J criteria; they will be denoted as a vector λ:

$$\lambda = (\lambda_1, \ldots, \lambda_J)'. \tag{5.1}$$

Clearly, usually the vector λ does not contain purely cardinal tradeoffs, but ordinal or binary weights. Most recently developed multiple criteria methods take explicit account of the "soft" nature of weights. The next step is the treatment of preference statements and impact matrices. As mentioned before, one may subdivide multicriteria methods into "hard" and "soft" evaluation problems. Hard problems deal with information measured at a cardinal (quantitative) level, whereas soft problems are based on information measured at an ordinal or binary (qualitative) level. Both information levels will successively be discussed.

5.1.1. *Quantitative information*

In the past, *cost–benefit analysis* has been the most commonly used method for evaluating discrete alternatives based on hard data. This approach was especially applied to so-called "single-step" evaluation problems. However, many projects or plans are concerned with outcomes or consequences which cannot be treated in terms of prices, and this makes the cost–benefit approach quite inappropriate for complex public decision making [see Nijkamp (1980) for an extensive criticism]. Related methods such as cost–effectiveness analysis [see, among others, Teitz (1968)], the planning-balance sheet method [cf. Lichfield et al. (1975)], and the shadow project approach [cf. Klaassen (1973)] are significant improvements over traditional cost–benefit analysis for complex planning purposes, but provide no satisfactory solution to the problem of judging incommensurate and intangible outcomes. Therefore, alternative (sometimes complementary) methods have been developed. The following hard data methods will be considered here: the weighted summation method [Schimpeler and Grecco (1968), Schlager (1968), Kahne (1975)], the discrepancy analysis technique [Nijkamp (1979)], the goals-achievement method [Hill (1973)], and the concordance approach [Guigou (1974), Roy (1968), Van Delft and Nijkamp (1977)].

The *weighted summation method* assigns quantitative weights to the criteria and treats these weights as "quasi-probabilities" which must add up to 1. Thus the expected value of the outcomes of each alternative plan can be calculated by multiplying the value obtained for each criterion by its appropriate weight and then summing the weighted values for all criteria. Thus the weighted score for a specific alternative i can be written as:

$$s_i = \sum_j \lambda_j p_{ij}. \tag{5.2}$$

Essentially, the weighted summation method calculates the weighted average of all (standardized) criterion scores in the evaluation matrix. This method implies a rather rigid approach since it assumes a perfect linear substitution of the values of the various criteria, which is seldom true in practical applications.

Another method for "hard" evaluation problems is *discrepancy analysis*. This approach attempts to rank the alternatives according to their discrepancy from a (hypothetical) optimum alternative. This optimum alternative achieves a set of predefined goals. Statistical correlation coefficients can then be used to identify the alternative most similar to the reference alternative. Although this method can be very attractive in combination with computer graphics, it should be used with care because the various discrepancies in the outcomes of an alternative plan or project cannot be made sufficiently explicit.

A method which is related to discrepancy analysis and which is often applied in planning practice, is the *goals-achievement method*. This method links each criterion to a quantitative achievement level or target value (see Section 4.4). Evaluation essentially involves taking the achievement score for each criterion, and aggregating these to give a total achievement score for each alternative plan. The values are aggregated using a weighted summation procedure similar to that described above for the weighted summation method. Hence, a similar criticism holds for this approach. However, this approach can be quite attractive for evaluation problems which need to be treated with very simple and straightforward methods, e.g. in approval procedures for governmental premiums.

The *concordance approach* is also widely used. This method is based on a pairwise comparison of alternatives, thus using only the metric interval characteristics of the various scores in the evaluation of the impact matrix. The basic idea is to measure the degree to which the scores and their associated weights confirm or contradict the dominant pairwise relationships among alternatives. The differences in weights and the differences in evaluation scores are usually analyzed separately.

The central concept in a concordance analysis is the so-called concordance index $c_{ii'}$. This index represents the extent to which alternative i is better than alternative i'. This index may be defined as the sum of weights attached to the criteria included in the so-called concordance set $C_{ii'}$; this is the set of all evaluation criteria for which alternative i in the impact matrix P is at least equally attractive as alternative i'. Clearly, this set can be determined irrespective of the degree of information on the impact matrix. Hence, the concordance index can be defined as follows:

$$c_{ii'} = \sum_{j \in C_{ii'}} \lambda_j. \tag{5.3}$$

A dominating alternative can now be found by employing threshold values, relative dominance indicators, or other concepts from graph theory.

In an analogous way, one may define a discordance index. This index reflects the extent to which alternative i is worse than i'. Instead of using weights in this index, the corresponding relative pairwise differences from the impact matrix are then taken into consideration. By combining the results from the concordance and discordance approach, final inferences on the ranking of alternatives may be made.

5.1.2. Qualitative information

In recent years, much attention has been paid to the development of evaluation techniques which are capable to deal in a consistent way with "qualitative" or "soft" evaluation problems. Many operational soft discrete multicriteria methods are now available [cf. Hinloopen et al. (1983)]. The following approaches will be discussed here: the extreme value method [Kmietowicz and Pearman (1981)], the permutation method [Paelinck (1976)], the regime method [Hinloopen et al. (1983)], the geometric scaling approach [Voogd (1983)], and the mixed data approach [Voogd (1983)]. The latter two approaches are especially designed to deal with "mixed" qualitative–quantitative evaluation problems.

The *extreme value method* can be regarded as an extension of the weighted summation method discussed above. It is still assumed that the scores achieved by each plan with respect to each criterion have quantitative properties, but in addition it is postulated that the probabilities (weights) are only known in a qualitative sense, i.e. only their ordinal properties are given. In essence, the aim of this approach is to determine the alternative with the maximum or minimum expected value. This is done by transforming the discrete problem into a linear programming problem, with the ordinal probabilities as constraints. Some elementary operations lead to maximum and minimum expected values for the alternatives under consideration, which may be used to arrive at a final assessment. However, as has been elaborated by Rietveld (1982), this assessment should not be made solely on the basis of the extreme values, but should also take into account certain expected values for alternatives generated for intermediate values of the probabilities.

The *permutation analysis* addresses especially the question: which rank order of alternatives is (after a series of permutations) in harmony with the ordinal information contained in P and λ? In case of I alternatives, the total number of possible permutations will be equal to $I!$ Each permutation can be numbered as p ($p = 1, \ldots, I!$). In the permutation analysis, each rank order from the permutations is confronted with the ordinal information contained in each of the J columns of the impact matrix. Then Kendall's rank correlation coefficient is used in order to compute the statistical correlation between the $I!$ rank orders and the J columns of P. This leads then to $I! \times J$ rank correlation coefficients denoted by τ_j^P. Clearly, a certain permutation p (i.e. rank order of alternatives) is more attractive as the value of τ_j^P is higher.

The next step is to relate this information to the weighted vector λ. If λ were cardinal, an ordinary weighted summation method might be applied in order to calculate the value of τ_j^P. In the case of ordinal information on λ, the following programming model is used:

$$
\left.
\begin{aligned}
&\max_{P} \; \sum_{j=1}^{J} \lambda_j \tau_j^P, \\[4pt]
&\text{subject to} \\[2pt]
&\lambda_1 \geqq \lambda_2 \geqq \cdots \geqq \lambda_j, \\[2pt]
&\sum_{j=1}^{J} \lambda_j = 1.
\end{aligned}
\right\}
\tag{5.4}
$$

The constraints in (5.4) reflect the available information about the λ_j, and are used as follows. First, all extreme points that are in agreement with the constraints on the weights are generated: $(1, 0, \ldots, 0)$, $(1/2, 1/1, 0, \ldots, 0)$, $(1/3, 1/3, 1/3, 0, \ldots, 0)$, $(1/J, 1/J, \ldots, 1/J)$. Next, a set of combinations of weights reflecting interior points of the above-mentioned extreme area are generated. Then one may calculate for each of these combinations which permutation p yields the maximum value of the objective function in (5.4). On the basis of this information, one may try to identify a rank order that is in agreement with the ordinal information from P and λ.

This approach also has some limitations. For instance, the weights λ, are dealt with in a rather unusual way by relating them to the coefficients τ_j^P instead of to the criterion impacts. This implies that the size of the weights cannot be linked with the size of the impact scores.

Regime analysis bears a certain resemblance to the concordance analysis. The starting point of regime analysis is the concordance index $c_{ii'}$, defined in (5.3). Given the definition of this index, $c_{ii'} - c_{i'i}$ can be interpreted as an indicator of the relative attractiveness of alternative i compared with i'. Since it is assumed that the weights λ_j are ordinal, it is impossible to find a unique numerical value for $c_{ii'} - c_{i'i}$. Therefore regime analysis focuses on the *sign* of this indicator rather than on its size.

It can be shown that in certain cases, ordinal information on weights is sufficient to determine this sign, so that a final ranking of alternatives can be derived from the pairwise comparison matrix, consisting of values $+1$ and -1. In other cases, this sign cannot be determined unambiguously, however. It can be shown that in such cases a partitioning of the set of cardinal weights can be derived, being in agreement with the ordinal information on the weights, such that for each subset of weights again the sign of $c_{ii'} - c_{i'i}$ can be determined. The final result of the method is a complete and transitive ranking of all alternatives, for each of the above-mentioned subsets of weights. In addition, the method produces the relative size of each subset so that one knows the relative importance of each subset.

The *geometric scaling approach* is based on the principles of nonmetric multidimensional scaling. The basic idea of this approach is to transform a large amount of ordinal data into a small amount of quantitative (cardinal) data, such that the new cardinal configuration is as close as possible (i.e. has a maximum goodness-of-fit) to the ordinal data. One limitation of this elegant approach is that it requires a fairly complicated computational algorithm. In addition, evaluation problems treated by this method should have a sufficient number of degrees of freedom to allow geometric scaling. This implies that unless sufficient ordinal information is available, no metric data can be extracted.

It is clear that several concepts from scaling analysis may also be applicable to ordinal multiple criteria problems. Various approaches can be imagined in this case. In the first place, one may use a scaling technique in order to transform a qualitative impact matrix into a cardinal matrix with less dimensions. Then the cardinal configuration of the initial qualitative matrix provides a metric picture of the Euclidean distances both between the alternatives and between the effects. This is a normal standard operation.

Second, one may also apply a scaling analysis jointly to a qualitative impact matrix and a qualitative weight vector. In that case, both the impacts and the weights have to be transformed into a cardinal metric scale. Though this is mathematically fairly difficult, one may ultimately arrive at cardinal results for both impacts and weights. The final result of this analysis is that one is able to indicate precisely which rank order of alternatives is consistent with a certain rank order of ordinal weights.

Most of the soft multicriteria methods mentioned above have been used in the (regional and urban) planning practice, despite the fact that they have only recently been developed. However, one serious and persistent criticism of these techniques is that only the ordinal characteristics of the available quantitative information are utilized. Therefore most recent research in this field has concentrated on the development of methods capable of dealing with "mixed data", i.e. evaluation matrices containing both quantitative scores and qualitative rankings. Voogd (1983) has developed a *mixed-data* method based on the geometric scaling approach (which obviously suffers from the same limitations as the simpler version mentioned above). This approach involves the construction of two measures: one dealing only with ordinal information and the other with cardinal information. By combining these steps, the information from these measures can be aggregated into one appraisal score for each alternative.

5.1.3.   Concluding remarks

The preceding subsection has shown that a whole series of discrete multicriteria methods is now available, each method having its own particular assumptions. It illustrates that there is no universal method for solving every type of plan or project evaluation. Besides, there always remains uncertainty regarding the applicability of a method, due to its implicit and explicit assumptions. Not all methods give the same results, which can be overcome in practice by performing some kind of a sensitivity analysis on the methodological assumptions of the discrete evaluation methods being used [see for more details Voogd (1983)].

5.2.   Continuous methods

Much attention has been given in the past to the development of continuous evaluation methods. Especially "hard" evaluation problems have been investigated, which resulted in a variety of optimization methods. The following methods will briefly be considered here: utility function approaches [Fishburn (1974)], penalty models [Theil (1968)], goal programming [Spronk (1981)], min–max approaches [Rietveld (1980)], and reference point approaches [Wierzbicki (1983)].

5.2.1.   Quantitative information

Utility methods start from the assumption that the entire set of relevant criteria or objectives can be translated through a weighting procedure into one "utility function" (see also Sections 3 and 4). Such a utility function reflects all tradeoffs and priorities (weights) attached to the successive criteria. Then this utility function has to be optimized given the constraints of the evaluation problem concerned. The utility approach is a theoretical instrument which has often been used in many neoclassical optimization problems. It is an elegant approach, but it has also obvious drawbacks. For instance, it presupposes complete prior quantitative information about all weights and tradeoffs among the whole range of feasible values of all criteria.

Penalty models assume the existence of a set of desired achievement levels ("ideal values") for the criteria under consideration. Any discrepancy between an actual criterion value and an ideal value incurs a penalty calculated through some kind of a penalty function. Evidently, the main difficulty in applying this kind of model is lack of information about appropriate penalty functions. For algorithmic reasons (ease of differentiation) often a quadratic function is used; however, this implies the introduction of an additional "weight" to the deviations, which can be very debatable. A special case of penalty models is the *goal programming* model discussed already above.

Min max approaches are based on the use of a matrix representing the payoffs between conflicting objectives as well as their feasible ranges. In a similar way as in game theory, one may next calculate the equilibrium solution from the payoff matrix. This equilibrium solution reflects the best compromise choice for the evaluation problem. A drawback is again that there are several ways to arrive at an equilibrium solution, so that there is no guarantee that the compromise solution is unique. Here again an interactive procedure may be helpful. This approach is especially appropriate when it is necessary to take into account different views of a problem in some explicit way. Each view is represented by a criterion function (or objective function) and the information given in the payoff matrix may then be used to help the decision committee to arrive at a compromise solution.

Reference point approaches are based on the concept of an ideal point (or utopian point). This ideal point is defined as a vector whose elements are the maximum values of the individual criterion functions. The closer the criterion values of an alternative is to the values of the ideal point, the better the alternative. The compromise solution is defined as the alternative in the set of efficient solution for which the distance to the ideal solution is minimal. An efficient solution (or Pareto solution) is a solution for which the value of one criterion (or objective) cannot be improved without reducing the value of a competing criterion (or objective). It should be noted that there are also reference point approaches which are formulated in a goal programming framework, where the reference point represents a set of aspiration levels. This approach is only appropriate if the reference points can be modified during the course of the analysis. It should therefore also be used in an interactive way (see also Section 6).

5.2.2. *Qualitative information*

The continuous methods described above all deal with "hard" evaluation problems. "Soft" continuous approaches, however, did not receive much attention in the past. Apart from some work in the field of fuzzy sets hardly any elaborative work can be reported on qualitative continuous evaluation methods. An interesting contribution however can be found in Leung (1983).

5.2.3. Concluding remarks

For global and macro decision problems, hard continuous evaluation methods have reached a stage of sufficient maturity, hence they can be and actually are applied in a wide variety of policy analyses. They are especially appropriate in planning processes in which feasible solutions within certain constraints are to be found, e.g. the capacity of drinking water supply, of municipal waste disposal centres, and so forth. Continuous methods may also be used to scan problems and to identify the main alternative lines of action. However, in empirical research practice one often faces non-quantitative information. Further research in this area is therefore certainly justified, also given the qualitive nature of many decision problems in practice.

6.   Interactive methods

6.1.   Introduction

Various multiple objective decision methods have been used in an interactive context. In each step of an interactive decision-making process, information is exchanged between the analyst and the decision maker. The analyst provides information on the set of feasible solutions, whereas the decision maker expresses information on his preferences by giving his reactions to the feasible solutions proposed to him. Thus, interactive methods deal with both design and selection of alternatives.

  The major point to be addressed in interactive decision methods is how the rules have to be formulated to achieve a successful cooperation. Some general criteria to be taken into account have already been mentioned in Section 4.7. Of special importance is that the information produced by the analyst in each step is digestible for the decision maker. Also, the interaction must be convergent in some sense: it must lead to the determination of a most preferred solution or to the selection of a certain range of attractive alternatives. The rules also have to guarantee that the analyst has a neutral role in the process: the analyst should not be able to manipulate the decision maker. For surveys and reflections on interactive decision methods we refer to Hwang and Masud (1979), Rietveld (1980), White (1983) and Wierzbicki (1983).

  Interactive decision methods as presented here differ in an essential way from the interactive estimation of weights discussed in Section 4.3, as in the latter approach the aspect of providing information on feasible solutions to a decision maker is not an intrinsic element.

6.2. *Interactive decision making by imposing minimum requirements*

A wide variety of interactive methods has been developed. In this section we will present a method with a relatively simple structure. The distinguishing feature of the method is that the decision maker expresses his preferences in terms of minimum requirements (see Section 4.5). Methods similar to this one can be found in Fandel (1972). Extensions and alternative methods will be discussed in the next section.

The method consists of a number of steps, while each step consists of two stages. In stage (a) the analyst provides information on the set of feasible solutions to the decision maker. In stage (b) the decision maker gives his reaction on this information. More specifically, these stages can be described as follows:

(a) The analyst provides the decision maker with three pieces of information:

(1) the maximum attainable levels of each objective (ideal solution) given the set of feasible solutions as well as preference statements of the decision maker, expressed in previous steps;

(2) the minimum attainable level for each objective given the constraints under 1;

(3) a compromise solution reflecting the wish to do justice to all objectives to a maximum extent taking into account the constraints under 1.

(b) The decision maker gives his opinion on the compromise solution by indicating for which variables it gives rise to unsatisfactory levels. If all objectives are satisfactory, the procedure can be terminated. If there is not any satisfactory objective, the conclusion must be that the problem does not allow an acceptable solution. If some objectives attain unsatisfactory levels, the analyst adds constraints to the constraint set used in the preceding step, indicating that the performance of the objectives concerned must be better than the values attained in the compromise solution.

The maximum and minimum attainable levels produced in stage (a) serve as a frame of reference for the decision maker to give him a firm background for evaluating the compromise solution. These levels are obtained via the payoff matrix discussed before, which is based on the maximization of each objective separately. There are several ways of operationalizing the notion of compromise solutions. Here we present one version reflecting the idea that a good compromise is as near as possible to the ideal solution, taking into account the differences in the dimensions of the objectives. This compromise can be obtained by solving the

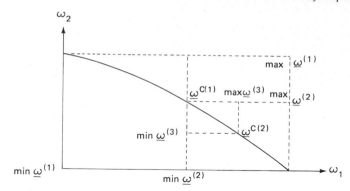

Figure 6.1. Example of an interactive procedure.

following mathematical programming problem:

$$
\left.
\begin{aligned}
\min_{x} ! \sum_{j} & \left(\frac{\max \omega_j - \omega_j(x)}{\max \omega_j - \min \omega_j} \right)^{p} \\
\text{subject to:} \quad & g_i(x) = 0 \qquad i = 1, \ldots, I \\
& \omega_j(x) \geq m_j \qquad j = 1, \ldots, J.
\end{aligned}
\right\}
\tag{6.1}
$$

Note that a standardization of objectives according to (4.6) has been carried out by using the term $(\max \omega_j - \min \omega_j)$ in the denominator. The parameter p may assume all values larger than or equal to 1. When $p \to \infty$, (6.1) becomes a min–max problem. The side-conditions imposed by the decision maker in earlier steps are represented by the minimum requirements m_j $(j = 1, \ldots, J)$. The solution of (6.1) will be denoted as x^c, giving rise to values $\omega_j^c = \omega_j(x^c)$ for the various objective functions.

In Figure 6.1 the essential features of the method can be found for the case of 2 objectives. Let the vectors with maximum attainable values and compromise values in step s be denoted as $\max \omega^{(s)}$, $\min \omega^{(s)}$ and $\omega^{c(s)}$, respectively. The figure shows that the rectangle implied by $\max \omega^{(1)}$ and $\min \omega^{(1)}$ contains all relevant feasible solutions. One of them, $\omega^{c(1)}$ is selected as an initial compromise solution. In the second phase of the first step, the decision maker gives his opinion on the compromise. Assume, that he wants the first objective to be improved. This means that the side-condition $\omega_1(x) \geq \omega_1^{c(2)}$ is added to (6.1). Obviously this will lead to a lower value for the second objective.

In the second step, the analyst computes the maximum and minimum attainable values taking into account the new side-condition.

The levels found show that the imposition of the side-condition gives rise to a considerable reduction of the set of feasible options. We assume in this figure that according to the decision maker the performance of the second objective in the compromise solution is unsatisfactory, which gives rise to the imposition of the constraint: $\omega_2 \geq \omega_2^{c(2)}$. The ensuing maximum and minimum values in the third step are already very near to each other, illustrating the convergence property of the method.

6.3. Alternative interactive decision methods

The interactive method sketched above is one out of a large group of possible methods. Alternative approaches can be found with respect to both stage (a) the information produced by the analyst, and stage (b) the decision maker's response to this.

The compromise solution in (6.1) is generated by minimizing the distance from the ideal point, making use of a distance metric for normalized objectives. As already noted in Section 4.2, also other ways of normalization can be used, giving rise to other compromise values. In addition, other approaches have been proposed to generate a compromise solution, for example based on compromise weights [see Fandel (1972)].

There exist several ways for the decision maker to express his opinion on the proposed compromise solution. In addition to imposing minimum standards, the decision maker may also relax aspiration levels in view of the compromise solution. An example is the method of displaced ideal, proposed by Zeleny (1982). Another possibility is that the decision maker indicates a relaxation level for some of the satisfactory objectives in the compromise solution in order to give scope for an improvement of the less satisfactory objectives [see Benayoun et al. (1971)].

There are also methods (usually assuming linear constraints) in which the analyst provides the decision maker with a limited set of non-dominated solutions. Then the decision maker may indicate which of these alternatives he prefers. This information can be translated by the analyst in terms of weights of a linear utility function (cf. Section 4.3). The improved knowledge on the weights can be used in the next step to generate a new set of non-dominated solutions, which gives a better representation of the decision maker's preferences [see, e.g. Zionts and Wallenius (1976) and Steuer (1976)]. Interactive methods can be conceived of as learning methods. They enable the decision maker to survey the set of feasible solutions in a user-oriented way. During the interactions, decision makers may find that in an earlier step they imposed a side-condition which too much reduces the set of feasible solutions. Such results are part of the learning process: how to deal sequentially with conflicting objectives in complex situations? In principle, the methods must be flexible enough in order to adjust a priori imposed side-conditions that are later regarded as too rigid.

The final result of an interactive procedure is not necessarily a unique solution. Usually, within a limited number of steps (say 5 or 10), the range of alternatives that is still feasible, is so small that it is not interesting any more for the decision maker to proceed any longer. In such a case one ends up with a (small) range of preferred alternatives. In Section 7 an illustrative application can be found of an interactive multiple objective decision method to industrial complex analysis.

7. The use of multiple objective decision methods in regional economics

7.1. Relevance of multiple objective decision analysis for regional economics

The foregoing survey has exhibited a wide variety of multiple objective decision methods being used as operational tools in planning and conflict management problems. Such methods are of utmost importance in regional economics due to various reasons:

(i) regional economics deals with concrete spatial economic problems at a practical level, in which usually many conflicts are involved between policy agencies, interest groups, decision makers, etc. (for instance, a conflict between regional industrialization and environmental quality);

(ii) a regional system is usually an open system, so that any development in the one component exerts an influence on other components of a spatial system. Such spillover effects may be complementary, but in many cases they evoke conflicts among entities of a spatial system (for instance, a multiregional conflict between efficiency and equity);

(iii) in many countries one observes an increasing trend toward integrated planning approaches at the regional or urban level. Such endeavours lead – by necessity – to a simultaneous consideration of many policy objectives, even sometimes far outside the realm of economic variables. Such a broader view on planning requires the use of principles from multiple objective decision analysis.

Altogether the conclusion may be drawn that multiple objective decision analysis provides regional economic policy problems with a relevant and operational foundation.

The operational significance of multiple objective decision methods for regional economic problems is also reflected in a variety of applications. A growing number of operational policy analyses has been carried out along the lines of multiple objective decision methods in the area of regional and urban planning. Usual themes covered in these analyses are the conflicts among various policy

fields: evaluation of regional policy, assessment of merits of investment alternatives, applications in the field of environmental protection, distributional issues in
urban planning, etc. Various examples can be found among others in Nijkamp
(1979, 1980), Rietveld (1980) and Voogd (1983).

A relatively new development is the introduction of multiple objective decision
methods in the context of multiregional models. Here we mention as examples:
Despontin (1982), Despontin et al. (1983), Hafkamp (1984), Lesuis et al. (1983),
and Lundqvist (1981). Through this development an important dimension could
be added to the conflicts mentioned above, viz. interregional and/or national–
regional conflicts.

Another field in which special attention is paid to spatial aspects of conflicting
objectives is transportation and location, both at the interregional level (see, e.g.
Ratick, 1983) and the intra-urban level [see, e.g. Lundqvist (1982)]. Conflicting
objectives in the accessibility of urban facilities are dealt with by Miller (1981)
and Massam and Askew (1982). Examples of multiple objective decision methods
in land use planning can be found in Shoou-Yuh Chang et al. (1982) and Voogd
(1983). In conclusion, there is a rich variety of multiple objective decision
methods that have been applied in the area of regional and urban economics. The
next section will be devoted to a brief empirical illustration of the use of a
particular type of multiple objective decision method.

7.2. An illustration of an interactive discrete multiple objective method for industrial complex analysis

At the western side of the greater Rotterdam area in the Netherlands, a large
industrial site has been created in the 1970s. The area (called the Maasvlakte) has
a considerable size (more than 1000 hectares) and it is accessible for deep-draught
sea vessels. Public discussions arose on the industries to be admitted on the site
given the unacceptable high level of air pollution in the area. For further details
on this issue we refer to Rietveld (1980).

A number of 8 candidate activities had been listed for a location in this area,
among others steel works, a tank storage plant, an oil refinery and a container
terminal. Given the space requirements for each industry, not all activities could
be allotted a place in this area. After a combinational analysis it was found that
151 different combinations of industries were in principle feasible. Four policy
fields played a role in the evaluation of the alternatives: economics, labour
market, spatial–physical planning, and environmental management.

The objectives were specified as follows:
economic variables:
   (1) value added (millions of Dfl. per year);
   (2) contribution to the differentiation of the economic structure (index);

(3) port revenues for the harbour authorities (millions of Dfl. per year);
labour market variables:
(4) total demand for labour (man-years);
(5) qualitative discrepancy between labour demand and supply (index);
(6) demand for foreign labour (percentage of total labour demand);
spatial – physical variable:
(7) occupation rate of the area (percentage);
environmental variable:
(8) air pollution (tons of particulates and SO_2 per year).
The variables 5, 6 and 8 were considered as variables to be minimized, whereas
the other ones are to be maximized.

The relevant information on the decision problem can be represented by means
of a matrix of size (151×8), which is rather large. Therefore, an interactive
procedure is likely an adequate tool for the analysis of the conflicts involved in
the decision problem. The interactive method described in Section 6.2 has been
used in cooperation with the delegate in charge of economic affairs of one of the
main governmental bodies concerned. As Table 7.1 shows, convergence has been
reached in 7 steps. In the first steps especially the objectives 4 (labour demand)
and 8 (air pollution) were apparently emphasized by the decision maker.

The application of the method used showed that its mechanism was easy to
understand. A short introduction period appeared sufficient to teach its basic
principles to the decision maker at hand. Especially the absence of the need for
specifying policy weights was regarded as one of the stronger points of this
method.

7.3. Outlook

A major advantage of multiple objective decision methods is their contribution to
a more explicit treatment of tradeoffs in policy analysis, so that they may create
an increased awareness of the interdependencies between actors or between
regions in a complex spatial economic system. In this respect, multiple objective
decision methods should not be in the first place regarded as optimization tools,
but as learning and communication tools in order to rationalize decisions. This
approach has important implications, as this leads to the necessity to pay
adequate attention to the specification of a representative set of objective
functions, to the generation and definition of a representative and feasible set of
alternatives, to the operationalization of weights and preferences in the planning
process, and to the dynamics in regional economic development planning.

Especially in recent years, much progress has been made in decision support
systems (DSS), aiming at an interplay between experts and decision makers on
the basis of man–computer interactions. Such decision support systems are also

Table 7.1

Stepwise presentation of results of an interactive multiple criteria decision procedure for industrial complex analysis.

Step	Total number of feasible solutions	Type of solution	ω_1	ω_2	ω_3	ω_4	ω_5	ω_6	ω_7	ω_8
						Values of decision criteria				
1	151	ideal	1389.9	100.0	90.0	15520.0	−6.9	0.0	100.0	0.0
		minimum	0.0	0.0	0.0	0.0	−91.0	−10.0	0.0	−157.8
		compromise	787.3	56.7	77.5	7740.0	−13.2	−7.1	98.9	−43.6
2	41	ideal	1389.9	91.4	82.5	15520.0	−12.5	−6.8	100.0	−41.3
		minimum	790.5	46.7	15.0	8000.0	−14.0	−10.0	55.6	−157.8
		compromise	879.3	52.1	62.5	8220.0	−12.6	−7.1	94.4	−131.1
3	21	ideal	1288.5	91.4	65.0	14720.0	−12.5	−8.6	100.0	−41.3
		minimum	919.0	72.9	15.0	12000.0	−13.5	−10.0	55.6	−60.1
		compromise	1198.5	76.8	35.0	14100.0	−12.8	−8.9	77.8	−45.6
4	10	ideal	1288.5	88.4	65.0	14720.0	−12.8	−8.6	100.0	−41.3
		minimum	1028.2	72.9	40.0	12500.0	−13.5	−9.7	82.2	−60.1
		compromise	1191.3	77.2	45.0	14120.0	−13.0	−8.9	94.4	−45.6
5	7	ideal	1288.5	87.8	65.0	14720.0	−12.8	−8.6	100.0	−45.6
		minimum	1029.4	72.9	50.0	12500.0	−13.5	−9.6	82.2	−60.1
		compromise	1211.7	75.3	50.0	14440.0	−13.3	−8.8	98.9	−45.6
6	3	ideal	1077.4	87.8	55.0	12820.0	−12.8	−9.5	93.3	−55.8
		minimum	1029.4	85.4	50.0	12500.0	−13.5	−9.5	82.2	−55.8
		compromise	1029.4	85.7	50.0	12720.0	−13.5	−9.5	82.2	−55.8
7	1	compromise	1077.4	85.4	55.0	12820.0	−13.1	−9.5	93.3	−55.8

Notes: (1) $\boxed{X}$ means that $\omega > X$ is imposed as a side condition in the next steps.

(2) The objective 5, 6 and 8 have been premultiplied with a factor −1, so that all objectives are to be maximized.

capable of including qualitative and less structured views from decision makers. Such systems do not aim at an optimal solution, but at structuring and rationalizing complex choice problems by highlighting the qualitative dimensions and impacts of the decision makers' views. A major advantage of such a system is the direct availability of consequences of alternative options. This new trend is essentially an outgrowth of recent developments in information systems for planning [see Nijkamp and Rietveld (1984)]. In this context, the input side of decision problems (e.g. the problem definition, the assessment of data) is receiving much attention. There is a growing awareness that the demands placed on highly technical and advanced decision methods tend to become lower as the quality of information systems increases.

Another merit of multiple objective decision analysis stems from its flexibility in a practical decision context: it provides an operational foundation for collective choice, it can be used for conflict analysis and conflict resolution, it may clarify the motives of strategic choice behaviour, and it may contribute to integrated regional (economic) planning. Furthermore, such methods can be linked in various ways to the regional and urban decision-making process; various modes of multiple objective decision models may be distinguished in this context, such as the rational actor model, the sequential and procedural decision model, the incremental decision model, the integrated network decision model, the "satisficing" or even "justifying" decision model, the cognitive process model, the conflict resolution model, the organizational procedure model, the communicative learning model or the contingency theory model. Each of these models is able to generate decision and choice rules in a multiple objective decision context. Altogether, multiple objective decision analysis opens a fruitful possibility for improved decision making in a regional and urban context.

References

Arrow, K. J. (1951) *Social choice and individual values*. New York: John Wiley.
Aumann, R. J. (1964) 'Subjective programming', in: M. W. Shelley and G. L. Bryan, eds., *Human judgment and optimality*. New York: Wiley, 217–242.
Benayoun, R., J. de Montgolfier, J. Tergny and O. Larichev (1971) 'Linear programming with multiple objective functions: step method (STEM)', *Mathematical Programming*, 1:366–375.
Blair, P. D. (1979) *Multiobjective regional energy planning*. Boston: Martinus Nijhoff.
Blin, J. M. (1977) 'Fuzzy sets in multiple criteria decision making', in: M. K. Starr and M. Zeleny, eds., *Multiple criteria decision making*. Amsterdam: North-Holland, 129–146.
Bowman, V. J. (1976) 'On the relationship of the Tchebycheff norm and the efficient frontier of multiple-criteria objectives', in: H. Thiriez and S. Zionts, eds., *Multiple criteria decision making, Jouy en Josas, 1975*. Berlin: Springer, 76–86.
Brill, E. D. (1976) 'The use of optimisation models in public sector planning', *Management Science*, 25:413–422.
Chankong, V. and Y. Y. Haimes (1983) *Multiobjective decision making*. Amsterdam: North-Holland.
Cochrane, J. L. and M. Zeleny, eds. (1973) *Multiple criteria decision making*. Columbia: University of South Carolina Press.
Cohon, J. L. (1978) *Multiobjective programming and planning*. New York: Academic Press.
Dawes, R. M. (1980) 'The robust beauty of improper linear models in decision making', *American Psychologist*, 15:132–148.
Debreu, G. (1959) Theory of value. New York: Wiley.
Despontin, M. (1982) 'Regional multiple objective quantitative policy: a Belgian model', *European Journal of Operational Research*, 10:82–89.
Despontin, M., J. Moscarola and J. Spronk (1983) 'A user-oriented listing of multiple criteria decision methods', *Revue Belge de Statistique, d'Informatique et de Recherche Opérationelle*, 23, no. 4 (special issue).
Despontin, M., P. Nijkamp and J. Spronk, eds. (1984) *Macroeconomic planning with conflicting goals*. Berlin: Springer Verlag.
Eckenrode, R. T. (1985) 'Weighting multiple criteria', *Management Science*, 12:180–192.
Fandel, G. (1972) *Optimale Entscheidung bei Mehrfacher Zielsetzung*. Berlin: Springer.

Farquhar, P. H. (1983) 'Research directions in multiattribute utility analysis', in: P. Hansen, ed., *Essays and surveys on multiple criteria decision making*. Berlin: Springer, 268–283.

Fiacco, A. V. and G. P. McCormick (1968) *Nonlinear programming: SUMT*. New York: Wiley.

Fishburn, P. C. (1974) 'Lexicographic orders, utilities and decision rules, a survey', *Management Science*, 20:1442–1471.

Frisch, R. (1976) 'Co-operation between politicians and econometricians on the formalization of political preferences', *Economic Planning Studies*, Dordrecht: Reidel, 41–86.

Gal, T. (1983) 'On efficient sets in vector maximum problems—a brief survey', in: P. Hansen, ed., *Essay and Surveys on Multiple Criteria Decision Making*. Berlin: Springer, 94–114.

Geoffrion, A. M. (1968) 'Proper efficiency and the theory of vector maximization', *Journal of Mathematical Analysis and Applications*, 22:618–630.

Guigou, J. L. (1974) *Analyse des données et choix à critères multiples*. Paris: Dunod.

Hafkamp, W. A. (1984) *Economic–environmental modeling in a national–regional system*. Amsterdam: North-Holland.

Hansen, F. (1972) *Consumer choice behaviour, a cognitive theory*. New York: The Free Press.

Hill, M. (1973) *Planning for multiple objectives*, Monograph Series no. 5, Regional Science Research Institute, Philadelphia.

Hinloopen, E., P. Nijkamp and P. Rietveld (1983) 'Qualitative discrete multiple criteria choice models in regional planning', *Regional Science and Urban Economics*, 13:77–102.

Hollnagel, E. (1977) 'Cognitive functions in decision making', in: H. Jungermann and G. de Zeeuw, eds., *Decision making and change in human affairs*. Dordrecht: Reidel, 431–444.

Hwang, C. L. and A. S. M. Masud, eds. (1979) *Multiple objective decision making — methods and applications*. Berlin: Springer.

Hwang, C. L. and K. Yoon (1981) *Multiple attribute decision making — methods and application*. Berlin: Springer.

Ignizio, J. P. (1976) *Goal programming and extentions*. Lexington, Mass.: Lexington Books.

Johnsen, E. (1968) *Studies in multi-objective decision models*, Monograph No. 1, Economic Research Center in Lund, Lund, Sweden.

Johnson, C. R. (1980) 'Constructive critique of a hierarchical prioritization schema employing paired comparisons', *Proceedings IEEE Conference on Cybernetics and Societies*. Cambridge: Cambridge Univ. Press, 373–378.

Kahne, S. (1975) 'A contribution to decision making in environmental design', *Proceedings of the IEEE*: 518–528.

Katona, G. (1951) *Psychological analysis of economic behavior*. New York: McGraw-Hill.

Keeney, R. L. (1968) 'Quasi separable utility functions', *Naval Research Logistics Quarterly*, 15:551–565.

Keeney, R. L. and H. Raiffa (1976) *Decisions with multiple objectives: preferences and value tradeoff*. New York: Wiley.

Kendall, M. G. (1955) *Rank correlation methods*. New York: Hafner Publishing Company.

Klaassen, L. H. (1973) 'Economic and social projects with environmental repercussions: a shadow project approach', *Regional and Urban Economics*, 3:83–102.

Klaassen, L. H. and T. H. Botterweg (1974) 'Evaluating a socio-economic and environmental project', *Papers of the Regional Science Association*, 33:155–175.

Kmietowicz, Z. W. and A. D. Pearman (1981) *Decision theory and incomplete knowledge*. Aldershot, U.K.: Gower.

Koopmans, T. C. (1951) 'Analysis of production as an efficient combination of activities', in: T. C. Koopmans, ed., *Activity analysis of production and allocation*. New Haven: Yale University Press, 33–97.

Kornai, J. (1971) *Anti-equilibrium*. Amsterdam: North-Holland.

Kuhn, H. W. and A. W. Tucker (1951) 'Non-linear programming', in: J. Neyman, ed., *Proceedings of the second Berkeley symposium on mathematical statistics and probability*. Berkeley: University of California Press, 481–493.

Lancaster, K. (1968) *Mathematical economics*. London: MacMillan.

Layard, R., ed. (1972) Cost–benefit analysis. Harmondsworth: Penguin.

Lesuis, P., F. Muller and P. Nijkamp (1983), 'An interregional policy model for energy environmental management', in: T. R. Lakshmanan and P. Nijkamp, eds., *Systems and models for energy and environmental analysis*. Aldershot, U.K.: Gower, 59–69.

Leung, Y. (1983) 'Urban and regional planning with fuzzy information', in: L. Chatterjee and P. Nijkamp, eds., *Urban and regional policy analysis in developing countries*. London: Gower, 231–249.

Lichfield, N., P. Kettle and M. Whitbread (1975) *Evaluation in the planning process*. Oxford: Pergamon Press.

Luce, R. D. and H. Raiffa (1957) *Games and decisions*. New York: Wiley.

Lundqvist, L. (1981) *A dynamic multiregional input – output model for analyzing regional development, employment and energy use*, Dept. of Mathematics, Report TRITAT-MAT-1980-20, Royal Institute of Technology, Stockholm.

Lundqvist, L. (1982) 'Goals of adaptivity and robustness on applied regional and urban planning models', in M. Albegov, A. E. Andersson and F. Snickars, eds., *Regional development modeling: theory and practice*. Amsterdam: North-Holland, 185–203.

Massam, B. H. and I. D. Askew (1982) 'Methods for comparing policies using multiple criteria: an urban example', *Omega*, 10:195–204.

May, K. O. (1954) 'Transitivity, utility and the aggregation of preference patterns', *Econometrica*, 22:1–13.

McLoughlin, J. B. (1969) *Urban and regional planning, a systems approach*. London: Faber.

Meehl, P. E. (1954) *Clinical versus statistical prediction*. Minneapolis: University of Minnesota Press.

Miller, D. H. (1980) 'Project location analysis using the goals achievement method of evaluation', *Journal of the American Planning Association*: 195–208.

Miller, D. H. (1981) *Plans and publics: assessing distribution effects*, Planologisch Memorandum 81-2, Dept. of Urban and Regional Planning, Delft University of Technology.

Mishan, E. J. (1971) *Cost – benefit analysis*. London: Allen & Unwin.

Nievergelt, E. (1971) 'Ein Betrag zur Lösung von Entscheidungsproblemen mit Mehrfacher Zielsetzung', *Die Unternehmung*, 25:101–126.

Nijkamp, P. (1979) *Multidimensional spatial data and decision analysis*. New York: Wiley.

Nijkamp, P. (1980) *Environmental policy analysis*. New York: Wiley.

Nijkamp, P. and P. Rietveld, eds. (1984) *Information systems for integrated regional planning*. Amsterdam: North-Holland.

Nijkamp, P. and W. H. Somermeyer (1973) 'Explicating implicit social preference functions', *The Economics of Planning*, 11, no. 3:101–119.

Osgood, C. E., G. J. Suci and P. H. Tannenbaum (1957) *The measurement of meaning*. Urbana: University of Illinois Press.

Paelinck, J. H. P. (1976) 'Qualitative multiple criteria analysis, environmental protection and multiregional development', *Papers of the Regional Science Association*, 36:59–74.

Pekelman, D. and S. K. Sen (1974) 'Mathematical programming models for the determination of attribute weights', *Management Science*, 20:1217–1229.

Pitz, G. F. (1977) 'Decision making and cognition', in: H. Jungerman and G. de Zeeuw, eds., *Decision making and change in human affairs*. Dordrecht: Reidel, 403–424.

Quirk, J. and R. Saposnik (1968) *Introduction to general equilibrium theory and welfare economics*. New York: McGraw-Hill.

Ratick, S. J. (1983) 'Multiobjective programming with related bargaining games', *Regional Science and Urban Economics*, 13:55–76.

Reitman, W. R. (1964) 'Heuristic decision procedures, open constraints, and the structure of ill-defined problems', in: M. W. Shelley and G. L. Bryan, eds., *Human judgments and optimality*. New York: Wiley, 282–315.

Rietveld, P. (1980) *Multiple objective decision methods and regional planning*. Amsterdam: North-Holland.

Rietveld, P. (1982) 'Using ordinal information in decision making under uncertainty', Research memorandum 1982-12, Department of Economics, Free University, Amsterdam.

Rietveld, P. (1984) 'The use of qualitative information in macro-economic policy analysis', in: M. Despontin, P. Nijkamp and J. Spronk, eds., *Macroeconomic planning with conflicting goals*. Berlin: Springer, 263–280.

Rittel, H. W. J. and M. M. Webber (1973) 'Dilemmas in a general theory of planning', *Policy Sciences*, 4:155–169.

Roy, B. (1968) 'Classement et choix en présence de points de vue multiples (la méthode ELECTRE)', *R.I.R.O.*, 2:57–75.

Saaty, T. L. (1977) 'Scaling method for priorities in hierarchical structures', *Journal of Mathematical Psychology*, 15:234–281.

Schimpeler, C. C. and W. L. Grecco (1968) 'The expected value method, an approach based on community structures and values', *Highway Research Record*, 238:123–152.

Schlager, K. (1968) 'The rank-based expected value method of plan evaluation', *Highway Research Record*, 238:153–158.

Shepard, R. N. (1964) 'On subjectively optimum selection among multi-attribute alternatives', in: M. W. Shelley and G. L. Bryan, eds., *Human judgments and optimality*. New York: Wiley, 257–281.

Shoou-Yuh Chang, E. D. Brill and L. D. Hopkins (1982) 'Efficient random generation of feasible alternatives: a land use example', *Journal of Regional Science*, 22:303–314.

Simon, H. A. (1957) *Models of Man*. New York: Wiley.

Sinden, J. A. and A. C. Worrell (1979) *Unpriced values*. New York: Wiley.

Skull, F. A., A. L. Delbecq and L. L. Cunnings (1970) *Organizational decision making*. New York: McGraw-Hill.

Spronk, J. (1981) *Interactive multiple goal programming for capital budgeting and financial planning*. Boston: Kluwer Nijhoff.

Steuer, R. E. (1976) 'Linear multiple objective programming with interval criterion weights', *Management Science*, 23:305–316.

Takayama, A. (1974) *Mathematical economics*. Hinsdale: Dryden Press.

Tarascio, V. J. (1968) *Pareto's methodological approach to economics*. Chapel Hill: The University of North Carolina Press.

Teitz, M. B. (1968) 'Cost-effectiveness', *Journal of the American Institute of Planners*, 34, no. 4: 303–312.

Theil, H. (1967) *Economics and information theory*. Amsterdam: North-Holland.

Theil, H. (1968) *Optimal decision rules for government and industry*. Amsterdam: North-Holland.

Torgerson, W. A. (1958) *Theory and method of scaling*. New York: Wiley.

Tversky, A. (1972) 'Elimination by aspects: a theory of choice', *Psychological Review*, 79:281–299.

Van Delft, A. and P. Nijkamp (1977) *Multicriteria analysis and regional decision-making*. Dordrecht: Martinus Nijhoff.

Vickrey, W. (1960) 'Utility, strategy and social decision rules', *Quarterly Journal of Economics*. 74:507–535.

Voogd, H. J. (1983) Multicriteria evaluation for urban and regional planning. London: Pion.

White, D. J. (1983) 'The foundations of multi-objective interactive programming—some questions', in: P. Hansen, ed., *Essays and surveys on multiple criteria decision making*. Berlin: Springer, 181–203.

Wierzbicki, A. P. (1983) 'Critical essay on the methodology of multiobjective analysis', *Regional Science and Urban Economics*, 13:5–30.

Winkler, R. L. (1982) 'Research directions in decision making under uncertainty', *Decision Sciences*, 13:517–533.

Zeleny, M. (1982) *Multiple criteria decision making*. New York: McGraw-Hill.

Zionts, S. (1974) *Linear and integer programming*. Englewood Cliffs: Prentice Hall.

Zionts, S. (1981) 'A multiple criteria method for choosing among discrete alternatives', *European Journal of Operations Research*, 7:143–147.

Zionts, S. and J. Wallenius (1976) 'An interactive programming method for solving the multiple criteria problem', *Management Science*, 22:652–663.

Chapter 13

REGIONAL LABOR MARKET ANALYSIS

ANDREW ISSERMAN, CAROL TAYLOR,
SHELBY GERKING and UWE SCHUBERT

1. Introduction

Regional labor market analysis entails a synthesis of economic and demographic modeling. Migration alters population levels and, thus, together with labor force participation rates determines labor supply. Population change also affects demand for goods and services within the region, thereby affecting the demand for labor. Together labor supply and demand determine wage, unemployment, and employment levels, which, in turn, have an effect on migration. Given these interdependencies and the spatial context of regional growth, regional labor market analysis draws on concepts and approaches from applied econometrics, macroeconomics, labor economics, and quantitative geography, as well as regional economics and demography.

This chapter provides a discussion of the theoretical foundations and modeling approaches involved in studying labor force supply, labor force demand, and wage determination. One section is devoted to each topic, followed by concluding observations regarding the proper treatment of labor market conditions within economic models intended for policy analysis.

Given its emphasis on regional macroeconomic modeling, this chapter is not a comprehensive survey of the rich field of labor economics and policy. For instance, there is no discussion of the heterogeneity of labor with respect to skills, occupation, and education, of institutional factors related to labor unions, collective bargaining, or job training programs, of discrimination based on age, sex, race, or ethnic group, or even of the literature related to labor market and migration decisions of individuals.

As is generally the case in regional analysis, the definition of region is important in studying regional labor markets. One common procedure is to work

Handbook of Regional and Urban Economics, Volume I, Edited by P. Nijkamp
©Elsevier Science Publishers BV, 1986

with administratively defined areas within which labor market relevant policy measures can be taken by planning authorities, such as federal states. This strategy has the advantage of data availability for these regions. The disadvantage consists in usually having to cut and subdivide functionally linked labor market areas, which often do not follow administrative boundaries. The disregard of functional interdependencies can have serious repercussions on the validity of the parameter estimation of theory-based labor market models [see, for example, Openshaw (1977), Baumann et al. (1983)].

Functional labor market regions are usually preferred on theoretical grounds, although there are several drawbacks with this concept in practical modeling situations. One follows from the remarks above, i.e. such regions may be under the planning authority of several governmental institutions which makes the formulation of the relevant policy variables in the model a rather difficult task. A second disadvantage is constituted by the arbitrariness of the cut-off points for the region defining variable. To illustrate, the most common variable used to define functional labor market regions is the level of commuting to the core region. A sub-zone is defined to belong to a labor market region when more than a certain percent of the local labor force commutes to the core of the region. In the case of the use of more than one variable for regionalization, the task becomes more complex and more intricate regionalization methods have to be applied [see, for example, Slater (1976), Fischer (1982), Masser (1980)].

When considering more than one region, additional problems arise. A decision has to be made whether a disjoint or overlapping spatial framework is appropriate. In the case of disjoint labor market regions each point in space belongs to only one region, which presents a problem for areas that lie between two strong cores or where cross-commuting is rather common. On the other hand, overlapping regionalization schemes make modeling far more complex because of the need to assure consistency in the treatment of the areas included in more than one region.

2. Labor force supply

2.1. Population change

Economic–demographic modeling for regions, states, provinces, or metropolitan areas is more difficult than national modeling because of trade and population flows within the country. For example, national models can focus on natural increase (births and deaths) in explaining population change because foreign immigration tends to be a small part of the total change. On the other hand, regional models must consider births, deaths, and internal migration, with the latter typically being a far larger proportion of population change than natural increase. To compound the difficulty, data available for national modeling efforts often are not reliable or even tabulated on the regional level. Consequently modeling strategies and methods must be invented that recognize and compensate for these data limitations. The models themselves then are the product of an intricate interplay of theory, data, and method.

2.1.1. *Theoretical perspectives on migration*

2.1.1.1. Human capital. In the human capital approach, migration is seen as an investment to increase the productivity of human resources. The present value of migration from one place to another is the difference in the present value of lifetime earnings at the destination and the origin, minus the costs of migration. The conceptual framework can be readily extended to consider all costs and benefits of migration, including psychic costs, such as leaving behind friends [Sjaastad (1962)]. If discounted benefits exceed discounted costs, "investing" in migration will increase utility.

Some neoclassical theories of regional growth have a narrower perspective on migration. Individuals are posited to move in response to wage-rate differentials [for example, see Borts and Stein (1964), Ghali et al. (1978), Smith (1974, 1975)]. These models, however, assume full employment with wages changing until the labor market clears. In the absence of full employment and such wage flexibility, wages as a measure of the expected earnings at the destination must be multiplied by the probability of gaining employment.

Measuring the probability of obtaining employment is a key problem in migration research. The basic concept is simple. Data are needed on job vacancies (employment opportunities or supply of jobs) and on the number of people seeking employment (employment competition or demand for jobs). Unfortunately, data on job vacancies are generally not available. Also, observed unemployment as a measure of expected employment competition ignores (1) discouraged workers who are not searching actively but may move directly into employment if job opportunities become available, (2) natural increase or aging of the labor force, that is, the entry of teenagers and the retirement of elderly, and (3) other migrants attracted by the same employment opportunities.

Since the desired measures are not available, various proxies for the probability of gaining employment have been used in the literature. Measures of opportunity include population [Greenwood and Sweetland (1972), Levy and Wadycki (1974), Miller (1973), Rogers (1967)], the employment-to-population ratio [Dahlberg and Holmlund (1978)], the growth in employment [Duffy and Greenwood (1980), Todaro (1969, 1976)], and the rate of new hirings [Fields (1976, 1979)]. The measure of competition for those employment opportunities typically is unemployment, but Blanco (1963) constructs the "prospective change" in the number of unemployed, which adjusts for aging of the labor force and changes in college enrollment and military levels.

Almost all empirical studies have used measure of employment opportunity and competition individually in migration equations. Fields (1976, 1979), Gleave and Cordey-Hayes (1977), Plaut (1981), and Todaro (1969), on the other hand, developed transformed variables to represent the probability of gaining employment. Fields used the ratio of the new hiring and unemployment rates, Gleave and Cordey-Hayes used the ratio of vacancies to unemployment, and Plaut used the ratio of employment growth to unemployment.

2.1.1.2. Distance and previous migration. Geographical studies of migration have long observed an inverse relationship between migration and distance. Although not always discussed in that context, distance can be incorporated into the human capital approach. It can represent a proxy for transportation costs, psychic costs, and uncertainty [Greenwood (1975b)]. Psychic costs may result from separation from family and friends; the greater the distance of the move, the lower the frequency of reunion and the higher the psychic costs [Schwartz (1973)]. Since information declines with distance, uncertainty increases and with it the expected value of the income stream at the destination. Empirical estimates of migration-distance elasticities ranged from -0.50 to -1.50 in eleven studies with a median value of -1.06 [Shaw (1975, p. 83)].

The information and psychic costs arguments also can be used to include variables measuring past migration in a human capital framework. The migrant stock (the number of persons born in state i but living in state j) is a measure of information flow back to i from j; also the presence of friends and relatives from home provides support to new in-migrants and reduces the psychic costs of moving to a new environment [Greenwood (1969)].

Demographers have noted that a large proportion of migrants are repeat migrants or return migrants. Thus high in-migration is likely to be reflected in high out-migration of repeat migrants; ostensibly, psychic costs of out-migration are lower for people who recently migrated into an area than for long-time residents. Likewise, previous out-migration may lead to in-migration of return migrants who incur lower psychic costs in returning than moving to another destination. Thus, previous in-migration has been used to predict out-migration and vice versa [for example, Greenwood (1975a)].

2.1.1.3. Socioeconomic factors. Demographers and economists also have observed differences in migration rates by age, sex, race, education, and labor force status. For example, young adults in their early twenties have the highest migration rates, with a monotonic decrease beyond that age except for possibly a minor peak at retirement age; the migration rates of children mirror the rates of their parents [Rogers (1979)]. These observations are consistent with the human capital approach, too, because older people have less time to reap the differential earnings from migration [Lewis (1967)] and may have more psychic investment at home. As Lowry (1966, p. 27) notes, younger people are "less encumbered with family and community responsibilities, real estate ownership, and vested interest in job seniority," so their costs in moving are lower. Similarly, recent studies indicate that the probability of interstate migration is lower for families with working wives [Lichter (1980), Long (1974), Sandell (1977)].

Empirical studies have found that economic variables such as employment growth, unemployment, and wages are less successful in explaining migration flows of women and nonwhites [for example, Rogers (1967)]. Quite possibly, this result stems from an aggregation problem. Aggregate figures may not adequately reflect economic opportunities and wages available to blacks and women, an argument made in the case of nonwhites in the South by Greenwood and Gormely (1971).

The human capital approach suggests that economic conditions at the origin and the destination have similar roles in explaining migration between two places. For example, income levels at each place are involved in calculating the present value of the differential income streams associated with moving and staying. Nevertheless, variables measuring economic conditions at the origin, including income, unemployment, and wages, frequently have been found insignificant in cross-section studies [for example, Fields (1979), Levy and Wadycki (1974), Lowry (1966), Miller (1973), Rogers (1967)]. Furthermore, a positive relationship is often observed between in-migration and unemployment rates at the destination [Greenwood (1975b)].

Misspecification often is the problem when end-of-period economic conditions are used in such studies, but DaVanzo (1978) suggests a more general possibility for the unexpected or insignificant findings. Although families whose heads are employed may be insensitive to aggregate unemployment at the origin in deciding whether to migrate, the migration decision of unemployed persons can be expected to be far more dependent on economic conditions there. Indeed, Herzog and Schlottmann (1984) found that the premove unemployment rate of migrants is approximately three times that of nonmigrants. Since the unemployed constitute a relatively small part of the population, the studies that indicate little sensitivity of migration to unemployment at the origin may be suffering from overaggregation of the underlying data.

2.1.1.4. Alternative opportunities. Another important concept in modeling migration is alternative opportunities, a type of opportunity cost. The likelihood of selecting a particular destination depends in part on conditions at alternative destinations. Some disagreement exists in the literature on the definition of the appropriate set of alternatives, but various measures have been incorporated successfully into cross-section studies of migration flows. [Levy and Wadycki (1974) and Wadycki (1979)] use the highest population, lowest unemployment rate, and highest average wage from among all regions that are no further away from the origin region than the destination. They speculate that, since information is likely to be inversely related to distance, a migrant moving 600 miles away also knew of opportunities less than 600 miles away [Levy and Wadycki (1974, p. 206)]. However, as Feder (1979, 1980) points out, increased distance may reduce the attractiveness of alternatives and limit information about them, but it need not eliminate them from consideration. Therefore, he proposes a measure which weights conditions at all possible destinations inversely to their distance from the origin.

2.1.1.5. Quality of life. Last, several studies of migration have incorporated measures of the quality of life and amenities. Liu (1975) constructed an index of the quality of life for each state of the USA from more than 100 variables grouped into nine categories. For example, the "individual status" category included fourteen variables, among them the labor force participation rate, the number of motor vehicles per capita, expenditures on education per capita, and a "quality index of medical service." The "living conditions" category included a crime index, the percentage of families in poverty, recreational acres per capita, telephones per capita, library books per capita, symphony orchestras per capita, motor vehicle deaths per capita, the average number of sunshine days, the average annual humidity, and ten other variables. Each variable in each component was given an equal weight and the components were weighted equally in constructing the overall index. Liu regressed 1960–70 net migration rates for each state on its 1970 index, but was able to explain only 8 percent of the variation in the rates (albeit 52 percent in the nonwhite rate). Similarly, Cebula and Vedder (1973) and Cebula (1979) found that economic variables are far more important than quality-of-life, environmental, or climatic variables in cross-section regression studies. Also, five measures of climate were rarely significant in seventeen cross-section studies of net migration into Bureau of Economic Analysis areas from 1958 to 1975 [Duffy et al. (1979)]. On the other hand, Alperovich et al. (1975), Clark and Ballard (1980), Graves (1980), and Miller (1973) were successful in partially explaining either in- or out-migration or both with climatic variables in cross-section studies, and Milne (1981) used population density successfully in a time-series analysis.

An alternative to the neoclassical and human capital view of the role of wage differentials in migration has been presented by Graves and Linneman (1979) and Graves (1980). Wage differentials represent compensation for differences in climate and amenities.

The demand for climate and amenities, like any other good, is expected to change with relative prices and income. For example, with increasing incomes, the demand for outdoor leisure activities increases and with it the desire to locate in more "appropriate" amenity-rich environments. Migration then takes place as a result of changing demand for location-fixed amenities. Graves argues that "one would not expect income differentials to lead to migration since those differentials reflect compensation for climate differences, i.e. equilibrium consumption choices.... This theoretical point accounts for the difficulty experienced by some authors...in finding significant income and unemployment coefficients of the correct sign" (1980, p. 229).

Although this claim may be overstated, viewing climate and other amenities as highly income-elastic consumption goods (so-called superior goods) is potentially useful for forecasting migration within the human capital framework. In fact, Plaut (1981) finds that net migration into Texas, ostensibly an amenity-rich state, increases with per capita real income in the USA.

In summary, many factors combine to create migration flows. The social science literature has documented the roles of economic conditions, demographic characteristics, distance and previous migration patterns, alternative opportunities, climate, amenities, and other aspects of the quality of life.

2.1.2. Migration models

2.1.2.1. A demographic method. The U.S. Bureau of the Census (1979) forecast in-migration and out-migration for each state on the basis of (1) 1965–70 interstate migration reported in the 1970 Census of Population and (2) estimated 1970–75 migration rates derived from the 1965–70 age pattern and estimated 1970–75 total net migration by state. Migration of college students and military personnel is modeled separately, but otherwise no distinction is made between labor force and nonlabor force migration.

In keeping with its strategy of making "illustrative" projections rather than forecasts, the Census Bureau extrapolates separately both the 1965–75 and the 1970–75 migration rates. Out-migration is projected by applying out-migration rates by age, sex, and race for each state to the relevant population subgroups in the state. Then the resulting national sum of out-migrants is allocated back to individual states as in-migration on the basis of the states' shares of national interstate migration during the relevant historical period, 1965–75 or 1970–75.

Such demographic approaches can be considered atheoretical, in that observed rates are simply extended into the future. Thus, changes in the spatial pattern of total net migration over time result entirely from changes in population composition, that is, the number of people in each age, race, and sex cohort in each state.

Economic conditions and other factors thought to affect migration decisions are not incorporated into the projection process.

2.1.2.2.   Time-series models. Time-series models must use annual migration data to be compatible with the econometric models to which they most likely would be linked. No reliable annual time-series data exist for interstate migration flows in the USA [see Isserman, et al. (1982)], and the situation is similar for most countries. Time series of net migration can be generated by estimating population for each year to derive population change and then using data on births and deaths to estimate net migration as a residual:

net migration = estimated population change − births + deaths.

Since data on births and deaths are registered vital statistics and presumably quite accurate, errors in the population estimates are reflected almost entirely in the net migration data. Given the similar magnitudes of the errors in estimating population change and the rates of annual net migration (both average between 1 percent and 2 percent for the states of the U.S.) errors of 50 percent or more in the migration data can be expected [Isserman et al. (1982)].

Despite such errors, net migration has been used in at least three economic–demographic modeling efforts in the USA. Ledent (1978) forecast net migration into the Tucson Standard Metropolitan Statistical Area as a function of change in total employment and the lagged regional and national unemployment rates, and Milne (1981) forecast interregional net migration among the nine Census regions as a function of relative wages, relative unemployment, and relative population density ("a proxy for crowding problems" related to the quality of life). Plaut (1981) has come closest to modeling the human capital theory explicitly. In his model of Texas, expected income is represented by relative wages and the relative vacancy-to-unemployment ratio (using data on employ-ment advertisements in newspapers to measure vacancies). National real per capita income is included as a measure of changing responsiveness to environ-mental conditions, and lagged population is included as a result of positing a partial adjustment model. Spatial factors and demographic detail, however, are missing from among those factors discussed in the previous section.

These various equations do not fit the historical data particularly well. Ledent reported an R^2 of 0.83, Milne a range from 0.66 to 0.90, and Plaut one of 0.88. All three statistics are very disappointing for time-series equations. The mean absolute percentage error for five years beyond the sample period was 22.5 in Plaut's model. Plaut's theoretical structure is appealing, but applied to two other states it fared poorly [Isserman (1985)].

The implicit net migration modeling approach of Ballard et al. (1980) is also worth mentioning. No attempt is made to model migration rates directly. Instead, the estimates of population are themselves modeled in five age groups. For instance, the population aged 18–44 is a function of itself lagged, a two-year moving average of the region's share of national employment, relative per capita income, and a time trend. The employment term represents job opportunity, income represents "an inducement to migrate," and the time trend represents "historical changes in environmental attractiveness" (p. 51). Note how similar this population equation is to Plaut's migration rate equation. Here the coefficient of the lagged population term, however, measures natural increase rather than lags in migration.

In dynamic simulations the average mean absolute percentage error in a sample from 1963 to 1976 for all fifty states was only one percent of total population. Yet, this summary statistic is less impressive than it might seem because the annual rate of population change did not exceed 1 percent for 26 states from 1970 to 1975. In short, Ballard et al. have modeled natural increase and migration implicitly by including their determinants as independent variables. The regression coefficients essentially are crude replacements for demographers' painstakingly derived death and migration rates. This approach does not preserve any of the advantages and information of demographic accounts.

2.1.2.3. Dynamic economic–demographic transition rate models. Much of regional economics entails the invention of methods to overcome limited data availability. The histories of the economic base model, nonsurvey input–output models, and regional econometric models are cases in point. Migration modeling is similar. Since the nature and periodicity of published data on migration vary widely from country to country, so do the methods suitable in each. A recently generated data series for U.S. internal migration, for example, makes possible a method that incorporates advantages of the demographic approach and the theoretical framework from economics. The data are created by matching income tax returns between two periods and comparing the respondents' addresses. Data on annual total migration flows currently are available for selected years. They suffice to model migration in a way compatible with regional econometric models based on annual time series data.

This economic–demographic approach involves the transition rates associated with multiregional demography. A transition or Markov matrix contains the probability that an individual in one region will remain in the region for another period and the probabilities that the individual will migrate to each of the other regions in the system. These probabilities usually are based on past rates. In aggregate terms estimated migration from region i to region j (M_{ij}) is based on the following equation:

$$M_{ij}(t) = P_i(t-1)\left[M_{ij}(b)/P_i(b-1)\right] \tag{2.1}$$

where P_i refers to population in region i in year $(t-1)$ surviving to year t, and b is a base year. The term in brackets is the migration rate observed in the base year. It is assumed to remain constant into the projection period.

Roger (1968, p. 85) has noted that the empirical results of using Markov chains to project future population totals have been disappointing as a result of "the restrictive assumption of unchanging movement probabilities," and Rogerson (1979) has demonstrated that linear adjustment of the probabilities by using two or more transitional matrices can lead to greater accuracy. Feeney (1973) has recommended adjusting the transition probabilities to reflect the changing spatial distribution of economic opportunity. A method for doing so was developed by Isserman et al. (1985). Its key equation is:

$$\frac{M_{ij}(t)}{P_i(t-1)} = \frac{M_{ij}(b)\left[\dfrac{A_j(t-1)}{A_j(b-1)}\right]^{\gamma}}{\sum_k M_{ik}(b)\left[\dfrac{A_k(t-1)}{A_k(b-1)}\right]^{\gamma}} \tag{2.2}$$

where k includes the entire set of regions, M_{ii} refers to people who remain in region i ("stayers"), A refers to an index of attractiveness, and γ is a parameter that measures the magnitude of the migration response to changing attractiveness.

With two sets of migration-flow matrices, γ can be estimated, for instance, to minimize the root square error between estimated and observed transition rates in the second year. Note that all transition rates are interdependent; migration probabilities from region i to region j change if there are no changes in the attractiveness of either region i or region j, when there are changes in the attractiveness of any other regions in the system.

When this approach was implemented using a crude attractiveness index consisting of employment opportunity (change in jobs plus separations) relative to employment competition (unemployed plus separations) and data on migration flows for 1975–76 and 1976–77 to project 1978–79 migration flows, it had a projection error 20 percent less than the standard demographic Markov model.

In using the economic–demographic transition-matrix approach, one must assume that γ is stable. As more years of IRS migration data become available in the USA or when the approach is used in the few countries with annual time series of migration flows, the properties of γ can be assessed empirically and perhaps even be modeled as an endogenous variable. Unfortunately, the absence of good time-series data on migration within most countries means, quite simply, that the nature of the phenomenon being modeled is still unknown. Regional economists are left to devise methods to exploit what little data are available, in effect to model a puzzle with many missing pieces.

2.2. *Labor force participation*

Modern analysis of labor supply still broadly conforms to the conceptual framework outlined in the seminal work of Lionel Robbins published over five decades ago [Robbins (1930)]. In simplest form, observed labor supply reflects consumer choice between goods purchasable with income and leisure. While regional labor force participation analysis is distinct from microeconomic models of labor supply, contributions of the latter significantly influence the former and hence are reviewed here briefly.

It is useful to distinguish two supply concepts: (1) the decision to participate in the labor force (a binary choice) and (2) the number of work hours offered assuming a positive decision to participate. The two choices are depicted in Figures 2.1 and 2.2. The horizontal axis shows hours available for leisure, T being the maximum amount, and the vertical axis measures income. Y_n is the

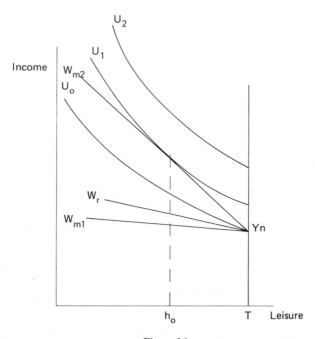

Figure 2.1

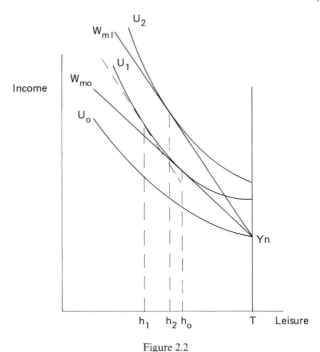

Figure 2.2

consumer non-labor income and the set of U_i curves depict consumer preferences between leisure and income (derived from underlying preferences between leisure and goods/services purchasable with income). For the participation decision (Figure 2.1), a critical parameter is the absolute value of the slope of the line w_r, the tangent to the indifference curve at zero hours of work and non-labor income Y_n. This slope is the consumer's reservation wage (or shadow wage at zero hours of work) and is dependent upon both Y_n and consumer preferences between income and time available outside the work place. The consumer choice set, the objective trade-off possible between income and leisure, is shown by the line emanating from (T, Y_n) with absolute slope w_m, where w_m is market wage. For $w_m < w_r$ (i.e. W_{m1} in Figure 2.1), the consumer maximizes utility at the corner solution (T, Y_n), i.e. at non-participation in the labor force. For $w_m > w_r$ (e.g. W_{m2} in Figure 2.1), participation occurs with a non-zero level of hours supplied to the work place ($T - h_0$ for w_{m2} in Figure 2.1).

Note that an increase in w_m must have a non-negative impact on the labor force participation decision. Participation indicates only whether the consumer maximizing solution is at the corner (T, Y_n), reflecting non-participation, or whether it is at an interior point to the left of leisure $= T$, reflecting participation.

For all $w_m \leq w_r$, the solution is the corner one and for all $w_m > w_r$, the solution is interior so an increase in w_m can only leave the participation decision unchanged or switch it from non-participation to participation.

This same result is not true for the impact of a wage increase on hours supplied, given an initial interior solution. The situation is depicted in Figure 2.2. At initial market wage, w_{m0}, $T - h_0$ hours are supplied to the work place. A wage increase from w_{m0} to w_{m1} has two conflicting effects. The compensated wage effect, the impact on hours supplied with initial utility level held constant, is unambiguously positive since the wage rate rise increases the price of leisure. In Figure 2.2, the compensated wage effect on hours supplied of the change from w_{m0} to w_{m1} is an increase in hours worked of $h_0 - h_1$. However, the wage change also has an income effect on hours supplied. It is generally assumed to be negative, reflective of the assumption that leisure is not an inferior good. In Figure 2.2, the income effect is the reduction in hours supplied to the work place or increase in leisure consumed of $h_2 - h_1$. The net effect of a market wage change on hours supplied may thus be either negative or positive depending upon the relative magnitudes of the compensated wage or substitution effect and the income effect.

The theory predicts that the same set of variables determines labor supply whether the latter is denoted by the labor force participation decision or by hours supplied. In both cases, critical parameters are determinants of preferences between leisure and income, market wage, and non-labor income. However, estimated wage impacts are not necessarily similar, the wage impact on the participation decision being positively biased relative to the wage impact on hours supplied. Indeed, "labor supply" wage elasticities estimated from labor force participation data are generally higher than those estimated with hours data [see Keeley (1981)].

While the simple analysis above provides a general framework, many modifications to it have been introduced. Major conceptual contributions (as opposed to issues of empirical variable measurement and econometric estimation techniques) focus on:

(1) *"Non-market time" vs. "leisure."* Becker (1965) recognized that time is allocated not simply between "work" and "leisure," but between, "market work," "non-market work," and "leisure." Non-market work is time spent in producing "home goods" (child care, clean house, mowed lawn, etc.). It is the home goods themselves which provide utility, not necessarily the time spent in producing them, the latter being an input into the household production function. In contrast, leisure is true recreational time entering positively into the utility function. The importance of Becker's distinction is two-fold: (i) all hours not spent in the market place do not enter the utility function on a parallel basis; (ii) the efficiency of the household production function is a factor affecting labor supply; a higher utility level embodying jointly more market hours worked and

more true leisure may be attainable at a given market wage if productivity of time spent in household work is increased. Rigorous analysis of the impact of (i) on labor supply to the market is microeconomic in nature, requiring an explicit household utility function. Using such a context, Wales and Woodland (1977) have shown that empirical estimates of market wage impact on labor supply are affected by the distinction between how hours are used outside the market place, e.g. the estimated elasticity of female labor market supply with respect to either own wage or husband's wage is changed if the housework/leisure distinction is imposed and housework is endogenized. For more aggregated analysis, part (i) has been interpreted to suggest that at least some non-market hours may be an inferior good, yielding a potentially positive income effect of a market wage increase on labor supply. For macroeconomic time series analysis, part (ii) can be identified as a trend component in labor supply with increasing availability of "housework saving" devices impacting labor force participation and hours offered.

(2) *Context of decision making.* The simple model outlined above is for an individual and implicitly a single potential-worker household. Many labor supply decisions, however, are made within the context of a potential two-earner household. Recognition of the family as the basic decision unit and the jointness of the husband/wife labor supply decision has spawned a vast literature investigating the implications of the family context for wage and income specification, interpretation, and estimation in labor supply models of particular population subgroups, e.g. married females. [These many studies are summarized in Keeley (1981).] Of primary importance from this literature is the expansion of the set of pertinent wage rate variables; own market wage rate and non-labor income must be supplemented by market wage rates of additional household workers.

(3) *Multiperiod analysis.* The implicit single-period time horizon of the above analysis has been expanded to investigate labor supply within a life-cycle context. Formally, such models posit a multiperiod, lifetime utility function with arguments $C(t)$ and $L(t)$ which respectively denote consumption and leisure at time t. The utility function is maximized subject to a budget constraint of the form initial assets equal the present value of the stream, of lifetime excesses of consumption over earnings [for example, MaCurdy (1981) or Heckman and MaCurdy (1980)].

Two particularly interesting results emerge from these analyses. First, for a single time period, the reservation wage is not necessarily independent of the market wages as assumed in traditional one-period models. Higher current market wages tend to be associated with higher reservation wage yielding the possibility of an inverse correlation between market wages and labor force participation, a phenomenon that has been observed in some empirical analyses [Heckmann (1978)]. Second, analysis of the formal intertemporal models cast some doubt on the theoretical basis for attempting to distinguish "transitory" and "permanent" wage effects in empirical labor supply studies. Traditionally, incorporation of these concepts in labor supply models has been more by general analogy to Friedman's (1957) classic analysis than by a correspondingly rigorous derivation. Heckman and MaCurdy (1980) demonstrate that Friedman's analysis of the consumption function cannot in fact be directly carried over to labor supply. The crux of the problem is that in the income/consumption model the exogenous income receipts enter the maximization problem only as a discounted sum, the latter thus being a scalar summarizing all the pertinent information about the income flow and forming the basis for the permanent income concept. However, no such simple summary scalar for the wage profile falls out of a formal model of life-cycle labor supply; the consumption/leisure choice at each age is a function of the entire time structure of wages.

(4) *Uncertainty*. Implicit in the simple model of labor market participation and labor supply is the assumption that should the individual choose to participate, there is a job at the market wage available for him or her. However, the decision to participate is more precisely a decision to undertake a job search and the costs of search and the probability of successful search may itself affect that participation decision. The impact of costs of labor market entry on labor supply has been primarily analyzed in a microeconomic context, but the impact of changing probabilities of successful search has contributed to specification in more aggregated models.

The most commonly used measure of this probability is the unemployment rate, although it is recognized that this may not adequately represent labor market conditions. For example, there are historical periods in which the unemployment rate was almost constant, but vacancies increased, the latter suggesting increasing market tightness. The "discouraged worker" hypothesis contends that an increase in labor market slackness as manifested by a rise in a general unemployment rate discourages persons from labor market entry and job search. However, the implied negative correlation between the unemployment rate and labor force participation may not be observed empirically. In particular, receiving much discussion in the 1930s, was what has become known as the "additional-worker" hypothesis, namely, unemployment of one family member may lead other family members to seek employment in an effort to maintain household income. Under the additional-worker hypothesis, the implied correlation between unemployment rate and labor force participation is positive. Most evidence from empirical estimates of labor force participation indicates dominance of the discouraged-worker hypothesis, i.e. a negative correlation between labor force participation and unemployment rate [Tella (1965), Dernburg and Strand (1966), Barth (1968), Bowen and Finegan (1969), Wachter (1972)].

A broad interpretation of probabilities of successful job search has resulted in inclusion of a variety of other area characteristics in labor force participation models. For example, Bowen and Finegan (1969) include industry mix measures and degree of urbanization in regional cross-section analysis of age/sex labor force participation based on 1960 U.S. Census data.

With the exception of item (4), many of the issues in labor supply have been analyzed primarily with micro data sets. Explicitly regional analysis, however, typically is focused on aggregated labor force participation rates in either a cross-section context or a single-region time series context. The transition from the micro analysis to this more aggregated regional analysis is not clear. In particular, there has been considerable debate as to exactly what regional labor force participation rates measure. One interpretation views them as measures of quantity of labor supplied [Mincer (1966), Cain (1966), Ashenfelter and Heckman (1974)]. Suppose a population is characterized by equal tastes and individuals (or households) offer the same amount of labor at a given wage rate and a given level of income. This amount is some proportion of total time available over the longer reference period for individual utility maximization, e.g. the lifetime. If the timing of this labor force participation is random, then the expected value of the aggregate labor force participation rate at a given point in time is equal to the proportion of time an individual plans to spend in the labor force. The aggregate rate then measures a quantity of labor supplied expressed as a proportion of total available time.

Ben-Porath (1973) and Lewis (1967), however, argue that the value of the aggregate labor force participation rate at a point in time reflects the proportion of people who want to work at the current wage, a macroeconomic analog of the microeconomic participation decision. If individual tastes differ, then at a given market wage some individuals choose to work and others don't and the aggregate labor force participation rate measures the proportion choosing to work.

The pertinency of this unresolved debate for regional analysis is two-fold. The Mincer interpretation implies that the appropriate variables for aggregated regional analysis are those which determine the supply of hours in a micro model but the Ben-Porath/Lewis interpretation clearly suggests that the relevant variables are those derived from microeconomic analysis of the labor force participation decision. Although there is considerable overlap in these two sets of variables (e.g. market wages, non-labor income, determinants of preferences between goods and leisure), some of the factors considered under item (4) above, e.g. the unemployment rate, are difficult to interpret in Mincer's context. More significantly, the two hypotheses substantially differ in implied interpretation of empirically estimated parameters. Under the first hypothesis, estimates of wage and income coefficients from regional labor force participation equations may be used to derive compensated wage elasticities and interpreted in this context; the data are presumed to measure quantity variations in a set of internal solutions of the theoretical labor supply model. Such an interpretation is not valid under the

Ben-Porath/Lewis analysis; the data are presumed to measure variations in population proportions of corner solutions in the theoretical labor supply model.

Assuming appropriateness of the unemployment rate in equation specification, it should be recognized that the regional context does not permit interpretation of the sign of that variable simply in terms of the discouraged-worker hypothesis vs. the additional-worker hypothesis. Mincer (1966) emphasizes that a negative regression coefficient on the unemployment rate variable in a regional analysis may reflect some selectivity of migration, a tendency for older, more job-determined individuals (with high levels of attachment to the labor force) to move to areas of improved economic opportunity. However, recalling some of the inadequacies of the unemployment rate as a measure of job opportunity, considerations of regional migration also suggest a possible positive correlation between regional unemployment rates and regional labor force participation rates. In particular, areas of expanding job opportunity (as measured, for example, by job vacancy data) and high net in-migration of labor force-attached households, may have high labor force participation rates and high unemployment rates. The latter may be reflective of a large amount of frictional unemployment as a relatively large proportion of individuals are temporarily between jobs because of recent movement to the area and/or because the rapidly expanding job market encourages increased quits and search for improved jobs by resident population.

In summarizing the analysis for empirical regional labor force participation estimation, it is necessary to distinguish the possible modeling situations in terms of (1) the age/sex data disaggregation; (2) time series or cross-section data. Typically, these two delineating factors are not independent, the more extensive age/sex detail being associated with cross-section analyses. The average labor force participation rate varies substantially among age/sex cohorts in the population because of the correlation between these demographic groupings and major factors affecting individuals preferences between labor market time and non-market time. Consequently, if aggregated data are analyzed, either in a cross-section or time-series context, a major factor affecting observed labor force participation may be variation in the underlying age/sex distribution of the population(s). Broadly controlling for these variations (e.g. proportion of population that is prime working age male or proportion of population over 65+ years of age), can substantially improve equation fit.

In cross-section studies, further disaggregation may permit isolation of groups by additional factors affecting general labor market attachment of the population, e.g. head of family status. Within these specific groups, cross-section data also often allow for specification to include a number of important variables determining labor market supply preferences and/or market wage, primary among these being color, average education level, and especially for married females, number of children and age distribution of these children. In more aggregated time series analysis, however, data constraints often preclude this precision of specification; the researcher is forced into the less satisfying situation of using summary trend variables which might capture significant intertemporal shifts in these variables [see, for example, the contrast in the time series and cross-section specifications in the extensive analysis of Bowen and Finegan (1969)].

After allowing for these extremely important population characteristic variables, pertinent labor market variables include wage(s), non-labor income, and objective labor market characteristics generally measuring probability of successful job search (e.g. unemployment rate, industry mix, degree of urbanization). In the simple theoretical model, wage and non-labor income are in real terms, but Friedman (1968) has argued for the allowance of a type of money illusion in labor supply so that simple divisions of nominal wage and income data by a price level may not be appropriate. In particular, workers contract in money wage so perceived money wage invariably equals actual money wage, but this is not always the case for real wages. Workers may implicitly evaluate money wages by a price level which is not the actual current one, but a distributed lag on past as well as current prices. Thus, if wages and prices increase proportionately at higher than historical average rates, the worker perceives a real wage increase. Some evidence of this phenomenon is found in Wachter (1972).

Returning to a focus on real wage, real non-labor income, and unemployment rate, it is useful to summarize expected empirical signs of these variables. In short, current theory permits any of the coefficients to be positive, negative or zero but not always in arbitrary combinations. The ambiguity of the sign of the unemployment rate variable has been extensively discussed above in terms of discouraged-worker and additional-worker hypotheses and correlations introduced by migration/labor market interdependencies. Consider a simple model

$$\ln L = \alpha_1 \ln w + \alpha_2 \ln Y_n + \alpha_3 X + \varepsilon \tag{2.3}$$

where L is regional labor force participation, w is real market wage, Y_n is real non-labor income, X is all other factors discussed above, ε is the random error term, and ln denotes natural logarithm. Theory allows for α_2 to be either positive or negative. Note that Becker's modification of the simple theoretical model to allow for distinction between true recreational leisure and "household production" time permits interpretation of a negative α_2 that does not require the dubious assumption that true recreational leisure is an inferior good.

Arguments with respect to the sign of α_1 in part depend upon how the regional labor force participation data are interpreted with respect to what they measure (the Mincer/Ben-Porath/Lewis debate above). If they measure quantity supplied, the coefficients 1 and 2 can be used to decompose aggregate wage elasticities into substitution and income effects:

$$\alpha_1 = \alpha^* + \alpha_2(E/Y_n) \tag{2.4}$$

where α^* is compensated wage elasticity and E is labor earnings. As noted earlier, theory implies the elasticity α^* is unambigously positive, the substitution effect of a wage increase is to raise hours offered to the market. If α_2 is positive, then under this interpretation of the labor force participation data, the gross wage effect, α_1, must also be positive. If α_2 is negative, α_1 may be either positive or negative.

The simple theory implied that the gross wage effect on the labor force participation decision is unambiguously positive. However, this does not mean that if a Ben-Porath/Lewis interpretation of regional labor force participation data is maintained, then α_1 must be positive regardless of the sign of α_2. The simple model was one-period; results of the life-cycle models summarized above allow for a possible negative correlation between the labor force participation decision and current wages.

While theory indicates what variables should be considered in empirical studies of regional labor force participation, it does not suggest functional form. The latter is a determinant of appropriate estimation technique, so little general econometric guidance can be offered. However, several functional form/econometric techniques issues should be briefly mentioned. First, many of the more complex estimation methodologies (complex relative to ordinary least squares) which permeate the general labor supply literature are not pertinent to estimation at the more aggregated regional level. They deal with problems particular to micro data sets. For example, if we try to estimate a probability of labor force participation from a micro data set, the problem is one of trying to estimate a continuous probability function from binary data (all we know about any individual is whether or not he participates in the labor force). It is the binary nature of the data which yields the necessity for probit or logit estimation techniques in this case. However, with aggregated regional data on labor force participation we do not have binary observations. Rather, we have what may be viewed as continuous observations on population probabilities.

Given no theoretical reason to pick one functional form over another, a particularly convenient one for regional labor force participation is the logistic probability functional form:

$$L = f(\alpha + \beta X) = 1/[1 + e^{-(\alpha + \beta X)}] \tag{2.5}$$

where L is labor force participation, X is the vector of determinants of L, α is a constant, and β is a coefficient vector. It is straightforward to derive that (2.5) implies

$$\ln[L/(1-L)] = \alpha + \beta X \tag{2.6}$$

and allowing for a random error term, ε, additive to (2.6):

$$\ln[L/(1-L)] = \alpha + \beta X + \varepsilon. \tag{2.7}$$

Equation (2.7) is linear in the parameters and is estimable by ordinary least squares under the usual assumptions about the error term. The benefit of this particular formulation is that any estimated value for L must lie within the logical bounds (0, 1). This feature is particularly desirable in a forecasting context when out of sample data might otherwise potentially yield absurd labor force participation rates.

3. Labor demand

Analysis of regional labor demand is typically based on a statement or set of statements which permits derivation of a link between production output and factor inputs. Under certain simplified conditions, statement of the production function alone, which describes technological conversion of inputs to outputs, is sufficient. Under more general conditions, the cost function which describes minimum cost of production as a function of output level and factor price inputs is sufficient. Finally, explicit statement of the cost function may not be necessary if statement of the production function is combined with a statement determining firm market behavior. The majority of empirical regional labor demand analyses focuses on the first and third situations, although in general, the second approach (statement of the cost function) may be the least restrictive.

Only under particular conditions is statement of the production function sufficient to derive labor demand. Several common formulations which permit such a simplified approach include:

(A) A single-factor (labor) production function. If production is described by $Q = f(L)$ with Q output and L labor input, then the production function itself fully specifies the linkage between labor demand and output, $L = f^{-1}(Q)$. Given Q, L is determined.

(B) A two-factor production function (capital and labor), but, capital assumed fixed in the short-run. In this model $Q = f(K, L)$, but in the short-run, K is fixed at K^*, so the labor demand problem reduces to that of (A), $L = f^{-1}(K^*, Q)$. With separate specification for determination of the growth path of the capital stock, L may be derived directly from the production function given Q and K.

(C) A Leontief multi-factor production function,

$$Q = \min(\alpha_L L, \alpha_1 M_1, \dots, \alpha_{n-1} M_{n-1}),$$

where M_1 to M_{n-1} are non-labor factors of production. Clearly, the production function implies, $L = Q/\alpha_L$.[1] This particular formulation, which allows for multiple factors of production, but reduces to simple specification for utilization of a particular factor, has widespread empirical application in regional analysis.[2]

The critical feature common to solutions (A)–(C) is that contemporaneous substitution between labor and other inputs to the production process is not permitted. Once such substitutions are allowed, the production function alone is insufficient to specify labor demand; an optimizing rule which allows for determination of the choice of input mix is necessary.

The simplest such rule is industry cost minimization. Given the production function and set of factor input prices, the cost function may be derived. However, it is equally permissible to simply start with a statement of the cost function, taking advantage of the fundamental principle of duality in production. In particular, any positive homogeneous, nondecreasing, concave function of factor prices is the cost function for some well-behaved technology. As Varian (1978, p. 180) indicates, statement of a theoretically acceptable cost function may be much simpler and afford more flexibility than an attempt to directly specify the production function.

Given the cost function, conditional labor demand may be directly derived using Shephard's lemma.[3] In particular, if $C(Q, I)$ is the cost function relating output Q and vector of input prices I, then assuming differentiability of C,

$$L = \partial C(Q, I)/\partial w = h(Q, I) \tag{3.1}$$

where L is labor demand and w is price of labor. Since C is positively linearly homogenous of degree one in I, h is homogeneous of degree zero in I. Consequently, L may be written:

$$L = h(Q, I') \quad \text{where } I' = I/w. \tag{3.2}$$

That is, labor demand is a function of output and price of labor relative to other inputs.

As noted above, this straightforward application of economic theory is rarely used as a basis for empirical regional labor demand analysis, perhaps because of its requirement of data on more than non-labor input costs.[4]

---

[1] Technically, going from the production function to $L = Q/\alpha_L$ does assume minimization of cost, but the step is trivial.

[2] For example, multiregional models utilizing this production function are summarized in Issaev et al. (1982).

[3] Derivation of conditional factor demand functions is covered in such standard texts as Varian (1978) and Henderson and Quandt (1980).

[4] An exception is Taylor (1982), which uses a conditional labor demand formulation, approximating relative labor factor cost by labor cost relative to a wholesale price index.

Besides the assumption of a Leontief production function, the most common empirical approach to regional labor demand analysis is statement of a production function combined with a statement of market output determination. In particular, assume the regional industry acts like a single profit maximizing firm in a competitive market. If $Q = f(L, M_i)$ is the production function with L denoting labor and M_i denoting a set of other factor inputs with associated costs w and p_i, and P is exogenous output price, then industry behavior is described by:

$$\max_{[Q, L, M_i, \lambda]} H = P \cdot Q - wL - \sum_i p_i M_i + \lambda(Q - f(L, M_i)) \tag{3.3}$$

or

$$\max_{[L, M_i]} Pf(L, M_i) - wL - \sum_i p_i M_i. \tag{3.4}$$

Differentiating (3.4) with respect to L, setting the derivative to zero, and rearranging terms, yields:

$$\partial f(L, M_i)/\partial L = w/P. \tag{3.5}$$

Expressed in general terms, (3.5) does not appear particularly useful for regional labor demand analysis. While it does not contain prices for non-labor inputs as (3.2) does, the maximizing condition generally does include the levels of all non-labor inputs, data often not available at a regional level. However, judicious choice of the production function, f, can yield a particularly simple expression for (3.5) involving only labor, L, output, Q, and w/P. In particular, such simple forms result whenever a Cobb–Douglas or constant elasticity of substitution (CES) production function is specified. For example, it is straightforward to show that if f is a generalized CES production function, i.e.

$$f = \gamma \left[\alpha L^{-\rho} + \sum_i \beta_i M_i^{-\rho} \right]^{-1/s} \tag{3.6}$$

then (3.5) implies:

$$L = \gamma^*(w/P)^{-1/(p+1)} Q^{(s+1)/(p+1)} \tag{3.7}$$

where $\gamma^* = (s\gamma^s/p\alpha)^{-1/p+1}$. Taking natural logarithms of (3.7) yields the readily estimable functional form:

$$\ln L = a_0 + a_1 \ln(w/p) + a_2 \ln Q \tag{3.8}$$

where

$$a_0 = \ln \gamma^*, \quad a_1 = -1/(p+1), \quad a_2 = (s+1)/(p+1). \tag{3.9}$$

The equation in (3.8) may be estimated with regional data on L, w, P, and Q, a result accounting for widespread use of this functional form (or a special case of it based on the Cobb–Douglas production function) in regional analysis.[5]

However, there can be numerous problems associated with using the development of (3.4)–(3.8). It is a much more restrictive framework than the conditional labor demand formulation in (3.2) which assumes only that the industry minimizes input cost for a given level of output. The present formulation assumed in addition that market output behavior is characterized by the maximization problem in (3.4). First, the estimated parameters must be consistent with that underlying maximization problem. In particular, for (3.5) to be a valid representation of behavior, the second order conditions for maximization as well as the first must be satisfied. A homogeneous production function with increasing returns to scale violates these second order conditions. In the homogeneous CES model $p/s \lessgtr 1$ indicates the returns to scale. From the definition of the coefficients in (3.8), it is clear that estimated a_2 is going to directly imply industry returns to scale. Estimated $a_2 < 1$ yields an empirical result which conflicts with the underlying theoretical model, a problem which unfortunately often does not concern the researcher utilizing the approach.

A way out of this problem is to respecify the market structure so that instead of being competitive the regional industry acts like a profit maximizing monopolist and to assume that the demand function facing that monopolist is characterized by a constant price elasticity. It is straightforward to carry through the maximization and derive a functional form similar to (3.8), but the constant term is complicated by including the constant price elasticity of demand. The theoretical formulation is now consistent with empirically estimated increasing returns to scale.[6] Besides the questionable assumption that the regional industry is in a market position to act like a monopolist, estimation is now complicated by the fact that price determination is endogenous to the regional industry. There is little basis for assuming that regional output price is well approximated by national data series and empirical estimation requires regional data on output price.

Although sometimes the labor demand formulations are the focus of interest per se, in typical application they are part of a broader regional model which includes industrial output estimation as well as labor demand. It is important to recognize that if the market behavior postulated in (3.3) defines determination of

---

[5] In a very few instances, (3.5) has been used with a production function which does not fortuitously eliminate all other inputs. The problem is then one of obtaining data for those other input levels. For example, Duobinis (1981) uses (3.5) with a bivariate (capital, labor) translog production function. The capital variable remains in the equation creating the need to either generate that data on a regional basis or specify an investment function that allows for the replacement of the capital variable with a more readily available regional variable.

[6] There are some second-order condition restrictions on the relative magnitude of the returns to scale and the elasticity of demand that essentially ensure that if marginal cost is declining it cuts the marginal revenue curve from below.

regional industrial labor demand, then it also defines determination of regional industrial output unless constant returns to scale are assumed. Maximization of H in (3.3) yields not only input levels, but also output levels. In most empirical applications, (3.4)–(3.8) is used to derive a specification for regional industrial labor demand, but is completely neglected when it comes to specifying output levels even though the estimation of regional labor demand indicated non-constant returns to scale. If output is not also selected so as to maximize H in (3.3), there is no reason to suppose that regional labor utilization satisfies (3.5). Such a model is internally inconsistent. The problem does not arise if labor demand is specified using traditional conditional factor demand analysis. Taken by itself, the latter is silent about determination of Q; it only assumes that whatever Q is, the industry minimizes cost in producing it.

If there is infinite elasticity of regional industry supply, then it is correct to view output as "demand determined." Other than in this case, however, a simultaneity of determination in Q and L must generally be presumed whether or not the formulation of regional labor demand makes that simultaneous determination explicit. Consequently, consistent parameter estimation in empirical regional labor demand analysis typically requires a simultaneous equations estimation technique. Even if regional infinite elasticity of supply is presumed, an assumption which may be reasonable in trade and services sectors characterized by small easily replicated firms, simultaneity between Q and L may emerge as a result of the regional income generation process. If labor employed by the industry constitutes a significant fraction of total area employment and the industry wage bill is a significant fraction of the area wage bill, then simultaneity between L and Q results if regional income is a determinant of demand for area output.

In empirical application of the theoretical models of regional labor demand, two other problems frequently arise. Often there are no data on Q, regional output. It is theoretically possible to specify regional labor so that regional output does not appear as a determinant of labor demand. If the market structure is completely specified, then the demand for labor can in principle be derived as a function of price variables exogenous to the industry [this is the factor demand function which conventional microeconomic theory contrasts with the conditional factor demand function formulation in (3.2)].

However, analytically the approach may be intractable and consequently there is emphasis on labor demand formulations linked directly to output.

The literature basically takes one of two approaches to lack of data on Q. One is to formally construct the series from available local data using techniques such as the Kendrick–Jaycox (1965) methodology and extension of it [e.g. L'Esperance et al., (1969), Moody and Puffer (1969), Glickman (1971, 1977), Hall and Licari (1974), Chang (1979), Rubin and Erickson (1980), Duobinis (1981)]. Alternatively, Q may be replaced by a proxy for Q (e.g. deflated construction awards in the case of the construction industry) or a vector of determinants of Q [e.g. Ratajczak (1974), Friedlaender et al. (1975), Latham et al. (1979), Taylor (1982)]. The constructed data series permit more direct estimation of the theoretical derivations and use of a "vector of determinants" may introduce multicollinearity into the estimated equation. However, the second approach avoids introducing errors into the analysis which arise from the limited accuracy of available techniques for constructing the regional output data.

A second empirical problem arises with the meaning of the variable L. In the theoretical model, "labor input" should be in person-hours. At a regional level, often the only available data are numbers of people employed. Hours and employees do not necessarily change proportionately, especially over a business cycle. Skilled labor may be retained, but not utilized intensively during low periods of production to avoid costs of rehiring and retraining when fuller utilization is required. There are generally two approaches to the problem, both widely used individually and in combination. First, a direct cyclical measure may be included in the labor demand formulation (e.g. a national capacity utilization measure). Second, a partial adjustment process may be specified which introduces the lagged dependent variable into the labor demand formulation.

4. Wage determination and wage differentials

Wage determination across space is a key issue both in regional labor market theory and in the specification of regional econometric models. However, due in part to problems in using aggregated data at the regional level, this issue is seldom analyzed using explicit labor demand and supply equations. Theoretical and empirical models used in regional science have instead relied on macroeconomic and institutional concepts such as wage diffusion and the Phillips curve. These two approaches are discussed in this section and contrasted in terms of their differing implications for the existence of interregional wage differentials. Empirical estimates of the extent of interregional wage differentials also are reviewed and a simple general equilibrium model showing the relationship between interregional wage differences, factor mobility, and commodity trade is presented.

4.1. The Phillips curve and wage diffusion

The Phillips curve, which shows a negative relationship between the rate of wage inflation and the rate of unemployment, was first presented almost thirty years ago in a now-famous paper by A. W. Phillips (1958). Although the main thrust of Phillips' paper was to document an empirical phenomenon in the UK, this relationship can be rigorously justified using equation (4.1)

$$\frac{Dw}{w} = \alpha\left(\frac{d-s}{s}\right)$$ (4.1)

where Dw/w denotes the time rate of change in wages in percentage terms, d denotes the demand for labor, s denotes the supply of labor, and $\alpha > 0$ is an adjustment parameter. Equation (4.1) embodies a commonly accepted law of supply and demand stating that the rate of price change in a market is proportional to excess demand. Lipsey (1960), however, noted that data measuring excess demand for labor are not available, requiring the use of a proxy variable such as the rate of unemployment. Thus, when $d = s$, the unemployment rate will be positive given nonzero frictional or structural unemployment; when $d > s$, the unemployment rate falls; and when $d < s$, the unemployment rate rises. In other words, because Dw/w is positively related to excess demand in the labor market it must be negatively related to change in the unemployment rate.

The Phillips curve relationship has been extensively discussed and tested from both a national and a regional perspective. Santomero and Seater (1978) have written an excellent review of work on the Phillips curve at the national level and Beaumont (1984) has concisely summarized the literature from a regional labor market point of view. As Beaumont indicates, empirical estimates of the Phillips relationship at the regional level have produced mixed results. Izraeli and Kellman (1979), for example, examine the specifications shown in (4.2) and (4.3):

$$W_i^0 = \beta_0 + \beta_1 P_{i,-2}^0 + \beta_2 UR_1^0 + \beta_3(1/UR_i)$$ (4.2)

$$W_i^0 = \beta_0 + \beta_1 P_i^0 + \beta_2 UR_i^0 + \beta_3(1/UR_i)$$ (4.3)

where W_i^0, P_i^0, and UR_i^0 denote the percentage changes in wages, prices and unemployment rates in region i, $(1/UR_i)$ is the reciprocal of the unemployment rate in region i, and $P_{i,2}^0$ is the percentage change in prices lagged two periods. These equations were estimated using annual data covering the period 1961–77 for 21 SMSAs. The coefficient of $(1/UR_i)$ generally was significant but with an unexpected negative sign. This finding, which corroborates the earlier work of Bowen and Berry (1963), Rees and Hamilton (1967), Metcalf (1971), and Mathur (1976), indicates that the time trend in the unemployment rate may better represent the behavioral relationship between wage changes and measurable labor market conditions.

An important feature of (4.2) and (4.3) is that they specify that wages in an SMSA are determined only by local factors. Izraeli and Kellman argue that this specification is consistent with their theory. However, this theory implies that labor markets are geographically segmented and that substantial interregional wage differentials may exist. One way to test whether regional labor markets are best treated in geographic isolation is to include a wage diffusion or transmission variable in the empirical analysis. Marcis and Reed (1974), for example, examined an equation similar to (4.3) except that a fourth explanatory variable ($W_{i,2}^*$) was added measuring the ratio of wages in city i to the average level of wages in the five urban labor markets they considered (Houston, Los Angeles, Portland, San Francisco, and Seattle). This variable was included to allow for interregional feedback effects on a city's wage determination process. In their estimations, using Zellner's seemingly unrelated regressions method, simultaneous equations methods, and ordinary least squares, Marcis and Reed found the coefficients of P_0 and $W_{i,2}^*$ to be positive and highly significant while neither the coefficients of UR_i^0 nor of $1/UR_i$ were significant. Reed and Hutchinson (1976) and Rubin (1979) also reached similar conclusions after incorporating interregional wage transmission variables into the analysis.

The leading region–leading sector approach represents a particularly interesting way of viewing the wage transmission and diffusion process. This approach is based on the idea that earnings changes in a leading market, determined by excess demand for labor, are passed on, in whole or in part, to lagging markets. Thus, unlike the Phillips curve, the leading region–leading sector hypothesis predicts that interregional wage differentials will be eliminated. There are two possible, but quite dissimilar, mechanisms that could bring about this outcome. First, the process by which lagging regions catch up may be largely an institutional one in which employees bargain for wage increases that are similar to those obtained in other regions irrespective of local labor market conditions. Second, wage increases in lagging regions may simply reflect the effect of competition in product markets and the mobility of factors of production in driving the economy toward equilibrium. Although the leading region–leading sector approach has appeal in light of successful applications by Hart and MacKay (1977) and Beaumont (1983, 1984) an important problem still remains: There does not appear to be an unambiguous or unique way to identify the leading sectors or regions. Various methods have been used including population size [Reed and Hutchinson (1976)] and key industry groups [Eckstein and Wilson (1962)]; however, Mehra (1976) argues with considerable justification that any ranking procedure will be arbitrary.

4.2. Interregional wage differentials

Interregional differences in average wages and earnings have motivated a large number of empirical studies to explain why those differentials have been maintained. Reasons often cited include impediments to capital and labor mobility as well as interregional differences in union strength, production techniques, living costs, industrial and occupational mix, racial discrimination, endowments of and returns to human capital, and amenities [Hanna (1951), Fuchs and Perlman (1960), Easterlin (1961), Segal (1961), Galloway (1963), Scully (1969, 1971), Coelho and Ghali (1971, 1973), Ladenson (1973), Hanushek (1973), Goldfarb and Yezer (1976), Hoch (1977), and Moriarty (1978)]. However, Bellante (1979) argued that analyses of the North–South wage differential require an explicit recognition of the heterogeneous nature of labor. In other words, there may be several types of labor which are paid different equilibrium wage rates and are not perfect substitutes in production. As a consequence, to the extent that those types of labor comprise different percentages of the workforce in each region, the finding of a wage differential may only reflect an aggregation error. Bellante then used 1970 Census of Population data to show that after carefully adjusting for differences in workers' schooling, age, and race, as well as living costs, the ratio of pay in the North to pay in the South was very close to unity.

While Bellante's point may seem obvious, it takes on greater meaning after considering the nature of the data typically used to establish the existence of interregional wage and earning differentials. Aggregate data taken from the Census of Manufactures and the Bureau of Labor Statistics, Area Wage Survey, have been used almost exclusively.[7] The strength of these data lies in their accessibility and comprehensive coverage of selected subpopulations, but their weakness is that aggregation problems are difficult to eliminate. Types of labor distinguished on the basis of varying amounts of human capital may end up being lumped together because insufficient information on that variable is given.[8] Census of Manufactures data, for example, contains no direct measurements on the human capital of workers and the users of the BLS data only can control for human capital differences by stratifying their observations by occupation.

Gerking and Weirick (1983) and Dickie and Gerking (1985) recently have extended Bellante's analysis in their examination of two microdata sets. In both papers, hedonic wage equations are estimated for four regions of the United States. Gerking and Weirick use observations on household heads drawn from the 1976 Panel Study in Income Dynamics (PSID), whereas Dickie and Gerking obtained their data from a national mail survey conducted in 1984. These samples, like others drawn from micro data sets, are not representative of the U.S. population. As a result, unqualified generalizations of the estimates presented should not be made to that larger population. Nevertheless, the estimates reported still are of interest because these data contain unusually detailed measures of an individual's education, work experience, and occupation, as well

---

[7]An exception is Hanushek's analysis of enlisted men departing from the US Army.
[8]Another weakness of data from the *Census of Manufactures* is that they only apply to the manufacturing sector.

as supplementary information on workplace and job characteristics. Thus, a more complete specification of the wage equation is permitted, particularly in comparison with other interregional wage differential studies. The conclusion in both studies is that the structure of wage equation used shows no tendency to shift between the four US regions considered. That is, the rewards to attributes relevant in determining wages are apparently independent of region of residence, a result consistent not only with Bellante's empirical work but also with the theory of hedonic prices as applied to the labor market [Thaler and Rosen, (1975)].

These results, however, conflict with the findings of investigators who have examined alternative microdata sets. Grilliches and Mason (1972), using a 1964 sample of military veterans, regressed the natural logarithm of nominal income on a group of explanatory variables chosen to measure education, ability, and current location, in addition to other personal background characteristics. Two dummy variables, indicating whether the respondent currently lives in the South or West, were both statistically significant at the 1 percent level, a result suggesting that there is a difference between regions in wages paid to individuals with similar characteristics.[9] Also, Brown (1980) reports several regressions based on National Longitudinal Survey Data, in which either a residence in South dummy or a residence in West dummy or both had a significant effect upon nominal wages at the 5 percent level. However, neither of these studies attempted to adjust their estimates for geographic differences in cost of living.

Other factors that could have been responsible for the finding of significant interregional wage differentials include an inadequate specification of the determinants of wages and the inclusion of part-time workers in the sample. Hanushek (1973) estimated a simple equation where earnings was specified as a function only of education, ability, and experience. Substantial variation in nominal wages was observed across seven US regions. Maier and Weiss (1986) reached a similar conclusion for Austrian regions although they considered additional explanatory variables including occupation and gender of respondent.

Sahling and Smith (1983) regressed real wages as an even more complete set of explanatory variables measured in the Current Population Survey data and found that real wages in the South exceeded real wages in other regions. However, none of these authors was able to include variables measuring work place characteristics and they were forced to use an indirect measure of work experience (years of age minus years of education minus size). Also, separate treatment was not given to part-time workers for whom the wage determination process could be considerably different than for full time workers.

---

[9] The South dummy was negative and the West dummy was positive.

4.3. Theoretical implications

The wage diffusion concept and the empirical estimates inspired by Bellante's research also provide a useful perspective through which to view the more theoretically oriented literature on interregional wage differentials. That literature, which is based upon applying a general equilibrium model frequently used by international trade theorists, consists of papers of two types: (1) those which attempt to explain how such differentials might be perpetuated over time [Batra and Scully (1972), Bradfield (1976)] and (2) those which incorporate a wage differential into an interregional general equilibrium analysis of other issues [Yu (1979, 1981)]. In the four papers referenced, the authors not only assume that one homogenous type of labor receives a different wage in each of two regions, but also that one homogeneous type of labor is interregionally immobile and inelastically supplied. To produce the interregional wage gap, each of the models is specified somewhat differently from the traditional two sector–two region (country) Heckscher–Ohlin type framework in which certain well-known assumptions guarantee factor price equalization even if those factors are interregionally immobile.[10] For example, Batra and Scully relaxed the identical technology assumption and Yu has pointed to different intensities of union activities among regions. Also, Bradfield (1976, p. 247) concluded that, "Labor immobility must be coupled with imperfections in at least one other market in order to generate an equilibrium wage differential between the two regions." However, if there are no differences in the reward structure to the various labor attributes, those justifications for the existence of a wage differential are difficult to defend. Furthermore, the long-run view adopted in each of the models does not appear to be entirely consistent with the assumed interregional impediments to the flow of factors or knowledge. Alternatives to these models, therefore, are worth considering.

A particularly useful approach is the neoclassical type of general equilibrium model analyzed, for example, by Batra and Casas (1976) and Jones (1971). That perspective suggests a model where each region produces two goods using three factors of production. Of course, such a specification cannot be applied in all situations and the topic to be treated largely dictates exactly how those goods and factors should be defined. However, the additional factor in the neoclassical model is compared with the two factor specification generally adopted in Heckscher–Ohlin type model.

The attractiveness of the neoclassical type of model in capturing interregional differences in average wage is easily demonstrated using an example based on specific factor formulation proposed by Jones (1971). In that formulation,

---

[10] Those assumptions are: (1) constant returns to scale in production, (2) interregionally identical technologies in producing like goods, (3) non-reversibility of factor intensities, (4) zero commodity transport costs, and (5) no distortions either in input or output markets.

production functions exhibit constant returns to scale and all markets are distortion free and always in competitive equilibrium. Those two assumptions imply that factors are fully employed and entrepreneurs earn zero profits. Algebraically, the full employment conditions can be expressed as:

$$C_{N1}^j X_{ij} = N_j \qquad (4.4)$$

$$C_{S2}^j X_{2j} = Sj \qquad (4.5)$$

$$C_{L1}^j X_{1j} + C_{L2}^j X_{2j} = L_j \qquad (4.6)$$

and the zero profit equations are

$$C_{N1}^j w^j + C_{L1}^j r^j = p_{1j} \qquad (4.7)$$

$$C_{S2}^j q^j + C_{L2}^j r^j = p_{2j} \qquad (4.8)$$

where C_{ik}^j is an input–output coefficient denoting the average amount of factor i ($i = N, S, L$) used to produce good k ($k = 1,2$) in region j ($j = A, B$), X_{kj} denotes the amount of good k produced in region j, N denotes the amount of unskilled labor available in region j, S_j denotes the amount of available skilled labor in region j, L_j denotes the amount of land available in region j, w_j denotes the wage rate paid to N_j, q_j denotes the wage rate paid to S_j, r_j denotes the rental rate of return to L_j, and p_{kj} denotes the price of good k in region j. The specification shown implicitly assumes all three factors are interregionally immobile and there is no trade in goods. In addition, within each region, land is intersectorally mobile whereas the two types of labor are sector specific factors used only in the production of one of the region's two goods.[11]

Now suppose that trade in goods can occur with zero transport costs, i.e. $P_{kA} = P_{kB} = P_k$ ($k = 1,2$), and there is a free flow of knowledge so that production technologies are interregionally identical. In a Heckscher–Ohlin type model, with an equal number of goods and factors, the assumptions made to this point would be sufficient to guarantee factor price equalization. For factor price equalization to occur in a neoclassical framework, however, at least one of the three factors would have to be completely mobile interregionally. That is, in the above model, the zero profit equations alone cannot be used to determine factor prices, once goods prices are known. Instead, factor prices depend not only on goods prices, but also on the factor supplies given by the full employment equations.

Factor price equalization in the neoclassical model, however, can be guaranteed by imposing the additional and, in a regional context, very plausible

---

[11] The specific factor characterization easily could be relaxed, but the additional complications introduced would not alter any of the statements to be made regarding how to model the existence of interregional wage differentials.

assumption that at least one of the two labor factors is interregionally mobile. For the moment, assume that only skilled labor is mobile. In that case, the wage paid to each factor would be equalized interregionally. Nevertheless, even if $w_A = w_B = w$ and $q_A = q_B = q$, the neoclassical model still would allow for an interregional difference in average wages paid to labor. To illustrate, *average* wages in region A are obtained by computing a weighted sum of w and q where the weights show the proportion of unskilled workers and skilled workers, respectively, in the total regional labor force. Even after allowing for interregional migration of skilled labor, the percentage of the two types of workers in the labor forces of each of the two regions would be the same only by luck. That situation easily can be seen since the initial regional endowments of land probably would differ. Therefore, assuming that $q > w$ the region with the highest percentage of skilled labor in its workforce also would have the highest average wage. Finally, that gap in average wages would be eliminated in the model described if both types of labor were interregionally mobile. In the complete labor mobility case, factor price equalization still would prevail; however, factor supplies in region A would end up being constant multiples of those in region B. Hence, in formulating a model where an interregional gap in average wages is an important feature to capture, a neoclassical approach with only skilled labor mobility might be chosen. From that viewpoint, a wage gap can be introduced without assuming complete labor immobility, the existence of impediments to the transmission of knowledge or factor flows, or imperfections in any market.

5. Conclusion

The complexity of modeling regional labor markets should be apparent from the previous sections, even without considering occupations, skills, and institutional factors. The various components of a labor market system are shown in Figure 5.1. Although the existence of these economic–demographic interrelationships may seem obvious in that they constitute a considerable simplification of the functioning of labor markets, demographers and economists very rarely model population and the economy as if they were interconnected.

Demographers generally have ignored both the economic consequences and determinants of population change in favor of extrapolating to the future carefully measured age-, sex-, and race-specific rates of fertility, migration, and mortality. In terms of Figure 5.1, demographic models of population change have focused almost exclusively on the lowest portion, boxes 5, 6, and 7.

The models built by regional economists are mostly incomplete too.[12] They vary in their approaches. Some economic models ignore population entirely; they

---

[12] Some notable exceptions are discussed in Isserman (1986)—see in particular the chapters by Plaut, Greenberg and Renfro, Taylor, Beaumont et al., and Williamson.

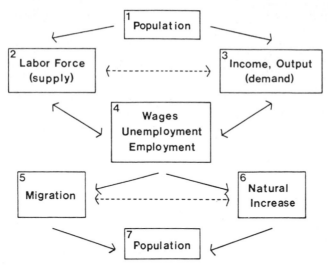

Figure 5.1

contain only boxes 2, 3, and 4. Other models treat population as exogenous, meaning they consist of boxes 1, 2, 3, and 4 and incorporate the consequences of population change but not its causes. Still others ignore the causes and only partially model the consequences of population change; they incorporate boxes 1, 3, and 4, the demand effects of population change, but not its supply effects. Finally some include the economic determinants of population change, but they do not model fertility or natural increase explicitly and they ignore population's effect on economic conditions; they consist of boxes 2 and/or 3, 4, and 7, typically by simply adding a population equation to the main economic model. Without more meaningful representations of regional labor markets, the contributions of such regional economic models to labor policy analysis will and ought to remain very limited.

References

Alperovich, G., J. Bergman and C. Ehemann (1975) 'An econometric model of employment growth in US metropolitan areas', *Environment and Planning*, *A*7:833–862.

Ashenfelter, O. and J. Heckman (1974) 'The estimation of income and substitution effects in a model of family labor supply', *Econometrica*, 42:73–85.

Ballard, K., R. Gustely and R. Wendling (1980) *NRIES: national-regional impact evaluation system.* Washington, DC: US Government Printing Office.

Barth, P. S. (1968) 'Unemployment and labor force participation', *Southern Economic Journal*: 375–382.

Batra, R. and F. Casas (1976) 'A synthesis of Heckscher–Ohlin and neoclassical models of international trade', *Journal of International Economics*, 6:21–33.

Batra, R. and G. Scully (1972) 'Technical progress, economic growth, and the north-south wage differential', *Journal of Regional Science*, 12:375–386.

Baumann, J. H., M. M. Fisher and U. Schubert (1983) 'A multiregional labour supply model for Austria: the effects of different regionalisations in multiregional labour market modelling', *Papers of the Regional Science Association*, 52:53–83.

Beaumont, P. M. (1983) 'Wage rate specification in regional and interregional econometric models', *International Regional Science Review*, 8:75–83.

Beaumont, P. M. (1984) 'ECESIS: an interregional economic-demographic model of the United States', Ph.D. dissertation, University of Pennsylvania, Philadelphia, PA.

Beaumont, P., A. Isserman, D. McMillen, D. Plane and P. Rogerson (1986) 'The ECESIS economic-demographic model of the United States', in: A. Isserman, ed., *Population change and the economy: social science theories and models*. Boston: Kluwer-Nijhoff Publishing.

Becker, G. S. (1965) 'A theory of the allocation of time', *Economic Journal*, 75:495–517.

Bellante, D. (1979) 'The north-south differential and the migration of heterogeneous labor', *American Economic Review*, 69:166–172.

Ben-Porath, Y. (1973) 'Labor force participation rates and the supply of labor', *Journal of Political Economy*, 81:697–704.

Blanco, C. (1963) 'The determinants of interstate population movements', *Journal of Regional Science*, 5:77–84.

Borts, G. and J. Stein (1964) *Economic growth in a free market*. New York: Columbia University Press.

Bowen, W. G. and R. A. Berry (1963) 'Unemployment conditions and movements of the money wage level', *Review of Economics and Statistics*, 45:163–172.

Bowen, W. G. and T. A. Finegan (1969) *The economics of labor force participation*. Princeton, NJ: Princeton University Press.

Bradfield, M. (1976) 'Unemployment conditions and movements of the money wage level', *Review of Economics and Statistics*, 45:163–172.

Brown, C. (1980) 'Equalizing differences in the labor market', *Quarterly Journal of Economics*, 96:113–134.

Cain, G. C. (1966) *Married women in the labor force*. Chicago, Il.: University of Chicago Press.

Cebula, R. (1979) *The determinants of human migration*. Lexington, Mass.: D.C. Heath.

Cebula, R. and R. Vedder (1973) 'Some determinants of interstate migration of blacks, 1965–1970', *Western Economic Journal*, 11:500–505.

Chang, S. (1979) 'An econometric forecasting model based on regional economic information system data: the case of Mobile, Alabama', *Journal of Regional Science*, 19:437–447.

Clark, G. and K. Ballard (1980) 'Modelling out-migration from depressed regions: the significance of origin and destination characteristics', *Environment and Planning*, A12:799–812.

Coelho, P. and M. Ghali (1971) 'The end of the north-south wage differential', *American Economic Review*, 61:757–762.

Coelho, P. and M. Ghali (1973) 'The end of the north-south wage differential: reply', *American Economic Review*, 63:757–762.

Dahlberg, A. and B. Holmlund (1978) 'The interaction of migration, income, and employment in Sweden', *Demography*, 15:529–266.

Da Vanzo, J. (1978) 'Does unemployment affect migration?: evidence from microdata', *Review of Economics and Statistics*, 60:502–514.

Dernburg, T. and K. Strand (1966) 'Hidden unemployment 1953–62: a quantitative analysis by age and sex', *American Economic Review*, 56:71–95.

Dickie, M. and S. Gerking (1985) 'Interregional wage differentials: an equilibrium perspective', manuscript, University of Wyoming, Laramie, Wyoming.

Duffy, M. and M. Greenwood (1980) 'Explorations in migration forecasting: time series and cross-sectional evidence', paper presented at the Western Regional Science Association annual meeting, Monterey, California.

Duffy, M., M. Greenwood and J. McDowell (1979) 'A cross-sectional model of annual interregional migration and employment growth: intertemporal evidence of structural change, 1958–1975', paper presented at the Regional Science Association meeting, Los Angeles.

Duobinis, S. F. (1981) 'An econometric model of the Chicago standard metropolitan statistical area', *Journal of Regional Science*, 21:293–319.

Easterlin, R. (1961) 'Regional income trends, 1840–1950', in: S. Harris, ed., *American economic history*. New York: McGraw-Hill.

Eckstein, O. and T. A. Wilson (1962) 'The determination of money wages in American industry', *Quarterly Journal of Economics*, 76:379–414.

Feder, G. (1979) 'Alternative opportunities and migration: an exposition', *Annals of Regional Science*, 13:57–67.

Feder, G. (1980) 'Alternative opportunities and migration: evidence from Korea', *Annals of Regional Science*, 14:1–11.

Feeney, G. (1973) 'Two models for multiregional population dynamics', *Environment and Planning*, A5:31–43.

Fields, G. (1976) 'Labor force migration, unemployment and job turnover', *Review of Economics and Statistics*, 58:407–415.

Fields, G. (1979) 'Place-to-place migration: some new evidence', *Review of Economics and Statistics*, 61:21–32.

Fischer, M. M. (1982) 'Some fundamental problems in homogeneous and functional regional taxonomy', in: A. Kuklinski, ed., *Societies — regions — boundaries*. New Babylon: UNRISD and Mounton Publishers (in press).

Friedlaender, A. F., G. I. Treyz and R. Tresch (1975) 'A quarterly econometric model of Massachusetts and its fiscal structure', study funded by the Massachusetts Senate Ways and Means Committee and the Executive Office of Administration and Finance, June 30, 1975.

Friedman, M. (1957) *A theory of the consumption function*. Princeton, NJ: Princeton University Press.

Friedman, M. (1968) 'The role of monetary policy', *American Economic Review*, 58.

Fuchs, V. and R. Perlman (1960) 'Recent trends in southern wage differentials', *Review of Economics and Statistics*, 42:292–300.

Galloway, L. (1963) 'The north-south wage differential', *Review of Economics and Statistics*, 45:264–272.

Gerking, S. C. and W. N. Weirick (1983) 'Compensating differences and interregional wage differentials', *Review of Economics and Statistics*, 65:483–487.

Ghali, M., M. Akiyama and J. Fujiwara (1978) 'Factor mobility and regional growth', *Review of Economics and Statistics*, 60:78–84.

Gleave, D. and M. Cordey-Hayes (1977) 'Migration dynamics and labour market turnover', *Progress in Planning*, 8:entire issue.

Glickman, N. J. (1971) 'An econometric forecasting model for the Philadelphia region', *Journal of Regional Science*, 2:15–32.

Glickman, N. J. (1977) *Econometric analysis of regional systems*. New York: Academic Press.

Goldfarb, R. and A. Yezer (1976) 'Evaluating alternative theories of intercity and interregional wage differentials', *Journal of Regional Science*, 16:345–363.

Graves, P. (1980) 'Migration and climate', *Journal of Regional Science*, 20:227–237.

Graves, P. and P. Linneman (1979) 'Household migration theoretical and empirical results', *Journal of Urban Economics*, 3:383–404.

Greenberg, C. and C. Renfro (1986) 'An economic-demographic model of New York State', in: A. Isserman, ed., *Population change and the economy: social science theories and models*. Boston, Kluwer-Nijhoff Publishing.

Greenwood, M. (1969) 'An analysis of the determinants of geographic labor mobility in the United States', *Review of Economics and Statistics*, 51:189–194.

Greenwood, M. (1975a) 'A simultaneous-equations model of urban growth and migration', *Journal of the American Statistical Association*, 70:797–810.

Greenwood, M. (1975b) 'Research on internal migration in the United States: survey', *Journal of Economic Literature*, 13:397–433.

Greenwood, M. and P. Gormely (1971) 'A comparison of the determinants of white and nonwhite interstate migration', *Demography*, 8:141–155.

Greenwood, M. and D. Sweetland (1972) 'The determinants of migration between standard metropolitan statistical areas', *Demography*, 9:665–681.

Grilliches, Z. and W. Mason (1972) 'Education, income, and ability', *Journal of Political Economy*, 80:s74–s103.

Hall, O. P. and H. A. Licari (1974) 'Building small region econometric models: extension of Glickman's structure to Los Angeles', *Journal of Regional Science*, 14:337–353.

Hanna, F. (1951) 'Contribution of manufacturing wages to regional differences in per capita income', *Review of Economics and Statistics*, 34:18–28.

Hanushek, G. (1973) 'Regional differences in the structure of earnings', *Review of Economics and Statistics*, 55:204–213.

Hart, R. A. and D. I. MacKay (1977) 'Wage inflation, regional policy and the regional earnings structure', *Economica*, 44:267–281.

Heckman, J. J. (1978) 'A partial survey of recent research on the labor supply of women', *American Economic Review*, 68:200–206.

Heckman, J. J. and T. E. MaCurdy (1980) 'A life cycle model of female labor supply', *Review of Economics Studies*, 47:47–74.

Henderson, J. M. and R. E. Quandt (1980) *Microeconomic theory*. New York: McGraw-Hill.

Herzog, H. and A. Schlottmann (1984) 'Labor force mobility in the United States: migration, unemployment, and remigration', *International Regional Science Review*, 9:43–58.

Hoch, I. (1977) 'Climate, wages, and the quality of life', in: L. Wingo and A. Evans, eds., *Public economics and the quality of life*. Baltimore: Johns Hopkins University Press.

Issaev, B., P. Nijkamp, P. Rietveld and F. Snickers, eds. (1982) *Multiregional economic modeling: practice and prospect*. Amsterdam: North-Holland.

Isserman, A. (1985) 'Economic-demographic modeling with endogenously determined birth and migration rates: theory and prospects', *Environment and Planning*, A17:25–45.

Isserman, A., ed. (1986) *Population change and the economy: social science theories and models*. Boston: Kluwer-Nijhoff Publishing.

Isserman, A., D. Plane and D. McMillen (1982) 'Internal migration in the United States: an evaluation of federal data', *Review of Public Data Use*, 10:285–311.

Isserman, A., D. Plane, P. Rogerson and P. Beaumont (1985) 'Forecasting interstate migration with limited data: a demographic-economic approach', *Journal of the American Statistical Association*, 80:277–285.

Izraeli, O. and M. Kellman (1979) 'Changes in money wage rates and unemployment in local labor markets: the latest evidence', *Journal of Regional Science*, 19(3):375–387.

Jones, R. (1971) 'A three-factor model in trade, theory, and history', in: J. Bhagwati, et al., eds., *Trade balance of payments and growth: essays in honor of C. P. Kindleberger*. Amsterdam: North-Holland.

Keeley, M. C. (1981) *Labor supply and public policy*. New York: Academic Press.

Kendrick, J. W. and C. M. Jaycox (1965) 'The concept and estimation of gross state product', *Southern Economic Journal*, 32:153–168.

Ladenson, M. (1973) 'The end of the north-south wage differential: comment', *American Economic Review*, 63:754–756.

Latham, W. R., K. A. Lewis and J. H. Landon (1979) 'Regional econometric models: specification and simulation of a quarterly alternative for small regions', *Journal of Regional Science*, 19:1–14.

Ledent, J. (1978) 'Regional multiplier analysis: a demometric approach', *Environment and Planning*, A10:537–560.

L'Esperance, W. L., L. G. Nestel and D. Fromm (1969) 'Gross state product and an econometric model of a state', *Journal of the American Statistical Association*, 64:787–807.

Levy, J. and W. Wadycki (1974) 'What is the opportunity cost of moving?: reconsideration of the effects of distance on migration', *Economic Development and Cultural Change*, 22:198–214.

Lewis, H. G. (1967) 'On income and substitution effects in labor force participation', unpublished manuscript, University of Chicago.

Lewis, W. (1977) 'The role of age in the decision to migrate', *Annals of Regional Science*, 11:51–60.

Lichter, D. (1980) 'Household migration and the labor market position of married women', *Social Science Research*, 9:83–97.

Lipsey, R. G. (1960) 'The relation between unemployment and the rate of change of money wage rates in the United Kingdom, 1862–1957: a further analysis', *Economica*, 27:456–487.

Liu, B-C. (1975) 'Differential net migration rates and the quality of life', *Review of Economics and Statistics*, 57:329–337.

Long, L. (1974) 'Women's labor force participation and the residential mobility of families', *Social Forces*, 52:342–348.

Lowry, I. S. (1966) *Migration and metropolitan growth: two analytic models*. San Francisco: Chandler.

MaCurdy, T. E. (1981) 'An empirical model of labor supply in a life-cycle setting', *Journal of Political Economy*, 89:1059–1085.

Maier, G. and P. Weiss (1986) 'The importance of regional factors in the determination of earnings: the case of Austria', *International Regional Science Review*, 10, no. 3 (in press).

Marcis, R. G. and J. D. Reed (1974) 'Joint estimation of the determinants of wages in subregional labor markets in the United States: 1961–1972', *Journal of Regional Science*, 14:259–267.

Masser, I (1980) 'The analysis of spatial interaction data', TRP 31, Department of Town and Regional Planning, University of Sheffield.

Mathur, V. K. (1976) 'The relation between rate of change of money wage rates and unemployment in local labor markets: some new evidence', *Journal of Regional Science*, 16:389–398.

Mehra, Y. P. (1976) 'Spillovers in wage determination in U.S. manufacturing industries', *The Review of Economics and Statistics*, 58:300–312.

Metcalf, D. (1971) 'The determinants of earnings changes: a regional analysis for the U.K., 1960–1968', *International Economic Review*, 12:273–282.

Miller, E. (1973) 'Is outmigration affected by economic conditions', *Southern Economic Journal*, 39:396–405.

Milne, W. (1981) 'Migration in an interregional macroeconomic model of the United States: will net outmigration from the northeast continue?', *International Regional Science Review*, 6:71–83.

Mincer, J. (1966) 'Labor force participation and unemployment: a review of recent evidence', in: R. A. Gordon and M. S. Gordon, eds., *Prosperity and unemployment*. New York: Wiley.

Moody, H. T. and F. W. Puffer (1969) 'A gross regional product approach to regional model-building', *Western Economic Journal*, 7:391–402.

Moriarty, B. (1978) 'A note on unexplained residuals in north-south wage differential models', *Journal of Regional Science*, 18:105–108.

Openshaw, S. (1977) 'Optimal zoning systems for spatial interaction models', *Environment and Planning*, A9:169–184.

Phillips, A. W. (1958) 'The relation between unemployment and the rate of change of money rates in the United Kingdom, 1861–1957', *Economics*, 25:283–299.

Plaut, T. (1981) 'An econometric model for forecasting regional population growth', *International Regional Science Review*, 6:53–70.

Plaut, T. (1986) 'Economic-demographic interactions in the growth of Texas', in: A. Isserman, ed., *Population change and the economy: social science theories and models*. Boston: Kluwer-Nijhoff Publishing.

Ratajczak, D. (1974) 'Data limitations and alternative methodology in estimating regional econometric models', *The Review of Regional Studies* 4:51–64.

Reed, J. D. and P. M. Hutchinson (1976) 'An empirical test of regional Phillips curve and wage rate transmission mechanism in an urban hierarchy', *Annals of Regional Science*, 10:19–30.

Rees, A., and M. T. Hamilton (1967) 'The wage-price-productivity perplex', *Journal of Political Economy*, 75:63–70.

Robbins, L. (1930) 'On the elasticity of demand for income in terms of effort', *Economica*, 10:123–129.

Rogers, A. (1967) 'A regression analysis of interregional migration in California', *Review of Economics and Statistics*, 49:262–267.

Rogers, A. (1968) *Matrix analysis of interregional population growth and distribution*. Berkeley: University of California Press.

Rogers, A. (1979) 'Migration patterns and population redistribution', *Regional Science and Urban Economics*, 9:275–310.

Rogerson (1979) 'Prediction: a modified Markov chain approach', *Journal of Regional Science*, 19:469–478.

Rubin, B. M. (1979) 'Further evidence on the metropolitan region labor market unemployment-inflation adjustment mechanism', Paper presented at the Regional Science Association Meetings, Los Angeles, 1979.

Rubin, B. M. and R. A. Erickson (1980) 'Specification and performance improvements in regional econometric models: a model for the Milwaukee metropolitan area', *Journal of Regional Science*, 20:11–36.

Sahling, L. and S. Smith (1983) 'Regional wage differentials: has the South risen again?', *Review of Economics and Statistics*, 65:131–135.

Sandell, S. H. (1977) Women and the economics of family migration', *Review of Economics and Statistics*, 59:406–414.

Santomero, A. M. and J. J. Seater (1978) 'The inflation-unemployment trade-off: a critique of the literature', *Journal of Economic Literature*, 15:499–544.

Schwartz, A. (1973) 'Interpreting the effect of distance on migration', *Journal of Political Economy*, 81:1153–1169.

Scully, G. (1969) 'Interstate wage differentials: a cross-section analysis,' *American Economic Review*, 59:757–773.

Scully, G. (1971) 'The north-south manufacturing wage differential, 1869–1919', *Journal of Regional Science*, 11:235–252.

Segal, M. (1961) 'Regional wage differentials in manufacturing in the postwar period', *Review of Economics and Statistics*, 43:148–155.

Shaw, P. (1975) *Migration theory and fact*. Philadelphia: Regional Science Research Institute.

Sjaastad, L. (1962) 'The costs and returns of human migration', *Journal of Political Economy Supplement*, 70:80–93.

Slater, P. B. (1976) 'A hierarchical regionalization of Japanese prefectures using 1972 interprefectural migration flows', *Regional Studies*, 10:123–132.

Smith, D. (1974) 'Regional growth: interstate and intersectoral factor reallocations', *Review of Economics and Statistics*, 56:353–359.

Smith, D. (1975) 'Neoclassical growth models and regional growth in the US', *Journal of Regional Science*, 15:165–181.

Taylor, C. A. (1982) 'Econometric modeling of urban and other substate areas', *Regional Science and Urban Economics*, 12:425–448.

Taylor, C. (1986) 'The effects of refining demographic-economic interactions in regional econometric models', in: A. Isserman, ed., *Population change and the economy: social science theories and models*. Boston: Kluwer-Nijhoff Publishing.

Tella, A. (1965) 'Labor force sensitivity to employment by age and sex', *Industrial Relations*, 4:69–83.

Thaler, R. and S. Rosen (1975) The value of saving a life: evidence from the labor market, in: N. Terleckyj, ed., *Household production and consumption*. New York: NBER.

Todaro, M. (1969) 'A model of labor migration and urban unemployment in less developed countries', *American Economic Review*, 59:138–148.

Todaro, M. (1976) 'Urban job expansion, induced migration and rising unemployment', *Journal of Development Economics*, 3:211–225.

United States Bureau of the Census (1979) 'Illustrative projections of state populations by age, race, and sex: 1975 to 2000', Current Population Reports series, P-25, Number 796. Washington, DC: US Government Printing Office.

Varian, H. R. (1978) *Microeconomic Analysis*, 2nd ed. New York. W. W. Norton and Co.

Wachter, M. L. (1972) 'A labor supply model for secondary workers', *Review of Economics and Statistics*: 141–152.

Wadycki, W. (1979) 'Alternative opportunities and United States interstate migration: an improved econometric specification', *Annals of Regional Science*, 13:35–41.

Wales, T. J. and A. D. Woodland (1977) 'Estimation of the allocation of time for work, leisure, and housework', *Econometrica*, 45:115–132.

Williamson, J. (1986) 'Regional economic-demographic modeling: progress and prospects', in: A. Isserman, ed., *Population change and the economy: social science theories and models*. Boston: Kluwer-Nijhoff Publishing.

Yu, E. (1979) 'On the theory of interregional wage differentials and technical change', *Journal of Regional Science*, 19:245–256.

Yu, E. (1981) 'Regional factor specificity, wage differential, and resource allocation', *Regional Science and Urban Economics*, 11:69–79.

Chapter 14

REGIONAL ENERGY AND ENVIRONMENTAL ANALYSIS

T. R. LAKSHMANAN and ROGER BOLTON

1. Introduction

A basic feature of economic activity is the extraction of materials from the environment, their transformation during production and consumption and their final restoration to the environment. The economics of environmental resources focuses on the types, forms, and quantities of materials returned, their destinations, and the laws, institutions and markets governing their return to the environment. Energy economics is concerned with similar issues pertaining to the removal and use of energy resources from the environment. There are many unusual characteristics of energy and environmental resources that require distinctive economic analysis of the markets and policies affecting their use. Some of those characteristics make *regional* economics one useful approach to studying the markets and policies. In this chapter, we explain how regional economics is useful in that respect.

The chapter has the following organization. In the remainder of this introduction, we describe just what we mean by energy and environmental resources. In Section 2 we describe the special characteristics of them that we believe make the regional implications of their production important, and in Section 3 we review some important theoretical issues. In Section 4 we describe at some length the effects of energy markets and the importance of energy rents, in the interregional distribution of income, and, more briefly, the role of environmental rents in the interregional distribution. The analysis of the distributional effects of energy and environmental resources is an important example of how regional economics is a fruitful approach. Finally, in Section 5 we describe a number of the available formal theoretical and empirical models for the analysis of regional effects of the production and use of energy and environmental resources.

It is useful to put energy and environmental resources in the context of the whole array of "resources" available to an economic system. The major groups of resources are: natural resources, labor, physical capital and human capital.

Handbook of Regional and Urban Economics, Volume I, Edited by P. Nijkamp
©Elsevier Science Publishers BV, 1986

The list is similar to the classical economists' "land, labor, and capital", except that here we give land the more descriptive label of natural resources and we add human capital. The boundaries between the kinds of resources are blurred; the one between labor and human capital, while it does not concern us here, is notably blurred, and so is the one between natural resources and physical capital. However, the taxonomy is useful.

Natural resources include the following: land, in the common usage sense of soil and space; air space; fresh air; fresh water and salt water bodies, including rivers and estuaries; solar energy; fossil and nuclear energy deposits; mineral deposits; plant life; animal life. Some of these are potential "energy resources," and will become actual energy resources in the right circumstances of preferences, technology, and markets; they are solar energy, water to the extent movements of it can be converted into usable energy, fossil fuels, nuclear energy ores, and the parts of plant life which are "biomass fuels," plus the land, space, and soil which are used for energy extraction and conversion and growth of biomass fuels.

In this chapter, we deal with two subsets of natural resources: environmental resources and energy resources. By environmental resources, we mean here natural resources that are used in production and consumption processes that accomplish one or more of the following: *create basic life support and protect human health, absorb wastes from human activity, and provide amenity*. Thus, land space, soil, fresh air and fresh water, salt water, air space, plant and animal life all may be environmental resources in that sense. Sometimes they are goods consumed directly; for example, fresh air of some minimum quality is necessary for everyday human activity. Sometimes they are intermediate inputs; for example, land space and soil, fresh air and fresh and salt water are all used at times for disposal of wastes from production, and the waste disposal function is crucial for efficient production.

Several additional comments are necessary. First, one of us is a geographer, the other an economist. Our conception of the environment is the economist's, and is considerably narrower than that of the geographer, who tends to use "environment" in an all encompassing way to include every aspect of the natural setting for human activity. Second, the boundary between natural resources and physical capital is fuzzy, because the quality of a resource can be augmented by investment. Third, we are excluding some important natural resources from either energy or environmental resources. Wood and minerals used as materials, and natural resources used in food production, are the chief examples. We do this merely to limit the scope of the chapter, which is not primarily concerned with natural resources as they are converted into material inputs, and is concerned more with the non-food aspects of life support and human health than with the food aspects. Fourth, some natural resources are both energy and environmental resources. Forests and mountain rivers are examples. Each can be used for either energy or for amenity, and especially in the case of rivers there are intense controversies over the choice. Fifth, some uses of environmental resources compete with each other. "Pollution," for example, seems best defined as the use of environmental resources for waste disposal to a degree such that the resource's value for life support or amenity is impaired. Finally, we focus on the more generic environmental and energy issues in the various world regions, eschewing an alternative approach that may have drawn attention to where and why different energy and environmental concerns receive different emphasis in different nations (e.g. the firewood issue in many low income countries). We thus point to the possible contribution of regional analysis to various energy and environmental issues.

2. Special characteristics of natural resources for regional analysis

What are the special characteristics of energy and environmental resources, that have stimulated the creation of whole subfields within economics and whole bureaucracies within governments? Why have the subfields developed much later than subfields which concentrate on other natural resources – land economics, mineral economics, and agricultural economics? And, finally, which of those special characteristics make *regional* economics a fruitful approach to studying them?

A traditional emphasis in the economic analysis of environmental resources is, of course, externalities. A great deal of the contents of a companion volume in this series of Handbooks deals with that subject, so we do not feel it an efficient use of our space here to review the basic theory. We concentrate more on some other characteristics that are especially relevant to regional analysis. Of course, the externalities are also relevant in regional analysis, so we must include them in our discussion in later sections.

The following seem to be important in this regard.

(a) Energy resources occur in specific locales. Historically, they localized economic activities near their place of occurrence before investments in social overhead capital brought energy transportation costs down. Even after transportation costs fell and production and consumption centers multiplied, the extraction and early conversion stages of energy were largely spatially concentrated in certain resource-oriented regions. Large scale production of primary energy in some regions results in regional specialization. In times of uncertain and short supply (as in the 1970s) large price increases lead to accrual of economic rent to these regions (for example, the OPEC countries and energy-producing states and provinces in the United States and Canada in the 1970s). The many policy questions and analytical issues raised by the price increases stimulated the development of a new subfield in economics.

(b) Environmental quality is also highly variant over space, because of differences among regions in: (i) the level of emissions which is dependent on industrial mix; (ii) the density of population and the consequent levels of damage from a given level of pollutants; (iii) the assimilative capacity of the environment; (iv) residents' preferences for environmental quality. If there is not such perfect factor mobility so as to adjust for differences in environmental quality, we may expect differences among regions in the policy to abate pollution. There will be regional differences in environmental quality target standards and in policy instruments.

The environment includes several subsystems (e.g. water quality, air quality, noise level) that vary considerably in terms of their spatial interdependence, their spatial extent, and their consequences. Many environmental resources such as amenity goods are local public goods, their extent restricted to regions. Consequently, the process of allocating scarce environmental resources optimally among competing uses needs to be differentiated by environmental medium and the instruments used. In a case where environmental damage is largely regional and interregional diffusion is negligible (e.g. noise pollution, or water quality basins where the region is conterminous with the domain of the water quality problem), there is an argument for planning at the regional level. A regional environmental authority, with responsibility for specific environmental problems, may be efficient even in a nation where there are national uniform standards to cope with other environmental problems.

(c) Energy resources are often inelastically supplied in the short run. One result is large market price fluctuations. Another is that a major portion of the returns to their owners is a form of "rent." That has implications for efficiency: price is completely demand-determined and not cost-determined, and taxes on rent can be efficient. It also has, for many people, implications for equity: some believe that rent is "undeserved" and eminently suitable for taxation on moral grounds as well as efficiency grounds.

The population in an energy-specialized region is likely to receive a disproportionate share of its income as rent (in accounting terms, of course, some of it comes as wages, some as profits, and some as rent in the more usual sense). This is an important feature of the *interregional* distribution of income in a nation. The rents are also attractive tax bases for both national and subnational governments, and so are relevant to the redistribution (interpersonal and interregional) of income through the public sector. Energy resource taxes can be significant sources of revenue for state or provincial governments. Regionally concentrated rents and the taxation of them raise policy issues at the national level, as shown by controversies over state severance and other taxes, Federal tax and leasing arrangements, and Federal energy pricing policies in the United States and Canada.

(d) Environmental resources are inelastic in supply, and they also produce economic rent that is unevenly distributed in space. The rent is received in a wide variety of forms: nonpecuniary income (amenity) or cost savings (lower health care costs) to households; land values in cases where the environmental quality is a feature of a particular site; cost savings in business firms (lower wages due to household benefits, lower costs for "cleaning" materials – as in water treatment – and for disposing of wastes). These rents seem to attract less attention politically, perhaps because they are not monetary, and because there has not been a recent dramatic run-up in the "prices" of the environmental resources in question. It is also the case that they are not concentrated in broad regions, with resulting political consequences but are spread over many smaller regions or even localities.

(e) Since commodities and pollutants are mobile across regions, production and environmental disruption in one region will have repercussions on environmental quality in other regions. Rivers and winds transport pollutants across regions. If one region specializes in the production of pollution-intensive commodities which are traded with another region with stricter environmental standards, interregional trade will influence regional environmental quality.

Because of the high income elasticity of superior environmental quality, factors of production may over time migrate across regional boundaries in response to differences in factor income and/or environmental quality. The mobility in turn will influence target environmental standards in regions. Further, decentralized regional decisions, in such cases where there are technological externalities or spatial spillovers, are not optimal. For instance, residents of high income metropolitan areas often prefer high environmental quality in pristine, sparsely settled, recreation areas. The political system may give such weight to those residents that the other regions must give up economic growth without compensation payments for those demanding the environmental quality benefits. This free rider problem and other deficiencies of decentralized environmental policy suggest the need for a national environmental policy, but one that is regionally differentiated.

(f) Until recently, the economic theory of energy demand and supply was essentially aspatial. In the classic theory of resource utilization, consumer sovereignty in demand for final goods leads back via production schedules and intermediate demands to primary production of energy resources. Economists implicitly had in mind a nation when developing this theory. If prices increase, markets everywhere call for increases in supply and factor and fuel substitution, and anticipated future demands determine the rate of exhaustion of resources. Economists did not pay sufficient attention to regional variation in this scheme.

In the decade of the energy crisis, the necessity for large scale investments to assure energy security focused the attention of economic analysis on the supply side and on the regional dimension. Supply side problems include the need to balance the energy production increases with the objectives of environmental quality, full employment, and price stability. There was concern with the problems of developing capacity in energy producing regions – physical, social, and economic infrastructure – to support the rapid growth of energy production. It was recognized that national policies of energy development, as, for example, in synfuels in the U.S., must be heavily influenced by regional analysis of economic, environmental, and social consequences of energy development.

It was also recognized that some energy resources have a finite, exhaustible supply even in the long run, or nearly enough so as to warrant different analysis from that used for reproducible goods. Assume region A has deposits that have lower extraction cost than region B's, but B's cost puts an absolute upper limit on A's price [B's resource is the "backstop" in the sense of Nordhaus (1973)]. Then a theoretical model predicts steady extraction in A until its deposits are totally exhausted. Expectation of exhaustion certainly affects the long-term growth path of A. Some type-A regions defend their heavy rent taxes as a necessary means to finance their attempts at diversification to insure their survival after the resource is exhausted, so this characteristic interacts with one mentioned above.

3.   Theoretical issues

3.1.   Environmental resources

As noted earlier, most environmental resources render both production and consumption services to a variety of users largely in a non-exclusive manner. Since many users share these services provided by environmental resources that are not subject to private ownership, and thus are available at zero price, their assimilative capacity can be reached, beyond which point the quality of these services will deteriorate for many if not all users. If the quality of the shared uses of environmental resources is to be maintained, either the usage levels must be restricted below assimilative capacity or the latter augmented by private or public action. Thus the environment suggests a number of theoretical problems: positive and negative externalities, congestion, common property resources, and public goods, among others.

The traditional approach is to frame it as a problem of externalities and investigate alternative mechanisms that allow society to correct, partially or fully, for the allocative distortions caused by externalities. While a variety of such solutions – moral persuasion, direct controls, public production and price incentives – exist, economic analysis stresses the role of policy tools operating through the price system. A handful of programs that utilize some or all of the elements of an environmental charges approach have been implemented in a number of countries. West Germany, East Germany, Hungary, Czechoslovakia, France and the Netherlands use different versions of effluent charges for water and air pollution control. Singapore has implemented a central area road pricing system and Japan and Malaysia are exploring road user charges in order to reduce transport congestion. Oregon, Michigan, Massachusetts, New York, Vermont and Maine have established beverage container deposit programs.

In these cases, from an efficiency point of view, the best level of pollution is the one at which the marginal damage of pollution just offsets the marginal costs of pollution abatement activity. Since the environment is defined over space, it can be shown that the application of this efficiency criterion requires a spatial specification of polluters and receptors. This can be demonstrated, following Tietenberg (1979), by a simple, static general equilibrium model, that identifies the various factors that define the optimal commitment of resources for pollution abatement and the production of other desired goods in the economy.

Assume that there exist regions $i = n$ in a country with consumers $c = 1, \ldots, m$, and production units $q = 1, \ldots, s$. The output levels in each of the regions is determined by a production function:

$$Y_{q,i} = G_{q,i}(W_{q,i}) \tag{3.1}$$

where $Y_{q,i}$ is the output level of the qth firm in the ith region and $W_{q,i}$ is the vector of factor inputs h, $(h = 1, \ldots, u)$ committed to the production of consumption goods.

Let the pollution generated during the course of production of the various goods in the n regions be represented by R, an n-dimensional vector of concentration levels of a single nonreactive pollutant. One element of this R vector, r_k, can be defined as:

$$r_k = {}_i a_{i,k} \left[{}_q f_{q,i}(Y_{q,i}, Z_{q,i}) \right] \tag{3.2}$$

where $f_{q,i}$ is the rate of emission of the pollutant by the qth firm in the ith region, which is a function of the output level of the firm $Y_{q,i}$ and $Z_{q,i}$ is a vector of amounts demanded of resources for pollution abatement. The linear coefficient of diffusion $a_{i,k}$, converts emissions in the ith region to a pollution concentration level in the kth region.

The production side can be further specified by two equilibrium conditions. In the product market, the supply must match the demand:

$$\sum_i Y_{q,i} = \sum_c X_c X_{c,q} \tag{3.3}$$

where $X_{c,q}$ is the good produced by the firm q and consumed by the consumer c.
On the factor market side,

$$\sum_q (W_{q,i,h} + Z_{q,i,h}) = \bar{Z}_{h,i} \tag{3.4}$$

where $\bar{Z}_{h,i}$ is the vector of factor endowments in the ith region.

Assume that the consumers in the country have utility functions of the following form:

$$U_c = U_c(X_c, R).$$ (3.5)

The arguments of the utility function include not only consumer c's X vector of goods but also the pollution concentration vector R.

Any efficient allocation in such a system can be viewed as an allocation (X, Z, W) that maximizes:

$$\theta = \sum_c \alpha_c U_c(X_c, R)$$ (3.6)

subject to the constraints (3.1), (3.2), (3.3) and (3.4) and where α_c is a coefficient of social worth. After appropriate substitutions and combinations, the equations that characterize the efficient allocation are:

$$\sum_c \alpha_c \left[\sum_i \frac{\partial U_c}{\partial r_i} \cdot a_{k,i} \cdot \left[\frac{\partial f_{q,i}}{\partial Z_{q,i,h}} - \frac{\partial f_{q,i}}{\partial G_{q,i}} \cdot \frac{\partial G_{q,i}}{\partial W_{q,i,h}} \right] \right] = \frac{\partial G_{q,i}}{\partial W_{q,i,h}} \cdot p$$ (3.7)

where p is the shadow price associated with (3.3). Equation (3.7) is a formal statement of the familiar notion that efficient factor allocation must equate the marginal damage with the marginal opportunity cost of pollution abatement. An examination of these components suggests that the efficient level of pollutants or the ambient standards will vary from region to region even though these concentration levels are public goods and even though regional residents may care about pollution levels in regions other than their own. A major reason is that the diffusion of emissions (and hence the resultant damage) will depend upon the spatial patterns of emitters and receptors.

From (3.7) it can be seen that the factors contributing to these regional differences in efficient ambient standards or emission charges are:

(i) the number of residents adversely affected by the pollution concentrations in the different regions;

(ii) the intensity of their disutility flowing from the pollution in the regions; and

(iii) the costs of abating the emissions in the region, which are related to the spatial relations between emitters and receptors of pollution. The contributions any particular emitter makes to the concentration level at a location is related both to the level of emissions and the location of the emitter. For a particular level of emissions, closer emitters contribute more heavily to concentrations than do faraway emitters. Hence the need for regionally differentiating policy instruments.

By extension, it can be shown that the imposition of uniform restrictions on emitters even *within* a region regardless of location (as for example uniform tax rates or transfer fees for saleable rights) will impose identical controls over different externalities and cause uniformity losses [Tolley (1975)]. In the limit, every emitter will face a unique emission charge that reflects the number of receptor locations affected by the particular emitter and the variations in the meteorological parameters, $a_{i,k}$.[1]

Given this preference in the theoretical literature for spatially differentiated policy targets and policy instruments, two further questions arise: Is it desirable to have regional or local jurisdictions decide entirely on environmental standards or effluent charges? Second, what is the impact of a regional environmental policy on interregional resource mobility and equity and other policy areas (e.g. industrial policy)?

It was noted earlier, that decentralized decisions do not lead to optimal solutions, given the interdependence in regional environmental welfare functions and the free rider program. Hence the issue whether environmental policy should be undertaken by autonomous regional authorities or by a national authority. Both solutions have disadvantages from the point of view of efficiency; the decentralized solution brings with it the danger that competition between regions could slow down or block pollution abatement; on the other hand, given the greater costs of information, the centralized solution may lead to answers that are too schematic [Frey (1979)].

What is needed is either an administrative area large enough to internalize all externalities or a mechanism to monitor interregional diffusion and to place an appropriate shadow price on pollutants crossing regional borders. Further, the solution to this assignment problem will vary with the characteristics of the environmental medium or the instruments used. In the case of water quality management, the use of regional authorities operating within the restraints of interregional diffusion norms seems to offer a practical solution. The problem of control of toxic wastes, on the other hand, may require national control both in terms of product norms and liability.

Differences in regional environmental quality may over time lead to interregional resource mobility and interregional policy competition. Residents may leave regions that ignore environmental protection and polluting industries move in. On the other hand, regions that greatly improve environmental ambient standards may attract residents. In the short run, people with homogeneous

---

[1] The empirical case for such an intrajurisdictional differentiation in the U.S. has been made by Atkinson and Lewis (1974). When they examined the costs of meeting a prespecified SO_2 ambient standard with and without intrajurisdictional differentiation of emission charges they concluded that spatial differentiation reduced the costs by about 50 percent from the allocation that would have resulted with only interjurisdictional differentiation.

environment–per capita income preferences may sort themselves into spatial groupings in the regions (à la Tiebout).

More likely in the long run, population shifts in response to regional differences will cause changes both in the X-vector and R-vector of (3.5) (i.e. structure of goods production and environmental concentration). Regions with low growth prospects begin to lose their ardour for environmental protection and weaken environmental controls in order to attract jobs. Fast growing regions exhibit newer capital stock, which, given the character of technical change, is likely to be environmentally benign. Thus interregional competition resulting from environmental policy induced resource mobility affects interregional equity.

The theoretical discussion so far provided some general propositions giving us valuable insights into economically efficient methods of pollution and congestion abatement. However, practical work in connection with policy and planning decisions requires greater sophistication about the empirical and behavioral complexities in the field. First, when we focus on the removal of one pollutant or residual and a single environmental medium, we ignore the laws of conservation of energy and matter which suggest that most forms of pollution abatement change the form of the pollutant and its medium of discharge. Thus SO_2 and particulates trapped in an electrostatic precipitator end up eventually as residuals in water bodies or land. Consequently, given the scale, structure and technology of production and consumption, discharge into an alternate medium or recycling materials into productive uses are the typical operations for protecting the environment. So, pollution problems must be viewed in a broader regional or national economy–wide context rather than as isolated problems of disposal of liquid, solid, gaseous, or energy discharges.

Second, a focus on the cost functions for emission reductions leads to a concern with end-of-the-pipe treatment rather than alternatives that are comprised of reduced generation of residuals. Examples of the latter are newer production processes induced by changes in relative material (or other input) prices. The consideration of such inducements that can be provided by government policy requires again a broader framework of analysis than we have presented so far.

Finally, it has been suggested that a wide variety of policy options for pollution control exist, with different instruments being appropriate depending upon the character of environmental circumstances [Baumol and Oates (1975)]. An "optimal" policy in this context may well be the design of a hybrid policy that needs to be assessed under particular circumstances.

In the light of the above considerations, many recent investigators have adopted a broad approach that reflects the interconnections between residuals, firms and environmental media on the one hand and production and consumption processes on the other. A number of such models that capture the quantitative patterns of interaction between economic activities and residual production and abatement have been developed as tools to support decisions on managing environmental quality at the regional and national geographical scales. We turn to a discussion of such economic–environmental policy models in Section 5 of this chapter.

3.2. Energy resources

Since energy resources are used as inputs to the production process and as a fuel for transport of supplies to the production site and of outputs to markets, the location of energy resources has always played a role in industrial location. In the early stages of industrialization, regions with large energy resources attracted economic activities. As technical change in the transport sector brought down costs of energy transport, most industries have been relatively free to locate without regard to energy. However, certain industries such as aluminum smelting remain sensitive to the cost of process energy and for many others, energy costs incurred in the access to markets continue to be significant.

Energy and disparities in its price among regions exert broader influences than those associated with the selection of particular sites. Historically, in the U.S., there have been considerable regional differences in energy prices (generally declining in a Northeast to Southwest direction), which in turn has led to corresponding spatial variations in energy intensity of production [Lakshmanan (1981)]. Thus the manufacturing sector of Louisiana, a major energy producing state, uses 15 times the BTU input per dollar of output as New York, an energy importing (high price) state, and adds 1/9th the value added for a given level of energy inputs (Figure 3.1). Thus the industrial mix in the states with higher energy prices is weighted more heavily to the less energy intensive sectors. Even within the five major energy intensive sectors – food and kindred products, paper, chemicals, stone, clay and glass, and primary metals – the high energy price Northeastern regions specialize in less energy intensive subsectors (Figure 3.2).

What has been the effect of the steep energy price increases in the last decade? First, there has been a reduction in the intensity of energy use and much capital investment in conservation – e.g. wind deflectors on trucks, more fuel efficient boilers, waste heat recovery systems, fuel efficient processes, etc. Second, there has been some switching to more abundant fuels like coal. Third, industry has been substituting other factors of production for energy. This pattern of fuel and factor substitutions (labor for energy, working capital for energy, materials for energy) varies not only among manufacturing sectors but also among regions [Lakshmanan (1983)]. Such differences in factor substitution among regions in one sector appear to be related to regional differences in the vintage of capital stock [Lakshmanan et al. (1984)].

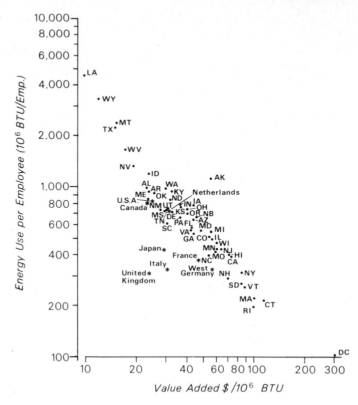

Figure 3.1. Energy intensity in manufacturing in the U.S. and selected industrial countries 1976.

The direct effect of all these changes arising from prices changes on the location of industry is unlikely to be dramatic for most industries [Schmenner (1984)]. First, for most manufacturing plants where energy is important, locations have been selected in the past with energy in mind. Since energy costs for most industries are a small fraction of the value of shipments, large disparities in prices may have limited effect on relative profits of firms. Second, regional disparities in energy prices have greatly narrowed in the U.S. in the last decade, suggesting that energy prices will be even less of a factor in plant locations in the future. Third, the direct effect of energy considerations on plant locations is further weakened by large scale conservation processes underway.

While the direct effects of energy prices on locations may be limited, indirect effects may be considerable. As energy prices increase, transport costs to markets increase leading over time to smaller market areas [Klaassen (1976)]; this in turn will exert an effect on locational decisions. Miernyk (1982) analyzes the changes

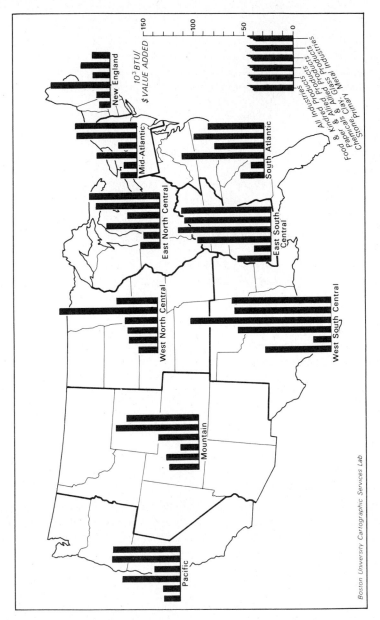

Figure 3.2. Regional patterns of energy intensity in all manufacturing and in energy intensive industries 1976.

in incomes of producing regions caused by recent increases in energy prices. These income effects in turn can lead to a variety of indirect or general equilibrium effects – changes in the demand for goods, labor and other inputs – and also affect input prices and in turn the location of firms. The full regional effect of changes in the prices and availability of energy resources can be significant, and is so complicated that only general equilibrium analysis can capture the full picture (see Section 5).

4. Effects on the interregional distribution of income

Income distribution analysis is fundamentally concerned with incomes of individuals. However, in this chapter we are concerned primarily with the aggregate incomes of individuals in different *regions*, or with what we call the interregional distribution of income. We will not discuss the effects on the size distribution of income within regions.

In this section we first make some general comments on the difficulty of defining a region, in the sense of defining the population of a region whose aggregate income is being analyzed. Then we describe at some length the regional income effects of a useful example, a change in national energy markets. That description makes abundantly clear the many complexities of analysis, which seem to us to point to the clear need for general equilibrium models of a certain kind. As such the discussion is important background for our discussion of the available models in Section 5. Although there have not been any completely satisfactory general equilibrium analyses of the interregional distribution effects of energy markets, there have been some useful examples of partial empirical analyses of them. We review a selected few such empirical analyses, in order to give the reader a better sense of the range of issues and analytical approaches, and also of the importance of distributional changes in policy making and in national policy controversy. Our chief examples are: The "terms of trade" effect often discussed by Miernyk; the distribution of energy rents in Canada, where geography and politics have combined to make the distribution of rents an unusually interesting subject; and the recent attention to state government "fiscal capacity" in the United States. We conclude Section 4 with a brief mention of a somewhat less important, or certainly less controversial topic, the interregional distribution of rents from environmental resources.

Energy markets affect each person qua producer and qua consumer, or, in Musgrave's terms, through the sources side and through the uses side of his budget [Musgrave (1959, p. 217)]. "Sources" are sources of income, net of taxes; "uses" are expenditures on goods and services. All individuals are affected on the uses side because all consume energy directly or indirectly through final products. And in a general equilibrium system the prices and quantities of all goods and services, no matter how energy intensive their production, are potentially affected. Some persons are also directly affected on the sources side because they are "producers," i.e. they work or own capital or land in energy industries. But again general equilibrium connections assure that producers in all industries, no matter how extensive their direct and indirect consumption of energy, are potentially affected. How a *region* is affected by all these connections thus depends heavily on the nature of its population.

Unfortunately, the composition of a region's population is difficult to define, because energy markets eventually stimulate migration, so that a region is not the same collection of people both before and after some change in energy markets. There is an important question: whose income "counts" in the aggregate that is identified with any particular region? [This section is an adaptation of part of Bolton (1982a).] Assume some change in markets at time $t = t_0$ creates adverse impacts on the people residing in region i. It may be clear to all that some present residents (but not which ones) will have to leave the region before some later date, t_n, and that some will leave only at considerable cost (i.e. leaving is their optimal adjustment to a bad situation). Thus, many people are immediately put at risk, and some actually suffer. Some other people will migrate into the region before t_n, to exploit various general equilibrium effects of the initial adverse energy change.

Which collection of people is the "region"? Is it: (a) People living there at t_0? (b) People who will live there at t_n including inmigrants and excluding outmigrants? (c) People who live there at t_0 and remain until t_n, excluding both inmigrants and outmigrants? or (d) All individuals who live there at any time, but with their income counted only when they are there?

Some theoretical analysis assumes definition (a), some assumes definition (d). Some political debate about prospective market and policy changes assumes (a), some assumes (d), and there is often confusion because the participants in political debate do not make clear which definition they are using. Regional income and employment data are always for definition (d). However, an attractive alternative definition is (d) plus people who suffer high costs when they leave, counting the latter for the *entire period* between t_0 and t_n, even though they live part of it out of the region. That would increase the complexity of empirical analysis of history considerably, because available regional data do not include people who have left the region. There is a need for research on the implications of selectively including some people who have left the region.

This problem of definition, of course, pervades long-run regional policy analysis and is not unique to analysis of changes due to energy or environmental developments.

It is interesting to note that for the regional planner, the residents of a region are a fundamentally different client group, from the owners of a corporate firm who are the client group for the firm's managers. [This section is based on Bolton

(1984).] In the corporate firm, at a first approximation, the managers can confine themselves to attempts to increase the market value of the firm; only market value matters, and the managers need not even know who the owners are. The reason for this is that owners can exit from the firm's client group quickly and at relatively low cost in the event they disagree with the firm's policies. Although they cannot avoid all negative effects from managerial mistakes, the ease of selling out reduces the costs of mistakes: *no owner is an involuntary participant in the firm for very long*. It is fundamentally different for the residents of a region, for whom the adjustment costs – both in time and monetary – are far greater. In a region, we may have many residents who are unwilling participants in the regional economy for a long time. Because of that, both national and regional planners must feel concerned for the welfare of many specific individuals. The distribution of income matters.

4.1. Sources and uses sides

The sources side is clearly a major importance. On the *uses* side, however, the costs that residents of each region pay for energy is a matter for special attention and distinctive analysis only if we hypothesize an alternative situation which is desirable or forecastable. For example, if energy is produced and sold in competitive markets, and we expect no significant changes in markets, then it does not seem productive to separate out expenditures for energy and to analyze their "incidence." It is when there is monopoly or other "distortions" that we analyze the incidence in order to make an explicit comparison to a preferable situation, and it is when we forecast changes that we analyze the incidence through the uses side in order to design adjustment of offsetting redistributive policies.

On the *sources* side, however, there seems to be inherent interest in the regional distribution of energy rents, even if rents are the result of purely competitive markets and even if no changes are forseen. The distribution reflects the economic specialization of regions, so it would be interesting for that reason alone. But even more important is the significant feeling that rents are "undeserved," or can be taxed away with little efficiency losses. That feeling is a legacy of a long tradition in economic analysis, even ignoring the recommendations – too extreme to gain popularity – of Henry George [Bolton (1985b)].

This all suggests that our emphasis in this discussion of distribution should be on the regional distribution of: (1) energy rents, including both where they are produced and where they are received as income whether or not the markets are competitive; (2) changes in energy rents and changes in energy costs that would result from a change in energy markets.

It is interesting that the core results of the theory of extractive resource exploitation are of little value in analyzing the things of primary interest here. Assume that energy markets are competitive. Let the costs of extracting a resource in year t be:

$$C_t = C(X_t, S_t) \tag{4.1}$$

where: C = total cost of extraction, X = outputs, S = stock of resource remaining unextracted. Then standard economic analysis derives these equilibrium results [this section is based on the exposition in Fisher (1981, ch. 2)]:

$$P_t = \frac{\partial C}{\partial X_t} + R_t \tag{4.2}$$

where R is a rent on the marginal unit of output, reflecting the marginal opportunity cost, in terms of future revenue, incurred by extracting the marginal unit now rather than waiting until later. The time path of the rent must be:

$$\frac{dR}{dt} = iR_t + \frac{\partial C}{\partial S_t} \tag{4.3}$$

where i is the rate of interest. This merely says that the change in royalty must equal the opportunity return which would be earned by leaving the marginal unit in the ground, plus the addition to marginal extraction cost caused by the stock depletion effect. The absolute level of R, however, and thus of P, must be determined by additional considerations, perhaps assumptions about the stock remaining when extraction ceases (one simple model assumes that depletion is complete, but that the price of the last unit is limited by the price of some substitute – the "backstop" resource). The time path of price is determined by differentiating (4.2) with respect to t:

$$\frac{dP}{dt} = \frac{d(\partial C/\partial X_t)}{dt} + \frac{dR}{dt} \tag{4.4}$$

or,

$$\frac{dP}{dt} = \frac{\partial^2 C}{\partial X_t^2}\frac{dX}{dt} + \frac{\partial^2 C}{\partial S\,\partial X}\frac{dS}{dt} + iR_t\frac{\partial C}{\partial S_t}. \tag{4.5}$$

Substituting $-X_t$ for dS/dt:

$$\frac{dP}{dt} = \frac{\partial^2 C}{\partial X^2}\frac{dX}{dt} - Xt\frac{\partial^2 C}{\partial S\,\partial X} + iR_t + \frac{\partial C}{\partial S_t}. \tag{4.6}$$

Some simple special cases are: (1) costs are negligible, so that $P = R$ and both rise at the rate of interest [(4.2) and (4.6), assuming that C is always zero]; (2) costs are not negligible, but marginal cost is constant and not affected by the stock, so that R rises at the rate of interest and P rises less rapidly [(4.3) and (4.6), assuming that $\partial C / \partial X$ is constant and $\partial C / \partial S = \partial^2 C / \partial S \, \partial X = 0$].

This sets the stage, but for our purposes it is more interesting to look at Y, the aggregate rents in a period, not R, the marginal rent. Aggregate rent is $Y = PX - C$, so its movement over time obviously depends on X, which depends on the demand function, and on the difference between price and average extraction cost, which depends on the shape of the cost function. Whether the aggregate rises or falls over time cannot be determined without more information. [This uncertainty is discussed in Campbell et al. (1976).]

For an imperfect competition case, current price and royalty are higher, by an amount which might be called the monopoly rent. The equilibrium conditions on R's time path are the same, but now the level of P, and of course of Y, depends on the nature of the demand curve and how it changes over time. [Some possibilities are discussed in Devarajan and Fisher (1981).]

Even if a country's energy industry has many noncollusive firms, its energy producing regions will earn monopoly rents if there are imperfections in the world market which raise prices above the competitive level. Energy producing regions in the country can share in the monopoly benefits created by foreign cartels or distortion policies.

Energy rents may be a significant part of the income received by individuals who own energy resources, and the capitalized rents a significant part of their wealth. Some individuals may also receive rents on other inputs – physical and human capital – employed in energy extraction and conversion. Those other rents may be a large part of individuals' incomes and their capitalized value a large part of wealth. As such, they are useful indicators of economic specialization (and vulnerability) even if they do not arouse equity concerns. However, such rents are seldom given special attention in economic theory because they are felt largely to be temporary departures from competitive equilibria in labor and capital markets. (An exception is the case where the distortion effects of inefficient taxation of physical capital are analyzed.)

4.2.   Location and ownership patterns

Another reason why the traditional theory of resource extraction is of limited value for present purposes is that much of energy and physical capital rents are not received in the region where the resources are located. A region is "energy producing" if energy extraction takes place there, but it is "rent receiving" to the extent its residents are owners of resources, no matter where located. A region may be an important rent receiving region even if it has no energy production. Absentee ownership is an important complication in any analysis of interregional trade and capital flows.

In any producing region, subnational governments (states, provinces, localities) are by definition "resident." They can tax rents, directly or indirectly, and thus appropriate a share of the gross rent even if private owners of the resources are residents of other regions.

4.3.   Effects of a change in energy markets

Some of the complications we have described can be illustrated by a description of the effects of a change in energy markets. For illustrative purposes we discuss an increase in energy prices. The result is a shift in the "terms of trade" between energy producers and energy consumers, to use a term popularized by Miernyk (1982). There will be the following effects.

First, there are "immediate" effects, defined as the increases or decreases in real income caused by changes in relative energy prices, calculated on the assumption that no adjustments in production and consumption of energy products can take place. An increase in prices, for example, raises the rents received by energy producers and lowers the real income of energy users. (However, if one assumes that quantities of energy are constant, then *either* one is assuming accommodating macroeconomic policy, and quantities of other goods are constant as well, or one is rather oddly assuming that sufficient time elapses to allow quantities of other goods to change but not energy quantities.) The regional distribution effects will depend on the regions of residence of resource owners and consumers.

These immediate effects may be almost purely hypothetical, if consumers and producers begin to adjust so rapidly that the immediate effects are ephemeral.

Second, there are "short-run" adjustments in consumption and production patterns, that can soften or accentuate the initial changes. They are adjustments within the constraints of a constant capital stock and population in every region. Adjustments by both consumers and producers partially reverse the initial price changes in energy products, but inevitably cause new price changes in other products. For example, consumers shift expenditures away from energy intensive products and toward others; producers shift resources away from other products and toward energy products. These changes take place in both national and regional markets, and, especially in an economy with widespread absentee ownership, the regional effects of them are difficult to predict a priori.

These changes partially reduce the adverse impact on consumers and the favorable effect on producers, compared to the initial changes described above. For example, given some time to change the consumption of energy, households can reduce the adverse effect. However, again it is dangerous to jump to conclusions about *regions*. One must know the effects of the changes on non-energy products, and one must know the regions in which owners of energy land and capital reside. To take an extreme example, assume: households in region A accomplish all their short-run adjustments by increasing consumption of products consumed in A but produced in other regions; A's residents own A's energy land and capital; no A residents own the non-energy land and capital that are favorably affected in other regions. Then the adjustments would shift the adverse effects on to other consumers in A and energy resource owners in A, but not produce any compensating positive effects on A residents as land and capital owners.

One can think of other extreme examples. While only illustrative, they show how difficult it is to argue convincingly for any particular pattern, once one allows for the production and consumption of many goods in each region, for interregional trade, and for absentee ownership of land and capital. Simple models which produce more definitive answers are characterized by simplifying assumptions which eliminate those complications. When all the complications are allowed for, one can easily hypothesize extreme combinations, as we did above, but one can also hypothesize mixed cases, in which a region has some of the favorable characteristics but not all, so that the net effect of these changes is not clear.

The implication is that a complex general equilibrium model, incorporating both interregional trading patterns and interregional ownership patterns, is required in order to analyze fully the effects of a change in energy markets on the interregional distribution of income. As discussed below, there are not yet any completely satisfactory models of this kind. Therefore any analysis must remain somewhat partial and fragmentary.

Still another complication is the effect of rents on fiscal capacity and public goods production. To the extent that state (or provincial) and local governments can tax rents accruing to non-residents, they can increase public goods production and/or decrease taxes on residents. The result will probably reinforce the changes in real income of residents. It is crucial whether the governments can tax away rent that would otherwise go to non-residents. That is likely to be the case in small energy producing regions with relevant tax power. We return to the issue of the regional distribution of energy tax revenues below.

The third set of effects are "long run" ones, with migration of people and changes in capital stocks. The direction and extent of these changes obviously depends on the short-run effects described above: it is the rents and quasi-rents earned in the short run, and the public goods that are financed by taxes on those rents, that attract new investment and migration in the long run. In many energy producing regions, there will be new investment and new population, but it is not clear whether the rate of return on old capital and the real wage of existing residents will rise or fall. In general the rents on land will rise, and the rents on various kinds of physical capital – the kinds which can be expanded only very slowly – will also rise. Whether these flow through to the local residents depends again on ownership. The rents on some kinds of human capital will also rise and remain high for some time, but the real wages of some workers can easily fall. Workers in energy production may enjoy higher real wages for extended periods, but residents in occupations *not* closely related to energy production may suffer due to rising local prices and increased supply of competing workers from inmigration [Helliwell (1981)].

There has been considerable discussion of possible inefficiency caused by migration seeking lower taxes and/or greater public goods in regions whose governments can tax rent. The discussion has been especially prominent in Canada [Helliwell (1981), Scott (1976b), Courchene (1976), Boadway and Flatters (1983)] for discussion about the U.S. see McLure and Mieszkowski (1983), Mieszkowski and Toder (1983), Cuciti et al. (1983). If people migrate because their net fiscal advantage (value of public goods minus tax payments) is greater in one region than in another – "rent seeking migration" – then the marginal product of labor can be lower, in equilibrium, at the destination than at the origin, violating a condition of national efficiency. This is not a problem if a person's location is not a factor in whether he or she can benefit from the rents. That requires either that rents are totally private, so they show up in private income no matter where one person lives, or are appropriated by the national government and used to benefit persons independent of where they live [Helliwell (1981)].

4.4. Results of some partial analyses

While a complete analysis is obviously difficult, there have been analyses of some important pieces of the total picture, using partial analysis. We review here a few of the especially interesting examples, simply to give a flavor of the research issues.

4.4.1. Effects of average income level

Lower income households spend a much larger proportion of income directly on energy than higher income households do, so the initial impact of an energy price rise is regressive. When expenditures on energy embodied in other products and services are added, regressivity is less, but still present [see studies reported in Beebout et al. (1982)]. It is unlikely that the regressivity disappears when the initial impact is adjusted for consumer adjustments. In general, we conclude that poorer regions would suffer a greater impact, relative to average income, than richer regions with the same climate.

4.4.2. Terms of trade effect

Miernyk has discussed the terms of trade effect often [Miernyk (1982, 1984), Miernyk et al. (1978)]. These references contain a wealth of information about regional variation in energy production, consumption, and prices, as well as about recent patterns of regional growth in the U.S. They also contain very interesting samples of large changes in exchange ratios in the 1970s for pairs of specific products, for example the amount of West Virginia coal or Texas natural gas that must be exchanged for a unit of Illinois corn or sulfuric acid. He concluded that the terms of trade effect caused a significant interregional transfer of real income in the U.S. in the 1970s – greater than did the relocation of manufacturing – and thus was one, but only one, factor causing the South and West (broadly speaking) to grow faster than the Northeast and Midwest.

Miernyk classified each U.S. state as energy surplus or energy deficit, by comparing production to consumption (in BTUs), and found a positive relationship between surplus and relative growth rate in per capita income. He did not attempt to measure the interregional redistribution in dollar terms, nor did he explain the growth rates by a formal economic model. And the positive relationship is far from perfect, suggesting, as Miernyk recognizes, that energy is not the sole factor. For example, over the 1959–79 period, the Southeastern region grew faster than any other major region, despite a substantial energy deficit, and New Mexico, Montana, and Utah declined relative to the national average despite being surplus states.

Miernyk argues that the energy price changes in the U.S. imposed their greatest effect by accelerating a movement, already underway, of economic activity nearer markets. Population was shifting to the West and Southwest, regions with many energy-surplus states, in any event; the terms of trade effect increased income in those regions and pulled market oriented activities even faster toward them. That effect is more important than energy availability or the effects of energy prices on production cost [Miernyk (1984) partly relying on Giarratani and Socher in Miernyk et al. (1978, pp. 103–116)].

4.4.3. Regional rents in Canada

The regional redistribution caused by rising energy prices in the 1970s was especially great in Canada. There has also been great controversy over federal vs. provincial powers, and the Canadian federal fiscal arrangements are extremely complex, so Canadian economists have been especially concerned with the interregional distribution. [Much of the following discussion is based on Helliwell (1981).] Most of the oil and gas in the provinces in owned by provincial governments, and some provinces also receive substantial rents on hydroelectricity production. On the other hand, the national government owns Arctic and offshore resources, can regulate exports and imports of energy, can fix energy prices, and has great taxation powers. *Foreign private* interests own the lion's share of the physical capital in energy production. Finally, there is a fiscal equalization tradition, so that when the tax bases of energy-rich provinces rise, there is pressure on the Federal government to transfer resources to other provinces.

Therefore, the distribution of energy rents to persons and to regions is the result of very complex political and market interactions. Like many other governments, Canada's has often sought to keep prices to domestic consumers low. But market prices have been high enough that a few provinces, notably Alberta, have been able to appropriate much of the rent as owner of the resources. Using a large model of regional primary energy demand, production, and prices, Helliwell calculated that in 1980 the value of net real economic rents to residents of Alberta ranged between 90 and 120 thousand dollars *per capita*. With the recent depression in relative prices, the estimates would undoubtedly be less now. While Helliwell's model takes account of many energy interactions, it is not a general equilibrium model incorporating extensive industrial location and migration responses.

The Canadian experience, and to some extent the Alaska experience in the U.S., shows the *range of discretion* open to the few subnational governments that own or tax large energy rents. That requires departure from the typical "small nation" assumptions in studies of regional change and national policy. The number of such fortunate regions is small, but the few that exist are important enough to affect their entire national economies.

Such a fortunate regional government has a number of options. It can distribute rents to current residents or it can invest them in various financial or real assets in order to build up a public "fund", which in one way or another benefits future residents. Future residents will not be exactly the same group of people as the current residents. The effort to save rents for future generations may be partly frustrated by increases in prices of housing and other inelastic goods and services that accompany immigration and that benefit current residents [Borcherding (1984)]. The government's decisions affect the intergenerational distribution of rents. The government has discretion in encouraging inmigration and new industry – "region-building." Fundamentally, it can either encourage new population only for the period of time required to exploit the resource or it can use rents to finance a new permanent diversified economic base. Its choices affect other regions, the intergenerational distribution of income, and national efficiency. In a federal system, the region *may* also have discretion in using its political power to attempt to alter basic constitutional and fiscal arrangements. For example, Alberta has considerable political power to do this, but Alaska does not. [Helliwell (1981) discusses these options in more detail for Alberta.]

4.4.4. *Fiscal capacity*

We have already noted the importance of uneven distribution of tax base. Many recent analyses use the notion of "fiscal capacity" which is essentially the same as "tax base" but is defined as a relative magnitude: it is the amount of per capita revenue a government can raise *if* it levies taxes on all its tax bases at some assumed tax rates (usually the average rate for all governments being compared), *relative* to the fiscal capacity of all governments combined in the group being compared. Thus:

$$\text{Absolute fiscal capacity of region } k = C_k = \left(\sum_j \bar{t} B_{kj} \right) / n_k$$

$$\text{(4.7)}$$

$$\text{Relative fiscal capacity of region } k = C_k \Big/ \left(\sum_i C_i \right)$$

where: $i = 1, \ldots, k, \ldots, K$ subscripts for K different regions;
           $j = 1, \ldots, M$ Subscripts for M different tax bases (income, sales, property, profits, energy production, etc.);
           $\bar{t} =$ hypothetical tax rate assumed equal in all regions;
           $B_{kj} =$ value of tax base j in region k; and
           $n =$ population.

Fiscal capacity is a weighted average of tax bases, the weights being equal to the hypothetical tax rates $\bar{t}$. The measure suggests the range of discretion open to a government, and it gives the region a potential advantage over other regions in attracting business and population, whether or not capacity is used to produce public goods. Of course, one cannot see the complete picture without knowing how each region actually uses its capacity.

This measure of fiscal capacity has shortcomings. The tax base is not totally exogenous; it may be affected by the tax *rate* itself and by other government policies. For empirical application, the definitions of tax bases in the formulae must be by statutory definitions, which are *not* the same as pure rents. They include some part of income that is the normal, opportunity cost return to a mobile factor, taxation of which will erode the tax base in the long run. Thus the discussion is usually identified as one of interregional distribution of energy "revenues" rather than of energy rents. The formula does not take account of the interregional incidence of taxes. Two states, for example, may have the same energy resources tax base, but interregional and international markets and ownership patterns may allow one of them more easily to shift taxes forward and backward on to other regions; then that one certainly has greater effective capacity than the other. The empirical analysis of interregional tax incidence of energy taxes has not proceeded very far, and we know of no comprehensive estimates [for a discussion of the issues, see McLure (1983) and Church (1981)]. Finally, a region may have to spend a lot of money to maintain the quality of the physical and social environment in the face of expanding energy production, but the capacity measure takes no account of that.

Some parts of fiscal capacity, the tax bases connected with energy property and production, are especially unevenly distributed. In Canada, some part of energy tax bases is included in fiscal capacity calculations that determine equalizing revenue flows from the Federal government to provinces with relatively low capacity [for discussions of the Canadian equalization grant system, see Scott (1976), Courchene (1976), Boadway and Flatters (1983)]. In the U.S., capacity measures so far have no official status in federal grant or revenue sharing formulae, but the uneven distribution of capacity has attracted much attention, and an independent commission occasionally publishes its estimates of capacity [Advisory Commission on Intergovernmental Relations (1985) presents estimates for 1982, but they do not include all energy tax bases]. Here, we are concerned only with the effect of energy resources on that uneven distribution; it goes without saying that many other tax bases are also unevenly distributed.

Cuciti et al. (1983) report calculations of the effect of oil, gas, and coal revenues of fiscal capacity in 1980 in each state in the U.S. (a state includes all the local governments in it). They included severance taxes, lease payments (many states own land containing energy resources and/or receive a share of the Federal government's lease income), property taxes, and corporate income taxes. We cannot summarize all that here, but perhaps the most notable one is that the coefficient of variation (population weighted) across states of energy capacity is nearly forty times as great as that for all the rest of capacity (4.168 compared to 0.116). The coefficient for energy is more than twenty times as great as that for any one of the major nonenergy bases (personal income, nonenergy corporate profits, nonenergy property, and sales). Finally, the coefficient of variation is nearly twice as great for total capacity, including energy capacity, as it is for nonenergy capacity alone (0.222 compared to 0.116). Thus, if one accepts the coefficient of variation as a measure of inequality of fiscal capacity, the ability to tax energy resources nearly doubles the inequality. Differences in capacity had narrowed somewhat through the early 1970s but then widened after the energy price increases.

The same authors also calculated capacity for thirteen special states; the group's nonenergy capacity was almost identical to the U.S. average but their energy capacity was so great that their total capacity was nearly 20 percent higher than the remaining states (there is considerable variation within the group of thirteen states, however).

Another interesting result is that energy capacity is almost uncorrelated with per capita income, a global economic value that is sometimes used as a rough measure of fiscal capacity (population weighted $r = 0.08$). Nonenergy capacity, on the other hand, is much more closely related to per capita income ($r = 0.89$).

The thirteen energy-rich states could, on average, finance the national average of per capita expenditures with a tax rate on nonenergy tax bases about 20 percent lower than in the other states. That is one interesting indicator of the fiscal advantage of the energy-rich states. Again, we remind the reader of the shortcomings of the fiscal capacity measure. For example, some states, with strong market power, could undoubtedly raise the same per capita revenue with an even lower tax rate than this average.

4.4.5. *Environmental resources and interregional distribution*

Rents to environmental resources are also unevenly distributed, but there has not been the same political controversy as over energy rents. Some of the same problems complicate empirical analysis, however. For example, if rents are capitalized in land values, and some owners of land are non-resident national corporations or other owners, then the interregional distribution of rents is affected by ownership patterns.

There has been some empirical work on the spatial distribution of environmental quality, but for good reasons, it has not focused on very large regions in the way energy research has. Rather, it has concentrated on showing the poor environmental quality, especially air quality, in smaller regions – indeed in urban areas, or even neighborhoods (often ones with low-income residents) within urban areas [Freeman (1972, 1977), Zupan (1973), Gianessi et al. (1977), Harrison and Runbinfeld (1978)]. For that reason, regional analysis of environmental impacts needs little review in this section of the chapter, but naturally receives major attention in the next section, where single-region analysis is a prominent topic.

Gianessi et al. (1977) estimated the distribution, in 1970, over U.S. regions (metropolitan areas and other groups of counties) of the *damages* from air pollution, as a guide to the areas which would gain the most from reduction in emissions. As they point out, the authors did not simultaneously consider the costs of reducing emissions. A major assumption was that reduction in air quality is highly correlated, over regions, with the rate of emission of pollutants. That assumption ignores differences, due to meteorological conditions, in assimilative capacity, and ignores spillovers from one region to another. It also ignores regional differences in preferences for air quality.

There has been concern with the regional effects of *national policies* to improve the environment. Nationally uniform effluent standards, or water and air quality standards, impose very different costs on households and firms in different regions, and produce very different benefits to residents. Cost differences may be due to industrial composition: a region with a base of heavy, polluting industry will have, as a region, higher cost burdens, and thus more difficulty in competing for consumers' dollars in general, than a region with a base of less polluting industry. Or, they may be due to different assimilative capacity of the environment. Benefits may differ due to differences in preferences, or due to initial quality of the environment. For example, reducing automobile emissions by a nationally uniform amount will produce much less benefit to people in sparsely populated and relatively unpolluted regions than it will to people in heavily urbanized, polluted regions. On the other hand, the costs to households in the former areas will be similar to the costs in the latter, so that the net benefit to the former may be negative. In the next section we describe a multiregional model designed to predict the effects of national air pollution control strategies on income and employment in different metropolitan areas in the U.S. However, the concern with the regional distribution of net effects from policies has been decidedly less than the concern with the effect on the size distribution of income [Freeman (1972, 1977), Dorfman (1973, 1975), Baumol (1975, ch. 13)].

In the next section we move on to review a number of formal mathematical models relevant to regional analysis of energy and environmental problems. Our chief concern there is not the interregional distribution of resource rents and other income. Rather our concerns are with models that do the following:

(1) describe the energy–environment–economy linkages and interaction within a single region;

(2) delineate trade-offs that are important to consider in policy analysis;

(3) describe the employment, labor income, and environmental effects of national policies on different regions, in a less-than-full general equilibrium analysis manner.

5. Environment and energy policy models

A major direction of recent research in regional environmental and energy analysis is the development of models that embed the problem of environmental quality in the broader context of overall allocation of scarce resources including energy. These models attempt to capture the quantitative pattern of interactions between the economy, environment and energy resources. They link the various economic activities (including production and use of energy) by functional relationships and delineate the magnitudes of different residuals generated by various economic activities. By laying bare the necessary trade-offs between environmental and nonevironmental outputs, these models contribute to a sophisticated understanding of the complex environmental problem. They help assess the consequences of various economic changes (e.g. economic growth, shifts in the output composition, patterns of energy supply) and determine the impacts of alternative types and levels of public policy choices.

Models that capture the interdependencies among various segments of the economy have a long tradition – from the Tableau Economique of Quesnay in the eighteenth century to Walras's General Equilibrium model of a perfectly competitive economy in the nineteenth century. The broad result of General Equilibrium Theory as developed in recent times by the work of Pareto, Hicks, Samuelson, Arrow and others is the proof that exchange in a static competitive economy will yield an equilibrating set of prices for resources and outputs and an associated allocation of resources corresponding to a Pareto optimum. A major assumption in this derivation is that all production functions of firms and utility functions of consumers are independent. Since there are pervasive externalities from pollution emissions from production and consumption, this assumption fails to hold. An innovative extension of the general equilibrium framework under these conditions of pervasive externalities has been recently attempted by Ayres and Kneese (1969) [see also Kneese et al. (1970)].

The central idea of the Ayres and Kneese model is that of materials balance, which suggests that except in the production of atomic power, materials withdrawn from the environment and introduced into production and consumption processes are neither destroyed nor created. Economic production invariably involves waste products that are either returned to the environment or recycled back into the production process. The traditional Walrasian model allows for transfers of materials except for the unpriced withdrawals from the environment and disposal of waste by firms and households into the environment. Ayres and Kneese attempt to incorporate these externalities into the Walrasian system by introducing two sectors through which all materials enter and exit the economic system. The "environmental sector" provides all the raw material via both market and nonmarket channels to production and absorbs waste products that are not recycled. The "final consumption" sector utilizes all the goods supplied to final demand and produces the waste products that may be recycled or discharged into the environment. These two sectors are intended to balance the flows of physical materials in the system.

Kneese et al. (1970) expand on this analytical framework for "second best" problems [Davis and Whinston (1965)] in order to tease some policy proposals out of this approach. While specific elements of this model have been criticized [Victor (1972), Norton and Parlowe (1972), Wilen (1973)] the Kneese–Ayres–D'Arge model has been useful in highlighting economic–environmental interactions and a variety of analytical implications. The model is, however, severely limited in its empirical application in view of the extravagant demands for data – a typical problem for general equilibrium models.

It is not surprising therefore, that the Leontief input–output simplification of the Walrasian framework has served as the point of departure for a number of formulations of economic–environmental–energy interactions [for early examples see Cumberland (1966), Daly (1968), Isard (1969), Victor (1972)].[2] Before we proceed to a discussion of the various models, it is useful to identify a general typology of economy–energy–environmental interactions and the relevant models. Viewing the multiplicity of the economic–environmental reactions in an I–O framework (Figure 5.1), it can be readily seen that Quadrant 1 at the upper left captures the scope of the traditional Leontief I–O model of interactions between various economic sectors. By contrast, Quadrant 4 is concerned entirely with the interactions in the environmental sector – among the different environmental media (air, water and land) and the different ecological sectors. The analytical processes of interest in Quadrant 4 are exemplified by Russell (1975), TRW (1971):

- Physical dispersion models
  (e.g. for bio-chemical oxygen
  demand or for suspended
  particulates) $\left.\right\}$ yield → Ambient concentrations
  of residuals
- Chemical reaction models
  (e.g. for photochemical smog)

- Biological systems models
  (e.g. for ecosystems in water) yield → Ambient concentrations of
  residuals and species populations

Quadrants (2) and (3) provide the links between economic and ecological processes. Quadrant (2) presents all the services provided by the environment to production and consumption agents. The analytical processes of interest pertain to the removal of energy and nonenergy resources from the environment to the economy, the provision of environmental amenity services, the environmental damages and the accrual of rents to various economic agents from these services. Quadrant (3) is concerned with the discharge of wastes from economic activities and their absorption into different media and various biological receptors of pollution in these media.

The various models proposed to describe the economic–energy–environmental interactions and relevant policy issues are in effect combinations of parts of the

---

[2] The Cumberland model is noteworthy as the first extension of the I–O framework in order to incorporate economic–environmental–interactions by including rows for environmental benefits and costs (though no clues for their estimations are provided). The Daly model is a conceptual framework to bring purely economic interactions, purely environmental interactions and interrelations between the economy and the environment into an I–O framework. Isard provides the broadest framework for organizing economic and ecological relationships. The Victor (1972) model is a rectangular commodity–industry I–O model that has been elaborated to include ecological commodities. The Wilen (1973) model is an extension of the Ayres–Kneese materials balance notions into the ecological system.

ECONOMIC SECTORS			ENVIRONMENTAL SECTORS	
Energy	Non Energy Production	Final Demand	Media	Bio Sectors

<table>
<tr><td rowspan="3">ECONOMY</td><td>Energy Sectors</td><td colspan="2">Energy Flows</td><td colspan="2">Emissions and Assimilation of Wastes into media and biota</td></tr>
<tr><td>Non Energy</td><td colspan="2">I-O Model Interactions</td><td colspan="2"></td></tr>
<tr><td>Primary Inputs</td><td colspan="2" style="text-align:right">Quadrant 1</td><td colspan="2" style="text-align:right">Quadrant 3</td></tr>
<tr><td rowspan="4">ENVIRONMENT</td><td>Air</td><td colspan="2">All Services of Environment</td><td colspan="2">Physical Dispersion Models</td></tr>
<tr><td>water</td><td colspan="2">to Firms and Consumers</td><td colspan="2">Chemical Reaction Models</td></tr>
<tr><td>Land</td><td colspan="2">Amenity Services</td><td colspan="2">Biological Systems Models</td></tr>
<tr><td>Bio-Sectors</td><td colspan="2">Economic Rents from Environmental Services

Quadrant 2</td><td colspan="2" style="text-align:right">Quadrant 4</td></tr>
</table>

Figure 5.1. A Schematic view of economic–energy–environment interactions.

four quadrants. Four types of models can be recognized in terms of their analytical scope:

(1) *Regional economic–environmental model.* This is a large class of models that is concerned with the economic consequences of pollution abatemant and thus with the analytical agenda of Quadrants (1) and (2) and to a limited degree of Quadrant (3).

(2) *Models of regional environmental quality management.* These are comprehensive environmental policy models that are helpful in assessing and ranking a number of alternative options of managing environmental quality according to some economic criterion. Their analytical scope encompasses all 4 Quadrants of Figure 5.1 and have the following components:

(a) an economic model of production and consumption (Quad. 1);

(b) a model of residuals and emissions (Quad. 3);

(c) an environmental model that translates the temporal and spatial pattern of residual discharges into temporal and spatial states of natural environment (e.g. Gaussian plume type model of atmospheric dispersions of SO_2 and particulates or aquatic ecosystem models that estimate residual concentrations or population levels of biota) (Quad. 4);

(d) a model of the effects of such concentrations on receptors in terms of damage functions, control costs (Quad. 2); and

(e) an analytical component on management strategies that compares the benefits and costs associated with alternative environmental management strategies.

(3) *Regional energy policy models.* These models focus on a variety of economic consequences ensuing from changes (e.g. in prices or supply systems) in the national or regional energy systems in terms of

(a) changes in the energy sector itself;

(b) changes in the rest of the economy; and

(c) macroeconomic impacts.

(4) *Integrated regional models of economy, energy and environment* that link models of energy sector, models of the national–regional economy and models of environmental emissions in order to assess interrelated energy supply, environmental quality and economic policies.

5.1. Regional economic–environmental models

We describe here two models that are illustrative of the scope of this class of models that assess regional economic effects of environmental policies.

The first model is an extension of the input–output framework to incorporate pollution emissions and pollution abatement activities [Leontief (1970)]. Leontief introduces:

(a) an extra row (or rows) to indicate the flow of pollutants from the economy to the environment using pollution coefficients (a_{gi}). He ignores the materials balance principle in not considering the reverse flows of materials from the environment to the economy;[3]

(b) an antipollution industry (or industries) which with given quantities of inputs (a_{ig}) from other sectors in the economy can remove a technologically determined level of pollution (Table 5.1). The model, expanded in this manner, can be used to determine the level of activity of each sector in the economy including antipollution sectors, that is necessary for the production of a specific level of final demand.

Notation

$$A_{11} = [a_{ij}], \qquad A_{12} = [a_{ig}], \qquad A_{21} = [a_{gi}] \qquad A_{22} = [a_{gk}]$$

$$X_1 = \begin{bmatrix} x_1 \\ x_2 \\ \vdots \\ x_m \end{bmatrix} \qquad X_2 = \begin{bmatrix} x_{m+1} \\ x_{m+2} \\ \vdots \\ x_n \end{bmatrix}, \qquad Y_1 = \begin{bmatrix} y_1 \\ y_2 \\ \vdots \\ y_m \end{bmatrix}, \qquad Y_2 = \begin{bmatrix} y_{m+1} \\ y_{m+2} \\ \vdots \\ y_n \end{bmatrix}$$

[3] Victor (1972) has implemented for Canada a variety of rectangular commodity–industry I–O models that make explicit use of the principle of materials balance.

Table 5.1
The Leontief system including pollution-related activities.

	Production Sectors	Antipollution Industry	Final Demand	Totals
	1,2,3...............m	m+1.........n		
Production	1			
Sectors	2			
	3	a_{ii}	a_{ig}	
	⋮			
	m			
Pollutants	m+1			
	m+2	a_{gi}	a_{gk}	
	⋮			
	n			
Value Added				
Total Outlays				

where $i = 1, 2, 3, \ldots, m$ production sectors; and

g, $k = m + 1, m + 2, \ldots, g, \ldots, k, \ldots, n$ pollutants.

Then the Leontief physical I–O balance is given by:

$$\begin{bmatrix} X_1 \\ \overline{X_2} \end{bmatrix} = \begin{bmatrix} I - A_{11} & -A_{12} \\ \hline A_{21} & -I + A_{22} \end{bmatrix}^{-1} \begin{bmatrix} Y_1 \\ \overline{Y_2} \end{bmatrix}. \tag{5.1}$$

Leontief (1970) demonstrates how his model can be used to examine the price effects of alternative pollution abatement technologies and policies. In a later work Leontief and his associates (1976) extended this framework to an I–O model of the world divided into 15 regions. The model for each region is analogous to Table 5.1 Interregional economic flows are handled through a dummy region from and to which import and export coefficients are computed. No interregional flow of pollutants is considered in this study.

The second example of this model type is an econometric model of the open metropolitan economies of the U.S., that is designed to assess the economy-wide effects of air pollution control strategies [Lakshmanan and Lo (1972)]. It is a Keynesian type regional econometric model with over 211 equations organized into a production block, an income block, a labor market block and an energy use block and linked to a national input–output model.

A Cobb–Douglas production function, and investment equation, a capital stock identity and a wage equation make up the production block.

$$V_{ijt} = A_j N_{ijt}^{\alpha} K_{ijt}^{1-\alpha} \tag{5.2}$$

$$\pi_{ijt} = (1 - \alpha) V_{ijt} \tag{5.3}$$

$$I_{ijt} = f(\pi_{ijt}, K_{ijt-1}) \tag{5.4}$$

$$K_{ijt} = K_{ijt-1} + I_{ijt} - d_j K_{ijt} \tag{5.5}$$

$$W_{ijt} = f(W_{ijt-1}, U_{it}) \tag{5.6}$$

where i is the ith metropolitan region ($i = 1, 2, \ldots, i, \ldots, 91$) and j subscripts the manufacturing sector ($j = 1, 2, \ldots, 19$), t stands for the tth time period, V is value added, N is employment, K is capital stock, π is gross profit, I is investment, W is the average wage and U is regional unemployment, d is depreciation rate.

In the income block, the manufacturing activities are viewed as export base activities determining regional income along with regional consumption and local government expenditure – both of which are endogenized by simple formulations.

$$Y_{it} = f\left(\sum_j V_{ijt}, C_{it}, G_{it}\right) \tag{5.7}$$

$$C_{it} = f(Y_{it}, C_{it-1}) \tag{5.8}$$

$$G_{it} = f(T_{it}) \tag{5.9}$$

where Y is metropolitan personal income, C is regional consumer expenditures and G is local government revenues in the metropolis.

In the labor market, nonmanufacturing sectors are treated as a residual activity. A regional employment identity, an unemployment equation and a labor force supply equation comprise the labor market block.

$$\bar{N}_{it} = f\left(Y_{it} - \sum_j V_{ijt}\right) \tag{5.10}$$

$$N_{it} = \bar{N}_{it} + \sum_j N_{ijt} \tag{5.11}$$

$$U_{it} = \frac{L_{it} - N_{it}}{L_{it}} \tag{5.12}$$

$$L_{it} = f\left(U_{it}, P_{it}, \frac{\sum_j W_{ij} N_{ij}}{\sum_j N_{ij}}\right) \tag{5.13}$$

where $\bar{N}$ and N are nonmanufacturing employment and total employment, respectively, L is labor force, P is population.

The energy block (not detailed here) provides the demand for different fuels and electricity in the industrial and residential sectors.

A national I–O model (aggregated to 42 sectors) is introduced to serve the role of an external market for each metropolitan economy and to capture regional feedbacks. Under the assumption that the regional share of the national market by industry – or location quotient – is relatively stable in the short run, we have:

$$b_{ij} = \frac{X_{ij}}{X_j} \tag{5.14}$$

where b_{ij} is the regional market share or location quotient of the jth industry in the ith region, X is output

$$X = BX \tag{5.15}$$

where $X = [X_{ij}]$ is the regional share of demand for manufacturing products in the national market, $B = [b_{ij}]$ is the regional market share matrix and X is a vector of national demand by industry.

If a vector of final demand changes representing the net pollution benefits from pollution control is available the impacts of these benefits are captured by:

$$X = (I - A)^{-1} Y \tag{5.16}$$

and allocated to each metropolitan region by (5.15) above.

The model was used to assess the economic effects of three pollution control strategies differing in their incidence of costs among industries and consumers. The model simulates the consequences of pollution control costs – capital and operation – incurred by industries and regional electric utilities and benefits incurred from pollution control in terms of a variety of production, income, labor market and energy use indicators.

While this model provides empirical estimates of economic effects of pollution control policies, their utility is weakened by several deficiencies in the specification of the regional economic model. Some of these drawbacks have been overcome in recent improvements (e.g. specification of flexible production functional forms, more explicit ways of capturing interregional access to markets and raw materials, of modeling regional public expenditures, of modeling labor markets, of modeling energy demand by end use sector) in this class of regional economic models [Rose (1982), Ballard and Wendling (1979), Lakshmanan (1983), Issaev et al. (1982)].

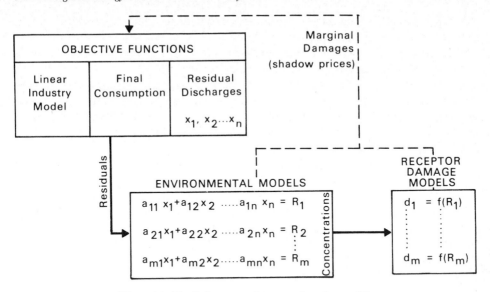

Figure 5.2. The Delaware environmental quality model.

5.2. Models of regional environmental quality management

As noted earlier, this class of models has economic and environmental components as well as a module for management decision criteria. The last component is usually in the form of objective functions that may be explicitly embedded in the framework of the model or may be exogenous to the model serving to guide the application of the model in complex multiobjective contexts. We present in this section an example for each of the two situations.

The Delaware Region model is the pioneering and best known of these economic and environmental models applied in a resource management context – i.e. in a conceptual framework aimed at developing information and tools which could be used for management [Russell and Spofford (1972), Kneese (1977), Thoss and Wiik (1974), Kohn (1970), Russell (1975)]. The main contribution of this model of the industrialized Delaware basin is the linking of a model of waste degeneration and reaeration for multiple points of discharge to an economic optimization model (Fig. 5.2).

While the quality of a body of water is affected by several variables, one of the most central is Dissolved Oxygen (DO). DO is affected by meteorological and hydrological variables and by the discharge of organic wastes and is often viewed as a surrogate measure of other quality variables. Assume m homogeneous segments characterizing the river basin and let C_i represent the improvement in water quality required to meet the DO target in segment i. The target vector C of

m elements can be obtained by changes of inputs to the waterbody in the m segments. Let there be other vectors X ($= x_1, x_2, \ldots, x_n$) where each vector is a vector of n residuals in each of m segments. These discharges are obtained from a linear economic model of production and consumption which permits choices among production processes, raw material inputs, residual recycling, etc., so that the quantity of discharges can be varied. In the feasible solutions of the programming problem, the vector X represents the waste discharges at various points in the river in order to meet the target vector C [Russell and Spofford (1972), Kneese (1974)].

The environmental models are essentially transformation functions converting a vector of residuals to a vector of ambient concentrations of DO. These functions are derived from Streeter–Phelps oxygen balance equations and are of the form:

$$AX = R \qquad (5.17)$$

where A is the matrix of transfer coefficients and R is a vector or DO concentrations under steady-state conditions. The model includes in addition to DO other degradable materials.

Recalling that C is a vector of target improvements, we have two restrictions on X, namely $AX \geq C$ and $X \geq 0$. If we define D as a row vector where $d_j =$ unit cost of X_j ($j = 1, 2, \ldots, n$) then the model problem is:

$$
\begin{aligned}
\text{minimize} \quad & d\,X \\
\text{subject to} \quad & AX \geq C \\
& X \geq 1
\end{aligned}
\qquad (5.18)
$$

This model was used (a) to analyze the total and incremental costs of achieving different levels of water quality, (b) to assess effluent charges – uniform and zone-specific and (c) to obtain a range of quantitative benefits of water recreation.

This pioneering model has several deficiencies. Among them is the limited range of technological options for water management (e.g. it did not consider the production function extensively) and the neglect of stochastic aspects of water quality. While some of these were addressed in the Potomac study (Kneese 1974) there is the troublesome issue of partial equilibrium description of the regional economy, in particular the lack of links with the national economy. It is in this area of national–regional links that the second model represents an interesting development [Hafkamp and Nijkamp (1983)].

The main contribution of the Hafkamp–Nijkamp model (1983) lies in its explicit consideration of the two way links between the national economic system and regional environmental quality system. Hafkamp and Nijkamp propose a triple layer model – a linked set comprising a national–regional economic model, a regional labor market model and an environmental model. The last component estimates regional environmental emissions and ambient concentrations of SO_x, NO_x and particulates. The noteworthy aspect of the model is the range of top-down (e.g. government sector, monetary sector) and bottom-up (e.g. those relating to consumption, prices, wages, investments) linkages between the national and regional economies.

The Hafkamp–Nijkamp model is a simulation model for analyzing the consequences of alternative policy options for the Netherlands. A multiple objective multidecision-maker problem to assess several goal variables (e.g. regional income, environmental quality and employment opportunities) can be solved. Several alternative measures to finance antipollution can be assessed.

5.3. *Regional energy policy models*

Two types of models for regional economic analysis of energy trends and policies exist.

The first type focuses on the regional differences in energy production and energy use consequent upon changes in energy prices or supply sources. Some of these models analyze the structure of energy flows taking into account the complex interdependencies between productions and final demand in different regions. A good example is the Beutel (1983) model which estimates the total energy content of goods.

In values units,

$$
E = B \quad (I - A)^{-1} \quad Y
$$

$$
= \begin{bmatrix} A_1 & A_2 \\ \hline 0 & 0 \end{bmatrix} \cdot \begin{bmatrix} I - \begin{matrix} A_1 & A_2 \\ \hline A_3 & A_4 \end{matrix} \end{bmatrix}^{-1} \cdot \begin{bmatrix} \hat{Y}_E \\ \hline Y_{NE} \end{bmatrix} \tag{5.19}
$$

where E is the energy content, and the A matrix of technical coefficients and Y matrix of final demand are subdivided into energy production and nonenergy production activities. Viewing input–output analysis as a special statement of a linear programming model, the traditional quantity and price models of $I-1$ analysis are transferred into a linear optimization model with a substantial gain in information for users. Beutel's objective is to analyze the structural differences in energy production and use in France, West Germany, Italy and Denmark.

Other models of the same type are concerned with the patterns of fuel and factor substitution in production, consequent on energy price changes. Building on recent developments in duality theory and flexible production functional forms [as illustrated in the work of Hudson and Jorgenson (1974) and Berndt and

Wood (1975)] there have been analyses of regional patterns of fuel and factor substitution in the Netherlands and U.S. [Lesuis et al. (1981), Lakshmanan (1983), Lakshmanan et al. 1984)]. The latter models using translog cost functions show the variations in the patterns of factor and fuel substitution among different sectors and regional locations in U.S.

The second type of economic analysis is exemplified by the analysis of energy supply sector responses to prices, regulations, tariffs or to new technologies. An early example of this is the intermediate-term energy sector model such as the U.S. Project Independence Evaluation System (PIES) [Hogan (1975)]. Comprising an energy demand model, a collection of supply models, and an integrating model, PIES projects energy prices and quantities. PIES can handle a variety of regulatory functions in the energy sector, and estimates the consequences of various policies such as import tariffs, import quotas, conservation measures, etc.

The Brookhaven energy system model (BESOM) focuses on the technical, characteristics of energy conversion, delivery, and utilization processes that comprise the total energy system [Hoffman (1972), Kydes et al. (1979)]. It is structured around a reference energy system (RES) that displays the flow of energy from a resource to the end-use point. The specialized format of RES indicates the detailed technological structure of the energy system, together with coefficients to characterize technical efficiency and emissions from the various energy supply processes. BESOM can be used in either the optimization or simulation mode [Kydes et al. (1979)]. In the former, when constraints on resource availability, market penetration of various technologies, and electricity generating capacity are specified, BESOM calculates the optimal supply–demand configuration. In the simulation mode, the model is constrained so as to duplicate desired supply–demand systems and to estimate the corresponding total system costs and environmental impacts. BESOM has been used to assess the contribution of clean, renewable resources (e.g. solar or wind power) and their related impacts on costs, social concerns, etc.

The major limitation of all the above three classes of models is their focus on one or two policy issues. Such individual issues may pertain either to economy–environment links, economy–energy growth linkages or to energy supply sector responses to prices or regulations, or technology or environmental assessment. Yet a full assessment of major policy choices in the economic, energy and environmental areas (e.g. the scale, composition, location and timing of large-scale energy developments) has broader scope. It requires at the same time an understanding of all of the above changes in the energy sector (in terms of demand–supply and technological process analyses), changes in regional and national production and consumption structures, as well as the environmental impacts of energy projects. In order to respond to such comprehensive information needs a few such models have been developed in the last few years by linking many of the models described above.

5.4. Integrated models for economic–environmental–energy assessment

These models appear to have taken the form of drawing models from different analytical traditions (e.g. energy system modeling, national and multiregional modeling, local public finance modeling, urban housing and infrastructure modeling), and linking them in the form of integrated impact models. These models share some common features: they all have some version of a macroeconomic model, and they represent, to varying degrees, production and consumption; they attempt multiregional analyses; they contain a reference energy supply system and depict energy technologies, demands, and prices, and finally, there are clear linkages between the energy sector, the rest of the economy and the environment.

We review here two such integrated models identifying their strengths, their degrees of analytical coverage and their shortcomings.

The Strategic Environmental Assessment System (SEAS) model for the U.S. was initially developed as an economy–environment model to provide a systematic assessment of emissions and the abatement costs associated with economic growth and various pollution policies [Lakshmanan and Krishnamurthi (1973)], and later broadened to include specification of energy supply, demand, and investment components [House (1977), Lakshmanan and Ratick (1977, 1981), Watson (1981)]. The component modules of SEAS are interrelated within and between the three substantive areas (of the economy, environment and energy) by functional relationships and data matrices to form a large, medium-term (15–21 years) model (Figure 5.3).

The core model of SEAS is a 211-sector dynamic I-1 forecasting model called INFORUM (interindustry forecasting model of the University of Maryland), and developed by Clopper Almon. It endogenizes the major final demand sectors by sophisticated econometric modeling and generates annual forecasts of sectoral activity in the context of some macroeconomic assumptions and final demand. Given the environmental focus of SEAS, the 211 sectors were disaggregated into many more product and technological subsectors (expressed in physical terms) in the INSIDE module, in order to delineate different polluting emissions. The ABATE module computes the capital and operation costs of pollution abatement in any one year, for feedback into INFORUM in order to obtain the relevant economic impacts for the next year.

The energy subsystem incorporates the reference energy system in the energy system network simulator (ESNS), three end-use energy demand models, and an energy investment model. The investment requirements corresponding to the energy supply technologies in the ESNS feed back to the energy demand modules and INFORUM.

The environmental modules estimate emission levels by type of pollutant and by type of technology from all production and consumption processes. REGION converts in a "top-down" fashion national economic and pollution forecasts into

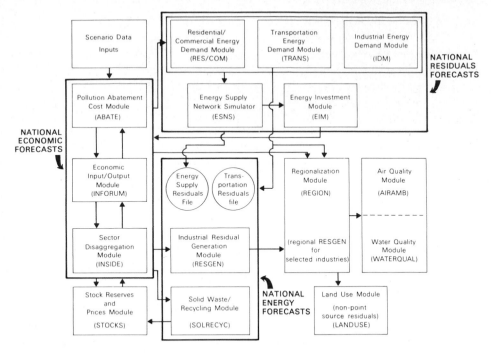

Figure 5.3. The SEAS model system.

a variety of geographical areas – states, metropolitan areas, and spatial units relevant to air and water quality control.

SEAS provides an elaborate set of conditional forecasts of the effects of alternative energy and environmental strategies. However, the regional analysis – given its simple "top-down" allocations of national totals – is rather primitive.

There is an elaborate regional–national modeling system in Sweden. It has several components–macoeconomic, multiregional, regional energy demand and supply – that permit regional–national and, to some degree, international interactions, as well as traditional linkages between the energy sector and the national economy [Johansson and Snickars (1985), Lakshmanan (1985b)].

The macroeconomic model is Bergman's computable general equilibrium model for an open economy which generates estimates of sectoral levels of employment, production, investment, energy uses, etc. [Bergman (1981)].

The multiregional model is MORSE, which has eight regions and nine sectors [Lundqvist (1981)]. This hybrid model uses a bottom-up approach with regard to consumption and most production sectors and a top-down approach for energy consumption, capital formation, and international trade. A variety of models drawn from analyses of housing and employment, building structures, and land-use planning help to define the future spatial distribution of energy demand. The system has been used to plan for the wide range of energy impacts in the Stockholm metropolitan region, and some models were drawn from earlier Stockholm planning studies. The energy supply system is detailed by adapting an energy network model (MESSAGE) to the Stockholm region. [For a detailed appraisal of the Swedish model in the context of both traditional and emerging regional planning concerns, see Bolton (1985a).]

5.5. *Future directions for economic–environmental–energy analysis*

While such models represent a beginning in integrated modeling, a number of key analytical issues in economic impact analyses remain unresolved: distributional issues; dynamic adjustment processes; regional, national, and international linkages; and the modeler–decision maker interface. [This section is based on Lakshmanan (1985a).]

A number of distributional issues arise when there is an increase in energy supply or fuel switching or a new environmental standard or charge in a region. For instance, the development of an energy resource frontier would lead to an uneven distribution of benefits and costs – depending on whether one owned resource assets, or whether older residents on fixed incomes get caught in boom town expansion, or whether there is curtailment of public services or labor dislocations. Indeed, it could be argued that much of the conflict between "old" and "new" groups in "boom towns" results from a failure to take these distributional outcomes into account and to incorporate them in politically responsive planning processes. As we noted in Section 4, both modeling and planning must take account of both intraregional and interregional distribution changes, and must take account of complications for both raised by absentee ownership.

In the case of a large-scale fuel switching and development of new energy forms in a metropolitan (e.g. Stockholm) market, the interactions between energy supply options and demand densities will generate energy price responses whose effects on different economic groups may well be uneven. It is therefore important to model the income distributional effects of these energy developments at the local and regional levels. Most multiregional models (including MORSE or the REGION module of SEAS) do not possess the capability, and could build upon the recent microsimulation modeling tradition [Orcutt et al. (1976)] for this purpose.[4]

In addition, the distribution of adjustment costs in an important concern [Bolton (1985)]. Like the energy market changes we discussed in Section 4,

---

[4] The MATH (Microanalytical transfer of households) and CHRDS (Comprehensive human resource data systems) models in the U.S. Department of Energy consider such distributional outcomes.

policies to improve energy supply, and environmental quality initiate a variety of adjustment processes – short term, medium term and long term. These responses will clearly differ markedly with industrial sector, type of household, and public agency. The various economic, behavioral, and technological relations incorporated in regional and national economic models will vary for each dynamic adjustment process. Fixed model parameters in the short term become variables in longer adjustment periods (e.g. if gasoline prices climb steeply, in the short term consumers will take a car type as given and will reduce their driving distances; over a 3–4 year period, they will change their capital stock by buying more fuel-efficient cars). Since economic, social, technological and urban development phenomena in the real world embody such dynamic adjustment processes, satisfactory economic models must incorporate them for the time periods over which they are believed to be appropriate; otherwise conditional or policy analysis predictions made from the model will be grossly inaccurate. Important things happen during the adjustment process, so a comparative static model is not adequate.

Econometric and I–O models obtained by fitting historical data assume that the estimated parameters are constant. Mathematical programming, based on engineering estimates of processes, can incorporate technological processes at future points in time, but they do not easily make the transition from the present to the future. Some economic models distinguish between short- and long-term price elasticities, while others let I–O coefficients vary with relative prices [Hudson and Jorgenson (1974)]. While these developments are relevant, they are only a partial treatment of structural change processes to which energy prices or large-scale energy developments are likely to lead in the form of changing technological and industrial mixes, and the location of population and production.

Some recent modeling efforts have begun to address this problem. The ideas of Berndt et al. (1979) in developing dynamic adjustment models of industrial demand have been applied at the regional level [Lakshmanan (1982), Anderson and Lakshmanan (1983)] and could be easily incorporated into regional–national models. Another example is the specification of adjustment processes via vintage modeling techniques as in MACROINVEST [Persson and Johansson (1982)]. Thus there is a potential for better specification of economic adjustment processes than is currently the case at the national and multiregional levels.

At the intraregional level, knowledge of the dynamics (interaction of variables and speed of adjustment) in models of employment, housing, and land use (whether in boom towns or the Stockholm region) is primitive. Generally, the interactions of variables are myopic (with current decisions entirely dependent on the outcomes of current parameter values) and adjustments are close to instantaneous. At the local level, dynamic processes of stock adjustment have not yet been analytically explored. Housing stock turns over slowly; productive and human capital much faster, leading to stock mismatches and disequilibria, with potential impacts on the quality of the urban environment. Analytical improvements in this area are a research frontier in urban and metropolitan modeling.

Most of the models dealing with the economy, energy processes, or the urban environment are derived from a neoclassical framework that does not pay much attention to technological innovation, yet dynamic processes such as innovation, innovation diffusion, and capital investment are obviously part of the adjustments to energy-related developments. Behavior-oriented models of households and firms that depict information generation, flows, communications and processing are needed, and could lay the foundation for the understanding necessary to identify dynamic adjustment processes in the various components of a large-scale energy system [Nelson and Winter (1983)].

The need for the regional–national interactive linkages is a staple of contemporary multiregional modeling literature [Bolton (1982b)]. The key point is that economic impact models should build in such two-way regional–national linkages. The multiregional, multisectoral model MORSE used in the Swedish case study provides an example of such desired regional–national linkages.

A second major component of model linkages relates to the international dimension. Major developments in conservation and domestic energy production will affect not only the prosperity of oil exporters such as Mexico or Venezuela, but also (through their effects on world oil prices) the economies of affluent (e.g. Sweden) and poor (e.g. India) nations. Thus large-scale import reductions in a large consumer such as the U.S. have a "public good" character that requires consideration by others. While the Bergman model captures some of these relationships between the Swedish economy and the rest of the world, this is as yet a poorly explored field.

In spite of the widely touted contribution that economic modeling can make to energy and environment decision making, the interface between the producers and users of models has been a bothersome barrier to its success. Differences in knowledge, functional roles, and time scales of operation between modelers and decision modelers and decision makers account for this barrier.

Policy issues in large-scale energy developments tend to be complex, ill-structured, and amorphous. Model systems are rather monolithic in the sense that the overall objective function determines optimality, while the real world has pluralistic decision structures, is interactive, and full of conflicts. These models thus tend to be useful in centralized decision contexts (as in typical operations research contexts). More often, in the public arena, economic modeling is inadequate in that it does not yet provide a method for strategic analysis that allows, in a context of advisory procedures and bargaining, an orderly approach to balancing model results and judgment.

What is needed is greater clarification of the institutional context of large modeling systems [Russell et al. (1974)], fresh developments in interactive multilevel modeling [Despontin et al. (1983)] and in decision analysis that sharpen the process of mutual understanding and learning among modelers and decision makers.

References

Advisory Commission on Intergovernmental Relations (1985) 1982 *Tax capacity of the fifty states*. Washington, D.C.: The Commission.

Anderson, F. R., A. V. Kneese, R. D. Reed, R. B. Stevenson and S. Taylor (1977) *Environmental improvement through economic incentives*. Baltimore: The Johns Hopkins University Press.

Anderson, William and T. R. Lakshmanan (1983) *A model of regional dynamic adjustment in U.S. manufacturing*. Boston University, Department of Geography Working Paper.

Atkinson, S. E. and D. H. Lewis (1974) 'A cost effectiveness analysis of alternative air quality control strategy', *Journal of Environmental Economics and Management*, 1:237–251.

Ayres, R. V. and Allen V. Kneese (1969) 'Production consumption and externalities', *The American Economic Review*, LIX:282–297.

Ballard, K. P. and R. M. Wendling (1979) *Projection and multiregional and national economic impacts of energy development*. Paper presented at the Southern Regional Science Association, Nashville, Tennessee.

Barkley, Paul (1982) 'The impacts of rising energy prices in rural areas', in: Hans Landsberg, ed., *High energy costs*, 266–287.

Baumol, William J. and Wallace E. Oates (1975) *The theory of environmental policy*. Englewood Cliffs, N.J.: Prentice-Hall.

Baumol, William J. (1975) 'Environmental protection and income distribution', in: Harold Hochman and George Peterson, eds., *Redistribution through public choice*. New York: Columbia University Press.

Beebout, Harold et al. (1982) 'The distribution of household energy expenditures and the impact of high prices', in: Hans Landsberg, ed., *High energy costs*, 1–36.

Bender, Susan, Joseph P. Kalt and Henry Lee (1984) 'The regional income effects of natural gas decontrol: the Northwest vs. the rest of the U.S.', Discussion Paper 1134, Harvard Institute of Economic Research, Harvard University, Cambridge, MA, January, mimeo.

Bergman, L. (1981) 'The impact of nuclear power discontinuation in Sweden', *Regional Science and Urban Economics*, 11:269–286.

Berndt, E. R. and David Wood (1975) 'Technology, prices and the derived demand for energy', *Review of Economics and Statistics*, 57(3):259–268.

Berndt, E. R., M. A. Fuss and L. Waverman (1979) *Dynamic adjustment models of industrial demand*. Palo Alto: Electric Power Research Institute.

Beutel, Jorg (1983) 'Interregional analysis of energy flows', *Papers of the Regional Science Association*, 53:83–114.

Boadway, Robin and Frank Flatters (1983) 'Efficiency, equity and the allocation of resource rents', in: Charles McLure Jr. and Peter Mieszkowski, *Fiscal federalism and the taxation of natural resources*, 99–124.

Bolton, Roger (1982a) 'An expanded portfolio analysis of regional diversification.' Paper read at meeting of Regional Science Association, Pittsburgh, Pennsylvania, November. Williams College, Department of Economics, Research Paper No. RP-52, December.

Bolton, Roger (1982b) 'The development of multiregional economic modeling in North America: multiregional models in transition for economies in transition', in: Boris Issaev et al., *Multiregional economic modeling: practice and prospect*. Amsterdam: North-Holland, 157–170.

Bolton, Roger (1984) 'Strategic planning by regions versus strategic planning by firms and households', Paper read at International Institute for Applied Systems Analysis's Workshop on Strategic Regional Policy, Warsaw, December.

Bolton, Roger (1985a) 'The Swedish case study,' in T. R. Lakshmanan and B. Johannson, eds., *Large-scale energy projects: assessment of regional consequences*. Amsterdam: North-Holland, 163–173.

Bolton, Roger (1985b) 'Three mysteries about Henry George', in: Stephen R. Lewis, Jr., ed., *Henry George and contemporary economic development*. Williamstown, MA: Williams College, 7–24.

Borcherding, Thomas E. (1984) 'Natural resources and transgenerational equity', unpublished working paper, Claremont Graduate School, Claremont, California.

Campbell, Harry F., W. D. Gainer and Anthony Scott (1976) 'Resource rent: how much and for whom?', in: Anthony Scott, ed., *Natural resource revenues: a test of federalism*, 118–136.

Church, Albert M. (1981) *Taxation of nonrenewable resources*. Lexington, Mass.: Lexington Books, D.C. Heath.

Cooper, Mark (1982) 'Conceptualizing and measuring the burden of high energy prices', in: Hans Landsberg, ed., *High energy costs*, 43–59.

Courchene, Thomas J. (1976) 'Equalization payment and energy royalties', in: Anthony Scott, ed., *Natural resource revenues: a test of federalism*, 73–117.

Crandall, Robert W. (1983) 'Pollution, 1983, environmentalists, and the coal lobby', in Roger G. Noll and Bruce Owen, eds., *The political economy of deregulation: interest groups in the regulatory process*. Washington: American Enterprise Institute for Public Policy Research, 84–96.

Cuciti, Peggy, Harvey Galper and Robert Lucke (1983) 'State energy revenues', in Charles McLure Jr. and Peter Mieszkowski, ed., *Fiscal federalism and the taxation of natural resources*, 11–61.

Cumberland, J. H. (1966) 'A regional inter-industry model for analysis of development objectives', *Regional Science Association Papers*, 17:65–95.

Daly, H. E. (1968) 'On economics as a life science', *The Journal of Political Economy*, 76:392–418.

Davis, Otto and A. Whinston (1965) 'Welfare economics and the theory of the second best', *Review of Economic Studies*, 32, January.

Deaton, Brady (1982) 'Assessing the impacts of high energy costs on small rural communities: discussion', in: Hans Landsberg, ed., *High energy costs*, 288–292.

Despontin, M., P. Nijkamp and J. Spronk (1983) *Macro-economic planning with conflicting goals*. Berlin: Springer.

Devarajan, Shantayanan and Anthony Fisher (1981) "Hotelling's 'Economics of exhaustible resources': fifty years later", *Journal of Economic Literature*, XIX, 1:65–73.

Dorfman, Nancy (1973) 'Who bears the cost of pollution control?: the impact on the distribution of income of financing federally required pollution control', Report prepared for the Council on Environmental Quality, Washington, processed.

Dorfman, Nancy, assisted by Arthur Snow (1975) 'Who will pay for pollution control – the distribution by income of the burden of the national environmental protection program, 1972–1981', *National Tax Journal*, 28:111–115.

Downs, Anthony and Katherine L. Bradbury, eds., *Energy costs, urban development, and housing*. Washington, D.C.: Brookings Institution.

Fisher, Anthony (1981) *Resource and environmental economics*. Cambridge, U.K.: Cambridge University Press.

Forsund, Finn R. and Steinar Strom (1974) 'Industrial structure, growth and residual flows', in J. Rothenberg and I. G. Heggie, eds., *The management of water quality and the environment*. London: The MacMillan Press, 21–69.

Freeman, A. Myrick, III (1972) 'The distribution of the environment', in Allen V. Kneese and Blair T. Bower, eds., *Environmental quality analysis: theory and method in the social sciences*. Baltimore: Johns Hopkins University Press.

Freeman, A. Myrick, III (1977) 'The incidence of the costs of controlling automotive air pollution', in: F. Thomas Juster, ed., *The distribution of economic well-being*. Ballinger, for the National Bureau of Economic Research, Cambridge, Mass.:163–193.

Freeman, A. Myrick, III, Robert H. Haveman and Allen V. Kneese, *The economics of environmental quality*. New York: John Wiley and Sons.

Frey, Rene L. (1979) 'Interregional welfare comparisons and environmental policy', in: H. Siebert, I. Walter and K. Zimmerman, eds., *Regional environmental policy*. New York: New York University Press, 97–118.

Gianessi, Leonard P., Henry M. Peskin and Edward Wolff (1977) 'The distributional implications of national air pollution damage estimates', in: F. Thomas Juster, ed., *The distribution of economic well being*. Cambridge, Mass.: Ballinger (for the National Bureau of Economic Research).

Hafkamp, Wim and Peter Nijkamp (1981) 'An integrated interregional model for pollution control', in: T. R. Lakshmanan and Peter Nijkamp, eds., *Economic–environmental–energy interactions: modeling and policy*. Boston: Martinus Nijhoff, 149–171.

Hafkamp, W. and Peter Nijkamp (1983) 'National-regional interdependencies in integrated economic-environmental energy models', in: T. R. Lakshmanan and Peter Nijkamp, eds., *Systems and models for energy and environmental analysis*. London: Gower Publishing, 71–79.

Harrison, David and Daniel Rubinfeld (1978) 'Housing values and the willingness to pay for clean air', *Journal of Environmental Economics and Management*, 5:81–112.

Helliwell, John F (1981) 'Using Canadian oil and gas revenues in the 1981s: provincial and federal perspectives', in: Terry Barker and Vladimir Brailovsky, eds., *Oil or industry?* New York: Academic Press, 45–71.

Hoffman, K. C. (1972) 'A unified planning framework for energy system planning', Ph.D. thesis, Polytechnic Institute of Brooklyn, New York.

Hogan, W. W. (1975) 'Energy models for project independence', *Computer and Operations Research*, 2, 251–271.

House, Peter (1977) *Trading off environment, economics and energy*. Lexington, Mass.: D.C. Heath.

Hudson, E. A. and D. W. Jorgenson (1974) 'U.S. energy policy and economic growth 1975–2111', *Bell Journal of Economics and Management Science*: 461–514.

Isard, Walter (1969) 'Some notes on the linkage of the ecologic and economic systems', paper delivered to the Regional Science Landscape Analysis Project, March 27, Dept. of Landscape Architecture, Harvard University.

Issaev, B., Peter Nijkamp, P. Rietveld and F. Snickars, eds. (1982) *Practice and prospects for multiregional modeling*. Amsterdam: North-Holland.

Johansson, B. and F. Snickars (1985) 'The Swedish case study', in: T. R. Lakshmanan and Borje Johansson, eds., *Large-scale energy projects: assessment of regional consequences*. Amsterdam: North-Holland.

Kalt, Joseph P. (1984) 'The political economy of coal regulation: the power of the underground coal industry', Discussion Paper 1147, Harvard Institute of Economic Research, Harvard University, Cambridge, Mass., March (mimeo).

Klaassen, Leo H. (1976) 'Energy, environment, and regional development', in: M. Chatterjee and P. V. Rompuy, eds., *Environment, regional science and interregional modeling*. Berlin: Springer-Verlag.

Kneese, A. V. (1977) *Economics and the environment*. Harmondsworth: Penquin.

Kneese, Allen V., R. U. Ayres and Ralph C. D'Arge (1970) *Economics and the environment: a materials balance approach*. Washington, D.C.: Resources for the future.

Kneese, Allen V. and Michael Williams (1979) 'Environmental aspects of resources policy in a regional setting', in: H. Siebert, Ingo Walter and Klaus Zimmermann, eds., *Regional environmental policy*. New York: New York University Press, 187–216.

Kohn, R. E. (1970) 'A linear programming model for air pollution control: a pilot study of St. Louis', *Journal of the Air Pollution Control Association*, 20, 78–82.

Kydes, A. S. et al. (1979) *The Brookhaven TESOM BNL 21223*. Upton, New York: Brookhaven National Laboratory.

Lakshmanan, T. R. (1981) 'Regional growth and energy determinants: implications for the future', *Energy Journal*, April.

Lakshmanan, T. R. (1982) 'Integrated regional modeling for the USA', in: B. Issaev et al., eds., *Multiregional economic modeling: practice and prospects*. Amsterdam: North-Holland, 171–188.

Lakshmanan, T. R. (1983) 'A multiregional model of the economy, environment and energy demand in U.S.', *Economic Geography*, July.

Lakshmanan, T. R. (1985a) 'National and regional models for economic assessment of energy projects', in: T. R. Lakshmanan and B. Johansson, eds., *The regional consequence of large energy projects*. Amsterdam: North-Holland, Chapter 6.

Lakshmanan, T. R. (1985b) 'National and regional models for economic assessment of energy projects', in: T. R. Lakshmanan and Borje Johansson, eds., *The regional consequences of large energy projects*. Amsterdam: North-Holland.

Lakshmanan, T. R., W. Anderson and M. Jourabchi (1984) 'Patterns of fuel and factor substitutes in U.S. manufacturing', *Regional Science and Urban Economics*, August.

Lakshmanan, T. R. and Fu Chen Lo (1972) 'A regional economic model for the assessment of effects of air pollution abatement', *Environment and planning*, 4:73–99.

Lakshmanan, T. R. and S. Krishnamurthi, eds. (1973) *The SEAS test model*. Washington, D. C.: Environmental Protection Agency.

Lakshmanan, T. R. and Samuel Ratick (1977) 'The economic and environmental effects of energy development scenarios', Paper presented at the Seminar on Urban Development, Northwestern University, Evanston, May (mimeo).

Lakshmanan, T. R. and Samuel Ratick (1981) 'integrated models for economic–energy–environmental impact analysis', in: T. R. Lakshmanan and Peter Nijkamp, eds., *Economic–environmental–energy interaction: modeling and policy analysis*. Boston: Martinus Nijhoff, 7–39.

Landsberg, Hans H., ed. (1982) *High energy costs: assessing the burden*. Washington, D.C.: Resources for the Future, Inc.

Leontief, W. (1970) 'Environmental repercussions and the economic structure: an input–output approach', *Review of Economics and Statistics*, LII:262–271.

Leontief, W. et al. (1976) *The future of the world economy*. Oxford: Oxford University Press.

Lesuis, P. J. J., F. Muller and Peter Nijkamp (1981) 'Operational methods for strategic environmental and energy policies', in: T. R. Lakshmanan and Peter Nijkamp, eds., *Economic–environmental–energy interactions: modeling and policy analysis*. Boston: Martinus Nijhoff, 41–73

Lundquist, Lars (1981) 'A dynamic multiregional input–output model for analyzing regional development, employment and energy use', Paper presented at the European Regional Science Congress, Munich.

McLure, Charles E., Jr. (1983) 'Tax exporting and the commerce clause', in: Charles E. McLure Jr. and Peter Mieszkowski, eds., *Fiscal federalism and the taxation of natural resources*, 169–192.

McLure, Charles E., Jr. and Peter Mieszkowski, eds., (1983) *Fiscal federalism and the taxation of natural resources*. Lexington, Mass.: Lexington Books, D.C. Heath.

Melvin, James R. and David T. Scheffman (1983) *An economic analysis of the impact of oil prices on urban structure*. Toronto: University of Toronto Press (for the Ontario Economic Council).

Miernyk, William (1982) 'The differential effects of rising prices on regional incomes and employment', in: Hans Landsberg, ed., *High energy costs*, 297–331.

Miernyk, William H. (1984) 'Energy and regional development', in: A. Downs and K. L. Bradbury, eds., *Energy costs, urban development, and housing*, 226–286.

Miernyk, William H., Frank Giarratani and Charles F. Socher (1978) *Regional impacts of rising energy prices*. Cambridge, Mass.: Ballinger.

Mieszkowski, Peter and Eric Toder (1983) 'Taxation of energy resources', in: Charles E. McLure, Jr. and Peter Mieszkowski, eds., *Fiscal federalism and the taxation of natural resources*, 75–92.

Musgrave, Richard A. (1959) *The theory of public finance*. New York: McGraw-Hill.

Muth, Richard F. (1984) 'Energy prices and urban decentralization', in: A. Downs and K. L. Bradbury, eds., *Energy costs, urban development, and housing*, 85–119.

Nelson, Richard and Sidney Winter (1983) *An evolutionary theory of economic change*. Cambridge, Mass.: Harvard University Press.

Nijkamp, Peter (1977) *Theory and application of environmental economics*. Amsterdam: North-Holland.

Nordhaus, William D. (1973) 'The allocation of energy resources', *Brookings Papers on Economic Activity*, 3:529–571.

Norton, G. A. and J. W. Parlowe (1972) 'The economic philosophy of pollution: a critique', *Environment and Planning*, 4:3–11.

Orcutt, F. J. et al. (1976) *Policy exploration through micro-analytical simulation*. Washington, D.C.: The Urban Institute.

Persson, Hakan and Bjore Johansson (1982) *A dynamic multisectoral model with endogenous formation of capacities and equilibrium prices: an application to the Swedish economy*, Laxenburg, Austria: International Institute for Applied Systems Analysis, 82–89.

Rose, Adam (1982) 'Modeling the macroeconomic impact of air pollution abatement', Research Institute, West Virginia University Working Paper No. 5, March.

Rothenberg, Jerome (1979) 'On regional differentiation of environmental policy', in: H. Siebert, I. Walter and K. Zimmerman, eds., *Regional Environmental Policy*. New York: New York University Press, 109–117.

Russell, Clifford S., ed. (1975) 'Ecological modeling', working paper, Resources for the Future, Washington, D.C., July.

Russell, Clifford S. and W. O. Spofford Jr. (1972) 'A quantitative framework for residuals management decisions', in: Allen V. Kneese and Blair T. Bower, eds., *Environmental quality analysis: theory and method in the social sciences*. Baltimore: The Johns Hopkins University Press, Chapter 4.

Russell, Clifford S., Walter O. Spofford, Jr. and Edwin Haefele (1974) 'The management of the quality of the environment', in: J. Rothenberg and I. G. Heggie, eds., *The management of water quality and the environment*. London: MacMillan Ltd., 224–272.

Schmenner, Roger W. (1984) 'Energy and the location of industry', in: A. Downs and K. L. Bradbury, eds., *Energy costs, urban development, and housing*, 188–225.

Scott, Anthony, ed. (1976a) *Natural resource revenues: a test of federalism*. Vancouver: University of British Columbia Press.

Scott, Anthony (1976b) 'Who should get natural resource revenues?', in: Anthony Scott, ed., *Natural resource revenues: a test of federalism*, 1–51.

Small, Kenneth (1982) 'Energy prices and real income distribution: the urban sector', in: Hans Landsberg, ed., *High energy costs*, 226–251.

Spofford, Walter O. (1975) 'Ecological modeling in a resource management framework: an introduction', in: Clifford S. Russell, ed., Ecological modeling, working paper, Resources for the Future, Washington, D.C., July, 13–48.

Thoss, Rainer and Kjell Wiik (1974) 'A linear decision model for the management of water quality in the Ruhr', in: J. Rothenberg and I. G. Heggie, eds., *The management of water quality and the environment*. London: MacMillan, 104–133.

Tietenberg, Thomas H. (1979) 'On the efficient spatial allocation of air pollution control responsibility', in: H. Siebert, I. Walter and K. Zimmermann, eds., *Regional environment policy*. New York: New York University Press, 79–93.

Tolley, George (1975) 'The resource allocation effects of environmental policies', in: Edwins S. Mills, ed., *Economic analysis of environmental problems*. New York: National Bureau of Economic Research, 133–163.

TRW, Inc. (1971) *Air quality implementation planning program*. Washington, D.C.: Environmental Protection Agency, Vols. 1 and 2.

Victor, Peter A. (1972) *Pollution, economy and environment*. London: George Allen and Unwin Ltd.

Watson, William D. Jr. (1981) 'Costs and benefits of water pollution control', in: T. R. Lakshmanan and Peter Nijkamp, eds., *Economic–environmental–energy interactions*. Boston: Martinus Nijhoff, 74–116.

Wilen, J. E. (1973) 'A model of economic system-ecosystem interaction', *Environment and Planning*, 5:419–421.

Zupan, Jeffrey M. (1973) *The distribution of air quality in the New York region*. Baltimore, Johns Hopkins University Press.

Chapter 15

INNOVATION AND CHANGES IN REGIONAL STRUCTURE*

E. J. MALECKI and P. VARAIYA

1. Introduction

Innovation or technological change is a principal source of change in the economic structure of regions and nations.[1] Although innovation has been studied as a critical variable in the production and management of firms and nations, technology has remained for the most part a "black box" within economic research [Rosenberg (1982)]. See Stubbs and Metcalfe (1980) for a comprehensive bibliography of the economies of technical change, and Malecki (1983) for a survey of the regional economic research. Within regional economics, theoretical and empirical research have diverged in recent years as much empirical work has emphasized policy concerns relating to labor and regional development.

Section 2 reviews the theoretical and model-based research on this topic, and emphasizes attempts to explain regional differences in productivity. Section 3 suggests that labor inputs are considerably more heterogeneous and variable than traditionally considered. Section 4 surveys the wide range of empirical studies that have contributed to our knowledge of the effects of technology on regional structure and change. In Section 5, some effects of technology on regional development are outlined. The organization of multiregional firms and their use of technology as an explicit strategic variable adds further complication to conventional theoretical treatments of urban and regional change. This review of the available empirical evidence on these topics focuses primarily on experience in the USA and Western Europe. Section 6 presents some comparisons between firms and regions in the context of innovation.

*The assistance of research grants from the U.S. National Science Foundation is appreciated.

[1] The concept of "region" in this chapter refers chiefly to a separately defined unit of space, usually an area within a national economy. Regions differ from each other in the node or dominant city around which each is centered, as well as in their historical concentration of some resource or factor of production that consequently evolved into specialization in a certain type of industry (e.g. steel) or a type of activity (e.g. R & D). See Richardson (1978a, pp. 17–29) and Hekman and Strong (1981).

Handbook of Regional and Urban Economics, Volume I, Edited by P. Nijkamp
©Elsevier Science Publishers BV, 1986

2. Regional growth and the role of technology

The study of technology in regional economic growth has grown directly from questions concerning national economic growth. The aggregate production function dominates the description of regional economic structure, toward which several streams of research have been directed. In this section, we review recent developments that build upon the factors of production and broaden their interpretation for changes in regional structure.

2.1. Technology as a residual

At the level of the national economy, a problem was posed by output growth that exceeded what could be expected from growth in capital stock and growth in labor service inputs. This question was addressed in neoclassical economics by introducing a new "factor", namely technological progress [Solow (1957)]. It was incorporated in the conventional Cobb–Douglas two-factor (capital and labor) production function as

$$Y = e^a K^b L^c. \tag{2.1}$$

Taking logarithmic derivatives and using lower case letters to denote the logarithms of the various quantities gives

$$y = a + bk + cl. \tag{2.2}$$

Using data for y, k, and l, one obtains estimates for the unknown parameter a; alternatively, a priori values of b and c are imposed and a is calculated directly as a residual. This is interpreted as the amount of growth rate attributable to "technical progress". Observe that technical progress measured this way is a residual. It is simply the growth rate that cannot be attributed to growth in capital and labor. Regional growth rate differences will then be attributable to differences in regional rates of technical progress. However, this leaves unexplained the differences in regional production functions. Presumably, they are due to variations in resource endowment (increasingly less important), in product mix, and in previous capital investment.

2.2. Technology embodied in capital equipment

For technical progress to be merely a residual prompted efforts to measure it and explain it more directly. Several directions have been pursued. One was to conceptualize technical change as the result of innovation in process or manufacturing techniques, with these innovations being built into or "embodied" in new capital equipment. This procedure leads to making capital heterogeneous, with different equipment being distinguished by vintage or model year. The idea is that equipment of more recent vintage is more "productive" in the sense of the following production function

$$Y(t) = \sum_{v \leq t} a(v) f[k(t,v), L(t,v)] \tag{2.3}$$

where $K(t, v)$ is the stock of capital of vintage $v \leq t$ in place in year t and $L(t, v)$ is the amount of labor working that stock. The multiplicative term $a(v)$ represents technological progress that is embodied in equipment of vintage v, and presumably $a(v)$ increases with v. The total output in year t, $Y(t)$, is the sum over the outputs corresponding to all vintages present in year t [Varaiya and Wiseman (1978)]. An implication of (2.3) is that if two regional economies have the same aggregate capital stock and labor, then the region whose capital stock has more recent vintages will have a larger output. If technical progress is assumed to be embodied in new equipment, as in (2.3), then differences in regional growth rates can be attributed to differences in the vintage structure and, ultimately, to the differences in the investment history of regions. This is done by Varaiya and Wiseman (1978, 1981). However, they do not explain why the latest techniques embodied in current investment may differ across regions due, perhaps, to differences in product mix, in wage rates, and in labor skills. In any event, regions in which "best practice" technology operates will have a competitive advantage over the other regions [Le Heron (1973)].

Note that the vintage approach also is open to the objection that no distinction is made between new technology that changes processes and that which changes products. As Stoneman (1983) points out, in an interrelated economy one industry's new products can be another's new processes [cf. Scherer (1982)], but in a regional context the development of such a product need not take place in the same region as its utilization in production.

2.3. Regional differences in productivity

Empirical analyses of technical progress that rely on variations in capital investment require detailed data on regional capital stocks and investment that are frequently unavailable at the regional level. Consequently, a second direction has been pursued to measure the impact of technical progress. The rate of technical progress in an industry (or economy) is assumed to be related directly to the rate of R & D investment, or indirectly to the rate of growth in output (under the

assumption that the latter is positively correlated with R & D expenditures).
Most emphasis in regional economics has focused on the relationship between
regional productivity increases and growth in regional output, termed the
Verdoorn–Kaldor "law" [Casetti and Jones (1983), Swales (1983), Thirlwall
(1983)]. This association leads to a model of "cumulative causation" – increased
investment occurs in faster growing regions, thereby reinforcing their higher
growth.

It is important to observe that, for cumulative causation to persist in a
multiregional economy where there is mobility of labor and investment, it is
necessary that the increased investment resulting from higher growth in a region
be located in the same region. This requires that returns to capital be higher in
that region. Two mechanisms would permit this condition, one in the short run
and the other in the long run.

In the first of these explanations for regional differences in rates of return on
capital, one region may have a lower wage rate, and a correspondingly higher
return on capital. As more investment flows into this low-wage region, it
increases labor's marginal product, hence the wage rate, until the differences in
wage disappears. This is the neoclassical paradigm expounded by Borts and Stein
(1964). Note that this paradigm denies the possibility of any long-term cumulative causation.

A second explanation permits differences to persist. It is based on the insight
gleaned from urban economics that spatial concentration of economic activity
can produce externalities – agglomeration effects. One would expect that regions
with large urban concentrations show greater technical progress. Thus in addition
to differences induced by heterogeneity of capital stock [as in (2.3)], another
source of heterogeneity is the degree of urban concentration. In a simple model
this would be specified as

$$Y = D^a K^b L^c \tag{2.4}$$

where D is a measure of urban density or concentration. Observe that if, upon
estimation, a turns out to be positive, this would indicate agglomeration economies; on the other hand, if a turns out to be negative, this would indicate
congestion effects.

Agglomeration economies imply that the same capital equipment and labor in
a plant operating in a larger urban environment will produce more than the plant
in a smaller urban environment. Thus, it is the environment that "contributes" to
higher productivity. Agglomeration economies play a multiple role: they promote
technical progress and higher productivity; they attract industry and capital
because they imply higher profits; and they influence interregional migration
[Richardson (1978b, p. 10)]. To attribute regional differences in technology to
agglomeration economies [Lande (1978)] is still to treat technology as a "black

box". Large urban areas are expected, ceteris paribus, to have higher rates of innovation, more rapid adoption of innovations, and higher proportions of skilled workers than smaller places, but technological change itself is not endogenous.

Alternatives to neoclassical growth models typically focus on urban size as an operational surrogate for these advantages of agglomeration, i.e. both increasing returns and greater innovativeness, and more rapid adoption of innovations [Richardson (1973)]. Thirlwall (1974, p. 6) notes that cumulative causation "is nothing more than the phenomenon of increasing returns in the broadest sense". Thus, models (based on the Verdoorn–Kaldor law) that propose an alternative to neoclassical growth models rely on increasing returns as a perhaps more plausible, but an equally mechanistic approach to regional change [e.g. Dixon and Thirlwall (1975)].

Finally, another explanation for regional differences in productivity is offered by Siebert (1969). He argues that higher output leads to more investment in R & D. The resulting new innovation is contained in new knowledge which offers certain initial advantages to the region. This, in turn, leads to higher output, and more R & D. Siebert notes that new technical knowledge tends (at least initially) to be polarized at the point of research or at a few other points in space, even if information and knowledge are mobile. The "polarizing incidence of technical progress" also leads to polarization of capital and labor, because of the initial advantage (profits) obtained from innovation. Wage rates and profits tend to be increased in order to induce the needed capital and/or labor toward the location of invention. Siebert summarizes the process:

> This process of polarization is increased if we take into account…economies of scale. The existence of these internal and agglomeration economies will intensify the polarizing effects…. The more mobile capital and labor, the stronger are the polarizing effects which technical knowledge induces with respect to these determinants [Siebert (1969, p. 40)].

In terms of an overall effect on regional structure, then, innovation "can be expected to have not a structure-preserving but a structure-changing function" (p. 41).

The persuasive arguments in favor of polarization are reinforced by the model of Krugman (1979), set in the context of international trade. Even with technology transfer to a non-innovating nation (or region), the advantage of initial innovative ability results in cumulatively larger interregional differentials in growth and income. Nelson and Norman (1977) attribute this type of advantage to the agglomeration of skilled workers for R & D and process improvement work associated with the early stage of the product life cycle, to be discussed in Section 3. Thus, although it remains a small body of research (and frequently originating outside regional economics), theoretical work appears to reinforce the disequilibrium notions of polarization and cumulative causation. The disequilibrium, however, may be associated with structural changes and fluctuations over time that may be quite unstable or even transitory [Nijkamp (1982), Nijkamp and Schubert (1985); see also Chapter 6 of this Handbook].

Polarization is of course ameliorated by the process of innovation diffusion, whereby new products and processes spread to potential users, who in this context will usually be other firms, some of which will be in other regions. Pre-eminent among regional factors determining the timing and rate of acceptance of new technology is city or region size (population), because it represents the spatial concentration of entrepreneurs and industry as well as market potential [Brown (1981)]. In addition, large urban regions are the focus of communication and transportation networks, mobile capital, and the decision-making locations of firms [Richardson (1978a, pp. 125–131)]. Thus, innovations spread among regions in a sequence that, in general, begins with larger, or more populous, regions and only later includes smaller regions. In developing countries, however, the gap in the levels of urban amenities and agglomeration economies between a nation's urban core and its periphery is typically very large. Clapp and Richardson (1984) show that, in this situation, widespread diffusion is unlikely to occur and polarization will tend to persist over time (see also Chapter 16 of this Handbook).

3.   Technology and the heterogeneity of labor

In explanations of technical change, labor is usually considered homogeneous, and technical change is either "disembodied" or it is "embodied" in new equipment. There is another model based on the concept of "human capital" which differentiates between different types of labor, depending on education and skills. Skills may be acquired on the job, through "learning by doing".[2] If learning by doing is significant, then one again sets up a reinforcing mechanism. The greater the investment, the more workers learn, the greater their productivity, the more the output, the greater the investment. This " virtuous circle" can easily be given a regional dimension. Innovations in one region are "acquired" by the workers in that region, and so on. Presumably the pace at which workers learn is faster than the pace at which innovations can diffuse to other regions, thus maintaining regional differences in productivity, output and investment.

---

[2] Bell (1984) identifies several levels of "learning" by which skill and technical knowledge are acquired by organizations and their workers and managers. These range from the rather traditional learning by operating to learning by searching for information and disembodied knowledge.

Different skill levels or education levels may result in differences in wage rates among regions, and this is perhaps the most important consequence of heterogeneous labor. The product life cycle model makes use of these differences to suggest regional specialization of economic activity over at least the medium run [Vernon (1966), Krumme and Hayter (1975), Thomas (1975)]. In the early or *innovation* stage of a product's life cycle, production requires R & D and skilled labor for refinements and improvements. The second or *growth* stage permits production to be less skill-intensive and to take place away from R & D centers. The final or *standardization* stage is characterized by shifts of production to low cost (especially low wage) locations. The same pattern results from the more comprehensive "manufacturing process cycle" of Suarez-Villa (1984). Such models provide an insight into regional economic structure that is based on the level of technology and skills needed on the part of labor in each stage [Storper and Walker (1983, 1984)]. The labor skills common to each region are reinforced by the fact that generally only jobs requiring that level of skill are attracted to such a region, and workers are unable to improve their skills through learning by doing in higher skill jobs. Demand for skilled labor is low in routine production, and firms find it advantageous to continue R & D activities in the parent region alone [Seninger (1985)]. An alternative, but related view, is that what matters in the regional allocation of investment is not wage differences but worker attitudes shaped by cultural (hence, long-lasting) patterns. These attitudes may be reflected in levels of union activity or marked variations in worker productivity that enhance output and attract further investment.

At first glance, it would seem that skill levels could not vary greatly among regions. In any large metropolitan area, for example, the variation in the distribution of labor skills probably is equal to the variation across a nation. However, in addition to labor skill enhancing productivity, skilled workers (more specifically, scientists, engineers, and technical workers) also generate new products or product improvements. Although process innovation, resulting in productivity increases, forms the basis of most neoclassical and cumulative causation theories, it is product innovation that is associated with observed phenomena such as regional industrial specialization and innovative activities in the innovation stage of the product cycle model. As Dixon and Thirlwall (1978, p. 98) state: "Technology impinges...on the price and income elasticity of demand for a region's exports, particularly through the process of product innovation, and...it is on product innovation that we would lay much greater stress as a prime source of regional growth rate differences." R & D expenditures by firms are predominantly for new or improved products, as distinguished from processes [Scherer (1982)]. The actual flow of causation from product R & D to growth rate increases is difficult to trace in practice. Product innovations in one sector (and one region) may well be used principally in other sectors and in other regions [Scherer (1982), Thwaites (1982)].

Finally, although skilled workers are more mobile then unskilled workers (because they are more responsive to regional wage differentials and because they have greater information about employment opportunities), skilled workers tend to concentrate in space. Especially in a setting of institutionalized R & D, the number of places where innovative activity occurs is limited. Even within this set of alternative locations, R & D workers have locational preferences that enhance the overall skill level of some regions over that of other regions. This mobility of skilled labor increases the effect of polarization associated with technical change noted in Section 2.3. The net result is a "partial polarization" [Siebert (1969)] of innovative ability, through the reinforcing locational decisions of capital (R & D facilities) and labor (skilled workers).

4. Empirical studies of innovation and regional structure

Empirical studies on this topic have been of two general types. The first has developed from the neoclassical model and its concerns and addresses questions related generally only to capital and labor inputs. Varaiya and Wiseman (1981) is an excellent example of this type, since it goes beyond considering only the conventional homogeneous capital input and instead develops a vintage model of investment and employment. The amount of annual investment per worker required to sustain employment in manufacturing in the United States was estimated and found to increase markedly as labor-saving technology is embodied in new capital equipment. At the same time, technology is rather unidimensional, embodied in capital and improved over time. Technology influences labor via capital investment and associated learning by doing but is not endogenous or influenced by labor.

A second broader, but less rigorous, line of research has attempted to document the interregional variation in labor skills, wages and labor force growth. Much of this work emphasizes the organization of multilocational firms, rather than formal models of capital and labor inputs [Malecki (1983)]. Regional specialization of firms' activities is the cumulative outcome of mergers and acquisitions, branch plant location, and the location of R & D and administrative functions. Each of these processes involves a degree of reallocation of industrial activity and control that alters regional economic structures. Mergers and acquisitions inevitably redistribute and consolidate administration, R & D, and other corporate functions differently than was the case before merger. A series of studies provide evidence of this for Great Britain, where corporate control and R & D have become increasingly concentrated in the South-East [see Gudgin et al. (1979), Hamilton (1978) and Leigh and North (1978)].

Two types of employment implications result from this research. First, rationalization and plant consolidation and location are processes that tend to reduce the need for labor in some plant locations and increase it in others, typically resulting in an overall reduction of employment. Thus, their effect is the same as that from labor-saving capital investment and usually takes place simultaneously. Second, as control over production and decisions at the plant level become farther removed from peripheral regions, these regions also lose the ability either to innovate or to generate new firms [Watts (1981)]. In part, the latter effects are a result of "de-skilling", a reduction in the levels of skills required for work at the plant level, which decreases the number of engineers and other workers associated with new firm formation [Massey and Meegan (1982)]. The regional outcome of these individual structural changes has been termed a "spatial division of labor" which largely separates high skill, high wage administrative and innovative jobs in different locational settings from low skill, low wage jobs in standardized production [Clark (1981), Massey (1984)]. Aydalot (1978, 1981) and Lipietz (1980) provide descriptions of similar patterns in France.

It must be stressed that much of this research is based on case studies, or even anecdotal observations, for which few theoretical frameworks have been available. Some synthesis of the empirical work is developing, centered either around the role of labor [Seninger (1985), Storper and Walker (1983, 1984)] or around the actions of global corporations in the context of technological change [Friedmann and Wolff (1982)]. The product life cycle has served as a major focal point for empirical research, although primarily for its resultant pattern of regional specialization rather than on the mechanisms that would produce such a pattern within a neoclassical framework [Hekman (1980c)].

The findings concerning regional specialization, however, are provocative in their suggestion of a tendency toward long-term patterns. For example, Hekman (1980a) suggests that American computer firms have kept their nonroutine activities – R & D and administration – in only a few places, like California, Massachusetts, Minnesota, and New Jersey, while they have moved their production facilities to the southeastern states to take advantage of lower labor costs. Koch et al. (1983) assert that the highly publicized growth in recent years in this "Sunbelt" region is illusory – it consists almost entirely of standardized production and assembly operations that have moved into small towns and rural areas [cf. Park and Wheeler (1983)]. Production facilities that produce standardized products seem increasingly to locate in Third World nations where labor costs are even lower than in the rural Southeast [Bluestone and Harrison (1982)].

In contrast, manufacturing of products that remain nonroutine throughout their lives rely on skilled and professional labor inputs. Hekman (1980b) also looked at the American medical instruments industry, which is characterized by relatively small production volumes. Since most production in that industry cannot be standardized in large plants, most manufacturing takes place near medical research centers, such as Boston and Chicago, where the industry's R & D also is concentrated. A study by Oakey (1981) on the British instruments sector yielded similar findings with respect to skilled workers, who largely determined the location of production. Even the services conform to this pattern, as recent work by Hall et al. (1983) has found in the American computer software sector. Work tasks are becoming polarized into "supertech" professional jobs, which are likely to remain concentrated in the Los Angeles and San Francisco urban regions, and paraprofessional jobs for more standardized programming tasks. Firms are attempting to disperse the routine work to other, lower cost parts of the country.

At present, there is little theoretical guidance for the study of corporate organization as it is related to innovation and regional economic structure. The possibility that regions may differ primarily because of differences in the location of corporate functions or stages of a product's life cycle does not correspond well to notions of either regional industrial mix (based on products produced) or of production functions (based on capital and labor). Hansen (1980) has shown that low-skill labor is the principal human input in standardized production in many industries, but capital intensity remains high because large amounts of specialized equipment are used. Hansen suggests that the product life cycle and spatial filtering – the relocation of aging industries in lower-wage areas – provide a better framework for the study of multilocational firms.

5. Effects of technology on regional development

In a dynamic setting, local and regional economies, like national economies, stand to lose routine production jobs to areas whose low wages or more efficient automated operations allow competitive pricing in global markets. This Schumpeterian competition affects most those regions where are concentrated industries that produce standardized products in large volumes [Hansen (1979)]. Employment in these large-volume sectors has been large historically, but is now relatively dispersed around the world, often with devastating impact on local areas. On the other hand, regions with R & D and small-volume production, especially of new innovative products and products that are continually improved, are likely to withstand global competition. This is due partially to the beneficial effects of product innovation, in contrast to the impact of labor-saving process innovations, and partially to the very different labor skill configurations often associated with each region.

The empirical findings concerning the "spatial division of labor" generally support cumulative causation conceptualizations of regional growth.[3] The agglomeration of skilled workers and their R & D activity and product and process

---

[3] See also Schmenner's (1982) detailed empirical work on corporate location, which reinforces the generalization that routine and nonroutine activities of firms are spatially separated.

innovations and improvements (all activities that characterize the early stage of the product cycle) are an explicit or implicit stimulus in such models of regional growth, as discussed in Section 2 [Nelson and Norman (1977), Pred (1977)]. The ability of a region to innovate and retain its competitiveness is at the heart of emerging Schumpeterian conceptualizations of regional development [Thomas (1983)].

If we attempt to isolate R & D and nonroutine activities as the primary forces affecting regional economic change, what regional development effects can be identified? As Buswell (1983) notes, the conventional economic reasoning – that R & D leads to a rise in innovative capacity, to a lowering of production costs and to greater regional competitiveness – is more often wrong than correct. One underlying reason for this is the emphasis traditionally placed on capital-embodied process innovation and competitiveness as indicated by production efficiency and cost reduction. The emphasis is misplaced for two reasons. First, as Scherer (1982) has found, three-fourths of all corporate R & D is for product innovation and improvements, as is nearly all government R & D. This suggests not that process innovation is unimportant, but that a much greater amount of corporate innovative effort goes toward innovation that is not addressed by conventional approaches. Second, the process innovations themselves frequently originate either at sites of equipment suppliers or at a firm's R & D locations, whereas they may be put into use at the widespread locations of the firm's branch plants.

The regional impact of competition based on new products is quite different from that of process innovation. Thwaites (1983) reports consistent job losses in British manufacturing establishments where process innovations are incorporated, but even larger job losses in noninnovating plants. Of course, most process innovation is the incorporation of new products developed by other firms, such as equipment suppliers and, given marketing practices, there is little reason for any geographical association to be expected between the location of R & D and the location of production cost savings. There also is a marked propensity for new product production to take place near (if not at) the sites of R & D [Thwaites (1982, 1983)]. The nature of interregional competition more closely follows dimensions related to the professional–technical labor market, rather than capital investment variations emphasized in the conventional wisdom.[4]

The labor market for professional and technical workers is different from that for production workers [Clark (1981)]. The locational preferences of technical personnel, in fact, exert a large influence on the location decisions for R & D [Malecki (1980, 1984), Oakey (1981, 1983)]. These workers favor attractive urban

---

[4]It should be pointed out that the conventional wisdom also is strongly tied to the experience of the manufacturing sector, whereas recent empirical research also frequently looks at the service sector [Noyelle (1983)].

regions where cultural, educational, and alternative employment opportunities are abundant. Thus, although this group of workers is highly mobile in the sense that their propensity to change employers and even residences is rather high, they are not footloose in that their location preferences rule out a large number of locations in favor of relatively few urban areas. A possible explanation for this geographical concentration is that technical workers are attracted by urban amenities which change only slowly so that some areas retain a higher supply of such technical labor. In general, the empirical evidence tends to reinforce cumulative causation notions of regional change, although the mechanisms are much more complex than theoretical frameworks have yet been able to capture effectively.

6. Some thoughts on the microeconomics of technology at the regional level

Regional variations in routine and nonroutine activities and in the efficiency of the capital stock are the composite of the actions of many individual firms. Although industry-wide commonalities are present to some extent, each firm has its own attributes, including a unique pool of technological knowledge, an organizational structure, and a stock of production processes which falls within the range from the best practice to worst practice [Nelson (1981)]. As a result, firms have different capabilities for making technological changes, whether in products or processes. In addition, many changes are incremental, and firms exhibit different abilities to exploit these [Nelson and Winter (1977), Rosenberg (1982)]. They also vary significantly because of differences in strategy that lead to an emphasis on new products, new low-cost processes, or narrow niches that prove to be profitable [Porter (1980)].

Individual plants or establishments are a cumbersome set of elements for regional analysis, but it is of course only at individual locations that investment and disinvestment, employment and unemployment take place. As dynamic international competition makes technological change more prominent and more rapid, the viability of individual plants depends on their status vis-à-vis industry best-practice and on their product mix and its prospects for sales growth. In the first instance, numerous incremental improvements (often not related to formal R & D) tend to be made to production processes [Carlsson (1981)]. These improvements are typically made to capital-intensive plants for which long-term utilization is likely or desired. Some of the improvements are planned in advance; others are the result of "learning by using" [Rosenberg (1982)] and continuous work along certain "natural trajectories" for the firm [Nelson and Winter (1977)].

This extremely disaggregated perspective of regional economic change is no one-to-one substitute for the rigorous models based on aggregate regional production functions. But, as Nelson and Winter (1982) note, economic *change* as an evolutionary process is more difficult to model than are equilibrium situations. The notion of evolution of regional economies may prove to be somewhat similar, but it may more accurately describe the continuities and evolving structures of regions [Clark and Gertler (1985), Hekman and Strong (1981)]. On the other hand, it is not clear whether sudden castastrophes or regular long waves describe regional structure better than smooth evolutionary progression [Nijkamp (1982)].

Regions are different from firms, but perhaps not fundamentally so. Both typically see growth as their primary goal, and both are made up of establishments whose viability is determined by exogenous variables (such as the actions of competitors and governments) and endogenous variables (including product mix, infrastructure, and R & D). The birth of new products, firms, or product-line divisions are a source of growth only if internal to the firm or region. However, firms can eliminate outside threats by acquisition; regions are bounded and can only try to attract sources of growth after they are created. If mobile, these tend to be routine manufacturing activities, albeit often in growing sectors and firms. Alternatively, firms and regions may reorient their long-term strategies, focusing on improving their capabilities for generating new products and for being competitive producers [Porter (1980)]. In the case of regions, improvements in educational, research, and cultural activities can be elements of a regional strategy, since these are amenities that attract both professional workers and firms.

Empirical studies of the location of R & D, headquarters, high-technology industry, or other indicators are not sufficient for understanding the role that technology plays in regional change, but they add a perspective not found in neoclassical models [Hansen (1980)]. Familiar variables and models are little help in assessing regional development, because many of the causes of regional economic change are qualitative and structural in nature [Stöhr (1982), Watts (1981)]. This is essentially the same point made by Nelson (1981) and Nelson and Winter (1982) in rejecting the "orthodox" approach to economic change. The larger problem concerning innovation in regional economies, however, may be quite different. Regional economic status (growth, development, and so on) is indicated by the diversity of available jobs, the incomes they provide, and the continual shedding of obsolete and noncompetitive jobs to be replaced by newer products, services and production methods. The overall problem is a thorny one, all the more so in light of a process such as technological change whose impacts are only partially understood, especially in the long run [Leontief (1983)].

7. Conclusions

The complex interplay of technology with other factors of production has progressed only slightly toward incorporation of the dynamic context in which technology operates. The traditional focus on capital investment as the embodi-ment of technology has provided useful insights into the nature of process innovation, capital–labor substitution, and best-practice technology. Cumulative causation models rely instead on technology as a continual process of innovation, although they too tend to rely on rather mechanistic operationalizations. A dynamic role of technology is at odds with neoclassical theory, in that each region is characterized by different technical relationships in productions (i.e. different production functions), rather than producing at different points along the same production function [Gertler (1984), Lande (1978)]. Part of the regional uniqueness of production results from the fact that regions vary both in the products which they produce (i.e. regional specialization) and in the stage of the overall production cycle at which they are producing. In addition, the level as well as the preferred destinations of investment may affect the regional product mix. When investment in the development and production of new products (as a subset of total investment) varies spatially, it further distorts over time the assumption of identical regional production functions.

Regional attributes such as skilled and unskilled labor are influences on economic activity in a region, and they also affect the nature and magnitude of future regional economic activity [Massey (1984)]. These complications, along with explicit corporate strategies, locational specialization, and competition based on product innovation, make the regional context especially difficult to model. Empirical research on technology and regional structure and change has pro-gressed more boldly and broadly than theoretical approaches. Technology and innovation in a regional context appear at present to be more appropriately modeled by cumulative causation frameworks than by the neoclassical perspec-tives that have tended to dominate [Richardson (1978a), Stöhr (1982)]. The study of innovations and regional economic structure is quite young, however, and remains open to the variety of useful approaches found both in economics and in related fields.

References

Aydalot, P. (1978) 'L'aménagement du territoire en France: une tentative de bilan', L'espace Géographique, 7:245–253.
Aydalot, P. (1981) 'The regional policy and spatial strategy of large organizations', in: A. Kuklinski, ed., Polarized development and regional policy: tribute to Jacques Boudeville. The Hague: Mouton, 173–185.
Bell, M. (1984) "'Learning' and the accumulation of industrial technological capability in developing countries", in: M. Fransman and K. King, eds, Technological capability in the third world. New York: St. Martin's Press, 187–209.
Bluestone, B. and B. Harrison (1982) The deindustrialization of America. New York: Basic Books.
Borts, G. H. and J. L. Stein (1964) Economic growth in a free market. New York: Columbia University Press.
Brown, L. A. (1981) Innovation diffusion: a new perspective. London: Methuen.

Buswell, R. J. (1983) 'Research and development and regional development: a review', in: A. Gillespie, ed., *Technological change and regional development*. London: Pion, 9–22.

Carlsson, B. (1981) 'The content of productivity growth in Swedish manufacturing', *Research Policy*, 10:336–355.

Casetti, E. and J. P. Jones (1983) 'Regional shifts in the manufacturing response to output growth: sunbelt versus snowbelt', *Urban Geography*, 4:285–301.

Clapp, J. M. and H. W. Richardson (1984) 'Technical change in information-processing industries and regional income differentials in developing countries', *International Regional Science Review*, 9:241–256.

Clark, G. L. (1981) 'The employment relation and spatial division of labor: a hypothesis', *Annals of the Association of American Geographers*, 71:412–424.

Clark, G. L. and M. Gertler (1985) 'An adjustment model of regional production', *Environment and Planning*, A17:231–251.

Dixon, R. and A. P. Thirlwall (1975) 'A model of regional growth-rate differences on Kaldorian lines', *Oxford Economic Papers*, 27:201–214.

Dixon, R. and A. P. Thirlwall (1978) 'Growth rate stability in the Kaldorian regional model', *Scottish Journal of Political Economy*, 25:97–99.

Friedmann, J. and G. Wolff (1982) 'World city foundation: an agenda for research and action', *International Journal of Urban and Regional Research*, 6:307–343.

Gertler, M. (1984) 'Regional capital theory', *Progress in Human Geography*, 8:50–81.

Gudgin, G., R. Crum and S. Bailey (1979) 'White-collar employment in U.K. manufacturing industry', in: P. Daniels, ed., *Spatial patterns of office growth and location*. New York: Wiley, 127–157.

Hall, P., A. R. Markusen, R. Osborn and B. Wachsman (1983) 'The American computer software industry: economic development prospects', *Built Environment*, 9:29–39.

Hamilton, F. E. I. (1978) 'Aspects of industrial mobility in the British economy', *Regional Studies*, 12:153–165.

Hansen, N. (1979) 'The new international division of labor and manufacturing decentralization in the United States', *Review of Regional Studies*, 9:1–11.

Hansen, N. (1980) 'Dualism, capital–labor ratios and the regions of the U.S.: a comment', *Journal of Regional Science*, 20:401–403.

Hekman, J. S. (1980a) 'The future of high technology industry in New England: a case study of computers', *New England Economic Review* (January/February):5–17.

Hekman, J. S. (1980b) 'Can New England hold onto its high technology industry?', *New England Economic Review* (March/April):35–44.

Hekman, J. S. (1980c) 'The product cycle and New England textiles', *Quarterly Journal of Economics*, 94:697–717.

Hekman, J. S. and J. S. Strong (1981) 'The evolution of New England industry', *New England Economic Review* (March/April):35–46.

Koch, D. L., W. N. Cox, D. W. Steinhauser and P. V. Whigham (1983) 'High technology: the South reaches out for growth industry', *Economic Review, Federal Reserve Bank of Atlanta*, 68 (September):4–19.

Krugman, P. (1979) 'A model of innovation, technology transfer, and the world distribution of income', *Journal of Political Economy*, 87:253–266.

Krumme, G. and R. Hayter (1975) 'Implications of corporate strategies and product cycle adjustments for regional employment changes', in: L. Collins and D. F. Walker, eds., *Locational dynamics of manufacturing activity*. New York: Wiley, 325–356.

Lande, P. S. (1978) 'The interregional comparison of production functions', *Regional Science and Urban Economics*, 8:339–353.

Le Heron, R. B. (1973) 'Best-practice technology, technical leadership, and regional economic development', *Environment and Planning*, 5:735–749.

Leigh, R. and D. J. North (1978) 'Regional aspects of acquisition activity in British manufacturing industry', *Regional Studies*, 12:227–245.

Leontief, W. L. (1983) 'Technological advance, economic growth, and the distribution of income', *Population and Development Review*, 9:403–410.

Lipietz, A. (1980) 'Inter-regional polarization and the tertiarisation of society', *Papers of the Regional Science Association*, 44:3–17.

Malecki, E. J. (1980) 'Corporate organization of R and D and the location of technological activities', *Regional Studies*, 14:219–234.

Malecki, E. J. (1983) 'Technology and regional development: a survey', *International Regional Science Review*, 8:89–125.

Malecki, E. J. (1984) 'High technology and local economic development', *Journal of the American Planning Association*, 50:262–269.

Massey, D. (1984) *Spatial divisions of labour: social structures and the geography of production*. London: Macmillan.

Massey, D. and R. Meegan (1982) *The anatomy of job loss*. New York: Methuen.

Nelson, R. R. (1981) 'Research on productivity growth and productivity differences: dead ends and new departures', *Journal of Economic Literature*, 19:1029–1064.

Nelson, R. R. and V. D. Norman (1977) 'Technological change and factor mix over the product cycle: a model of dynamic comparative advantage', *Journal of Development Economics*, 4:3–24.

Nelson, R. R. and S. G. Winter (1977) 'In search of useful theory of innovation', *Research Policy*, 6:36–76.

Nelson, R. R. and S. G. Winter (1982) *An evolutionary theory of economic change*. Cambridge, Mass.: Harvard University Press.

Nijkamp, P. (1982) 'Long waves or castastrophes in regional development', *Socio-Economic Planning Sciences*, 16:161–171.

Nijkamp, P. and U. Schubert (1985) 'Urban dynamics', in: J. Brotchie, P. Newton, P. Hall and P. Nijkamp, eds., *The future of urban form: the impact of new technology*. London: Croom Helm, 79–92.

Norton, R. D. and J. Rees (1979) 'The product cycle and the spatial decentralization of American manufacturing', *Regional Studies*, 13:141–151.

Noyelle, T. J. (1983) 'The rise of advanced services: some implications for economic development in U.S. cities', *Journal of the American Planning Association*, 49:280–290.

Oakey, R. P. (1981) *High technology industry and industrial location*. Aldershot, U.K.: Gower.

Oakey, R. P. (1983) 'New technology, government policy, and regional manufacturing employment', *Area*, 15:61–65.

Park, S. O. and J. O. Wheeler (1983) 'The filtering down process in Georgia: the third stage of the product life cycle', *Professional Geographer*, 35:18–31.

Porter, M. E. (1980) *Competitive strategy*. New York: Free Press.

Pred, A. R. (1977) *City-systems in advanced economies*. New York: Wiley.

Richardson, H. W. (1973) *Regional growth theory*. New York: Wiley.

Richardson, H. W. (1978a) *Regional and urban economics*. Harmondsworth: Penguin.

Richardson, H. W. (1978b) 'The state of regional economics: a survey article', *International Regional Science Review*, 3:1–48.

Rosenberg, N. (1982) *Inside the black box: technology and economics*. Cambridge, Mass.: Cambridge University Press.

Scherer, F. M. (1982) 'Inter-industry technology flows in the United States', *Research Policy*, 11:227–245.

Schmenner, R. W. (1982) *Making business location decisions*. Englewood Cliffs, N.J.: Prentice-Hall.

Seninger, S. F. (1985) 'Employment cycles and process innovation in regional structural change', *Journal of Regional Science*, 25:259–272.

Siebert, H. (1969) *Regional economic growth: theory and policy*. Scranton: International Textbook.

Solow, R. M. (1957) 'Technical change and the aggregate production function', *Review of Economics and Statistics*, 39:312–320.

Stöhr, W. (1982) 'Structural characteristics of peripheral areas: the relevance of the stock-in-trade variables of regional science', *Papers of the Regional Science Association*, 49:71–84.

Stoneman, P. (1983) *Economic analysis of technological change*. Oxford: Oxford University Press.

Storper, M. and R. Walker (1983) 'The theory of labour and the theory of location', *International Journal of Urban and Regional Research*, 7:1–41.

Storper, M. and R. Walker (1984) 'The spatial division of labor: labor and the location of industries', in: L. Sawers and W. K. Tabb, eds., *Sunbelt/snowbelt: urban development and regional restructuring*. New York: Oxford University Press, 19–47.

Stubbs, P. C. and J. S. Metcalfe (1980) 'Bibliography', in: T. Puu and S. Wibe, eds., *The economics of technological progress*. New York: St. Martin's Press, 258–332.

Suarez-Villa, L. (1984) 'Industrial export enclaves and manufacturing change', *Papers of the Regional Science Association*, 54:89–111.

Swales, J. K. (1983) 'A Kaldorian model of cumulative causation: regional growth with induced technical change', in: A. Gillespie, ed., *Technological change and regional development*. London: Pion, 68–87.

Thirlwall, A. P. (1974) 'Regional economic disparities and regional policy in the Common Market', *Urban Studies*, 11:1–12.

Thirlwall, A. P. (1983) 'A plain man's guide to Kaldor's growth laws', *Journal of Post Keynesian Economics*, 5:345–358.

Thomas, M. D. (1975) 'Growth pole theory, technological change, and regional economic development', *Papers of the Regional Science Association*, 34:3–25.

Thomas, M. D. (1983) 'Growth and structural change: the role of technical innovation', paper presented at the North America Meetings of the Regional Science Association, Chicago, November.

Thwaites, A. T. (1982) 'Some evidence of regional variations in the introduction and diffusion of industrial products and processes within British manufacturing industry', *Regional Studies*, 16:371–381.

Thwaites, A. T. (1983) 'The employment implications of technological change in a regional context', in: A. Gillespie, ed., *Technological change and regional development*. London: Pion, 36–53.

Varaiya, P. and M. Wiseman (1978) 'The age of cities and the movement of manufacturing employment, 1947–1973', *Papers of the Regional Science Association*, 41:127–140.

Varaiya, P. and M. Wiseman (1981) 'Investment and employment in manufacturing in U.S. metropolitan areas 1960–1976', *Regional Science and Urban Economics*, 11:431–469.

Vernon, R. (1966) 'International investment and international trade in the product cycle', *Quarterly Journal of Economics*, 80:190–207.

Watts, H. D. (1981) *The branch plant economy*. London: Longman.

Chapter 16

REGIONAL POLICIES IN DEVELOPING COUNTRIES

HARRY W. RICHARDSON and PETER M. TOWNROE

1. Introduction

There are about one hundred countries in the world which may be regarded as "developing", excluding the small island states and principalities with populations of under one million. This total encompasses a huge range of geographical and economic diversity, from the high-income Middle Eastern oil exporting countries, to the prosperous city states of Hong Kong and Singapore, the emerging middle-income South American and Mediterranean countries, and the low-income high-density Asian countries. This diversity is compounded by marked differences in government structures, in social objectives, and in cultural values and traditions. Some countries have high levels of urbanization with only low levels of industrialization. Others have very centralized urban hierarchies and spatially concentrated economies. Yet others have a spatial distribution which reflects strong tribal divisions or ethnic diversity. All commentary on economic development issues runs the risk of facile generalization, because there always appear to be exceptions to any attempt to discern a pattern.

Diversity in the regional problems of developing countries and in the social and economic policies designed to alleviate these problems reflects not only different levels of development and systems of government but also geography, history and tradition, and societal goals. In any country, developed or developing, what constitutes a regional "problem" differs among social groups. In the developed industrial market economies, regional problems are rarely defined in terms of absolutes. *Relative* imbalances in indicators of the social and economic conditions of different regions induce regional policy responses from the centre. A regional problem can be defined only in the context of the country's dominant social and political values. In many developing countries, on the other hand, the interregional imbalance factor is often given a low priority in the portfolio of national economic and social policies. Development and economic growth in the national setting are much more likely to be the dominant policy objectives, with the spectre of rapid population growth often lurking near the foreground.

Handbook of Regional and Urban Economics, Volume I, Edited by P. Nijkamp
©Elsevier Science Publishers BV, 1986

In the developing country context, a distinction has to be made between regional policies which are primarily a response to political pressures and regional policies which are essentially regionally based or focused on economic development programmes, often within the framework of a national economic development strategy. Political pressures for differentials in public expenditure favouring a given region or group of regions may reflect the supporters of the ruling party or elite and their geographical base. The central government may also need to smooth tribal, ethnic or religious divisions with regional aid programmes. A sensitive frontier region may also be favoured, not only in logistically useful infrastructure investments (e.g. military roads and airbases) but also in the provision of government services. In federal states, the revenue-raising powers of individual states may be reinforced or distorted with differential federal government grants and subsidies. Non-federal states, which tend to have more primate urban hierarchies [Henderson (1982)], may favour expenditures in the largest city or cities; or may favour the smaller cities if the primate city is perceived to be "too big". Although political pressure is exercised on behalf of both *places* and social *groups*, regional economic development policies tend to be place-specific, focusing only indirectly on target groups.

The economic case for regional economic policies in developing countries follows the well-established case made out for such policies in developed countries. The case rests partly on the development and utilization of economic resources, including human resources. It also relies on the imperfect operation of factor markets and the tendency for levels of economic prosperity between regions to widen as national per capita incomes rise [before subsequently converging again, Williamson (1965)]. Policy intervention may be necessary to keep the disparities in check. Intervention may also be justified on the grounds that social costs (benefits) are different from private costs (benefits) for both households and firms as a result of rapid urban growth and strong interregional factor flows. Within regions targeted for development, increasing returns to scale implies selectivity in growth (by sector, urban place, or expenditure programme).

The economic case for regional economic policies is also supported by both the "top-down" and the "bottom-up" schools of development planning. On the one hand, the "region" is a useful bureaucratic layer for the application of national policies which require factory or farm gate or doorstep delivery; on the other, it is a vulnerable economic, social and political entity buffeted by strong external forces. For top-down planners, the region is an administrative and managerial convenience, not as subject to local pressures and influence as a municipality but insulated from the centre and day-to-day political control. For bottom-up advocates, the region has to be designed as a political entity with considerable autonomy, seeking the opportunities while avoiding the dangers of closer contacts with the national and the world economic system. Simplifying greatly, both sides view regionally based economic development policies as an effective mechanism towards more rapid overall development, although each defines development in a different way.

One key feature dominates the less-developed nations of the world in contrast to the smaller group of industrialized nations, apart from differences in levels of Gross National Product per capita. This is relatively high rates of population growth, and even faster growth of urban populations. Between 1970 and 1981 [World Bank (1983)], the average annual percentage growth rate of urban population in thirty-four low income nations (GNP per capita of less than 400 U.S. dollars in 1981) was 4.4 (and 5.3 for nations in this group other than India and China). In thirty-nine lower middle income nations (up to $1,700 per capita), the growth rate was 4.3 percent. In twenty-one upper middle income nations (up to $5,500 per capita), the rate was 3.8 percent, and in the four large Middle Eastern oil exporting states, the rate was 8.2 percent. In contrast, in the industrial market economies the rate averaged 1.4 percent, and in Eastern Europe the rate was 1.8 percent. Developing country population growth rates are currently much higher than the growth rates experienced by the now developed countries in their early industrialization phase.

Any attempt to use the experience of developed countries as a springboard for discussion of regional policy problems in developing countries is subject to major constraints. First, as already pointed out, the demographics are so different. Regional policies in countries with rapidly growing populations are focused more on problems associated with the absorption of people in the markets for labour, housing and public services. In countries with stagnant populations, on the other hand, many regional problems are concerned with the effects of depopulation on local economies. The "typical" problem in a developing country is how to generate economic development (and jobs) in a hitherto underdeveloped region relying on traditional agriculture supported by a hierarchy of urban service centres; in developed countries the typical problem is how to revitalize a chronically depressed old-established industrial region (job creation remains important because the rate of job loss often exceeds the rate of population decline).

Second, the environment in which interregional economic change takes place varies so much between developed and developing countries. In many developed countries economic activities could relocate with minor efficiency losses. Even lagging regions have growth potential (many of them grew rapidly in the past) because they have skilled labour forces, infrastructure, agglomeration economies in their cities, and entrepreneurship. Also, they are well connected to the rest of the national space economy via comprehensive interurban transport and communication networks. Moreover, many industries in developed economies are footloose and can operate at a large number of locations at similar cost and with more or less equal access to national markets. If firms remain reluctant to relocate to peripheral regions, the reasons may be more non-economic than economic. In developing countries, on the other hand, comparative costs may vary widely among locations, access to national markets is often very low outside the core region, and the supply of infrastructure may be very inadequate. Thus, the economic costs of a peripheral location may be too high to be bridged by affordable location subsidies.

A third difference between developed and developing countries is in regional policy objectives and priorities. In developing countries there may be substantial emphasis on promoting economic development and on stabilizing rural regions. In developed countries interregional equity objectives may be dominant, and regional policies may be used to pursue goals such as environmental protection, resource conservation and the control of inflation. The goals adopted in developing countries frequently result in active intervention in rural development strategies by the private sector. The industrial decentralization policies that may exist on paper are only rarely pursued vigorously. The trade-off between growth and spatial distribution goals may be difficult to reconcile. In developed countries the policy goals are much more likely to be compatible. For example, measures to reduce interregional income disparities may have side benefits in moderating the effects of external diseconomies in the prosperous regions and in alleviating inflation [Higgins (1973)].

Of course, in many developing countries spatial equity considerations are given a high priority among regional policy objectives. Examples include Brazil where for more than two decades the Federal government has consistently attempted to promote economic development in the much poorer North East region, and the Philippines where each region has a regional executive office under the National Economic Development Authority (NEDA) and an Integrated Area Development Plan focusing especially on the rural areas. Interestingly, these two cases illustrate a more general hypothesis that countries which emphasize interregional equity tend to have inequitable income distributions.

This raises the possibility that the priority given to regional development policies in some countries may reflect an attempt to substitute spatial equity for interpersonal equity. On this view, regional policies are a smoke screen to divert attention from the economic and social problems that result from the heavily skewed distribution of income.

Section 2 of this chapter discusses the key themes which link thinking about regional development to the process of economic growth. Section 3 refers to the policy implications of these theories. Section 4 argues for the relevance of the urban dimension in regional policy analysis. In Section 5 the discussion turns to four major aspects of regional development strategy: experience with national and regional planning agencies; the role of infrastructure; policies to promote industrial development in lagging regions; and the roles of communications and human resource investments. Section 6 draws some lessons from regional development experience in developing countries in the past two decades. Finally, some conclusions on the effectiveness of past policies and implications for the future are presented in Section 7.

2. Alternative theories of regional development and economic growth

Several countries have adopted regional development strategies in *all* regions as a policy base for national social and economic development. These countries include Chile, Peru, Venezuela, the Philippines, Tanzania and Zambia. In federal countries, however, the constitutions often give much of the responsibility for subnational development planning to state ministries and agencies. In some cases, a more piecemeal regional approach is adopted, emphasizing the planning of metropolitan regions (e.g. Bombay, Lagos, São Paulo), or resource-rich areas (e.g. the Nabouk Valley in Malaysia, Ciudad Guayana in Venezuela), or river basins (e.g. the Lerma in Mexico, the Euphrates in Syria).

Much of the thrust for regional development strategies and policies in all of these approaches has derived from the need for a multisectoral approach to development, coordinating the skills of architects, engineers, planners and economists and the activities of sectoral agencies at both the national and local levels. In addition, links have been developed between the administrative hierarchies of each country and the structure of political power and control. The specific solutions adopted, however, are different from country to country. Behind all the country differences, an almost universal perception is of a lack of regional "balance" and of spatial distortions in the pattern of national economic growth. In most countries, a regional policy rests on much more than an administrative game plan for more efficient economic growth.

2.1. Spatial disparities

The idea of spatial "distortion" stems from the observation that the geography of economic growth in all nations is uneven. For some, this in itself is undesirable. Over time, the *relative* prosperity of the inhabitants of some localities falls behind, apparently for reasons beyond their control. Political demands develop for corrective action. In particular, "excessive" primacy of urban growth in the largest city or cities is identified as resulting in both economic inefficiencies and social inequities. Lack of "balance" results in strong and polarized migration flows and the possibility of social turmoil.

This dissatisfaction with uneven development may be sufficient grounds politically to identify a regional "problem" and to introduce regional development policies and/or urban development strategies, directed at changing the spatial distribution of population and economic activity. However, in the absence of explicit social goals and in the absence of analysis as to why the pattern of development is uneven, this can hardly constitute a rigorous case for policy intervention. It is very difficult to argue analytically that social welfare will be unambiguously improved by one pattern of population distribution rather than another, given all the relevant and varied exogenous parameters operating at a specific point in time in a given country.

What analysis in this field has been able to do is to offer reasons why development is likely to be uneven, pointing in particular to three factors: increasing returns to scale, constraints on the free operation of factor markets, and the role of government in an industrializing economy. The economic consequences of these three factors provide economic grounds for policy intervention. It is important to note that analysis in this area has not always observed the distinction between the positive and the normative. The contribution of regional economics to diagnosis has at times become mixed up with the policy guidance of urban and regional planners and policy makers.

The initial prosperity of the majority of third world countries was based on the export of minerals, raw materials and foodstuffs, an orientation frequently associated with colonialism. Economic growth was concentrated on a relatively narrow range of products and was restricted to a small number of urban centres. These centres grew, often as ports or transport interchanges, and a pattern of spatial imbalance developed. Urban primacy and regional concentration resulted from international trade. Profits were derived from natural resource locations and from agricultural areas, and remitted overseas or used to build up capital in the cities. Spatial concentration followed from the distribution of income and wealth and from increasing returns to early infrastructure investments (e.g. railways). Early stages of industrialization followed this pattern, with urban and foreign capital often being used to undercut indigenous producers of simple household goods and farming equipment.

This fact of initial concentration is reflected in the theory of the export base and local multiplier impacts. However, this perspective is too limited once a nation is launched on a path of industrialization and commercialization of agriculture, particularly against the background of continuing high birth rates and falling death rates. Three alternative economic viewpoints may then be taken as to why a spatially uneven pattern of development persists and gets more marked, and may eventually result in a slowdown in the rate of economic growth and a deceleration in the growth of aggregate social welfare.

2.2. Cumulative causation and core–periphery models

The first viewpoint began to be defined by Myrdal and Hirschman, and was given prominence by Friedmann in his studies of Venezuela [Friedmann (1966)]. In

Myrdal's analysis a region begins to develop with a "growth trigger" such as a mineral discovery or development of a new export food crop. Rising real wages and high returns to capital reflect increasing returns to scale and the development of spatial external economies of agglomeration, manifested in rising labour and capital productivity as a function of the growth rate of regional output [Kaldor (1970), Oates et al. (1971), Richardson (1973), Dixon and Thirlwall (1975)]. Limits to the increase in the growth rate may be explained by inadequate capacity or external diseconomies. Regional economic growth is, in effect, a process of cumulative causation, in which the high value cards are dealt to those regions which already hold a favoured hand. Any allocation of public expenditure among regions which seeks to maximize returns to the growth of the national product will tend to reinforce regional disparities. Market forces and state spending join in increasing rather than decreasing the inequalities among regions.

Both Myrdal and Hirschman influenced thinking about processes of economic growth among countries as well as among regions within a single country. These ideas were also linked to those of Perroux (1955) whose Schumpeterian theories of innovation were given a geographical focus by Boudeville (1966) and others to explain the processes by which groups of interrelated industries in individual cities or subregions took off onto a path of self-sustaining relatively rapid growth. The literature on growth poles and growth centres is now voluminous. This theory of unbalanced growth has been widely used for policy prescription.

Friedmann's view of the generation of regional inequalities extended the range of relevant factors away from the narrowly economic. His core–periphery model (1966, 1972–73, 1973) views lagging regions as a periphery, standing in a colonial relationship to the core, dependent and lacking economic autonomy. Ideas, technology, capital, attitudes favourable to economic development: all are generated in the core, or received in the core from overseas. Spatial dualism emerges and is reinforced over time. The model incorporates imbalances in political and economic power, and asymmetry among regions in rates of cultural change. These forces influence patterns of innovation diffusion, investment, the allocation of resources by the state and migration. Eventually, however, the disparities among regions begin to narrow. The core–periphery dichotomy becomes blurred as markets expand, communications improve, attitudes change, and urban growth disperses. Key issues are whether this turnaround will ever occur without active policy intervention, and if so whether it makes good sense to try to accelerate the process.

2.3. *Radical interpretations*

The notion of regional dependency at the heart of the core–periphery model has led to a second viewpoint on regional imbalances. The thinking behind the cumulative–causation approach, and its reflection in the core–periphery model, has been criticized on several grounds [Gilbert and Gugler (1982)]. The role of foreign influences is underplayed, the poverty issue is neglected, the precolonial history of nations is ignored, and governments are assumed to operate "in the public interest". These lines of criticism from neo-Marxist writers [e.g. Stuckey (1975), Santos (1979)] argue for a recognition that the geography of development is a reflection of class interests, the extraction of surplus value over space, and the role of the state in supporting private capital. The driving force of the economy is capital accumulation and this imperative results in the co-existence of dominant core areas and subordinate peripheral regions. The dynamic national centre is in turn dependent upon the financial and industrial capitals of developed nations. The hierarchy is strengthened by the activities of social and political elites, making strong countervailing policies unlikely. Regional convergence has to wait for political and social development as well as for economic development.

Another normative model usually associated with radical views is the "agro-politan" view of regional development, also advocated by Friedmann [Friedmann and Douglass (1978)]. A key element is "selective regional closure", which implies a high degree of economic and political autonomy in a region, even at the expense, at least in the short run, of aggregate income growth [Stöhr and Tödtling (1978)]. This is combined with advocacy of the maximum possible decentraliza-tion of decision making. Agriculture and other indigenous natural resources are emphasized strongly in the development process.

2.4. Neoclassical models

A third viewpoint rests on a much narrower vision of the dominant forces in an economy. At its neoclassical simplest, this view takes regions as aggregated production units among which an equilibrium of income and employment emerges from the smooth working of factor markets. Imbalances merely reflect lags in the adjustment towards equilibrium (recognizing that the target may be moving faster than the arrow) or imperfections in market processes. In newly industrializing nations, it is easy to point to numerous reasons why one or both of these conditions may hold. A more developed neoclassical view allows for increasing returns and new technology, the influence of public-sector supporting investment, and a more dynamic perspective [e.g. Borts and Stein (1964), Romans (1965), Siebert (1969)]. It is then possible to develop this into a view of urbanization which rests on economies of agglomeration broadly defined, involv-ing nodal rather than homogeneous regions [e.g. von Böventer (1970), Richardson (1973)].

This approach is the one with which the majority of regional economists feel most comfortable. However, critics point to the narrow explanation of regional growth patterns, an excessive emphasis on the formal manufacturing sector as the prime agent of change, and the relative neglect of social and political factors. Also, systems of government and the complexities of state interventions in the economy found in all modern states have major locational consequences. These range from the physical location of the large public sector workforce to the hierarchy of power in the allocation of public expenditures and in the determination of tax rates and charges, to sites of access for permissions, permits, finance and protective subsidies, and to the spatial consequences of macro and sectoral policies.

3. Policy implications of the theories

The three approaches – cumulative causation, radical and neoclassical – are not mutually exclusive. Although they offer alternative theories of regional development, suggestive elements for regional economic development policies can emerge from all three. Approaches to policy design, however, tend to have a different emphasis from one theory to another. Crudely, the neoclassical view leans to incentives to steer productive factors, especially in the formal manufacturing sector. Cumulative causation theory leads to policies for growth centres and improvements in infrastructure, transport and communications, and education. The radical views suggest an emphasis upon regional closure and greater regional autonomy. A policy package can obviously contain elements of all these approaches, without a specific commitment to any of the theoretical under-pinnings.

3.1. Manufacturing bias

In the LDC context, however, two other aspects of economic development have been relatively neglected in discussions of regional policies. The first is the emphasis given in many national economic development strategies to the manufacturing sector, whether in import substitution or export promotion, in comparison with the resources devoted to the development of commercial agriculture. The message of Schultz (1964) and others, advocating higher prices and stronger policies to support innovations and farm-based investments generating large multiplier effects, has taken two decades to become the conventional wisdom in development economics [Little (1982), Tolley et al. (1982), Schultz (1978)]. The impact of active pro-agricultural policy measures has not been incorporated into regional development theory, although it has influenced the practice of Integrated Rural Regional Development planning.

3.2. Primate city and core region bias

The second area of neglect is very much related: it is that of the ("implicit") spatial impacts of non-spatial policies. Protectionist and subsidy policies for specific industrial sectors, infrastructure investment policies in response to need (rather than potential), policies for the uniform pricing of public services, and tax policy: all have locational effects. These effects are very difficult to identify, but where serious efforts have been made to quantify their impact [e.g. Tyler (1983)] the policies appear heavily biased in favour of the prosperous core region and the primate city.

3.3. The dubious relevance of developed countries' experience

An interesting question, which will be hotly debated [Chatterji (1982), Richardson (1980)], is the value of regional economics techniques and models for regional policy analysis for developing countries. Answers to this question raise several distinct issues. The first is whether the behavioural assumptions which underpin most regional models as applied to developed countries, particularly the modes of economic rationality that are most easily summarized as neoclassical assumptions, are appropriate to developing countries. Although tradition and culture may play an important role, for example in the agricultural and informal manufacturing sectors, there is increasing evidence that firms and households in developing countries respond to economic incentives in much the same way as in developed countries. On the other hand, the public sector is more interventionist in most developing countries (e.g. as a direct participant in production or as a price controller) which suggests that optimization models may be more useful than market models.

A second issue is whether developing countries have the data base and information systems to permit the application of sophisticated quantitative models. If not, new types of models using "soft" approaches such as applications of multidimensional scaling methods involving cross-impact matrices and other qualitative assessments [Nijkamp and Van Pelt (1983), Nijkamp (1983), Voogd (1981)] may be more relevant in developing country contexts. However, the range and quality of data varies widely among developing countries, from some African countries which have never had a population census to countries such as Brazil which have better regional and urban data than many developed countries. Nevertheless, in many developing countries subnational economic statistics are so rare or weak that innovative approaches in the use of qualitative information will be needed to evaluate regional policies, both ex ante and ex post.

A third problem is whether the assumptions about the stability of economic structures which underpin most regional economic models are relevant in developing countries where a primary objective of regional policy may be to transform the regional economy very rapidly indeed. Take, for example, interregional input–output models [Hewings (1983), Richardson (1985)]. The assumptions that interindustry and interregional trade coefficients remain constant or change in predictable ways may be invalid in developing countries, especially at the regional level. Of course, the operational flexibility of regional input–output models is so great that this limitation has not prevented their use in developing countries. Where data problems are compounded with inappropriate assumptions, however, the results can be unfortunate. A striking example is the 11-region input–output model developed in prerevolutionary Iran by the Battelle Institute. All the coefficients in this model were estimated using "Delphi methods". In practice, this involved asking informed people familiar with the individual sectors for their estimates of coefficient values. It is a little unkind but not inaccurate to say that all the coefficients in the model were invented!

4. Urban dimensions of regional policy

Regional problems in developing countries are an inevitable consequence of economic growth. If economic growth is dependent upon the links between a given country and the world economy, then regional economic differences within the nation are likely to be wider than in a closed economy. These economic forces also influence the pattern of urban development within the nation. The particular pattern of urban growth experienced may then influence in turn the relative economic fortunes of different regions. It is to this interdependence that we turn next.

In many countries strong interregional differences in the rate of expansion of towns and cities have emerged. This has led to concern with the dominance or primacy of one or a few major cities, and/or with pressures of expansion on individual cities which challenge the managerial abilities of urban authorities. Frequently, governments have attempted to influence the interurban distribution of this population growth. They have tried to slow down the growth of large cities, to decentralize growth, to promote the growth of secondary cities, to expand agricultural service centres or to generate industrial growth complexes. Increasingly, these policies are integrated under the banner of "National Urban Development Strategies" or "Population Distribution Policies" [Richardson (1981)]. These policies are complementary to regional economic development policies, each reinforcing the other. The two policy sets are analytically rather different, however.

Although regional development policy is the primary concern of this paper, we have not been able to avoid intermittent references to urban development. This invasion of the territory of a companion volume requires some justification. This is not difficult. Almost every regional economist favours the concept of the nodal or polarized region to that of a homogeneous region, and nodal regions emphasize the linkages among urban centres both within and between regions. To the extent that regional development strategies focus on promoting manufacturing and quaternary services, these strategies must pay some attention to urban structure and facilities because most establishments in these sectors are located within urban centres. A key aspect of the growth centre concept is the relationship between the centre (or pole) and its hinterland [Richardson (1976)] which, in effect, makes the urban and regional dichotomy impossible. In geographically small countries interregional effects can barely be understood outside the context of the system of cities; even in very large countries ignoring this context is possible only in very special cases (e.g. sparsely populated frontier regions with very few urban centres such as the Amazon regions of Brazil or Peru). A final and compelling justification is that regional policy analysts may have to deal with urban–regional interactions by default, because urban economists often treat the city as an isolated production and consumption unit whose connections with the rest of the system (its home region, other cities and regions, the international economy) are not considered to be of interest except in the form of exogenous flows.

The spatial thrust of any regional economic development policy is seen in the relative growth rates of cities and urban areas, region by region. While urban growth is not always synonymous with economic growth, cities with rapidly growing populations usually experience a rapid growth of economic activity. If the spatial distribution of these growth rates is changing, both between regions and within regions, a major determinant of these changes is the growth of the formal manufacturing sector. In most regional development policies in the industrializing nations, priority is given to instruments which will influence the location of manufacturing. In only a minority of cases is there a complementary effort to promote development in the agricultural sector or the service sectors. There is a danger, therefore, in measuring regional development only in terms of new factories and the jobs they provide. However, investments in urban infrastructure and urban-based services af all kinds, which are required to promote manufacturing, also assist and induce development in other sectors. Urban growth is not just a multiplier consequence of manufacturing.

Pressures of population growth in nearly all developing countries not only present policy makers concerned with issues of spatial distribution with major operational problems (problems which may overwhelm informed and longer-term strategic choices); these pressures also provide an opportunity for influencing the geographical distribution of development. This opportunity rarely exists in the typical fully industrialized nation with a static population. United Nations estimates in 1980 [Hauser and Gardner (1980)] suggested that between 1980 and the year 2000 there will be a 78 percent rise in the urban population worldwide, an increase of 1,400 million people, nearly three times the estimated rural increase. Three-quarters of this growth will occur in the less developed nations of the world, with an average rate of urban growth of 3.9 percent per annum. Although the growth rates in many countries have begun to decelerate, the absolute increments to urban populations remain very large. A major component of the "regional problem" in many developing countries is how to accommodate this expansion.

Urban growth, even when primarily fueled by natural increase rather than by net in-migration, presents opportunities for developing industry, raising productivity and incomes, and reducing poverty. Both internal and external economies of scale are exploited, innovations spread more rapidly, and the concentration of economic and political power [Friedmann (1972–73)] reinforces the advantages of the larger cities. However, there is widespread concern that the processes of urban growth, especially in the larger cities, are excessively rapid and costly. Rightly or wrongly, economic inefficiencies and inequities are seen as being increased by the continuing growth of large urban areas. Policies designed to improve regional "balance" would, on this argument, also serve an efficiency goal in seeking to redistribute urban growth. But most economic commentators are wary about supporting a regional development policy on these grounds. It is unjustifiable under strict economic efficiency criteria to advocate one urban size or one particular city size distribution across a region or a nation as being preferable to another.

In colonial and precolonial times, the cities of the low and middle income nations were centres of government, ports or agricultural trading centres. Industrial development has in many cases supplemented these historical roles, usually reinforcing the advantages of city size. This pattern of growth has had three consequences for regional development policies. One is a high degree of primacy, i.e. the concentration of urban and industrial growth in the single largest city (and hence in a single region). A second is a focus of urban growth in cities that are already large. A third is that a region may lag in urban growth because of its history rather than because of any inherent unsuitability for industrial development. In such cases, industrial development may be stimulated by improvements in transport and communications or by the opening up of agricultural and mineral resources to the market.

Against the background of these three urban growth consequences of industrial development, most advocates of regional development policies have insisted upon an urban growth strategy as a central component of a regional policy [e.g. Renaud (1981), Rondinelli (1983)]. This is in contrast to the industrial-development-focused policies of many developed countries. Different developing countries face contrasting situations in their levels of development and their geography, as the classification of Renaud (1981) makes clear. But all face a choice of urban growth strategy. Richardson (1981) presents ten alternatives, from development axes to the promotion of secondary cities or smaller growth centres, recognizing that a hybrid strategy will most likely be appropriate for any given country. All strategies, except a laissez-faire approach, involve selectivity among cities for infrastructure allocations and development incentives. Indeed, the selection of too many centres as candidates for promotion, an understandable reaction to political pressures, has probably been the single most undermining factor in experiences with regional development policies to date. Competition between places and areas in claiming favoured treatment is a central feature of all regional policies, a conflict which perhaps diverts attention away from intra-area inequities and the levels of relative deprivation at the household level under which the goals of the policy are normally defined. Urban growth strategies can also have a built-in conflict. The most effective strategy for slowing the growth of a metropolitan core area in an economy is often the promotion of major secondary cities in the core region, i.e. intraregional decentralization. This at once conflicts with attempts to build up peripheral regions by diverting public sector urban-based expenditures and new industrial investments from the core region as a whole.

The linking of regional economic development to urban growth planning emphasizes the twin notions of layer and perspective in drafting a policy to respond to regional problems in developing countries. Friedmann (1975) has offered a list of issues of regional development planning:

(i) Regional coordination of national investment policies and programmes.

(ii) Excessive centralization in the territorial organization of power.

(iii) Growing urban primacy and underutilization of natural resources on the periphery of major core regions.

(iv) Underutilization of manpower and human talent.

(v) The incorporation of internally dominated peripheral regions into a single national economic system on a basis of greater equality of living levels and reciprocity in exchange.

(vi) Dualistic development of rural and urban economies.

(vii) Destructive use of land resources.

To these, we would add:

(viii) Efficient use of scarce skills in regional development and urban management.

(ix) Concern with the social effectiveness of urban infrastructure investment.

(x) The implicit spatial impact of non-spatial policy decisions.

This set of issues has to be addressed by national policies, but those policies have to be delivered at subnational levels (region, city, rural area and village). Regional economic development planning can be seen as offering a coordinating framework to associated policy areas at these various layers. In each policy area, however, a decision has to be reached about which functions and responsibilities should be left to the control of each layer, and this is linked to decisions about levying taxes and allocating the revenues generated. It is here that perspective is important, not only for different views about the devolution of political power and the appropriate extent of administrative decentralization, but also in the diagnosis of the problems to be addressed. Much of the earlier writing in regional economics was non-spatial, in which regions were treated as discrete entities, in effect as competing economies. The influence of quantitative geography and regional science has since become important. The spatial structure of the national economy is now heavily stressed when defining regional problems, and the spatial structure of the region is taken into account in prescribing a policy response. In addition to these perspectives, more attention is being given to distributional issues, to be considered as equally important as economic efficiency and growth. The new visibility in the literature given to the internal management of cities in developing countries as an important determinant of the direction of urban growth makes a link to regional development analysis which has yet to be fully exploited [Linn (1983), Gilbert and Gugler (1982)].

5. Policy instruments and strategies

The instruments for promoting economic development in selected regions (and their major urban centres) include cash subsidies to capital and to labour, indirect protection from the tax system and import controls, the allocation of public sector investments, intervention in the location of public sector employment, licensing arrangements, the sponsorship of growth centres and new towns, and administrative decentralization. Direct controls over migration have been tried [and mostly failed; Simmons (1981)]. Granting a degree of political and fiscal autonomy to regions has been recognized as a means of giving an impetus to local economic development. Choosing an appropriate policy mix among the many options is not easy, although governments rarely experiment in regional policy innovation. This section of the chapter discusses these issues in the light of developing country experience in the last two decades.

5.1. Regional planning agencies

The need for a specialist development agency in a designated region will depend not only upon the formal structures of central, state and local governments but also upon their capacities. Relatively little appraisal of the performance of specialist agencies has been undertaken, taking into account the governmental context within which they work. The mere existence of an agency tends to give it an ex post justification which may be difficult to identify ex ante. Nevertheless, the relative success stories in regional development planning may be linked to the creation of a multisectoral agency with special powers and responsibility. The examples of SUDENE in North East Brazil and SUDAM in the Amazon region are frequently quoted, though many local observers remain unconvinced that these particular agencies have worked well in practice.

Key elements in the success of specialized agencies are the size of their financial resources and the extent of their powers to decide the levels and scope of subsidies to industry and allocations for key infrastructure investments. Their role is most important in developing countries where governmental power and control is highly centralized. In such cases, little cross-referencing to other ministries takes place and the coordinated delivery of a carefully planned programme in a development region rapidly fragments. The need for coordination is one reason why regional development agencies are often not placed under a single central government or state government ministry but have been attached to the office of the prime minister or state governor.

In the typical developing country a regional economic development policy, whether or not it operates through a special agency, has two major coordination roles. The first is to coordinate planning for agricultural development and planning for industrial development, striving to exploit the potential linkages between the two sectors. The second is between sectoral planning and planning for urban growth. The difficult balance to be achieved in urban policy is between planning for the growth of services in response to excess demand and the need to take a strategic view of the allocation of urban investments to promote the growth in agricultural and industrial output (i.e. the trade-off between social infrastructure and economic infrastructure).

The coordination roles of special agencies in regional development can make their political control a difficult and contentious issue, with the clear temptation to place them under a form of executive board at arms length from politicians. This is particularly difficult when the agency is a central government creation, operating in both the geographical and the functional territory of a state or local government. The lower-tier authority may have been required to surrender powers to the agency. The potential for bureaucratic conflict is serious. The central government may have chosen to create the agency in response to a poor performance by lower-tier authorities as much as in response to lagging development or the identification of economic potential. Or the agency may also have been created in response to pressures from outside international lending agencies, such as the World Bank. An international institution, a foreign aid programme or an international commercial bank will try to minimize both its administrative costs and its risk. Not only is it simpler to deal with a single bureaucracy, but the financial accounting is more straightforward. The opportunities for the lender to press for policy reforms will also be greater than if the borrowed funds were channelled through several government departments.

5.2. The role of infrastructure

A major issue for regional policy in developing countries is the balance between economic infrastructure and social infrastructure in the allocation of scarce investment resources. One argument is that this should vary by region and over time. Hansen (1965) adopted a threefold classification of regions (congested, intermediate and lagging) and argued that infrastructure policy should focus on economic infrastructure in intermediate regions and on social infrastructure in lagging regions in the early phases of development. This view was supported by a case study of Mexico [Looney and Frederiksen (1981)]. First, public infrastructure investment on these lines appeared to stimulate GRP. Second, the emphasis on economic infrastructure in intermediate regions and on social infrastructure in lagging regions had a favourable effect on regional income disparities: thus, "the implicit trade-off between growth and minimizing differences in income need not exist" [Looney and Frederiksen (1981, p. 295)]. This last point is particularly important because it is well known that interregional disparities in social indicators (such as social service facilities, e.g. hospital beds, schools) are much wider in developing countries than disparities in per capita income. This provides a rationale for social infrastructure provision in peripheral areas. Side benefits might include: better prospects for the immigration of managers, professionals and technical workers into the periphery; and a reduction in the overall rate of periphery-to-core migration as a result of the narrowing of interregional *welfare* differentials. However, the linking of economic infrastructure investments to intermediate regions is consistent with arguments elsewhere in this chapter that infrastructure strategies have to be spatially selective and that regional policies should vary in focus from one kind of region to another. Finally, the overall scarcity of investment resources implies that the adoption of appropriate (usually lower) infrastructure standards and cost recovery mechanisms are as critical issues as the *type* of infrastructure to be emphasized. Reducing standards and recovering costs are important for both economic and social infrastructure (e.g. building access roads to industrial estates that are too wide is no more excusable than supplying water to households at prices that are too low).

5.3. Industrial promotion policies

It will be difficult for a regional development policy to help agricultural and industrial enterprises to be permanently viable unless initial financial injections and technical assistance are subsequently supported by an active commercial banking system. These banks could be in the public sector or the private sector, and they could be investment or development banks rather than consumer-oriented banks. The important issues are their accessibility for commercial and industrial clients in the development region and the rules under which loans are given. The problems are more serious in rural regions without a large city. Many governments have recognized banking as a constraint on development in rural areas and small towns (e.g. the Nigerian Rural Banking Scheme, the Brazilian Rural Credit Outposts, and the Indian Regional Rural Banks).

The choice of policy instruments in a regional development programme has to be made within the contexts of existing urban and industrial policies, the level and pattern of economic development, and the government structure. The choice of instruments will also be influenced by the criteria used to measure their impact. Typical criteria include the generation of output or jobs, the leverage effect on private investment, the use of scarce budgetary resources, the degree of administrative complexity, the bias introduced into resource allocation, or anticipated local multiplier effects. There are marked differences on how different instruments score against these criteria [Townroe (1979, p. 118)].

Some hold the view that regional development in a country experiencing rapid economic expansion and population growth at the national level can be supply-led. This particularly North American sentiment was one of the reasons why such a large part of the regional development expenditures in Appalachia ended up in concrete for roads [Hansen (1972)]. It also explains why overinvestment in serviced industrial land has been so common in lagging regions in developed and developing countries alike. The policy conflict is clear. Infrastructure investments form necessary preconditions for all but the largest industrial investments to take place. The service or facility must exist before industrial operations can commence. But infrastructure investments typically exhibit strong economies of scale with large discontinuities in the cost function. Add the embarrassment of a failure to supply and the temptation to overinvest is clear. Infrastructure investments are also the controllable end of a regional development programme. The expenditures do not have to wait for a private sector response.

The most extreme case of supply-led infrastructure is the industrial estate. Industrial estates have been established in all parts of the developing world. In some countries, such as Thailand and Kenya, specialist agencies have been set up with the sole function of developing industrial estates. The concept of an industrial estate is basically sound. The spatial juxtaposition of industrial establishments, especially if they are from a similar set of industries or linked sectors, permits economies of agglomeration in the form of reductions in unit infrastructure costs and avoids higgledy-piggledy land use patterns. The problem is how to plan industrial estates in line with effective demand so that scarce investment resources are not tied up in underutilized infrastructure. The alternative approach – building a large estate from scratch and, after completion, sitting back and waiting for the firms to turn up – is very risky. The supply of industrial infrastructure may be a necessary condition for regional industrial development, but it is far from a sufficient condition.

Although many industrial estates in developing countries, especially in the primate city or its core region, are filled very quickly, there are many, many more which remain more or less empty for years. The main reasons for overbuilding are the poor quality of market analysis (overestimating the demand for new industrial space) and proliferation in the number of industrial estates in response to local political pressures. Too many industrial estates built too fast on sites which are too large but are often badly located (e.g. where cheap public land exists rather than at the optimal locations from the point of view of accessibility to interurban highways or workers), and using infrastructure standards that are too high or are otherwise inappropriate to needs: this is the story of industrial estate failures everywhere. The success rate could be improved dramatically by phasing, in terms of both the number of estates and the rate of construction of each estate. This is the only way of making an industrial estates programme compatible with economizing on scarce infrastructure resources. Also, it is unrealistic to expect even the more promising industrial estates in the peripheral regions of developing countries to be successful without supplementation with other measures, such as location subsidies.

5.4. Communications and human resource investments

Two important aspects of regional development which frequently fall outside the direct control of a regional development agency are communications and education. As a country starts to industrialize and both the road system and the telecommunications network are relatively underdeveloped, a lagging or peripheral region receives a measure of protection against industry and commerce in the core region from the friction of distance. Further investment in communications in and around the core region, on the other hand, increases its relative agglomeration advantages, developing secondary cities *within the region* as effective industrial locations competitive within the core city. Peripheral regions then suffer from their relatively restricted access. These regions require upgrading of their roads and other transport services and of their telephone networks if companies based there are to compete effectively for the core (or export) markets. But this upgrading simultaneously increases the exposure of the regional market to outside companies. Examples of the locational impact of major road developments and of the introduction of microwave telecommunication systems on industrial development can be found in many countries, e.g. Nepal [Blakie (1981)], or São Paulo State in Brazil [Dillinger and Hamer (1982)].

A familiar argument is that the task for regional policy makers will be made easier in the future as a result of technological advances, especially in the communications sector. This argument has three strands. First, technological progress diffuses over time through the national space economy, and this will give the peripheral regions a chance to catch up (e.g. plants locating in the periphery will, on average, be newer and embody more recent technology). Second, a major obstacle to economic development in the periphery is the lack of economic infrastructure, such as transport and communications, and increasing wealth permits governments to invest in the periphery's infrastructure. Third, advances in communications are facilitating economic penetration of the periphery, by relaxing constraints on location. An implication is that even quaternary industries such as the information-processing industries will no longer have to rely on face-to-face contacts and hence to cluster in core region metropolises. They can become footloose and disperse to other regions, with relocation motivated by locational preferences or other reasons.

Whatever the merits of these arguments, it is doubtful whether they apply with much force to developing countries. A recent paper shows that, counterintuitively, as long as unit transport, communication and contact costs are higher in the periphery than in the core, the impact of technological progress in the information-processing sector will tend to widen core–periphery disparities rather than to narrow them [Clapp and Richardson (1984)]. This result is reinforced by the periphery's deficiencies in communications infrastructure, the locational pull on business services of the manufacturing sector which is heavily concentrated in the core region, the reluctance of professional and technical personnel to leave the primate city and its social and cultural amenities, and the inability of poor countries to pay international wage rates for computer programmers and similar skilled workers. Furthermore, adding capital in the form of computers and other electronic data-processing equipment will widen core–periphery income differentials by raising skilled wages in the core (reflecting capital-skilled labour complementarity) and depressing unskilled wages in the periphery (migration from the periphery to the core will slacken as a result of the substitution of capital for unskilled labour at the core).

The policy implications implied by this scenario are: heavy investment in interurban (interregional) telecommunications infrastructure; location incentives for business services and information-processing industries not only for manufacturing; and a national programme of human resource investments to increase the constrained supply of technicians in the business services sector. The underlying hypothesis is that eventually the high-order services sectors will become as important in the economic structures of developing countries as they are proving to be in the developed countries.

Manpower planning has had a chequered history in countries at all stages of development and it is difficult to advocate precise policies designed to generate skills in a workforce in advance of new industry expanding to take up the supply. At the same time, skill shortages have formed a major constraint on regional development initiatives, and many countries have felt a need to include an industrial training element in a regional development policy package. The local multiplier effects of expenditures on training are high, unless the acquisition of a skill forms an incentive to migrate, an incentive which is obviously increased if there is no local opportunity to apply the skill. Hence the attraction of tying subsidies for skill training to on-the-job training or to company-specific off-the-job programmes rather than promting specific industrial skill training in colleges in advance of need.

All of the indirect and infrastructure elements of a regional development programme seek to attract external industrial investment and to foster local companies. Four questions have to be asked of each element: What is the appropriate scale of expenditure at each location? What level of quality is required for effectiveness? Can or should a price (or tax) be charged for the service? How important is consistency in delivery? The incentive effect of these expenditures on training, communications, utilities, and industrial parks is low but, to a greater or lesser degree, they form preconditions for development. It may not be necessary to match what is available in the core region, but it is necessary to provide enough infrastructure and services to allow industrial development to take place.

6. Recent regional development experiences in developing countries

Regional development incentives aim to attract mobile industrial investment from other regions or abroad as well as to promote the more rapid growth of indigenous firms. In some countries, incentives available in lagging regions have been combined with taxes or licensing procedures in the more prosperous areas, hoping to induce a flow of footloose plants away from the centre. The range of incentives available and their principal strengths and weaknesses have been reviewed in several studies of regional policy for developed countries [Armstrong and Taylor (1978), Richardson (1979), Emanuel (1973), Hansen (1974)]. Comment is limited here to issues which refer specifically to regional development in developing countries.

A serious practical problem in the design of locational incentives (and disincentives) is most easily understood in the context of the core–periphery model. In effect, the core–periphery model divides the national space economy into *two* regions (or two sets of region), namely the core and the periphery. A locational subsidy is intended to encourage industrial growth in the periphery (and, especially if it is combined with a locational tax, to discourage growth in the core region). But in geographical terms the two-region framework implies that where the core region ends the periphery begins. If the subsidy applies to all parts of the periphery, core region firms can obtain its benefits without bearing the higher risks and costs of a peripheral location by establishing plants a short distance across the core region boundary. This "boundary problem" distorts the impact of locational incentive schemes in many developing countries. Examples include:

the 50 kilometer ban on industrial development around Manila which has induced artificial industrial growth in secondary cities a few kilometers further out; the rapid buildup of industry at the Hub industrial estate where Karachi firms can obtain the subsidies offered to the backward province of Baluchistan; the growth of industries at Mirzapur in Bangladesh adjacent to Dhaka district which is excluded from industrial incentives; and many more. The solution to this problem, rarely adopted, is to create a buffer zone between the core region and the periphery in which no incentives are offered. However, to avoid discrimination against this buffer zone, disincentives (taxes) need to be imposed on industrial development in the primate city and the core region so that zero incentives within the buffer zone place it in an intermediate neutral position between encouraged industrial growth in the periphery and discouraged growth in the core.

The target group of firms for an incentive policy, even in the largest developing countries, is relatively small. The number of companies in the core region which might be tempted to decentralize or establish a branch plant unit in a peripheral region will be no more than a few score, even in cities the size of SãoPaulo, Bombay, Cairo or Bogota. The number of established companies within a designated region which might be encouraged to expand faster will be even smaller. The limited universe of manufacturing enterprises in the formal sector of these economies presents both a problem and an opportunity. The problem is the lack of choice and the scarcity of managerial skills in the companies able to respond to incentives and to the difficulties of multiplant operation. The opportunity lies in the limited number of contacts that have to be made and the possibility of tailoring incentives to the situation of individual companies. Both state-owned companies and multinational corporations bringing in investment from outside may receive special treatment. Many developed countries have found MNCs particularly receptive to regional incentives. This may be less true in developing countries. MNCs are typically at the high-technology and strong export ends of the industrial spectrum, and the relative agglomeration advantages (including access to government offices and agencies) of the core region outweigh any cost differentials resulting from subsidies to the periphery. For both multinationals and domestically owned concerns, the size of subsidies and the degree of protection available at the national level for new operations may be so large as to pose a severe visibility problem for even generous regionally based payments. This problem suggests that regional incentives should take a distinctively different form from any national incentives.

In developing countries government involvement with industry is strong, placing a premium on contacts with officials (and politicians). Extensive licensing is common for investment, imports, and the use of foreign exchange. For an expanding enterprise, the single most important constraint may be foreign exchange, introducing a new potential policy lever. A further feature of many developing countries is a strong political commitment to economic growth, with the result that policy makers may be reluctant to introduce measures which inhibit economic growth and impair the efficient use of fiscal resources and capital. Unemployment or under-employment might be expected to make governments resist incentive policies which increase the relative capital intensity of projects, but administrative simplicity and a belief in relatively fixed factor proportions leads to the opposite conclusion. An intermediate response is to attach an employment creation, or cost-per-job, condition to capital subsidies.

Capital subsidies have been the prime instrument used to influence the location of manufacturing industry. One interesting variant is the points system used in North East Brazil by SUDENE. Under the 34/18 program [Goodman (1975)], capital subsidies have been available up to 75, 60, 50, 40 and 30 percent of total project investment costs, depending upon such factors as employment creation, the specific industrial sector, import substitution, export generation, local purchasing, location within the North East region, labour intensity, and the pattern of ownership. Similar ideas have been used in Malaysia [World Bank (1975)], linking regional development payments to national priority sectors, the Malaysian content of the product, and employment generation. A highly discretionary approach to incentives poses problems in the need for trained, skilled, knowledgeable and incorruptible civil servants to administer the scheme, and also violates Friedmann's (1972) requirement that the policy be simple, pragmatic and easy to understand. Experience with regional economic policies in both developed and developing countries has shown the need for a medium-to-long-term political commitment, avoiding frequent changes in either the form or intensity of the incentives payable.

One key finding of studies of industrial location decision making in developed nations is the importance of "non-economic" costs in locational choice. Large companies have to consider whether their top managers are willing to transfer to the new location. For the owner–manager, the upheaval of a household relocation may be too much to countenance on top of a plant relocation. Any policy oriented to industrial mobility in a newly industrializing country will face similar constraints. For example, in the 1980 São Paulo Industrial Location Survey [Townroe (1983)], "Personal and family reasons of the owner" were cited by 20 percent of firms decentralizing out of the São Paulo Metropolitan Area as a major or decisive factor in locational choice. This proportion rose to 29 percent for new firms, and to 42 percent for firms moving from locations in secondary cities in the State (the majority of this group consequently moved *within* the same secondary city). The factor "Favourable environment for attracting management staff" was not as important, however, being cited as a major or decisive factor by 19 percent of the decentralizing group, only 8 percent of the firms moving out to the suburbs but staying within the metropolitan area, and by 12 percent of the secondary city movers. The importance of these factors varies by size of firm, and whether a branch plant or a complete transfer is being contemplated. However, in general, the "psychic distance" of a relocation from the primate city region of a developing country to a peripheral region is relatively greater than that facing a manager or owner in a highly integrated industrialized nation.

A United Nations working group on policy instruments for decentralized industrialization [UNCRD (1976)] suggested satisfactory results could only be obtained with direct subsidies, strong fiscal incentives, the development of financial intermediaries, pushing of foreign investors to less developed areas and the pricing of public utilities to support decentralization. This conclusion, however, appears excessively influenced by the experience of West European regional development policies of the 1960s and early 1970s, failing to recognize the severe constraints of limited public sector resources in LDCs on the feasibility of alternative regional policy proposals.

Advocates of selective regional closure as the key to development and improved regional balance, in the attempt to swing the pendulum more towards bottom-up approaches rather than top-down policy initiatives, run the risk of overturning economic and institutional relationships in an economy in order to satisfy limited regional development objectives. However, policy elements implied by this perspective, which emphasises "territory" rather than "function", extend the range of policy instruments for the promotion of regional economic development.

For example:

"(1) Provision of broad access to land and other territorially available natural resources as the key production factors in most less developed areas....

(2) The introduction of new, or revival of the old, territorially organized structures for equitable communal decision-making on the integrated allocation of regional natural and human resources....

(3) Granting a higher degree of self-determination to rural and other peripheral areas....

(4) Choice of regionally adequate technology oriented towards minimizing waste of scarce, and maximizing use of regionally abundant, resources....

(5) Assignment of priority to projects which serve the satisfaction of basic needs of the population....

(6) The introduction of national pricing policies which offer terms of trade more favorable to agricultural and other typically peripheral products....

(7) ...external assistance (national or international) would be solicited but should be mainly considered as compensation for the eroding effects of previously emerging dependencies....

(8) Development of productive activities exceeding regional demand...
should be promoted only to the extent that they lead to a broad
increase in living levels of the population of the territorial unit....

(9) Restructuring of urban and transport systems to improve and equalize
access of the population to all parts of the country to them, rather than
strengthening such systems oriented to the outside....

(10) Improvements of rural-to-rural and rural-to-village transport and communication facilities (rather than the present priority given to rural-to-
large-urban communities) should have preference....

(11) Egalitarian societal structures and a collective consciousness are im-
portant prerequisites for a strategy for development "from below"."
[Stöhr (1981, p. 64), see also Stöhr and Tödtling (1977, 1978), Lo and
Salih (1981), Friedmann and Weaver (1979)].

It is difficult to envisage these policies applied to one or two selected regions and
not to all. The discussion of bottom-up strategies therefore shades into arguments
about appropriate national government structures. It is also not clear from the
arguments put forward by this school of thought how decentralization and
greater regional autonomy would reduce interregional equity as opposed to
making existing spatial inequities more tolerable. Also, the cost in terms of
national economic growth may not be acceptable to a national government.
Selective spatial closure theorists have broadened the debate on the content of a
regional development program, but the issues raised are more ethical and
political than economic [Weaver (1981, p. 93)].

Without broadening the regional policy issue to national dimensions, there are
four other policy avenues via which faster growth in a lagging region might be
promoted. The first is a set of instruments directed at the urban and industrial
complements to agricultural development, fostering services and agro-related
urban-based manufacturing to accelerate the growth of agricultural output. The
second is the use of public sector manufacturing industry as propulsive plants or
sectors in designated growth areas, with the possible risk of underwriting locations that may be inefficient *intra*sectorally. The third avenue lies in the promotion of entrepreneurship in small-scale industry. Experience suggests that
small-firm programmes are best delivered at the regional rather than the national
level. These programmes require a rather delicate mix of advice, finance and
credit, the provision of work spaces, and ongoing relationships between the small
firms and the sponsoring agency. The last avenue is the decentralization of public
sector employment, overcoming the objections of employees and relocating
hospitals, universities, and government offices involved in routine clerical work to
peripheral regions. There are probably communications diseconomies involved,
but these activities are large employers with strong local multiplier effects. A
"decentralization of government establishments" strategy is much more spatially

selective than administrative decentralization in general which involves the transfer of functions and personnel to *all* subnational government units. The latter's benefits are more political rather than economic. The choice between the two depends upon institutional constraints and policy objectives. Either is much preferable to a third type of government locational change, namely relocation of the national capital. Experience in Brazil and Pakistan suggests that this is a very expensive way of achieving limited regional development objectives.

7. Conclusions

In developed and developing countries alike, the world-wide recession of the early 1980s illustrated the difficulty of running an effective regional economic development policy in an environment of slow national economic growth [Richardson and Turek (1984)]. Most regional policies rely heavily on new industrial investments as a precondition for success.

However, in developing countries economic recession did not have a significant impact on the scale or pattern of urbanization. The underlying dynamic remains the fertility and mortality experience of the existing urban population rather than a slowdown in the growth rate of the GNP. Data are not yet available to test whether the deceleration in the growth of the large-scale manufacturing sector modified the migration streams from the rural areas and the small towns to big cities and from peripheral regions to core regions.

One lesson from the past two decades however is that the economic fortunes of a lagging region, and the potential for a policy intervention, are governed by external forces and institutions as much as by internal structures. One important external force has been a changing policy stance towards agriculture. Food production is now more highly regarded as a major contributor to economic development rather than being treated merely as a source of cheap sustenance, tax revenue and labour for urban manufacturing. The social benefits from land reform and higher agricultural prices are maximized if supported by investment in commercial inputs and by spending on rural services [electricity, water supply, transport, health, education, and technical assistance; see Johnson and Kilby, (1975) and Little (1982)]. This has implications for the urban development of rural regions [Rondinelli and Ruddle (1978)]. In the rural areas of Africa and Asia "Integrated Rural Regional Development" is interpreted increasingly in these agricultural support terms [e.g. Livingstone (1979), Hazlewood and Livingstone (1982), Belshaw (1977)].

The recent emphasis on rural planning reflects the more general problem of the difficult balance in regional development policies in developing countries among physical planning, public sector economic planning, and stimulus to an often unpredictable private sector. Policy instruments such as the provision of infrastructure or locational incentives cannot dominate or counter the commercial requirement of access to markets or to resources. A regional economic policy cannot be deterministic, and regional "blueprints" for development are an inappropriate conception of effective strategy. Regional development planning needs to be comprehensive in its coverage without the pretence of being comprehensive in what can be directed or coordinated.

Changes in thinking about the nature of regional economic planning and about the effective promotion of rural development are reflected in the cyclical attitude to the growth pole concept. Hansen (1981, p.34) suggests three phases: "(1) Optimism with respect to possibilities for inducing growth in a few centres and to the subsequent generation of spread effects; (2) pessimism when the expectations of the early phase failed to materialize; and (3) a broader view of growth centres as one aspect of more comprehensive development planning." Richardson (1978) also returned to a defence of the growth centre approach in the context of both rural development and national urban policy.

The growth pole approach has to be treated very cautiously in developing countries. There are many unsatisfactory experiences resulting from a careless transfer of growth pole policy ideas from developed countries with little adjustment to indigenous conditions. The most extreme cases have been based on heavy industrial complexes with negligible linkages with the hinterland and minimal employment generation. An alternative strategy might begin with the fact that most growth poles in developing countries are located in rural regions. Such poles might emphasize the growth of agro-based industries to expand the market for hinterland output, and hence to stimulate rural productivity and income, and the generation of higher-order services [Richardson (1978)]. This is not quite the same as the agropolitan development planning approach, because it implies intermediate-size centres somewhere between the large industrial poles implied by traditional growth pole theory and the small agropolitan centre.

Some aspects of growth pole theory are especially applicable in developing countries. The development axis concept [Pottier (1963)], for example, where the promotion of multiple growth poles (initially at the endpoints of the axis, but subsequently at intermediate distances along the axis) helps to generate the cost reductions and agglomeration economies associated with opening up a transportation corridor, may provide a successful means of integrating growth pole strategies and interregional transport investments. Similarly, countermagnet strategies work better in situations where cities grow rapidly via in-migration from rural areas than where people are reshuffled within an established urban hierarchy in a highly urbanized society. The idea of strengthening a regional metropolis as a counterweight to the primate city is more effective if the city size distribution is still evolving than in countries where the urban hierarchy has become fossilized. Unfortunately, the primate economies where countermagnets are most needed (e.g. Thailand, Peru, Chile, Argentina) lack the large candidate cities for countermagnets, while those countries which have strong second and third cities (e.g. India, Malaysia, the Philippines) have little reason to adopt a countermagnet strategy. Also, a successful countermagnet may replicate the adverse spatial impacts of primacy in another part of the country.

The evolutionary character of national urban hierarchies in developing countries has another major implication for the implementation of growth pole strategies. Too often, growth poles have been selected in a piecemeal manner as "points" of development with little regard for each pole's role in the cementing of urban hierarchies, both national and regional. Growth pole policies cannot be implemented successfully outside the broader context of a national urban development strategy. Agglomeration economies are urban in character [both intra-urban and interurban; von Böventer (1975)], and the promotion of national urban development strategy will have direct repercussions on regional development, both within and among regions. Growth pole strategies, whatever their weaknesses, help to integrate urban and regional development.

After an earlier preoccupation with the role of metropolitan centres and small towns and villages in regional development, recent attention has focused on policies to improve the development prospects of medium-sized (secondary, intermediate) cities. This attention reflects the desire of national governments to diffuse urbanization spatially, but it also reflects a realization that secondary city policies can be a mechanism to reduce regional inequities as well as to improve administrative efficiency, raise urban productivity and reduce urban poverty [Rondinelli (1983)]. The scope of these programs (e.g. Brazil, Thailand, Indonesia) has included the improvement of local government managerial capacity, greater local financial autonomy, physical infrastructure investments, and the promotion of the economic base of each city. The economic dynamics of the growth of a system of secondary cities with different economic structures and roles and their regional implications is poorly understood. A recent empirical study of Brazil is an attempt to locate the sources and interactions of growth in these cities in rapidly industrializing regions which are larger than in most countries [Henderson (1983)].

As suggested above, many recent commentators on regional economic policy in developing countries have stressed non-economic institutional and political aspects of development planning, especially in rural areas. This has been a reaction to the apparent failure of Western urban–industrial models of regional development to reduce regional inequalities and rural poverty. This reaction has stressed several layers of dualism, between rural areas and urban areas in many developing countries, between the formal and informal sectors of the economy and between the industrialized and industrializing countries [Lo and Salih (1981)]. One benefit has been a greater understanding of the significance of political structures and the relevance of alternative administrative modes [e.g. Hinchcliffe (1980) on Papua–New Guinea]. A more dubious result has been advocacy and polemics [e.g. Weaver (1981), Friedmann and Douglass (1978)], especially because of a refusal to acknowledge the role of innovation diffusion and the gains from trade, while playing down efficiency considerations in favour of redistribution and political devolution.

This paper began with a standard warning about the dangers of generalization. The regional problems of countries with large industrial sectors, whether middle-income nations such as Brazil or Mexico or poorer nations like India or China, will be rather different from the regional problems of nations with relatively small industrial sectors, such as Bangladesh or the Ivory Coast. However, the common problems of large agricultural sectors in the economies of all developing countries and of more or less rapid urbanization allow many perspectives to be transferred with some qualifications from country to country. The dominant task of regional economists in the medium-term future continues to be to build bridges between research in development economics and new insights in regional analysis and the economics of urban growth. The literature in this area is thin on long-term empirical studies of individual developing countries. The stage of merely applying techniques and policy findings generated in the developed countries is over.

References

Armstrong, H. and J. Taylor (1978) *Regional economic policy and its analysis*. Deddington: Philip Allan.

Belshaw, D. G. R. (1977) 'Rural development planning: concepts and techniques', *Journal of Agricultural Economics*, 28(3):279–291.

Bertrand, T. (1978) 'An analysis of industrial incentives, and location in Nigeria', World Bank, mimeo.

Blakie, P. (1981) 'Nepal: the crisis in regional planning in a double dependent periphery', in: W. B. Stöhr and D. R. Fraser Taylor, eds., *Development from above or below? The dialectics of regional planning in developing countries*. Chichester: John Wiley.

Borts, G. H. and J. L. Stein (1964) *Economic growth in a free market*. New York: Columbia University Press.

Boudeville, J.-R. (1966) *Problems of regional economic planning*. Edinburgh: Edinburgh University Press.

Chatterjee, L. and P. Nijkamp, eds. (1983) *Urban and regional policy analysis in developing countries*. Aldershot: Gower.

Chatterji, M. ed. (1982) *Regional science for developing countries*. Boston: Kluwer-Nijhoff.

Chatterji, M. et al., eds. (1983) *Spatial, environmental and resource policy in developing countries*. Aldershot: Gower.

Clapp, J. M. and H. W. Richardson (1984) 'Technological change in information-processing industries and income differentials in developing countries', *International Regional Science Review*, 9:241–257.

De Bruyne, G. and P. Van Rompuy (1982) 'The impact of interest subsidies on the interregional allocation of capital', *Regional Science and Urban Economics*, 12:121–138.

Dillinger, W. and A. M. Hamer (1982) 'Sources of growth in manufacturing employment in non-metropolitan areas', Report No. UDD 13, Water and Urban Development Department, The World Bank.

Dixon, R. and A. P. Thirlwall (1975) 'A model of regional growth rate differences on Kaldorian lines', *Oxford Economic Papers*, 27:201–214.

Emanuel, A. (1973) *Issues of regional policy*. Paris: O.E.C.D.

Friedmann, J. (1966) *Regional development policy: a case study of Venezuela*. Cambridge, Mass.: MIT Press.

Friedmann, J. (1972-73) 'The spatial organization of power in the development of urban systems', *Development and Change*, 4:12–50.

Friedmann, J. (1973) *Urbanization, planning and national development*. Beverly Hills: Sage.

Friedmann, J. (1975) 'Regional development planning: the progress of a decade', in: J. Friedmann and W. Alonso, eds., *Regional policy readings in theory and applications*, Cambridge, Mass.: MIT Press.

Friedmann, J. and M. Douglass (1978) 'Agropolitan development: towards a new strategy for regional planning in Asia', in: F. Lo and K. Salih, eds., *Growth pole strategy and regional development policy: Asian experiences and alternative strategies*. Oxford: Pergamon Press, 163–192.

Friedmann, J. and C. Weaver (1979) *Territory and function: the evolution of regional planning*. London: Arnold.

Gilbert, A. and J. Gugler (1982) *Cities, poverty and development: urbanization in the third world*. Oxford: Oxford University Press.

Goodman, D. (1975) 'Fiscal incentives for the industrialization of North East Brazil and the choice of techniques', *Brazilian Economic Studies*, 1:201–225.

Hansen, N. M. (1965) 'Unbalanced growth and regional development', *Western Economic Journal*, 4:3–14.

Hansen, N. M. (1972) *Growth centers in regional economic development*. New York: The Free Press.

Hansen, N. M., ed. (1974) *Public policy and regional development*. Cambridge, Mass.: Ballinger.

Hansen, N. M., ed. (1976) *Public policy and regional economic development: the experience of nine western countries*. Cambridge, Mass.: Ballinger.

Hansen, N. M. (1981) 'Development from above: the centre-down development paradigm', in: W. B. Stöhr and D. R. Fraser Taylor, eds., *Development from above or below? The dialectics of regional planning in developing countries*, Chichester: John Wiley.

Hauser, P. M. and R. W. Gardner (1980) 'Urban future: trends and prospects', in *United Nations Fund for Population Activities, International Conference on Population and the Urban Future, Documents*, Rome, 7–78.

Hazlewood, A. and I. Livingstone (1982) 'Integrated rural development: a Tanzanian case study', in: I. Livingstone, ed., *Approaches to development studies: essays in honour of Athole Mackintosh*. Farnborough: Gower Press.

Henderson, J. V. (1982) 'The impact of government policies on urban concentration', *Journal of Urban Economics*, 9:64–71.

Henderson, J. V. (1983) 'Urban development in Brazil', Report No. UDD 30, Water Supply and Urban Development Department, The World Bank.

Hewings, G. J. D. (1983) 'Regional and interregional accounting systems for development planning', in: M. Chatterji and P. Nijkamp, eds., *Urban and regional policy analysis in developing countries*. Aldershot: Gower, 181–202.

Hewings, G. J. D. and M. C. Romanos (1981) 'Simulating less-developed regional economies under conditions of limited information', *Geographical Analysis*, 13:373–390.

Higgins, B. (1973) 'Trade-offs and regional gaps', in: J. Bhagwati and R. S. Eckaus, eds., *Development and planning: essays in honour of Paul Rosenstein Rodan*. London: Allen and Unwin, 152–177.

Hinchliffe, K. (1980) 'Conflicts between national aims in Papua New Guinea: the case of decentralization and equality', *Economic Development and Cultural Change*, 28(4):819–838.

Hirschman, A. O. (1958) *The strategy of economic development*. Yale University Press, New Haven.

International Labour Organization (1973) *Fiscal measures for employment promotion in developing countries*. Geneva: International Labour Organization.

Johnson, B. F. and P. Kilby (1975) *Agriculture and structural transformation: economic strategies in late-developing countries*. New York: Oxford University Press.

Kaldor, N. (1970) 'The case for regional policies', *Scottish Journal of Political Economy*, 17:337–348.

Kuklinski, A. ed. (1978) *Regional policies in Nigeria, India and Brazil*. New York: Mouton.

Lakshmanan, T. R. and A. Elhance (1984) 'Infrastructure and economic development', mimeo.

Linn, J. F. (1983) *Cities in the developing world: policies for their equitable and efficient growth*. Oxford: Oxford University Press.

Little, I. M. D. (1982) *Economic development. theory, policy and international relations*. New York: Basic Books.

Livingstone, I. (1979) 'On the concept of 'integrated rural development planning' in less developed countries,' *Journal of Agricultural Economics*, 30:49–53.

Lo, F. and K. Salih (1981) 'Growth poles, agropolitain development, and polarization reversal: the debate and search for alternatives', in: W. B. Stöhr and D. R. Fraser Taylor, eds., *Development from above or below? The dialectics of regional planning in developing countries*. New York: John Wiley.

Looney, R. and P. Frederiksen (1981) 'The regional impact of infrastructure investment in Mexico', *Regional Studies*, 15:285–296.

McLure, C. (1980) 'Administrative considerations in the design of regional tax incentives', *National Tax Journal*, 33:177–188.

Myrdal, G. (1957) *Economic theory and underdeveloped regions*, London: Duckworth.

Nijkamp, P. (1983) 'Qualitative impact assessments of spatial policies in developing countries', *Regional Development Dialogue*, 4:44–65.

Nijkamp, P. and M. J. F. van Pelt (1983) 'Urban and regional impact analysis in development programming', in: L. Chatterjee and P. Nijkamp, eds., *Urban and regional policy analysis in developing countries*. Aldershot: Gower, 171–181.

Oates, W. E., E. P. Howrey and W. J. Baumol (1971) 'The analysis of public policy in dynamic urban models', *Journal of Political Economy*, 79:142–153.

Perroux, F. (1955) 'Note sur la notion de pôle de croissance', *Économie Appliqueé*, 7:307–320.

Pottier, A. (1963) 'Axes de communication et développement économique', *Revue Economique*, 14:58–132.

Renaud, B. (1981) *National urbanization policy in developing countries*. Oxford: Oxford University Press.

Richardson, H. W. (1973) *Regional growth theory*. London: MacMillan.

Richardson, H. W. (1976) 'Growth pole spillovers: the dynamics of backwash and spread', *Regional Studies*, 10:1–9.

Richardson, H. W. (1978) 'Growth centers, rural development, and national urban policy: a defense', *International Regional Science Review*, 3(2):133–152.

Richardson, H. W. (1979) *Regional economics*. Urbana: University of Illinois.

Richardson, H. W. (1980) 'The relevance and applicability of regional economics to developing countries', *Regional Development Dialogue*, 1:57–75.

Richardson, H. W. (1981a) 'National urban development strategies in developing countries', *Urban Studies*, 18:267–283.

Richardson, H. W. (1981b) 'Industrial policy and regional development in less-developed countries', in: M. E. Bell and P. S. Lande, eds., *Regional dimensions of industrial policy*. Lexington, Mass.: Lexington Books, 92–120.

Richardson, H. W. (1985) 'Input–output and economic base multipliers: looking back and forward', *Journal of Regional Science*, 25:607–661.

Richardson, H. W. and J. H. Turek (1984) *Economic prospects for the Northeast*. Philadelphia: Temple University Press.

Romans, J. T. (1965) *Capital exports and growth among U.S. regions*. Middletown: Wesleyan University Press.

Rondinelli, D. A. (1983) *Secondary cities in developing countries: policies for diffusing urbanization*. Beverly Hills: Sage.

Rondinelli, D. A. and K. Ruddle (1978) *Urbanization and rural development: a spatial policy for equitable growth*. New York: Praeger.

Santos, M. (1979) *The shared space: the two circuits of the urban economy in underdeveloped countries*. London: Methuen.

Schultz, T. W., ed. (1978) *Distortions of agricultural incentives*. Bloomington: Indiana University Press.

Schultz, T. W. (1964) *Transforming traditional agriculture*. New Haven: Yale University Press.

Siebert, H. (1969) *Regional economic growth: theory and policy*. Scranton: International Textbook Company.

Simmons, A. (1981) 'A review and evaluation of attempts to constrain migration to selected urban centres and regions', in: United Nations, *Population distribution policies in development planning*. New York: United Nations, 87–98.

Stöhr, W. B. (1975) *Regional development in Latin America: experience and prospects*. The Hague: Mouton.

Stöhr, W. B. (1981) 'Development from below: the bottom-up and periphery-inward development paradigm', in: W. B. Stöhr and D. R. Fraser Taylor, eds., *Development from above or below? The dialectics of regional planning in developing countries*. Chichester: John Wiley.

Stöhr, W. R. and F. Tödtling (1977) 'Evaluation of regional policies—experiences in market and mixed economies', in: N. M. Hansen, ed., *Human settlement systems*. Cambridge, Mass.: Ballinger, 85–119.

Stöhr, W. B. and F. Tödtling (1978) 'Spatial equity—some antitheses to current regional development strategy', *Papers of the Regional Science Association*, 38:33–53.

Stuckey, B. (1975) 'Spatial analysis and economic development', *Development and Change*, 6:98–101.

Tolley, G. S., V. Thomas and C. M. Wong (1982) *Agricultural price policies and the developing countries*. Baltimore: Johns Hopkins University Press.

Townroe, P. M. (1979) 'Employment decentralization: policy instruments for large cities in less developed countries', *Progress in Planning*, 10(2):85–154.

Townroe, P. M. (1983) 'Location factors in the decentralization of industry. A survey of Metropolitan Sao Paulo, Brazil', World Bank Staff Working Paper No. 517.

Tyler, W. G. (1983) 'The Brazilian sectoral incentive system and the regional incidence of non-spatial incentive policies', Report UDD 31, Water Supply and Urban Development Department, The World Bank.

UNCRD (1976) *Growth pole strategy and regional development planning in Asia*. Nagoya, Japan.

Von Böventer, E. G. (1970) 'Optimal spatial structure and regional development', *Kyklos*, 23:903–924.

Von Böventer, E. G. (1975) 'Regional growth theory', *Urban Studies*, 12:1–29.

Voogd, H. (1981) *Multi-criteria analysis in urban and regional planning*. London: Pion.

Weaver, C. (1981) 'Development theory and the regional question: a critique of spatial planning and its detractors', in: W. B. Stöhr and D. R. Fraser Taylor, eds., *Development from above or below? The dialectics of regional planning in development countries*. Chichester: John Wiley.

Williamson, J. G. (1965) 'Regional inequality and the process of national development: a description of the patterns', *Economic Development and Cultural Change*, 13:3–45.

World Bank (1975) 'Industrial growth and economic progress in Malaysia', Report 861-MA, World Bank, Washington, D.C.

World Bank (1983) *World Development Report*, Washington, D.C.: The World Bank.

AUTHOR INDEX

SUBJECT INDEX